EDUCATIONAL PSYCHOLOGY
FROM THEORY TO APPLICATION

D0084016

WITHDRAWN

WITHDRAWN

EDUCATIONAL PSYCHOLOGY
FROM THEORY TO APPLICATION

BRUCE W. TUCKMAN

Florida State University

370.15

T 898E

8/94

Harcourt Brace Jovanovich College Publishers

Fort Worth   Philadelphia   San Diego   New York   Orlando   Austin   San Antonio
Toronto   Montreal   London   Sydney   Tokyo

CUYAHOGA COMMUNITY COLLEGE
EASTERN CAMPUS LIBRARY

SEP 0 6 1994

To Bob Gagné,
mentor, colleague, friend

Acquisitions Editor: Julia Berrisford
Manuscript Editor: Cate DaPron
Production Editor: Sheila Spahn
Designer: Cathy Reynolds
Art Editor: Cindy Robinson
Production Manager: Diane Southworth
Permissions Editor: Eleanor Garner

COVER: TIB/WEST/Charles Allen © 1991

ILLUSTRATIONS: Bob Yochum and Asterisk Group, Inc.

Copyright © 1992 by Harcourt Brace Jovanovich, Inc.

All rights reserved. No part of this publication may be reproduced or transmitted in any form or by any means, electronic or mechanical, including photocopy, recording, or any information storage and retrieval system, without permission in writing from the publisher.

Requests for permission to make copies of any part of the work should be mailed to Permissions Department, Harcourt Brace Jovanovich, Inc., 8th Floor, Orlando, Florida 32887.

ISBN: 0-15-520871-3

Library of Congress Catalog Card Number: 91-72172

Printed in the United States of America

Text credits and photo and figure credits appear on pages 473–74, which constitute a continuation of the copyright page.

Preface

Textbooks can grow cluttered over time. Fundamentals get buried and duplication becomes unavoidable. *Educational Psychology: From Theory to Application* is for instructors who want a book that is simple and uncluttered. This book, while containing the major topics of educational psychology — classroom management, instructional design, development, and motivation — is designed to be covered in a one-semester course.

But, you say, educational psychology is "the world." It includes everything; no aspects of psychology are bypassed, except perhaps the physiological and clinical. How can we get it all into one book that can be covered in a single course? The answer is to return to theories, the comprehensive and seemingly timeless frameworks that help us organize and understand an entire field like learning, or instruction, or cognitive development. Treating theories as primary and facts and extrapolations as secondary is what makes this book different from its competitors.

The theories covered are psychological theories, not curricular or administrative ones. Among them are the approaches of Skinner, Gagné, Piaget, Bandura, and Weiner, the basics of how people learn, think, grow, interact, and direct and motivate themselves. They contribute to education by contributing to the foundation of education. Once they are presented and learned, applications can be formulated and proposed from them.

So this is a theoretical book — *theoretical* meaning "underlying principles" and *underlying principles* meaning "explanatory." Students are likely to forget a multitude of facts, but they are likely to remember the basic explanations of how children learn, think, grow, interact, and become directed and motivated. If they remember the explanations, they can use them as teachers when the opportunity comes along.

Educational Psychology: From Theory to Application contains applications as well, most apparently in the myriad of "boxes" in each chapter. For instructors who want to cover testing, another area of great strength for applications is Part Three. It explores in depth how to write and evaluate tests and then how to score, grade, and interpret the results of their use. And the book, like a good teacher itself, practices what it preaches: abstraction, organization, elaboration, advance organizers, and mathemagenics throughout. Some obvious examples in each chapter are objectives, headings that make the discussion easy to follow and specific material easy to find, tables that condense pertinent discussions and figures that crystallize them, a comprehensive summary, and a list of resources for further reading. But there are less obvious devices as well: frequent examples and metaphors; key words and points emphasized with italics; and detailed information on study skills, test-taking, learning from text, and self-motivation — all of which students can use on themselves.

For, after all, who are the primary targets of this book? Not the public-school children whom we hope most of these prospective teachers will someday teach, but the prospective teachers themselves — whose classroom experience to-date is as students, not as teachers. What you are trying to do as their teacher, this book is trying to do as well: Say to them "Prospective teacher, learn to teach yourself." Here in *Educational Psychology: From Theory to Application* are the theories and applications to help you — and them — do it.

The Instructor's Manual to accompany *Educational Psychology: From Theory to Application* provides a wealth of material, all classroom-tested and successful. Its intent is to help design and present a course in which students learn to use the theories in the textbook to solve problems and envision their own applications. For each chapter there is an overview of the main ideas, to maintain the focus on content; a more extensive section on points of emphasis, to help guide the discovery and discussion processes; and plentiful activities to provide the "raw" or case material from which students can "construct" meaning by applying theories covered in the textbook. The Instructor's Manual also contains tests of approximately 60 multiple-choice items per chapter, four tests through which to test the whole course, and 100 transparency masters.

Acknowledgments

I am grateful to the reviewers of the manuscript for *Educational Psychology*: Juliet Baxter, Oregon State University; Lester A. Beckland, San Diego State University; and Michael S. Meloth, University of Colorado, Boulder. I would particularly like to acknowledge my good friend and colleague, Harold J. Fletcher, who shared with me some of his innovative approaches to teaching this course; my first editor, Julia Berrisford, who got me going on this project; my second editor, Cate DaPron, who helped me finish it; and my wife, Darby, whose continual encouragement helped fuel the fire that a task like this requires. I would also like to thank all those young women and men who pass through our halls and our educational psychology classrooms en route to teaching the children of the next generation.

Bruce W. Tuckman

About the author

Bruce W. Tuckman is Professor of Educational Psychology and former Dean of the College of Education at Florida State University in Tallahassee, Florida. His books include **Conducting Educational Research** (three editions), **Testing for Teachers** (two editions), and **Evaluating Instructional Programs** (two editions). He has researched and published extensively in the areas of student motivation, instructional design, group processes, test construction, and exercise and health. When not researching, writing, and teaching educational psychology to undergraduate and graduate students, he race-walks, swims, and watches baseball for fun.

Contents

Part Two

🍎

Development, Interaction, and Motivation   167

Part Three

🍎

Testing and Evaluation   331

Chapter
1

The Study of Educational Psychology

Objectives

1. Identify practical and intellectual reasons for studying human behavior.
2. Identify and distinguish between the characteristics of facts, principles and theories.
3. Identify the relationships between facts, principles, theories and hypotheses.
4. Define deduction and induction.
5. Describe experimental research methodology.
6. Describe observational research and contrast it to experimental research.
7. Describe the role of models in formulating plans of action.
8. Identify the different target areas of principles, theories, and models covered in this book.

Why Study Human Behavior?

Human behavior is not random. It follows patterns and in many cases is predictable. When someone is yelled at, he or she will often yell back, and may feel hurt or hold a grudge. When an idea is explained well to someone, he or she will understand it. When a child cries, someone who cares for that child will often console him or her. When hungry people are offered food, they will eat it.

Some of these regularities in behavior are known to most people based simply on their experiences. As children grow up, they naturally learn these things. However, some of these regularities are not necessarily noticed, because (1) they are subtle, (2) it is hard to behave and analyze what is going on at the same time, or (3) most people have not learned to attend to behavior and its causes. Also, many of the factors that help explain behavior go on inside people, based on experiences they have already had, rather than outside where they can be observed at that moment. Often, what is observed is not necessarily an accurate reflection of what is going on inside a person. Many people smile even though they are sad, or laugh even when they do not find something funny.

While much behavior has patterns and explanations and relationships to other behavior, both within people and between them, you may not always be aware of all the behavior that is going on. People are sometimes naive about their own feelings and motives, to say nothing of the feelings and motives of others. And since some feelings and motives are covert or hidden inside, you may not know how your behavior affects other people, even after you perform it.

As a result of this lack of knowledge or awareness, this naivete, people may affect other people in ways different from those intended, and may fail to affect them in ways they want to. A teacher may hurt students' feelings when he or she really wants to make them feel better, or may fail to help students understand something even though he or she is trying hard to convey the information necessary to make them understand.

This is the *practical* side of knowing educational psychology, the science of human behavior applied to teaching and learning. Such knowledge can help make people more aware of their thoughts and actions and the effects of these on themselves and others. It can also help make teachers more effective. Teachers have to help people, usually young people, learn and understand ideas at the same time that they help them feel good about themselves and about the experience of learning. Teachers have to motivate students to want to learn; they have to communicate with students or create the necessary experiences so that students can learn. Teachers have to do all this in ways that make students' attitudes or feelings about learning and their own capabilities as learners positive. To do so requires knowledge and awareness on the part of teachers, that knowledge and awareness being the product of studying human behavior and knowing what to do (and not do), what to look for and where to look.

There is also an *intellectual* side to knowing educational psychology, as there is to knowing anything. Such knowledge expands a person's own capabilities for thinking and for knowing. It enhances mental discipline and problem-solving skills. In a very real sense it makes people smarter.

Limitations of the School Setting

It is important to realize that the relationship between knowledge of educational psychology and either practical or intellectual skills is not one-to-one. The study of educational psychology will not provide recipes for being either a scholar or a successful teacher. A teacher operates within very real restrictions. Groups of students to be taught are organized into *classes*, often of relatively large size, and teaching and learning are often confined to *classrooms*. What is to be taught is usually prespecified in the form of a *curriculum* or a *course* of study, and the amount of time during which teaching and learning can take place is further delimited by the *clock* to distinct class periods and by the *calendar* to days, weeks, semesters, and school years.

Given all these restraints, even if there were a formula for successful teaching, it would be hard to follow. Imagine if educational psychology taught that people learned better when there was a practical problem to solve rather than when learning was being done either for its own sake or for the purpose of passing a course or getting a degree. If that were true, it might be hard for a teacher to apply educational psychology when the course was one like history or algebra, with a seeming lack of practicality. A history teacher or a math teacher would still have to teach the concepts of these courses, even if they were inherently hard to teach. But knowledge of educational psychology may yield some insight into how to go about teaching these difficult concepts.

Similarly, a teacher may learn from educational psychology that she can best teach her material by allowing the students to experiment with it directly and discover what it is about. However, that teacher may be teaching a class of 35 students in a lecture room for one hour a day, and the material in question may constitute only a small part of the curriculum for that course. Under these conditions, a hands-on discovery approach to teaching may be highly impractical. Yet, knowing what she knows, the teacher may still

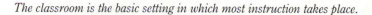
The classroom is the basic setting in which most instruction takes place.

elect to slant her approach to make great use of question-asking in preference to straight lecturing, thus putting her knowledge of educational psychology to some use.

Educational psychology is not studied to discover the formulas or recipes for success, because such formulas or recipes do not exist, and even if they did, they would be hard to apply in the real world. Educational psychology is studied to learn principles and theories of human behavior, because these principles and theories may help teachers determine the best way for them to behave in different situations or may help them figure out how to determine what the best way is.

School Learning Versus Real-World Learning

There is also a difference between the way learning typically takes place in school and the way it occurs in the "real world." Resnick (1987) has pointed out that school learning focuses on *individual performance* because students are evaluated as individuals and most often learn by themselves. Real-world learning, by comparison, focuses on *socially shared performance* because people work in teams and contribute to only a portion of the final outcome. Knowing about educational psychology research on the advantage of having students work in groups (see Chapter 10) should help teachers include opportunities for socially shared performance in their teaching approach.

In school, children are grouped by age, but in the "real world," younger children often learn from older ones.

Resnick (1987) also suggests that school learning typically fosters *unaided thought*, or thought done entirely in the head, while real-world learning involves *the use of cognitive tools* such as books or calculators. Moreover, schools primarily attempt to cultivate *symbolic thinking*, while in the real world people engage directly with *objects and situations*. In other words, school problems are more abstract — that is, students try to solve them because teachers pose them — while in the real world people solve problems because they must be solved to accomplish some purpose. In the real world, people work with the problem itself, rather than with a representation of it as in school. However, recent advances in teaching problem-solving skills (described in Chapter 7) provide students with a more tool-based, concrete, real-world view of problems and their potential solutions.

Resnick (1987) also sees school learning as focusing on *general skills and knowledge* in contrast to the *situation-specific competencies* of the real world. Horticulturalists, for example, the people who grow flowers, would need to know a lot about which plants grow best under which conditions, but would not necessarily need a great knowledge of general biology. Yet the general biology teacher can apply some of the techniques of expert systems (described in Chapter 7) to the teaching of many aspects of biology.

Again, educational psychology can provide some broad strategies or approaches for the classroom teacher to take within the limits of the nature of school learning. What the teacher will find most difficult to both remember and use are specific facts or details about learning and school performance, because they may be hard to fit into the classroom situation. What is needed are broader and more flexible representations of psychological processes that apply to the educational setting.

Why Principles and Theories?

There are *facts* that are discrete pieces of knowledge and information — say, that expecting to be in a stressful situation makes a person anxious. Then there are *principles* that expand upon facts or connect them to other facts — say, that anxiety, a general feeling of apprehension, can be provoked in a person if he or she is led to expect an unpleasant situation, or that when someone is experiencing anxiety, being with others who share the same expectation is preferable to being alone (perhaps an elegant way of saying "Misery loves company"). The principle is more general and more inclusive than the fact by virtue of including many facts, and so there will be fewer principles than there are facts. Consequently, it will be easier to remember principles and easier to adapt them to a variety of situations. Encyclopedias are collections of facts; but while they are excellent reference sources, their contents are seldom read from cover to cover or easily remembered.

Theories are collections of principles (which are based on facts) and are even more general and more inclusive than principles. They are what may be called *comprehensive* because their scope and range are inclusive enough to enable people to use them to better understand the world around them.

A theory that says that people use other people to help them judge and understand their own capabilities and feelings (called social comparison theory by Festinger, 1954) would help teachers comprehend the relationship between perceived stress and the desire to be with others. By watching the reactions of others and sharing their feelings with them, students in a stressful situation can determine either that there is nothing to worry about or that it is all right to be worried (Schachter, 1959). Teachers might then be inclined to use a group approach when the assigned task is likely to prove anxiety-provoking (such as making a class presentation or preparing for a test) so that students would have ready access to others for comparison purposes. Teachers might also be less inclined to ask John why he could not do his work as well as Joan did if they knew the power and importance of social comparison to John's sense of well-being.

Sometimes there is a tendency to hear the word *theory* and think "useless" or "abstract" or "irrelevant" because it is part of the word *theoretical*. But *theoretical* means speculative, that is, explanatory of why a particular fact or set of facts occurs. In other words, theories are not only comprehensive, they are also *speculative*. They attempt to explain the why of something, not merely to note its existence. Students sometimes get anxious; that is a fact. They often get anxious when they expect something they do not like (like a test); that is another fact. When students get anxious, many of them like company; third fact. Why do people like company when they get anxious? *Perhaps* because they can see then whether it is okay to be anxious — they can use social comparison. This last statement is not a fact. It is an attempt at an explanation. It is speculative. It is theoretical.

But is this theoretical explanation useless and irrelevant? The answer is NO if it helps teachers know how to handle stress situations that arise in their classes. If the theory can be translated into action, then it becomes practical. What is also practical is that there will be many fewer theories than facts, because theories both subsume or include facts as well as explain them. Facts fill encyclopedias while theories only fill books. Through an understanding of a small number of theories, most of the behavior that goes on in classrooms (and probably in life as well) can be explained.

Hence, the focus on theories has three bases. The first is that theories are comprehensive or inclusive and so each one can subsume or include a lot of facts. The second is that because they are so broad-based, only a small number of theories need to be learned. The third is that theories are speculative or explanatory and so can be used to explain, in a wide variety of situations, what will happen, why it will happen, and how to be able to deal with it when it does happen. Learning about theories, therefore, helps learners organize information better and use it more easily than simply learning a collection of facts.

The relationship between facts, principles, and theories is illustrated in Table 1.1.

Table 1.1 🍎 What We Know: Facts, Principles, and Theories

Facts	Principles	Theories
Based on observation	Based on inference	Based on speculation (about facts)
Discrete, specific and numerous	Fewer in number than facts	Comprehensive and fewest in number
Elemental and unitary	Made up of connected facts	Made up of connected principles
Actual behavior that can be seen	Help relate behaviors to one another	Help explain behavior

How Do We Know if a Theory Is Accurate?

Since theories are based on facts, we can test them by gathering facts that relate to them. On the basis of theories, *hypotheses* or predictions are made about what is expected to happen or what facts are expected to be observed in a given situation. We can then test these hypotheses by making the necessary observations (that is, by collecting the necessary facts). The pattern looks like this:

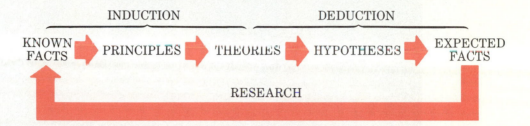

When specific facts are used to think up more general theories that explain those facts, that process is called induction. Taking a variety of facts about how people are observed to behave in anxiety-provoking situations and then thinking up the explanation that their behavior is based on social comparison is an example of induction.

When general theories are used to think up specific facts that will help test those theories, that process is called deduction. Using social comparison theory to think up the hypothesis that people will choose to be with other people who are similar to them rather than dissimilar ("Birds of a feather flock together") is an example of deduction. We induce theories from facts, and then we deduce what new facts are needed to test their accuracy.

The process used to test whether the facts that theories tell us to expect are actually true is research. Doing research means making observations or collecting data (in contrast to induction and deduction, which are modes of thinking). The purpose of this research is to test the hypotheses or hunches about what will happen in a given situation based on the explanatory power of a theory. Supportive evidence collected by research helps validate the theory being tested.

Schachter (1959), for example, tested the hypothesis, deduced from social comparison theory, that people who anticipated being stressed (from electric shock) would choose to be with others rather than be alone because they would then be able to see that being anxious was a commonly shared, and therefore appropriate, feeling. When Schachter created this situation and collected the facts, he discovered that his speculation or hypothesis was correct.

The approach used to test a theory is called a paradigm. A paradigm is a design or framework that can be used repeatedly for testing the relationships within a set of variables or factors that affect behavior. In subsequent chapters some specific research paradigms will be presented. Here the two general ones, experimental research and observational research, will be described.

Teachers are not expected to be researchers in the specific sense of the term, but they are expected to interpret and apply some of the research that they learn about in courses such as educational psychology. In evaluating some bit of knowledge, it is helpful

Theories tell us that people often choose to be with others to whom they are similar.

for teachers to know how it was discovered and if it is likely to apply under the circumstances in which they may use it. Teachers are also likely to draw their own conclusions about students as well as about the circumstances of their behavior, and so it is important that they realize what factors affect the validity of these conclusions.

Making Judgments.   Two factors that affect the accuracy of judgments are called internal and external validity, or *certainty* and *generality* (Tuckman, 1988b). *Certainty* refers to the confidence one holds in the conclusion that the teacher's or researcher's action, rather than some other variable, has caused the student to behave or perform differently. How certain can you be that variable A has caused the observed change in variable B? To conclude that variable A is indeed the cause of the change in variable B when in fact a third factor, variable C, is the true cause is to make a false judgment. It is important to try to maximize certainty in order to decrease the chances of a false judgment.

Consider a new program for teaching reading that a teacher is trying for the first time. If the students taught by this program perform better on a subsequent reading test than last year's students did on the same test after being taught by the old program, can the teacher conclude with certainty that the new program works? Perhaps not! Perhaps this year's students were brighter or more motivated than last year's. Perhaps the teacher was more enthusiastic about the new program than the old and devoted more effort to teaching it. Perhaps the teacher expected it to work better (see Box 1.1). The new program may indeed work better than the old one, but it is difficult to be certain about that conclusion under the given circumstances.

Box 1.1

Expectations Can Affect Outcomes

Rosenthal and Fode (1963) told half of their student experimenters that the rats they were to study had been selectively bred to be bright. The other half were told that their rats were dull. In fact, the two groups of rats were identical. Each student experimenter was instructed to train his or her rats, bright or dull, to run through a maze as fast as they could to get a bit of food. The timing device on the maze was completely automatic. It went on automatically when the rat left the start box and went off automatically when the rat entered the goal box; there was no way to artificially influence the timing. Nevertheless, the "smart" rats ended up outperforming the "dull" ones. And the "smart" ones were liked more by their student experimenters. Get the picture? Somehow the experimenters must have treated the "smart" rats better.

Rosenthal and Jacobson (1968) then tried the same thing with schoolchildren. They circulated to teachers a list of names of students who were expected to "bloom" that year based on results of an IQ test. In fact, the children on the list were no different from their classmates. However, teachers must have believed they were and changed their expectations, because those children gained more in IQ over the course of the year than their classmates did. As the children on the list improved, their teachers reported them to be more interesting and better adjusted. When other children improved—those who were not expected to (their names were not on the list)—they still were seen by their teachers as being less interesting and less well-adjusted. Something that is expected to happen is indeed more likely to happen than something that is not expected to happen. This is called the self-fulfilling prophecy.

In addition to wanting to be certain about conclusions, we also want to be able to have them apply again, under other circumstances—that is, to have *generality*. If a teacher concludes that the new reading program works better than the old one, should other teachers try it? Can they conclude that it is likely to work for them too? What if they are not as enthusiastic as the original teacher was, or what if their students are not as bright or as motivated? Is it accurate to say that the judgment of program superiority can be made again? If not, then there is no point in training teachers to use the new program or in having them use it to teach to other students.

Educational psychology, as has already been said, focuses on attempting to discover and transmit knowledge about student behavior and performance. That means transmitting information about the factors that affect student behavior and performance for which there is a high degree of certainty and generality. To understand if the findings on which educational psychology theories are based have adequate certainty and generality, it is useful to examine the manner in which these findings are determined.

Doing Experiments.   One way to do research or test a hypothesis is to do an experiment. In an experiment, the impact or effect of one variable or factor on another variable or factor is studied. For example, say that the following hypothesis is to be tested: When they are anxious, in contrast to when they are not anxious, people are more likely to choose to be with other people than to be alone. The two *variables* or factors to be related here are (1) presence or absence of anxiety and (2) whether people choose to be alone or with others (called affiliation). A researcher could wait around until some people got anxious and observe whether they chose to be alone or with others, but that may happen very infrequently or under varied conditions that would affect the certainty and generality of the conclusions.

In an experiment the researcher attempts to maximize certainty by controlling what people experience. The researcher does not wait for the causative or *independent* variable to occur naturally or under its own initiative. Instead, the researcher makes the independent variable happen by imposing (by manipulation) a *treatment* or *intervention*. For example, in the anxiety–affiliation example above, the researcher imposes a manipulation or treatment intended to create anxiety, such as telling students that they are going to take a test.

If the manipulation or treatment is applied to *all* of the students and it makes *all* of them anxious, and then they all choose to be with other people, the researcher will not know whether the result of choosing to be with others might also have happened if no one were made anxious. To be certain about whether induced anxiety caused the outcome or *dependent variable* of choosing to be with others rather than alone, the researcher must cause anxiety for only some of the students rather than for all of them. In this way the two groups can be compared to see whether the manipulation or treatment has actually caused a change in the outcome. In the previous example of the new reading program, not all of the students should be given the new program. Some should be given the old one so that the two groups can be compared. The structure of an experiment is shown in Figure 1.1.

Figure 1.1 🍎 The Structure of an Experiment

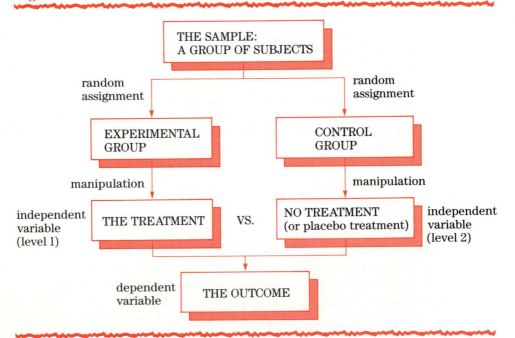

In addition, insofar as possible, everything must be exactly the same for and about both groups — the one that receives the treatment and the one that does not. If any aspect of the experience other than the presence or absence of the treatment differed between groups, the researcher would not know which aspect had caused the difference in the outcome. Additional possible causes would then "confound" the relationship between the independent and dependent variables and reduce certainty.

In determining which students should be given the treatment and which ones should not, the researcher should pick the names out of a hat, to ensure that one group is not smarter or more motivated than the other. Random assignment is important because it increases the likelihood that one group will not be different from the other to begin with. If students are permitted to pick their own groups, then the groups might not start out on an equal footing.

Let us return to the reading program example. Comparing two classes, one that uses the new program and one that uses the old one, would not result in an accurate or certain conclusion if the students in one class were brighter or already had better reading skills than the students in the other class. In that case, one program might appear to be more effective than the other, but only because the students who used it were more capable; those students would probably do well regardless of which reading program were used. It would be better to have originally assigned students to the two classes on a random basis so that they would be likely to be the same, or to assign the new program to half of the students in each class, chosen by chance, with the remaining halves using the old program. In that way, any differences in outcome would be more certainly a function of program differences than of student differences.

It is also important, especially for generality, that students not be aware that anything special or out of the ordinary is being done when a treatment is being tried. That lack of awareness is called being *blind* to the treatment. When people realize that they are being given special treatment, they often respond differently than they ordinarily would. The teacher using the new reading program in the above example would be advised to avoid having the students respond to their treatment as being new or special.

One way to make the experimental and control group experiences equivalent in all respects other than the presence or absence of the treatment is to give the control group a treatment, too, but one that is unrelated to the desired outcome. This could be called a *placebo* treatment. The original placebo was a salt tablet that was given to patients in drug evaluation studies to find out if the mere fact of getting medication, rather than the nature of the medication itself, was resulting in any change in symptoms. When patients got better from the placebo pill, researchers saw that it was not what was in the pill that mattered. In the example of the study of the effect of the new reading program on test performance, the placebo treatment would be the old reading program.

Another example of a placebo treatment might be a study to determine the effect of computers on learning. Students whose performance was to be compared to that of students who learned on computers were given a book or magazine to read or a game to play rather than having nothing at all to do. If the computers had not mattered, both groups would have performed equally well on the test at the end.

It is useful not only to keep the persons who are and are not receiving the treatment in the blind, but to keep the persons who are administering the treatment in the blind as well. This is called the *double-blind* technique. The teacher or teachers who are providing the real treatment and the placebo treatment should not be told which one is which, so that they cannot thereby unduly influence the behavior of the students. Often, unfortunately, this is impossible to do, but without it the generality of a finding may be seriously questioned. For an illustration of the powerful effect of potential experimenter or teacher influence on the outcome of an experiment, see Box 1.1.

The five requirements of experimental research are shown in Table 1.2. Meeting these requirements gives the researcher sufficient *control* over the potential variables in a study to be able to conclude with a reasonable degree of certainty that the outcome of the experiment was probably caused by the treatment (Tuckman, 1988b).

Let us illustrate this again with another example. Suppose the hypothesis to be tested is that the more time students spend studying, the more they learn. The researcher might manipulate the study time by creating a two-hour study hall treatment before an exam for one group of students and showing a two-hour movie before the exam for a second group of students. The movie is a placebo. It also helps increase the likelihood that the second group does not have time to study. Everything else is to be held constant across both groups. For example, students are assigned randomly to either the study hall or the movie group. Students in both groups then take the same exam at the same time. Finally, neither students nor teachers should know which of the two experiences is the treatment and which is the placebo control. Insofar as possible, neither group should even know about the experience the other group is having.

Table 1.2 🍎 The Five Requirements of Experimental Research

Requirement	Elaboration
1. Make the independent variable happen by manipulation.	Do not just wait around for it to occur. Create the treatment that you want.
2. Include a control group.	Compare the treatment group to a group that receives no treatment, or include a placebo treatment, to see whether the outcome might have occurred even without the treatment.
3. Except for the treatment itself, handle experimental and control groups the same.	Do not allow any other variable to vary between groups, because then it, rather than the treatment, may be what accounts for any difference that might occur.
4. Assign subjects randomly to experimental and control groups.	Do not assign already-existing groups and do not allow subjects to choose their own group, because then the two groups may not be the same to start with. Pick names out of a hat. Then any differences at the end cannot be attributed to initial differences because there will not have been any.
5. Keep subjects unaware of what group they are in and teachers unaware of what group they are teaching.	Use the double-blind technique as a safeguard to ensure that any differences between groups are real and not the result of the research being perceived as "only an experiment."

Observational Research.   While the formal tests of our theories may come in the form of experiments, the foundations on which theories are built are often based on less formal, observational research. Merely observing behavior in various naturally occurring situations is less precise and more subjective than doing controlled experiments, but it is accomplished more easily. If such observations can be made without altering the behavior being observed, then the researcher can be confident that the behavior is real and not being staged for his or her benefit (or detriment). Unlike experimental research, where subjects may behave differently because they know they are in an experiment (see Box 1.1, for example), observational research provokes no such effect if the researcher is unobtrusive enough. Thus, observational research is less intrusive but also more subjective than experimental research.

Consider the observational work of Smith and Geoffrey (1968) in an inner-city school where Geoffrey was a teacher. Smith spent every day of the whole school year sitting in Geoffrey's classroom observing what went on. Their purpose was to develop a model of the classroom and to learn more about how a middle-class teacher would cope with a group of lower-class children. They tested a number of hypotheses, such as

> As amount of personalized interaction increases, then both pupil satisfaction and esteem for teacher increase; and as pupil satisfaction and esteem for teacher increase, then classroom control increases. (Smith & Geoffrey, 1968, p. 19)

Both men kept detailed field notes, one as a participant and the other as a nonparticipant. They then compared and combined their notes to produce their research results.

Their analysis of the field notes (Smith & Geoffrey, 1968, p. 15) consisted of (1) reading them through, looking for "insightful" comments; (2) abstracting the incident that precipitated the comment and elaborating on its significance; (3) showing the teacher, Mr. Geoffrey, the report of the incident and asking him to explain it and to react to the elaboration; (4) rereading one another's comments and generating new interpretations; (5) including occasional insignificant incidents "to keep the other honest."

They discovered teaching techniques like the following to produce pupil enthusiasm and the joy of knowing: (1) teach a lesson that has content *low enough in difficulty* for all students to understand, but at the same time make sure that the content is both *clear* and *important*; (2) to teach the lesson, use a *variety* of activities that include *pupils actually doing things* that will provoke their *interest* and that have a *gamelike quality*; (3) keep the *frequency of teacher interaction* with pupils *high* and include *banter* (personal, humorous conversation or byplay).

In a lesson dealing with making compound words out of simple ones (one of the simple ones being *girl*), Smith and Geoffrey (1968) recorded the following incident:

> Geoffrey sends Elma to the board to call on people and write down their answers. She's highly embarrassed about calling on people at first but Elma soon finds this is fun and calls on them by pointing. There is much humor as they call out particulars. Joe K. suggests "Tom girl." This brings down the house. They list some more. Billy suggests "sexy girl" and Elma with big chuckle writes it on the board. Geoffrey finally says "enough of that nonsense" and has Elma erase it — along with the rest. (p. 196)

Formulating Models

After researchers have tested principles and theories, by testing hypotheses deduced from them, and the principles and theories have been found to have some degree of accuracy, the next step is to try to apply them to practice. For this, the principles and theories need to be translated into a framework that will help teachers determine how to change classroom behavior in desirable ways. *These practical frameworks are called models*, and they are used for designing experiences, materials, and programs to use in educational settings.

Let us now see how a model might be developed for the earlier example of social comparison theory (page 9). Remember, *social comparison theory* says that people use other people's behavior and performance as a way of judging their own (Festinger, 1954). Based on social comparison theory, a model might be derived that says that if you want people to be attracted to other people, the way to do it is to create a state of uncertainty. This could be called the *uncertainty–attraction model* (Jones & Gerard, 1967). Teachers could use it to motivate students to work in groups by creating a situation in which every student has some of the information necessary to complete a task but is also missing some. Some of the information that one student is missing would be in the possession of another student. Since no student has all the information, each will experience a degree of uncertainty, being unsure if he or she can complete the task alone. This uncertainty, however, will — according to the model — cause students to be attracted to one another, hence to work in groups. The model, therefore, can be translated into a specific plan of action.

Different Target Areas of Principles, Theories, and Models Covered in This Book

In this book a number of theories and explanatory principles, and models based on them, will be covered — all different in what they try to explain and how they try to explain it. They vary in how they try to explain something because there are always different ways to explain an outcome or a phenomenon, depending on your point of view. They vary in what they try to explain because no theory, and especially no single principle, is likely to apply equally well to all aspects of behavior nor is any one model likely to be universally useful. Some fit certain aspects of behavior better than others. As each of the following aspects of behavior relevant to teaching is covered, the theories and explanatory principles that help make that aspect of behavior understandable and the models that help make it most manageable will be explored.

Classroom Management and Control.   Getting students to learn to behave properly is a major task for teachers. In fact, according to some surveys, this is the single most important task they face. To provide teachers with a mechanism for teaching students how to control their behavior, reinforcement theory and its applied model, behavior modification, will be examined. The initial focus will be on understanding the principles of behavioral control, followed by a consideration of how to apply them in a classroom.

Planning and the Design of Instruction.   Once the students have learned to behave themselves, the teacher can turn to the lesson. That lesson should be planned and designed in advance to be maximally effective. Instructional design theories provide a basis for understanding how people learn in relation to how they can be most effectively instructed. A nine-phase instructional design theory helps provide a context for some models for guiding both the planning and the design and sequencing of instructional materials.

Learning, Teaching, and Studying.   Since the purpose of teaching is to produce learning, it would be most advantageous to teach in a way that is based on and consistent with the way students learn. In other words, a theory of teaching should really be a theory of learning, and teaching models should really be learning models. A cognitive approach to learning is presented that focuses on the mental encoding and storage processes that go on during rote learning and those that go on during the learning of meaningful material. The metacognitive principles of learning that are presented form the basis not only for a model of teaching but also for a model of studying (or study skills), since studying represents, in essence, the process of teaching oneself.

Thinking and Problem-Solving.   Beyond learning are thinking and problem-solving, higher cognitive processes that teachers would hope to stimulate and enhance. To teach thinking and problem-solving requires that teachers understand the factors or principles by which these mental processes operate. Higher mental processes, called metacognitive processes, are used to teach students to learn, think, and problem-solve. Principles and models that describe these processes will be examined.

Development.   Since schooling is a developmental process, teachers must understand the changes that take place in people over time as they advance from infancy through childhood and adolescence. What to expect at the different ages and stages and how to facilitate growth as these ages and stages occur must be principal concerns of teachers. Development will be viewed as an adaptation process, and a theory for understanding the capabilities and characteristics of youngsters as they adapt over the years from nursery school through college will be presented.

Social Interaction.   Students are not educated in isolation; they are educated as members of groups. Understanding how people react to one another and how they behave in groups provides a basis for using models of group-centered instruction and fostering cooperative learning. Some principles of interaction and their application to the social events and opportunities encountered by teachers will be presented.

Motivation.   To perform a task successfully requires two things. One is to have the necessary skills or capabilities. The second is to have the desire or motivation, the wish or inclination, to succeed. Much teaching time is spent trying to motivate students. Moreover, almost all interactions between teachers and students, and a majority of experiences students have in school, have an impact on motivation. A number of theories are presented, including one based on self-beliefs and another on perceptions of why things turn out as they do, to explain the whys and wherefores of motivation. Each provides models of how teachers can try to motivate their students.

Individual Differences.   How are students different and how do we tend to differentiate between them? Relatively stable characteristics such as intelligence, aptitude, race, and social class will be covered, as well as a wide range of acquired skills, achievements, and attitudes. This information forms a basis for understanding how differences occur, how they are detected, and how they are to be dealt with.

Assessment.   Teachers must judge student achievement and behavior. To do so they often use tests, the construction of which is, for many, beyond their training and comprehension. Carter (1984) found that teachers spent little time editing or revising their tests, in part because they felt insecure about the strength of their background in testing. In this book, the treatment of assessment will be threefold. The first topic will be how to construct tests, both multiple-choice questions and essay questions, to measure knowledge, comprehension, and the higher cognitive processes. The second topic will be how to evaluate and improve tests in terms of both what they measure and how accurately they measure it. The third topic will be how to interpret test results, on both an absolute and a relative basis, in order to assign grades or make diagnostic or instructional decisions or recommendations.

Summary of Main Points

1. Human behavior follows patterns, many of which are subtle or otherwise escape our notice because people are too busy behaving to also be observers. Moreover, what goes on inside people does not necessarily show on the outside. By not being aware of behavioral patterns, teachers may affect people, particularly children, in ways other than those intended.

2. Studying educational psychology can help increase our awareness of how certain behaviors affect other people. This is a practical reason for such study. There is also an intellectual reason—namely, to expand our knowledge and awareness of the world around us.

3. Studying educational psychology, however, will not provide a formula for success in teaching. Teachers are restricted because schools and the educational process are structured into classes and classrooms, curriculums and courses of study, and are regulated by the clock and the calendar. Hence, teachers cannot control all aspects of their environment.

4. Moreover, school learning and real-world learning tend to be different in a number of ways. Even if formulas for success existed, and they do not, teachers would not necessarily be able to convert them into the appropriate action at the appropriate time.

5. In this book, the approach is to focus on principles and theories rather than on a much larger number of discrete facts. Principles are more general than the connected facts that make them up, and theories, by combining principles, are more comprehensive yet.

6. Theories have the additional feature of being speculative: They attempt to explain the why of something, not merely to note its existence. Theories help both to organize information and to apply it in a variety of situations (unlike facts, which simply represent information itself).

7. In order to determine whether theories are accurate, we can deduce hypotheses or predictions from them and then test these by doing research. The models used to do research or collect data are called paradigms.

8. One of these paradigms is the experimental method. In this method, a group that receives a particular treatment, the experimental group, is compared to a group that

does not, the control group. Using a control group helps establish the certainty of the experiment, that is, whether the outcome would have occurred even without the treatment.

9. Beyond that, experimental and control groups should be treated the same. Students should be assigned to the two groups on a random basis, to increase the certainty that they are the same to begin with.

10. It is important to keep subjects unaware of, or blind to, which group they are in, to increase the generality or applicability of a study. Students in the control group should be given an alternative treatment, called a placebo, that cannot affect the outcome other than by indirectly making the subjects expect or believe that it will make them change. It is also a good idea to keep the persons in charge of delivering the treatment and the placebo unaware of, or blind to, which one is which. This is called the double-blind technique.

11. An alternative paradigm that is less conclusive but also is less intrusive and less likely to artificially influence the phenomenon being studied (and, hence, yields more generality) is observational research. In observational research, researchers observe and keep records of naturally occurring behavior in a real setting. The theories presented in this book have been subjected to both types of research.

12. Not only are theories tested, but they are also used as a basis for formulating models, practical frameworks that help practitioners such as teachers see what to do in different situations. This book will include such models, where they exist, to help teachers translate comprehensive theories into practice.

13. This book will cover the following target areas: (1) classroom management and control; (2) planning and design of instruction; (3) learning, teaching, and studying; (4) thinking and problem-solving; (5) development; (6) social interaction; (7) motivation; (8) individual differences; and (9) assessment, or testing.

Suggested Resources

Edmonds, R. R. (1986). Characteristics of effective schools. In U. Neiser (Ed.), *The school achievement of minority children*. Hillsdale, NJ: Lawrence Erlbaum.

Good, T. L., & Brophy, J. E. (1988). *Looking in classrooms* (4th ed.). New York: Longman.

Good, T. L., Biddle, B. J., & Brophy, J. E. (1975). *Teachers make a difference*. New York: Holt, Rinehart & Winston.

Goodlad, J. I. (1984). *A place called school*. New York: McGraw-Hill.

Marx, R. W., & Walsh, J. (1988, January). Learning from academic tasks. *Elementary School Journal*, 207–219.

Pyke, S. W., & Agnew, N. M. (1991). *The science game: An introduction to research in the social sciences* (5th ed.). Englewood Cliffs, NJ: Prentice-Hall.

Tuckman, B. W. (1988). *Conducting educational research* (3rd ed.). San Diego: Harcourt Brace Jovanovich.

Part One

Learning
and
Instruction

Chapter 2

Early Behavioral and Cognitive Approaches

Objectives

1. Identify fundamental differences between behavioral and cognitive approaches to learning and behavior.
2. Describe Pavlov's classical conditioning paradigm including unconditioned and conditioned stimuli, unconditioned and conditioned responses, and their interrelationships.
3. Describe other conditioning phenomena, including extinction, secondary conditioning, inhibition, generalization, and discrimination.
4. Describe and illustrate Thorndike's connection learning model based on the law of effect.
5. Describe the general Gestalt explanation for learning and behavior based on the whole configuration.
6. Describe Köhler's experiments with chimpanzees, including solving problems that involve detours and implements.
7. Describe the characteristics and features of insightful problem-solving and the basis for its discovery by Köhler.

Behaviorism and Cognitivism

The basis for learning and behavior has been debated for some time. In general, there are two points of view.

The first one focuses on the connection between specific behaviors (called responses), the situations in which these behaviors occur (called stimuli), and the consequences that follow these behaviors. This point of view is the *behavioral* one, since in it discrete behaviors and patterns of behavior are examined and explained in terms of connections to situations and consequences. By changing the situation and the consequence, we can, according to the behavioral approach, change the behavior or response that has been connected or conditioned to occur under those circumstances.

Those who pursue the behavioral approach, called *behaviorists*, focus only on what has happened, what is happening (that is, the behavior), the circumstances under which it is happening, and what will happen next. By controlling the circumstances, behaviorists control behavior. They have little interest in what goes on in between, inside the head of the person whose behavior is being controlled.

Contrast this with the *cognitive* approach to learning, in which the emphasis is primarily on what goes on inside the learner's head. *Cognitivists* view the learner's active part of the process not as just responding to circumstances but as organizing and reorganizing incoming information in ways that have come to be called thinking and problem-solving. In the cognitive approach, learning involves using mental structures to process information, often with a unique or insightful result.

Thus, we have two fundamentally different views of learning. For the behaviorist, learners must be taught connections and contingencies. In other words, learners will learn to perform a certain behavior under particular conditions because of the consequences of that behavior or the connections that have been established between conditions and behavior. Control of learning is ultimately external to the learner, and the results of exercising this control are quite predictable. Why the behavior occurs is not necessarily understood at this time, but the behaviorists are satisfied with the regularity of the outcome. They believe that eventually the causes of learning will be discovered at the physiological level.

The cognitivists, on the other hand, venture into the mind of the learner to try to puzzle out how he or she transforms information, stores it in memory, and retrieves it to solve a problem or recall a fact. While the cognitivist poses questions that are harder to answer than those of the behaviorist, the answers may reveal more about how complex materials are learned.

The issue here, however, is not who has the right answer to the question of how people learn or what determines their behavior. Depending on what you are trying to teach, and to whom, one approach may work better than the other. Change the purpose and the audience and you may have to change the approach as well. Our effort will focus on trying to understand both models and the ways that each may be used most productively. We will begin by looking at the modern beginnings of both approaches and end by contrasting them again.

Pavlov (center) in his laboratory with his assistants, his apparatus, and one of his dogs.

An Early Behavioral Model: Classical Conditioning

Ivan Pavlov was a Russian physiologist who experimented with dogs in order to try to understand how the nerve pathways in their brains worked. The behavior he chose to study was salivation as it occurred reflexively or automatically at the presentation of food. Let a dog see or smell food and it will salivate. The salivation reflex is not learned; it occurs automatically and provides the juices needed in the mouth to chew food.

Pavlov (1927) detached the salivary duct from the inside of a dog's mouth and fastened it to a point in the dog's cheek where a hole had been made. This caused any saliva that was secreted to flow not into the dog's mouth but through the hole in the cheek into a glass bulb that had been attached to the outside of the cheek. The bulb had calibrations on it so that the amount of saliva secreted could be measured. When food was presented to the dog, the dog salivated into the glass bulb. Pavlov called the food the *unconditioned stimulus* (UCS) and salivation the *unconditioned response* (UCR), since the connection between them was reflexive (that is, automatic or unlearned). The connection looked like this:

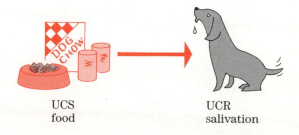

UCS
food

UCR
salivation

The Classical Conditioning Paradigm.   In this paradigm or model, Pavlov (1927) presented a sound (the gong of a bell or the click-click of a metronome) before presenting the food. After he did this a few times, the dog began to salivate at the sound, even before the food appeared. This pairing of sound and food caused the animal to become conditioned to, or establish a connection between, the sound stimulus and the salivation response. We call this approach to learning *classical conditioning*. (It is also referred to as Pavlovian or respondent conditioning.) The sound becomes the *conditioned stimulus* (CS) and the salivation to the sound becomes the *conditioned response* (CR). It looks like this (the diagrams are to be read from left to right):

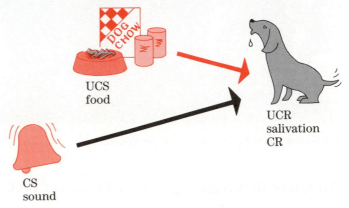

And eventually, after conditioning, the sound comes to elicit the salivation all by itself:

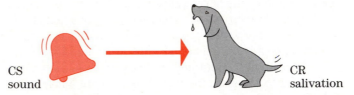

The picture of classical conditioning can be drawn a different way to represent the time sequence of the stimuli and responses. It would look like this:

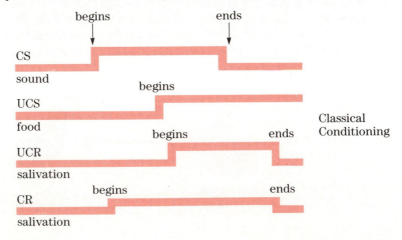

Classical Conditioning

The sound comes on before the food appears, continues until after the food appears, and then goes off. After classical conditioning has taken place — that is, after the sound and the food have been paired a number of times — salivation begins right after the sound begins and before the food appears. Thus, the sound is *eliciting* salivation or causing it to occur.

Another way to test whether conditioning has occurred is to present the sound without the food and see what happens. If the result is

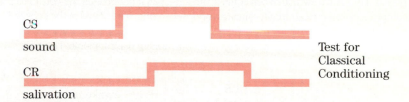

CS

sound   Test for

CR   Classical

salivation   Conditioning

then conditioning has occurred.

What, then, are the conditions or requirements for classical conditioning to take place? According to Pavlov (1927), there are four:

1. CS and UCS must overlap in time, with CS starting first;
2. the animal must be alert but not disturbed;
3. the animal must be healthy;
4. CS must not be so strong or unusual as to cause the animal to initially react to it by itself.

An example of human conditioning appears in Box 2.1.

Extinction. What happens if we condition an animal to salivate in response to the sound and then present the sound by itself (that is, without the food) continually thereafter? Initially, the animal will salivate as it has been conditioned to do (as shown in the above diagram of the test for classical conditioning). But eventually the animal will stop salivating when it hears the sound. This unlearning is called extinction, and the conditioned response is said to have been extinguished. Unconditioned responses can never be extinguished (food will always elicit salivation), but conditioned responses will disappear if the conditioned stimulus is presented by itself enough times. The number of trials it takes before extinction occurs depends upon the strength of the conditioning (which, in turn, is based on how many conditioning trials have occurred). The stronger the conditioning, the greater the resistance to extinction of the conditioned-stimulus–conditioned-response connection.

Secondary Conditioning. Pavlov (1927) discovered that a strongly established or well-learned connection between a conditioned stimulus and a conditioned response could be used to enable a different stimulus to be conditioned to that same response

Box 2.1

🍎

An Example of Human Conditioning

In 1938, O. H. Mowrer developed a conditioning procedure for the elimination of bed-wetting, based not on getting children to control themselves but on getting them to awaken in response to bladder tension. The child sleeps on a special, heavy cotton pad containing bronze screening that acts as a moisture switch. When liquid strikes the pad it penetrates the cotton to the screening and completes an electrical circuit, causing a doorbell to ring. The sound of the doorbell wakes the child, who then can go to the bathroom. After training, the child learns to awaken at the feeling of bladder tension — before the accident occurs. The conditioning diagram looks like this:

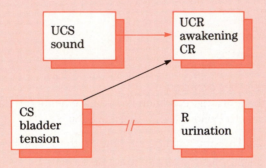

without the unconditioned stimulus ever being presented. He called this phenomenon secondary conditioning, and it looks like this:

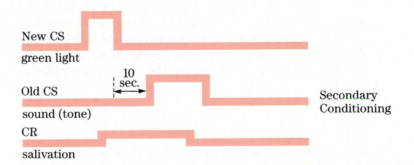

Suppose that the dog had already been conditioned to salivate at the tone. Now Pavlov preceded the tone with the appearance of a green light. The green light always came on before the tone, but the food was not used at all. Because the tone had been strongly conditioned to elicit salivation, it served in place of the food to establish a connection between the green light and salivation. By virtue of the new association of the light and the tone, the light also came to elicit salivation (as shown above). But Pavlov (1927) found that secondary conditioning would work only if there were a delay of 10 seconds between the time the new CS (the green light in the example) went off and the time the old CS (the tone) came on.

It would be similar to always clearing your throat before you clapped your hands to get your students' attention, or to the click that the school clock makes before it rings at the end of the class before lunch period. Because of secondary conditioning, your mouth may start watering for lunch immediately after you hear the click. Secondary conditioning frees us from a dependence upon the constant presence of the unconditioned stimulus (in this case, the smell of food).

Inhibition.   As a physiologist, Pavlov was primarily interested in the effect of learning on neural connections in the brain. What would happen, he wondered, if the new stimulus and the old CS were on at the same time? Would they block one another out in the dog's nervous system? Indeed, Pavlov (1927) found that overlapping the new CS and the old CS blocked or inhibited the old CS from eliciting the CR (although the old CS still elicited the CR when it was paired with the UCS). He called this learned interference *conditioned inhibition*, as shown below.

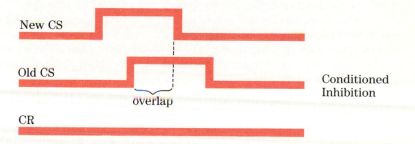

In the previous example, if the green light and the tone (or the throat-clearing and hand-clapping, or the clock clicking and the bell ringing) occurred at the same time, rather than the secondary stimulus occurring before the other came on, the result would not be salivation or attention or whatever the conditioned response was. The new stimulus would interfere with the old one rather than becoming connected to it.

Pavlov (1927) believed that the old CS–CR connection was blocked in the brain by the new, overlapping CS. He differentiated between conditioned inhibition based on neural blocking and what he called *external inhibition*, which was simply caused by a new stimulus of intensity sufficient to draw the animal's attention away from the old CS.

Generalization.   What if you vary the CS a little every time and pair each variation with the UCS (food)? In other words, change the tone of the sound or the number of clicks of the metronome on each trial but always pair it with food? The animal learns to generalize from one stimulus to another. That is, the animal learns that a lot of different sounds go with food. Even if you present a totally new variation of the CS sound on the test trial (the trial without the UCS), the dog will salivate if the CS has been varied in the training trials.

Box 2.2

🍎

The Substitute Teacher and Pavlov's Classical Conditioning

A new substitute teacher was asked to take over five science classes for a teacher who would be out for two and one-half months. After having accepted the position, the sub was told that, in all but one of her classes, the regular teacher herself could not control the students.

After enduring a first week of what might be called typical "test the sub" days, the substitute teacher was nearly ready to throw in the towel. She had tried praise, rejection, and all the other methods she could think of, when, much to her delight, she gained control of the classroom quite by accident.

On this particular day, the students' loud and unruly behavior caused the substitute teacher to become so enraged as to look for something to use as a gavel to demand order. The ruler on the counter seemed to fill the bill. While banging the ruler on the desk, she noticed that everyone came to attention and covered their ears. The students later asked her not to beat the ruler because it hurt their ears.

Appreciating their attention and silence, when they again became unruly she grabbed the ruler. They again became silenced and covered their ears. By the third time, all she had to do was *reach* for the ruler and everyone quickly covered their ears and became silent.

Pavlov would call the loud, smacking sound of the ruler the unconditioned stimulus and the pain in the ears the unconditioned response. The substitute teacher's students had learned to associate the sight of the ruler in her hand (the conditioned stimulus) with painful ears. (Then, following Thorndike, they had learned to quiet down to avoid that painful alternative.)

Think of how you "salivated" at the anticipation of food when the school bell rang to signal the end of the last period before lunch. Even if you changed to a new school where the bell was louder or softer, or even where a buzzer was used instead of a bell, your response would be similar, its degree of similarity depending on the similarity of the sound of the new bell to the old one. This is generalization. It happens when the test CS is similar to the training CS, and it is facilitated when the training CS is varied a little during training. The more similar the training and test stimuli, the more similar the training and test response. This is called the *gradient of generalization*.

Discrimination.   What if the CS varies a little during training, but when it varies, it is never paired with the UCS? The animal learns to respond to the original, exact CS and not to respond to any other form of the CS. That is, the animal learns to discriminate between the real CS — which goes with food — and the other stimuli — which do not go with food. On the test trial only the real CS will elicit the CR. Those stimuli that are different, even if similar, will elicit nothing. Thus, discrimination requires that one stimulus be paired with the UCS and all others be presented by themselves (without the UCS).

If your school has a fire bell that sounds different from the bell that signals the end of the period, the fire bell will not make you salivate, even if it occurs shortly before lunch time, because you have learned to discriminate between the two based on what follows them — lunch or lining up and marching outside.

What Have We Learned from Pavlov?   Pavlov demonstrated that learning took place when the subject formed connections between stimuli and responses. Admittedly, the level of the learning was low, because his work was limited to the study of reflexes. However, he had shown, in a very systematic and scientific way, that learning can be caused by outside events, that the results can be predictable, and that we can vary the amount or even the possibility of learning by varying the nature of the circumstances under which it takes place.

While today we may not be as concerned with classical conditioning as a fundamental behavioral model of learning, it did provide some basic behavioral concepts that we use today: (1) conditioning and secondary conditioning, (2) extinction, (3) inhibition, (4) generalization, and (5) discrimination. Moreover, B. F. Skinner redubbed it "respondent conditioning," to contrast with his "operant conditioning," described in Chapter 3. In describing the learning of new behaviors (or the learning of feelings and emotions), it is important to be able to account for how that learning occurs and how it can be varied. Pavlov provided a useful framework for explaining many simple learning phenomena. (For a classroom example of classical conditioning, see Box 2.2.)

Thorndike's Behavioral Approach: Trial-and-Error Learning

Edward Thorndike was an American educational psychologist who began his research by studying the behavior of cats in what he called a puzzle box. Thorndike's (1911) puzzle box was actually a wooden cage with a door in it that was kept closed by a latch. A hungry cat was placed in the puzzle box and some cat food was placed immediately outside the box. Not knowing how to get out of the box to get the desired food, the cat thrashed about, clawing and pushing the walls of the box. Eventually, by chance, the cat bumped the latch that controlled the door to the box, causing the door to open and freeing the cat to get the food.

Thorndike then quickly placed the cat back in the box and relatched the door. This time, and each time thereafter, the cat approached the latch more quickly and got out to get the food. Eventually, the cat learned to push the latch immediately to free itself from the box and get the food.

The Law of Effect.   Thorndike (1913) cited what he called the *law of effect* to explain the basis for the cat's learning the appropriate behavior to get out of the box and get the food. The law of effect states that *"when a modifiable connection is made and is accompanied by or followed by a satisfying state of affairs, the strength of the connection is increased; if the connection is made and followed by an annoying state of affairs, its strength is decreased"* (p. 2). Applied to the cat in the puzzle box, the law of effect looks like this:

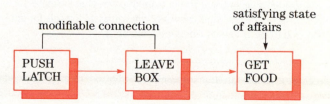

The cat uses a pattern of trial-and-error behavior to learn the connection between pushing the latch and being able to leave the puzzle box. The connection between pushing the latch and leaving the box is learned because it is followed by getting food, which, to a hungry cat, is a satisfying state of affairs.

Thus, we have early, fundamental behaviorism. If you want to change from trial-and-error to a specific behavior (such as pushing a latch), just wait around till the behavior occurs and then follow it with a satisfying state of affairs. The satisfying state of affairs will strengthen the connection between the behavior and the situation in which it occurred. If you want to eliminate a behavior, follow it with an annoying state of affairs. Animals (and people as well) will learn to perform those behaviors that lead to a satisfying state of affairs under a particular set of circumstances and not to perform others that lead to an annoying state of affairs.

Aftereffects of a Connection in Human Learners.   Thorndike did not spend all of his time studying cats. In fact, most of his research was done with human learners. With human learners, the aftereffects Thorndike used were the words *right* and *wrong*, rather than food. Those responses Thorndike wanted to strengthen were followed by "right"; those he wanted to weaken were followed by "wrong." For example, Thorndike (1931) presented learners with the letters "bo _ t." The learners were to fill in the blank with a letter to make a word. Initially, most learners filled in the blank with the letter *a* to make the word *boat*. However, the word *boat* was responded to by the experimenter as "wrong." Eventually, all learners filled in the blank with the letter *l* to make the word *bolt*. This connection occurred because the word *bolt* was responded to by the experimenter as "right."

Box 2.3

🍎

Connection Building, Thorndike Style

Fill in the blank space with the letters *i* and *e* to make a word. For example, good _ _ s would be *goodies* (not *goodeis*).

f _ _ ld	read _ _ s
tr _ _ s	al _ _ n
bel _ _ ve	dec _ _ t
rec _ _ ve	fr _ _ nd
rec _ _ pt	

Now check your answers at the bottom of page 34 in footnote 1.

Once you have checked your answers, can you write the rule for determining when the order of the letters should be *ie* versus when it should be *ei*?

_____

The answer to this question appears at the bottom of page 34 in footnote 2.

Thorndike regularly found that all responses that were always followed by the word "right," even ones that were very weak initially, became stronger to the point of being made every time. However, the announcement of "wrong," he found, did not produce a weakening effect in nearly the same proportion as the strengthening effect of "right." In fact, the announcement of "wrong" turned out to have no weakening effect. It appeared to only when it was used with "right," as in the *boat–bolt* experiment above. All of the effect was actually coming from the announcement of "right." So Thorndike modified the law of effect to apply only to the strengthening of connections as the result of satisfying aftereffects.

To see how connections can be built up to form a higher-order rule for spelling, read Box 2.3.

The Early Cognitive Approach: Gestalt Psychology

Gestalt psychology originated in Germany among a group of psychologists who chose its name to represent their emphasis on the "whole" configuration, in contrast to the behaviorists' preoccupation with discrete stimuli and responses. Gestaltists believed that learning involved organization and reorganization of the entire perceptual field in terms of figure and (back)ground and that this process occurred as a unitary one at one time, taking into account the total field. Behavior was not built up in small steps based on its effects, starting from trial-and-error, these psychologists contended. Rather it either occurred or failed to occur depending on the occurrence of the necessary perceptual processes and their cognitive organization. And so the Gestaltists set out to prove that the behaviorists were wrong. Some Gestalt research involved having children solve problems (such as the matchstick problems in Box 2.4). Of particular note, however, was research done with chimpanzees by the Gestaltist Wolfgang Köhler. It is to Köhler's work that we now turn.

The Study of Chimpanzees.   Köhler set up his research center in the remote Canary Islands off the coast of Africa in 1920. There he studied a group of chimpanzees that had been recently captured. He chose to study chimps rather than human beings because he was sure that he could create problem-solving situations that required solutions the animals had never used or encountered in the wild. To the primates, the use or construction of implements or the solving of roundabout or detour problems would be completely foreign, while to human beings, even to relatively young children, some aspects at least would be familiar. Köhler needed organisms with the intelligence to solve problems but not the experience. Chimps seemed perfect.

Why was it so important to Köhler that he study organisms that had little or no prior experience, direct or indirect, of the problems he used? The answer is that Köhler had set for himself the task, as he saw it, of trying to disprove behaviorism. To do so, he felt, he must demonstrate that organisms could solve problems not on the basis of trial-and-error and the serendipitous building up of small stimulus–response connections, as had Thorndike's cats, but on the basis of reorganizing the whole perceptual field — or "thinking." Köhler needed creatures that were smart enough to do this, yet totally inexperienced with the potential problem solutions themselves. So he created his laboratory and populated it with chimps.

Box 2.4

Gestalt Matchstick Problems

One of the tasks used by George Katona (1940), a Gestalt psychologist, was the matchstick problem. In the drawing below, 16 matchsticks have been placed in the positions you see.

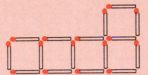

The problem is to make four squares out of the five squares by moving three and only three matchsticks. All of the 16 matchsticks must be used in the solution and each of the resulting four squares must be the same size as each of the original five.

Give it a try and see how many of the four possible solutions you can come up with. The solutions appear at the bottom of page 36 in footnote 3.

Katona (1940) gave these matchstick problems to three groups of students. The first group (controls) had never seen them before (like you). The second group (memorization) had been shown the problem and four versions of the same solution. The third group (examples) had seen six different solutions to a problem. Then each group was given problems to solve that none of them had seen before. Four weeks later they were given more problems to solve. On both testings the memorization group did a little better than the control group and the examples group did between three and four times better than the control group. Obviously, seeing some solutions helped.

If you cannot solve the matchstick problem above, look at the solutions on page 36 in footnote 3. Then try again with the matchsticks below and see if you can do better — like Katona's third group. The answers are on page 36 in footnote 4.

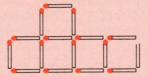

Detours and Implements.   To test the problem-solving capability of the chimps, Köhler devised problems that could be solved only by taking an indirect or detour route to the goal, in each case a banana, or by using an implement like a stick to reach it. In one instance, a banana was thrown out of the window and the chimp had to exit through a door on the wall opposite the window, go down a hallway and out of the building, and make a turn to reach the outside of the window.

---

[1]Answers to words in Box 2.3: field, tries, believe, receive, receipt, readies, alien, deceit, friend.
[2]Answer to rule in Box 2.3: *i* before *e* except after *c*.

You can't keep a good chimp down! Faced with the problem of reaching a banana suspended high overhead, the chimpanzee at left has managed by balancing a long stick beneath it and quickly climbing up. The chimpanzee at right has hit upon the "insight" of piling three boxes one atop another as a makeshift step stool (Köhler, 1925).

The vast majority of the problems involved the use of sticks as reaching implements. In the simplest problem, a stick placed at the back of the cage had to be used to reach a banana that was outside the front of the cage and beyond arm's length. Without the stick, the banana was too far away to reach, but with the stick, the banana could be moved close enough to the bars of the cage to grab. In a variation of this problem, the banana was hung from the ceiling of the cage beyond the chimp's leaping range. A box placed at the far end of the cage was needed as a "launching pad" to bring the banana within reach. However, the box helped only if it was moved to a position approximately underneath the hanging banana.

Köhler then made the problems more difficult by requiring some alteration of implements or implements in combination. In the two-stick problem, the chimp had to use a shorter stick inside the cage to reach a longer stick outside the cage and then use the longer stick to reach the banana. Or, in a variation, the chimp had to join two sticks together to form a single stick long enough to reach the banana. This type of implement-making problem was also extended to boxes. In one version, the chimp had to remove heavy stones from the box before it could be moved to a position underneath the suspended banana. In another, the chimp had to pile two boxes one on top of the other to reach the hanging banana.

Finally, the most difficult problems involved both implement and detour, by requiring that the chimp move the banana in a direction other than toward itself in order to reach it. By blocking the opening in the cage bars with wire mesh in the area nearest the banana, Köhler forced the chimp to use the stick to push the banana sideways to a point beyond the mesh, where it could then be reached. Or, the chimp was placed outside the front of the cage and the banana within it, and only the back of the cage was not enclosed in mesh; the chimp actually had to push the banana directly away from itself and toward the more open back of the cage in order to reach it.

The Discovery of Insight.   What did all these problems have in common? In order to solve them, the animal (1) had to use a component that seemed *irrelevant* or carry out an action that seemed *contradictory*, that is, that led away from the goal, even though (2) all of the components could not be seen simultaneously. In other words, a minor objective had to be attained, such as getting the stick or the box, before an attempt could be made to reach the major objective, the banana. Moreover, the attainment of the minor objective required movement away from the major objective. To accomplish this indirection, the chimp had to see each problem step as a part of the *whole*. This view of the whole was particularly difficult to accomplish since Köhler designed each problem so that "the structure of the situation in itself had no power whatever directly to determine conduct appropriate to it" (Köhler, 1959, p. 168). In other words, the problem design could not cause the appropriate behavior to occur, even by accident, since the attainment of the intermediate objective required such a different action from the attainment of the final one.

Yet many of Köhler's chimps succeeded in solving each problem. Initially, a chimp would go directly for the banana and often have a temper tantrum when, even after repeated attempts, it could not be reached. The animal would then sit and seemingly

---

[3]Answers to first matchstick problem in Box 2.4:

[4]Answers to second matchstick problem in Box 2.4:

Box 2.5

Two Chimpanzees Solve the "Banana" Problems

Nueva was tested three days after her arrival (11th March, 1914). She had not yet made the acquaintance of the other animals but remained isolated in a cage. A little stick is introduced into her cage; she scrapes the ground with it, pushes the banana skins together into a heap, and then carelessly drops the stick at a distance of about three-quarters of a meter from the bars. Ten minutes later, fruit is placed outside the cage beyond her reach. She grasps at it, vainly of course, and then begins the characteristic complaint of the chimpanzee: She thrusts both lips — especially the lower — forward, for a couple of inches, gazes imploringly at the observer, utters whimpering sounds, and finally flings herself onto the ground on her back — a gesture most eloquent of despair, which may be observed on other occasions as well. Thus, between lamentations and entreaties, some time passes, until — about seven minutes after the fruit has been exhibited to her — she suddenly casts a look at the stick, ceases her moaning, seizes the stick, stretches it out of the cage, and succeeds, though somewhat clumsily, in drawing the bananas within arm's length. Moreover, Nueva at once puts the end of her stick behind and beyond the objective, holding it in this test, as in later experiments, in her left hand by preference. The test is repeated after an hour's interval; on this second occasion, the animal has recourse to the stick much sooner, and uses it with more skill; and, at a third repetition, the stick is used immediately, as on all subsequent occasions. (p. 31)

(March 26th): Sultan is squatting at the bars, but cannot reach the fruit, which lies outside, by means of his only available short stick. A longer stick is deposited outside the bars, about two meters on one side of the objective, and parallel with the grating. It cannot be grasped with the hand, but it can be pulled within reach by means of the small stick. Sultan tries to reach the fruit with the smaller of the two sticks. Not succeeding, he tears at a piece of wire that projects from the netting of his cage, but that, too, is in vain. Then he gazes about him (there are always in the course of these tests some long pauses, during which the animals scrutinize the whole visible area). He suddenly picks up the little stick once more, goes up to the bars directly opposite to the long stick, scratches it towards him with the "auxiliary," seizes it, and goes with it to the point opposite the objective, which he secures. From the moment that his eyes fall upon the long stick, his procedure forms one consecutive whole, without hiatus, and, although the angling of the bigger stick by means of the smaller is an action that *could* be complete and distinct in itself, yet observation shows that it follows, quite suddenly, on an interval of hesitation and doubt — staring about — which undoubtedly has a relation to the *final* objective, and is immediately merged in the final action of the attainment of this end goal. (pp. 155–156)

SOURCE: Köhler, W. (1959). *The mentality of apes.* New York: Vintage.

---

stare at the banana until all of a sudden it would appear that "it was beginning to dawn on him." And then the animal would go straight for the box or stick and use it to reach the banana, the solution appearing as *"a single, continuous occurrence, a unity in space and time."* Time after time Köhler noted that the solution, when it did appear, appeared as a complete attempt with reference to the whole layout of the field rather than as the product of accidentally connected parts. (See Box 2.5 for two examples of actual solutions.)

And so Köhler chose the term *insight* to describe the continuous and unified solution process, in contrast to the behaviorist concept of conditioning or connecting. When a solution requires two steps, and the first appears to move in a direction opposite to the final objective of the second, then, contended Köhler, this first step could not possibly have been developed by itself but only in conjunction with the second since together and only together do they achieve the final objective. Discovering the whole solution, he argued, requires insight, the ability to reorganize and provide closure for the total field — not a series of chance occurrences cemented together by the ultimate attainment of a satisfying end state, as early behaviorists would contend.

(Do you want to see if you can use insight to solve a problem? Try the one in Box 2.6.)

Gestalt Psychology with Humans.   Not all of the Gestalt psychologists restricted themselves to the study of animals as Köhler did. Some, like Katona, studied human learning and problem-solving (see Box 2.4). Another, Michael Wertheimer (1945), studied productive thinking as it would apply to the classroom teaching situation. After he discovered that the solutions to certain geometry problems were taught to students by teachers using rote or memory techniques (see Box 2.7), he undertook a series of informal experiments with young children. He first taught the children how to find the area of a rectangle by breaking it down into *a* columns and *b* rows of little squares, and then he showed them how multiplying *a* times *b* resulted in the same number as counting the squares. Then he gave them the task of finding the area of a parallelogram.

Some children folded the parallelogram and others cut off its ends with scissors in an effort to convert the parallelogram into rectangles. Wertheimer saw such attempts as insightful, arising not from mere recall of past experience or blind trial-and-error but instead from the requirements of the problem. The thinking processes used were not the sum of several operations, he contended, but the emergence of "one line of thinking-out the gaps in the situation" in an effort to "get at the good inner-relatedness" or to straighten out the situation "structurally" (p. 50). Wertheimer was thus applying the concept of insight to the solving of complex problems by children as Köhler had before him to the solving of simpler problems by chimpanzees. His recommendation to teachers would be to teach students to see the relatedness of the parts of the problem to the whole, or gestalt, in order to be able to apply insight to the solution of similar problems.

We will return to these kinds of thinking problems in Chapters 6–8.

Box 2.6

An Insight Problem: Missionaries and Cannibals

Five missionaries and five cannibals who have to cross a river find a boat, but it is so small that it can hold no more than three people. If the missionaries on either bank of the river are outnumbered at any time by cannibals, they will be eaten. Find the simplest schedule of crossings that will allow everyone to cross safely. At least one person must be in the boat at each crossing.

The solution appears at the bottom of page 40 in footnote 5.

Box 2.7

🍎

A Lack of Productive Thinking in the Classroom

Wertheimer (1945) visited a classroom where the teacher was reviewing with his pupils the method for finding the area of a rectangle, namely, taking the product of the two sides. The teacher went on to draw parallelogram A (below), dropped two perpendiculars, and labeled the sides. He then proceeded to prove the theorem that the area of a parallelogram is equal to the product of the base times the altitude. The students were told to study this well so that they would know it.

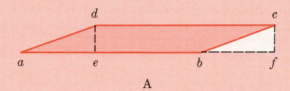

A

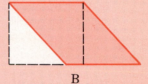

B

The next day, in the same classroom, a student was called to the board and performed the proof exactly as taught. Wertheimer was told that the student was only average. But Wertheimer was concerned whether students had *understood* the procedure or were just repeating it blindly. He drew parallelogram B (above) and asked the students to explain how to determine its area. While they knew that its area was equal to the base times the altitude, they were not able to show why it was true in this case. Some complained that they had not had that yet; others tried to blindly copy the procedure for parallelogram A that their teacher had shown them.

A few students, though, after some puzzlement, suddenly smiled and rotated parallelogram B 45 degrees, making it the equivalent of the original. They could now solve the new problem. The others had apparently learned a rote procedure rather than learning to understand what was accomplished, so they were not able to transpose the solution, in gestalt terms, from the training situation to the new one.

Behavioral and Cognitive Approaches Compared Again

Most basically, the behavioral approach focuses on external behaviors rather than on internal mental states and explains these behaviors as being based on the connection between elements, that connection being strengthened by its effect. For Pavlov, the elements were stimuli and responses, connected initially through the reflex and changed by means of conditioning. For Thorndike, the elements were likewise stimuli and responses; the connections between them, which were initially based on trial-and-error, were strengthened by their aftereffects. Even for higher mental processes, Thorndike (1931) turned to elements and their connections for his explanation:

> The compositions of forces which determine the direction of thought are highly elaborate and complex; but the forces themselves are very simple, being the elements in the situation and the connections leading from those elements and various combinations thereof which the past experience and present adjustment of the thinker provide. (pp. 159–160)

Contrast this with the Gestalt approach, in which the unit of analysis was the configuration or pattern rather than the element, and the whole was greater than (or at least different from) the sum of its parts rather than equal to it. For the Gestaltists, behavior not only represented unity but also was aimed at achieving unity in that behavior sought to be complete (called by the Gestaltists the *law of closure*). For the behaviorists, behavior may have appeared to be continuous yet was analyzed into discrete, simple connections — and connections between those connections. A comparison of how behaviorists and cognitivists (like the Gestaltists) deal with a wide range of topics is shown in Table 2.1.

Where Do We Go from Here?

It is useful to understand the differences between behavioral and cognitive approaches because subsequent examination of and explanation for a wide variety of behavior are based on one approach or the other. Maintaining classroom discipline, preparing a lesson

---

[5]Solution to missionaries (O) and cannibals (X) problem in Box 2.6:

Table 2.1 🍎 Comparing Behavioral and Cognitive Approaches

	Behaviorism	Cognitivism
Early proponents	Pavlov, Thorndike	Gestaltists (e.g., Köhler, Katona, Wertheimer)
Components	Elements (stimuli, responses)	Whole configuration
Learning basis	Connections, aftereffect	Reorganization, relatedness, closure, insight
Focus of learning	Product (outcome)	Process
Goal	Satisfaction	Understanding
Motivation	External	Internal
Purpose of feedback	To control or change	To inform
Learning outcome	Competency (skill)	Capability
What is learned	Specific behavior	General idea
Measure of learning	Response rate, response magnitude, generalization	Transfer (ability to solve class of problems)
Learner orientation	Empirical (to figure out "how")	Theoretical (to figure out "why")
Route to goal	Direct	Indirect
Initial behavior	Trial-and-error	Exploratory

plan, presenting instruction, motivating students, and helping them learn and develop — all topics of major concern and interest to educational psychology — will be explained as the result of external behavioral control, internal mental organization, or both. Both explanations may have merit and credence in any situation, but one tends to work better than the other in some situations but not in others.

The behavioral approach has been used successfully in business and athletics to improve various forms of performance, therapeutically to help people overcome personal problems such as fears or phobias (see the discussion of drive theory in Chapter 12), and instructionally to enhance learning (see the discussion of individualized instruction in Chapter 5). We will begin by looking at the most significant behavioral approach, reinforcement theory, as set forth by Skinner, and describing its use primarily in an area where it seems to be used most often: classroom management.

The Gestalt approach in particular, as an early cognitive explanation for behavior, can be seen as a precursor of today's cognitive theories of memory, meaningful learning, and problem-solving. These current cognitive or information-processing theories, based on what goes on inside the learner's head, are covered in detail in Chapters 6 and 7, following the discussion of behaviorism.

Summary of Main Points

1. Two approaches to learning are contrasted, one behavioral and one cognitive. Behaviorists focus on performance outcomes, which are learned through combining or connecting of elements (such as, "In this situation this is the response to perform") and then are repeated if they result in satisfying aftereffects. Cognitivists focus on the learning process, namely, thinking or insight, which requires a reorganization of perceptions and ideas. (The two approaches are contrasted in Table 2.1.)

2. An early behavioral model was classical conditioning as proposed by Ivan Pavlov, a Russian physiologist. Dogs learned (or were conditioned) to salivate at the sound of a tone (the conditioned stimulus) when it was paired with food (the unconditioned stimulus). Salivation, initially elicited as the unconditioned response to the food, came to be elicited as a conditioned response by the sound of the tone alone, after sufficient pairings of tone and food, but only if the tone preceded or overlapped the food in time. After conditioning, repeatedly presenting the tone alone ultimately resulted in the loss of conditioning—called extinction.

3. Pavlov also demonstrated various other conditioning phenomena, such as secondary conditioning (using an already conditioned stimulus in place of an unconditioned stimulus in order to condition the response to occur to an entirely new stimulus), conditioned inhibition (using a new stimulus that comes on before and overlaps with the conditioned stimulus to block it from eliciting the conditioned response), generalization (conditioning the animal to respond to a range of different, yet similar, stimuli by varying the conditioned stimulus during training and pairing all variations with the food), and discrimination (conditioning the animal not to respond to similar stimuli by never pairing them with the food during training).

4. Edward Thorndike, meanwhile, demonstrated in both animals and humans that the connection between specific behaviors (or responses) and the situations (or stimuli) that were to provoke them could be learned if the aftereffect of such behavior were satisfying. He termed this the law of effect and used it to explain how hungry cats became able to escape from cagelike puzzle boxes to acquire some food.

5. The other approach, the cognitive one, was pursued by a group of German psychologists calling themselves Gestaltists (from gestalt, a word that means "whole array" or "whole configuration"). Principal among them was Wolfgang Köhler, who studied the problem-solving behavior of chimpanzees recently brought in from the wild. These animals proved able to circumvent detours and not only to use implements, such as sticks and boxes, to get bananas, but to combine them, when necessary, to attain a remote goal.

6. *Insight* was the name Köhler gave to the process of discovering a single, unitary, and continuous solution, even when it required moving away from the goal to get a necessary implement or reach a needed opening. Insightful learning was different from the conditioning or trial-and-error learning of behaviorism, according to Köhler, because it depended on reorganization of the perceptual field rather than on the aftereffects of random connections.

7. This early work set the stage for more contemporary approaches of both behavioral and cognitive types, to account for learning and behavior. These newer approaches are covered in the succeeding chapters.

Suggested Resources

Glover, J. A., Ronning, R. R., & Bruning, R. H. (1990). *Cognitive psychology for teachers*. New York: Macmillan.

Köhler, W. (1959). *The mentality of apes*. New York: Vintage.

Ormrod, J. E. (1990). *Human learning*. Columbus, OH: Merrill.

Pavlov, I. P. (1960). *Conditioned reflexes*. New York: Dover.

Thorndike, E. L. (1931). *Human learning*. New York: Century.

Chapter
3

A Behavioral Approach to Learning

Objectives

1. Describe operant conditioning as a way of changing behavior based on the use of discriminative stimuli and differential reinforcement.
2. Identify different types of reinforcers, including primary and secondary; positive and negative; and social, token, and activity.
3. Describe different schedules of reinforcement (ratio and interval, fixed and variable) and their effects.
4. Identify procedures for behavior modification (that is, the application of operant conditioning), including the use of prompting, chaining, and shaping techniques.
5. Describe the application of the behavior modification approach to effective classroom management, incorporating the principle of specify-praise-ignore.
6. Identify circumstances and techniques for the effective use of punishment and aversive control in the classroom.
7. Describe the application of reinforcement theory to teaching.

Introduction

The purpose of this chapter is to introduce a powerful behavioral approach for managing and controlling outcomes in a classroom. It is called *reinforcement theory*, and it is primarily based on the work of a psychologist named B. F. Skinner. In essence, the teacher who uses reinforcement theory controls the effect of a student's behavior by choosing whether or not to follow that behavior with a positive experience — called a reinforcer. The effect or reinforcement becomes *contingent* on, or depends on, whether or not the appropriate behavior occurs.

This decision to reinforce or not reinforce a behavior can be called *contingency management*. This means managing or controlling the likelihood of recurrence of a specific behavior by following it or not following it with a reinforcer. The teacher can be the contingency manager by giving or withholding reinforcement selectively, depending on the student's behavior. By focusing on changing behavior through selective reinforcement, we are continuing on with behaviorism and the law of effect as described in the previous chapter.

Operant Conditioning

Skinner (1938) termed the basic type of learning *operant* (or Type *R*) *conditioning* and defined it as a "reinforcing stimulus being contingent upon a response" (p. 19). Operant conditioning means learning to perform a specific behavior, called an operant (such as raising your hand in class) based on the occurrence that immediately follows it, that is, its consequences (for example, being praised by the teacher). Behaviors that are followed by positive consequences increase in their frequency and probability of occurrence: They are learned and are repeated. People learn to operate on their environment to attain or achieve positive consequences. This is called operant conditioning, and it is the basic principle of Skinner's reinforcement theory. The principle of reinforcement is an outgrowth and refinement of Thorndike's law of effect.

Operant conditioning is different from classical conditioning as proposed by Pavlov, which Skinner renamed Type *S* conditioning. In classical, or Type *S*, conditioning, the response or respondent is elicited or evoked initially by the unconditioned stimulus and eventually by the conditioned stimulus. In Skinner's words, Type *S* conditioning is "defined by the operation of the simultaneous presentation of the reinforcing stimulus and another stimulus" (1938, p. 19). *In other words, the reinforcing stimulus (UCS), in classical conditioning, is connected to another stimulus (CS).*

In operant, or Type *R*, conditioning, the response is emitted initially on a low-frequency basis; but as it continues to occur and be reinforced, its frequency increases. The cause of the behavior in operant conditioning is the consequence that follows it — the reinforcement — rather than some automatic or learned stimulus that precedes it and hence triggers it. (Many behaviors occur without any preceding or triggering stimulus.) *The reinforcing stimulus, in operant conditioning, is connected to a response.*

The Discriminative Stimulus.   There is, however, a stimulus that can serve as a signal or cue in operant conditioning, rather than as a trigger in classical conditioning, thereby increasing the likelihood that the operant response will be emitted (Skinner,

1953). Rather than having to wait around for the operant response to be emitted on a random basis, the teacher can cue the students to behave in a certain way if they want to receive reinforcement. Skinner called this signal the *discriminative stimulus* (S^D) and represented its relationship to the operant response and consequent reinforcement this way:

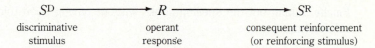

$$S^D \longrightarrow R \longrightarrow S^R$$

discriminative   operant   consequent reinforcement
stimulus   response   (or reinforcing stimulus)

When the teacher tells the class members that to get called on they must wait until she calls for questions before raising their hands, this instruction serves as a discriminative stimulus. Her call for questions, the discriminative stimulus or S^D, does not cause students to raise their hands. It simply directs or signals them to do so at that time if they wish to experience a positive consequence — being recognized and perhaps subsequently praised by the teacher. It is important to recognize that the behavior is ultimately controlled by or is contingent upon the consequence, not the signal, but the signal helps cue or guide the learner to choose to perform the appropriate response, the one upon which reinforcement is contingent.

What happens if children raise their hands at a time when the teacher is lecturing and has not called for questions, that is, in the absence of S^D? Skinner calls a stimulus that signals not getting reinforced S^Δ, or S delta. Lecturing would be an example of S^Δ. Calling for questions would be an example of S^D. If the operant response is made in the presence of S^Δ, it is ignored. If the operant response is made in the presence of S^D, it is reinforced.

The mechanism that makes a stimulus or signal a discriminative one is called differential reinforcement. *Differential reinforcement* means reinforcement that is given following the operant response *only when that response is preceded by the discriminative stimulus S^D, never when it is preceded by S^Δ*. That means that when the operant response occurs but has not been preceded by the discriminative stimulus, no reinforcement follows. It also means that when any response other than the operant response follows the discriminative stimulus, it is not reinforced or rewarded either. The only combination that yields reward is the discriminative stimulus followed by the operant response.

As an illustration of this point, imagine that the appropriate discriminative stimulus (S^D) is the teacher's instruction "Take out your spelling books," and the operant response (R_1) is the students responding by taking out their spelling books and then sitting quietly, waiting for the spelling lesson to begin. When this happens, the teacher praises the class, which serves as the reinforcement (S^R). Thus,

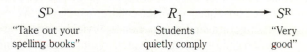

$$S^D \longrightarrow R_1 \longrightarrow S^R$$

"Take out your   Students   "Very
spelling books"   quietly comply   good"

However, taking out the spelling books when told to take out the reading books results in no reinforcement:

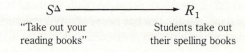

$$S^\Delta \longrightarrow R_1$$

"Take out your   Students take out
reading books"   their spelling books

Also, talking and playing after being told to take out the spelling books results in no reinforcement:

$$S^D \longrightarrow R_2$$

"Take out your   Students talk
spelling books"   and play

Finally, taking out the spelling books without having been told to do so results in no reinforcement:

$$R_1$$

Students take out
their spelling books

It is only the combination of the discriminative stimulus (S^D) and the operant response (R_1), as in the first illustration, that yields reinforcement (S^R).

Types of Reinforcers

Different kinds or types of reinforcers can be used to modify or control behavior. In this section, they are described and compared.

Primary Versus Secondary

Some reinforcers are inherently or automatically satisfying. Called *primary* reinforcers, they include such things as food and protection, and people do not have to learn to like them. Since it would be hard to provide such primary reinforcement in a classroom on a regular basis, teachers have come to rely instead on reinforcers that students have learned to like. These learned preferences are called *secondary* reinforcers, and they include praise, money, and the opportunity to play. Such secondary reinforcers have probably come to have reinforcement value because they have been associated early and often in our lives with primary reinforcers.

Positive Versus Negative

It is also possible to distinguish between *positive* reinforcers, those nice experiences or stimuli people desire to have, and *negative* reinforcers, those aversive experiences or stimuli people desire to terminate, escape from, or avoid. When children are given candy, praise, or a good time for their behavior, they have attained something positive and desirable and will be inclined to repeat that behavior in order to regain or reexperience the positive consequence. When children's behavior allows them to escape from a painful, embarrassing, or aversive experience, it yields negative reinforcement and will also tend to be learned and repeated. (Negative reinforcement is different from punishment, as will be seen later, because it represents a "good" consequence while punishment represents a "bad" one. See Table 3.3 on page 61.)

In learning research done with animals, the escape from or avoidance of electric shock was often used as a negative reinforcement to teach a particular response such as pushing a bar. Initially, the bar press allowed the animal to escape from the shock, but if the shock was preceded by a discriminative stimulus, the animal learned to push the bar before the shock came on and thereby avoided the shock entirely. In Skinner's early research, he used an obnoxiously bright light that the rat could turn off by pushing the bar. The bar press response was thus negatively reinforced when the rat terminated the unpleasant brightness of the light.

Social, Token, and Activity Reinforcers

There are three kinds of reinforcers that can be used with reasonable ease in the classroom. The first of these, *social* reinforcers, represents desirable interactive experiences with other people, either the teacher or other students. Social reinforcers that teachers can use with students include complimenting them, smiling at them, patting them on the back, or even hugging or kissing them. "Good work" and "You're pretty smart" and "Way to go" are all phrases that serve as social reinforcers.

Token reinforcers are things that can be "traded in for" or converted to some other, more basic form of reinforcer. Gold stars and points can work as token reinforcers. Often, token reinforcers come to have reinforcement value of their own because of their common association with other, more primary reinforcers such as social ones. Money is such a token reinforcer: For many people, it has come to be desirable in its own right, independent of what it might buy.

Finally, *activity* reinforcers are desirable things to do, such as going out to play, having recess, being a monitor, going on a field trip, or getting to use a computer. The

Getting to play is a good activity reinforcer.

effective use of activity reinforcers was illustrated by the psychologist David Premack (1965), giving rise to what is most often referred to as the *Premack principle*. This principle states that any high-frequency behavior (something that a child likes to do) that is contingent upon, or that will only be allowed to happen in the classroom following the occurrence of, a low-frequency behavior (something that the child does not like to do) is likely to increase the occurrence of the low-frequency behavior. Put more simply, children will learn to do things that they might not like very much, such as seatwork, reading, or recitation, if the consequence of doing these things is to get to do something that they like a lot, such as playing. The more preferred activity thus becomes the reward or reinforcement for carrying out the less preferred activity.

Consistent with the Premack principle is the idea that the teacher need not guess at what a more preferred activity or activity reinforcer might be for a child or group of children. The best strategy would be to ask each child what he or she would like to do as a reward for completing the seatwork or reading or other classwork activity. In other words, tailor-made or individualized activity reinforcers could be used to reward each child's classroom work. The teacher must be sure, though, that the student likes the "rewarding" activity, because it will be rewarding only if the student perceives it as such. An example of the actual application of the Premack principle in a classroom situation is given in Box 3.1.

Box 3.1

Using the Premack Principle to Get Brian to Do His Schoolwork

Mrs. Ripken had tried everything she could think of to get second-grader Brian to complete his assignments on time—to no avail. This was no new problem. Brian's first-grade teacher had told Mrs. Ripken that she too had tried everything she could think of. Most recently, Mrs. Ripken had kept Brian in from recess numerous times, thinking this would help. But it turned out that this form of punishment meant nothing to him.

Another approach Mrs. Ripken had tried was writing notes to his grandmother about his work not being turned in. This had failed too. Instead of sympathizing with Mrs. Ripken's problem, Brian's grandmother told her about all the problems *she* was having with Brian. Since Brian's mother was not living with him anymore, the grandmother could do nothing with him. This was discouraging, to say the least.

As a last resort, Mrs. Ripken turned to corporal punishment (which happened to be legal in the state where she was teaching). Being a "tough" kid, however, Brian wasn't bothered by this either. The fact was, Brian was quite capable of performing the work; he just wasn't motivated.

School was well into the second six weeks and Brian had made no progress. Mrs. Ripken was about to give up when a visit to the teacher's lounge one day changed everything. Mrs. Grant, the music teacher, made a casual remark about how much Brian loved music. She went on to say that she had no discipline problems with him during music class. This surprised Mrs. Ripken, because in addition to not finishing his work, Brian liked to annoy his classmates. After Mrs. Grant left the lounge, Mrs. Ripken thought with amusement that maybe she should let Brian listen to music all day.

Schedules of Reinforcement

Sometimes, such as when learning or operant conditioning is first taking place, reinforcement must be given every time the operant response occurs. This is called *continuous reinforcement*, and it is necessary if learning is to occur. If, on the other hand, no reinforcement is given, a response that has already been learned will stop occurring. This unlearning process is called *extinction*. Continuous reinforcement, which produces learning, and no reinforcement, which produces extinction, represent the extreme schedules or patterns of reinforcement. There are other schedules in between (Ferster & Skinner, 1957; Walker & Buckley, 1974), as described below.

Intermittent Reinforcement: Ratio Versus Interval

Ratio Reinforcement Schedule.   It is possible to provide reinforcement following the performance of the operant response some specific number of times (such as five times) rather than every time. In other words, a child would have to do five problems rather than just one to gain the reward, or an animal would have to push the bar five times rather than just once to get food. The ratio of responses to reinforcements would be five to one (5:1). Whenever the response must occur some number of times before reinforcement is forthcoming, a *ratio* reinforcement schedule is being used. If the

Later on, the thought came back to her, and she decided to purchase some popular music tapes and put them in the classroom learning center. Only the children who finished their work were permitted to go to any of the learning centers. Up to this point, Brian had never gone and hadn't seemed to want to. This now changed. Brian was eager to listen to the tapes, so Mrs. Ripken made a deal with him: If he would finish his reading worksheet on time each day, he could go to the center and listen to the music on tape.

First thing the next morning, she put the tapes in the center. When Brian arrived in class, he went immediately to his desk. It was time for reading. The seatwork was about to start. To Mrs. Ripken's surprise, Brian finished his assignment—ahead of time. Then he headed for the center, put on the earphones, and gave a wide grin of satisfaction. You would have to know Brian to appreciate that smile.

He wanted to go to the learning center again in the afternoon, but workshop time was only in the morning from 10:00 to 10:30. Then Mrs. Ripken thought, If it worked for reading, why not use the same method to get him to finish his math? Again she made a deal with Brian. It really amazed her that something so simple as getting to listen to music could work so well.

Brian's story is a perfect example of how positive reinforcement can outweigh punishment as a motivator. Since each child is unique, though, there are no set rules or guarantees. Basically, it takes trial and error to find the perfect solution. But for a busy, caring teacher, that perfect solution is well worth the effort.

response must occur three times for a reinforcement, then the ratio schedule is 3:1, and so on. Since reinforcement is given not for every response but for every *n*th response, a ratio schedule represents intermittent or occasional reinforcement rather than continuous reinforcement.

Interval Reinforcement Schedule.   Another way to give reinforcement intermittently is to give it for the first response that occurs after a given *interval* of time has elapsed. For example, a reinforcement could be given for the first response that occurs after a minute has elapsed or two minutes or three minutes, and so on. This is called an interval schedule. The problem with an interval schedule is that a child or even an animal quickly learns that the reinforcement will occur only every so many minutes, no matter how many responses are made; so the child or animal slows the response rate to zero during the interval. It is only as the end of the interval approaches that rapid responding is likely to occur.

Variable Versus Fixed Reinforcement Schedules

In order to increase both response rate (the number of responses per minute) and resistance to extinction (the number of responses that will occur with no reinforcement at all), Skinner invented the idea of a variable reinforcement schedule in contrast to a fixed one.

Table 3.1 🍎 Four Kinds of Intermittent Reinforcement Schedules

Type of Schedule	Description of Schedule	Effects on Behavior	
		Schedule in Operation	*Schedule Terminated (Extinction)*
Fixed Ratio (FR)	Reinforcer is given after each preset number of responses.	High response rate.	Irregular responding. More responses than in continuous reinforcement, fewer than in variable ratio.
Fixed Internal (FI)	Reinforcer is given for first response to occur after each preset number of minutes.	Subject stops working after reinforcement; then works hard just prior to time of next reinforcement.	Gradual decrease in responding.
Variable Ratio (VR)	Reinforcer is given after an average number of preset responses.	Very high response rate. Higher ratios yield higher rates.	Very resistant to extinction. Maximum number of responses before extinction.
Variable Interval (VI)	Reinforcer is given for first response to occur after an average number of preset minutes.	Steady rate of responding.	Very resistant to extinction. Maximum time to extinction.

In a *variable* schedule, the number of times a response must be made before a reinforcement is received, or the interval of time that must elapse before a reinforcement is received, changes after every reinforcement. In other words, for a variable ratio schedule, the schedule could be two responses followed by a reinforcement, then four responses before the next reinforcement, then three responses, and so on. The average ratio might be 3:1, but the actual ratio would vary each time rather than being fixed or constant.

Similarly, for a variable interval schedule, the first reinforcement might occur after one minute, the second after three minutes, the third after two minutes, and so on, with an average interval of two minutes but an actual interval that varied from reinforcement to reinforcement. With such a variable schedule, the child or animal could not predict exactly when a response would be followed by a reinforcement, and so would keep the response rate high in order to maximize the possibility of receiving reinforcement. (The four kinds of intermittent reinforcement schedules are summarized in Table 3.1.)

Intermittent reinforcement schedules, particularly variable ones, add a high degree of practicality to the practice or use of reinforcement theory in managing behavior. It is neither necessary nor even desirable to give reinforcement after each performance of the operant response, other than when it is being learned in the first place. Once the behavior has been learned, variable ratio or variable interval reinforcement schedules can be used to maintain the performance of the operant response at a high rate of occurrence.

Behavior Modification

The use of selective or contingent reinforcement, as described by behaviorists such as Skinner, to manage or control naturally occurring behavior is called *behavior modification*. In behavior modification, a target behavior is selected and discriminative stimuli and differential reinforcement are used either to increase that behavior or to decrease it (Phillips, 1971). (One teacher's behavior modification project is described in Box 3.2.)

Basically, then, behavior modification requires that the teacher carry out the following four steps:

STEP ONE: Identify a desired or target behavior (R).
STEP TWO: Give clear signals of when to perform (S^D) and when not to perform (S^Δ) the target behavior.
STEP THREE: Ignore disruptive or nontarget behavior.
STEP FOUR: Reinforce (S^R) the target behavior when it occurs.

To help accomplish this, some particular techniques can be used, as follows.

Prompting, Chaining, and Shaping

Prompting.   Prompting means adding familiar discriminative stimuli that are likely to signal the desired response, rather than merely waiting for the desired response to occur on a chance basis. Prompting may mean, for example, a teacher telling the class what behavior to perform and when to perform it. He might do such prompting when presenting his rules for classroom behavior. Prompts are established $S^D \longrightarrow R$ relationships that can be used to facilitate learning new $S^D \longrightarrow R$ relationships.

Box 3.2

A Classroom Teacher Uses Behavior Modification

Two months after the new school year had begun, Mrs. Thomas was still having a problem keeping her third-grade class under control. She seemed to be spending less and less time teaching and more time handling discipline problems, such as excessive talking, and students being out of their seats rather than doing their assignments. She knew she had to do something to restore order to her classroom and bring her students under control if she was ever going to do her teaching.

Her first effort was to bring in a video camera and videotape the children. Then she played back the tape so they could see how bad they were being. But what this did, in fact, was increase the disruptive behavior, because now all the students *wanted* to be on the video so they intentionally acted up. As the tape was being played back to the students, they weren't paying any attention to the bad behavior they were seeing—only to *who* got on the video. Mrs. Thomas had positively reinforced the bad behavior, and so it increased.

Mrs. Thomas quickly threw the videotape idea out the window, and came up with a new idea: giving out stickers to those students who were quiet, did their work, raised their hand before speaking, and carried out the other good behaviors she had asked for. She carried stickers in her pocket, and as she walked around the room observing the students, she would immediately reward the ones who acted appropriately. Those who were "being good" had a sticker placed on their desk. The students collected the stickers throughout the day, and at the end of the day the five students with the most stickers were rewarded by a grand prize.

After about a week of doing this, Mrs. Thomas had cut her discipline problems in half. By the end of two weeks, she had only a few scattered problems left. The students' undesirable behaviors had been extinguished by being ignored, and rewarded behaviors had replaced them. Mrs. Thomas' discipline problems were finally under control.

Prompting is commonly used in the teaching of reading. When a child has trouble reading a word, the teacher may help the child sound it out. Giving clues or help to make the unfamiliar become more familiar represents prompting.

In prompting, there are two important ideas or rules to remember. First, *the normal S^D should occur before the prompting S^D.* In other words, extra help should not be given before the student tries to complete the task without extra help. If the teacher helps or prompts first—by sounding out a word, for example—the student will come to rely on the prompt rather than on the normal discriminative stimulus, the appearance of the word on the page. The student will not learn to respond without prompting if it always comes first.

Second, *prompts should be faded or withdrawn as soon as possible* so that the student learns to perform without constant help or reminders. Gradual withdrawal is best.

Thus, prompting is a way of helping the student to know what response will be right, and prompting will lead to the correct response in a given situation. Prompts can help increase the likelihood of the student emitting reinforceable responses at the start of learning, but they should be gradually eliminated so that they do not become a necessary element of the performance situation.

Sometimes a little prompting can help a student perform successfully.

Chaining. This represents a technique for connecting simple responses in sequence to form a more complex response that would be difficult to learn all at one time. In a chain, simple behaviors under the control of discriminative stimuli are joined into a sequence of behavior, which is then reinforced at its completion. A chain might look like this:

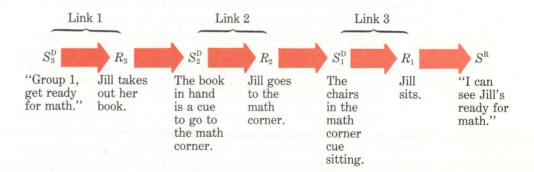

Link 1		Link 2		Link 3		
S_3^D	R_3	S_2^D	R_2	S_1^D	R_1	S^R
"Group 1, get ready for math."	Jill takes out her book.	The book in hand is a cue to go to the math corner.	Jill goes to the math corner.	The chairs in the math corner cue sitting.	Jill sits.	"I can see Jill's ready for math."

Each S^D in a behavior chain tends to acquire a reinforcing function for the response that precedes it and a discriminative function for the response that follows it.

The most common method for establishing a behavior chain in the classroom is first to prompt each step in the chain and then to fade the prompts. For example, the chain for going to the math group, shown above, could initially have been made up of three separate instructions:

1. "Get out your math books."
   "Good. Everyone has a book out."
2. "Now walk quietly to the math corner."
   "Good."
3. "Let's all sit in our chairs."
   "You got ready quickly. I like that."

After several repetitions, it would have been unnecessary to say more than "Get ready for math," because the students would now have known what to do.

Shaping.   This is used when the target or desired response is not one the student can perform already (that is, the desired response is not in the student's repertoire) or when there is no way to prompt the response.

Skinner (1953) gives the following laboratory example of shaping:

> To get the pigeon to peck the spot as quickly as possible we proceed as follows: We first give the bird food when it turns slightly in the direction of the spot from any part of the cage. This increases the frequency of such behavior. We then withhold reinforcement until a slight movement is made toward the spot. . . . We continue by reinforcing positions successively closer to the spot, then by reinforcing only when the head is moved slightly forward, and finally only when the beak actually makes contact with the spot. We may reach this final response in . . . two or three minutes. (p. 92)

There are two keys to shaping. The first is *differential reinforcement* — reinforcing only those behaviors that meet a given criterion and not behaviors that fail to meet that criterion. (This, of course, is a standard practice in all behavior modification.)

The second key to shaping is to use a *shifting criterion for reinforcement*. That means gradually changing the response criterion for reinforcement in the direction of the target behavior. The researcher or teacher starts shaping by reinforcing any behavior that approximates or is vaguely similar to the target behavior (such as doing one math problem), and ends up reinforcing only the exact target behavior (such as doing ten math problems). Between start and end, she gradually imposes the requirement that, to be reinforced, the student's behavior must move closer and closer to the target behavior.

Thus, the technique of shaping reinforces successive approximations to the target behavior, each getting closer to it than the one before. Care must be taken not to stay with each new requirement any longer than is necessary to meet the criterion, or else the student's behavior will stop there.

In shaping, the teacher follows these steps: (l) define the target behavior (for example, do ten math problems independently and without distraction); (2) decide what behavior to build from (do one math problem with help); (3) establish a reinforcer (earning points to be used toward a play period); (4) outline the program of steps (1 math problem with help, 1 problem without help, 2 with help, 2 without help, 5 without help, 8 without help, 10 without help); (5) start training with the first criterion; (6) decide when to shift to a new criterion; (7) if the criterion is not met, return briefly to an earlier step or add a new step in between and try again; (8) repeat steps 6 and 7 until the target behavior is achieved. (An anecdotal illustration of shaping is given in Box 3.3.)

Effective Classroom Management

On the first day of school, a teacher wrote the following five rules on a corner of the chalkboard for permanent display:

RAISE YOUR HAND WHEN YOU WISH TO TALK.

WALK IN THE ROOM AND HALLS.

KEEP YOUR HANDS AND FEET TO YOURSELF.

BE POLITE.

WHEN YOU FINISH YOUR WORK YOU MAY FIND SOMETHING TO DO
   FROM THE BACK OF THE ROOM.

The teacher reminded the children of the rules by (1) having them read them each morning, (2) making praise comments contingent on their being followed and referring to the rule in the praise comment (for example, "I called on Tim because he raised his hand"), and (3) attending to only that behavior that is within the limits of the rules (Becker, Engelmann, & Thomas, 1975, pp. 117–18). This story illustrates the basic strategy for effective classroom management using reinforcement theory.

Specify, Praise, Ignore.   The first principle of effective classroom management is to *specify*, in a positive way, the rules that are the basis for reinforcement. The rules serve as prompts; as children learn to follow them, they can be repeated less frequently (faded). Good classroom behavior, however, should continue to be reinforced. The rules represent the discriminative stimulus.

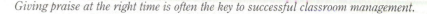

Giving praise at the right time is often the key to successful classroom management.

Box 3.3

A Teacher Tries Shaping (and a Few Other Things) with Little Dwayne

The class rules were Speak quietly, Stay in your seat, Keep your hands away from others, Don't hit or swear, and Respect the belongings of others. Little Dwayne would go down the list and seemingly try to break them all, one or two at a time. For a second-grader, he had quite a reputation. He swore, hit the other children, was out of his seat most of the time, and his hands were always busy, throwing pencils in the classroom or food in the lunchroom. Once, when a student's mother was volunteering in his classroom, she stayed and ate lunch with the children. They all showed her a biscuit stuck on the wall where Dwayne had thrown it the day before. He beamed when she expressed shock.

Each time he broke a rule, he was sent to a "time out"* section of the office with his unfinished worksheets (which he could do in a few minutes when he wanted to). He often had company from other classrooms, and since these children were left unsupervised most of the time, time-out was quite a treat for Dwayne — a reward rather than the punishment it was intended to be. In the regular classroom he was always being punished for his antics, and the other children shunned him. It was more desirable to him to be sent to the time-out room.

His teacher finally woke up to the fact that her punishment was having little effect on Dwayne's behavior when one day she went to check on him in the time-out room and found him and a child from another class dipping snuff that he had smuggled into school that day. She decided something else must be tried. She had read an article on shaping, so she decided to begin such a program for him. First, she focused on getting him to just remain in his seat. She had a difficult time ever catching him in it, but when she did she reinforced him with a piece of candy and praise. (The rest of the class would look on with amazement, seeing Dwayne being rewarded for something they had been doing all along.) To keep his interest, she varied her reinforcement to include stickers and free time. He seemed to thrive on the attention he received.

Soon, Dwayne began staying in his seat. But he was still continually making contact with the other students by throwing things at them, talking loudly, and swearing at them. This was very hard for the teacher to ignore. So she concentrated next on getting him to not throw things. Here, she used some prompting. She told him that if he wouldn't throw anything at anybody for a week, she would let him be the official fish feeder for a whole week. He had never earned this privilege before; it was usually given out daily to a deserving student. He was very excited at the prospect and helped the teacher decorate a chart with his name and the days of the week on it. The whole first day he restrained himself from throwing things, but the next day he forgot. So they started over. This happened for about a week. When the second week began and by Monday afternoon he had not thrown anything at all, the entire class cheered for him. So that whole second week he didn't throw anything, and he sat in his seat most of the time. Imagine his face (and his classmates') when he got to feed the fish all of the next week!

In the last half of the year, the teacher began to work on Dwayne's swearing. While she had diminished the frequency of her rewards for sitting and not throwing things, her praise and attention for his good actions seemed to be even more rewarding to him. By the end of the school term, he had even stopped swearing. Well, almost. Once, when a student volunteer was there, he swore. Then he clapped his hand over his mouth and his eyes grew very big!

*Time-out is described on pages 61–62. It refers to being punished by spending time away from the class.

The second principle is to *praise* desirable behavior. Teachers should catch children being good rather than waiting for them to misbehave. The focus should be on reinforcing or praising behavior that is important for the development of social and cognitive skills. Teacher behaviors such as relating children's performance to the rules, being specific, and praising the behavior rather than the child him- or herself are recommended. Becker, Engelmann, and Thomas (1975) provide these examples of effective praise (p. 120):

> "You watched the board all the time I was presenting the example. That's paying attention."
>
> "That's a good answer. You listened very closely to my question."
>
> "Jimmy is really working hard. He'll get the answer. You'll see."

Some additional examples are given in Table 3.2.

It is also important that improvement, rather than just the absolute or final level of performance, be rewarded. Students should be praised for doing better as a way of shaping their behavior in the direction of doing well.

Table 3.2 🍎 Some Examples of How to Praise Acceptable Behavior Rather Than Criticize Unacceptable Behavior in Different Classroom Situations

Classroom Situation (*S*)	Teacher Response (*R*)
The children have just returned from recess, and several are still out of their seats or talking rather than starting on the next assignment.	Praise the children who are in their seats and working.
In class discussion, the children are required to raise their hands if they wish to answer, but some do not.	Ignore the children who blurt out. Say "Billy's got his hand up. What answer would you give, Billy?"
The children are going to the bathroom. Some are walking quietly down the hall, but others are running and laughing.	Praise the children who are walking quietly and ignore those who are running. (Note that it may be necessary to back up the praise by some more powerful reinforcer.)
The class is standing in line to go into the lunchroom. Some of the children push in at the head of the line rather than waiting their turn.	Praise the children who wait in line, and back up the praise by picking them to go into the lunchroom first. Do not censure the children who break into line.
The class is doing written assignments. You notice that one of the children is copying.	Ignore the child who is copying. Praise a child who is doing his own work. After the child who has been copying begins to do his own work, you should praise him for working hard.

SOURCE: Adapted from Becker, W. C., Engelmann, S., & Thomas, D. R. (1975). *Teaching 1: Classroom management* (p. 72). Chicago: Science Research Associates.

Praise has also been shown to be an effective way of changing teachers' behavior. Cossairt et al. (1973) found that teachers who were praised by an observer for using praise themselves dramatically increased their subsequent use of praise.

The third principle is to *ignore* disruptive behavior unless someone is getting hurt. When a behavior problem persists, someone, usually the teacher, is inadvertently reinforcing it. Often, the reinforcement comes in the form of giving attention to a student who craves it and attempts to gain it by acting out. Ignoring such behavior is preferable to punishing it.

Madsen et al. (1968) discovered that the more the teacher said "Sit down," the more the children stood up. In other words, the less teachers ignored students' standing up and instead scolded or criticized them by ordering them to sit down, the more often students stood up. The "Sit down" response served as a reinforcement for standing up. Because the children sat down after being told to do so, the teacher thought that the "Sit down" response was working, but instead the response was causing more students to stand up. Criticism represents teacher attention being given to off-task behavior, and it is like a trap. The more a teacher criticizes, the more likely it is that the criticized behavior will occur; then the teacher has to criticize even more. A vicious circle has been created.

Reinforcement theory advises that the teacher should ignore off-task behavior and, instead, praise sitting and working. The sequence is (1) to *specify* that students should keep seated, (2) to *praise* sitting and working, and (3) to *ignore* standing up idly.

Also, reinforcement should occur immediately, because if it is delayed it may follow and thereby strengthen behaviors other than the target behavior. Any behavior that is immediately followed by reinforcement will become more likely to occur. Skinner's pigeons sometimes walked around in a circle before pecking the key and getting food. Thereafter, they would always make a circle before pecking even though reinforcement was not contingent on this circling behavior. When a reinforcement occurs accidentally — say, a child finds some money while walking home from school — any behavior that happened to precede this stroke of good luck will be reinforced and, hence, repeated. The lucky youngster may continue to follow the same route home or may walk looking down, even though finding the money was not predictably contingent on either behavior. Skinner (1953) called this *superstitious behavior*.

Every instance of the target behavior should be reinforced (continuous reinforcement) until it is mastered. Thereafter, intermittent, variable reinforcement schedules can be used.

Finally, as reinforcing agents teachers must be in control of themselves or else they will not be able to control their students. Their use of praise must be consistent, as must their inclination to ignore disruptive behavior. A teacher's loss of temper will be likely to lead to ineffective classroom management and, like scolding or criticizing, will only increase (rather than decrease) undesirable behavior.

Punishment

According to reinforcement theory, effective use of reinforcement should make the use of punishment unnecessary. The most effective technique for weakening behavior is to use nonreinforcement — to ignore it. The next best approach is to use negative reinforcement — to allow punishment to be avoided or escaped if the undesirable behavior is terminated (Skinner, 1953). Punishment is not a preferred method for changing behavior, because the person being punished usually does not extinguish the undesirable behavior. Rather, he or she simply resists the punishment or waits and performs the undesirable behavior at another time. The behavior is merely suppressed and may reappear later under different circumstances (Skinner, 1953, 1968). Moreover, the punisher may serve as a model for future aggressive behavior on the part of the person being punished, and the current situation may turn into a battle of wills between the teacher and the youthful "offender."

However, there are two circumstances when punishment, as a last resort, may be used effectively. The first is when undesirable behavior is so *frequent* that there is virtually no desirable behavior to reinforce. Extreme aggressiveness in a child sometimes leaves no room for reinforcement. The second is when the problem behavior is so *intense* that someone, including the child himself, may get hurt. Again, aggressiveness can be an example of such intense behavior.

Types of Punishment

There are two types of punishment. Type 1 involves the presentation or use of aversive or painful events, such as scolding. Type 2 punishment involves taking away or stopping reinforcers, and it is usually referred to as *response cost*. The person's undesirable response costs him or her privileges or money (for example, a fine). Cutting out a student's potential reinforcers and access to all possible reinforcement by having him or her sit alone (called *time-out*) is an example of Type 2 punishment. The two types of punishment can be related to the two types of reinforcement, as shown in Table 3.3.

Using Punishment Effectively

Research by Azrin and Holz (1966) has shown that if punishment is used effectively, it can be expected to weaken behavior, just as reinforcement strengthens it. In using punishment effectively, one must *prevent avoidance and escape from the source of punishment*.

Table 3.3 🍎 The Relationship Between Two Types of Punishment and Two Types of Reinforcement

Effect on Behavior	Procedure	
	Present Stimulus	*Terminate Stimulus*
Strengthens	Positive reinforcement (getting candy)	Negative reinforcement (not getting scolded)
Weakens	Type 1 punishment (getting scolded)	Type 2 punishment (not getting candy)

SOURCE: Adapted from Becker, W. C., Englemann, S., & Thomas, D. R. (1975). *Teaching 1: Classroom management* (p. 255). Chicago: Science Research Associates.

Withdrawal of positive reinforcers, as in Type 2 punishment, is generally regarded to be the more effective form of punishment (Burchard & Barrera, 1972) as long as clear-cut steps are provided for earning the reinforcement back. In other words, once a procedure like time-out begins, it cannot be avoided or escaped; but by subsequently behaving properly, the student can earn back the lost rewards and avoid future time-outs. Note in Table 3.3 the arrow connecting Type 2 punishment and positive reinforcement. By behaving acceptably, students can avoid time-out and earn positive rewards in its place.

Secondly, it is important to *minimize the need for future punishment*. The teacher can do this by using a warning signal, which, when paired with a punishment, becomes a conditioned punishment. That is, the warning signal alone comes to cause the person to

Box 3.4

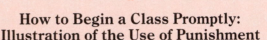

How to Begin a Class Promptly:
Illustration of the Use of Punishment

Problem

The children in my class had some difficulty in settling down when they came into the classroom. Frequently, many were still out of their seats when the last bell rang. I decided to attempt to change this situation by arranging things a little differently in the classroom.

Method

I began by simply counting the number of children not in their seats at the last bell, both at the beginning of the morning and afternoon school sessions. In my class of 21, frequently as many as half of the children were not seated at the last bell. I kept this record without letting the children know that I was doing it for a total of eight days. On the ninth day, I told the children what I was doing and what would happen to them if they were not in their seats when the last bell rang. The punishment was that each child who was not in his seat would miss five minutes of Physical Education time. He would go to the Physical Education class but would have to remain standing at the back of the room for five minutes before he could enter into the games. I issued this warning both on the ninth and tenth day, with no appreciable effect on their behavior. On the eleventh day, the contingency went into effect.

Results and Discussion

As you can see by the graph, the number of children out of their seats at the last bell has decreased considerably. This has proven to be an effective way to lessen the confusion and increase the instruction time at the beginning of school.

behave properly. Also, reinforcing behavior that is incompatible with the objectionable behavior will cause the objectionable behavior to be replaced by the desirable behavior. In other words, students cannot talk and be quiet at the same time.

Finally, the punisher, or person administering the punishment, must be *calm and consistent* and the punishment must be *matter-of-fact* and *directed at the behavior*, not at the child. Moreover, it must be *immediate*. The punisher must not be angry and aggressive, nor must the punishment function as a retaliation or put-down; because otherwise the receiver of the punishment will be exposed to an aggressive model who is likely to be imitated (see the discussion of modeling in Chapter 11). An illustration of the effective use of punishment in changing classroom behavior is shown in Box 3.4.

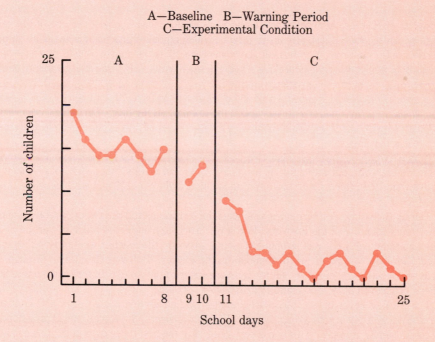

A—Baseline   B—Warning Period
C—Experimental Condition

Number of children who failed to be seated by the final bell

SOURCE: Jill Stiltner, in Wood, W. S. (1971). The Lincoln Elementary School projects: Some results of an in-service training course in behavioral psychology. In W. C. Becker (Ed.), *An empirical basis for change in education*. Chicago: Science Research Associates.

Time-out can be an effective punishment, particularly for young children, but it must involve *cutting off all reinforcement for a period of time*. Removing a child from a situation that is unpleasant does not constitute a punishment. In fact, it represents a negative reinforcement and so strengthens the behavior that led to its occurrence (see Table 3.3 and refer back to Box 3.3 for a concrete example of this effect). For example, sending a child to the principal's office may actually reinforce the behavior that caused the child's ejection if the classroom represents an aversive environment to the child. Objectionable behavior will be weakened by ejection only if the child thereby loses the chance to gain immediate positive reinforcement. For that to occur, the child must want to stay in the classroom.

Box 3.5

🍎

The Digit Reverser

Bob was an eight-year-old enrolled in a Basic Skills class. He was considered one of the better students by his teacher. But nearly every time he added numbers producing a two-digit sum, he would reverse the numerals. For example, he would write 31 as the sum of 5 and 8. Because of this behavior, Bob received several neurological and eye examinations. He was also given lots of extra help by several teachers. The problem remained.

A check of Bob's skills showed he could discriminate 31 from 13, 24 from 42, and so on. In fact, he would point out reversals on his paper if the teacher missed them. On several occasions he was seen erasing a correct answer and replacing it with a reversal. An experiment was undertaken to see what was going on.

Sets of twenty problems yielding two-digit sums were made up for each day. They involved the same kind of work, but with different examples. Over four weeks' time, each possible sum was used seven times. Problems with sums having identical digits (11, 22) and with sums of 10 were not used.

During the study, Bob raised his hand when he had completed the twenty problems and his teacher would then check the answers. For seven days (baseline), the teacher marked C if an answer was right and X if it was wrong. For wrong answers, the teacher would say, "This one is incorrect. You see, you reversed the numbers in the answer." Bob was then taken through each problem he missed and "helped" to get the right answer with the aid of counters and number lines. For these first seven days, Bob made *18 to 20 errors each day*.

For the next seven days, Bob's teacher simply marked all correct answers C. No comments were made nor help given with wrong answers. For right answers, the teacher might give Bob a pat on the back, a smile, and say, "This one is very good." For the first three days under this condition, Bob's errors remained near 20. Then for the next four days they *dropped to 5, 1, 4, and 0*.

There could be little question that the teacher had been caught in the "being helpful" trap.

SOURCE: Becker, W. C., Engelmann, S., & Thomas, D. R. (1975). *Teaching 1: Classroom management* (pp. 78–79). Chicago: Science Research Associates.

Aversive Control

Although not advocated by Skinner (1953), aversive control is a procedure that many practitioners of his theory use to alter the behavior of children. It begins as Type 1 punishment when the child's undesirable behavior, having become difficult or impossible for the teacher or parent to ignore, is punished by a scolding or by the application of some other aversive stimulus. After a few such aversive results, the child learns to avoid the aversive stimulus or scolding by performing an acceptable behavior rather than the punishable one under the same set of circumstances. Thus, punishment gives way to negative reinforcement (see the arrow between punishment 1 and negative reinforcement in Table 3.3). When the parent says "Go to bed," for example, or the teacher says "No talking now," the child goes to bed or stops talking in order to avoid being spanked or yelled at. Occasionally, the child will slip as a result of extinction of the desirable behavior, but another punishment will quickly restore the negative reinforcing value of acceptable behavior.

In effect, aversive control means control of behavior by the threat of punishment, rather than by the punishment itself. Its practical weakness lies partly in the fact that the undesirable behavior is not unlearned or forgotten, merely suppressed, and may manifest itself in other forms (like going to the bedroom but playing instead of going to bed, or talking "behind the teacher's back"). Its major weakness is that, for it to be effective, punishment *must* be forthcoming whenever the bad behavior occurs, or else the threat is not a real threat at all. If a child can sometimes perform the bad behavior and not be punished (or see other children who do it not punished — as in some modeling examples in Chapter 11), then the alternative, good behavior, will not be negatively reinforced. Aversive control breaks down because of adult inconsistency.

Skinner on Teaching

Skinner (1953, 1968) applied reinforcement theory to the process of teaching (a topic to be covered again in Chapter 5, in the context of the design of instruction). The application is quite direct and straightforward and follows from the principles covered in this chapter. It can be summarized by the points below.

1. Provide for an active *response* by the learner. (Merely listening is not enough; the learner must perform a response.)
2. Follow the performance of a correct response with *positive consequences* (such as "You are correct," or "Good answer"); ignore incorrect responses. (See Box 3.5.)
3. Provide optimal *contingencies* of reinforcement for correct performance: positive, immediate, and frequent; initially continuous and then intermittent.
4. Maximize the likelihood of correct responses and minimize the likelihood of errors by *shaping* behavior through the use of small instructional steps.
5. *Avoid* aversive control (do not punish errors; see Box 3.5).
6. Use *cues* to signal and *prompt* the correct performance.
7. *Reinforce* the exact performance that you want the learner to learn.

8. *Program the environment* (for example, teach by using instructional materials and experiences to manage the contingencies). This is also called "stimulus control" (Skinner, 1969). Design the materials to do the teaching (see Chapter 5).

9. Begin with *contrived reinforcers*, but prepare the learner for the *natural reinforcers* of the real world.

Summary of Main Points

1. *Operant conditioning* refers to responses that are emitted and learned because they lead to or are followed by positive consequences, called *reinforcement*. People learn to operate on their environment to gain reinforcement.

2. Even though operant responses are emitted randomly, they can be signaled by signs called *discriminative stimuli, or S^D*. People learn that if they perform the behavior after the discriminative stimulus has been presented, they will get the reward, but if they perform it following any other stimulus, or S^Δ, they will not. Reinforcement that follows only a discriminative stimulus is called *differential reinforcement*.

3. There are many types of reinforcement. Some, called *primary*, have automatic reinforcement value; others, called *secondary*, must be learned to be liked. Food is a primary reinforcer, while money is a secondary one. *Positive* reinforcers are those that people like to get (such as candy), while *negative* reinforcers are those that people would like to escape or avoid (such as electric shock).

4. *Social* reinforcers are interpersonal pleasures, such as praise; *token* reinforcers are points that can be traded in for something better; and *activity* reinforcers are good things to do, like play. The *Premack principle* states that children will do things they don't like very well, such as study, in return for getting to do something they like a lot, such as play.

5. For learning to occur, reinforcement must occur every time the target behavior occurs, that is, it must be *continuous*. If it never occurs, the learned behavior will cease to occur. That is called *extinction*.

6. Once a behavior has been learned, the teacher or researcher can maintain its occurrence by reinforcing it *intermittently*, that is, after so many occurrences (called *ratio* reinforcement) or after so much time has elapsed (called *interval* reinforcement). Moreover, the number of occurrences or the amount of time between reinforcements can stay the same (be *fixed*) or change (be *variable*).

7. Using reinforcement theory to manage naturally occurring behavior is called *behavior modification*. It involves teaching someone to perform a target behavior as a response to a signal or discriminative stimulus in order to gain a reinforcement. Behaviors other than the target behavior are ignored.

8. Giving the learner additional signs or signals in the form of more discriminative stimuli is called *prompting*. Such prompts should eventually be removed or faded out to avoid the learner becoming dependent on them. Connecting simple responses together to form a complex act is called *chaining*.

9. If a learner cannot initially perform a target behavior according to a particular performance criterion, the teacher can *shape* that behavior by initially reinforcing approximations of it and, little by little, requiring that the performance attain the final criterion in order to be reinforced. Thus, shaping can be used to achieve gradual mastery of a difficult behavior.

10. A teacher can use reinforcement theory to be an *effective classroom manager*. Desired behaviors such as rules should be *specified* in advance, performing these behaviors should be *praised*, and not performing them should be *ignored*.

11. However, in extreme cases of unacceptable and potentially harmful behavior, *punishment* may be used. The potentially most effective form of punishment is the removal of opportunities for reinforcement — called *response cost*.

12. The avoidance of punishment, or aversive control, can also be used to deter undesirable behavior. Desirable behavior will be negatively reinforced if the child is allowed to avoid punishment. However, the inconsistent application of punishment can make aversive control ineffective, even as a behavior suppressant.

13. Skinner's theory has been applied to teaching. The teacher must provide the learner with the opportunity to respond, and then must prompt and shape that response so that it is likely to be correct. The correct response should be followed by a reinforcer. Instructional materials should be designed to help do the teaching, and aversive control should be avoided.

Suggested Resources

Becker, W. C. (1986). *Applied psychology for teachers: A behavioral cognitive approach.* Chicago: Science Research Associates.

Skinner, B. F. (1978). *About behaviorism.* New York: Knopf.

Skinner, B. F., & Epstein, R. (1982). *Skinner for the classroom.* Champaign, IL: Research Press.

Skinner, B. F. (1968). *The technology of teaching.* New York: Appleton–Century–Crofts.

Sulzer-Azaroff, B., & Mayer, G. R. (1986). *Achieving educational excellence: Using behavioral strategies.* New York: Holt, Rinehart & Winston.

Chapter
4

The Conditions of Learning

Objectives

1. Identify and describe eight phases or processes that help define the conditions of learning.
2. Describe the specific learning conditions embodied in each of the steps or events of the instructional sequence.
3. Identify and describe five outcomes of learning.
4. Describe the role of learning analysis and learning hierarchies in specifying necessary instructional tasks.
5. Describe a model for the systematic design of instructional materials such as guides and manuals.

Introduction

This chapter will focus on a theory of learning developed by Robert M. Gagné (1985; Gagné & Driscoll, 1988) that describes learning as a sequence of processes or phases, each of which requires that different conditions be met for learning to take place. Because this theory can be applied to both lesson planning and the delivery of instruction, it might more accurately be called a theory of instruction. It focuses on (1) the phases or *processes* that learners go through while learning meaningful material, and the *conditions* that facilitate each phase, as a way of understanding the learning process; (2) the various *outcomes* of learning—that is, the specific competencies to be acquired as a result of learning; and (3) the *events* that must occur in order for learning to proceed successfully. By incorporating into his or her instruction the events and the conditions called for in each event, the teacher can facilitate the various learning outcomes. Hence, Gagné's theory provides us with a framework for determining those conditions that are most conducive to learning and that should therefore be provided through instruction. The relationship of the parts of Gagné's model to one another is shown in Table 4.1.

The Processes of Learning

The processes are shown in sequence in Figure 4.1. Together they represent an attempt to explain the entire learning process, beginning with the reception of a stimulus and ending with the results of an action. For example, a traffic light turns red, your receptors perceive this and send a message via your sensory register to your short-term memory to be recorded. Long-term memory tells you that red means stop, and so your response generator tells your foot to hit the brakes. Later in this chapter we will see how the processes may be applied to the necessary events of classroom instruction.

Attention.   For learning to begin, stimulation must be received, and such reception requires that the learner attend to or focus on the stimulation. If the learner does not pay attention to instruction, it will not be received and no learning will take place. Students who are talking to one another while the teacher is instructing are not attending to instruction and so will not receive its message.

The teacher could gain students' attention by changing the intensity of his voice or waving his arms, as in hailing a taxi. But most characteristically he will gain it by giving students verbal directions, such as "Look carefully at what I've written on the board" or, even more directly, "This is important; you'd better pay close attention." College stu-

Table 4.1 🍎 Component Parts of the Gagné Theory

Before Learning	During Learning	After Learning
Learner with entering capabilities	Learning phases (internal conditions)	Learning outcomes: verbal information, intellectual skills, cognitive strategies, attitudes, motor skills
Learning analysis (to identify competencies)	Instructional events (external conditions)	

dents often become quite adept at knowing what it is that they had better pay attention to — such as anything the professor says twice or writes on the board and then underlines. For younger students, constant efforts to gain or maintain attention may be required.

Motivation.   An early learning process is motivation, specifically incentive motivation, in which the learner strives to reach some goal and then receives something for the result. Most individuals are believed to have the urge or desire to achieve or perform in a competent manner (White, 1959); if they are to be engaged in the learning process, this desire must be activated.

     In order to establish motivation based on the incentive to achieve a particular goal, Gagné advocates establishing in learners an *expectancy* of what they will gain as a result of engaging in learning or participating in instruction. The teacher establishes this expectancy by telling learners what it is they will be able to do at the completion of learning (Gagné & Driscoll, 1988). Motivation, therefore, is established by creation of an expectancy of learning, which, in turn, is based on the anticipation of being able to know or do something new at the completion of instruction. "When I'm done teaching this unit, you'll be able to solve problems involving fractions" is a statement of expectancy designed to motivate learners. Motivation does not ensure learning, but it does prepare someone to learn from subsequent instruction.

Selective Perception of Features.   What students must attend to in order to learn is more than a mere impression of the information that is presented. Students must focus on the pattern of new information. This focus or perception is selectively based on the goal or expectancy that has motivated it. As Gagné and Driscoll (1988) illustrate, in written material such as this textbook, the reader focuses on the words and their meaning, not on the size, shape, darkness, and texture of the printed type. The reader

The author, left, with Robert M. Gagné.

Figure 4.1 🍎 Relation of Learner Structures and Processes in an Act of Learning   From R. M. Gagné, 1985.

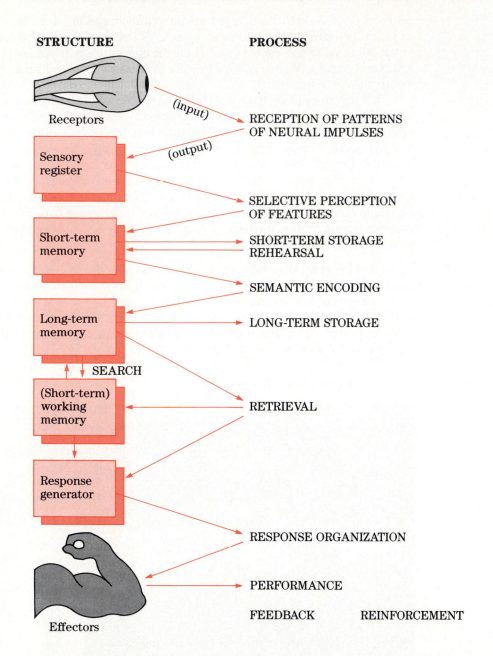

selectively perceives some aspects of what he is presented with, as opposed to others, because the perceived aspects are relevant to the purpose of the reading.

Furthermore, selective perception of the features of a stimulus situation requires that the learner be able to discriminate or distinguish between the various features, the appearances, the letters, the words, the meanings. You, as a learner, must be able to discriminate between the main points and the less important or supportive material so that you can selectively perceive or pay more attention to the former. When you go through a textbook and highlight the key points, you are selectively perceiving the features relevant to your learning goal.

Once students have selectively perceived the key features, they must store this information in *short-term memory*. For material to be stored, it must be transformed into a form that is most storable and subsequently recognizable. One difficulty is that short-term memory has a limited capacity, limited in terms of both (1) the amount of time that something can remain in it — approximately 20 seconds according to Anderson (1985); and (2) the number of items that can be stored simultaneously — seven, plus or minus two, according to Miller (1956). To overcome the time limitation, students can repeat the stored material over and over to themselves (called *rehearsal*), as you would a phone number. To overcome the number-of-items limitation, students can combine units into groups or clusters (called *chunking*) and then remember the groups, as you might the members of a baseball team or the cast of a movie. (Rehearsal and chunking will be encountered again in Chapter 6 on information processing.)

Semantic Encoding.   New information must be transformed again if it is to enter into long-term memory. The process of organizing new information meaningfully to make it more memorable — and hence lasting — is called semantic encoding. There are many ways that semantic encoding can be accomplished (most of which will be covered in Chapter 6 on information processing). Some examples are connecting words into sentences (Jensen & Rohwer, 1963) or providing pictures along with words (Levin & Kaplan, 1972). Often, learners will learn or develop their own ways of accomplishing the semantic encoding process, especially when they are given little guidance in the instructional process.

Storage in Long-Term Memory.   The new information that has just been semantically encoded now enters into long-term memory. It may be remembered for a while and then fade, or information entered after it may interfere with its being remembered. Review and practice are activities that help maintain information in long-term storage.

Search and Retrieval.   When a person needs to use a piece of information that has been stored in long-term memory, that information must be searched for among all the stored information and, once found, must be retrieved or recalled. *Cues* can be used to jog someone's memory, that is, to help him or her recall something previously learned. Even though learners should be taught to be responsible for their own recall, designers of instruction would be well-advised to provide cues to stimulate or activate the retrieval process.

Performance.   In order (1) to verify that learning has taken place and (2) to provide an opportunity for feedback, Gagné proposes that the next process in the learning sequence be performance. The actual nature of the performance represents a learning outcome (which is described in a later section). To be sure that learning has occurred, it is usual for the teacher to require more than a single performance.

It is often important that the performance situation not be exactly the same as the learning situation, in order to ensure that learning can be applied in a variety of contexts. Being able to perform in a variety of situations is called *transfer* and is typically an important goal of learning.

Feedback.   It is also important that learners be able to discover whether or not their performance has satisfied the requirements of a given situation or met a given goal, so that they can confirm or discontinue the expectancy they established in the first phase. Feedback represents the knowledge of the adequacy or inadequacy of the given performance. It also represents what Skinner (in the preceding chapter) refers to as reinforcement. In Gagné's theory, however, reinforcement simply confirms an expectancy and hence closes the learning loop — rather than strengthening the tendency to respond in a given way to a given situation, as in Skinner's theory. Thus, feedback or reinforcement is seen by Gagné as primarily having informational value rather than functioning as an automatic strengthener. With feedback a student can tell whether he or she has done the task right, either by seeing the obvious results, as in trying to hit a target with a dart, or by being told, as in getting a test back and seeing the grade and the teacher's comments.

Performance is a key process in learning. It helps the student show what she has learned and provides the teacher with a chance to give her feedback.

The Events of Instruction

The most concrete aspect of Gagné's theory is the events of instruction: the nine experiences or sets of conditions that must occur in an instructional sequence or lesson to ensure that the desired learning takes place. If you apply the nine processes of learning already described to the five learning outcomes, you come out with the nine events. The events incorporate each of the necessary processes into a lesson so that each type of learning outcome may be mastered. Knowing the events of instruction provides a solid basis for designing instruction or constructing a lesson plan. Knowing how students learn (that is, the processes) provides a basis for deciding how to teach them (the events). Each event will be described in turn. (The relationship between the processes and the events is shown in Table 4.2.)

Table 4.2 🍎 The Relationship Between the Learning Processes and the Instructional Events

Process	Event	Example
Attention	Gaining learner's attention	"You know how important it is to get a job. Listen up because we're going to learn something that helps you get one."
Motivation	Informing learner of objective	"Now you're going to learn how to write a job application letter in business format."
Selective perception of features	Stimulating recall of prior learning	"You've already learned how to write a business letter."
	Presenting the stimulus	"A job application letter is a business letter that describes your background, interests, qualifications, and job desires."
Semantic encoding / Storage in long-term memory	Providing learning guidance	"Here's an example of a job application letter. Let's go over it together and identify and describe each of its parts."
Search and retrieval / Performance	Eliciting performance	"Now I want you to write your own job application letter."
Feedback	Providing feedback	"I have read each of your letters and written my comments on them."
	Assessing performance	"Now I am going to test you on your ability to write this kind of letter."
	Enhancing retention and transfer	"Here is a case of an actual student. I want you to write a letter for that student."

Event 1. Gaining Attention.   The first condition of learning, according to Gagné — the first thing to be done in teaching a lesson — is to get the students' attention. Often, this is done by means of a verbal instruction: "This is important." "I want you to pay particular attention to this." "This will be on the test." However, teachers should also think of other attention-getting devices, such as a demonstration or the use of some strong stimulus (for example, a light or sound).

Event 2. Informing the Learner of the Objective.   The second condition of learning is an expectancy for what the end state of learning will be. Telling the student the *aim* or *objective* of instruction helps establish such an expectancy. "This is what you will be able to do when this unit is completed." It may be to recite the state capitals, measure the volume of a gas, or analyze a poem; but whatever the objective is, students are more likely to achieve it, according to Gagné, if they are told in advance what it is.

It may also be motivating to a student to try to master an objective if the *relevance* of that objective to the student's subsequent learning or performance is made clear (Keller, 1983). Finally, students cannot tell when they have accomplished a learning task and experience the satisfaction of that accomplishment unless they know what final performance is expected of them. It is the objective that tells students what final performance is expected. (We will encounter objectives again in the next chapter.)

Event 3. Stimulating Recall of Prior Learning.   The third condition of learning is that the learner has already mastered the essential skills on which the new material builds. New learning invariably builds on prior learning. Therefore, the success of the new learning will depend on whether (1) the necessary prior learning has already taken place, (2) the student knows what prior learning to try to remember and apply, and (3) the student can remember the necessary prior learning. To accomplish this learning event, the teacher must first determine what prior learning is relevant to the new learning and then must either point it out ("Remember that you have already learned how to convert a mixed number to an improper fraction") or reinstate it ("You need to remember how to convert a mixed number to an improper fraction, so I want us to go over that again quickly"). The teacher may then reteach the old material or have the students try to perform the previously taught task themselves.

Tasks that must be learned before new ones can be learned are called *prerequisites*. Without both learning and remembering prerequisites, new learning cannot occur. Therefore, many subjects must be taught in sequence and the teacher must ensure that previously learned prerequisite tasks are retrieved from memory by students before presenting new tasks that depend on these prerequisites. According to Gagné, the teacher should not depend on the learner to determine which previously learned tasks are relevant. The teacher should point them out.

Event 4. Presenting the Stimulus.   The fourth condition of learning is that what is to be learned must be presented to the learner in some fashion. Learning requires the presentation of new information. It is the old information and the new information combined that enables an attentive, expectant student to achieve mastery of a task. Providing new information means providing students with a new stimulus. This may take the form of pointing out to students the *distinctive features* of the stimulus. ("These fractions have the same denominator so they can be added or subtracted.") The stimulus may take the form of a definition or a rule. It may be a proposition (a piece of declarative knowledge) or a production (instructions about how to do something). In any event, it will be a stimulus, it will be new, and the teacher's task is to present its distinctive features so that it can enter the students' short-term memory. The teacher must determine (1) what new stimulus information is required by an objective and (2) how to present that new stimulus information so that students can perceive and retain it.

Event 5. Providing Learning Guidance.

The fifth condition of learning is that all the components of the task to be learned be combined in the necessary way. To properly combine old and new information and to make it possible for the result to be entered into long-term memory, students must be given help or guidance. This help should focus on ways that the combined information can be semantically encoded. Gagné (1985) has referred to this as *integrating instructions* that supply the learner with the rule or model for using all the relevant information to perform the task properly. Examples, demonstrations, diagrams, and step-by-step instructions (such as recipes) all serve to help the learner combine, store, and retrieve all the information in a way that will be suitable or appropriate for performing the objective.

Teachers need to plan what techniques they will use to guide the learners in a given task and how they will present these techniques. Sometimes it is best to let students try to discover how to use the information they have been taught to perform the task. At other times, prompting or cuing may be required, and occasionally only explicit step-by-step instructions will do the job. Teachers may want to plan to try more than one approach.

Event 6. Eliciting Performance.

The sixth condition of learning is that the combined components of the learning task actually be carried out by the learner. The preceding steps ensure that learning has taken place, that new information or skills have been encoded into long-term memory. The sixth step serves as an opportunity for learners to demonstrate (to themselves and their teachers) that the new learning has, in fact, occurred. Now is the time for learners to actually complete the task they have been just taught to do.

Performance is elicited when students complete a worksheet, do homework, answer questions in class, complete an experiment, or take on any other form of practice that gives them the chance to try out what they have learned.

Event 7. Providing Feedback.

The seventh condition of learning is the opportunity to find out how successful or accurate the performance has been. Hence, the follow-up to practice is feedback — information about the student's performance that tells him or her how good it is or how it could be improved. Successful performance yields positive feedback, which serves as a reinforcement for performance of the task. Students now know that they have developed the capability set forth in the original objective. Those whose performance needs improvement and who realize, from the feedback, what improvements to make should be allowed to practice some more and should again be provided with feedback. Eventually they will experience success and be reinforced for their efforts.

Event 8. Assessing Performance.

The eighth condition is that learning be evaluated so that decisions about subsequent learning can be made. Now that the performance has been practiced and reinforced, it is time to test it. This time students have to demonstrate their learning to the satisfaction of the teacher before they can be deemed ready to continue on to new work. Moreover, the test situation will confront the students with circumstances and details that are not precisely the same as those previously encountered, to ensure that understanding rather than mere memorization has taken place.

Event 9. Enhancing Retention and Transfer.   The ninth and last condition of learning is that experiences occur that will enable new learning to generalize to other situations and be used again. Hence, the last step features review and application. Reviewing the material helps ensure that it will be remembered. Applying it in a variety of contexts and situations helps ensure that it will transfer, that it will be useful beyond the specific situation in which it was originally learned. Adding fractions and mixed numbers may have been learned in the abstract, for example, but it would be useful to have this knowledge transfer or apply to real situations, such as measuring pieces of lumber to build a doghouse or dollhouse. To facilitate such transfer, the teacher must show students how and when to apply their newly learned skills.

Thus, we have the teaching/learning sequence according to Gagné. It forms — as we shall soon see, here in this chapter and again in the next — a highly useful model for instructional design. Its application to the design of an actual lesson is shown in Table 4.2, again in Box 4.1, and a third time in Box 4.2.

The Outcomes of Learning

Gagné has identified five categories of learning outcomes that represent ways of classifying performance. The value of the classification process is that it enables us to group together performances that have common features and thereby enables us to focus on those common features or conditions that must be met to facilitate instruction. In other words, learning how to ride a bike is more similar to learning how to sew than it is to learning the capitals of the states, or than learning how to sew is to learning how to solve personal problems. Isolating the common features or necessary conditions of the learning performances or outcomes described below helps teachers determine what they must do to ensure that such outcomes are mastered.

Verbal Information

Verbal information represents knowledge, that is, what a person knows. It is made up of facts that have been learned and remembered and that can then be recalled later. Verbal information includes such facts as telephone numbers, lines of a poem, football rules, names of the planets, and the multiplication tables. When students are asked to *name*, *list*, or *state* something, they are usually being asked to provide verbal information.

Declarative Knowledge.   A unit of verbal information may be considered to be a fact or, alternatively, an idea — an idea being a connection between facts. E. D. Gagné (1985) refers to ideas as *propositions* and uses the proposition to represent what she calls declarative knowledge, or knowledge that "something is the case." A proposition contains a noun, called the argument, and a verb, called the relation (R). Arguments are further divided into subject (S), objects (O), and recipients (r). In the proposition "Tony gave Herb a ride," *Tony* would be the subject, *Herb* the recipient, and *a ride* the object. The relation would be *gave*.

Box 4.1

Teaching First-Graders to Read the Calendar

Instructional Event	Classroom Activity
1. Gain attention.	Ask students to raise their hand if they know when their birthday is.
2. Inform learner of the objective.	Explain that they are going to learn how to read a calendar.
3. Stimulate recall of prior learning.	Ask the students if they remember what the days of the week are. Ask the students if they remember what the twelve months of the year are. Ask the students to count to 31 by ones.
4. Present distinctive stimulus features.	Show the students a large calendar. Discuss how it is made. Talk about the number in the first square and the number in the last one. Then count out all the numbers on the calendar.
5. Provide learning guidance.	Show the name of the current month as well as the names of the other months. In addition, ask the students what the dates of their birthdays are. Also, ask the students the dates of any holidays they might know. Then discuss marking the days with appropriate symbols. For example, a birthday cake could symbolize a child's birthday. Ask the children to look at the calendar each day and determine which child's birthday or holiday is next.
6. Elicit performance.	Ask each student to make his own copy of the large calendar. Ask him to mark his calendar each day using the appropriate symbols. Give him worksheets and ask him to answer various questions about his calendar orally.
7. Provide feedback.	Check the calendar the student has made and make any necessary corrections. Tell her orally if the answers she gives to the worksheet exercise are correct.
8. Assess performance.	Give the students a new calendar and ask them to answer questions to see if they can read it correctly.
9. Enhance retention and transfer.	Ask the students to help make a classroom calendar. Dates can be marked for important events such as visitors, field trips, and special school occasions.

Box 4.2

Gagné's Events of Instruction Implemented in the Exciting Game of Soccer

It's 9:00 on a gorgeous summer morning—the first day of soccer camp in Seattle, Washington. I'm an instructor here. Before me are six sprawling, manicured soccer fields, and milling about on the nearest of them are 180 very lively children.

gaining attention

A whistle blows, loudly. Nearly all 180 pairs of eyes turn toward the noise. "Come in, please!" Walter Schmetzer—the camp director—shouts with a thick German accent. Once the children are gathered and quiet, Walter says, "This morning all of you, at the end of the first session, will be able to dribble a soccer ball effectively, or at least will know how to." The youngsters look at him incredulously.

informing kids of objective

"Have any of you ever kicked a can while you were walking down the street?" Many heads nod "yes." "Well, the same principle applies; however, you must keep the ball close to your feet, and keep your head up so that you can see where you're going." We instructors then break into pairs, each pair responsible for 20 promising young soccer players.

stimulating recall of prior learning

presenting new information

Once in our assigned area, my fellow instructor, Jim, and I give further instructions. I begin: "This is how a player properly dribbles (I demonstrate) a ball." I offer *five* key points. Then the children attempt it—but only after a review of each key point.

providing learning guidance

The children are asked to incorporate the key points in a progressive (add one key point to another) manner. Once the children have attempted to assimilate the learning, Jim and I have them dribble past us, in two lines, so we can offer suggestions to improve dribbling ability. Usually, the children forget just one key element. "Keep the ball closer to you. Look up when you dribble! Only glance at the ball."

eliciting performance

providing feedback

Next, Jim and I divide the children into two teams. We briefly review and demonstrate the proper method of dribbling. After this, the children are tested; they are graded—from 1 to 10—after they dribble past us this second time.

assessing performance

Next we have a scrimmage, during which the children are offered praise and constructive criticism as to their demonstrating the correct dribbling skills. Thus, they are encouraged to bring their knowledge into a gamelike situation.

enhancing retention and transfer

Jim and I finish the session by stressing how important dribbling is to players during games, how vital it is that players retain possession of the ball when advancing it, and how having this skill makes them better players.

Figure 4.2 🍎 An Example of a Propositional Network

From Hayes-Roth and Thorndyke, 1979.

The Domestic Welfare Agency (DWA) distributes information about professional options. Information about professional options is distributed by means of computer terminals.

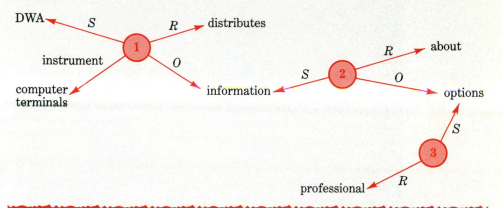

Propositions can be connected to form networks to help researchers understand how people may be able to remember as many ideas as they do. With propositional networks, related bits of information can be stored closer to each other than unrelated bits in order to increase the storage capacity of working memory. An example of a propositional network is given in Figure 4.2. (Another appears in Figure 6.1 in Chapter 6.)

Functions of Knowledge. Knowledge serves a number of functions for students. It may serve as a *prerequisite for further learning*, in the sense that learning is made up of building blocks of ideas. It may be of *practical importance in providing labels for everyday communication*. Some people carry a wealth of information in their heads and use it for a variety of purposes, including "making small talk." Finally, knowledge provides *"food" for thought*; that is, it provides the elements for thinking and for problem-solving.

Intellectual Skills

Whereas declarative knowledge means knowing *that* something is the case, intellectual skills represent knowing *how* to do something. Intellectual skills are also called *procedural knowledge* (by E. D. Gagné, 1985). They enable the learner to transform information from one form to another, that is, from a problem, such as how to find something, to a solution: finding it. Procedural knowledge is represented by *productions*, or condition–action statements. The condition is represented by an IF clause and the action by a THEN clause. For example, "IF the goal is to find out what kind of geometric shape something is, THEN count the number of sides."

Intellectual skills are important because if we had to learn everything as knowledge, there would be far too much to remember. Instead, we learn to use symbols to represent

The teaching of intellectual skills begins in the early grades.

entire classes or categories of object or event. These skills or productions then become the mechanism for transforming facts into acts.

R. M. Gagné (1985) identifies five kinds of intellectual skills, arranged (and described below) in order of complexity from simplest to most complicated.

Discriminations.   Discriminations represent the ability to distinguish one feature of an object or symbol from another. Said another way, the performance made possible by discrimination learning is the ability *to tell the difference among stimuli*. This does not necessarily mean being able to use or even name these stimuli, only being able to recognize that they are different. Discrimination is the mechanism involved in the process of learning that was previously described as the selective perception of features: separating what is important to you at the moment from what is not.

Here are two symbols:

$ 𝄞

One is smaller than the other and they are shaped differently. You may or may not know what they mean, but at least you know that they are different. You can discriminate between them. Below are pictures of two objects. Even if you do not know their names, you can see that they are different. They look different; hence you can discriminate between them.

Concrete Concepts.   Beyond the ability to tell that objects or events are different is the ability to identify, name, or label them. Above are a baseball bat and a tennis racket. We learn to recognize objects such as these by sight. The manufacturer or even the material from which they are made may vary, but their identity and hence their recognizability remain the same. They represent some of the many concrete concepts we learn to identify, usually as children. We also learn to recognize and name object qualities, such as smooth versus scratchy or round versus pointed. Relational concepts such as near and far, above and below, higher and lower are also learned.

   According to Gagné and Driscoll (1988, p. 50), the performance indicative of concrete concept learning is "the ability to identify a class of objects, object qualities, or relations by pointing out one or more instances of the class." The learner must know the name or label for the concrete concept (for example, those in the middle, the squares, the largest, the whales) and must be able to identify the class by means of its particular instances. Thus, upon seeing a picture of one whale, the student can either identify the class of whales as the name for both the instance and the entire class or can fit the label "whale," when provided by the teacher, to the appropriate picture.

Defined Concepts.   There are many objects, object qualities, and relations for which the student must be given a definition, at least initially, in order to be able to identify them. They cannot simply be looked at and recognized. "State capital" would be an example of one, as would "supermarket" or "chemical element." R. M. Gagné (1985) calls these more complex concepts *defined concepts*, and a principal activity of school learning is to acquire these defined concepts. Learners demonstrate the acquisition of a defined concept by being able to classify instances of the concept. Given an array of food merchandising establishments, students will point out the supermarkets; given a list of chemical substances, students will check those that are elements.

   The distinction between a concrete concept and a defined concept is that to use the latter, you must know what it means or what its essential features are. You cannot simply rely on being able to recognize every possible instance. To recognize the essential features of a class of objects, you must know what they are: You must know the definition.

Rules.   Performances using rules represent the ability to do something rather than simply describe how it is done. Rules, in E. D. Gagné's terms, embody procedural knowledge, or knowing how to do something. Rules are represented by IF–THEN statements or productions telling students what to do under particular conditions. Rules link actions to conditions.

There are many rules at work in reading and computing. Reading represents decoding of printed symbols, and we employ rules to pronounce words and determine their meaning. Carrying out operations on numbers also requires the extensive use of rules. Solving the equation $4X + 3 = 19$ for X requires a student to know the rule for transposing a number from one side of an equation to another and the rule for dividing both sides of an equation by the same number.

According to Gagné and Driscoll (1988), rules make it possible to connect a class of objects, events, or instructions with a class of performances. You do not need to learn a separate response to every equation you might be called upon to solve and carry them all around in your memory. Once you learn the rules for solving equations you can generate a solution to any equation that fits those rules, even equations you have never seen before. Thus, rules extend our mental capabilities enormously without requiring an equivalent extension of our memories.

Higher-Order Rules.   R. M. Gagné (1985) distinguishes between simple rules and more complex, or higher-order, rules that are made up of combinations of simple rules. When a teacher draws up a lesson plan for a class, she employs higher-order rules that tell her how to choose the material to be covered, how to prepare objectives, how to plan to present the material, and how to determine whether students have learned it.

To do mathematics problems, students must be given the guidance they need to learn the procedural rules.

Cognitive Strategies

Whereas verbal information and intellectual skills refer to *what* is learned, cognitive strategies refer to the *way* something is learned. Such strategies, including self-guidance and self-monitoring, may be called *executive control* processes. When a student skims a chapter in a textbook, or outlines it, or makes notes in the margin, he or she is utilizing cognitive strategies. In other words, cognitive strategies are ways to manage the learning process a person chooses to employ.

R. M. Gagné does not provide much detail about cognitive strategies, but we will encounter them again, in considerably more detail, in Chapter 6 on information processing.

Attitudes

Attitudes represent *preferences* or *likes* and *dislikes*. Like all of the outcomes previously described, attitudes are learned: Teachers try to influence or teach children to like school, to like learning, to like the subjects they are taught. Attitudes fall into what is called the *affective domain* (Krathwohl, Bloom, & Masia, 1964), or the area of feelings. In contrast, all of the preceding learning outcomes fall into the *cognitive domain* (Bloom, 1956), or the area of ideas. (Bloom's taxonomy will be described in the next chapter.)

General attitudes or feelings about things or people are referred to as *values*. Our values and our attitudes about ourselves constitute self-esteem and can be expected to have a great influence on school behavior and performance. Attitudes play a much greater role in social learning theories like those of Bandura and Weiner (to be encountered later) than they do in Gagné's theory.

Motor Skills

The final outcome area identified by Gagné is motor skills — precise, accurate movements involving our muscles that enable us to accomplish some task. Sports activities, such as shooting a basket, hitting a baseball, or getting a bulls-eye, require motor skills, as do various work activities, such as typing or driving a bus. Each of these activities may involve intellectual skills and attitudes as well, but the primary requirement to learn to carry out the performance smoothly and automatically would be in the motor area.

Analyzing the Requirements for Learning

In the sequence of learning events described on pages 76–78, three events represent the fundamentals or essence of the instructional process: events 3 (stimulating recall of prior learning), 4 (presenting the stimulus), and 5 (providing learning guidance). To determine exactly what prior learning must be recalled, what stimuli or new information must be presented, and how to guide the combination of old and new information, according to R. M. Gagné (1985), teachers must analyze the requirements for learning a specific task. First, the final learning task must be placed in one of the five learning outcome categories (verbal information, intellectual skill, cognitive strategy, attitude, or motor skill). Second, the task must be analyzed to reveal its *prerequisites*, the component skills that make it up. And third, the relationship between the learning task and all of the prerequisite skills must be set forth in the form of an organizational chart that R. M. Gagné (1985) has termed a *learning hierarchy*.

Learning Analysis and the Learning Hierarchy.   In developing a learning hierarchy, the teacher begins with the final task (called the *terminal objective*), asking the question, To learn this final task, what prerequisite tasks must the student have already mastered? The answer will yield the highest-level or most complex prerequisite tasks. The teacher then breaks down these tasks into prerequisites by asking and answering that same question about each of them.

This bears some similarity to the Skinnerian concept of shaping (covered in the previous chapter), except that it is more cognitive than behavioral. In both shaping and learning analysis, however, a final task must be subdivided into its necessary components to ensure that the components are taught and learned.

In its simplest form, a learning hierarchy would look like this:

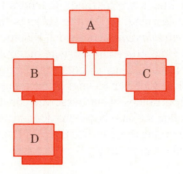

We would determine the hierarchy by asking these questions:

1. What activities must each activity precede? (*B*, for example, must precede *A*.)
2. What activities must precede each activity? (For *B*, *D* must precede it.)
3. What activities can occur at the same time? (*B* and *C* are parallel activities.)

For example, suppose task *A* was solving expressions involving fractions. An actual problem might be

$$\tfrac{1}{4} \times \tfrac{1}{2} + \tfrac{1}{8} - \tfrac{1}{4} \div \tfrac{3}{8} = \text{?}$$

To solve this type of problem, students would have to be able to perform task *B*, adding and subtracting fractions, and task *C*, multiplying and dividing fractions. To perform task *B*, adding and subtracting fractions, students would have to be able to perform task *D*, finding the least common denominator.

How can the hierarchy help? First of all, it helps the teacher determine the prerequisites that must have been mastered before the new learning can take place. Students who have not yet learned the prerequisites must be taught them before receiving instruction on the terminal objective. Second, the hierarchy tells the teacher what prerequisites the students must be reminded of in the third teaching event, the recall of relevant prior learning. Without this analysis, the teacher can only guess at the prerequisites and so

Figure 4.3 🍎 Intellectual Skills Subordinate to First Step in Psychomotor Skill of Putting a Golf Ball

From Dick and Carey, 1985.

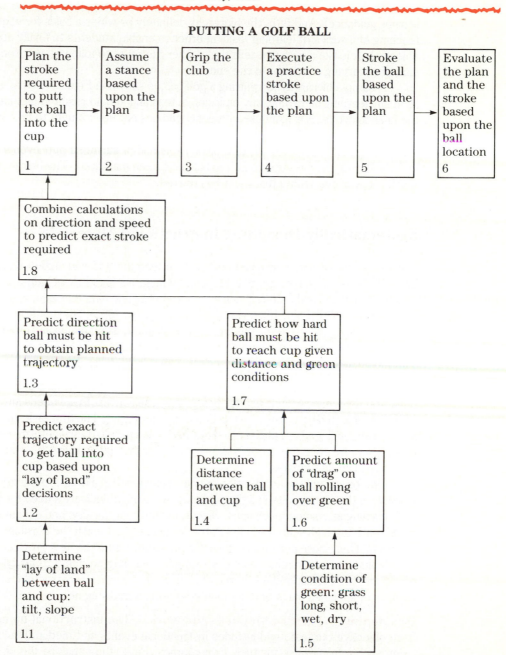

PUTTING A GOLF BALL

may fail to remind students of a necessary idea that has already been learned. Third, the hierarchy helps the teacher not leave anything new out in presenting the new stimulus information in event 4. Fourth, the hierarchy may help the teacher get ideas about how to help the students put the old and the new information together in event 5 (providing learner guidance). And fifth, the hierarchy definitely provides a basis for sequencing the teaching of a series of learning tasks in order to enable students to finally attain a major objective. It is like a map that tells the teacher the route to follow to get from the beginning of a learning sequence to the end.

A sample hierarchy, on putting a golf ball, is shown in Figure 4.3 (page 87). Here, as in any learning hierarchy, any omission in teaching should result in ultimate failure on the final objective. For example, someone who has not been taught to take into account the "drag" or speed of the green (that is, how much or how little the grass will slow down the moving ball — task 1.6) will have little likelihood of sinking a putt even if all the subtasks involving the direction to hit the ball have been mastered. The hierarchy helps the teacher cover everything that must be covered.

Systematically Designing Instructional Materials

Given the systematic, organized approach to learning and instruction that Gagné has provided, it is not surprising that he has extended his ideas to include a model for the design of instructional materials such as textbooks, teaching manuals, and instructional guides (Gagné & Briggs, 1979; see also Dick & Carey, 1985). His model advocates using specific learning objectives as the target of instruction, using media and other technology as instructional aids, and trying out and revising materials before implementing them. The model appears in Figure 4.4.

Developing the Curriculum Framework.   Developers of instructional materials must first determine what is needed before they can convert these needs into statements of course objectives for which instruction can be prepared. The first task, then, is a *needs assessment*, during which the instructional needs and purposes are determined. Next, the feasibility of meeting these needs is analyzed. Finally, curriculum goals and then course objectives can be prepared.

So, for example, if an aircraft plant has just opened in a local community, the people who live in that community and the new employers might indicate a need for high-school-level training in aviation mechanics. Discussing the cost, facility, and equipment requirements with the high school administration would help establish the feasibility of the new program. Then those persons responsible for constructing the new program would have to establish each curriculum goal (for example, teaching students to install new engine parts) and the corresponding course objectives (being able to correctly install each of a number of specified parts onto a mounted diesel aircraft engine).

Developing the Instructional Framework.   The instructional framework goes from objectives to tests and includes instructional events and media. Teachers can develop such a framework for their own courses. First, they analyze the objectives into subskills, using the process of learning analysis to produce a learning hierarchy. Then they identify instructional events to teach each of the subskills specified in the analysis. Then they choose media, where appropriate, for each instructional event. Last, they

Figure 4.4 🍎 **Phases of Development in the Gagné–Briggs Instructional Design Model**
From Gagné and Briggs, 1979.

Phase I: Developing the Curriculum Framework

STEP 1 Identify needs, long-range goals, and priorities

STEP 2 Identify the feasibility of attaining the goals

STEP 3 Establish curriculum goals

STEP 4 Derive target (end-of-course) objectives

Phase II: Developing the Instructional Framework

STEP 5 Analyze target objectives into procedures and component subskills

STEP 6 Write performance objectives for subskills

STEP 7 Identify instructional events for each objective

STEP 8 Select media for the instructional events

STEP 9 Develop tests for the objectives

Phase III: Installing the System

STEP 10 Teach training in use of the system

STEP 11 Do a formative evaluation of the system

STEP 12 Field test and revise

STEP 13 Do a summative evaluation of the system

STEP 14 Install and diffuse the system

prepare tests to measure the attainment of each objective. These procedures follow the Gagné model as previously described.

For example, some of the subskills needed at the aircraft plant might involve wiring, so students would need to be taught how to wire. Teachers might use computer-assisted instruction and demonstrations to teach wiring skills prior to having the students actually do the wiring themselves on an engine mock-up.

Installing the System.   Part of what makes this approach systematic is the way the instructional program is actually implemented. After teachers are trained in its use, it goes through a *field test* or *tryout*, which represents a process called *formative evaluation*. The purpose is to find out what students have missed. The results of this evaluation are used to revise the materials and improve their ability to help students master the objectives. Following this, a second evaluation, called *summative evaluation*, is completed, designed to demonstrate to all concerned parties that the new instruction really works. If this evaluation is a success, then the new instruction system is ready to operate in the schools and needs only to be installed and started up. It may also be appropriate to install the system in a variety of schools at the same time.

The Conditions of Learning on the Behavioral–Cognitive Continuum

R. M. Gagné's conditions of learning theory is primarily a behavioral theory because of its emphasis on external influences, but it includes an important cognitive component: semantic encoding. Because it focuses on behavioral objectives, predetermined prerequisite skills, learning analysis, repetition, practice, and feedback, the theory has many of the features of behavioral theory. But it is considerably more complex than Skinner's reinforcement or any of the early behavioral theories. And it goes beyond simple associations as the explanation for learning. Gagné embraces and includes aspects of what goes on inside the learner's head, albeit in considerably less detail than do the cognitivists who follow (Chapters 6 and 7).

Gagné has attempted to blend behaviorism and cognitivism, or at least to include cognitivism within behaviorism. Thus, he represents a transition between the two approaches. He has also proposed a theory that lends itself well to systematic instruction, as will be seen in the next chapter.

Summary of Main Points

1. Gagné's theory provides a framework for identifying the conditions under which learning takes place. It can thus serve as a theory of instruction, because clearly teachers would want to teach in the way that students learn. The learning process is described as having eight phases.

2. *Attention* and *motivation* are the first two phases: Learners must want to learn and must attend to incoming information if it is to register itself in their sensory systems.

3. Then come three information-processing phases, starting with the *selective perception* of features. To enter into a person's sensory register, the important, to-be-

learned aspects of incoming information must be selectively separated from all other aspects and must be perceived. But this information enters only into short-term memory. To go further, it must be *semantically encoded*, that is, be somehow reduced and "labeled" so that it can move into *long-term memory*.

4. When the learner is ready to use the information, it must be *searched* for and *retrieved* and then applied to a *performance*. That performance is followed by *feedback* so that it can be perfected or mastered. Feedback also serves as a source of reinforcement.

5. Applying the learning phases to the learning outcomes produces Gagné's nine instructional events. These are the steps the teacher must carry out to provide the conditions that will ensure that learning takes place.

6. The instructional events are *gaining attention, informing the learner of the objective, stimulating recall of prior learning, presenting the stimulus, providing learning guidance, eliciting performance, providing feedback, assessing performance*, and *enhancing retention and transfer*.

7. Gagné also classifies learning outcomes into five categories. The facts or declarative knowledge that are taught constitute *verbal information* or knowing "that," while *intellectual skills* or procedural knowledge represent knowing "how."

8. Intellectual skills, a major target of school teaching, are further subdivided into *discriminations* (telling things apart), *concrete concepts* (identifying things based on their appearance), *defined concepts* (classifying things based on their definitions), *rules* (applying information to solve problems), and *higher-order rules* (generating new rules by combining old ones).

9. Next come *cognitive strategies*, which represent ways of learning, followed by *attitudes* (choices based on preference) and *motor skills* (actual physical movements).

10. To find out what the component tasks or prerequisites are for a particular objective to be learned, Gagné proposes *learning analysis*. It asks, What must you have already learned in order to learn this objective, given nothing but definitions? The answer takes the form of a knowledge structure called a *learning hierarchy*.

11. The Gagné approach is also applied to the formal design of instructional materials, as follows: (a) A *curriculum framework* is developed, made up of course objectives produced as a result of needs assessment; (b) the *instructional framework* is built from a learning hierarchy to include and connect teaching materials and media to test items; (c) the *system is installed*, including two kinds of evaluation — the first kind to perfect it and the second to demonstrate to others that it works.

Suggested Resources

Bell-Gredler, M. E. (1986). *Learning and instruction: Theory into practice*. New York: Macmillan.

Gagné, E. D. (1985). *The cognitive psychology of school learning*. Boston: Little, Brown.

Gagné, R. M. (1985). *The conditions of learning* (4th ed.). New York: Holt, Rinehart & Winston.

Gagné, R. M., & Driscoll, M. P. (1988). *Essentials of learning for instruction* (2nd ed.). Englewood Cliffs, NJ: Prentice-Hall.

Chapter 5

The Design of Instruction

Objectives

1. Identify and describe the steps in the instructional design model proposed by Dick and Reiser (based on Gagné's theory) including how (a) to classify goals using Bloom's taxonomy, (b) to prepare instructional objectives, (c) to develop instructional activities, and (d) to choose media.

2. Identify the principles and characteristics of an individualized instruction approach based on Skinner's theory.

3. Describe Bloom's mastery teaching/learning model based on his theory of school learning, including its characteristics and effectiveness.

4. Describe the direct instruction model based on the process–product approach, including its recommended teaching behaviors.

5. Describe Bruner's model of discovery learning, the basis on which it works, and its variation, called guided discovery.

The Instructional Design Model

A classroom instructional design model for teachers most closely based on Gagné's theory of learning, described in the previous chapter, has been proposed by Dick and Reiser (1989). This model is shown in Figure 5.1 and has the following distinctive features:

1. Instruction is based on clearly stated objectives.
2. Tests are based on the same objectives as is instruction.
3. Instructional media are used as part of the instructional delivery system.
4. Instruction is evaluated based on student performance and is revised as needed prior to reuse.

Setting and Classifying Goals.   The goals of instruction are usually provided to teachers in the form of a curriculum. These goals have been established over time on the basis of experience and by consideration of statewide and national instructional goals as embodied in textbooks and testing programs. These goals can be divided into the different types of learning outcomes proposed by Gagné (see pages 78–85). They can also be divided on the basis of another, more commonly used classification system, *Bloom's taxonomy* (Bloom, 1956), which is shown in Figure 5.2. (This taxonomy applies only to the cognitive domain. Taxonomies for the affective and psychomotor domains are not shown here.)

The taxonomy includes six major categories, of increasing complexity: knowledge, comprehension, application, analysis, synthesis, and evaluation. Bloom (1956) suggests

Figure 5.1 🍎 The Dick and Reiser (1989) Model for Developing Effective Instruction

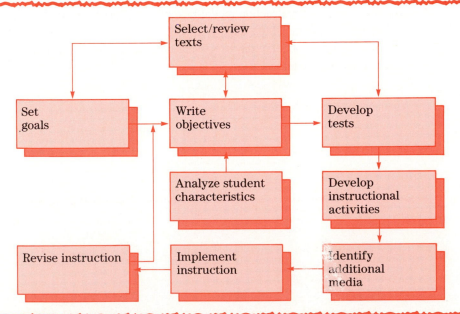

that taxonomies such as his will help teachers (l) define ambiguous terms like *understand* so that they can communicate curricular and evaluative information among themselves, (2) identify goals that they may want to include in their own curricula, (3) identify directions in which they may want to extend their instructional activities, (4) plan learning experiences, and (5) prepare measuring devices. It might also be added that taxonomies such as Bloom's may help teachers put instructional goals in their proper sequence because of their *hierarchical* nature, that is, the fact that taxonomies are organized into levels or ranks.

Figure 5.2 ✿ Taxonomy of the Cognitive Domain
From Bloom (1956).

1.00 KNOWLEDGE
   1.10 of Specifics
      1.11 of terminology
      1.12 of specific facts

   1.20 of Ways and Means of Dealing with Specifics
      1.21 of conventions
      1.22 of trends and sequences
      1.23 of classifications and categories
      1.24 of criteria
      1.25 of methodology

   1.30 of the Universals and Abstractions in a Field
      1.31 of principles and generalizations
      1.32 of theories and structures

2.00 COMPREHENSION
   2.10 Translation
   2.20 Interpretation
   2.30 Extrapolation

3.00 APPLICATION

4.00 ANALYSIS
   4.10 of Elements
   4.20 of Relationships
   4.30 of Organizational Principles

5.00 SYNTHESIS
   5.10 Production of a Unique Communication
   5.20 Production of a Plan, or Proposed Set of Operations
   5.30 Derivation of a Set of Abstract Relations

6.00 EVALUATION
   6.10 Judgments in Terms of Internal Evidence
   6.20 Judgments in Terms of External Criteria

Consider a middle-school or high-school social studies teacher who is interested in having students attain the goal of "knowing where to go to get information about a topic." In the taxonomy, this would be categorized as "1.00: Knowledge"; more exactly, "1.20: Knowledge of Ways and Means of Dealing with Specifics"; and within that, "1.25: Knowledge of Methodology." In other words, the teacher wants students not to learn about a topic (that would be "1.10: Knowledge of Specifics") but to learn ways and means of finding out about a variety of topics. This might take the form of interviewing or doing library research or making observations. Classifying the goal this way may make it easier to formulate specific learning objectives (see below), to determine when in the sequence to teach this unit (after, for example, teaching knowledge of specifics), and to decide about some possible instructional activities.

Keep in mind that taxonomies such as Bloom's are made by people, not by nature. While they often help to organize thoughts and observations, they are not guaranteed to include all possible learning goals or to ensure that all users will classify every goal the same way.

Writing Objectives.   An *objective* is a clear-cut statement of exactly what it is the teacher wants the student to be able to do as a result of instruction. It must be written in such a way that its attainment, or lack thereof, can be observed and measured. In other words, an objective is *not* a statement describing what the teacher will do to provide a learning experience; rather, it describes what the *student* will be able to do after completing a learning experience. Moreover, an objective does *not* specify what a student will know, think, or understand, because we cannot determine these outcomes directly. An objective does specify only *actions* that can be seen by the teacher, who can then validate that the objective has been attained.

Most objectives are written as *brief action statements* using an *action verb* (as are, for example, the objectives provided at the beginning of each chapter of this book). In more detailed form, objectives include two other parts: a statement of the *conditions* or *givens* under which the action is to be performed, and the *criteria* by which the action is to be judged. The objective or action statement, either by itself or in combination with the conditions and criteria, is a *descriptive statement of intended student performance using an action verb*. A list of possible action verbs to use in writing objectives based on the taxonomy of the cognitive domain is shown in Table 5.1. A much shorter list appears below.

Identify — Given a list of possible answers to a question (as in a multiple-choice item), circle the correct one.

State — Given a *specific* question calling for a specific fact (as in a completion item), provide that fact.

Describe — Given a topic or an object (as in an essay item), write about it.

Demonstrate — Given a problem (as in a problem-solving item), show how to solve it.

Construct — Given materials and a task (as in a performance item), use the materials to complete the task.

If, for example, one goal in a high school chemistry class were to teach the students Boyle's Law, a first glance might lead the teacher to say that the objective was to have the students understand Boyle's Law. But *understand* is not an action verb. What could the students do to show that they understood Boyle's Law? Suppose the teacher gave them the volume and temperature of a gas and asked them to find the pressure of the gas. If they could do this — if they could *demonstrate a procedure for finding the pressure of a gas given its volume and its temperature* — then the teacher could conclude that they "understood" Boyle's Law.

Let us try another example, this one from third-grade language arts. The goal deals with teaching students words that rhyme. The teacher wants them to "know" when words rhyme and when they do not rhyme. His objective, therefore, is this:

> Given a single word and a list of words, identify the word on the list that rhymes with the single word.

In seventh-grade English, a teacher wants her students to be able to tell about the characters in a story. So:

> Given a story, describe the characters in the story by writing descriptions that include physical characteristics, personality, and how they behaved in the story.

Note that in this last example it was necessary to include in the objective a detailed criterion — namely, what the descriptions of the story's characters were to include — because otherwise someone judging students' performance would not be able to distinguish success from failure. In each of the first two examples there was only one right answer, which could be specified in advance, while in the third example the determination of an answer's "rightness" required a judgment and hence a specific criterion.

Often, for convenience's sake, we write our objectives in their short form, that being the action that the student should succeed in learning to do. When we are preparing test items, however (see Chapter 14), or evaluating them (see Chapter 15), we include all three parts — action statement, conditions, criteria — in our objectives.

Identifying Student Characteristics.   The instruction to be designed, according to this model, depends on two things: the objectives to be learned and the characteristics of

Table 5.1 🍎 Action Verbs for Writing Objectives Based on the Taxonomy of the Cognitive Domain

Category	Alternative Action Verbs
knowledge	define, describe, identify, label, list, match, name, outline, select, state
comprehension	convert, defend, distinguish, estimate, explain, extend, generalize, give examples, infer, paraphrase, predict, rewrite, summarize
application	change, compute, demonstrate, discover, manipulate, modify, operate, predict, prepare, produce, relate, show, solve, use
analysis	break down, diagram, differentiate, discriminate, distinguish, identify, illustrate, infer, outline, point out, relate, select, separate, subdivide
synthesis	categorize, combine, compile, compose, create, design, devise, rewrite, summarize, tell, write
evaluation	appraise, compare, conclude, contrast, criticize, describe, discriminate, explain, justify, interpret, relate, summarize, support

the students to whom those objectives will be taught. The characteristics that are important in a particular instance are those that serve as *prerequisite* skills for the objectives to be taught. Prerequisite skills represent *what the students must already have learned and must be able to use in order to be able to master the objective given the appropriate instruction*. Since much learning is sequential, many units of instruction teach the prerequisite skills required for beginning subsequent units. All a teacher need do, then, is proceed in sequence from unit to unit.

However, we cannot always assume that all prerequisite skills have been mastered by all students. When there is any doubt, it is better to check. But in order to check, the teacher must be able to specify what the prerequisite skills are. For this, it is often helpful to use the learning analysis process described by Gagné to produce a learning hierarchy (see pages 85–88). Once the prerequisite skills have been identified, the teacher can assess them with a *diagnostic test*, a test given before instruction to detect the presence or absence of prerequisite skills.

Selecting Textbooks and Materials.[1]   Before selecting textbooks and other printed material, teachers should review them to determine the following (Dick & Reiser, 1989):

1. whether the content is accurate, up-to-date, understandable, and unbiased toward any particular group;
2. whether the format represents good writing at the proper grade level with main themes and sufficient illustrations;
3. whether the instructional design reflects components that match the teacher's objectives and will facilitate learning by the inclusion of summaries, practice activities, and motivational activities (see the next chapter for additional aspects of this feature);
4. whether data are available that indicate how effective the material has been, whether activities are included that can be carried out in the classroom, and whether supplementary materials are available.

Developing Instructional Activities.   The instructional plan, according to Dick and Reiser (1989), should include seven activities (based on and therefore closely reflecting Gagné's instructional events; see pages 75–78). These are (1) motivation, (2) objectives, (3) prerequisites, (4) information and examples, (5) practice and feedback, (6) testing, and (7) enrichment and remediation. An example of an instructional plan covering these seven areas appears in Box 5.1.

Choosing Instructional Media.   Dick and Reiser (1989) present three questions for choosing an instructional medium:

1. Is it practical (that is, is it available or obtainable)?
2. Is it appropriate for the students?
3. Is it well suited to present a particular instructional activity?

---

[1]The next step in the model is actually *Developing Tests*, but it is covered in detail in Chapter 14 and will not be repeated here.

Box 5.1

🍎

A Sample Instructional Plan

Goal: Solve mathematical word problems.

Objective(s): Solve word problems that involve rate, time, and distance by using the formula $D = R \times T$.

Sample Test Item(s): Walter has been running for thirty minutes at seven miles per hour. How much distance has he covered?

Instructional Activity	Content of Activity	Means of Presenting Activity
1. Motivation	Use highway travel and new speed limits.	Videotape and Teacher
2. Objective	Tell students they will solve word problems involving how far, how fast, how long it takes to travel.	Teacher
3. Prerequisites	Assume math, travel. Remind that travel takes time, and how to use algebraic equation.	Teacher
4. Information and Examples	Explain concepts of rate, time, and distance. Explain formula $D = R \times T$.	Textbook and Teacher
	Give examples involving each part of formula as unknown.	Teacher
5. Practice and Feedback	Group students to work on a variety of written problems.	Worksheet and Teacher
	Review results with class, before individual practice.	Teacher
6. Testing	Give a fifteen-item test, consisting of solving five problems each for rate, time, and distance.	Worksheet
7. Enrichment and Remediation	Pair students who mastered objectives with those who did not. Students who mastered serve as tutors for those who did not.	Students

SOURCE: Dick, W., & Reiser, R.A. (1989). *Planning effective instruction*. Englewood Cliffs, NJ: Prentice-Hall.

The medium should fit into and be suitable for one of the above seven instructional activities that constitute the plan. An example of how this might be done is also shown in the right-hand column of Box 5.1.

"Media" does not necessarily mean just TV, films, or computers. Many media—worksheets, other handouts, overhead transparencies—can be prepared and produced by the teacher. Textbooks, as well, represent a medium for instruction. Moreover, when the teacher delivers instruction, he or she is the medium; when the students present information, through prepared reports and discussion, they are the medium.

Implementing Instruction.   The instructional design model labels implementation as a necessary stage but has no unique perspective on how it is to be accomplished. Moreover, teaching teachers how to actually deliver instruction represents the content of education "methods" courses rather than educational psychology. However, educational psychology has produced some relatively unique implementation models, which will be described later in this chapter. This instructional design model can be applied most clearly to the design and evaluation of the lesson that is to be taught, rather than to the specific methods teachers use to teach that lesson.

Revising Instruction.   Key to the instructional design model are the notions (1) that instruction should be revised (that is, it should not just be developed and then always remain the same) and (2) that the basis for this revision should be the results of using the instruction with students and determining what works and what does not. Often, the tendency is to design a lesson and then teach it that way thereafter. However, good instructional designers evaluate their materials, not only by observing how students react to them, but also by seeing how well students do on the tests that accompany them. This is called *formative evaluation*. If all or nearly all students fail to master one of the lesson's objectives, as reflected in the test results, then the teacher as formative evaluator not only notes this but changes the instructional plan and materials to minimize the likelihood that this will happen again. Formative evaluation, then, becomes an ongoing process until the result meets with the teacher's satisfaction.

Individualized Instruction

In its earlier days, the individualized instruction model that was based on Skinner's reinforcement theory was referred to as *programmed instruction* (Skinner, 1968). Programmed instruction was delivered in print format through a device called a teaching machine or in the form of a programmed textbook. According to O'Day, Kulhavy, Anderson, and Malezynski (1971), the principles to develop programmed instruction were as follows:

1. Specification of the goal that the learner is to master.
2. Careful pilot testing of the material.
3. Self-pacing to allow learners to move through the material at their own rate.
4. The need for definite responses from the learner.
5. Immediate feedback so the learner will know if a response is correct.
6. Division of the overall task into small steps.

The feedback served as reinforcement, and each step, called a *frame*, was written in such a way as to ensure a high likelihood of a correct response. To accomplish this, the researchers made the steps quite small and used *prompts* frequently. This is in keeping with Skinner's (1954) emphasis on the critical importance of *reinforcement*. An example of the use of programmed instruction as developed by Holland and Skinner (1961) to teach an introductory psychology course is shown in Box 5.2.

Box 5.2

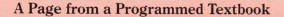

A Page from a Programmed Textbook

A doctor taps your knee (patellar tendon) with a rubber hammer to test your _____.

1-1

To avoid unwanted nuances of meaning in popular words, we do not say that a stimulus "triggers," "stimulates," or "causes" a response, but that it _____ a response.

1-9

In the patellar-tendon reflex, a forceful tap elicits a strong kick; a tap barely above the threshold elicits a weak kick. Magnitude of response thus depends on the intensity of the _____.

1-17

Onion juice elicits the secretion of tears by the lachrymal gland. This causal sequence of events is a(n) _____.

1-25

A response and its eliciting stimulus comprise a(n) _____.

1-33

The latency of a reflex is the (1) _____ between onset of (2) _____ and _____.

1-41

The layman frequently explains behavior as the operation of "mind" or "free will." He seldom does this for reflex behavior, however, because the _____ is an adequate explanation of the response.

1-49

Answers appear on page 102 in footnote 2.

SOURCE: Holland, J. G., & Skinner, B. F. (1961). *The analysis of behavior*. New York: McGraw-Hill.

The idea of programmed instruction was extended to the teaching of an entire course through the development of what was called the Personalized System of Instruction (PSI) or the Keller Plan (named for Fred Keller, its inventor). The teacher does little presentation of information in this plan because that would be too inefficient to do on an individual basis. (Some lectures are given, which students attend on a voluntary basis if they desire additional instruction.) Instead, students are given reading units, each with specific goals and study guides, which they read at their own pace to learn the course content (Robin, 1976). After completing a unit, students must present themselves for testing before being able to proceed to the next unit. Immediate feedback is also given. Because students mainly read the course content, rather than hearing it through lectures, they can work by themselves at times and rates of their own choosing, thereby making the instructional process individualized. The use of specific goals, small instructional steps, frequent testing, immediate feedback, and a high likelihood of success are the hallmarks of Skinnerian theory applied to instruction. Both programmed instruction and the Personalized System of Instruction have been found to be at least as effective as conventional instruction (Bangert, Kulik, & Kulik, 1983) and in some evaluation studies more effective (Kulik, Kulik, & Cohen, 1979).

Today, instructional content can be delivered by television or computer (thereby providing a discriminative stimulus or S^D). The computer can also be used to enable the learner to respond actively (R) as well as to provide testing and feedback (or consequences). Hence, if we so choose, we now have the technological capacity to provide individualized or so-called computer-assisted instruction (CAI) on a wider scale than ever before. Note the similarity between this approach and Skinner's operant conditioning. Gagné's approach can also be used to design the instruction to be provided by computer.

The Mastery Learning Model

The mastery learning model, a variation on the general theme of individualized instruction, is based on a theory of school learning proposed by Bloom (1976). The theory is shown in Figure 5.3.

School Learning Theory.   What the theory posits is that on a learning task the three learning outcomes — (l) level and type of achievement, (2) rate of learning, and (3) affective outcomes (principally attitudes) — are a function of three variables: (a) cognitive entry behaviors of students (what they know when they start), (b) affective entry characteristics of students (how they feel when they start), and (c) quality of instruction. In other words, school learning is proposed to be a joint function of the *learner's history* (what has already been learned and what feelings already exist) and the *quality of instruction*. Its proponents believe that *both can be modified*.

Bloom's theory of school learning is based in large measure on a theory originally proposed by John B. Carroll in 1963 (and updated in 1985) that hypothesized that the amount of student learning would depend on two factors: (1) how much time and instruction the student needed in order to learn and (2) whether the opportunity to learn and the quality of instruction were sufficient to meet those needs. In other words, if the time allotted for instruction and the quality of instruction given during that time are equal to what the student needs to learn, then learning will take place.

Both Bloom's theory and Carroll's theory lead to the inevitable and perhaps controversial conclusion that virtually *any student can be taught to complete any learning task successfully, given sufficient instruction*. First, the student would have to be taught the prerequisites in order to attain the necessary entry characteristics. Then the necessary instruction, necessary in terms of both amount and quality, would have to be provided. The result should be learning success, or *mastery* as termed by Bloom (1976).

In much of instruction, learning is sequential: Mastery of the first task is a prerequisite for the learning of the second task, mastery of the second task is a prerequisite for

---

[2]Answers to frames in Box 5.2: reflexes, elicits, stimulus (tap), reflex, reflex, time (interval), stimulus (and) response, stimulus.

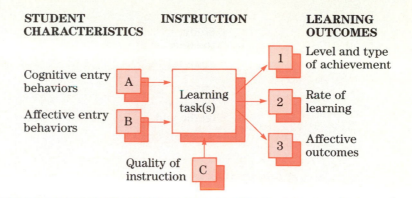

Figure 5.3 🍎 **Major Variables in the Theory of School Learning**
From Bloom, 1976.

the learning of the third task, and so on. Hence, the most critical tasks are the ones early in the sequence, because if they are not mastered, the student will have difficulty with all tasks that follow. If students are allowed to progress through the sequence without regard to whether or not they master each task, the result will be a greater incidence of differences in level and rate of achievement as more and more students fail at an increasing number of tasks. Alternatively, if students are not permitted to move from one task to the next unless and until they master the one they are on, the result will be a decreasing variation in level or rate of achievement because all students should succeed at each successive task.

Mastery Teaching.   Translated in a practical manner, this is the model of mastery learning (or, perhaps, more accurately, the model of mastery teaching), as shown in Figure 5.4. The teacher should provide sufficient instruction so that students will master each task, and should not allow them to proceed to the next task until they have mastered the one they are on. What will vary from student to student, as accurately predicted by Carroll in 1963, will be the amount of *instructional time* each student requires. Some will require extra instruction to ensure mastery; others will not. Instruction will need to be individualized if the mastery model is to be applied.

In other words, after providing all students with instruction on Unit 1, the teacher must test them to see if they have mastered all the objectives of Unit 1. Those students who have failed one or more Unit 1 objectives must be given additional instruction and then retested. If they fail again, the sequence must be repeated until they pass. As a result, all students should learn all units and, theoretically, they should not differ in final achievement. (See Box 5.3.) However, *different students will require different amounts of instructional time*. To operate this instructional model, therefore, teachers must be able to vary the amount of instructional time per unit from student to student.

The key, then, to mastery teaching is to provide as much instructional time and as much instruction as are necessary for each student to achieve mastery on each learning task before moving on to the next one. It is possible, therefore, to virtually guarantee mastery by each and every student on each and every learning task *if some students can be given different instruction than other students at the same time*. Traditional group or whole-class instruction necessitates teaching all students the same content at the same time and

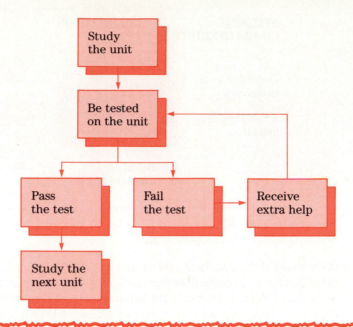

Figure 5.4 ❧ Bloom's Mastery Teaching Model

thus does not lend itself easily to the mastery teaching model (which can be expected to require a good deal of individualized or small-group instruction). The next model is more amenable to the limitations of the typical classroom.

The Direct Instruction Model

This approach, so named by Rosenshine (1979), utilizes teacher-directed activities (such as seatwork) and features clearly stated goals, an emphasis on the coverage of content, virtually all classroom time spent on-task, performance monitoring, and immediate feedback. The choice of instructional activities, materials, and tempo or pacing is made by the teacher.

Process–Product Research.   Where does the direct instruction model come from? It comes from research studies in which effective teachers were first identified based on their ability to affect an increase in student achievement as measured by nationwide achievement testing programs. Those teachers whose classes made clear gains on these tests, over and above their starting levels, were observed and their teaching behaviors recorded (Tikunoff, Berliner, & Rist, 1975). Similarly observed were teachers whose classes made no such gains. The purpose of observation was to identify those teaching behaviors carried out by the teachers whose classes gained in the tested achievement. The conclusion was that if other teachers were to carry out the same teaching *process* as the successful teachers, then they too would achieve a successful *product*.

Good and Grouws (1979) carried the process a step further with fourth-grade mathematics. After they identified the teaching behaviors that separated achievement-

Box 5.3

🍎

Mastery Versus Nonmastery Teaching:
A Comparison of Results

In 1976, Bloom reported on a number of studies comparing the effect of mastery and nonmastery teaching. In each case, two initially equivalent groups of students were taught the same subject matter by the same teacher. In the mastery class, students were given feedback and corrective help, if necessary, after taking a test on task objectives. In the nonmastery class, students were provided with neither feedback nor corrective help after testing.

The expectation was for the two classes to be about even after taking the test on Task 1 but for the mastery class to get further and further ahead on each successive task test because all of those students would have mastered the criterion entry behaviors for each task before they were allowed to start the next one. The graph below shows how well this expectation was borne out by the data. Note how the performance gap between mastery and nonmastery groups widened from the first to the fourth learning task.

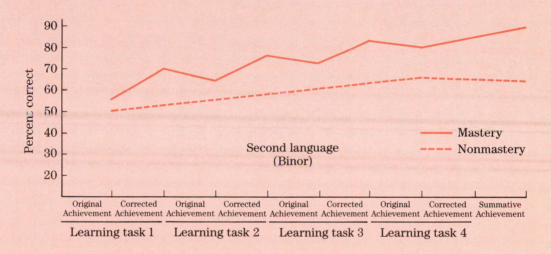

SOURCE: Bloom, B. S. (1976). *Human characteristics and school learning* (p. 59). New York: McGraw-Hill.

producing and non-achievement-producing teachers, they taught those presumed achievement-producing behaviors to a third group of teachers. This third group then used those behaviors in their subsequent teaching of mathematics and, lo and behold, the mathematics achievement of their students went up.

Direct Instructional Behaviors. The key behaviors identified through process–product research (Good, Grouws, & Ebermeier, 1983) are shown in Table 5.2. Clearly, a very heavy emphasis is placed on review, on presentation or lesson development, and on

In mastery teaching, extra instruction is given to those students who need it before they can move on to the next unit.

active participation by learners through seatwork and homework. Instruction is presented to the whole class at the same time, while seatwork and homework are individual activities.

It is important to point out an aspect of this instructional model that differentiates it from most of the others described in this book. Unlike the other models, the process–product approach is not a theoretical approach. It is based instead on observation. In other words, there is no explanation for why this model works, only evidence that it does work. A limiting factor is that most of the evidence that the model does work comes primarily from the elementary grades in the area of basic skills (reading and mathematics), areas for which nationwide achievement testing is routinely done. The model may not apply equally well to other subject-matter areas.

It is also important to recognize that the criterion for successful teaching on which the process–product model is based is limited to tested achievement, primarily of acquired skill and knowledge. There is no guarantee that this model will contribute equally

Table 5.2 🍎 Summary of Key Direct Instructional Behaviors

Task	Behaviors
Daily Review (First 8 minutes except Mondays)	1. Review the concepts and skills associated with the homework 2. Collect and deal with homework assignments 3. Ask several mental computation exercises
Development (About 20 minutes)	1. Briefly focus on prerequisite skills and concepts 2. Focus on meaning and on promoting student understanding by using lively explanations, demonstrations, process explanations, illustrations, and so on. 3. Assess student comprehension by a. Using process product questions (active interaction) b. Using controlled practice 4. Repeat and elaborate on the meaning portion as necessary
Seatwork (About 15 minutes)	1. Provide uninterrupted successful practice 2. Momentum—keep the ball rolling—get everyone involved, then sustain involvement 3. Alerting—let students know their work will be checked at the end of the period 4. Accountability—check the students' work
Homework Assignment	1. Assign on a regular basis at the end of each math class except Fridays 2. Should involve about 15 minutes of work to be done at home 3. Should involve one or two review problems
Special Reviews	1. Weekly Review/Maintenance a. Conduct during the first 20 minutes each Monday b. Focus on skills and concepts covered during the previous week 2. Monthly Review/Maintenance a. Conduct every fourth Monday b. Focus on skills and concepts covered since last monthly review

SOURCE: Good, T. L., Grouws, D., & Ebermeier, H.(1983). *Active mathematics teaching*. New York: Longman.

well to the development of thinking skills or to the enhancement of motives and attitudes. However, within its limits, direct instruction has proven quite effective. It seems to guarantee that young learners will get maximum exposure to and practice in the performance of basic skills.

Discovery Learning

Discovery learning, according to Jerome Bruner (1960), should provide problem situations that stimulate and encourage students to discover or figure out the structure of the subject matter for themselves. Structure refers to the ideas, relationships, and patterns of the subject matter, not to the facts and details. By arranging the learning environment and by introducing specific materials and tasks, teachers can increase the likelihood, but

Active participation by students is a key element of direct instruction. Asking questions is a good way to get students to participate in instruction rather than letting them just sit and listen.

not necessarily guarantee, that such discovery will take place. Hence, the approaches of discovery learning and direct instruction are reasonably opposite to one another. Direct instruction tells students what they need to know, as do instructional design and mastery learning — these being primarily behavioral approaches; the discovery approach creates the situations necessary for students potentially to figure out for themselves what they are expected to learn. Hence, discovery learning is a more cognitive approach.

The discovery approach according to Bruner should produce learning on an *inductive* basis, that is, going from the specific to the general or from facts and observations to more general principles and theories. In effect, discovery learning should make the student behave like a theorist. To accomplish this, teachers need to provide examples of specific facts from which students can make generalizations. Or the specific facts can come from observations that students themselves make of the phenomenon under study as they might in a laboratory, for example, and from which they induce the general principles that apply. An example of this for you to try yourself is given in Box 5.4. (We will encounter further examples in the chapter on development when we consider models of instruction to enhance development based on Piaget's theory.)

Box 5.4

An Example of Discovery Learning

Here is a game called The Prisoner's Dilemma. It is played by two persons, PRISONER ONE and PRISONER TWO. Each player may make either one of two possible moves—playing RED or playing BLUE—but neither player knows what move the other has made until after he or she has made his or her own move. Moreover, the players may never communicate with one another.

The *payoff matrix* below tells what the result will be for each player for each of the four possible combinations of moves.

The purpose of the game is to learn what the defined concepts of competition and cooperation mean in operational terms. In the classroom, students are paired off and actually play the game with (or against) one another. The teacher changes the payoff matrix a few times during the activity. The object is to win as much money as you can.

Think about the following questions and try to answer them by imagining yourself playing the game (or by actually playing it) with a friend.

1. Which response is competitive and how can you tell?
2. Which response is cooperative and how can you tell?
3. How would you change the payoff matrix to increase the likelihood of cooperation?
4. How would you change the payoff matrix to increase the likelihood of competition?
5. How does this apply to the real world? (In other words, what have you learned?)

Answers to these questions appear at the bottom of page 110 in footnote 3.

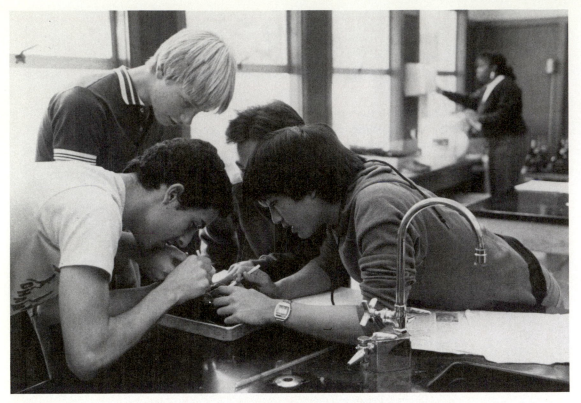

Discovery learning occurs when students are put in a situation in which they have to figure out something for themselves. A laboratory is the kind of place where students like these are likely to make discoveries.

Guided Discovery.   While true discovery learning requires a laboratory-type or hands-on approach to instruction, a version of discovery learning called guided discovery can be used for group instruction. Rather than telling students a particular principle, the teacher can present them with a carefully chosen set of illustrations that will *guide* them in the direction of the necessary principle and hence make it more possible for them to induce it. The illustrations, accompanied by helpful probing and prompting by the teacher, can lead right up to the principle or solution; or the teacher can choose to have

---

[3]Answers to questions in Box 5.4:
1. Blue, because you win and the other player loses and the difference between you is 15¢.
2. Red, because you both win and the amount you both win is the same.
3. By increasing the mutual payoff for each player playing red, increasing the mutual loss for both playing blue, and making the red/blue combination more costly for the player who plays blue.
4. By increasing the difference in payoff for a blue/red combination in favor of blue and against red, and reducing the joint cost of the blue/blue combination.
5. People will cooperate when it is sufficiently to their mutual gain and when not cooperating is sufficiently costly. Therefore, if we want cooperation we must increase mutual payoffs for cooperative behavior.

the illustrations fall short of the principle or solution so the students will be forced to use their *intuition* or imaginative judgment to arrive at the desired endpoint.

In an elementary-school unit on service occupations, for example, students are shown pictures of people in action, all of them wearing uniforms. The question is, Why do they wear uniforms? To answer it, students must separate the pictures into two groups: those who wear uniforms to be recognized (such as police officers) and those who wear uniforms to protect their clothing (such as exterminators). By choosing certain pictures and gently guiding the discussion, the teacher can lead the students to discover the different functions of uniforms.

There are other instructional design models, particularly cognitive ones. These include Ausubel's model, covered in Chapter 6, and a number of subject-matter-specific models as well as a general one for teaching problem-solving, in Chapter 7.

Summary of Main Points

1. The *instructional design model* proposed by Dick and Reiser (1989) (and derived largely from Gagné's theory) uses clearly stated objectives as the basis for instructional materials, performance tests, and instructional media. Instructional materials are also evaluated based on student performance and are revised prior to reuse.

2. The first step in instructional design is to set and classify *goals*. Goals can be classified, according to Bloom's (1956) taxonomy of the cognitive domain, as knowledge, comprehension, application, analysis, synthesis, or evaluation. Such classification helps teachers define ambiguous terms, decide which goals they want to use, choose and plan the appropriate instructional activities and learning experiences, build tests, and put goals and instruction in sequence.

3. The second step is to write *objectives*, which are clear-cut statements of exactly what the teacher wants the student to do as a result of instruction. An objective must describe an observable behavior of the student so that its achievement can be determined.

4. Most objectives are written as *brief action statements* that use an *action verb* such as *identify, state, describe, demonstrate*, or *construct*. More elaborately written objectives include a statement of the *conditions* under which the action will be performed and the *criteria* by which the action will be evaluated.

5. The third step is to identify *student characteristics* in terms of the attainment of prerequisite skills, that is, what the students must already have learned in order to be able to master the objective, given the appropriate instruction. The teacher can determine what those prerequisite skills are by doing learning analysis as described by Gagné, and can determine whether they have been mastered by giving a diagnostic test.

6. The fourth step is to select *textbooks* and *materials* based on the suitability of their content, format, and design and on whether evidence of their effectiveness is available.

7. Fifth is to actually *develop* instructional activities in the form of an instructional plan. Sixth is to choose instructional *media* based on considerations of practicality, appropriateness for students, and suitability for the chosen instructional activity.

8. *Implementing* instruction is seventh, followed by *revision* of instruction based on a *formative evaluation* using evidence from actual student performance.

9. *Individualized instruction*, originally called *programmed instruction*, is based on Skinner's reinforcement theory. The principles of this approach are to specify learning goals; break down instructional content into very small steps or frames; require that learners make definite responses — to questions that have been designed to ensure a high probability of success (based, in part, on considerable prompting); provide immediate feedback that reinforces correct responses; and carefully pilot-test the material.

10. With the advent of Fred Keller's *Personalized System of Instruction*, this approach was extended to cover entire courses. Students worked at their own pace and proceeded from unit to unit (using specially developed study guides) after successfully completing each end-of-unit test. Today, technology provides a ready basis for even wider use of this individualized instruction approach.

11. The *mastery learning/teaching model* is based on Bloom's (1976) theory of school learning, which proposes that learning outcomes are a function of students' *cognitive* and *affective entry behaviors* (that is, what they know and how they feel at the start) and the *quality of instruction*. Since both entry behavior and quality of instruction can be modified, Bloom concluded that any student can be taught to complete or master any learning task successfully, given sufficient instruction.

12. To achieve mastery, students are not permitted to proceed to a new unit until they pass a test on the current unit. Those who demonstrate mastery move on; those who fail receive additional instruction and are retested. This cycle is repeated as necessary until all students reach mastery.

13. While students will not differ in achievement if the mastery model is used, they will differ in the amount of instructional time they require, necessitating that the teacher be able to provide different amounts of instruction to different groups of students.

14. The *direct instruction model* utilizes behaviors identified through *process–product* research rather than from theories. Achievement-producing teachers are compared to non-achievement-producing teachers to see how they differ, and those teaching behaviors that were shown to contribute to achievement then become the model.

15. The model is called direct instruction because it emphasizes *teacher-directed*, -controlled, and -paced activities with a definite content orientation, such as review, lesson development and presentation, and student participation through seatwork and homework. Instruction is also *group-based* rather than individualized, and it works best for teaching basic skills to young learners.

16. Bruner's (1960) *discovery learning* utilizes the presentation of *problem situations* that stimulate and encourage students to figure out for *themselves* the *structure* or meaning of the subject matter.

17. Rather than being told what they are to know, students discover it through *inductive reasoning*—using examples or facts to help them think up a general principle or theory that explains the evidence. Teachers can help students make those discoveries by *guiding* them and encouraging them to use their *intuition* or imaginative judgment.

Suggested Resources

Brophy, J. E. (1988). Research linking teacher behavior to student achievement: Potential implications for instruction of Chapter 1 students. *Educational Psychologist*, 23(3), 275–276.

Dick, W., & Reiser, R. A. (1989). *Planning effective instruction*. Englewood Cliffs, NJ: Prentice-Hall.

Mager, R. F. (1984). *Preparing instructional objectives* (2nd ed.). Belmont, CA: Pitman.

Peterson, P., & Walberg, H. (1979). *Research on teaching: Concepts, findings, and implications*. Berkeley, CA: McCutchan.

Reiser, R. A., & Gagné, R. M. (1983). *Selecting media for instruction*. Englewood Cliffs, NJ: Educational Technology Publications.

Skinner, B. F. (1968). *The technology of teaching*. New York: Appleton–Century–Crofts.

Chapter
6

A Cognitive Approach to Learning

Objectives

1. Identify and describe a three-stage information processing model including sensory register, short-term memory, and long-term memory.
2. Identify and describe the factors that affect rote learning: meaningfulness, serial position, practice, organization, transfer and interference, and mnemonic devices.
3. Identify and describe the metacognitive processes that affect meaningful learning: abstracting, elaborating, schematizing, and organizing.
4. Identify and describe the metacognitive structures that affect meaningful reception learning, as set forth by Ausubel: advance organizers, signals, postlesson summaries and review questions.
5. Describe mathemagenic activities: notetaking and answering adjunct questions.
6. Describe the metacognitive strategies of monitoring and affecting.
7. Identify combinations of the above that constitute study skills.

Box 6.1

🍎

A Memory Experiment

To prepare for this experiment, take a piece of paper and write the numbers 1 through 12 down the left side. Draw a vertical line just to the right of the numbers and then draw four more vertical lines so the paper is divided up into four columns. Now you are going to test yourself to see how well you can remember each of four lists of words. Each list has 12 words and you must study each list for exactly 10 seconds. The lists each appear at the top left-hand margin of each of the next four left-hand pages.

When I say go, turn to page 118 and look at your watch. Then study the list of words at the top left corner of the page for 10 seconds. (You may need to have a friend or roommate do the timing.) At the end of 10 seconds, turn back to this page and, in the first column on your lined sheet of paper, write down as many of the words as you can remember. Then turn to the second list on page 120 and repeat the procedure; do the same with the third list on page 122, and finally the fourth and last list on page 124.

When you have tested yourself on all four lists, compare the printed lists to your own, and write down at the bottom of each column on your paper the number of words that you have correctly remembered (regardless of order). You should do this experiment before you read this chapter. Then, when you read the text, you will realize exactly what this experiment is all about.

Are you ready? Have you numbered and lined your paper? Do you have a stopwatch or a timer? OK, GO.

A Three-Stage Information Processing Model

As has already been proposed by Gagné in the preceding chapter, the processing of or acting on incoming information by the brain is not a single-step process. The information must first "get into" the brain and then must be kept or stored in the brain through a process called memory. Furthermore, it must be stored in such a way that it can be recalled or retrieved. Storing information in a retrievable form has been called *semantic encoding* by Gagné (1985) and others.

Sensory Register. The existence of three stages of information processing — (1) entry via a sensory register (which is also referred to as perception), (2) storage in short-term memory, and (3) storage in long-term memory — has been widely proposed (see, for example, Loftus & Loftus, 1976). The information we attend to and perceive with our eyes and ears is registered or received in our thinking process. It is then stored, temporarily, in short-term memory before being transferred to long-term memory. If you carried out the experiment in Box 6.1, then during the 10 seconds that you were studying each list, you were committing it to your sensory register (along with any markings in the book that you or others have made and any background sounds, such as conversation or TV, that might be going on while you study).

Short-Term Memory. Information that a person focuses on and chooses to retain enters into short-term memory, at least for a brief period of time. Unfortunately, short-term memory has a limited capacity. If someone is introduced to six people at a party, he or she may remember the names of only a few of them. Of course, part of the problem here may be attention. George Miller (1956) has shown that the capacity of short-term memory is about seven units of information. Of the twelve "words" on the first list in the Box 6.1 experiment (actually they were not words but so-called nonsense syllables — two consonants separated by a vowel), you probably were able to remember about seven of them, the limit of your short-term memory. Even though you may have repeated the list over and over to yourself in the 10-second period, a process known as *rehearsal*, this would enable you to reach only the upper limit of your short-term memory, again about seven or eight units of information.

However, people can expand their short-term memory capacity by increasing the size of each unit of information. This is called *chunking*. If someone were to combine an entire list of words into a meaningful chunk or sentence (such as the last list in the Box 6.1 experiment), then it could be remembered along with six or seven more chunks or sentences as well.

In summary, we can store information for longer periods in short-term memory through (1) *chunking*, that is, by connecting smaller pieces together to make larger pieces, or (2) continuous or repeated *rehearsal*. For example, if you repeat over and over a phone number you heard at a party, you can remember it until you get home and write it down; you can remember phone numbers you call frequently; you can remember phone numbers more easily if you can connect the numbers together.

Short-term memory is called *working memory*. It is the place where newly registered information is mixed with previously learned information during reading, thinking, and problem-solving. People with good short-term memories can shift their focus repeatedly from reading to thinking without having to reread the previous material to remember the gist of it. This is a major difference between skilled and unskilled readers (Chall, 1983).

Long-Term Memory.   Information that must be remembered for longer periods of time is transferred to long-term memory where it may remain for most of a person's life. The process of long-term memory storage is called semantic encoding because many psychologists believe that what is stored is not the information itself but some more efficient verbal representation of it. Thus, people do not usually store information in long-term memory by rehearsal or repetition, as was true for short-term memory, but by transforming the information into meaningfully and purposefully connected verbal chunks that have been referred to as *semantic networks* (E. D. Gagné, 1985). (An example of such a semantic network is shown in Figure 6.1.)

A semantic network is a set of interconnected and interrelated ideas in which one idea or element of an idea can trigger the memory of another idea. Entire sets of knowledge can be organized into such networks of ideas with common or shared elements. In this way, all of the ideas do not have to be in short-term or working memory but can still be accessible to it.

The ideas that are formed into semantic networks may be of two types (E. D. Gagné, 1985): (1) *propositions* or units of *declarative knowledge*, that is, knowledge about facts; and (2) *productions* or units of *procedural knowledge*, that is, knowledge about operations or how to do something. For example, the knowledge that the words *was* and *were* are verbs is declarative knowledge, whereas knowing which form of the verb to use with the singular pronoun *I* is procedural knowledge. We can represent procedural

List 1
gis
dep
tir
bez
yad
kol
wuk
jov
puh
hab
mij
lec

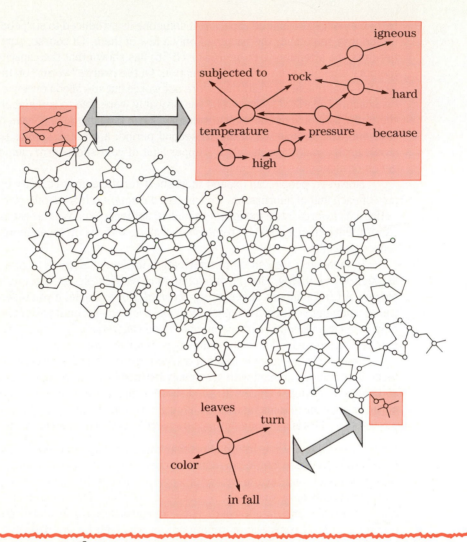

Figure 6.1 🍎 The Propositional Network
Each proposition, indicated by a node–link structure, is linked to other propositions through common ideas. Thus, all of declarative knowledge is interrelated in a vast network of propositions. (From E. Gagné, p. 74.)

knowledge as productions that are IF–THEN statements. An example: IF the subject of the sentence is *I*, THEN use the verb form *was*. IF the subject is *you*, THEN use *were*.

So far, only semantic networks of propositions and productions have been described as a means of representing or encoding information in long-term memory. An alternative form of long-term knowledge representation is the *schema*. A schema is a mental image or code that can be used to organize or structure information. (See Box 6.2 for an example of processing information with and without a suitable schema.) Some theorists (for example, Paivio, 1979) contend that information is stored in long-term

Box 6.2

The Value of Having the Right Schema

Read the paragraph below and try to figure out what it is about.

> With hocked gems financing him, our hero bravely defied all scornful laughter that tried to prevent his scheme. "Your eyes deceive," he had said, "an egg not a table correctly typifies this unexplored planet." Now three sturdy sisters sought proof, forging along sometimes through calm vastness, yet more often over turbulent peaks and valleys. Days became weeks as many doubters spread fearful rumors about the edge. At last from nowhere welcome-winged creatures appeared signifying momentous success. (Dooling & Lachman, 1971, p. 217)

Now that you have read it, cover it up and try to remember what it said and what it meant. Did it sound to you like it was about "Star Wars"? In fact, it was not, but in your effort to make sense out of it, you had to search for the right schema that would enable you to decode and then encode the content.

The real title of the paragraph appears in footnote 1 on page 120. Read the real title now and then reread the paragraph. Does it make more sense when you have the right schema to process it? Can you remember it better? Most people answer yes to both questions (Dooling & Lachman, 1971).

memory as *both* a semantic network and a schema. This is called the *dual-code theory*. The advantage of a dual code is that if one form is lost or forgotten, the other will still remain. In other words, two memories are better than one.

Factors Affecting Rote Learning

The consideration of cognitive factors impacting on learning will begin with rote learning. Rote learning is learning by repetition and memorization. Saying something over and over to oneself, called *vocalization* or *rehearsal*, places greatest reliance on short-term or working memory. There are many kinds of information that are likely to be learned this way, especially in preparation for tests. The Box 6.1 experiment, an example of rote learning, will be used as much as possible to illustrate the various factors that affect the ability to learn by rote.

Meaningfulness.   The more meaningful information is, the easier it is to memorize and retain. In addition, the more meaningful information can be made to be, the easier it will be to memorize and retain.

In the Box 6.1 experiment, this point is best illustrated by a comparison of your results on Lists 1 and 2. List 1 is made up of nonsense syllables (consonant–vowel–consonant nonwords). Nonsense syllables are meaningless. List 2 is made up of real words; words have meaning. Therefore, List 2 should be easier to remember than List 1, and you should have correctly recalled more words from List 2 than from List 1. Also, the

List 2
pen
our
whom
can
has
boy
fast
too
span
run
foot
wing

story in Box 6.2 should be more easily remembered after you have figured out or discovered the right schema, because the right schema helps give the paragraph meaning.

The memorability of information, such as a list of words, can be increased if you substitute more familiar, concrete words for unfamiliar, abstract words (Wittrock, Marks, & Doctorow, 1975). When you have new material to learn that involves new terminology or vocabulary, try to link the new terms to older, more familiar ones to make them easier to remember.

Serial Position.   Serial position effects result from the location of an item in a list, be it at the beginning, the middle, or the end. (These might also be called *sequence* effects.) Those items that come first tend to be remembered best (called the *primacy* effect), as do those that come last (the *recency* effect). When you are introduced to a group of people you do not know, you tend to "catch" the names of only the first few and last few people, while "losing" those in the middle. There is definitely a memory advantage for items having nothing before them (like those that come at the beginning) or nothing after them (like those at the end) over items surrounded by other items (like those coming in the middle). There may well be less interference at the two ends of a list than in the middle.

Go back to your results in Box 6.1. Chances are you always got the first two words on each list right, as the result of primacy. See if you also got the last two words on each list right. Chances are you did not. Sometimes more time is spent studying the beginning of a list at the expense of the words at the end, thereby giving the first few words the benefits of both primacy and recency. Remember, whatever is focused on last has the benefit of recency. If you practiced the list one and a half times, for example, the words in the middle would have been practiced most recently. Whatever word you had reached when you stopped would have the benefit of recency.

Practice.   Practice may not necessarily "make perfect," but, in general, the more people practice the more they remember. If you were given 20 seconds to practice the words in the Box 6.1 experiment, rather than 10 seconds, you would have remembered more words—although not necessarily twice as many. The corollary to this rule would be that the more you study, or the more times you read the assignment, the more of it you will remember.

However, there are two types of practice: *massed* practice, which is continuous, nonstop practice, and *distributed* practice, or practice spread over time with rest periods interspersed. When students study all night before an exam, they are engaging in massed practice. When they study two hours each night during the week before the exam, they are engaging in distributed practice.

Distributed practice has been shown to be more effective than massed practice, perhaps because it allows for the dissipation of fatigue, but also because it allows the learner to make associations or connections to more than one context (Glenberg, 1976). The implication is that "cramming" is a poor way to study because it represents massed practice. Frequent but short practice sessions with breaks in between are likely to lead to better memorization of information. In the Box 6.1 experiment, the instructions were intended to keep both the amount and the type of practice constant.

[1]Title to Box 6.2 paragraph: "Christopher Columbus Discovering America."

Practice contributes to memory. Going over or rehearsing key information before a test will make it easier to remember it later. But practice should be spread out or distributed over time, not all crammed into the night before the test.

Organization.   Remember from an earlier discussion (pages 116–117) that short-term memory was reported to have a capacity limited to about seven units of information. However, if several pieces of information can be organized into a single unit by means of a technique such as chunking, then more pieces of information can be remembered.

Consider Lists 3 and 4 in the Box 6.1 experiment. The words in List 3 all relate to the same topic, the house, so they possess some degree of topical organization or *semantic organization* by virtue of their common meaning. The words in List 4 have an even greater degree of organization. They form a sentence that provides *structural organization* so that each word can be directly connected to the words immediately before and after it. List 4 can be considered a single chunk, so it should be the easiest of all four lists to remember.

Your own performance on the four lists, therefore, should have become progressively better from List 1 to List 4 since the lists increase progressively in both meaningfulness and organization. These are two of the important factors that affect rote learning.

List 3
kitchen
house
door
attic
wall
stair
room
window
roof
garage
bath
floor

Taylor and Samuels (1983) have shown that children who are aware that reading material has been structured into main idea plus supporting detail can remember it better than children who are not aware of the text structure. For another example of the effect of organization on the ability to remember, see Box 6.3.

Transfer and Interference.   Transfer is the effect of prior learning on new learning. New information is easier to learn when other information has already been learned that has much in common with the new information. The atomic weights of elements in chemistry will be easier for students to learn once they have learned the atomic numbers, because the two sets of information have some commonalities. This is called *positive transfer*. However, sometimes prior learning makes new learning more difficult, as in learning to read Greek after learning English. Because some Greek letters look like the English letters to which they correspond (*A* and *Alpha*, for example), there will be positive transfer. But some Greek letters look like English letters to which they do not correspond (*Rho*, the Greek letter *R*, looks like a *P*), so there will also be significant *negative transfer*.

While transfer has to do with the effect of prior experience on learning something new, *interference* has to do with the effect of learning something new on remembering something from the past. Interference, as the name implies, does not have a positive side and a negative side, only a negative one. New information forces old information out of short-term memory, making the older information harder to remember. Hence, what is

These kids aren't chess masters yet, but the more experience they have playing the game, the better they will get at remembering the location of the pieces on the board, by remembering patterns or "chunks."

being learned may interfere with the ability to remember what has already been learned (although it may transfer positively — that is, help what will be learned next).

To prove this to yourself, take out a piece of paper and write down as many words as you can remember from List 2 of the Box 6.1 experiment. If you are like most people, you will remember fewer words than you did originally because what you have learned since then has interfered with your memory of List 2.

Let's say you are trying to remember a list of numbers, such as a telephone number, and a friend is teasing you by repeating random numbers aloud. The new numbers tend to interfere with the old ones, and may make you forget the phone number you are trying to remember or cause you to insert new, incorrect numbers in it so that you remember it incorrectly. When interference works backward like this, it is called *retroactive*. If, on the other hand, you are trying to remember a phone number and then you hear a second phone number and try to remember it as well, the first number may interfere with the second. This interference, working forward, would be called *proactive*. Proactive interference can also be considered negative transfer (described above).

Since rote learning depends so greatly on short-term memory, transfer effects are likely to be negative and interference effects are likely to be frequent. In massed practice situations, such as cramming for a test, last chapter's notes will negatively transfer to memorizing this chapter's notes (which is proactive) and memorizing this chapter's notes

---

Box 6.3

🍎

The Chess Masters Study

DeGroot (1965) conducted a classic study using a group of people who were among the best chess players in the world. These people had qualified as chess masters by earning victory points in national and international competitions. In this study they played not against other chess masters but against amateurs, except they played against a number of amateurs at the same time. (You may have heard of such demonstrations, where one master plays a number of chess matches simultaneously against local chess enthusiasts. The master walks up and down along a row of tables with an active chess game going on at each table. The idea is for the master to try to win every game.)

In the experiment, the masters were taken out of the room in the middle of the games and asked to correctly recall the location of the chess pieces on every board. The masters were remarkably accurate in their recall, much more so than the amateurs. Then, on another trial of the experiment, the chess pieces were placed on the board randomly rather than in the positions they would take as the result of actual moves. Suddenly, the masters had lost their advantage. Their recall of the random boards was no better than that of the amateurs.

Why could the masters remember the real boards so much better than the random ones? Obviously, it could not be a function of how good their memories were or they would have remembered both equally; rather, it seemed to depend on how they used their memories. It appeared that the masters "had recognized the structure of pieces on the board, coded it in memory in terms of the pattern, and used the coded pattern as the recall cue" (Taylor & Samuels, 1983, p. 518). In other words, the masters used their vast knowledge of the game to *chunk* the many pieces into a smaller, more memorable, number of units.

List 4
Charles
first
cousin
was
once
town
mayor
after
winning
the
close
election

will interfere with remembering last chapter's notes (which is retroactive). In trying to minimize negative transfer and interference effects, it is helpful (a) to space out or distribute practice, (b) to focus on meaningful learning (the subject of the next section of this book) rather than rote learning, and (c) to use mnemonic devices — the topic that will be covered next.

Mnemonic Devices.   These are techniques or "tricks" for aiding memory by associating less meaningful material with more meaningful or more memorable images, words, or sayings. Think about how you were taught to remember the musical notes that appear on the *lines* of the staff in treble clef. It may have been by being taught the mnemonic EGBDF, whose first letters correspond to the notes: *E*very *G*ood *B*oy *D*oes *F*ine. Chances are that you will remember this for the rest of your life because of the ease of learning and remembering the mnemonic phrase.

One of the most popular mnemonic techniques is the *Peg Method*, a useful way to remember numbered items in a list. Create the image of a rhyming word for each number and then form an image that combines the rhyming-word image with the word to be remembered. This technique is illustrated in Box 6.4. The rhyming words serve as the "pegs" or "hooks" on which the numbered words to be remembered are "hung." Of course, to use this technique you need to create for yourself and commit to memory a set of pegwords and images that you are sure you can remember. Research has shown that mnemonic techniques that rely on images to connect old words to new words make those new words easier to remember than they would be without the mnemonic images (McDaniel & Pressley, 1984).

Metacognitive Processes Affecting Meaningful Learning

Meaningful learning is less automatic than rote learning. It requires the use of systematic processes for coding and storing information in long-term memory and for retrieving it. These processes are called "metacognitive" because they represent ways of acquiring thoughts rather than the thoughts themselves. These processes are described below.

Abstracting.   This represents the technique of extracting the main point or gist of a passage or section of text, and we do it by skimming the passage for an overview and then writing down the phrase or sentence that best describes what the passage is about. The purpose of abstracting is to reduce the written material or text to an amount that can be understood and retained. Hence, the first principle for learning information from a textbook is to *reduce the information to a manageable amount by picking out the most essential elements.* The key ideas here are (1) to make more into less and (2) to have the "less" capture the essential meaning of the "more."

The product of abstracting is an *outline* or a *summary* of main points. This outline or summary itself can sometimes be abstracted to form a shorter, more concise outline or summary. The idea is to continually reduce information by making each outline "richer" in essential information than the one that preceded it. Creating a final product short enough to be contained within short-term memory would be a desirable result.

The idea of abstracting is somewhat analogous to creating a juice concentrate or freeze-dried coffee. Each represents the essence of what it started out as, but in considerably reduced form. However, importantly, the reduction has not been at the expense of essential ingredients; these have been retained. When the original substance is desired, water is added to the concentrate and, presto, the original is restored. With textbook information, the essential parts can be abstracted to form a "knowledge" concentrate. Later, these bits of information can be expanded to reproduce a more detailed account of what has been read.

Elaborating.   This process is somewhat the opposite of abstracting in that it produces more information rather than less. However, the additional information produced is different from the original in that, by virtue of having been produced by the learner, it is clearer to him or her than was the original. Moreover, the new version of the original idea or concept is typically more concrete, realistic, and familiar than the old. The elaboration can be an example, an illustration, a drawing, an analogy, a metaphor, or a rewriting of the idea in the reader's own words. Weinstein and Mayer (1985) describe elaborating as making connections between new material and more familiar material.

A good example of elaborating appears in the preceding subsection under abstracting. In order to facilitate understanding of the idea or concept of abstracting, the metaphor of preparing food concentrates such as frozen juice or freeze-dried coffee was used. The idea of abstracting or *reducing* ideas to their essence was elaborated upon or expanded on in a different form in that it was likened (or made analogous) to the idea of

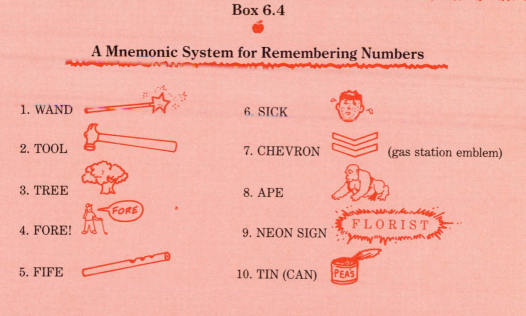

Box 6.4

🍎

A Mnemonic System for Remembering Numbers

1. WAND

2. TOOL

3. TREE

4. FORE!   FORE

5. FIFE

6. SICK

7. CHEVRON   (gas station emblem)

8. APE

9. NEON SIGN   FLORIST

10. TIN (CAN)   PEAS

If you need to remember, for example, that the fourth item in a list is the word *can* (see List 2 on page 120, which you studied in the Box 6.1 memory experiment), visualize a golfer hitting a soda can (instead of a golf ball) and shouting "Fore!" Images of action that connect the above "number pictures" with "pictures" of the words or ideas to be remembered make the connections easier to code into long-term memory.

reducing food substances like juice or coffee to their *essence*. Presumably, the elaboration in the form of a metaphor or an analogy helped make the description of abstracting more understandable.

When text material is read, it must be understood if it is to be learned, expounded on, and used. Moreover, since there is invariably too much information to be memorized verbatim, it must be understood if it is ever to be reduced or abstracted into its essential points. For this reason, elaborating on each new point helps to ensure that it is understood. This point is supported by Weinstein (1982), who found that students trained in elaboration (including rewriting the author's explanations in their own words) did better on tests than students who were not given this training.

How would you elaborate on the concept of "elaborating"? Does it seem to you like stuffing a pillowcase to make a pillow, or is it more like the cuckoo bird that springs out of the clock to cluck the hours so that you can hear the time in addition to seeing it? Is it the string you tie around your finger to help you remember something, or a pink elephant that can't be lost or hidden? Finding a way to help see a point increases the chances of both understanding it and remembering it. Maybe it is more like a bedtime story used to help children understand why they are being punished. Or it might be like the electric bulb that goes off in someone's head when something difficult has finally been brought to "light." Try elaborating on the sentences in Box 6.5.

Schematizing.   A schema (plural, *schemata*) (introduced on page 118 and in Box 6.2) is a framework or code for structuring information so that it can be both understood and stored in long-term memory. If information is coded, then when it is ready to be used, it can be found. Schemata, therefore, are a critical component of the metacognitive process used in learning meaningful material. In fact, in abstracting, it is schemata that help to diagnose what the main points of the passage to be outlined are, and what information can be disregarded. Moreover, the purpose of elaborating is to try to find or uncover the proper schema to use in making sense out of or decoding the text. Schemata are like mental forms or templates that are used to help us understand and retain what is being learned.

Researchers like Anderson (1984) have discovered how important schemata are. Most directly, schemata help learners (l) understand what they read and (2) focus on the

---

Box 6.5

Elaborating

Make believe that you are reading a story and you come to the following two sentences:

TIM WANTED A NEW MODEL AIRPLANE.

HE SAW THE CHANGE LYING ON HIS FATHER'S DRESSER.

As you read these sentences, think of how you might elaborate on them. Write three or four more sentences that come into your head that help make these two sentences into a story. Then look at footnote 2 on page 129 to see the elaborations that a researcher came up with.

most important parts. Less obviously, schemata also help learners (3) figure out what is implied but not directly said (in other words, read between the lines), (4) search through memory for what other information they must know in order to understand what is being read, (5) pick out the main points for long-term storage (which, as has already been said, is abstracting), and, finally, (6) fill in the gaps in memory when the main points are recalled later (a form of elaborating). Schemata, therefore, are important learning and thinking tools.

There are some very important general schemata that are used over and over to process information effectively. Sometimes these are referred to as *structures* because they help the reader to structure or interpret what has been read. Other times they are referred to as *levels* of processing because they help the reader go beneath the surface of the text to extract its true meaning.

Meyer (1975) has identified a set of five structures that can be used for processing or schematizing text in order to extract the main point or meaning:

> *antecedent/consequent* — structure that shows a cause and effect relationship between topics (for example, drinking before driving causes accidents);
>
> *comparison* — points out similarities and differences between topics (for example, the effects of drinking and taking drugs on driving are similar);
>
> *collection* — brings together and lists the components of a topic (for example, alcohol, marijuana, and cocaine are all mind-altering substances);
>
> *description* — gives a general statement along with supporting details or explanations (for example, the effect of drinking and driving is illustrated by the number of traffic fatalities in drunk driving cases); and
>
> *response* — presents a problem and solution or question and answer (for example, government can solve the problem of drunk driving by making the penalties for it more severe).

To see how these five structures actually work, read the material in Box 6.6 and try to use each one of the five structures to describe the passage or some aspect of it. Then check your answers against those given at the bottom of page 130.[3]

The value of using the structures (or schemata) to process information is that doing so makes it possible to abstract the main point more easily and to code, store, and retrieve it in memory (Meyer, Brandt, & Bluth, 1980). Learning and remembering seem to work much better when there is a focus on exactly what is to be learned and remembered, and when there is a mechanism, such as a structure or schema, that can be used to provide that focus.

Organizing. This involves imposing a structure on the material rather than trying to discover the "structures" within it. To organize the material, the reader subdivides it into sections and subsections. An additional feature of the imposed organization is that the parts, sections, or headings have a hierarchical relationship: Smaller parts fit into, or, when taken together, make up larger parts. For example, note how this book has been "organized." The major headings are parts, which in turn are made up of chapters and then sections. Sections have been further divided into subsections. You can get a "picture" of the organization of this (or any) book by looking at its table of contents.

Recall from Chapter 4 Gagné's learning hierarchies. These represented organizational structures that were derived from an analysis of a final or terminal learning task. The type of organization referred to here is a less formal one, in which the idea is simply to separate information into subsets that relate to a common point or idea. However, both Gagné's analytical approach to organization and the one here based on commonality of ideas are intended to make learning easier and more complete.

When information is organized, it is put into subsets, which enhances or adds to the capacity of working memory to store it. Glynn and DiVesta (1977) gave some college students the following outline for a passage on Minerals:

    I. Metals
        A. Rare metals
           1. Silver
           2. Gold
        B. Alloys
           1. Steel
           2. Brass
    II. Stones
        A. Gem stones
           1. Diamonds
           2. Ruby
        B. Masonry stones
           1. Granite
           2. Marble

Other students read the passage without the outline. Afterward, both groups tried to recall what they had read. Both groups recalled general ideas equally well, but the group with the outline recalled specific details better than the group without it.

Sometimes the material to be learned is already well organized, in which case it will be easier to learn (Thorndyke, 1977). However, when it is not organized well enough to be clear, organizing or reorganizing it yourself will make it easier to understand and remember. Organizing or reorganizing textbook material is a way of chunking it and schematizing it to make it easier to process. Consider, for example, the Supertanker passage in Box 6.6. One way of organizing it is shown in Table 6.1.

In the next section of this chapter, more will be said about organizing and organization effects as specific instruction aids in the context of meaningful reception learning.

Metacognitive Structures Affecting Meaningful Reception Learning

The instructional theorist David Ausubel coined the phrase "meaningful reception learning" to describe what happens when a learner is presented with instructional material or text in learnable, organized form. According to Ausubel, "the most important factor influencing the meaningful learning of any new idea is the state of the individual's existing cognitive structure at the time of learning" (Ausubel & Robinson, 1969, p. 143). In other words, content that is properly prepared and structured will be easiest for students to learn because it will provide them with the metacognitive structure they need

Box 6.6

The Supertanker Passage

A problem of vital concern is the prevention of oil spills from supertankers. A typical supertanker carries a half-million tons of oil and is the size of five football fields. A wrecked supertanker spills oil in the ocean; this oil kills animals, birds, and microscopic plant life. For example, when a tanker crashed off the coast of England, more than 200,000 dead seabirds washed ashore. Oil spills also kill microscopic plant life that provides food for sea life and produces 70 percent of the world's oxygen supply. Most wrecks result from the lack of power and steering equipment to handle emergency situations, such as storms. Supertankers have only one boiler to provide power and one propeller to drive the ship.

The solution to the problem is not to immediately halt the use of tankers on the ocean, since about 80 percent of the world's oil supply is carried by supertankers. Instead, the solution lies in the training of officers of supertankers, better building of tankers, and installing ground control stations to guide tankers near shore. First, officers of supertankers must get top training in how to run and maneuver their ships. Second, tankers should be built with several propellers for extra control and backup boilers for emergency power. Third, ground control stations should be installed at places where supertankers come close to shore. These stations would act like airplane control towers, guiding tankers along busy shipping lanes and through dangerous channels.

Use each of the five structures on page 127 to describe some aspect of this passage. (Answers are in footnote 3 on page 130.)

SOURCE: Meyer, B. J. F., Brandt, D. M., & Bluth, G. J. (1980). Use of top-level structure in text: Key for reading comprehension of ninth-grade students. *Reading Research Quarterly, 16,* 72–103.

to satisfactorily process it. Consider what some of the techniques might be for metacognitively structuring text material to ensure that it will be meaningfully received and learned by students.

Advance Organizers.   These are previews or summaries provided at the beginning of the text (Ausubel, 1960) that characterize the purpose of the text and the approach taken to fulfill that purpose. Moreover, advance organizers relate to what students have already learned to help them look for the salient points in the new material. Advance organizers essentially alert students to the cognitive structures or schemata that will be needed to process the new text information, and they do so in terms that are already familiar to them. The organizational outline of the Supertanker passage, shown in Table

---

[2]Box 6.5 elaborations: Reder (1976, p. 394) came up with the following elaborations: "Tim is about 8 to 12, has a crew cut; the father's dresser is just at Tim's eye level; the model airplane is silver with chevron decals; the father is the absentminded type who would not notice the change missing but who would be furious if he found out his son took it."

6.1, would be a useful advance organizer for the passage itself since it not only summarizes the passage but provides an organizational structure for representing the meaning of the passage as well. Instructional objectives that appear at the beginning of chapters also serve as advance organizers.

Ausubel (1968) reported that advance organizers are especially valuable when the material to be learned is poorly organized and the students have limited ability — which means they will have trouble organizing it themselves. In such cases, the material is more likely to go unorganized and hence unlearned without the assistance of advance organizers.

What makes the *best* organizers? According to Mayer (1979), the answer to that question is

- concrete models
- analogies
- examples
- sets of general, higher-order rules
- discussions of main themes in familiar terms

What makes the *worst* organizers? Again, Mayer (1979) answers:

- specific factual prequestions
- outlines
- summaries
- directions to pay attention to specific key facts or terms

Signals.   These are noncontent words placed within a passage to emphasize or call attention to either the organization or the meaning of a passage. If recognized, signals can cue the student to the most important points in the passage and their relationship to one another. Signals also represent what Skinner called (in Chapter 3) discriminative stimuli. Knowing the signals means knowing "when" to look and "what" to look for.

According to Mayer (1984), the three major types of signals are

1. cues to the structure of ideas in the passage and how they relate to one another ("the problem is," "the solution is," "first," "second," "third");

2. advance, abstracted statements of key information to follow ("the main ideas discussed in the chapter are"); and

3. point words that emphasize important information ("more importantly," "also," "for example").

---

[3]Structures illustrated for the Supertanker passage (Box 6.6):

   antecedent/consequent: "Lack of power and steering in supertankers" *leads to* "oil spills."
   comparison: "Ground control stations for supertankers" *are similar to* "control towers for aircraft."
   collection: *Three ways to improve supertankers safety are* "training officers," "building safer ships," and "installing ground control stations."
   description: *The fact that* "oil spills kill wildlife" *is supported by the example* "that 200,000 seabirds died."
   response: *The problem is* "that supertankers spill oil," *and the solution is* "to improve their safety."
Taken together, the five structures provide a reasonably complete account of the passage.

Table 6.1 🍎 Possible Organization of the Supertanker Passage from Box 6.6

I. PROBLEM: How to prevent oil spills from tankers

   A. Cause: Lack of power and steering

   B. Effect: Dead seabirds and plant life

II. RESTRICTION: Can't halt use

   A. Reason: Need oil and they carry it

III. SOLUTION

   A. Training: Train officers to maneuver

   B. Power: Build tankers with backup props

   C. Guidance: Create ground control stations

Reread the Supertanker passage in Box 6.6 and see if you can find the signals. Underline them. Note that the passage begins with "A problem of vital concern" and then states the solution. The second paragraph begins with "The solution to the problem" and then states what the solution "is not." It follows this with "Instead, the solution lies" and then states the solution. The details of the solution in the second paragraph are signaled by the words *first*, *second*, and *third*. In the first paragraph, details are signaled by the point words *for example* and *also*. If you can locate these eight signals, you can form an organized outline of the passage that contains its meaning.

Postlesson Summaries and Review Questions. Ausubel (1960) also points out the importance of cognitive structures that come at the end of text material and either summarize and interpret it for students or help them summarize and interpret it for themselves. The advantage of providing this structure in advance is that it helps students work through material themselves. However, should they fail to get the meaning of the material by the time they have finished reading it, they will be unprepared to continue without some final assistance. This is provided by the summary and review questions.

Combining Organizers. In Chapter 5, in the discussion of the design of instruction, primary focus was placed on the application of behavioral approaches. These approaches involved the systematic presentation of what is to be learned, an opportunity for the student to respond, and a reinforcement that is contingent upon the student's correct response. We can now modify this approach or change it dramatically by using instructional design principles based on the cognitive or metacognitive view of learning identified by Ausubel and described above.

If all of Ausubel's organizers are combined—advance organizers, signals, postlesson summaries, and review questions—the result is the old teaching adage: "Tell them what you are going to tell them; then tell them; then tell them what you told them." More specifically, this means doing the following:

1. beginning instruction with advance organizers such as previews, outlines, questions, or behavioral objectives;

2. making sure that new concepts and terms are defined and illustrated;

3. organizing and sequencing new material, using headings and signals so it can be followed;

4. keeping the student as active as possible during instruction by means of questions and activities;

5. ending instruction with a review of main points; and

6. following up instruction with questions or other assignments that require students to process and use the information they have just learned.

Note the similarities and differences between these points and Skinner's behavioral approach to instruction on pages 65–66. In Chapter 7, yet another approach to instructional design—based on a metacognitive view of learning as problem-solving—will be presented.

Mathemagenic Activities

Mathemagenic activities are activities that students undertake on their own initiative to prepare themselves for and assist in their own learning (Rothkopf, 1970). This includes two general kinds of activities, taking notes and answering adjunct questions, which will be discussed in turn.

Notetaking.   At best, this is a technique for outlining or abstracting main ideas presented in lecture or in written text (Mayer, 1984). It also includes the subcategories of

Taking notes like this—on what the teacher says—is one way students can assist in their own learning. It helps them organize and remember verbally presented information.

highlighting and making notes in the margins, neither of which provides the same level of processing as notetaking, but both of which are more effective than passive reading.

What advice can be given about notetaking? Armbruster and Brown (1984) suggest six rules for taking notes from written text:

1. delete trivial material,
2. delete redundant material,
3. substitute a superordinate (that is, more inclusive) term for a list of subordinate items when possible,
4. substitute a superordinate event for a list of subordinate actions when possible,
5. select a topic sentence if the author has provided one, and
6. write your own topic sentence if necessary.

For example, rather than writing out in detail the three ways to solve the oil spill problem in the Supertanker passage (Box 6.6), you could list two superordinate (that is, more inclusive) terms to cover the three detailed statements. These would be *power* and *guidance*. Remembering these terms should then cue you to remember more of the detailed information in the passage.

How should students go about taking lecture notes? Carrier and Titus (1981) recommend that they

1. distinguish between superordinate and subordinate information,
2. abbreviate words,
3. paraphrase in their own words, and
4. use an outline format.

It is much more efficient to focus on capturing main ideas and distinguishing between major headings (superordinate information) and minor ones or details (subordinate information) than to try to take down verbatim everything the lecturer says (Kiewra, 1985). It is also helpful to look and listen for schemata and structures, such as were presented on page 127, to use in processing information. Another set of structures, described by Cook (1982), can be very helpful in reading science texts. These structures are

1. generalization (look for a main idea followed by an explanation, a clarification, or an extension of that idea),
2. enumeration (look for facts listed one after the other),
3. sequence (look for a connected series of events or steps in a process),
4. classification (look for material grouped into categories), and
5. comparison/contrast (look for the relationship between two or more things).

These structures can be used to organize the notes taken from course reading. They can also be used to organize lecture notes.

In regard to notetaking from either lecture or text, but particularly from lecture, it is highly advisable to go over notes as soon as possible after taking them and organize them so that they represent accurate, processed information rather than just raw input. Notes are not intended to be a "soundtrack." They should be information that has been processed in the ways described in this chapter.

Answering or Writing Adjunct Questions.   Adjunct questions are questions about the text material that appear at the beginning or end of the text or somewhere within it, most typically at the end of a section or a chapter. These can be test questions or activities for the student to complete. It has been clearly shown that answering these questions or completing these activities helps students learn and remember what they have read (Reynolds & Anderson, 1982). Compared to those at the beginning, questions at the end of a segment or section are less likely to narrow the readers' focus and are more likely to enable them to encode the material in their own words (Sagaria & DiVesta, 1978).

Prequestions, as has already been said, can serve as advance organizers, and as such they should be as general as possible and focus on the main points of the material. Their purpose is to prepare students for the information to follow by providing structures and schemata to process it. The questions at the end serve a different purpose. They are most valuable when they direct attention to points that are typically misunderstood, that is, to so-called student misconceptions (McConkie, 1977).

Answering questions at the end of an instructional unit can help the student (1) to recall information explicitly stated in the text, (2) to make appropriate inferences that go beyond but are based on information that is stated, and (3) to activate schemata to draw conclusions about related issues that are neither included nor implied in the text (Wixson, 1984). This mathamagenic activity is most successful when text designers try to provide questions that will serve all three of these purposes. Of course, no purpose is served if students make no effort to answer these adjunct questions.

Students can also be helped to become more involved with and aware of text information by constructing their own test items to measure their own learning (Tuckman & Sexton, 1990). A homework assignment of constructing test questions that cover text material can help students process the content and concepts covered in the text.

Metacognitive Strategies

Metacognition is the internal master control of thinking behavior designed to make sure that learning takes place. It includes processes that help people learn and processes that help people know whether or not they are learning. If learning is not taking place, metacognition triggers other processes that will correct the situation. Metacognition involves activating all of the factors and processes that have been described in this chapter, such as abstracting, elaborating, schematizing, and organizing. Metacognition also includes two other strategic activities that can be carried out by students to help them learn and understand what they are reading or being taught.

Monitoring.   This is the process of continually keeping track of whether or not learning is taking place. To a certain extent the teacher does the monitoring, but this may turn out to be too little and too late. It is far better for students to do their own monitoring on a regular basis, that is, continuously, whenever they are in a learning situation.

Monitoring includes activities such as the following (Zimmerman, 1989):

1. *Self-questioning*: Asking oneself, "Do I understand this? Can I make sense out of it? Am I ready to take an exam on it? Do I need help? Do I need to study more?"

2. *Establishing goals*: Deciding for oneself, "What level of performance do I want to achieve?" If the goal is an A grade, then the answers to the self-questions may be different than if the goal is a grade of C.

3. *Self-testing*: Giving oneself a test to find out as accurately as possible how much has been learned and how much has not been learned.

4. *Searching the environment*: Looking at materials and listening to other students and teachers to help determine whether or not one understands something well enough to meet the goals established above. Something may seem well understood until someone else is consulted.

5. *Using feedback*: Using results on tests, homework assignments, and in-class activities to help determine what one understands and does not understand. Going over the mistakes on a test as soon as it is given back is a good way to determine exactly what is misunderstood.

Affecting. Once students find out where they stand, they need to do something about it. If they want to meet their goals, they need to use all the cognitive processes at their disposal. This should include such activities as

1. going to class
2. paying attention in class
3. taking notes in class
4. reading assignments before class
5. reading assignments after class
6. taking notes on the reading
7. doing their homework
8. correcting their test mistakes
9. answering questions in the textbook
10. studying for exams
11. keeping up-to-date on all assignments
12. managing their time
13. asking for help when they need it
14. joining a study group
15. choosing studious persons as friends

Jones (1984) studied disadvantaged college students who, unlike many of their peers who came from similarly difficult circumstances, were earning grades of A in college courses and were on the Dean's List of their respective colleges. What were their secrets of success, he asked these "overachieving" students. Their answers were all the same: "When you don't understand something, ask questions. Stay after class if necessary, and talk to the instructor or go to his or her office. Use all the resources at your disposal, such as libraries and study groups. Hang out with other A students, not with people who are always in some sort of trouble. Keep up with your work; don't fall behind and end up always playing catch up." These are sound strategies and are consistent with what has been said in this chapter.

In the next chapter, metacognitive strategies will be returned to in the context of problem-solving.

Study Skills

What has been described in this chapter? The answer is, How people learn. Students are people, so what has been described in this chapter is, How students learn. If you apply all that you have read in this chapter to yourself as a student, then you will have developed

A good learning strategy is to look outside of class for information that will help you better understand something you learned in class. Using all the available resources is the mark of a good student.

study skills. If you teach all that you have read in this chapter to your students, then they will develop *study skills*. Here are some points to remember:

- Practice what you want to remember, but space out the practice rather than cram.
- If you don't understand something you've read, make up an example or analogy or some other elaboration to help yourself understand.
- Use structures and schemata to help you make sense out of and organize what you read.
- Take notes on each chapter as you read it.
- Identify and write down the main points, and organize them in terms of superordinates and subordinates.
- Answer the questions at the end of chapters.
- Be aware of what you don't understand.
- If you don't understand something, don't ignore it. Ask for clarification.
- Look for signals to help you find the main points in a textbook or lecture.

Studying requires more than passive exposure to information and more than memory. It requires cognitive processing of the information to encode it into long-term memory and to be able to decode it back into short-term memory when needed. To learn, therefore, students need to do the kinds of cognitive processing described in this chapter.

Summary of Main Points

1. Incoming information enters first the sensory register and then the short-term or working memory, which has a very limited capacity. To be stored more permanently and then retrieved when necessary, incoming information must be semantically encoded into long-term memory.

2. New information may be chunked into semantic networks, which are interconnected units of declarative knowledge called propositions and interconnected units of procedural knowledge called productions. According to the dual code theory, information may also be stored in the form of mental images or codes called schemata.

3. Learning information by repetition or rehearsal so that it can be "memorized" or stored in limited short-term memory is called rote learning. How well people can learn this way is affected by how meaningful the information they are learning is to them; where in the order of presentation the information appears, that is, its serial position; how much they practice it and whether they mass all the practice together or distribute it over time; how well the information is organized; whether information like it has already been learned or whether after they learn it they then use their short-term memory to learn something else; and whether or not they use memory aids called mnemonic devices.

4. Rote material is best learned—is most likely to be remembered—if it (a) is meaningful; (b) appears at the beginning or end of the list to be learned; (c) is practiced a lot, but practice is distributed over time; (d) is organized into chunks; (e) is similar to

material already learned; (f) is tested immediately, before anything else is learned; and (g) is learned using a mnemonic device.

5. Information that is learned by processing or encoding into long-term memory so that it can be stored and subsequently retrieved is called meaningful learning. Students can enhance and facilitate meaningful learning by the following metacognitive processes: (a) abstracting the material to be learned, forming a summary or an outline of the main points; (b) elaborating it, creating examples, diagrams, images, analogies, metaphors, stories, and the like that will help them understand what the material means; (c) schematizing or structuring it, connecting it to specific schemata or structures that help give it meaning by representing what it is about (such as cause and effect or problem and solution); and (d) organizing it, using a system of headings and subheadings to subdivide it into parts and subparts (as in a table of contents).

6. "Meaningful reception learning" is the label Ausubel has given to the learning process that depends on the state of the individual's thinking structure or long-term memory at the time of learning. The structures that affect this, he contends, are (a) advanced organizers, that is, previews or summaries or objectives that appear prior to the students' reading of the material to be learned; (b) signals or key words and phrases (or words in italics or underlined) that call attention to the meaning or main points of a passage; (c) postlesson summaries, such as the one you are now reading; and (d) review questions, such as might appear at the end of a chapter.

7. Good instructional material, according to Ausubel's principles, therefore begins with an advance organizer to prepare the learner to process what is to follow, includes signals for the learner to process while reading, and ends with a summary and review questions to ensure that the necessary processing will be done.

8. Ausubel describes what the textbook writer can do to assist thinking and understanding; Rothkopf describes what the student can do, and names these student activities mathemagenics. They include taking notes, highlighting, and writing margin notes on text and lecture material; answering the adjunct questions in the textbook, and creating one's own questions to answer.

9. In addition to these mathemagenic activities, students can use metacognitive strategies to help themselves learn. They can activate their master control processes by monitoring or keeping track of what they are and are not learning. Self-questioning, establishing goals, self-testing, searching the environment for feedback, and using that feedback when they get it are ways students can keep track of or monitor their own learning.

10. The second metacognitive strategy is to affect or do something to facilitate one's own learning. Going to class, paying attention, asking questions, keeping up-to-date, and studying for exams are examples of the affecting strategy.

11. Following the techniques for rote and meaningful learning, taking advantage of the structures provided by authors for meaningful reception learning, engaging in mathemagenic activities such as notetaking and question-answering, and consistently employing the metacognitive strategies of monitoring and affecting: Taken together, these represent the sum total of what is meant by study skills.

Suggested Resources

Anderson, J. R. (1985). *Cognitive psychology and its implications* (2nd ed.). New York: Freeman.

Bourne, L. E., Jr., Dominowski, R. L., & Loftus, E. F. (1979). *Cognitive processes.* Englewood Cliffs, NJ: Prentice-Hall.

Gagné, E. D. (1985). *The cognitive psychology of school learning.* Boston: Little, Brown.

Glover, J. A., Ronning, R. R., & Bruning, R. H. (1990). *Cognitive psychology for teachers.* New York: Macmillan.

Mayer, R. E. (1987). *Educational psychology: A cognitive approach.* Boston: Little, Brown.

Ormrod, J. E. (1990). *Human learning: Theories, principles, and educational applications.* Columbus, OH: Merrill.

Chapter
7

Problem Solving and Creativity

Objectives

1. Identify general problem-solving strategies in terms of the heuristics or approaches used for attacking the problem and generating solutions.
2. Describe the differences in the ways experts and novices solve problems, particularly in terms of the role of domain-specific knowledge.
3. Describe the combination of general strategies and expert knowledge, especially as it affects the transfer of solution strategies.
4. Identify metacognitive models for teaching problem-solving skills in the domains of reading, social studies, and mathematics, as well as one general model.
5. Describe what creativity is, how it is determined, and how it is often regarded and reacted to.
6. Describe techniques and procedures for increasing creative performance, including reframing and brainstorming.

Introduction

The question of whether the key to problem-solving is the ability to use *general* strategies or the ability to use *context-specific* strategies has not been resolved. In some situations the more general strategy, the one that fits all problems, may be the better one. In other situations the context-specific strategy, the one that fits a specific problem or class of problems, may work better. It depends, in part, on the amount of knowledge the problem-solver has of the problem's context.

Both views, the general strategy and the context-specific one, will be presented. A partial synthesis of both views into a single one will be presented as well. Based on the various views, specific problem-solving skills will be described. In exploring the general strategy approach, we will examine techniques used by persons who are experts in the context of the problem, as contrasted to those used by novices or amateurs.

General Problem-Solving Strategies

Perkins and Salomon (1989) cite the situation of a fictitious remote country bounded by a neighboring country with aggressive intentions and superior force. To counteract this disadvantage, the leader of the remote country called upon its major "resource," the reigning world chess champion, to help him see how to outthink—and thus outmaneuver—the enemy. The leader's critics immediately pointed out that being a chess genius does not automatically make someone a genius in the military and political domains. But the leader held firm, arguing that "above all, a chess player is a problem-solver, needing to plan ahead, explore alternatives, size up strategic options, just as a politician or military tactician does" (Perkins & Salomon, 1989, p. 16). And so the leader continued to expect the chess master to find a solution to the problem.

The question of whether the leader has a right to expect the chess master to be a military and political tactician is the same question as, Is there a general problem-solving skill or strategy (just as there seems to be a general intellectual skill—see Chapter 13) and, if there is, what are its elements? The mathematician Gyorgy Polya (1957) argued that success in finding mathematical solutions for attacking the problem depended on using a variety of general strategies or *heuristics* rather than on having mathematical knowledge per se. He identified the following general problem-solving strategies or heuristics:

- breaking a problem into subproblems
- solving simpler problems that reflect some aspect of the main problem
- using diagrams to represent a problem in different ways
- examining special cases to get a feel for a problem

While Polya's approach was focused on mathematics, it clearly could be applied to problems of all sorts. He also proposed a stepwise procedure for attacking a problem, featuring the following steps (Polya, 1957):

1. understand what information the problem requires and what is given;
2. devise a plan, step by step, for connecting the given information to the unknown (using the four heuristics listed above);

3. carry out the plan, one step at a time; and

4. look back at the solution and make sure it actually solves the given problem while fitting in all of the given information.

After succeeding, the problem-solver should make a record of exactly how she went about solving the problem, because she may have invented a useful heuristic for herself.

A second approach to general problem-solving comes from the work on artificial intelligence (AI) and the design of computer programs like the "General Problem Solver" (Newell & Simon, 1972). This program used a heuristic called *means–end analysis*. Given the input of a beginning state (for example, the chess pieces on a board), an end state or goal (checkmating the opponent's king), and all allowable operations for changing one state into another, the program would pursue a chain of operations for transforming the beginning state into the end state. It did this by seeking an operation or means that would make the beginning state more like the end state. After carrying out that operation, it would seek another operation to reduce the difference still further, and would keep doing this until no difference existed at all. If it reached a dead end, it would back up and try another path.

Often, it was not possible to have the computer pursue all possible solution paths by performing all possible operations (called the *algorithmic* solution), because there were too many; instead, the operations that the computer performed represented heuristics or general-solution strategies (such as always moving the important pieces toward the center of the board, or always keeping pieces around the king, or never giving up a piece if it can be avoided). An example of a problem to solve using means–end analysis (or working backward) is shown in Box 7.1.

Heuristics or general strategies became the major feature of these problem-solving approaches; specific knowledge — like knowing the rules of chess — although considered necessary, was not considered very important because there did not seem to be very much of it. And although computers were used, it was not because of their capability to test out all possible combinations — the algorithmic solution — because that would be inefficient. Moreover, such an approach would not be representative of how human problem-solvers functioned. Human problem-solvers, at least successful ones, tended to use heuristics.

Experts Versus Novices: Specific Problem-Solving Strategies

Remember the chess masters, and how they chunked information so that they could remember so many more real chessboards than ones with randomly placed pieces (see Box 6.3 on page 123)? These results showed that chess masters knew something not only very powerful but also very specific to chess. Otherwise, they would have done well on the random layouts too. In fact, Chase and Simon (1973) figured out that chess masters knew something like 50,000 chess-specific configurations or schemata, and these provided the chunks that they used to plan chess moves.

In other words, chess masters were experts, and being experts meant they had a lot of very organized, domain-specific knowledge — in this case, knowledge of chess. Perhaps it was not their general problem-solving ability but their chess expertise that

Box 7.1

Using Means–End Analysis to Solve a Problem in Cryptarithmetic

Remember that means–end analysis involves these steps:

1. Find the difference between the goal and the current state.
2. Find an operation that will change that difference.
3. Perform that operation to reduce that difference.
4. Keep repeating the above three steps until you solve the problem.

Now consider this cryptarithmetic problem (from Newell & Simon, 1972). The goal is *to find what number to assign to each letter so that when added together and translated back to letters, they would produce the name ROBERT.*

$$
\begin{array}{r}
D\,O\,N\,A\,L\,D \\
+\ G\,E\,R\,A\,L\,D \\
\hline
R\,O\,B\,E\,R\,T
\end{array}
$$

Given: D = 5

As you try to solve this problem, think aloud and make notes of your thoughts. Try using means–end analysis as a heuristic. Since there are a third of a million possible answers to this problem (Simon, 1978), the algorithmic solution strategy would be a little time-consuming. The answer appears in footnote 1 at the bottom of page 146.

made them such good chess players. Rabinowitz and Glaser (1985) studied the performance of experts in other fields and discovered that their performance was characterized by such things as (1) a large knowledge base of domain-specific patterns, (2) rapid recognition of situations in which these patterns apply, and (3) reasoning that moves from such recognition directly toward a solution (called forward reasoning or working forward).

By comparison, novices tended not to see the relevant patterns, because they did not know them or did not know them well enough to rapidly recognize them. Novices based their reasoning on superficial problem content. And novices worked backward, rather than forward, by focusing on working from the unknowns to the givens. Novices used means–end analysis while experts used forward reasoning, and this was true in fields as diverse as physics (Larkin, 1982) and medicine (Patel & Groen, 1986).

In other words, experts depend not on general strategies but on a rich data base and on an elaborate structure into which those data are organized for rapid retrieval. Their major heuristic for problem-solving is working forward, or examining a current situation and performing operations to change it. Those operations, however, are not necessarily constrained or limited by the goal (as in means–end analysis). The working-forward technique works for experts but not for novices because experts have the data or knowledge (based in large measure on experience) to recognize which operation is likely to work in a given situation. Novices do not. A list of the many differences between

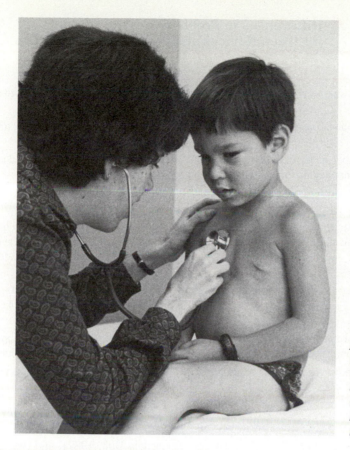

When it comes to solving certain types of problems, physicians are experts. This doctor will combine the information from her examination of this little boy with her domain specific knowledge of medicine to try to diagnose his illness.

experts and novices in solving problems appears in Table 7.1, and some suggestions on how to become an expert student in terms of your capability to read textbook chapters appears in Box 7.2.

The computerized approach to problem-solving, as in the study of artificial intelligence, also moved away from general problem-solving strategies and toward what are called *expert systems* (Wenger, 1987). These systems attempt to simulate the intelligence of an expert in a specific domain, such as medicine, by manipulating a large amount of organized, domain-specific knowledge. Such systems help physicians diagnose specific illnesses by utilizing medical test results and other information about symptoms. Compared to expert systems, general heuristics are regarded as weak methods for problem-solving.

Finally, if expertise and specific problem-solving strategies are not needed to solve problems but general strategies or heuristics will suffice, then, to go back to the original example, the fictitious chess master ought to be as good a political or military tactician as he is a chess player. However, just as it was long ago proven that learning Latin does not improve your mind's faculty (Thorndike, 1923), it has also been proven that teaching children to use general strategies has no clear benefits outside the specific domains in

Table 7.1 🍎 Differences in Problem-Solving Between Novices and Experts

Novice	Expert
Relies on raw memory.	Uses chunking and schemata to remember relationships and groups.
Classifies problems according to concrete similarities.	Classifies problems according to underlying principles.
Focuses on specific features of a problem and tries to link them to a memorized formula.	Focuses on the big picture and looks for relevant principles.
Relies on disorganized, general knowledge.	Relies on hierarchically (concrete to abstract) domain-specific knowledge.
Considers a large number of alternatives and works through all logical possibilities.	Cuts problem down to size by quickly identifying relevant schemata and then uses them (for example, analyze, categorize, solve).
Works backward (using means–end analysis).	Works forward: Uses shortcuts, estimates ballpark answers, converts unfamiliar problems to familiar ones.
Focuses on problem solution rather than problem-solving process.	Focuses on problem formulation and problem-solving process and knows solution will come.
Has little self-awareness of the strategies being used.	Has great self-awareness and a plan for the strategies being used.

which they are taught (Pressley, Snyder, & Cariglia-Bull, 1987), and that teaching students to write programs in a computer language does not necessarily make them better reasoners in general. Hence, the fictitious chess master will not necessarily give his leader the right advice to outwit the enemy if the contest between them is not carried out with chess pieces on a chess board.

Combining General Strategies and Expert Knowledge

Can it be concluded, therefore, that general strategies do not work and the fictitious chess expert will be helpless in the political and military domains? Not necessarily, even

---

[1]D = 5, T = 0, L = 8, R = 7, A = 4, E = 9, N = 6, B = 3, O = 2, G = 1. Here is one possible pattern of thinking: If D = 5, then T must equal 0 (5 + 5 = 10). That means that L + L + 1 (one was carried) equals R. L must be 1, 3, 4, 6, or 8 (we've already used 5 and 0; 2 would yield 5; 7 would yield 5; 9 would yield itself), in which case R would be 3, 7, 9, 3, or 7. Let's try R = 7 (it appears twice), which would make L either 3 or 8. Let's try L = 8. That leaves only 1, 2, 3, 4, 6, and 9 unused, so A can only be 1, 4, 6, or 9. Let's try A = 1; then E = 3, leaving only 2, 4, 6, and 9. So N can only be 2, which would make B = 9. Now only 4 and 6 are left. Since E = 3, O = 4 could not work (4 + 3 = 7), so O would have to be 6. But that would leave G = 4, and 4 + 5 are not 7. *So A = 1 and E = 3 was wrong.* Let's go back and make A = 4; so then E = 9. Now only 1, 2, 3, and 6 are left. So N must be 6 (6 + 7 = 13), which makes B = 3. Now only 1 and 2 are left. Since E = 9, then O must be 2 (remember that 1 was carried and 1 + 2 + 9 = 12). G must then be 1 (1 carried + 5 + 1 = 7).

Box 7.2

Becoming an Expert Student/Reader

Consider the difference between expert students and novice students or between expert readers and novice readers (Brown, 1980). When novice students read a textbook chapter, they just read it. When expert students read a textbook chapter, they first skim or scan it all; then they reread it and take notes on what they are reading. Moreover, these expert student/readers concentrate on reading for meaning, by focusing on the main points and monitoring their comprehension as they read. They check and review what they have gotten from their reading relative to their goals, and when they do not understand something, they take corrective action (such as looking up a word in a dictionary). Finally, when they are interrupted from their reading, they quickly recover and pick up where they left off.

Do you want to be an expert student/reader? Follow these rules:

1. SKIM the chapter before you read it, to see what it's about.

2. FOCUS on MEANING and MAIN POINTS when you read it through.

3. TAKE NOTES on main points while you are reading.

4. MONITOR YOUR COMPREHENSION as you read. If you don't understand something, REREAD IT.

5. CHECK and REVIEW what you've learned relative to your purpose for learning it.

6. LOOK UP words and ideas you don't understand in other reference sources or ask for help.

7. GET RIGHT BACK TO WORK if you're interrupted.

though experts are usually good problem-solvers only in their own domains where they have the necessary knowledge base. Most of the work on expert systems has dealt with experts solving only standard or common problems in their domain. What might happen if an expert were given an atypical or unusual problem in his or her domain (for example, a physician diagnosing an illness that has never been diagnosed before)? Clement (1989) has found that physicists fall back on more general strategies when attacking the unfamiliar. For example, (1) they use analogies to connect the unfamiliar problem to systems or related areas that they understand better, (2) they search for the areas or aspects in which the analogy does *not* fit, (3) they try to create visual images or pictures to help them understand how the given system might work if it were pushed to its limits, and (4) they construct a simpler problem of the same sort.

These approaches discovered by Clement represent heuristics or general strategies, and even the experts seem unable to solve some problems without them. However, these heuristics do not substitute for domain knowledge. Instead they seem to provide a basis for gaining access to and using domain knowledge. But will these heuristics or general strategies transfer from one area to another? Or, to return to our original question, will the chess master be a master of politics and military tactics as well?

That depends — according to Brown and Kane (1988), who studied the transfer of problem-solving strategies among three- and four-year-olds — on the following:

1. whether learners are shown how problems resemble each other;
2. whether learners' attention is drawn to the underlying structure of comparable problems;
3. whether learners are familiar with the problem domains or areas;
4. whether examples are accompanied by rules, particularly when those rules are formulated by the learners themselves; and
5. whether learning takes place in a social context (where students work together) and the interaction produces explanations, justifications, and principles that are then discussed and defended.

In other words, if the goal is for students to use general problem-solving strategies, supported by the necessary knowledge base or expertise, and to transfer those strategies to a variety of problem domains, they must be taught to do that. They must be taught to apply the principles stated above to facilitate the transfer of problem-solving strategies. To accomplish this, teachers must first look at the ways people can be taught to use or transfer problem-solving strategies. If we rely on just teaching people the knowledge base or expertise that these strategies are built on, they will not learn to be good general problem-solvers.

So it looks like our fictitious chess master would need to be taught something about politics and military tactics as well as something about how to transfer his chess strategies to these new domains. Unfortunately, by the time he has had all this training, it might be too late. His country's enemy may have already successfully made its move.

To see if you can transfer your problem-solving skills, try the problems in Box 7.3 (pages 150–151). Lehman, Lampert, and Nisbett (1988) found that students who did graduate study in psychology or in medicine were able to transfer the strategies they learned in courses on statistics and research methodology and in actually doing research to solving everyday problems that required similar kinds of reasoning. Samples of those problems appear in Box 7.3. Even though you have not done graduate study in psychology or medicine, you may want to "test" your reasoning skills against those who have. After you have done the problems in Box 7.3, try the one in Box 7.4 (page 152).

Applying Metacognitive Strategies to Teaching Problem-Solving Skills

There are a number of ways to teach problem-solving skills. These ways differ according to how problem-solving is viewed. One issue is whether problem-solving is a single skill or a set of component skills. Most teachers agree on the latter, that problem-solving requires a set of component skills. A second issue is whether the focus in problem-solving should be on process or product, that is, on the thought processes that are used versus merely getting the right answer. The predominant approach is to focus on the problem-solving process. The third issue is whether to teach problem-solving as a general course by itself or to integrate it into existing subject-matter domains. The tendency has been to teach it as part of the approach to an existing subject matter, which is what will be considered first.

In Chapter 5, instructional techniques built primarily on behavioral theories were described. In Chapter 6, instructional design was extended to include a cognitive approach based on the work of Ausubel (pages 128–132). Also in Chapter 6, the concepts of metacognitive processes (pages 124–128) and metacognitive strategies (pages 134–137) were introduced. These are processes and strategies that teachers and learners use to ensure that learning takes place. They include abstracting, elaborating, schematizing, organizing, monitoring, and affecting. These and similar techniques can also be used to ensure that problem-solving takes place. The techniques for teaching these metacognitive strategies, as applied to problem-solving in specific subject-matter contexts as well as generally, are described below.

Recall also that in Chapter 6 two techniques were presented for "schematizing" a textbook's content in order to understand its meaning. The first, on page 127, was related to the analysis of the Supertanker passage (Box 6.6); the second, on page 133, called structure training by Cook (1982), was related to reading and outlining science textbooks. Both can be considered problem-solving procedures related to solving the problem of interpreting textbook content. Other approaches are described below.

Reading.   Two approaches to teaching problem-solving as a way to improve reading comprehension are worth noting. (Textbook reading has already been discussed in the context of problem-solving in Box 7.2.) Meichenbaum and Asarnow (1979) describe a method for teaching reading comprehension skills to seventh- and eighth-graders with reading problems. It includes (1) breaking the text into manageable chunks, (2) determining the skills needed for each chunk, and (3) translating these skills into rehearsable self-statements. For each chunk of a story, students are taught to ask themselves the following three questions:

1. What is the story about (what is its main idea)?
2. What are the important details (such as the order or sequence of the main events)?
3. How do the characters feel and why?

Students are also taught to take pauses, to think of what they are doing, and to listen to (that is, monitor) what they say to themselves to make sure they are saying the right things. They are also taught not to worry about mistakes, but when they make them, to try again, and to be calm and relaxed while they read. And when they succeed, they are taught to be proud of themselves.

A second model, called reciprocal teaching, has been developed by Palincsar and Brown (1984) for use with the same group. Initially, the classroom teacher demonstrated or modeled four strategies: *summarizing* (what was the passage about?), *questioning* (who did what?), *clarifying* (what does it mean?), and *predicting* (what is likely to happen next?), always in that order. The students were taught to take turns at playing the teacher's role and asking the other students the four questions. When they faltered, they were prompted by the teacher; they were also given feedback and praise by the teacher when appropriate. This approach produced noteworthy and stable gains in reading comprehension that generalized and transferred both to other tests and to other tasks, indicating that teaching problem-solving strategies is a good way to teach reading.

Box 7.3

Test Your Problem-Solving Skills*

Statistical Reasoning—Everyday Life

After the first two weeks of the major league baseball season, newspapers begin to print the top ten batting averages. Typically, after two weeks, the leading batter has an average of about .450. Yet no batter in major league history has ever averaged .450 at the end of a season. Why do you think this is?

(a) A player's high average at the beginning of the season may be just a lucky fluke.

(b) A batter who has such a hot streak at the beginning of the season is under a lot of stress to maintain his performance record. Such stress adversely affects his playing.

(c) Pitchers tend to get better over the course of the season, as they get more in shape. As pitchers improve, they are more likely to strike out batters, so batters' averages go down.

(d) When a batter is known to be hitting for a high average, pitchers bear down more when they pitch to him.

(e) When a batter is known to be hitting for a high average, he stops getting good pitches to hit. Instead, pitchers "play the corners" of the plate because they don't mind walking him.

Methodological Reasoning—Everyday Life

The city of Middleopolis has had an unpopular police chief for a year and a half. He is a political appointee who is a crony of the mayor, and he had little previous experience in police administration when he was appointed. The mayor has recently defended the chief in public, announcing that in the time since he took office, crime rates decreased by 12%. Which of the following pieces of evidence would most deflate the mayor's claim that his chief is competent?

(a) The crime rates of the two cities closest to Middleopolis in location and size have decreased by 18% in the same period.

(b) An independent survey of the citizens of Middleopolis shows that 40% more crime is reported by respondents in the survey than is reported in police records.

(c) Common sense indicates that there is little a police chief can do to lower crime rates. These are for the most part due to social and economic conditions beyond the control of officials.

(d) The police chief has been discovered to have business contacts with people who are known to be involved in organized crime.

Conditional Reasoning—Permission Schema

You are a public health official at the international airport in Manila, capital of the Philippines. Part of your duty is to check that every arriving passenger who wishes to enter the country (rather than just change planes at the airport) has had an inoculation against cholera. Every passenger carries a health form. One side of the form indicates whether the passenger is entering or in transit, and the other side of the form lists the inoculations he or she has had in the past six months. Which of the following forms would you need to turn over to check? Indicate only those forms you would have to check to be sure.

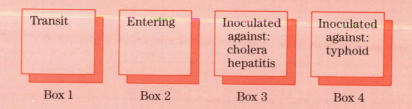

Transit	Entering	Inoculated against: cholera hepatitis	Inoculated against: typhoid
Box 1	Box 2	Box 3	Box 4

  (a) Boxes 2 & 3   **(d)** Boxes 2 & 4

  (b) Box 2 only   **(e)** Box 3 only

  (c) Boxes 2, 3, & 4

Verbal Reasoning

The new miracle drug Amotril has caused unforeseen side effects of a devastating nature; therefore, no new drugs should be released for public consumption without a thorough study of their effects.

Which of the following arguments most closely resembles the argument above?

(a) Because exposure to several hours of television a day has been shown to undermine children's interest in reading, children should be prevented from watching television.

(b) Because it is difficult to predict whether the results of pure research will be of practical benefit to human beings, the amount of money spent on such research should be sharply curtailed.

(c) The 1977 model of this compact station wagon has been shown to have a faulty exhaust system; therefore, it is urgent that this model be recalled immediately.

(d) Some of the worst highway accidents have been caused by teenagers between the ages of 16 and 18; therefore, only carefully screened members of this age group should be granted driver's licenses.

(e) Rising medical costs have put many routine medical procedures out of the reach of low- and middle-income families; therefore, doctors should prescribe only the most essential laboratory tests.

---

*Answers are in footnote 2 on page 152.

SOURCE: Lehman, D. R., Lampert, R. O., and Nisbett, R. E. (1988). The effects of graduate training on reasoning: Formal discipline and thinking about everyday-life problems. *American Psychologist, 43,* 431–442.

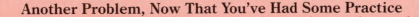

Box 7.4

🍎

Another Problem, Now That You've Had Some Practice

From Wason (1968) we have the following problem in deductive reasoning. Try it out and then compare your results to those of the students who did the problem originally. Answers appear in footnote 3 at the bottom of page 154.

For each of the above cards, a letter appears on one side and a number appears on the other. Which cards would you have to turn over to decide whether the following rule is true?

IF A CARD HAS A VOWEL ON ONE SIDE,
THEN IT HAS AN EVEN NUMBER ON THE OTHER SIDE.

Social Studies.   Armbruster and Anderson (1984) recommend teaching a particular problem-solving strategy or schema called a *goal frame* to help students comprehend what they read in history textbooks. The goal frame has four slots or components — goal, plan, action, and outcome — that represent the four steps or stages in explaining a historical event such as a war or passage of a law. The *goal* is what the principal persons or groups want to happen (such as independence or expansion); the *plan* is the strategy for attaining the goal (such as attacking or trading); the *action* is the actual behavior taken to implement the plan; and the *outcome* is the consequence of the action, which may or may not result in the goal being met.

For example, when the Pilgrims set off for the New World, their goal was to attain religious freedom, their plan was to establish a colony in the New World, their action was to set sail in the *Mayflower*, and the outcome was the establishment of the Plymouth Colony. Using the goal frame this way — to study history as a series of problems to be solved — is expected to make the subject easier for students to understand.

Mathematics.   Remember that heuristics are general strategies for solving problems of a particular kind. Schoenfeld (1979, 1985) tried to teach students to think the way real mathematicians do in solving real problems. He taught them the kind of heuristics mathematicians use. For example:

1. drawing a diagram to represent the problem;
2. considering a similar problem with fewer variables;

---

[2]Answers to problems in Box 7.3: a, a, d, d.

When one student helps another solve a problem, it represents a type of reciprocal teaching. Playing the role of the teacher is a good way to learn.

3. trying to establish subgoals;

4. looking for an inductive argument, a general explanation for all the facts;

5. arguing the contrapositive: instead of trying to prove that if X is true, then Y is true, trying to prove that if Y is false, then X must be false;

6. arguing by contradiction: assuming that the statement they are trying to prove is false, and then trying to prove that one of the given conditions in the problem is false, or that something they know to be true is false, or that what they wish to prove is true (and if they can do any of these, then they will have proved what they want).

Teaching students to use these heuristics or general strategies to solve sample mathematics problems more than tripled their success in solving similar mathematics problems.

Lampert (1986) has devised methods for teaching mathematics to fourth-grade students based on their understanding of the world beyond the classroom. She starts teaching multiplication, for example, by using simple coin problems, such as "How can you make 82 cents using only nickels and pennies?" This builds on the students' implicit knowledge of how to solve multiplication problems based on their everyday experiences with coins.

In the second phase of teaching multiplication through problem-solving, Lampert has her students create stories for multiplication problems, as illustrated in Figure 7.1. Through the stories, the students perform a series of decompositions or breakdowns of the problem and discover that it has no one "right" representation, just more and less useful representations depending on the context. Finally, in the third phase, students are introduced to the standard multiplication tables.

Using this technique, Lampert's students ended up with four kinds of knowledge: (l) intuitive — knowing the shortcuts or heuristics for solving problems, (2) computational — knowing how to do the computations, (3) concrete — knowing how to solve real problems, and (4) principled — knowing the mathematical principles involved. Most noteworthy is that this approach treats the learning of mathematics as problem-solving. It shows the students the real-world importance and value of what they have already learned. It also teaches them that mathematical problems often can be solved by more than one heuristic or strategy and helps them realize that they can create their own solution paths by behaving as a real mathematician would.

Lewis (1988) gave students word problems like the following:

> Musicland is selling the new REM tape for $6.99. This is 75 cents less than the Tape Shop is selling it for. How much does the new REM tape cost at the Tape Shop?

She first gave her students *representation training* so that they would learn how to represent such problems with diagrams, rather than relying on keywords like *more* or *less* to figure out whether to add or subtract. The procedure for diagramming or representing the solution to this problem is shown in Figure 7.2.

Representation training incorporates three principles for training students to problem-solve. First, it focuses on small component skills — in this case, ways to recognize and represent relational statements. Second, it models the appropriate process, namely, systematically translating problems into diagrams. Third, the training is part of a specific subject-matter domain: mathematics — or, more specifically, solving word problems through applied mathematics. Students who were trained to represent problems, such as the one about tapes shown above, by drawing diagrams did considerably better when given more complex problems to solve than did students who did not receive representational training (Lewis, 1988).

General Problem-Solving.

Perhaps the best known and proven program for teaching thinking and problem-solving skills is the *Productive Thinking Program* (Covington, Crutchfield, Davies, & Olton, 1974), which uses detective stories as the vehicle for helping fifth- and sixth-graders improve their problem-solving skill. Each story presents

---

[3]Answer to problem in Box 7.4 on page 152: E and 7. (The 4 card does not need to be turned over, because it does not matter if a vowel is on the other side: The rule does not make a prediction concerning whether or not there will be an even or odd number on one side if the other side does *not* have a vowel. In other words, it does not matter whether a vowel or consonant appears on the other side of the even number 4 because there is no rule that says that consonants cannot be paired with even numbers.) The right answer was chosen by only 7%. E and 4 was chosen by 55% and E alone by 24%.

Figure 7.1 🍎 Story Problems and Solutions for Teaching Multiplication From Lampert, 1986.

T: Can anyone give me a story that could go with this multiplication . . . 12 x 4?

S1: There were 12 jars, and each had 4 butterflies in it.

T: And if I did this multiplication and found the answer, what would I know about those jars and butterflies?

S1: You'd know you had that many butterflies altogether.

T: Okay, here are the jars. [*Draws a picture to represent the jars of butterflies—see diagram.*] The x's in them will stand for butterflies. Now, it will be easier for us to count how many butterflies there are altogether, if we think of the jars in groups. And as usual, the mathematician's favorite number for thinking about groups is?

S2: 10

T: Each of these 10 jars has 4 butterflies in it. [*Draws a loop around 10 jars.*] . . .

T: Suppose I erase my circle and go back to looking at the 12 jars again altogether. Is there any other way I could group them to make it easier for us to count all the butterflies?

S6: You could do 6 and 6.

T: Now, how many do I have in this group?

S7: 24

T: How did you figure that out?

S7: 8 and 8 and 8. [*He puts the 6 jars together into 3 pairs, intuitively finding a grouping that made the figuring easier for him.*]

T: That's 3 x 8. It's also 6 x 4. Now, how many are in this group?

S6: 24. It's the same. They both have 6 jars.

T: And now how many are there altogether?

S8: 24 and 24 is 48.

T: Do we get the same number of butterflies as before? Why?

S8: Yeah, because we have the same number of jars and they still have 4 butterflies in each.

Figure 7.2 🍎 Using Representation to Solve a Mathematical Word Problem

Problem: Musicland is selling the new REM tape for $6.99. This is 75 cents less than the Tape Shop is selling it for. How much does the new REM tape cost at the Tape Shop?

Step 1:   Locating known variable on number line.

————————— × —————————
           Msclnd, $6.99

Step 2:   Marking possible relationship of unknown variable to known variable.

—————————? ————————— × —————————? —————————
                    Msclnd, $6.99

Step 3:   Tentative placement of unknown variable.

—————————? ————————— × —————————? —————————
        Tape Shop   Msclnd, $6.99
This placement shows Tape Shop price 75 cents less than Musicland price.

Step 4:   Representation verification. Verification not found (since Musicland price is supposed to be 75 cents less than Tape Shop price).

Step 5:   Try other placement.

—————————? ————————— × —————————? —————————
                    Msclnd, $6.99   Tape Shop
This placement shows Musicland price 75 cents less than Tape Shop price.

Step 6:   Check again.
           Verification found (since Musicland price is supposed to be 75 cents less than Tape Shop price).

Step 7:   Plan arithmetic operation and solve.

—————————? ————————— × —————————? —————————
                    Msclnd, $6.99   Tape Shop
Addition: $6.99 + .75 = $7.74 (Tape Shop price)

clues and then asks students to generate ideas to explain and ultimately solve the mystery. Two of the characters in the stories are Jim and Lila, who try to solve the mystery as well as serve as models for students to emulate.

Because of the success of this program in improving the problem-solving capabilities of youngsters in areas other than the Jim-and-Lila mysteries (Mansfield, Busse, & Krepelka, 1978), it is worthwhile to consider the problem-solving skills that the program teaches. These appear in Box 7.5.

Box 7.5

🍎

Want to Be a Good Detective?
Use These Problem-Solving Skills from the Productive
Thinking Program

1. Decide exactly what the problem is that you are trying to solve before you begin working on it.
2. Get all of the facts first.
3. Follow a plan for working on the problem.
4. Don't jump to conclusions about the answer. Keep an open mind.
5. Think of as many ideas as you can, especially unusual ones. Don't stop with one idea.
6. To get ideas, think carefully about all the important persons and objects in the problem.
7. Think first of general solutions and then figure out more specific ideas for each one.
8. When you're trying to think of ideas, let your mind roam. Good ideas can come from anywhere.
9. Check each idea against the facts to make sure it fits.
10. If you get stuck, keep trying.
11. When you run out of ideas, try looking at the problem differently.
12. Review all the facts to make sure you haven't missed anything.
13. Make up an unlikely answer and see how it works.
14. Keep an eye out for odd or puzzling facts. Explaining them may lead you to the solution.
15. If there are a number of puzzling facts, try to find a single explanation that connects them all.

Creativity

What Is Creativity?   This book began by describing classical conditioning of simple reflexes and progressed through more complex conditioning, rote learning, meaningful learning, and problem-solving. We have now reached what some consider the pinnacle or zenith of the thinking process: creativity. *Creativity* refers to the ability to generate many *unique* yet *appropriate* responses to a problem for which there is no one right answer. Guilford (1967) calls creativity an example of *divergent thinking*, generating more than one acceptable solution to a problem, in contrast to *convergent thinking*, or generating the one correct solution. Creativity is different from intelligence, which is a measure of verbal knowledge and intellectual skills (see Chapter 13). It is also different from wisdom (Sternberg, 1985), from practical intelligence (Sternberg & Wagner, 1986), and from tacit knowledge (Wagner, 1987), each of which represents a combination of knowledge and thinking applied to finding correct answers for problems in the real world.

In other words, creativity is unique among the mental processes insofar as the others require going from the facts to the one solution while creativity requires going from the facts to the many solutions.

How Can Creativity Be Measured?   Psychologists such as Guilford (1967) and Torrance (1984), who have studied creativity extensively, detect it in one of three ways. One way is to give someone the name of a familiar object, such as a shoe, and ask him to generate as many uses for that object as he can. Take a minute to see how many different uses for a shoe you can think of. The only ones that count toward creativity are the ones that are *unusual* yet *appropriate*. If you said that a shoe could be used for walking, then you would not score a point because that answer is too obvious. But if you said that a shoe could be used as a paperweight, a bug killer, or a flower pot, you would get one point for each answer.

The second way to find out how creative people are is to give them an unusual situation and ask them to generate as many consequences of that situation as they can. Try this one: The earth's surface, except for the highest mountain peaks, will be entirely covered by water within three months. Write as many consequences as you can. Again, if you said that everyone will go out and buy a boat or move to the mountain peaks, you would not get any points because these are obvious consequences. But if you came up with some remote yet possible consequences, such as an increase in swimming lessons or a sudden shift to hydroponics (underwater farming) or a good time to go into the business of selling scuba gear, you would be demonstrating your creativity. And the more of these you came up with, the more creative you would be.

The third way to discover creativity is to look at people's drawings. For example, draw some pairs of parallel lines on a piece of paper and then make as many unique drawings from them as you can. Do not merely scribble or doodle. That is not creative. The drawings must be recognizable or representative in the eyes of the judges. Now compare your drawings to the ones in Figure 7.3. This is called *figural* creativity, in contrast to the *verbal* creativity measured by how many uses or consequences you can generate using words.

One further approach to the determination of creativity is worthy of note because it is different from the above three. Getzels and Jackson (1962) gave students fables with the last lines missing. Students were required to provide three different endings for each fable, one moralistic (having the connotations of good and bad), one humorous, and one sad. Scoring was based on the appropriateness of each ending, that is, on whether it followed the story. An example of a fable is given in Box 7.6.

Is Creativity Necessarily a Valued Capability?   Although people tend to express admiration and high regard for creativity and for those who exhibit it, this expression is usually either in the abstract or after the fact. Children who exhibit creativity in the classroom are often regarded as nonconformists by their teachers. Wallach and Kogan (1965) found that highly creative girls who were not equally high in measured intelligence had difficulty coping with the achievement demands of their teachers and carrying out the classroom behaviors that their teachers expected. In other words, while teachers expected conformity even in thinking, especially from their female students, they did not get it from the ones who were most creative. The teachers' reactions tended to make

Figure 7.3 🍎 Some Examples of Creative and Noncreative Drawings Made from Lines

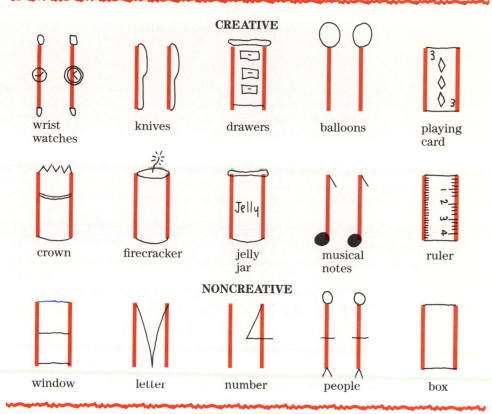

CREATIVE

wrist watches   knives   drawers   balloons   playing card

crown   firecracker   jelly jar   musical notes   ruler

NONCREATIVE

window   letter   number   people   box

these creative students defensive and undoubtedly resulted in the teachers viewing them less positively than they did their less creative classmates.

So it is the student with the creative response who often rubs the teacher the wrong way or is seen as a troublemaker or uncooperative. Similarly, in a work situation, even though creativity is given lip service as a universal good, it is usually the conformist who gets promoted and the truly creative employee who makes the boss uncomfortable. This, however, is not a desirable state of affairs, particularly in classrooms. Teachers should attempt not only to be open to creativity but also to stimulate and foster it as much as possible.

Increasing Creative Performance

Here are some general suggestions for increasing creative performance:

1. Challenge the rules. Don't always just go along with everything. Try asking "why."
2. Don't lock onto a single thought, because then you lock out all other possibilities.

Box 7.6

A Fable to Test Creativity

The Mischievous Dog

A rascally dog used to run quietly to the heels of every passerby and bite them without warning. So his master was obliged to tie a bell around the cur's neck that he might give notice wherever he went. This the dog thought very fine indeed, and he went about tinkling it in pride all over town.

But an old hound said . . .

Finish the sentence three times. Write a moralistic ending, a humorous ending, and a sad ending. Some sample answers are given in footnote 4 on page 162.

SOURCE: Getzels, J. W., & Jackson, P. W. (1962). *Creativity and intelligence: Explorations with gifted students.* New York: Wiley.

---

3. Try visualizing or conceiving a picture of the problem.
4. Forget what you know (the corollary of which is Don't assume).
5. Don't be complacent or comfortable with what you've got.
6. Do creative things, like exaggerating or distorting or looking at something backwards or upside down, to try to solve your problem.
7. Get some friends to help you think out loud.
8. Take a short break—that's when a good idea might come.
9. Be ambiguous. Try a lot of answers.
10. Try putting yourself in someone else's shoes and seeing their perspective.
11. Write down anything that pops into your head.
12. Avoid early criticism of ideas.
13. Lighten up. Use your sense of humor.

The above suggestions all serve to increase flexibility and pliability and give the creative side of the thinking capability an opportunity to work. Sometimes it is necessary for thinking to be analytical, verbal, rational, logical, and goal-oriented. Yet, people are still capable of thinking in a fashion that is visual, intuitive, spontaneous, artistic, and creative, especially when circumstances permit. The creative side seems to work, for example, while people are sleeping, drawing, or even exercising (Tuckman & Hinkle, 1986), which sometimes enables them to come up with creative solutions to problems that have previously defied solution. It has been suggested that the rational side and the creative side of thinking may be associated with different "sides" or hemispheres of the brain (Bradshaw & Nettleton, 1981).

There are two very special techniques to increase your ability to come up with creative solutions.

Reframing.   If you are trying to solve a problem and are getting stuck, a change in perspective, in how the problem is looked at, may be instrumental in your making progress instead of coming back to the same dead end. Trying to change perspective often requires reframing the problem. To do this, first think about all the positive aspects of the problem, and then think about all the negative aspects. Reframing includes thinking about the interesting aspects as well, then asking "What if?" questions, and linking the answers to these questions to the positive, negative, and interesting aspects of the problem. No idea or possible solution to the problem should be ruled out too quickly. It is especially important to try generating insightful solutions or ones you have not thought of before.

Brainstorming.   A very popular technique for generating creative solutions to difficult problems is brainstorming. Brainstorming usually involves a small group of people, with each person trying to come up with as many solutions as possible to a given problem. In brainstorming there are some basic rules:

1. Everybody gets a turn or turns.
2. As many solutions as possible should be generated.
3. Every possible solution gets written down.

Brainstorming is often a good way to come up with ideas. It is important, however, that none of the ideas be evaluated until every person in the group has had a chance to generate as many as he or she can.

Box 7.7

🍎

Brainstorming at Work

Problem: Doreen, a third-grader, keeps taking other children's things, like pencils and crayons. What can the teacher do about it?

Unprocessed Solution Possibilities

1. Talk to Doreen and explain to her that her behavior is inappropriate.
2. Give her gold stars for not taking other kids' stuff.
3. Punish her (with time-out) whenever she takes something.
4. Call in her mother and talk to her about it.
5. Seek the advice of the school psychologist.
6. Ignore the behavior and let the kids deal with it.
7. Give Doreen her own pencils and crayons.
8. Whenever Doreen takes something, firmly but gently take it from her and give it back to its rightful owner.
9. Teach a lesson on the importance of respecting other people's property.
10. Seat Doreen away from the other kids.
11. Try to get Doreen special counseling.
12. Have all the kids mark their own pencils and crayons for easy identification so that Doreen will feel embarrassed if she takes them.
13. Have all students leave their own pencils and crayons at home and use only communal ones.
14. Have students work in teams and share pencils and crayons.

Can you think of any more possible solutions? If not, can any of the above possible solutions be combined into a single solution? If not, then brainstorming is over and evaluation can begin. (In evaluation, you combine any similar solutions on your list and then identify the advantages and disadvantages of each solution, with the ultimate goal of selecting the solution or solutions to be tried.)

---

[4]Some sample answers to the Mischievous Dog fable in Box 7.6:

Moralistic: "Pride goeth before a fall." "It's false pride to be proud of one's faults." (not given credit: "Now you can't bite as you've done before.")

Humorous: "For whom does the bell toll now?" "Did you ring?" (not given credit: "Now you should learn to sing.")

Sad: "But the bell will get so heavy it will break his neck." "Now everyone will run away from you and you will be lonely." (not given credit: "The foolish dog is proud of his own faults.")

   4. All ideas are welcome, no matter how wild.

   5. People should build on other people's ideas.

   6. No idea should be evaluated or "put down" (at the time that it is offered).

This last rule is crucial. Criticism at this stage is premature. It will stifle creativity. Comments such as "It's a little too radical," "It sounds good, but . . . ," "We tried something like that once," "Let me play devil's advocate," "It's just not me (us)," "I wish it was that easy," or, worst of all, "It'll never work (fly)" set limiting conditions on the process of creativity. In brainstorming, the purpose is to create, not evaluate (or, in terms of Bloom's taxonomy, Figure 5.1, it is to put synthesis before evaluation).

Once brainstorming has run its course, and a wealth of possible solutions has been generated, then it will be necessary to cull the list to avoid redundancy, to combine similar ideas, and to identify the positives and negatives associated with each. This evaluation must eventually be done if the ideas are to be translated into action. Criteria like practicality and cost must be applied to reduce the list to a realistic number of alternatives from which the ultimate solution may be derived. Evaluation is the end stage of problem-solving, while creating solutions is the start. An example of brainstorming appears in Box 7.7.

Summary of Main Points

   1. Problem-solving strategies can be subdivided into *general* ones that can be used in many situations and *context-specific* ones that fit only one specific problem or class of problems.

   2. General strategies for attacking a problem are called *heuristics* and include such activities as breaking a problem into subproblems, solving simpler problems that reflect aspects of the main problem, using diagrams to represent problems, and examining special cases to get a feel for the problem. In solving the problem, then, one first attempts to understand it, then devises a solution plan, implements the plan, and checks the result against the givens.

   3. Computer experts working to develop a model of artificial intelligence attempted to create a general problem-solving program employing means–end analysis, a technique for transforming a beginning state into an end state one step at a time. This strategy also represented a heuristic, in contrast to the typical computer approach of trying all possible combinations or solution routes (called an algorithm).

   4. To study context-specific strategies for solving problems, researchers compared *experts* to *novices* to see the different way each group went about the problem-solving process. Experts used chunking, schemata, and underlying principles to classify problems and cut them down to size. They used their wealth of highly organized, domain-specific knowledge to develop shortcuts and plan their strategies. They knew enough about the problem to work forward in solving it, without constantly referring to the desired goal or end state for comparison.

   5. Novices, by comparison, considered many alternatives and relied on working backward from the desired end state to decide what the solution was. Lack of expert knowledge was clearly their limitation.

6. What happens when experts encounter problems that are out of the ordinary even for their field of expertise? Then they too seem to rely on more general strategies, although these strategies are now employed with the benefit of whatever expert knowledge can be applied. In order for students to function as true experts, they must be taught not only appropriate general strategies but also how to transfer these strategies or use them to solve a variety of problems.

7. Problem-solving skills or metacognitive strategies are best taught as a *set of component skills* (rather than as a single skill), with an emphasis on *process* or how to proceed (rather than on product or solution), in the context of a *specific subject-matter domain*.

8. When reading comprehension is treated as problem-solving, strategies such as *summarizing, questioning, clarifying*, and *predicting* help students determine what a story is about, what its important details are, and what the characters feel and why.

9. In social studies, the *goal frame* helps students treat history reading as problem-solving in that they look for the *goal, plan, action*, and *outcome* of each historical event.

10. In mathematics, students as problem-solvers are encouraged to use *diagrams*, to *scale* problems down, to establish *subgoals*, to look for *general explanations*, to *argue* the *contrapositive*, and to *argue* by *contradiction*—all procedures that mathematicians themselves actually use. A particularly successful approach for young learners is to use practical problem-solving situations and applications and to create stories to break the problem into more solvable parts. Finally, *representation training* can be used to teach students how to represent mathematical word problems using the number line, so that they can tell when to add and when to subtract.

11. There is also a general approach to teaching problem-solving skills, called the *Productive Thinking Program*, that uses detective stories as the teaching vehicle. Students are given a series of 15 rules to use in order to function as good detectives and solve the given problems.

12. Creativity requires a different kind of problem-solving: It uses divergent thinking—finding many solutions—in contrast to convergent *thinking*—finding the right solution. Being creative means generating as many *unique* yet *appropriate* responses to a situation or solutions to a problem as possible.

13. Creativity is measured in such ways as giving someone a familiar object and asking for *unusual* or *alternative uses*, giving a situation and asking for unusual or *remote consequences*, giving lines or circles and asking for a *variety* of drawings, and giving an *unfinished* fable and asking for an *ending*. Creativity seems to place a premium on using intuition in contrast to analysis.

14. Being creative is not as well-treated a talent as many people, including teachers, would have us believe it is. Creative students are sometimes treated as nonconformists and troublemakers and, unfortunately, are made to feel and act defensive. Nevertheless, creativity would seem to be a quality well worth cultivating.

15. To increase creativity, people should ask why (and not just follow suit), be open to new ideas, use visualization, think out loud with others, not pressure themselves, try a lot of answers, put themselves in others' shoes, write down their ideas, not be self-critical, and use their sense of humor. Two particular techniques are *reframing*,

which can help a person change perspective, and *brainstorming*, which can help produce new ideas.

16. In brainstorming, the goal is to generate as many solutions to a problem as possible, no matter how outlandish some may seem. In fact, the key to brainstorming is not to engage in premature evaluation. No idea can be judged or criticized until all participants have come up with every idea they can. Quick judgments or evaluations inhibit the creative process.

Suggested Resources

Gagné, E. D. (1985). *The cognitive psychology of school learning*. Boston: Little, Brown.

Glover, J. A., Ronning, R. R., & Bruning, R. H. (1990). *Cognitive psychology for teachers*. New York: Macmillan.

Hayes, J. R. (1989). *The complete problem solver* (2nd ed.). Hillsdale, NJ: Lawrence Erlbaum.

Newell, A., & Simon, H. A. (1972). *Human problem solving*. Englewood Cliffs, NJ: Prentice-Hall.

Polya, G. (1973). *How to solve it* (2nd ed.). New York: Doubleday.

Part Two

Development, Interaction, and Motivation

Chapter
8

Cognitive Development

Objectives

1. Describe the schema, the basic structure of cognitive organization according to Piaget.
2. Describe intellectual development as the process of adaptation, featuring the processes of assimilation and accommodation directed toward the attainment of equilibrium.
3. Identify intelligence as the capability to carry out operations that make possible the attainment of the concept of conservation.
4. Identify the factors that influence the course and pace of cognitive development.
5. Describe the sensorimotor stage of development, including its six periods, and the role of the three circular reactions.
6. Describe the characteristics of thinking during the preoperational stage.
7. Describe and illustrate the meaning of the concept of conservation.
8. Describe the characteristics of schemata developed during the stage of concrete operations.
9. Describe and illustrate the characteristics of schemata developed during the stage of formal operations in terms of experiments done to discover and explain them.
10. Apply Piaget's conception of cognitive development to the process of education.

The Developmental Psychology of Jean Piaget

The largest contribution to our understanding of cognitive (or intellectual) development (and even emotional development, as will be shown in the next chapter) has been made by a Swiss biologist named Jean Piaget (shown in Figure 8.1). Piaget, who died in 1980 at age 84, spent 60 years observing children and reporting on their growth in well over 200 books and articles. Although trained in biology and philosophy, Piaget turned to psychology to try to understand the development of intelligence in children. In this chapter, Piaget's major concepts and principles for explaining the behavior he observed are examined first, followed by the four developmental stages he hypothesized to exist. Next, some of Piaget's experiments are described, and last, his principles are applied to education.

It is important to point out that Piaget's method of doing research was to make meticulous observations and then report on what he observed (a technique called observational research in Chapter 1). He began with observations of his own three children and then expanded to observe many other children and young adults as they engaged in a variety of tasks, many of which he posed for them to deal with. From his extensive observations, he fashioned the detailed theory of development that is described in this chapter and the next.

The Basic Structure of Cognitive Organization: The Schema

Piaget, and others who followed him, perceived the schema to be the basic unit necessary for mental organization and mental functioning (see also Chapter 6 for discussion of the schema). Piaget (1952; also Flavell, 1963) defined a schema as "*a cohesive, repeatable*

🍎 **Figure 8.1**
The Child Psychologist Jean Piaget
Piaget is considered by many to be the father of modern child psychology. He died in 1980 at age 84.

action sequence possessing component actions that are tightly interconnected and governed by a core meaning." Wadsworth (1989) suggests that schemata be thought of as "index cards" on-file in the brain, each one telling the person how to identify and react to incoming stimuli or information. An infant has a small number of small index cards, all of which represent reflexive schemata such as grasping or sucking. Adults, by comparison, have large numbers of large index cards. They need to be large to keep track of the experiences associated with each schema and the refinements that might result from some of those experiences.

Schemata help people classify or categorize an object or event and decide how to act toward that object or react to that event. Often, the initial necessary act is to label or recognize a situation so that the appropriate response can be made. When you are given a list of grocery items and the cost of each and are asked what the total cost will be, you have a schema that enables you to recognize that addition is the appropriate arithmetic process and another schema that enables you to carry out the addition process to arrive at a solution.

Schemata, as described by Piaget, seem quite similar to productions or procedural knowledge, the "how to" or "IF . . . THEN . . ." statements of cognitive thought described in Chapter 6. Procedural knowledge is the representation of "action sequences" in the current cognitive or information-processing theory. When Piaget, whose work predated current information-processing theory, talked about the development of a person's mental processes, he was referring to increases in the number and complexity of the schemata that person had learned. Once learned, those schemata were available for the person to use to deal with, or identify and react to, whatever objects and events he or she encountered.

Intellectual Development as Adaptation

The basic tenet of Piaget's theory of development is that the organism interacts with the environment in a relationship called *adaptation*. In adaptation, the organism develops schemata that enable it to continue to function in that environment. The very essence of life is a continuing and repeatable interaction between the organism and its environment that enables the organism to function.

Think of the giraffe, which has evolved its long neck in order to be able to feed on the leaves of very tall trees. The long neck is the giraffe's adaptation to its environment that enables it to survive. Of course, physical adaptations of this sort take longer than intellectual ones. You learn quickly, when you want something that is stored on the top shelf of a cupboard or closet, to use a ladder. Even before learning about ladders, you learned to pile up boxes (like Köhler's chimpanzees; page 35) or to use a chair to climb up on the kitchen counter.

Assimilation and Accommodation.   Piaget (1952) posited two mechanisms to carry out adaptation. The first, assimilation, is a process used *to incorporate new information into existing schemata that are sufficient to understand it*. What this means is that when someone encounters something new, he or she will try to deal with it (that is, recognize it or react to it) by using an existing schema or action plan. As a result, the schema is not changed essentially, but it is expanded to include the new experience and the result of the reaction to it.

Assimilation is somewhat similar to the behaviorist's concept of stimulus generalization, in which an organism, after having learned to respond to one stimulus, responds similarly to other stimuli that are like the original. This tendency increases if the outcome of responding to the new but similar stimulus is as satisfactory as it was when the organism responded to the original.

Suppose you are teaching and a student who has not completed her work gives you an excuse you have never heard before. You already have a schema to deal with incomplete work, and you assimilate this experience into it and react to the student by giving her an additional assignment, as you would any other noncompleter, regardless of the circumstances. You have adapted to the new situation by using an already-existing plan for dealing with it. You have not added a new schema; you have simply made an existing one fit.

By contrast, accommodation, Piaget's second adaptive mechanism, is a process used *to modify an existing schema in order to be able to understand information that would otherwise be incomprehensible with existing schemata*. This time, the person having the new experience cannot deal with it by using an existing schema; none fits it closely enough. That person must change an existing schema to create an essentially new schema in order to be able to make an adaptive response. This is like concept learning or problem-solving in Chapter 7. When what is known does not work in a given situation, something new must be tried.

To continue the earlier illustration likening schemata to index cards, accommodation means that a person adds new index cards by finding the closest existing one and then modifying it. As a new teacher, you may not have a schema for dealing with a student's incomplete work, but you might remember how your supervising teacher dealt with this issue and then modify that approach to fit the situation you are facing. Once you have done this, you will then have a schema for dealing with incomplete work and will probably be able to use it to assimilate future instances when the problem arises again.

Assimilation and accommodation are processes that enable people to grow and adapt to their environment continually. Assimilation helps people make better use of the schemata they have, and accommodation helps them alter their schemata to fit new situations. In assimilation, the situation is made to fit existing schemata, and in accommodation, existing schemata are changed or new ones developed to fit the situation. *Play*, according to Piaget (1952), is an example of essentially pure assimilation in that something is done as it always has been, that is, as a simple, repetitive activity. *Imitation*, by comparison, is an example of essentially pure accommodation in that a person does something that he or she has never done before, by watching and copying it from someone else. All other experiences would fall somewhere in between.

Equilibration.   According to Piaget, a balance must exist between assimilation and accommodation as well as between oneself and one's environment. Life cannot be all play, because then nothing new would be learned. Neither can it be all imitation, because then there would be no self or stability. There must be enough accommodation to meet and adapt to new situations and enough assimilation to use one's schemata quickly and efficiently. In other words, a state of equilibrium must exist between these two processes, which, in turn, makes possible a state of equilibrium between oneself and one's environment. When equilibrium or balance does not exist, something must be done to achieve it.

That something is either accommodation or assimilation, depending on the circumstances. Carrying out these processes in an effort to restore equilibrium is called *equilibration*, and it represents the major source of motivation in Piaget's system.

The basis for development of the increasing intellectual capacity of a child is equilibration. As new experiences occur, the young child is motivated to develop new schemata to deal with them through accommodation. Once these new schemata are developed, the young child is then motivated to use them through assimilation. The "index card file" is continually expanding, with each new development laying the foundation for subsequent developments in an orderly and progressive way. Since equilibrium is always only momentary and each new encounter creates disequilibrium, the process of equilibration or trying to attain equilibrium serves as a constant motivator of intellectual development throughout childhood. (In Chapter 12, the concept of *drive* will be presented as another kind of motivating force.)

Intelligence.   To Piaget, intelligence is a combination of all of an individual's schemata. These schemata enable an individual to maintain equilibrium between him- or herself and the environment—to adapt to and deal with circumstances as they arise. Intelligence, therefore, is the regulating or adapting force, and as such is the result of assimilations and accommodations between a person and the surrounding world. Moreover, to Piaget intelligence does not represent content or the amount of knowledge a person has. Rather, it represents *structure* or how what is known is organized so that it can be used. The particular organizational structures of intelligence are schemata, structures formed as the result of assimilation and accommodation.

This view of intelligence as adaptability or capability of dealing with a changing environment is quite different from the more common view of intelligence (to be described in Chapter 13) as either general or specific knowledge. To Piaget, intelligence is more like procedural knowledge or knowing what to do than it is like declarative knowledge or simply knowing facts. (These types of knowledge were described in Chapter 6.)

Because intelligence is both the result of and the basis for assimilation and accommodation, it can be expected to vary considerably from age to age. As children have more and more experiences, they develop the structures or schemata that help them adapt to their environment. As shall soon be seen, Piaget divides the development of intelligence into discrete stages, each with its own intellectual challenges to equilibrium.

Operations.   What is intelligence used for, or, put another way, what are its outputs? For Piaget the answer is operations. Operations are *systems or coordinated sets of actions* for dealing with objects or events. Identification would be an operation, as would addition or classification. All of the actions a person can take within the systems of logic or mathematics constitute operations (Piaget, 1950). As individuals mature, their thinking gets organized into more and more well-defined systems. That is to say, as individuals grow, they can perform more and more operations and these operations become more and more complex.

Each of Piaget's four developmental stages is characterized by the attainment of a specific operation. Perhaps the most well-studied of these is the operation of conservation.

Conservation.   This is the development of a schema that enables a person to realize or recognize that *the amount of a substance stays the same even when its shape or arrangement is changed*. When a child performs the operation of conserving, that child recognizes that the quantity of matter is conserved or kept the same regardless of how it is divided up mechanically. If a fixed amount of water is poured into each of two glasses, one tall and one short, the amount of water is the same even though the tall glass may *look* like it contains more water.

Equal amounts of water

When ten buttons are lined up in either one row or two rows, the number of buttons remains the same even though the single-row arrangement may look like it contains more buttons.

Equal numbers of buttons

In other words, a child can use the operation of conservation if he or she can separate how something looks from the *logical* awareness that amounts remain unchanged regardless of how they may be arrayed or arranged. This is a concrete operation because it involves a distinction between what is and what appears to be, but it is a critically important operation because it reflects having the intellectual structure that makes it possible to think about amounts and quantities before and after they are rearranged. To be able to conserve, a child must be able to reverse an operation in his or her mind, to put things back together mentally after taking them apart. Once reversibility is attained as a schema, it can be used over and over again to solve conservation problems.

Developmental Factors.   Piaget's theory is a theory of development, or a theory of changes in intelligence over time. These changes, as we will see, are represented by stages that children go through and that are characterized by different adaptations as a function of existing schemata and the development of new schemata. Before these stages are described, it is useful to examine the four factors that Piaget (1961) cites as contributing to cognitive development.

The first factor is *heredity* or inheritance, which affects a person's rate of *maturation*. According to Piaget, maturation does not cause cognitive structures to develop. Rather, it determines the range of possibilities at a specific stage, that is, whether a particular structure can possibly develop at a specific stage, not necessarily whether it will. Hence, maturation places broad constraints on cognitive development. It provides the potential for the appearance of specific structures; but whether or not they do in fact appear depends on the next three factors.

The second factor is *active experience*, or the child's actions in his or her environment. These actions can be physical or mental and they can be with objects or people. Children who have a childhood rich in active experiences will be more likely to develop the structures that characterize each stage and to proceed through all four stages than will children whose experience base is limited or impoverished. Early school programs such as Headstart and participation or imitation-type television programs such as *Sesame Street* serve to increase the active experiences of children who, in particular, may lack the opportunity for such experiences in their everyday lives.

The third factor is *social interaction*, or the exchange of ideas among people. This is especially important in the development of ideas that do not have a physical referent, that cannot be seen or heard — like the idea of freedom or of fairness. Socially defined concepts depend very heavily on social interaction for their development. (This aspect of development will be covered in the next chapter.)

The fourth factor is *equilibration*, which has already been introduced. Equilibration, according to Piaget (1977), accounts for the coordination between the other three factors. But beyond that, equilibration serves as a self-regulating device that enables the individual to process new information through either assimilation or accommodation and to always be moving toward a balance with the environment.

These four factors, taken together, account not only for the continuous process of development but also for the dramatic changes that occur from one period or stage of development to another.

Four Stages of Cognitive Development

The four stages of development are not absolute in terms of either their timing or their characteristics. Rather, they represent a set of tendencies brought about by the four developmental factors described above. They are summarized in Table 8.1, and each is described below.

The Sensorimotor Stage (ages 0–2)

This stage extends from birth to the acquisition of language. At its inception, the newborn does not distinguish him- or herself from surrounding objects; at its close the young child recognizes him- or herself as one part of a much larger world (Piaget, 1967). The major themes of this stage relate to the progressive growth of the child's concepts of *object* (things outside of oneself) and *causality* or cause and effect. Piaget divides this stage into six periods, each of which features the appearance of more complex behaviors involving the connections between the *senses* (seeing, hearing, touching) and actual movements or *motor* behavior.

Table 8.1 🍎 Overview and Summary of the Four Developmental Stages

Stage	Age*	Overview
Sensorimotor	0–2	Behavior is primarily motor, involving action schemata such as reaching and grasping. Circular reactions feature learning by repetition. Preverbal and prethinking. Ends with object permanence.
Preoperational	2–7	Development of language and prelogical thought. Focuses on self and own perspective with no ability to vary one's point of view. Unable to reverse operations.
Concrete Operations	7–11	Development of ability to apply logic on basis of concrete correspondence between event and explanation. Ability to conserve is developed.
Formal Operations	11–15	Thinking structures reach their highest level of development, making possible the use of logical reasoning. Can think out explanations for events by considering combinations of variables.

*All ages are approximate.

The major assimilation activity of this stage is what Piaget (1952) called the *circular reaction*, in which the infant tries to reproduce interesting events or make interesting sights last. First the infant stumbles upon a new experience as a result of some act; then she tries to repeat the experience by repeating the original act in a kind of rhythmic cycle (Piaget, 1952). This repetition of events enables the infant to assimilate experience and to make new adaptations, such as increasing her awareness of the existence of specific objects, and understanding the relationship between cause and effect. Following a short *first* period of about one month after birth, during which the infant exhibits only reflex activity, a circular reaction makes its first appearance. In the *second* period, up to the fourth month of age, the *primary circular reaction* appears, with its focus on the infant's own body and directed toward the manipulation of some object.

Piaget's method for discovering the characteristics and features of this stage was to observe his own children (Laurent, Lucienne, and Jacqueline) and report on their behavior at different ages (indicated by three numbers — for example, 0;2(3) — that represent years–months–days). In the illustration of the *primary circular reaction*, below, Piaget's son Laurent is first observed on the third day of his second month of life and displays the repeated and rhythmical, self-initiated behavior of scratching and grasping. These behaviors would not be considered reflexive because they do not appear to be caused by specific external stimulation.

> Observation 53. — From 0;2(3) Laurent evidences a circular reaction which will become more definite and will constitute the beginning of systematic grasping; he scratches and tries to grasp, lets go, scratches and grasps again, etc. On 0;2(3) and 0;2(6) this can only be observed during the feeding. Laurent gently scratches his mother's bare shoulder. But beginning 0;2(7) the behavior becomes marked in the cradle itself. Laurent scratches the sheet which is folded over the blankets, then

grasps it and holds it a moment, then lets it go, scratches it again, and recommences without interruption. At 0;2(11) this play lasts a quarter of an hour at a time, several times during the day. At 0;2(12) he scratches and grasps my fist which I placed against the back of his right hand. He even succeeds in discriminating my bent middle finger and grasping it separately, holding it a few moments. At 0;2(14) and 0;2(16) I note how definitely the spontaneous grasping of the sheet reveals the characteristics of circular reaction—groping at first, then regular rhythmical activity (scratching, grasping, holding, and letting go), and finally progressive loss of interest. (Piaget, 1952, pp. 91–92)

In the *third* period, from about four to eight months of age, the *secondary circular reaction* appears and is a clear illustration of what Piaget calls *reproductive assimilation* or making interesting sights last. In addition to Piaget's illustration below, a somewhat more familiar one is the infant throwing a toy out of the crib, entreating someone to give it back, which they do, and immediately throwing it out again. The whole sequence is repeated over and over until it becomes tiresome.

Observation 95. — Lucienne, at 0;4(27), is lying in her bassinet. I hang a doll over her feet which immediately sets in motion the schema of shakes. But her feet reach the doll right away and give it a violent movement which Lucienne surveys with delight. Afterward she looks at her motionless foot for a second, then recommences. There is no visual control of the foot, for the movements are the same when Lucienne only looks at the doll or when I place the doll over her head. On the other hand, the tactile control of the foot is apparent: After the first shakes, Lucienne makes slow foot movements as though to grasp and explore. For instance, when she tries to kick the

The primary circular reaction of infants involves repeated scratching, grasping, and sucking.

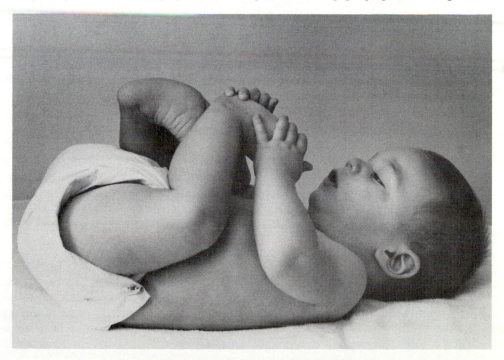

doll and misses her aim, she begins again very slowly until she succeeds (without seeing her feet). In the same way I cover Lucienne's face or distract her attention for a moment in another direction: She nevertheless continues to hit the doll and control its movements. (Piaget, 1952, p. 159)

Following a *fourth* period (age 8–12 months) that features the coordination of schemata and the appearance of intentionality of action, the *tertiary circular reaction* is exhibited in the *fifth* period (age 12–18 months), evidenced by the invention of new means, through active experimentation, to accomplish ends. The child now intentionally varies the repetitions to see if similar actions have the same effect. He may, for example, drop a rubber object and then wait for it to bounce. The child has discovered that people as well as objects can cause outcomes that are completely independent of his own actions, as seen in the following illustration:

Observation 152. — At 1;0(3) Jacqueline is before me and I blow into her hair. When she wants the game to continue she does not try to act through efficacious gestures nor even, as formerly, to push my arms or lips; she merely places herself in position, head tilted, sure that I will do the rest by myself. At 1;0(6) same reaction when I murmur something in her ear; she puts her ear against my mouth when she wishes me to repeat my gesture. (Piaget, 1952, p. 275)

The sensorimotor stage ends after the *sixth* period (18–24 months), during which time the child has begun to learn how to talk and has become able to represent objects and events mentally, by thinking about them. New learning can now be accomplished without active physical experimentation but by the representation of action through thinking.

A major capstone of the sensorimotor stage, representing an important state of equilibrium, is the emergence of schemata that make possible the realization that *objects have permanence*, even when they are out of sight and hearing. Heretofore, the child was unable to represent objects in the mind; hence, when they could no longer be seen or heard, they no longer existed. Now, with the emergence of the ability to store ideas, object permanence becomes a reality. The same is true for *causality*. The availability of thought makes possible the awareness of causality. (See Box 8.1 for examples of both object permanence and causality.)

The child has now reached age 2 and is quite different from the newborn infant. As the infant has proceeded through the six sensorimotor periods, new and more sophisticated capabilities have emerged, each making him or her better equipped to deal with life's demands. The development and use of each new schema through assimilation and accommodation is a reflection of the adaptive process that Piaget viewed the development of intelligence to be.

The Stage of Preoperational Thought (ages 2–7)

The ability to represent ideas in the form of symbols and signs, such as words and numbers, makes its appearance during this stage and helps distinguish the actual thinking of this stage from the mere sensory and physical coordinations of the preceding one. Piaget does not break this stage up into distinct periods. Instead, he describes the essential features of preoperational thought (Piaget, 1951, 1952; Piaget & Inhelder, 1969).

Box 8.1

Illustrations from the Sixth and Last Period of the Sensorimotor Stage

Object Permanence

Observation 64. — At 1;7(20) Jacqueline watches me when I put a coin in my hand, then put my hand under a coverlet. I withdraw my hand closed; Jacqueline opens it, then searches under the coverlet until she finds the object. I take back the coin at once, put it in my hand and then slip my closed hand under a cushion situated at the other side (on her left and no longer on her right); Jacqueline immediately searches for the object under the cushion. I repeat the experiment by hiding the coin under a jacket; Jacqueline finds it without hesitation.

II. I complete the test as follows: I place the coin in my hand, then my hand under the cushion. I bring it forth closed and immediately hide it under the coverlet. Finally I withdraw it and hold it out, closed, to Jacqueline. Jacqueline then pushes my hand aside without opening it (she guesses that there is nothing in it, which is new), she looks under the cushion, then directly under the coverlet where she finds the object. . . .

I then try a series of three displacements: I put the coin in my hand and move my closed hand sequentially from A to B and from B to C; Jacqueline sets my hand aside, then searches in A, in B, and finally in C.

Lucienne is successful in the same test at 1;3(14). (Piaget, 1954, p. 79)

Causality

At 1,4(4) . . . Laurent tries to open a garden gate but cannot push it forward because it is held back by a piece of furniture. He cannot account either visually or by any sound for the cause that prevents the gate from opening, but after having tried to force it he suddenly seems to understand; he goes around the wall, arrives at the other side of the gate, moves the armchair which holds it firm, and opens it with a triumphant expression. (Piaget, 1954, p. 296)

In a general way, therefore, at the sixth stage the child is now capable of causal deduction and is no longer restricted to perception of sensorimotor utilization of the relations of cause to effect. (Piaget, 1954, p. 297)

Egocentrism.   One of the principal features of preoperational thinking is a preoccupation with oneself and one's own particular point of view. Egocentric preoperational children cannot take another's point of view; they believe that everyone sees and thinks the same things as they do. Moreover, preoperational children do not question their own thoughts even when presented with evidence to the contrary. They believe, although not intentionally, that their ideas and perceptions are right. Hence, reasoning with them ranges from difficult to impossible. It is not uncommon for preoperational children to talk to themselves and to fail to listen to someone who is speaking to them.

Egocentrism is a factor that acts to limit development, and it manifests itself in some form in every stage. Just as the sensorimotor child is initially egocentric in failing to distinguish him- or herself as an object from other objects, the preoperational child is initially egocentric in failing to differentiate between his or her own thoughts and the thoughts of others. This tendency lessens as the child proceeds through this stage.

Centration.   When presented with a visual stimulus, the preoperational child tends to focus or *center* all of his attention on only one aspect or dimension of the stimulus at a time. Any thinking task is dominated by perception, or what things look like, since it is appearance on which the child is focused.

Consider the following two arrays.

Array 1   Array 2

When asked which array has more objects, the preoperational child typically picks Array 2, even though it has fewer objects and she "knows" that. Array 2 is seen as having "more" because the child is centered on the appearance or length of the two arrays and Array 2 looks longer.

Nontransformational Reasoning.   The preoperational child does not focus on the transformation of an object from an original state to a final state. Instead she focuses on the elements in the sequence or each successive state (at Time 1, Time 2, and so on), not on the changes that have occurred between states. For example, when four-year-old children were shown a glass of water that was then poured into another glass hidden behind a screen, many correctly realized that the unseen glass had as much water in it as the original glass. However, when the water in the first glass was poured into a smaller glass that the children could see, they all said that the second, shorter glass held less water than the original (Bruner, 1964). The preoperational children were focusing on only the original state and the final state, disregarding the transformation between them. Nontransformational reasoning makes logical thinking impossible.

Irreversibility.   The ability to reverse thought or follow a line of reasoning back to where it started is, according to Piaget (1954), one of the most important characteristics of intelligence. In order to realize that something that has changed in appearance has not changed in amount, a child must be able to reverse the operation of change in his mind and mentally restore that thing to its original appearance. If someone runs into your car and dents it, you can still tell that it is your car and can still imagine or visualize what it looked like without the dent. That is because operational thinking enables you to reverse an event, to think backward. Preoperational thinking does not. For a preoperational child, thinking is irreversible. Once something has changed, it is a "new" thing, different from the original.

If a preoperational child is given two equal-length rows of eight coins each, that child will recognize that the two rows are equal. If one of the rows is lengthened while the child is watching, the child will perceive that the lengthened row has more coins (Wadsworth, 1989). The preoperational child cannot reverse or undo the lengthening in her mind to "see" that it still contains the same number of coins it did *before*, only now they are further apart. The child at this stage cannot reverse an action and so depends solely on perception or appearance to make judgments.

Piaget's four concepts of egocentrism, centration, nontransformational thinking, and irreversibility are all closely related. When a child focuses on him- or herself, judges things by a single dimension, and ignores the transformations or actions that cause things to change, it surely follows that he or she will be unable to do reverse thinking or to visualize a thing as it once was. Since physical reality usually goes in one direction only — forward — the preoperational child lacks physical models for reverse thinking. It is only when maturation and experience combine to help the child overcome these egocentric, centered, nontransformational patterns that the mental capability for reverse thought becomes possible.

While thinking skills are still limited in the preoperational stage, physical coordination continues to improve.

Box 8.2

A Party for Children in the Preoperational Stage

A group of high-school students who were members of the student council in a K–12 school gave a small party for some kindergarten students. First, they played games, such as pin-the-tail-on-the-donkey and show-and-tell, which were supervised by the older students. The games made everyone hungry and thirsty, even the high-school students, so next they prepared the table for refreshments.

The 15 high-school students poured punch into different-shaped glasses. There were 15 very wide glasses and 15 narrow glasses. They filled them so that the narrow glasses were filled just a bit higher than the wide ones. When the kindergarten students went up to the table to get food and punch, they checked out the level of each glass. The kindergarten students quickly reached for the narrower glasses, laughing and saying that they had more punch than any of the high-school students.

The high-schoolers also served apples, and one of the kindergarten students wanted one. When asked whether he wanted it cut into six pieces or eight, he replied that he'd rather have it cut into six pieces, because "he wasn't hungry enough to eat eight." To a kindergarten child, an apple cut into eight pieces represented more fruit than an apple cut into six pieces, just as a narrower, taller glass appeared to contain more punch than a wider, shorter glass.

Conservation

Conservation is the idea or realization that the amount or quantity of something stays the same regardless of changes in any dimension irrelevant to the amount or quantity. (See Box 8.2.) A child can conserve when he or she can recognize that the number of pennies or dots in each of two rows is the same, even when those in one row are further apart than those in the other row (as shown below). This is called *conservation of number*.

$A + B$ above is seen as <u>equal</u> to $A + B$ below

But $A + B$ is seen as having <u>less</u> area here

than it does here (or <u>more</u> here than there)

A B

A B

A B

A

B

A child can also conserve when he or she can recognize that the area within two shapes is the same, even if the shapes are arrayed differently (as shown below). This is called *conservation of area*.

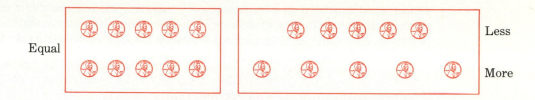

Finally, a child can conserve when he or she can recognize that the amount of water in two glasses of different shapes is actually the same, even though the level of one is higher (as shown below). This is called *conservation of volume*.

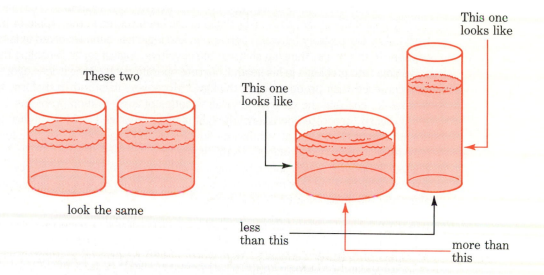

As the transition occurs from preoperational thought to concrete operational thought, the ability to conserve appears. It is not likely to appear while the child's thinking is strongly characterized by egocentrism, centration, nontransformational thinking, and irreversibility, because these patterns are antithetical to being able to perform a mental operation like conservation, which is both logical and independent of the way things look. Therefore, the ability to conserve does not appear until near the end of the preoperational stage and does not become developed until the child enters the stage of concrete operations.

Thus, the emergence of conservation is a gradual process. It stretches from ages of about 5 to 6, when conservation of number appears, to ages of about 11 or 12, when conservation of solid volume appears. Within this period, conservation of area and of liquid volume appears (ages 7 to 8). Hence, conservation somewhat overlaps two developmental stages.

Also, Piaget contended that conservation ability cannot be taught directly and cannot be acquired until the child is ready developmentally. He believed that development of conservation depended on a combination of maturation and relevant direct experience that enabled it to evolve "spontaneously." However, others have shown that the mastery of conservation skills can be accelerated somewhat through teaching (Pasnak, 1987; Pasnak, Brown, Kurkjian, Triana, & Yamamoto, 1987).

The Stage of Concrete Operations (ages 7–11)

This is the stage in which a child develops the capacity for *logical operations*, or *thinking characterized by mental actions or internalized thoughts that are reversible and therefore allow a child to arrive at logical conclusions.*

According to Piaget (1970), logical operations have four characteristics: (1) they are actions that can be carried out in the head, (2) they are reversible, (3) they assume some invariance or conservation, and (4) they are part of a system.

Up until this stage, the child's thinking has been rooted in the visible or perceptual world. Any discrepancy between perception and logic has been resolved in favor of perception. In this stage, thinking shifts to the cognitive, logical realm, enabling the child to solve concrete problems in his head. Concrete operational thinking is less egocentric and less centered than preoperational thinking. Moreover, it is both transformational and reversible, enabling the child to solve all varieties of conservation problems.

Clearly, concrete operational thought is more advanced and logical than preoperational thought. However, it still has its limitations. Its logic can be successfully applied only to real, observable objects in the immediate present (Piaget, 1972; Inhelder & Piaget, 1958). Its logic cannot be applied with the same degree of success to solve problems that are hypothetical or abstract, such as those that involve both multiple variables and the application of abstract principles.

Inversion and Compensation.   One form of reversibility used by concrete operational children Piaget (1967) called *inversion*. Inversion is the application of reversibility to problems of order or sequence. Wadsworth (1989) reports on a study in which three Ping-Pong balls were put in a tube: first a black ball, then a white ball, then a striped ball. Both preoperational and concrete operational children realized that the balls would both exist within the tube and exit the tube in the same order in which they entered: (1) black, (2) white, (3) striped. Then, the tube was inverted, turned upside down. Now, while the preoperational children still thought the balls would exit in the order they entered, the concrete operational children realized that because of inversion, the balls would exit in the opposite order: (1) striped, (2) white, (3) black.

Concrete operational thinking also features a second kind of reversibility called *compensation*, which reflects the logic of one dimension compensating equally for another. When the liquid is poured from the short, squat container into the tall, thin one (as on page 183), the concrete operational child realizes that the amount of water is the same because the increased height of the container is compensated for by its narrowness. There is a relationship between height and width as they affect volume. If height goes up and width compensates for it by going down, then volume can remain the same.

Seriation.   This is the ability to mentally arrange a set of elements in increasing or decreasing order along some dimension, such as size, weight, or volume. Typically, researchers test this by having children arrange a set of sticks in order of length. Preoperational children, because of their inclination toward physical centering, tend to align the sticks according to the heights of their tops, with little regard to the alignment of their bottoms, as shown below.

Preoperational
Seriation

Children at the stage of concrete operation order the sticks correctly by maintaining an equal alignment at the bottom, as shown below.

Concrete Operational
Seriation

To perform seriation correctly, children must understand the principle of *transitivity*. Transitivity, as illustrated in Box 8.3, is the realization that if *B* is greater than *A* and *C* is greater than *B*, then *C* is greater than *A*. Using transitivity, a child would recognize in the example in Box 8.3 that the correct increasing order of the three quantities would be *A*, *B*, *C*.

Classification.   This is the ability to put together objects that are alike, such as geometric shapes (Piaget, 1972; Piaget & Inhelder, 1969). To accomplish this task, children must understand the principle of *class inclusion*, namely, that objects of the same class or overlapping classes can be combined, and that a class includes all possible subclasses. Using a concept to label things that are alike in some respect — say, all kinds of fish — is an example of classification. Gagné (Chapter 4) included both concrete and defined concepts as categories of intellectual skills.

Consider this experiment by Piaget (1952): A child is given 20 brown wooden beads and 2 white wooden beads and is asked, Are there more wooden beads or more brown beads? Concrete operational children realize that the class "wooden beads" includes the classes of brown beads and white beads. There are 22 wooden beads (20 brown beads plus 2 white beads) compared to just 20 brown beads. The number in a total class includes the sum of the numbers in all of its distinct subclasses. This is class inclusion. Without this capability, preoperational children believe that brown beads outnumber wooden beads because they compare brown beads to white beads, not to total beads.

Box 8.3

🍎

**Demonstrating the Principle of Transitivity
in Solving Seriation Problems (Concrete Operational Stage)**

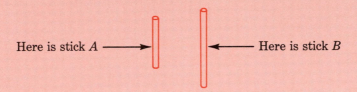

Here is stick *A* ⟶   ⟵ Here is stick *B*

1. Which one is longer, *A* or *B*?

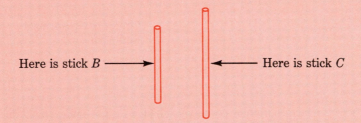

Here is stick *B* ⟶   ⟵ Here is stick *C*

(Cover up stick *A*.)

2. Which one is longer, *B* or *C*?

3. Which one is longer, *A* or *C*?

(Transitivity is required for students to be able to answer Question 3. Preoperational children are not likely to answer it correctly.)

This stage also features the development of the ability to combine dimensions such as time and distance, as illustrated in Box 8.4.

The Stage of Formal Operations (ages 11–15 and older)

In this stage, the student is able to reason in a logical manner using abstract schemata and can use this reasoning power to solve scientific problems. However, not all students reach this stage of logical reasoning. Only about half of the U.S. student population attain this level of formal operations, the remainder staying in the preceding stage of concrete operations (Schwebel, 1975).

Box 8.4
🍎

Demonstrating the Principle That Distance = Speed × Time
(Concrete Operational Stage)

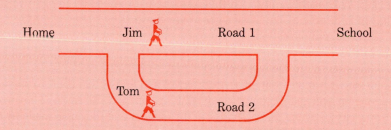

Tom and Jim are brothers. They leave home at the same time and arrive at school at the same time even though Jim takes Road 1 and Tom takes Road 2. Did they travel at the same speed? If not, which boy traveled faster? (Preoperational children are not likely to answer this correctly.)

Whereas concrete thought is limited to solving tangible problems in the present, formal thought makes it possible to go beyond experience to solve complex, hypothetical problems like the ones that will be illustrated later in this chapter. Using formal operations, a student can make hypotheses about what is going to happen based on general or abstract principles and then can test those hypotheses in a scientific manner. (The research process described in Chapter 1 is an example of this formal operation.)

According to Inhelder and Piaget (1958), formal operational schemata enable students to engage in (1) hypothetical deductive reasoning, that is, reasoning in which specific inferences or conclusions are drawn from a set of general premises; (2) scientific–inductive reasoning, or reasoning in which general conclusions are drawn from a set of specific facts; and (3) combinatorial reasoning, or reasoning about a number of variables at the same time. These processes (which were described in Chapter 1) cannot be carried out with concrete operational schemata.

Some of the formal operations of this stage are described below in the context of specific experiments conducted by Piaget and his co-workers to illustrate these operations (as reported by Inhelder & Piaget, 1958). These experiments can be recreated by both elementary and secondary school teachers in their classrooms to help their students discover and develop both concrete and formal operations.

Reciprocal Implication. The principle of compensation has already been introduced in conjunction with concrete operational thought. In solving conservation problems, the concrete operational child realizes that quantities can remain the same even though one dimension increases if a second dimension *compensates* for it by decreasing to the same degree. In formal thought, the conservation principle can be extended to more complex relationships in which one dimension is the reciprocal of the other, being equal to and opposite from it. This is illustrated in the billiard game experiment shown in Figure 8.2.

Balls are shot from the plunger and banked off the cushion in an effort to hit balls positioned on the table. The operating principle, which the children must discover, is that the angle at which the ball hits the cushion (or angle of incidence) is equal to the angle at which the ball comes off the cushion (or angle of reflection). Each angle implies or leads to its own reciprocal or exact opposite. Preoperational children, in this as in all the experiments, can describe only what they see or what they do ("I think it works because it's in the same direction." "It always goes over there.").

Concrete operational children discover the *concrete correspondence* between what they do and what results from their action ("The more I move the plunger this way — to the left — the more the ball will go like that — on that sharp angle."). It is only at the stage of formal operations that students discover and report that the two angles, the one striking the cushion and the one coming off it, are, in fact, the same. They see the necessary reciprocity between the inclination of the plunger and the angle made by the trajectory of the ball off the cushion.

Figure 8.2 ❦ The Billiard Game

The principle of the billiard game is used to demonstrate the angles of incidence and reflection. The tubular spring plunger can be pivoted and aimed. Balls are launched from this plunger against the projection wall and rebound to the interior of the apparatus. The circled drawings represent targets that are placed successively at different points.

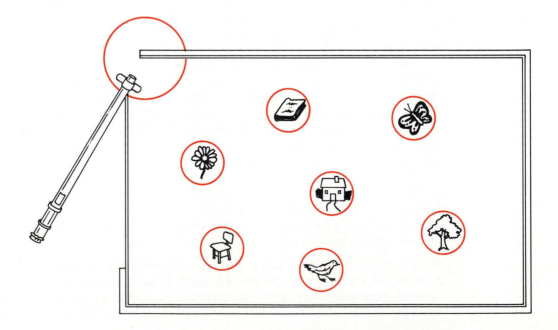

Separation of Variables.　　The flexibility experiment is used to illustrate the ability of formal operational students to separate out the independent effect of each of a number of variables at the same time. (Recall from the description of the way experiments are done, in Chapter 1, that the idea is to control the effects of all of these variables except one, the independent variable.) The apparatus is shown in Figure 8.3. The rods in Figure 8.3 can be thought of as diving boards. (Thinking of them as diving boards is an "elaboration," to use the terminology of Chapter 6.) The rods can be (1) extended in length (long) or retracted (short), (2) thick or thin, (3) round or square in cross-section, (4) wood or metal. At the unattached end they can have (5) a light object or a heavy object. The objective is to determine which combination of those five variables yields the greatest flexibility or bend. If each rod is thought of as a diving board, the question becomes, Which combination of variables would make a diving board that bends the most toward the water?

Again, preoperational children try random combinations and report what they see regardless of contradictions ("It doesn't work because it's too high."). Concrete operational students try different combinations but fail to see how one dimension compensates for another because they vary more than one dimension at a time. If the rods are made longer and thinner at the same time, it is impossible to tell whether both dimensions contribute to flexibility or only one does. If a rod is made longer and thicker at the same time, and there is no change in bend, the concrete operational student might think

Figure 8.3　🍎　The Flexibility Experiment

Diagram A illustrates the variables used in the flexibility experiment. The rods can be shortened or lengthened by varying the point at which they are clamped (see B for apparatus used). Cross-section forms are shown at the left of each rod; shaded forms represent brass rods, unshaded forms represent non-brass rods. Dolls are used for the weight variable (see B). These are placed at the end of the rod. Maximum flexibility is indicated when the end of the rod touches the water.

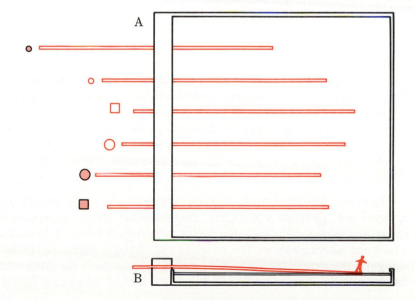

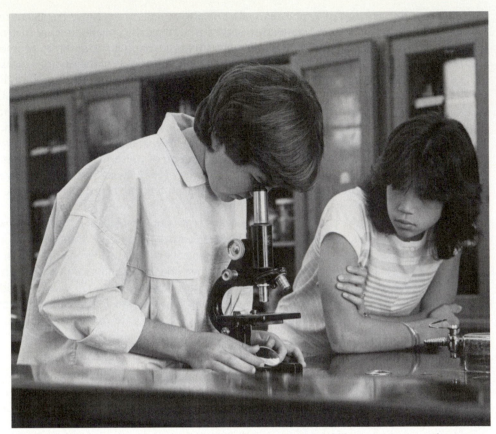

The development of formal operational thinking brings with it the ability to conduct experiments to learn about the operation of physical principles.

that neither matters; in fact, both do but the changes are actually compensating for one another.

The key to solving this experiment is discovered by formal operational students. They see that the key is to separate variables by testing or *varying one variable or dimension at a time while holding all the others constant* (as in the description of doing research, in Chapter 1). In this way they can discover, for instance, that "a rod made of the same material as another but thicker rod may bend an equal amount providing it is lengthened" (Inhelder & Piaget, 1958, p. 63). By being systematic and separating variables, these students figure out the extent to which one dimension can compensate for another.

Exclusion.   The principle of exclusion is illustrated by the pendulum problem, shown in Figure 8.4. To create a pendulum, the researcher simply suspends a weight from a string. The student then causes the weight to move back and forth, or oscillate, by pulling it back and applying a force. The variables that can be changed are (1) the length of the string; (2) the amount of weight at the end; (3) the height of the dropping point, that is, the distance the weight is pulled back (see the dashed lines in the figure); and (4) the

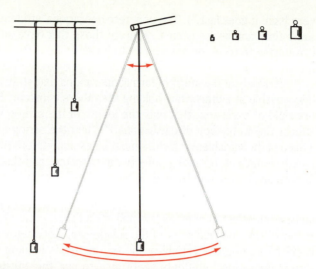

Figure 8.4 🍎 The Pendulum Problem

The pendulum problem utilizes a simple apparatus consisting of a string, which can be shortened or lengthened, and a set of varying weights. The other variables that at first might be considered relevant are the height of the release point and the force of the push given by the subject.

force with which the weight is pushed forward. The objective is to determine which variables affect the number of times the pendulum will swing back and forth (the frequency of oscillations).[1]

Think of the pendulum as a child's swing in the park (another "elaboration" to facilitate understanding). A parent is pushing the swing and wants to push it so that it swings back and forth the most number of times during the next full minute. The parent can vary (1) the length of the swing, by picking a short one or a long one; (2) the weight of the child (perhaps putting one child or two on the swing); (3) how far the swing is pulled back; and (4) how hard the swing is pushed forward. Which combination should the parent choose?

In this experiment, as in the preceding one with the bending rods, it is important that the student vary only one of the variables at a time, to avoid being misled by compensating relationships between variables. If length were increased and weight decreased, and length and weight happened to compensate for one another, the relationship would never be discovered because the result would be no change. Weight, pull distance, and push force must all be held constant while length is varied. Then length, pull distance, and push force must all be held constant while weight is varied, and so on, until each variable has been tested by itself, independent of the others. Only then can the effect of each variable be discovered. (Again, this is the basic principle of experimental research described in Chapter 1.)

The preoperational child cannot separate or dissociate the force he or she applies from the motion of the pendulum, which is independent of his or her action ("If you put it

---

[1]Note that the issue is not the size of the swing or how far the weight swings (the amplitude of oscillation), but rather the number of swings per minute or frequency of oscillations.

very high, it goes fast."). The concrete operational student varies several variables at the same time and hence cannot separate those that have an effect from those that do not ("You have to try to give it a push, to lower or raise the string, to change the height and the weight.").

It is only at the stage of formal operations that students realize they must vary only one variable at a time while holding the others constant. By so doing, they discover the principle of exclusion: that only the length of the string, not any of the other variables, affects the frequency of oscillations ("When the string is short, the swing is faster."). Three of the variables or factors must be excluded from the explanation because only the fourth, length of the string, affects the outcome, and this discovery can be made only if factors are tested one by one.

Disjunction.   As the preceding experiments have illustrated, sometimes the variables all have an effect in combination and sometimes some variables have no effect at all. In either event, the discovery of the relationship between variables and their effect always requires testing the variables one by one while holding the others constant, and only formal operational students seem able to use this strategy. In this next experiment, shown in Figure 8.5, the idea is to make the marble travel the fastest beyond the inclined plane by adjusting (1) the angle of the plane, (2) the point on the plane from which the marble is launched, and (3) the size of the marble.

The preoperational child, as has already been seen, describes what he or she sees and does ("Because it is heavy, it falls faster because it has a lot of force. I am going to put on the big one: It wants to go far because it is very steep."). The concrete operational child is able to exclude the factor of weight, which bears no relation to the desired outcome, and settles on the conclusion that slope and distance of roll together affect the amount the marble jumps at the end.

Only the formal operational student is able to realize that slope and distance always vary together or in combination. Therefore, slope and distance must be disjoined or

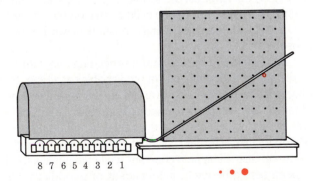

8 7 6 5 4 3 2 1

Figure 8.5 🍎 The Inclined Plane

We can raise or lower the inclined plane by moving the peg on which it rests to different holes in the board. These also serve as an index for measuring height. Marbles of varying sizes are released at different heights on this plane, hit a springboard at the bottom, bound in parabolic curves, and come to rest in one of the compartments (numbered 1 to 8). These are the subject's index to the length of the bound.

dissociated from their product, *height*. Slope, distance, and height are *not* three separate factors insofar as they effect the distance the marble "jumps." There is only one factor that counts and that is height, which is the product of slope times distance. Slope and distance *never* operate as separate factors. Height is the sole determining factor, while slope and distance compensate for one another by producing height.

Equilibrium and the INRC Group.   The last of the Piagetian principles combines all that have come before it in an experiment dealing with equilibrium or the balance of forces. Equilibrium is produced by conservation, compensation, or reciprocity, all of which mean changes that serve to neutralize or cancel one another out. The apparatus is the hydraulic press shown in Figure 8.6. It is, to elaborate again, like the lifts used in gas stations to lift a car so that someone can get underneath it and change the oil. There is a piston within vessel A, on which varying weights may be placed. It is connected to a tall tube (B) which is filled with a fluid, that fluid being alcohol, water, or glycerine, each of which varies in density from the others. The fluid in the tube flows in and out of vessel A depending on the weight of the piston. What must be discovered is the explanation of *the transmission of force as a function of weight and inversely as a function of the density of the fluid*.

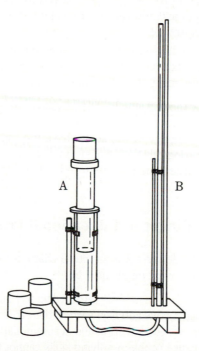

A   B

Figure 8.6 🍎 The Hydraulic Press

The equipment used for this problem in equilibrium involves two communicating "vessels" of different sizes and shape. Vessel A is provided with a piston that can be loaded with varying weights. We vary the amount of pressure exerted by the piston (which is dropped into the vessel by the subject) by adding weights.

While preoperational children describe ("It's the heavy ones that go lowest."), concrete children identify the observed correspondence between weight and the displacement of liquid without realizing that there is liquid resistance. It is not until the stage of formal operations that students realize that the liquid exerts a force in a direction opposite to the weight, the force being a function of the density of the liquid. The most dense liquid, glycerine, exerts the greatest force of resistance; the least dense liquid, alcohol, exerts the least force of resistance. Hence, we have equilibrium resulting from the principle of action and reaction — the reciprocity between the downward force of the weight (action) and the upward force of the liquid (reaction).

To figure out how this system works and thus attains equilibrium, the student must identify four logical transformations or ideas:

1. the action exerted by the pressure of the weight put on the piston — that is, the application or action of a force itself (called *Identity*);
2. the reduction or diminution of this action that occurs when weights are taken off the piston — that is, the removal, cancellation, or inverse of the above force (called *Negation*);
3. the reaction or resistance of the liquid, which is a pressure opposite to the force of the weight, is achieved by the addition of liquid or more dense liquid, and neutralizes or compensates for the force of the weight (called *Reciprocal*);
4. the reduction or diminution of the resistance of the liquid that occurs when liquid is removed or is replaced with less dense liquid that has the same effect as adding more weight (called *Correlative*).

Identity (adding weight) and negation (taking off weight) are equal and opposite, as are identity and reciprocal (increasing the density of the liquid). Identity and correlative (reducing the density of the liquid) have the same effect as do negation and reciprocal. Combining the logical INRC transformations in various ways allows equilibrium to be both offset or disturbed and then restored, which illustrates the power of formal operational thought.

Applying Piaget to Educational Practice

If one were to derive some practical characteristics of the schooling process from the work of Piaget, what might they be?

Learning by Exploration.   According to Piaget (1973), intellectual development depends on constructive activity, with all the errors that may result and the extra time that may be required. Assimilation and accommodation require an active learner, not a passive one, because problem-solving skills cannot be taught, they must be discovered (Piaget, 1958). Kamii and DeVries (1978) suggest many hands-on classroom activities for teaching students the operations that are appropriate to their level of development and hence enhancing the likelihood that they will develop necessary problem-solving skills.

Exploration also means experimentation. Building things, using things, trying them out, making them work, "playing" with them, and trying to answer questions about how and why they work is the essence of Piaget's approach to development. The opposite of his approach is simply transmitting knowledge to students verbally in lecture or "cookbook" form.

Lesson plans based on Piaget's work would not be simple summaries of content to be transmitted. They would include activities for children to engage in, demonstrations for them to watch, and questions for them to answer. Student roles would be both active and self-directed, much more like the model of discovery learning (pp. 107–111) than like the model of direct instruction (pp. 104–107) or the other models described in Chapter 5.

Learning Centers.   Not only the process of educating children would be oriented toward their self-controlled engagement with learning materials; the physical structure of the classroom would also be designed to enhance student activity and self-direction. The child-centered classroom would be divided into learning centers where students would go to interact directly with a set of specific learning materials. Walls separating rooms could be removed and chairs and tables rearranged around these learning or interest centers in

The Piagetian classroom is divided into learning centers where students do individual or small-group work on specific projects with selected materials.

which specific concepts could be taught in what might be called an experiential or hands-on fashion. Students would move from center to center to be exposed to and learn about different ideas. This model has been referred to as the open classroom (Blitz, 1973) or the informal classroom (Rathbone, 1974). It is also characteristic of the so-called developmental approach practiced in the British primary schools (Rogers, 1970).

One way to provide students with activities in conjunction with learning centers is to provide *task cards*. Each task card presents students with a concrete task that enables them to apply many of the Piagetian processes appropriate to their grade level. Tasks should be relevant to the children's experiences, inherently motivating to do, and connected to topics and content that are important for the children to learn. Examples of task cards are shown in Box 8.5.

One learning center might be a place where a young child can listen to a favorite story—learning to connect the words he hears with the words he sees. A learning center is a good place for positive reinforcement (recall Chapter 3).

Box 8.5

Sample Task Cards

Choose one living thing in your immediate school environment and keep a record of how it changes through the year. It can be plant or animal life.

See how many ways you can keep your record—pictures . . . stories . . . poems . . . models . . . How many more can you think of?

Make a list of opposite word pairs. Examples: light–heavy, dangerous–safe, beautiful–ugly.

Go inside or outside and find things that fit your word pairs. If they can't be brought back to the classroom, make pictures.

Make an OPPOSITES book or chart or display.

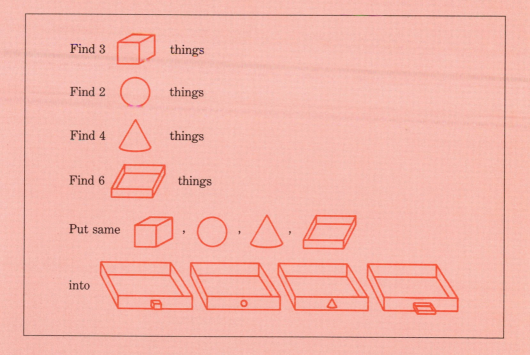

SOURCE: Newman, T. R. (1976). *Changeover: Breakthrough to individualization* (pp. 182, 184, 188). Wayne, NJ: Wayne Township Public Schools.

Box 8.6

Flowchart for the Theme "Family"

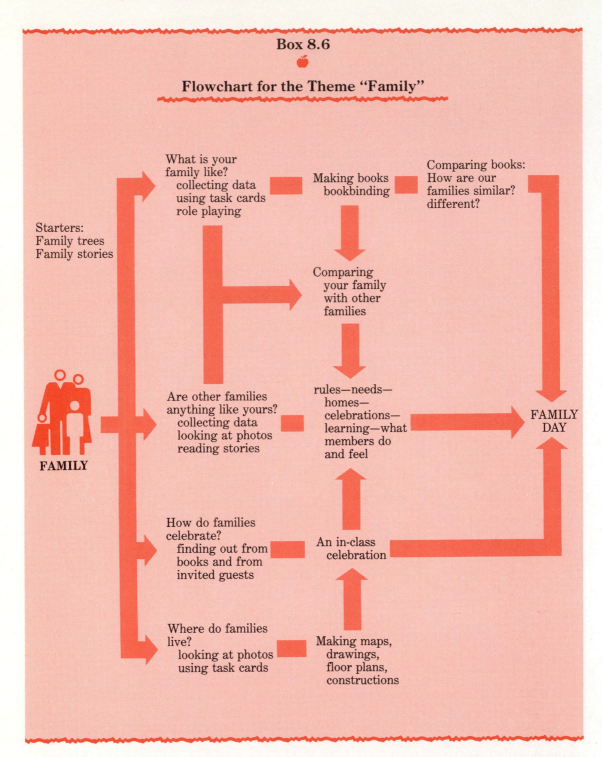

Starters:
Family trees
Family stories

FAMILY

What is your
family like?
   collecting data
   using task cards
   role playing

Making books
bookbinding

Comparing books:
How are our
families similar?
different?

Comparing
your family
with other
families

Are other families
anything like yours?
   collecting data
   looking at photos
   reading stories

rules—needs—
homes—
celebrations—
learning—what
members do
and feel

FAMILY
DAY

How do families
celebrate?
   finding out from
   books and from
   invited guests

An in-class
celebration

Where do families
live?
   looking at photos
   using task cards

Making maps,
drawings,
floor plans,
constructions

Use of Themes.   If one follows Piaget, then the resulting curricular emphasis will be less on discrete subject-matter knowledge and more on integrated, interdisciplinary topics or themes. Themes like probability, trees, ecology, the family, and the automobile provide vehicles for learning about and using science, mathematics, social science, and language arts in an integrated way. With a thematic approach, it is the process of acquiring information, rather than the information itself, that takes on the greatest importance. In other words, the important skills become the "how-to" skills. Box 8.6 shows a "flow-chart" for a unit on the theme of "family."

Child-Centered Orientation.   The child, rather than the curriculum or any national testing program, would be the basis for classroom instruction. Instructional choices, rather than a strictly defined or prescribed set of skills to be mastered, would reflect where the individual child was in the developmental sequence. The child-centered orientation would also be reflected in the approach to evaluation, which would be individualized and based primarily on observation rather than on any large-scale or lockstep testing program. As a result, many children would be working on different learning activities or tasks at the same time. Much learning would take place individually or in small groups rather than through whole-class instruction.

The child-centered approach also differs from direct instruction in that the teacher is not the primary deliverer of instruction (as is typically true in whole-class, lecture-type instruction), but instead functions as the "orchestrator" of instruction. The teacher is available to answer individual questions and to function as a guide while each small group of children engages in different learning tasks based on the various environmental sources.

Focus on Development of Schemata.   At the appropriate time developmentally, instruction in mathematics and science in particular would focus on helping children develop and use schemata to aid their problem-solving (see Chapter 7). In the early and middle elementary grades, for example, children could be taught to solve conservation problems correctly (Gelman & Gallistel, 1978). In the late elementary and early middle grades, the conceptual focus would be on tasks involving seriation, classification, inversion, compensation, and the use of concrete correspondence. Starting in the final grades of middle school and extending through high school, the emphasis would be on teaching logical reasoning and thinking rather than on rote memorization of facts and formulas. In every instance, the teaching focus would be on helping students to develop schemata that would enable them to understand and explain phenomena in the world around them.

Some examples of teaching concrete correspondence through measurement and comparison in the elementary grades are shown in Box 8.7. (Also see the story problems in Figures 7.1 and 7.2.) Such measurement activities help children develop the various schemata required for concrete operations. For the development of formal operational schemata, experiments patterned after those described on the preceding pages can be used. Other possibilities include problems of logic and reasoning, such as those shown in Boxes 2.5, 7.1, 7.3, and 7.4.

Finally, as a summary of how Piagetian concepts apply to the way people learn—and, hence, how they can be taught—the personal scenario in Box 8.8 is offered.

Box 8.7

**Examples of Teaching Concrete Correspondence
Through Measurement and Comparison**

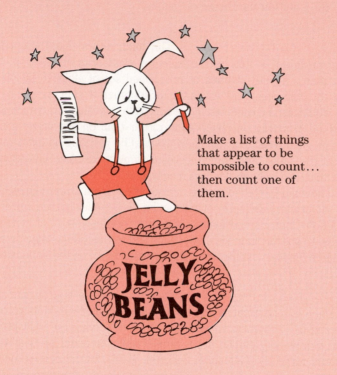

Make a list of things that appear to be impossible to count... then count one of them.

Volume of stone (a) is 3 "spinks"   Volume of stone (b) is 4½ "spinks"

Stone (b) is larger — 4½ : 3
4½ − 3 = 1½

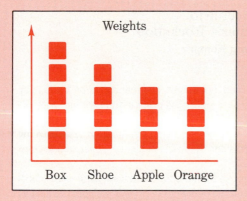

Weights

Box   Shoe   Apple   Orange

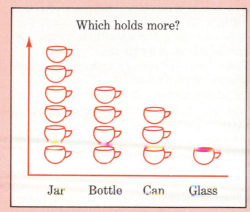

Which holds more?

Jar   Bottle   Can   Glass

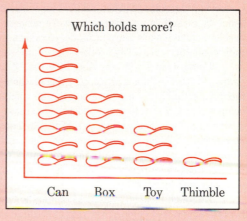

Which holds more?

Can   Box   Toy   Thimble

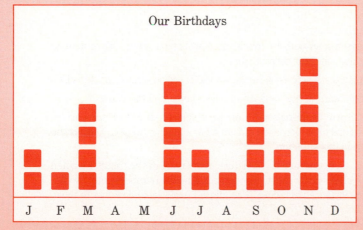

Our Birthdays

J F M A M J J A S O N D

Jan.	🧍🧍
Feb.	🧍
Mar.	🧍🧍🧍🧍
Apr.	🧍
May	
June	🧍🧍🧍🧍🧍
July	🧍🧍
Aug.	🧍
Sept.	🧍🧍🧍🧍
Oct.	🧍🧍
Nov.	🧍🧍🧍🧍🧍🧍
Dec.	🧍🧍

Box 8.8

A Personal Scenario:
Learning in My Father's Workshop
by Alicia Wolfgang Kemper

Piaget believed that problem solving skills were learned, not taught, and that hands-on learning by exploration is most conducive to the development of these skills. Experimentation without controls is necessary. I spent a great deal of time in grade school and high school in a learning situation replete with materials having nearly no controls and with no deliverer of instruction. The learning center was my father's garage, which housed the tools and materials of a small construction company that built houses and fabricated fine cabinetry.

My father left the house every day at 3:00 p.m., so from the time I arrived home from school until late evening I could entertain myself with the contents of the garage. I was welcome as long as I observed the rules of order, respect for tools, and no wanton destruction of materials. I had the space to myself; my siblings who were nearest in age to me were girls whose extracurricular problem-solving skills were being developed as they encountered difficulties with the contents of their cosmetics cases. My brothers were too young to be allowed in the garage.

Using what I will now label "themes," I interacted with the learning environment of the garage. A "theme" was a product, or thing I wanted to make. It was necessary to develop measurement skills (math) for length of boards and volume of paint or shellac. I developed motor skills in using the drill press, jigsaw, handsaw, miterbox, hand drill, and other tools. I learned to correct mistakes by jury rigging, and to realize when structure or aesthetics would be compromised by jury-rigging. With no teacher, I had to problem-solve my way through learning the nomenclature of wood- and metalworking. I used the dictionary to discover meanings. I selected materials for my products based on hands-on comparisons with other materials for texture, strength, durability, flexibility, hardness, etc.

Although I had no awareness of it at the time, I was developing concepts of seriation, classification, inversion, comparison, and concrete correspondence as I worked my way through to a finished product.

Some examples:

Seriation—grading textures smooth to rough, grading similar paint colors light to dark, replacing drill bits in their correct slots.

Classification—grouping types of screws, solvents, woods (based on some characteristics).

Inversion—working backward in my mind from a mistake to find the cause.

Comparison—nearly all of my materials and tools were selected based on comparison with other materials and tools because I did not have a teacher to say, "This is the proper thing to use in this situation."

Concrete correspondence—I generally had a picture in my mind of the things I wanted to make. It was a lectern, a toy chest, wooden block house numbers, etc.: something that I had seen instances of before. The things I made looked similar to those observed things.

Note: It takes a motivated learner to learn by this method as opposed to just dealing with problems as they come up.

Summary of Main Points

1. Piaget observed children from birth through adolescence, often gave them tasks or experiments to solve, and meticulously described the results. From these observations he formulated a theory of cognitive development with the *schema* as the basic unit, the schema being a repeatable action sequence governed by a core meaning. As development proceeds, schemata increase in number and complexity in order to direct the child's actions as he or she deals with objects and events.

2. The basic tenet of Piaget's theory is that the basis for intellectual growth and development is *adaptation*, or being able to deal with and function in a given environment.

3. The two adaptive mechanisms are *assimilation*, or incorporating new information into existing schemata, and *accommodation*, or modifying an existing schema when new information cannot be understood with existing schemata.

4. Assimilation helps people make better use of the schemata they have to cope quickly and efficiently with their environment, while accommodation enables them to expand their range of capabilities. Play is pure assimilation; imitation is pure accommodation.

5. A balance or equilibrium must exist between oneself and one's environment. In order to ensure this, people *equilibrate*; that is, they sometimes assimilate and sometimes accommodate in dealing with the situations they encounter. This force toward attaining and maintaining equilibrium is what motivates the developmental process.

6. What develops are schemata, the organizational structures that represent *intelligence*. Intelligence is used to carry out *operations* or coordinated sets of actions for dealing with objects and events.

7. The most critical operation is *conservation*, the ability to recognize that the amount of a substance remains the same even when its shape or arrangement is changed. In conserving, a child is able to recognize amounts that may look different but must, logically, be the same. The classic illustration is the same amount of water remaining equal when poured into a tall, narrow glass and a short, wide one, even though the tall glass looks like it contains more water.

8. Development is based on four factors: *heredity* (which affects *maturation*), *active experience*, *social interaction*, and *equilibration*. The result is four possible stages of cognitive development, ordinarily occurring at about the same spans of time for most children.

9. The *sensorimotor* stage (0–2 years of age) is made up of six periods, during which there is an appearance of progressively more complex behaviors involving the connections between the senses and motor behavior.

10. The major activity is the *circular reaction* (primary, secondary, tertiary) in which the infant stumbles upon a new experience as a result of some act and then tries to repeat the experience by repeating the original act. The infant progresses from the performance of only reflex actions at birth to the performance of actions intended to produce desired outcomes by age 2.

11. By the end of this first stage, the child has developed sufficient schemata to be able to recognize objects even in their absence (called *object permanence*).

12. The second stage, *preoperational thought* (2–7 years of age), is characterized by four features of prelogical thinking. First is *egocentrism*, a preoccupation with one-self and one's own point of view and a consequent inability to recognize the reality or legitimacy of any point of view other than one's own.

13. Second is *centration*, the focusing of all of one's attention on only one aspect or dimension of a stimulus at a time.

14. Third is *nontransformational reasoning*, focusing only on the successive states in a sequence (such as original and final) while ignoring the transformations that caused the change in state.

15. Fourth is *irreversibility*, the inability to reverse thought or follow a line of reasoning back to where it started.

16. These four characteristics of preoperational thought are closely related, and all combine to make it impossible for children to do the logical reasoning required for successful completion of *conservation* tasks. However, by the time this stage ends and the next, the stage of *concrete operations* (7–11 years of age), begins, children are able to do conservation of number, with conservation of area and of volume soon to follow.

17. Concrete operations are logical operations: They represent thinking, are reversible, assume conservation, and are part of a system, but they are still limited to dealing with what can be perceived. In other words, in this stage there is a *concrete correspondence* between thoughts and external, observed reality.

18. Based on the application of reversibility and conservation, concrete operations include *inversion* (reversing order or sequence in one's head), *compensation* (realizing that something will remain the same even though one of its dimensions increases, if its other dimension decreases proportionately), *seriation* (mentally arranging things in order based on increases or decreases along a single dimension), and *classification* (combining or grouping things that have common or overlapping features, that is, *class inclusion*).

19. The final stage, *formal operations* (11–15 years of age), is not attained by a large proportion of the population. In this stage, logical reasoning appears without concrete limitations, enabling students to solve both hypothetical–deductive and scientific–inductive problems (that is, to go either from the general to the specific or from the specific to the general).

20. To describe this stage, Piaget used a series of experiments involving sets of different apparatuses. In the billiard game, students in the stage of formal operations used the principle of *reciprocal implication*, the equal and opposite relationship between two dimensions, to discover that the angle of direction or incidence of a ball shot against a cushion is equal to the angle of trajectory or reflection of the ball off the cushion.

21. In the flexibility experiment, students in the stage of formal operations used the principle of *separation of variables*, testing or varying one of five variables at a time while holding the other four constant, to discover that the five variables could be directly combined to produce the most flexible "diving board."

22. In the pendulum problem, students in the stage of formal operations discovered the principle of *exclusion*: By systematically testing variables one at a time, they found that some variables could be excluded from the solution because their variability did not affect the outcome. The number of swings of the pendulum per unit time was affected only by the length of its string.

23. In the inclined plane experiment, formal operational students discovered the principle of *disjunction*: Variables that vary together to affect a third variable must be disjoined or disconnected in order that the third variable can be recognized. The ball's journey down the slide was governed by the slide's height, which was in turn a joint function of slope and distance.

24. Finally, in the hydraulic pump experiment, formal operational students realized that the *equilibrium* of the system was based on the principle of *action* and *reaction*, which in turn was based on direct and compensating relationships between four logical transformations or actions: *Identity* (the force added), *Negation* (the force removed), *Reciprocal* (the counterforce added), and *Correlative* (the counterforce removed).

25. To apply Piagetian principles to educational practice teachers would adopt the process of *learning by exploration*—by constructive, active engagement with learning materials—and would organize the learning environment into *learning centers* or locations where specific learning tasks can be undertaken.

26. In addition, the curriculum should feature the *use of themes* or integrated, interdisciplinary topics as a vehicle for teaching subject-matter-type skills. Moreover, instruction should be *child-centered* rather than either curriculum- or teacher-centered, and it should make great use of both individual and small-group instruction and evaluation.

27. Finally, instructional content would *focus on the development of schemata* such as conservation, seriation, and classification in the elementary and middle grades and formal, abstract problem-solving in the high school grades.

Suggested Resources

Flavell, J. H. (1963). *The developmental psychology of Jean Piaget*. Princeton, NJ: Van Nostrand.

Piaget, J., & Inhelder, B. (1969). *The psychology of the child*. New York: Basic Books.

Schwebel, M., & Raph, J. (1973). *Piaget in the classroom*. New York: Basic Books.

Sigel, I., Brodzinsky, D. A., & Golinkoff, R. M. (1981). *New directions in Piagetian theory and practice*. Hillsdale, NJ: Lawrence Erlbaum.

Wadsworth, B. J. (1989). *Piaget's theory of cognitive and affective development* (4th ed.). New York: Longman.

Chapter
9

Affective Development

Objectives

1. Describe Piaget's three stages of moral development — moral realism, mutuality, and autonomy — including his concepts of justice and punishment.
2. Describe the moral dilemma as a measure of moral reasoning.
3. Describe Kohlberg's six stages of moral development in terms of their orientations — punishment–obedience, personal reward, good person, law and order, social contract, and universal ethical principle — within three levels: preconventional, conventional, and postconventional.
4. Describe and illustrate procedures for enhancing moral development.
5. Identify and describe Erikson's eight stages of psychosocial development, that is, the development of ego identity, in terms of the developmental crises faced in each: trust versus mistrust, autonomy versus shame and doubt, initiative versus guilt, industry versus inferiority, identity versus confusion, intimacy versus isolation, generativity versus stagnation, and integrity versus despair.
6. Describe and illustrate procedures for helping to build initiative, industry, and identity in the school context.

Introduction

Up until now, the focus of this book has been on cognitive functioning: thinking, learning, and problem-solving. Now, the focus is going to shift to the other major aspect of human functioning: the *affective* domain or area. This is the *social* and *emotional* side of people, the side that includes *feelings*, *attitudes*, *beliefs*, and *values*. These are important human qualities that, like the cognitive qualities previously described, follow a pattern of development as people grow and mature. These affective qualities are also important determinants of how people function and perform in various situations, such as school. Not only must teachers deal with students as learners, thinkers, and problem-solvers; they must also deal with students as social and emotional beings, possessors of feelings and values. The nature of students' social interactions, motivational patterns, and moral characteristics will depend on their affective sides.

Three theories that cover the development of this affective side of people's being — their personality and their character — will be described. The first of these three was developed by Piaget and represents a counterpart of his theory of cognitive development covered in the preceding chapter.

Piaget's Stages of Affective Development

Piaget's focus in affective development was primarily on moral development or the development of *moral judgment*. This refers to children's conceptions of rules and the respect that children acquire for these rules (Piaget, 1932). To discover what children's conceptions of rules are at different ages, Piaget (1932) studied the game of marbles, the most popular children's game of his day, and questioned children about their perceptions of the rules by which the game is played.

He also constructed stories that contained an immoral act, such as a lie, but varied in their degree of *intentionality*, or whether or not the immoral act was intended to deceive someone. He asked children to tell him which child (in which story) was naughtiest and why. Consider these two sample stories:

> A. A little boy (or a little girl) goes for a walk in the street and meets a big dog who frightens him very much. So then he goes home and tells his mother he has seen a dog that was as big as a cow.

> B. A child comes home from school and tells his mother that the teacher had given him good marks, but it was not true; the teacher had given him no marks at all, either good or bad. Then his mother was very pleased and rewarded him. (Piaget, 1932, pp. 144–145)

Finally, Piaget (1932) studied children's ideas about justice and punishment by telling children stories like the one below and asking them whether the child in the story should be punished and how.

> A little boy is playing in his room. His mother asks him to go and fetch some bread for dinner because there is none left in the house. But instead of going immediately the boy says that he can't be bothered, that he'll go in a minute, etc. An hour later he has not gone. Finally, dinner time comes, and there is no bread on the table. The father is not pleased and he wonders which would be the fairest way of punishing the boy. He

thinks of three punishments. The first would be to forbid the boy to go to the Round-abouts [fair] the next day. . . . The second punishment the father thought of was not to let the boy have any bread to eat. (There was a little bread left from the previous days.) . . . The third punishment the father thinks of is to do to the boy the same thing as he had done. The father would say to him, "You wouldn't help your mother. Well, I am not going to punish you, but the next time you ask me to do anything for you, I shall not do it, and you will see how annoying it is when people do not help each other." (The little boy thinks this would be all right, but a few days later his father would not help him reach a toy he could not get by himself. The father reminded him of his promise.) . . . Which of these three punishments was the fairest? (Piaget, 1932, pp. 200–201)

Based on the pattern of responses by children of different ages to questions about rules, intentionality, and justice taken from the game of marbles and the two types of stories, Piaget (1932) identified the stages of affective development described below.

Stage 1: Moral Realism (ages 2–7)

In this stage, rules are taken literally and absolutely and must be respected. The child believes in *objective responsibility*, or being responsible for one's transgressions regardless of the intentions behind them. The child also believes that the severity of a transgression is directly proportional to its superficial magnitude. In other words, the bigger the lie, the worse it is. Rules are a reality of the outside, adult world, and the child has a sense of duty in following them. Consider the following examples.

In playing the game of marbles, each child plays for himself rather than competing with his companions and sharing a set of common rules. Each rarely looks at the other and each simultaneously follows his own conception of the rules of the game. Each strives to imitate an elder model rather than engaging in a socially interactive activity. Two children play two separate games, reflecting the egocentricity that has already been encountered at this age.

In evaluating a lie, as reflected in stories A and B above, the child at this stage reacts not to the intentions of the liar, but to the likelihood that the lie might be true. In other words, the more outrageous the lie, the worse it is, irrespective of the intention of the liar to deceive. So the little girl who said she saw a dog as big as a cow is naughtier than the one who said her teacher had given her good marks, because it (a dog as big as a cow) "could never happen," or "there's no such thing," or it is "the biggest lie." The child who told that lie should, in the judgment of children at this stage, be punished the most.

Moreover, in the stage of moral realism, actions are evaluated in terms of the material result and independently of motives. That means the worse the result, the worse the crime — as illustrated in Box 9.1, where the greater the number of items that are broken, even by clumsiness, the naughtier the act. This carries over to the idea of justice in which the moral realist believes that the worse the crime, the more severe the punishment should be. The moral realist hands out what Piaget (1932) calls *expiatory punishment*, which is strong and arbitrary and thereby allows the wrongdoer to expiate or pay penance for the wrongdoing. Painful punishment is expected to deter further rule-breaking. So, for the story of the child who would not get the bread (pages 208–209), children in the stage of moral realism choose the only punishment of the three they

Box 9.1

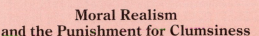

Moral Realism
and the Punishment for Clumsiness

The two stories of the broken cups were used to evaluate a child's level of affective development.

A. A little boy who is called John is in his room. He is called to dinner. He goes into the dining room. But behind the door there was a chair, and on the chair there was a tray with fifteen cups on it. John couldn't have known that there was all this behind the door. He goes in, the door knocks against the tray, bang go the fifteen cups, and they all get broken!

B. Once there was a little boy whose name was Henry. One day when his mother was out he tried to get some jam out of the cupboard. He climbed up onto a chair and stretched out his arm. But the jam was too high up and he couldn't reach it and have any. But while he was trying to get it he knocked over a cup. The cup fell down and broke. (Piaget, 1932, p. 118)

The basis for punishment in moral realism—the *magnitude* of the crime (objective responsibility)—is revealed in the response of George, age 6:

Have you understood these stories, George? — *Yes*. — What did the first boy do? — *He broke eleven cups*. — And the second one? — *He broke a cup by moving roughly*. — Why did the first one break the cups? — *Because the door knocked them*. — And the second? — *He was clumsy. When he was getting the jam the cup fell down*. — Is one of the boys naughtier than the other? — *The first is because he knocked over twelve cups*. — If you were the daddy, which one would you punish most? — *The one who broke twelve cups*. — Why did he break them? — *The door shut too hard and knocked them. He didn't do it on purpose*. — And why did the other boy break a cup? — *He wanted to get the jam. He moved too far. The cup got broken*. — Why did he want to get the jam? — *Because he was all alone. Because his mother wasn't there*. — Have you got a brother? — *No, a little sister*. — Well, if it was you who had broken the twelve cups when you went into the room and your little sister who had broken one cup while she was trying to get the jam, which of you would be punished most severely? — *Me, because I broke more than one cup*. (Piaget, 1932, pp. 120–121)

The basis for punishment in later stages—*intent*—is revealed in the response of Nuss, age 10:

[The naughtiest is] *the one who wanted to take the jam*. — Does it make any difference the other one having broke more cups, Nuss? — *No, because the one who broke 15 cups didn't do it on purpose*. (Piaget, 1932, p. 125)

George, the younger one, would punish the child who had, however unintentionally, broken the most cups, while Nuss, the older one, would punish the child who broke only a single cup but did it while trying to do something bad.

regard as at all severe, namely, not allowing the child to go to the fair. Punishment is morally necessary to make up or pay for the transgression and thus to prevent a relapse.

This view of justice is termed *retributive* justice ("an eye for an eye, a tooth for a tooth"), and it is based, according to Piaget (1932), on the child's perception that adult authority imposes respect for given orders and rules and that the laws themselves must be avenged when broken (which Piaget calls *adult restraint*).

In between retributive and distributive justice, developmentally, is *immanent justice* or the idea that if you do something bad, something bad will happen to you. In other words, there are automatic punishments that emanate from the events or acts themselves (for example, getting a stomachache from eating candy you were not supposed to have).

Stage 2: Mutuality (ages 7–11)

Mutuality means *equality* or following the "golden rule" of doing unto others as you would have them do unto you. Mutuality also means *reciprocity* or taking turns or sharing equally. If the ball goes over the fence, then each of the players should take turns retrieving it rather than the same one getting it every time. Hence, mutuality means *mutual respect*. It means sharing when only one has something or when everybody but one has something. If there is a chocolate bar to be divided between two sisters, each should get half.

When it comes to following rules, mutuality means *cooperation*. Cheating is bad because it is not fair to others. In regard to justice, one person who wrongs another must

Mutuality means sharing or taking turns. Playing well together involves mutuality.

be punished or made to give back what he or she has taken. That reflects reciprocity. In the game of marbles, the boy who cheats is excluded from the game for a time. Marbles unlawfully won are restored to their rightful owner or distributed among the other players. When the strong exploit the weak, they must be forced to make restitution. Punishment is neither automatic and absolute nor a means of making one pay for one's sins (as in retributive justice). Instead, it is a way of treating everyone the same and restoring equality (called *distributive justice*).

If a misdeed occurs and the perpetrator is unknown, as when someone throws something in class but the teacher cannot tell who, then mutuality dictates that no one be punished because it cannot be done fairly. On the other hand, moral realism requires that everyone be punished because there must be a punishment at all costs, even if it strikes the innocent as well as the guilty.

When it comes to lying, children in the stage of mutuality take into account the notion of fairness or the effect on other people, which makes them sensitive to intentionality. In response to the stories about lying on page 208 (the "big dog" versus the "good marks"), the worse lie to children in this stage is the one about the "good marks" because it was intended to mislead and gain something to which the liar was not entitled. Such deceit is not in keeping with the spirit of mutuality.

In the stories on clumsiness in Box 9.1, older children choose to punish an act of destruction, however small, if the child performs it while trying to take advantage of someone or something unfairly; they forgive an act of destruction of larger magnitude if it occurs accidentally.

Finally, in meting out distributive justice, children in this stage believe there should be reciprocity between the punishment and the crime. In the story about the child who would not help his mother by going out to pick up the bread, the punishment of choice is to not help the child when he asks for it, because he was not willing to help when asked. The punishment is designed to "fit the crime," showing that children at this stage realize the social consequences of their actions.

Stage 3: Autonomy (ages 11–15)

In this stage, rules are seen as set by mutual agreement and changeable through mutual agreement. There is an interest in rules, in an abstract or formal sense, as a code of conduct, and in codifying all possibilities. The rules serve to accomplish more than just guaranteeing cooperation; they maintain the spirit of the game or, in the case of marbles, ensure insofar as possible that outcomes will be a function of skill rather than luck. Hence, the young adult of this stage has been freed from or has become autonomous of the constraints of either adult-imposed reality or peer-imposed mutuality. Rules have become entities unto themselves that are made by people and can be changed by people through mutual consent. The enforcement of rules has passed from constraint to cooperation to mutual consent. The rule has become the rational rule as part of a system of legality involving rationally interlocking rules.

In the case of justice, the principle of equality, or "the same for all," gives way to the principle of *equity*. Equity means not automatically treating everyone exactly the same but rather taking into account each individual's particular circumstances. In equity there are shades of equality depending on factors such as age, size of contribution, need, and so on. Consider the following question (Piaget, 1932, p. 287): "Why must you not copy from

---

Box 9.2

The Idea of Justice

Two boys, a little one and a big one, once went for a long walk in the mountains. When lunchtime came they were very hungry. But when they took their food out of their lunch bags, they found that there was not enough for both of them. What should they have done? Given all the food to the big boy, all to the little one, or the same to both?

Moral Realism: "The big boy should have had most." *Why?* "Because he's the eldest."

Mutuality (Equality): "Each must be given the same. It would be fair."

Autonomy (Equity): "The little boy should have had more because he was smaller."

SOURCE: Piaget, J. (1932). *The moral judgment of the child* (pp. 309–311). New York: Harcourt Brace & World.

---

your neighbor?" Moral realists answer, "Because you get punished." Those in the stage of mutuality answer, "Because it isn't fair." Those in the stage of autonomy answer, "It isn't fair for those who can learn, but those who can't learn ought to be allowed to have a little look" (Piaget, 1932, pp. 287–288). Another example appears in Box 9.2.

So we see that the idea of *unfairness* develops from

1. moral realism, or behavior that is forbidden by either adults or the rules of the game, to
2. mutuality, or behavior that goes against equality, to
3. equity, or acts of economic or political injustice connected with adult society.

To the moral realist, some forbidden acts are lying, stealing, fighting, and breaking things. In the mutuality stage, the inequalities might be giving something better to one than to the other, punishing one worse than the other, and hitting someone who has done nothing to you. In the autonomy stage, inequities or social injustices include a teacher preferring a student because she is more clever than others, or students leaving other students out of their games because they are not well-dressed enough.

Hence, justice goes from *retributive* or requiring punishment to stamp out disobedient or unjust acts, to *distributive* or considering equality by treating everybody the same and maintaining harmony as the primary consideration, to *equity*, in which attenuating circumstances are taken into account. Piaget's stages of affective development are summarized in Table 9.1.

A Related Approach

Selman (1978) has described a sequence of levels of social thought that parallels Piaget's stages of logical thought (described in Chapter 8). At the lowest level, Level 0, children

Table 9.1 🍎 Piaget's Three Stages of Affective Development

Stage	Rules	Accidents	Lying	Justice
Moral Realism (2–7 years)	Games played in isolation; no cooperation or social interaction	Intentions not considered. Children do not take the view of others. Judgments are based on effects of actions.	Punishment is the criterion for a lie. No punishment = no lie. Lying is being "naughty."	Submission to adult authority. Arbitrary, expiatory punishments are considered just.
Mutuality (7–11 years)	Rules observed, though children lack agreement as to what the rules are.	Intentions begin to be considered. Children begin to take the view of others.	Lie = not true. Unpunished untruths are lies.	Justice is based on reciprocity. Equality is more important than authority.
Autonomy (after 11–12 years)	Rules known to all; agreement as to what the rules are; rules can be changed by consensus; rules are of interest for their own sake.		Intentions decide whether a false statement is not a lie. Truthfulness is viewed as necessary for cooperation.	Equality with equity. Reciprocity considers intent and circumstances.

SOURCE: Adapted from Wadsworth, B. J. (1989). *Piaget's theory of cognitive and affective development* (4th ed., p. 132). New York: Longman.

confuse their own perspectives with those of others. They are, therefore, egocentric, as were Piaget's preoperational children. At Level 1, children realize that other children have social thoughts and feelings that are different from their own. At Level 2, they consider others' attitudes and feelings. At Level 3, they view their own and other children's thoughts and feelings mutually and simultaneously, and at Level 4 they recognize that there is a general social viewpoint that goes beyond the perspectives of the individual child. These stages also parallel Piaget's affective stages.

By asking children to solve social dilemmas, Selman helps them consider more social perspectives than just their own. One such dilemma is whether to buy a close friend a dog for his birthday to replace his recently lost dog, even though he says he does not want a new dog because it would just make him miss his old one more. In this dilemma, the choice of buying the dog for the friend as a way of helping the friend is a more socially advanced response than not doing it for fear of losing a friend. The choice of buying the dog takes into account the friend's needs even beyond what the friend himself has acknowledged. It is based on the recognition that people's needs can be helped to change by acts of friendship.

Before considering the classroom implications of Piaget's theory of affective development, we will describe Kohlberg's theory of moral development, which is a refinement and expansion of Piaget's.

Kohlberg's Stages of Moral Development

Lawrence Kohlberg (1969, 1975, 1981) took Piaget's ideas about the development of the conception of justice in children and expanded them into a six-stage theory of moral development. He determined the characteristics of moral reasoning in children by presenting them with *moral dilemmas* or situations in which they had to choose between two desirable or two undesirable alternatives (where no choice is either absolutely right or wrong) and explain the reasons behind their choice. The above story about the dog is an example of a dilemma. Another example, used by Kohlberg, is this:

> A man's wife is dying. There is one drug that could save her, but it is very expensive, and the druggist who invented it will not sell it at a price low enough for the man to buy it. Finally, the man becomes desperate and considers stealing the drug for his wife. What should he do, and why?

How do children of different ages respond to a situation like this, and is there a pattern? Are there stages at which children say that it is absolutely wrong to steal the drug and stages at which it may be acceptable with qualifications? Kohlberg answered these questions by identifying three levels of progressive moral reasoning, each with two stages. Descriptions follow. See Table 9.2, page 217, for a summary.

Level 1: Preconventional Moral Reasoning

This level of moral reasoning conforms closely to Piaget's stage of moral realism and is typical of young preoperational children. Because of their egocentricity, or their focus on their own interests to the exclusion of the interests of others, young children's judgment of right and wrong is based on doing what is good for them. And what is good for them is primarily avoiding punishment. Young children acquiesce to the power of the rule-givers if they fear the consequences; if they do not fear the consequences, their behavior is likely to be relatively uncontrolled by moral considerations. In response to the drug story above, children at Level 1 are likely to say that it is wrong to steal the drug because you might get caught (or, alternatively, that it is OK to steal the drug if you think you can get away with it).

Preconventional moral reasoning is divided into two stages.

Stage 1: Punishment–Obedience Orientation.

Stage 1 individuals are limited in their own actions only by the fear of punishment. They do not act out of a sense of duty or because of personal values or ideals. They defer to power because to do otherwise is to risk being punished. Of course, when the likelihood of punishment is perceived to be slight, Stage 1 individuals will do most anything that pleases them.

In the normal course of development, most young children go through this stage. However, without appropriate role models and socializing agents, some children may never leave this stage. Their behavior will remain relatively uncontrolled except by the threat, and subsequent realization, of severe punishment. They will continue to believe that "good" means what you can get away with and "bad" means what you cannot get away with. They will lack any moral criteria for judging "right" and "wrong."

Stage 2: Personal-Reward Orientation.   At this slightly more advanced, preconventional stage, there emerges some limited sense of reciprocity, as in "You scratch my back and I'll scratch yours." Good is still defined as "what's good for me," which is taken to mean personal need satisfaction. But morality at this stage has become a very practical morality, a kind of "honor among thieves." In other words, a Stage 2 individual might try to strike up some sort of a deal with the druggist or else make a deal with a law enforcement officer to "look the other way" while he or she steals the drug. While this is a perfectly natural stage for children to pass through, those who never progress beyond it may well choose to spend their lives engaged in organized crime or in a career that is considered to be without "scruples."

Level 2: Conventional Moral Reasoning

At this level, moral reasoning is reasoning with a focus on the social perspective in that the child takes into consideration the viewpoints of others. The result is doing what is expected of her, doing her duty, doing what will please other people, and consequently gaining social acceptance. Conventional morality is an adherence to traditional values, to law and order, to loyalty to others and to society. This level corresponds roughly to Piaget's stage of mutuality and is characteristic of children in the upper elementary and middle grades but, for many people, represents the limit of their moral development.

In the conventional stage, individuals look beyond personal benefits and consider the effects of their actions on other people. Approval for one's beliefs and actions is sought and laws are considered to be of paramount importance.

Stage 3: Good-Person Orientation.   In this first conventional stage, the emphasis is on (1) being nice, (2) being approved of, (3) pleasing others, (4) performing "appropriate" behavior, (5) fulfilling mutual expectations, and (6) conforming. Trust and loyalty are important virtues, and the "golden rule" is observed. In response to the drug story, the Stage 3 individual would say that it is all right for the man to steal the drug because he is trying to help his wife. In other words, his intention is honorable, and to the Stage 3 moral reasoner, intentions are of great importance. Stealing the drug, therefore, is justified by the man's good intentions based on loyalty to his loved ones.

Stage 4: Law-and-Order Orientation.   In this second conventional stage, morality is oriented toward (1) respecting authority, (2) doing one's duty, and (3) maintaining the social order for its own sake. The concern enlarges to an awareness of the society's values, national values, and religious values that extends beyond the immediate primary groups of family and friends. However, there remains a tendency toward conformity along with a sense of duty and a belief in "doing the right thing." Laws and rules are to be upheld in order to fulfill one's responsibility to keep the system as a whole going. In response to the drug problem posed on page 215, law-and-order moralists would say that stealing the drug is wrong under any circumstances because it is wrong to steal.

Level 3: Postconventional Moral Reasoning

This third and highest level features a more abstract, principled, and individual view of rules and morals, not attained until the high-school years and even then not attained by many. It corresponds to Piaget's stage of autonomy. Moral principles are defined independently of either authority or group identification conditions, as in the preceding two levels. A Level 3 moral reasoner might say that stealing the unaffordable drug to cure one's dying wife is not wrong as long as the man is willing to suffer the consequences of his act and go to jail. However, the Level 3 person would also see a need to protect the right of the druggist, and so a better solution might be gained through legal recourse.

Stage 5: Social-Contract Orientation.   The belief here is that while laws are necessary, they are relative rather than absolute. Laws are perceived to reflect a social consensus or agreement among people to maintain social standards and to protect individual rights. Because laws are consensual rather than handed down, they may be changed democratically if they are no longer meeting society's needs. In other words, Stage 5 moralists believe that laws are not "carved in stone" but serve to protect individual rights in the society. The purpose of laws is to enable people to live in harmony and maintain a sense of community while not transcending such individual liberties as are set

Table 9.2 🍎 Kohlberg's Stages of Moral Reasoning

Level 1: Preconventional Moral Reasoning

Basis for judgment: rules and personal needs.

Stage 1: Punishment–Obedience Orientation
Rules are obeyed to avoid punishment. Actions are judged "good" or "bad" by their physical consequences.

Stage 2: Personal-Reward Orientation
"Right" and "wrong" are determined by personal needs. Favors are paid back as in "you do something good for me and I'll do something good for you."

Level 2: Conventional Moral Reasoning

Basis for judgment: traditional values, approval of others, loyalty, expectations, laws of society.

Stage 3: Good-Person Orientation
"Good" is determined by what is approved of by or pleases others.

Stage 4: Law-and-Order Orientation
Laws are absolute. Social order and authority must be respected and maintained.

Level 3: Postconventional Moral Reasoning

Basis for judgment: social standards, individual rights, conscience, human dignity.

Stage 5: Social-Contract Orientation
"Good" is determined by socially agreed upon and mutually acceptable standards of individual rights.

Stage 6: Universal-Ethical-Principle Orientation
"Good" is a matter of universal standards, based on abstract concepts of human dignity, justice, and fairness.

SOURCE: Adapted from Kohlberg, L. (1975). The cognitive–developmental approach to moral education. *Phi Beta Kappan, 56,* 671.

forth in the Bill of Rights of the U.S. Constitution. When a law is unjust, it is changed or discarded in order to help regulate society better. Laws serve people, rather than vice versa, and must not interfere with higher-order rights such as individual liberties.

Stage 6: Universal-Ethical-Principle Orientation.   Those few persons who reach this stage (epitomized by Jesus, Gandhi, and Martin Luther King, Jr.) have a clear vision of abstract moral principles like justice and fairness. They not only teach these principles to others but sacrifice their lives, if necessary, to stand up for them. Right is defined not by convenience or by mutual consent but by universal standards of justice. Right is abstract and ethical (such as the dignity of human beings) rather than concrete and moralistic. The right to equality is a major belief.

Stage-specific responses to the resolution of another moral dilemma are shown in Box 9.3.

Enhancing Moral Development

Distribution of Stages.   As a result of normal socialization and development, preconventional moral reasoning (Level 1) characterizes almost all children at age 7, about a quarter of all 13-year-olds, and slightly less than a quarter of all 16-year-olds. Conventional moral reasoning (Level 2) characterizes only a small number of 7-year-olds, but more than half of all 13- and 16-year-olds. Postconventional moral reasoning (Level 3) is virtually unseen among 7-year-olds, while it characterizes about one quarter of all 16-year-olds. Thus, 7-year-olds are primarily preconventional, while about half of 13- and 16-year-olds are conventional and the remaining half are split between preconventional and postconventional. This is true for children not only in the United States but in such diverse places as a Malaysian aboriginal village, a Turkish city and village, a Mexican city, and a Mayan village (Turiel, 1973). Can this be changed?

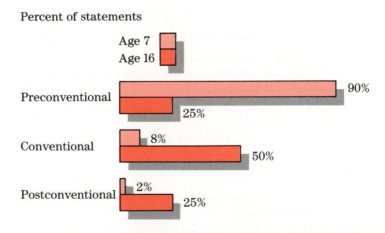

Training.   Schlaefli, Rest, and Thoma (1985) examined 55 studies that attempted to enhance moral development through training. These studies used a test called the *Defining Issues Test*, or DIT, in which students were given moral dilemmas to resolve. Instead of making up their own answers, they were required to choose given answers that were representative of the different stages of moral reasoning. Test-takers were given a score that placed them on the moral reasoning scale somewhere between the low end (preconventional or personal-consequences reasoning) and the high end (postconventional or principled reasoning).

Studies using the DIT have shown that (1) older people score higher than younger ones, (2) better-educated people score higher than less-well-educated people, (3) children of parents who use democratic yet warm childrearing practices score higher than children of parents who use dictatorial childrearing practices, (4) children of parents who practice rational behavior themselves score higher than children of parents who do not, and (5) there are no differences between major religious groups in level of moral reasoning.

Box 9.3

🍎

Resolving a Moral Dilemma

A firefighter in the midst of fighting a fire in an occupied building hears that his own house is on fire. Should the firefighter leave his post to help his own family members who may be in danger, or should he stay where he is and help others?

Level 1: Preconventional

Stage 1: *Punishment-obedience orientation*: The firefighter should stay, or else he'll be punished or fired by the head of the fire department.

Stage 2: *Personal-reward orientation*: The firefighter should go to his own family, or else he'll never stop worrying about what's happened to them.

Level 2: Conventional

Stage 3: *Good-person orientation*: He had better go to his own family because good parents care about their families.

Stage 4: *Law-and-order orientation*: He should stay where he is because that's exactly what the rules say he should do.

Level 3: Postconventional

Stage 5: *Social-contract orientation*: He probably should stay because that's what he agreed to do, but if he hears that his family is in real danger, that might justify his leaving.

Stage 6: *Universal-ethical-principle orientation*: He should stay because it is right and ethical to put the welfare of the many above that of the few—regardless of who they are. The people he is helping are someone's family members too, and he is bound to take care of them. To do less would be to sacrifice self-respect.

In the studies reviewed, when students of junior and senior high-school age discussed the moral dilemmas and their resolutions in a supervised class setting, the tendency to use principled reasoning increased significantly in comparison to that of students not participating in these discussion sessions. According to Oser (1986), what makes these discussions of morality effective in raising the level of moral reasoning is that they provide students with an opportunity (1) to focus on moral conflict in an effort to stimulate higher moral thought, (2) to analyze their own moral beliefs and reasoning, (3) to undertake moral role-playing and experience moral empathy, (4) to understand shared norms and the meaning of community, and (5) to directly consider moral action in relation to moral choice.

Classroom Applications.   Geiger and Turiel (1983) have found that students who score especially low in moral judgment are particularly likely to exhibit disruptive behavior in the school setting. For this reason, teachers should be motivated to stimulate moral growth and encourage moral development in their students. Along with this, teachers should help their students attain related affective goals, such as interpersonal skillfulness, self-discipline, independence, and enthusiasm for learning. Developing these skills will enable students to participate cooperatively and enthusiastically in classroom life. To teachers, having their students develop good moral behavior in the classroom should be every bit as important as having them acquire knowledge, so stimulating personal growth among students is as significant a classroom goal as teaching them facts and concepts.

How can teachers help students grow morally and emotionally? The answer lies in formal and informal efforts at *affective education*. Eisman (1981) suggests having *classroom discussions* of the kinds of *dilemmas* students are encountering in their lives, such as sibling rivalry, teasing, and prejudice among elementary grade students and cheating, drinking and drugs, conformity, and unpopularity among high-school students. For teachers carrying out such discussions, Eisman (1981) further suggests the following:

- Encourage students to see others' perspectives (perhaps by switching roles).
- Help students connect values and actions (and see inconsistencies where they arise).
- Make sure students are listening to one another (by having them acknowledge what others are saying).

These sound like the advanced stages described by Selman on pages 213–214.

It is essential that the teacher allow students to remain silent, if they so choose, and protect their right to privacy. It is also important that students learn to distinguish between administrative rules, such as coming to class on time, and more basic, moral rules, such as respecting another person's right to privacy.

Another classroom approach is for teachers to recognize the level or stage of moral reasoning of their students from a discussion of in-school problems (for example, "What was the worst thing that happened in school this week?") and then present conflicting arguments representative of the next higher stage. This technique is called *plus-one matching* (Lickona, 1977; Lockwood, 1978) and is based on the premise that people cannot skip a stage in their moral development. Therefore, by provoking disequilibrium and forcing change, the teacher can enhance a person's moral development from one stage to the next.

Alternatively, teachers may choose simply to guide a discussion of students' moral issues and record on the blackboard the reasons students give for behaving as they did. Students can then be called on to provide illustrations of the various stages of moral reasoning. A sample classroom activity for moral development is shown in Box 9.4.

Erikson's Stages of Psychosocial Development

Erik Erikson was particularly interested in how people developed their *ego identity* or their sense of who they really are. He saw ego identity as the essence of a person's

---

Box 9.4

A Sample Activity for Stimulating Moral Development

How do you make a decision when two of your values, say, honesty and loyalty, come into conflict? Consider the two stories below. For each one, decide what action you would take and what the consequences of this action are likely to be. (Also consider alternative actions and their consequences.) Do you feel good about the action you have chosen? Have you ever been in this situation or one like it before? What did you actually do then?

Bobby is taking a final in educational psychology. He has studied for the test but not as much as he knows he should have. When Bobby looks at the test questions he realizes that he is not adequately prepared. Bobby knows he needs a B in the final to get a C in the course, and he becomes panicky. If Bobby doesn't get at least a C, he'll have to take the course over in the summer and won't be able to work as a camp counselor.

Bobby has never cheated before, although he knows that it is a common practice among other students. He is sitting next to someone who always gets high grades, and the teacher is busy reading a magazine. Bobby does not like the idea of cheating, but he also does not like the idea of repeating the course.

Should Bobby cheat this one time or not? Why? Are there times when cheating is justified? Why or why not?

Sandy's class is having a big end-of-school party and she is dying to go. The party is only two weeks away and Sandy does not yet have a date. Then Drew calls and asks Sandy to go to the party, and even though Sandy doesn't really like Drew that much, she accepts. Two days later Robin, the guy Sandy really likes, calls and asks Sandy to go to the party. Sandy really wants to go with Robin and is excited that Robin called, but she doesn't know what to say. Sandy promises to call Robin back in an hour.

Should Sandy go with Drew because she already said she would, even though she's not crazy about Drew? Why? Or should Sandy break the date with Drew and go with Robin, the one she really likes? Why?

individuality, within the context of society and the demands of the culture. His view was that a person's identity is formed as the result of a series of developmental crises that occur naturally within the social environment at different stages of life. In dealing with each of these crises and attempting to master the challenges that they pose, individuals either grow toward greater *self-actualization* (meaning greater mastery, unity of personality, and accuracy of perception) or regress toward a more infantile resolution (Erikson, 1968).

Crisis, to Erikson, represented "a turning point or a crucial period of increased vulnerability and heightened potential" (Erikson, 1968, p. 96) rather than a threat or catastrophe. Each crisis, in each stage, represented an opportunity to develop another aspect of one's sense of self or identity in either a healthy or an unhealthy way. It is to each of these eight stages (Erikson, 1963, 1968) that the discussion now turns. (The desire for self-actualization as a motivational force will be encountered again in Chapter 12.)

Infancy: Trust Versus Mistrust

Infancy is a time of dependency on others, particularly on one's mother, for the satisfaction of basic needs. Food, shelter, security, and care cannot be provided by oneself but must be provided by another person. When these basic needs are fulfilled, infants learn to trust others as well as developing a fundamental sense of their own trustworthiness. When there is an estrangement or a distance between parent and child such that basic needs are not adequately met, infants develop a sense of mistrust, often accompanied by a tendency to withdraw into themselves. Hence, we can "regard basic trust as the cornerstone of a vital personality" (Erikson, 1968, p. 97).

It is true that newborns live through their mouths. To live, therefore, they must be met by the coordinated ability and intention of their mothers to feed them. But the infant's need to incorporate or take into itself soon extends to sensory and social stimuli as well. It is through such receiving and accepting that human infants first encounter their culture. It is also by "getting what is given" that a person develops the inclination to be a giving person. Erikson (1968) refers to the relationship between mother and infant as mutuality (a term already introduced by Piaget).

In the later part of infancy, the need to incorporate manifests itself as taking and holding onto things. As the mother begins to withdraw as part of weaning and becomes less involved in child care, the infant may feel abandoned. This feeling may produce a sense of mistrust. It is at this point that young children must begin to learn to depend on or trust themselves. Although the quantity of maternal care may be reduced, if the quality is maintained, the sense of trust is likely to survive this crisis.

Traditional child care, Erikson (1968) believes, is likely to produce the least conflict and hence the most trust. And with trust comes a gain in psychosocial strength along with the origin of later feelings of faith, hope, and optimism.

The Toddler: Autonomy Versus Shame and Doubt

As children grow, their needs grow too, along with new possibilities for satisfaction and frustration. At the same time, two other factors in the lives of children increase: the number and kind of people to whom they can respond, and their capacities and skills for dealing with their physical and social environment. *It is the experience with new encounters and the necessity to manage them, coupled with the sense of having to do it more and more by oneself, that evokes the developmental crisis of each period.* At this stage of life, the need to successfully manage the combined acts of holding on and letting go, associated with such tasks as toilet training and self-control, are critical to the child's development of an autonomous or independent will.

It is during the toddler period that children learn to delineate their world into "me" and "you," and "mine" and "yours." According to Erikson (1968, p. 109), "the matter of mutual regulation between adult and child now faces its severest test." If the parent is

Play satisfies impulses to explore and satisfies the child's growing curiosity. The development of initiative is the result.

overcontrolling, overdemanding, or overprotective, the child will be faced with defeat—represented by feelings of doubt and shame. The creation of these feelings now is often accompanied in later life by an excessive degree of conscience or compulsiveness. If the child is allowed to experience a sense of self-control without loss of self-esteem, feelings of free will or autonomy will be the positive result. The child will become convinced that she is a person in her own right. However, positive resolution at this stage, as at all others, presupposes positive resolution at all preceding stages. Hence, trust is a prerequisite for the development of autonomy or free will.

Early Childhood: Initiative Versus Guilt

Three relevant developments occur in early childhood that support the potential emergence of a realistic sense of ambition and purpose in the young child. These are (1) the opportunity for greater freedom of movement; (2) the development of language, making it possible for the child to question; and (3) an expanding of imagination and dreams (Erikson, 1968, p. 115). Out of this develops the anticipation of adult roles and the possibility of a sense of initiative, a vitality to explore and try new things. The child's learning leads away from the child's own limitations and into his or her future possibilities.

This is the stage of play and curiosity, of powerful impulses to explore and express. If these impulses are thwarted, frustrated, or condemned by adults, the result will be guilt—the pangs of conscience and of self-condemnation. And the morality of guilt can, according to Erikson (1968, p. 119), "become synonymous with vindictiveness and with the suppression of others" when it grows out of experiences with a parent who tries to get away with the very transgressions the child has been told are unacceptable. In later life, the absence of initiative will be represented by self-restriction and self-denial.

The necessary adult role is to offer children of this age models for action by example. Successful models offer their children appropriate avenues for exploration and mastery rather than providing them with an endless stream of "don'ts." The heroes of children's fantasies must come gradually to be replaced by realistic role models such as a parent or teacher who can function more like a companion than an overseer. Only then can the child establish the "steadily growing conviction, undaunted by guilt, that 'I am what I can imagine I will be'" (Erikson, 1968, p. 122). Models and their effects will be encountered again in Chapter 11.

School Age: Industry Versus Inferiority

When children enter elementary school, they are usually ready to learn to perform, to share obligations, and to apply discipline. They are also usually ready to work cooperatively, to share, and to imitate. Each child, in sum, is ready to make things and to make them well, to become a worker, to develop what Erikson (1968) has called a sense of industry. At this age, children seek to win recognition by producing things and accomplishing things.

If a child (1) is not prepared by family life to take on the responsibility of productiveness, (2) still wants to be a "baby," or (3) has had his wish and will to learn thwarted by criticism and lack of opportunity, then a sense of inferiority or unworthiness will develop at this stage. This is the feeling that one will never be any good. It is an important time for teachers to emphasize what children can do rather than what they cannot do, to help them avoid or overcome this feeling.

The child's optimal environment at this stage is one that features neither the extreme of restraint and the strict imposition of duty nor the extreme of autonomy and its total lack of structure. In other words, for industriousness to develop as part of a child's identity, the environment must fall somewhere in between total work and total play. Given the guided opportunity for learning the necessary skills to function in a school setting, a child can come to believe that "I am what I can learn to make work" (Erikson, 1968, p. 127).

Adolescence: Identity Versus Confusion

All of preceding development seems to coalesce in the period of adolescence. If everything has gone well thus far, adolescents will possess (1) trust in themselves and in others, (2) a sense of autonomy or free will in choosing their life directions, (3) the initiative and imagination to focus on what they might become, and (4) the industry to work in order to meet their goals. Taken together, these qualities create the potential for a sense of identity if they are present in an environment where expression is permitted, choices are available, and recognition and acceptance are forthcoming. Without these qualities or the opportunity to express them, the question of identity or "who I am" will become cloudy and confused.

Identity represents the image persons have of who they are, defined in terms of their abilities, likes and dislikes, hopes and expectations. Career choices, sexual choices, and beliefs about the surrounding world all grow out of the sense of identity.

How confident or sure are adolescents of their identity, or, alternatively, how confused are they? Some, though not many, according to Marcia (1980), have reached a state of *identity achievement*. They have experimented and explored and know, at least for now, what they want out of life. They have set their goals and have a plan for achieving them. Sometime later in life there may be detours or reversals, but at this point they have made some well-thought-out choices.

Other adolescents have chosen *identity foreclosure*. Rather than exploring the possibilities, they have simply chosen a predetermined path — often the career of a parent — and are committed to that choice. They have taken on or borrowed an identity and may experience much confusion in the future if that identity does not work.

Then there are many adolescents who experience *identity diffusion*. Some have thought about their future but reached no conclusion; others have avoided making choices at all. These are the confused ones. Should I go to college or to work? What should I major in? What school should I go to? Should I get married or stay single? They have many questions and few answers.

Finally, some adolescents are in a state of *moratorium*. They have simply postponed their decisions to a later time. They may be leaning in a certain direction, but they are not ready to firm up that choice.

How can the problems of adolescence be dealt with in oneself, in one's children, and in the students one teaches? As in many of the preceding stages, a balance must be struck between too little freedom and too much freedom, too much structure and too little structure. Neither total control nor total autonomy is conducive to resolving the identity crisis of adolescence. External control and externally imposed structure must be gradually decreased so that adolescents can set their own standards based on who they are. But adults must still help provide adolescents with some sense of limits and support for efforts gone awry as the process of identity formation begins to gel. The adolescents' transition to adulthood must be made possible, yet neither the adolescents nor their parents should expect their childhood to be instantaneously and totally abandoned.

A case study of an adolescent in crisis appears in Box 9.5.

Young Adulthood: Intimacy Versus Isolation

Intimacy represents a fusing of identities, a joining together or sharing by two people. It goes beyond sexual intimacy, because it includes sharing in many regards — combining sexual intimacy with friendship. Those choosing impersonal or highly stereotyped interpersonal relationships over genuine sharing develop or retain a deep sense of isolation or separation.

Adolescence is the period when previous developments are expected to coalesce. Sometimes, in an effort to develop a separate identity, teenagers take on highly distinctive styles of appearance and behavior.

Shared intimacy defines the meaning of love, according to Erikson (1968), and the result is shared identity between two people. Where individual identities have not yet developed, love is impossible. People who attain the stage of intimacy together believe that "we are what we love" (Erikson, 1968, p. 138).

Adulthood: Generativity Versus Stagnation

Generativity refers to a "concern for establishing and guiding the next generation" (Erikson, 1968, p. 138). It represents the parenting not only of children but of ideas. Its byproduct is productivity and the capability to live a satisfying and useful life. A lack of

---

Box 9.5

Leaving Our Parents' World: The Case of Ranny

Ranny replaced her alcoholic, sexually promiscuous mother as the responsible one in the family. She was her highly moral father's favorite, and before she left for college, they had long intellectual discussions.

During her first year in college, Ranny was a serious, dedicated science student. The next year, she acquired a reputation as a brilliant but erratic student, one who almost failed courses but always rescued herself at the last moment. She was known as a drinking "party girl" who dated only athletes; she pretended to be promiscuous, although she graduated still a virgin. Finally, in her senior year, Ranny became a serious student in a useful but not especially intellectual field. And she kept her fun-loving personality.

During her first year in college, Ranny slavishly imitated her father. In the next few years, she blindly mimicked her mother by living out a "party" life. But throughout she remained true to some inner voice and pulled it all together in her final year.

We form our adult consciousness slowly during these years. Step by step we abandon our parents as models and begin to construct our own identities. By about age 22 we have to leave the half-child, half-adult world in which we can be anyone and settle into being someone. Each time we replace a piece of childhood consciousness with adult consciousness, we become our own someone. The process is painful but also exciting and rewarding.

SOURCE: Gould, R. L. (1978). *Transformations: Growth and change in adult life* (pp. 68–69). New York: Simon & Schuster.

generativity yields boredom, dissatisfaction, even apathy, and a pervading sense of stagnation. Adults who are able to attain a sense of generativity through family and career represent caring, self-fulfilled, and contributing members of society.

Old Age: Integrity Versus Despair

In accepting oneself, one's life as it has been lived, and those people who have played a significant role in it, one develops a sense of integrity, of wholeness. Self-acceptance carries with it an acceptance of one's fate, of one's lifestyle and life cycle, and of the people and institutions of one's world. Those who lack this self-acceptance or acceptance of old

Old age has the potential to bring happiness and satisfaction as a result of being able to accept oneself and the life that one has led.

age and its circumstances experience disgust and a sense of despair. It is often hidden behind cynicism, hostility, displeasure, and contemptuousness.

Erikson (1968) calls the strength born of integrity "wisdom." And it manifests itself at this stage by the belief that "I am what I am."

Erikson's eight stages are summarized in Table 9.3.

Applying Erikson in the Classroom

Teachers need to create classroom environments that relate to the psychosocial stage of their students. This means helping preschoolers build initiative; helping elementary and middle schoolers build identity; and helping adult, returning students build generativity. Some specific suggestions for how to accomplish this are given in Box 9.6.

Table 9.3 🍎 Erikson's Stages of Psychosocial Development

Psychosocial Stage	Period of Life	Characteristics
Trust vs. Mistrust	Infancy	Fulfillment of basic needs leads to trust in oneself and others, along with a sense of faith and hope, rather than mistrust.
Autonomy vs. Shame	Toddlerhood	Opportunity for self-control leads to a sense of being autonomous rather than doubting one's selfhood.
Initiative vs. Guilt	Early Childhood	Opportunity to play and explore leads to learning initiative within limits rather than feeling guilty about one's behavior.
Industry vs. Inferiority	School Age	Opportunity to perform and succeed at "work" tasks yields a sense of oneself as industrious, not inferior.
Identity vs. Confusion	Adolescence	Opportunity for expression, choice, and acceptance leads to the development of a sense of who one is rather than to confusion over identity.
Intimacy vs. Isolation	Young Adulthood	Accepting the opportunity for openness and sharing with others results in intimacy and love rather than separation and isolation.
Generativity vs. Stagnation	Adulthood	Choosing to become the parent of children or the producer of a career effort represents the generative sense; to do otherwise is to stagnate.
Integrity vs. Despair	Old Age	Accepting oneself and one's life gives a sense of wholeness and completion rather than of disgust and despair.

SOURCE: Adapted from Erikson, E. H. (1968). *Identity: Youth and crisis*. New York: Norton.

Box 9.6

Helping to Build Initiative, Industry, Identity, and Generativity

Building Initiative in Preschool

- Let children make choices for themselves (especially of learning activities they want to engage in).
- Help children succeed at the activities they choose.
- Create activities that enable children to play different roles.
- Don't use adult standards to evaluate what children do.
- Be supportive of what children try to do even if it does not come out perfectly.
- Make children take responsibility for some aspect of their learning and play environment.

Building Industry in Elementary and Middle School

- Increase the amount of responsibility that students must take for their learning and play environment.
- Expose students to realistic occupational models.
- Identify positive aspects of the performance of each student.
- Provide students with encouragement regarding their ability to succeed.
- Give recognition for jobs well done.

Building Identity in High School

- Create a climate of trust and acceptance.
- Help students become aware of their values.
- Help students build their self-concepts.
- Give students the opportunity to set goals.
- Build choices for students into the curriculum.
- Exhibit patience and understanding when dealing with behavior.

Building Generativity in Returning Students

- Show respect for the student's "adultness."
- Build upon the many experiences adult students have already had.
- Recognize the other skills adults bring to the classroom.
- Relate to the adult student as a person.
- Help the adult student feel comfortable in the classroom context.
- Give the adult the opportunity to make a productive contribution.

Summary of Main Points

1. Affective development refers to the development of people's *social* and *emotional* side, their beliefs, attitudes and values. Piaget's conception of affective development focuses on how children learn to reason morally, or on their development of *moral judgment*.

2. Piaget presented children with moral choices that reflected different orientations to the concepts of *justice* and *punishment* and then examined their responses. He also questioned children about the rules of the game of marbles. His results led him to identify stages of development.

3. Piaget called the first stage *moral realism*, which is characterized by a belief in *objective responsibility*. This means believing (a) that one must take responsibility for one's transgressions, regardless of the intentions behind them, and (b) that the magnitude of the punishment should fit the magnitude of the crime. For example, a child who accidentally breaks five teacups is more culpable and deserves a stiffer punishment than a child who breaks only one cup while engaged in the act of theft. So too with lying: the more outrageous the lie, the worse it is, irrespective of the liar's intentions.

4. In the stage of moral realism, children evaluate outcomes in terms of the material result rather than the motive. Evaluation results in *expiatory punishment*, or penance paid for wrongdoing, and *retributive justice*, or "an eye for an eye and a tooth for a tooth." It is, therefore, *adult restraint* that controls children's behavior in this stage.

5. The second stage is *mutuality* or "doing unto others as you would have them do unto you." In the game of marbles mutuality means shared rules that are enforced by mutual consent; in judging wrongdoing it means *distributive justice* or treating everyone the same (*equality*). In lying, as in other transgressions, the intentions behind the act are taken into account; in fixing the punishment, the child at this stage applies the principle of *reciprocity*, meaning the punishment should fit the spirit of the crime.

6. In the third stage, *autonomy*, the more abstract notion of *equity* replaces the peer-imposed constraint of equality as the basis for judgment. Equity means judging everyone on an individual basis as a function of circumstances and reacting against social injustice. This may mean accepting some behaviors from some people, based on their unique unmet needs, but not from others.

7. Kohlberg elaborated on Piaget, converting his stages into levels — preconventional, conventional, postconventional — and dividing each level into two stages of *moral reasoning*. He detected these stages by posing *moral dilemmas*, or situations in which children must choose between undesirable alternatives (for example, letting a loved one die versus stealing to save her), and examining their responses.

8. The preconventional level is akin to moral realism, wherein children base their judgment of what is "wrong" on what they will get punished for doing (in *Stage 1*, the *punishment–obedience orientation*) and what is "right" on what is materially good for them (*Stage 2, personal-reward orientation*).

9. In Level 2, or conventional moral reasoning, the emphasis is on doing one's duty — that which is expected or that which will please other people (*Stage 3, good-person*

orientation) — or on respecting authority and maintaining the social order for its own sake (*Stage 4*, *law-and-order orientation*).

10. In Level 3, or postconventional moral reasoning, laws are taken as relative, reflecting a social consensus to maintain social standards and protect individual rights (*Stage 5*, *social-contract orientation*) or as abstract, ethical principles, defined not so much by mutual consent as by "conscience" (*Stage 6*, *universal-ethical-principle orientation*).

11. While the sequence of stages has been found to occur in many, diverse cultures, the transition from stage to stage is far from complete, with twice as many people ending up with conventional morality as with either the pre- or the postconventional levels. Moral development has been shown to relate to age, education level, and parents' childrearing practices but not to religious affiliation.

12. Discussions of moral dilemmas in junior and senior high-school classrooms have been found to stimulate moral thought and produce moral empathy. Ignoring moral development may be the same as ignoring disruptive behavior. Classroom discussions of relevant issues are encouraged, to help students exchange perspectives, connect values and actions, and learn to listen to one another. Teachers can help by presenting conflicting arguments at the next higher stage of moral reasoning, a technique called *plus-one matching*.

13. Erikson proposed eight stages of *psychosocial development* covering the entire life span. In each stage, a naturally occurring *life crisis* is resolved in a way that contributes to the development of *ego identity* or a person's sense of what he or she really is. Each crisis represents an opportunity to develop additional positive or negative aspects of one's sense of self or identity.

14. In *infancy*, the crisis or vulnerability is over satisfaction of one's basic needs, such as food, shelter, and security. Need fulfillment is accompanied by a sense of *trust* in others as well as in oneself. This is the cornerstone of a vital personality since it is the basis for subsequent faith, hope, and optimism. Weaning too soon or too late provokes instead a sense of *mistrust*.

15. The *toddler* faces a crisis over who is in control, or mutual regulation between child and parent, particularly as regards toilet training. The toddler who is enabled to experience a sense of self-control without loss of self-esteem has resolved the crisis by developing *autonomy*, while overdemanding or overprotective parents will cause the child to feel *shame and doubt*.

16. The preschoolers of *early childhood* must learn a realistic sense of purpose and ambition through play and curiosity, exploration and expression. In so doing, they develop *initiative*. Frustration and condemnation by adults provokes a sense of *guilt*. Children must learn to believe that they can be what they imagine themselves to be.

17. *School age* brings on the need to perform, to share obligations, and to apply discipline. Being provided with both the guided opportunity and the stimulus to be productive yields a sense of *industry*, a belief that one can learn to make things work, while too much restraint or too little structure results in a sense of *inferiority*.

18. In *adolescence*, all preceding development seems to coalesce. If all has gone well thus far and choices are available and expression has been encouraged, a sense of *identity*, rather than *confusion*, will result.

19. Optimally, *identity achievement* or knowing what you want out of life will develop — as opposed to *identity foreclosure* (automatically following a prescribed plan), *identity diffusion* (not knowing what you want to do), or *moratorium* (postponing your decisions). External control must be gradually reduced so that adolescents can experience the freedom necessary to develop a sense of self.

20. In *young adulthood*, choosing to share yields *intimacy*, while choosing impersonal or highly stereotyped relationships yields *isolation*.

21. In *adulthood*, the choice is between parenting, in the sense of family and of ideas, which yields *generativity*, and following a narrower, more fixed path into *stagnation*.

22. Finally, *old age* offers the choice between self-acceptance or *integrity* and disgust or *despair*.

Suggested Resources

Erikson, E. H. (1968). *Identity: Youth and crisis*. New York: Norton.

Gould, R. L. (1978). *Transformations: Growth and change in adult life*. New York: Simon & Schuster.

Howe, L. W., & Howe, M. M. (1975). *Personalizing education: Values clarification and beyond*. New York: Hart.

Piaget, J. (1965). *The moral judgment of the child*. New York: Free Press. (Original work published 1932)

Purpel, D., & Ryan, K. (Eds.). (1976). *Moral education . . . it comes with the territory*. Berkeley, CA: McCutchan.

Reimer, J., Paolitto, D. P., & Hersh, R. M. (1983). *Promoting moral development: From Piaget to Kohlberg* (2nd ed.). New York: Longman.

Chapter
10

Group Processes

Objectives

1. Describe a model of group dynamics to explain group processes in the classroom.
2. Describe the influence of teacher expectations on student expectations, called the self-fulfilling prophecy, and how these expectations are communicated.
3. Describe what group norms are and how they influence individual behavior.
4. Describe the effect of normative goal structures — cooperation, competition, and individualism — on student performance and explain how to implement these goal structures.
5. Identify different bases for leadership and how to use different leadership styles and techniques for effective classroom management.
6. Describe the effects that the communicator, the content of the communication, audience predisposition, and audience response have on the influence of the communication.
7. Identify effective and congruent communication skills.
8. Describe factors that make groups attractive to their members and outcomes or benefits that result from attractive groups.
9. Describe the components of an effective classroom climate.

Group Dynamics

A classroom is a social setting and a class is a social group insofar as the members of the class interact. Sometimes students in a class work interdependently: in pairs or small groups. Even when functioning as a single group, class members may interact with one another through discussions or various kinds of informal behavior (for example, passing notes). And, of course, they often interact with the teacher.

Classmates also share some common goals, such as learning (or perhaps just surviving), as well as developing their own sense of self and having a satisfying—and we hope enjoyable—time.

The interplay or interaction between the characteristics of the members of a group (such as expectations) and the characteristics of the group as a whole (such as norms or rules of conduct) produces various group processes (for example, development, communication, leadership, and conflict). These processes, in turn, produce various group outcomes (say, friendship, influence, and climate; Jewell & Reitz, 1981). This arrangement of interdependent parts, shown in Figure 10.1, represents a model of group dynamics.

For example, if class members have highly positive *expectations* about the experiences they will have in a class, and the *norms* or rules of the class are ones that permit a lot of freedom and interaction between class members, then the process of *communication* in the class is likely to be facilitated. This will tend to produce considerable *friendship* between class members and a positive *classroom climate*.

Of course, in a classroom, all of the participants are not equally influential. The teacher's role is more central than that of any individual student. Amidon and Hunter (1966) estimate that teachers talk about 70 percent of the time. They also make the rules. That is why, in applying the group dynamics model to the classroom, we will give particular attention to the teacher's role and influence on the interaction process.

Figure 10.1 ● A Group Dynamics Model of the Classroom

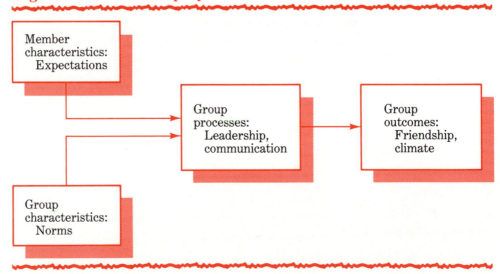

Expectations

Expectations are beliefs people hold about how they and others will behave in various situations and what the result of those behaviors will be. People hold many beliefs, but the beliefs they hold about themselves are particularly influential, and so will be a major topic of the next two chapters. In this chapter, the beliefs or expectations that teachers have for their students are examined, as well as how these beliefs can affect teachers' own behavior and what impact that behavior has on their students. These effects are discussed within the context of the classroom as a social community.

The Self-Fulfilling Prophecy.   The strong influence of one's expectations on one's own subsequent behavior as well as on the behavior of others is reflected in the concept of the *self-fulfilling prophecy*, first coined by Merton (1949). The self-fulfilling prophecy says that what someone expects (or prophesies) to happen will indeed come to pass. People's expectations will be fulfilled merely because they believe that they will. If you believe you are smart, you will act smart, and others will perceive you, based on how you have acted, to be smart. If you believe someone else is smart, you will probably, though unconsciously, treat him as if he were smart; he, in turn, will unconsciously "read the message you are sending him" — that he is smart — and will probably behave as if he were smart. Hence, your belief will provoke his behavior, which will reinforce your belief. This circular process is the self-fulfilling prophecy.

Rosenthal and Fode (1963) established that the self-fulfilling prophecy can apply to animals (see Box 1.1, page 11). In 1968 he and a colleague set out to prove that it can apply to schoolchildren (Rosenthal & Jacobson, 1968). Their study, *Pygmalion in the Classroom*, made reference to a story by George Bernard Shaw in which a plain girl from the slums of London is made into a "fair lady" by a doting professor. In the original Greek myth, Pygmalion, a beautiful statue, is transformed into a living woman through the belief of her adoring admirer, Galatea.

If a professor can turn a slum girl into a fair lady and an admirer can turn a statue into a live woman just by believing in them, then, thought Rosenthal and Jacobson, a teacher may be able to turn an ordinary student into a "bloomer." To test this hypothesis, they selected a group of students at random in a San Francisco school and told their teachers that these students were expected to bloom based on a test that had been administered at the start of the year. At the end of the year these students had, in fact, "bloomed" by exceeding normal expectations in tested reading, intelligence, and teachers' ratings of social and personal adjustment.

Although the results of this study were the subject of much controversy (see especially Thorndike, 1968), it has been generally concluded by Brophy and Good (1972) and others that the expectations of teachers influence the self-expectations of students and, hence, their performance in school. Schmuck and Schmuck (1988) refer to this effect as a *circular interpersonal process* and represent it as shown in Figure 10.2. It shows that your feelings and expectations about yourself and others influence your behavior, which, in turn, affects how others see themselves and you, and then affects how they behave toward you. Their behavior toward you then affects your feelings and expectations about yourself and others, making a big and never-ending circle.

Figure 10.2 🍎 The Circular Interpersonal Process

Adapted from Schmuck and Schmuck, 1988, pp. 83–85.

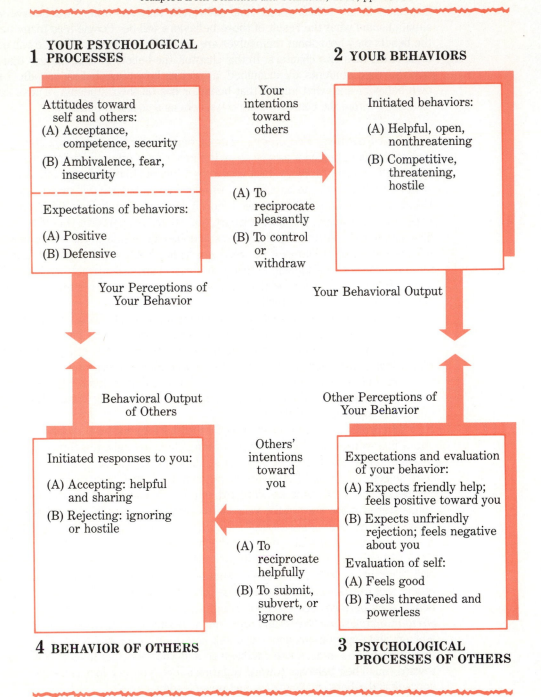

For example, suppose a new student feels fearful and insecure in the classroom because of her past school experiences with teachers who have threatened and embarrassed her. In her new classroom, she will expect the same thing to happen and it will make her defensive. As a result, she will withdraw from interactive situations or will behave in a hostile fashion. This behavior will cause teacher and classmates alike to begin to expect her to behave in an unfriendly manner, which will cause them to feel threatened by her and to form negative feelings toward her. These negative feelings will lead the teacher and many classmates to respond to her with hostility of their own. When she perceives their hostility, it will only intensify her original feelings of fear and insecurity and cause the whole cycle to continue, until and unless something can be changed. If the teacher does not perceive the student's withdrawn or hostile acts in a negative light, and so does not react to them negatively, it may be possible to alter the cycle.

Communicating Expectations.   How do teachers communicate their expectations to students? Good and Brophy (1984) found that students whom teachers perceived to have high ability received (1) more praise, (2) more help and coaching, and (3) more time in answering questions than those students believed to be of low ability. Teachers were more critical of those students believed to be of low ability, gave them little time to answer a question (since they believed they did not know the answer), and accepted poor-quality answers from them. Instead of waiting longer for the poorer students to answer questions, they waited longer for the better students to answer questions—reflecting greater patience and higher expectations. Similar findings were obtained by Rubovits and Maehr (1971).

Rosenthal (1973) described four ways teachers tend to communicate *positive* expectations for student performance:

1. Climate: warmth, attention, and emotional support
2. Feedback: encouragement and praise
3. Input: hints, rephrased questions, additional information
4. Output: encouragement and waiting for answer to be given

Cooper (1979) believed that teachers are concerned with the *performance* of high-expectation students but not of low-expectation students. With the latter group, they are concerned primarily with being able to *control* their behavior. Therefore, teachers praise and encourage high-expectation students, which enhances those students' performance and strengthens teachers' belief in their high expectations. Low-expectation students do not feel as personally in control of situations (which they are not, because teachers are trying to control them) so they perform less well, thereby strengthening their teachers' belief in the correctness of their low expectations. Hence, the circular interpersonal process is in operation again.

How can teachers break this negative circular interpersonal process in the classroom group? Some suggestions are given in Box 10.1. How can schools break the pattern? See Box 10.2 for one approach.

Box 10.1

Breaking the Cycle of Negative Expectations in the Classroom Group

When Carrying Out Discussion or Recitation Lessons

1. Purposely call on the students you believe are less able.
2. Give them more time to answer than other students.
3. Demand the same from them as from other students.
4. Give them as much help, praise, and encouragement as possible.

In Performance Situations

1. Have students estimate the performance expectations they have of themselves and of one another.
2. Have them compare actual performance to expected performance.
3. Talk to students about their self-image and performance expectations.
4. Give accurate and supportive performance feedback to all students.

In Classroom Interaction

1. Be friendly and warm to students regardless of your expectations for their academic performance.
2. Avoid criticism, rejection, and avoidance of those students from whom you expect less.

In General

1. Be aware of your feelings toward and expectations of each of your students.
2. Be aware of the messages you are sending out to individual students.

Norms

Norms are agreed-upon or shared beliefs by members of a group on such matters as (1) how to view the world around them, (2) what to think, (3) what to like or dislike, and (4) how to behave. Norms may be *formal* or *informal*, depending on whether or not they are carefully stated. In either case, they are adhered to by the group. They can be *static* or unchanging or, alternatively, *dynamic*. Some examples of the four types of classroom norms are given in Figure 10.3 on page 242.

Box 10.2

Ability Grouping and Expectations:
Galatea at Work in the School Community

Ability grouping or tracking is a commonly used school practice, particularly at the high-school level, where students are separated into homogeneous classes or levels based, presumably, on aptitude or prior academic performance. Since the circular interpersonal process tells us that others' evaluations will affect our evaluation of ourselves and hence our subsequent performance, it is possible, and even likely, that so-called ability grouping will set in motion the self-fulfilling prophecy and serve to keep students in their "places."

Tuckman and Bierman (1971), working within a small city high school — arbitrarily, randomly, and without the knowledge of either students or teachers, but with the concurrence of the school's administration — reassigned a certain percentage of students from the middle and lowest tracks to the next highest track. Some of the higher C track students were moved up to the B track, and some of the higher B track students were moved up to the A track. Since it was Galatea's admiration that turned Pygmalion from a statue into a woman, perhaps the apparent "recognition" of these students by their school would turn them from poorer students to better ones.

And, lo and behold, to a certain degree it worked. By the end of the year, more than half of the students who were arbitrarily moved up in track were recommended by their teachers to remain in the new, higher track. More than half had proven that they could do better if their school and their teachers believed in them enough. Even their scores on independent, standardized tests were beginning to show their new ability to perform.

Shouldn't Galatea be at work at more schools?

Norms Are Influential.   The fact that norms can affect how we see things is illustrated in a classic experiment by Asch (1952). Group members were asked to tell which of three lines was the same length as a given test line. The judgment was not difficult to make, but all of the members of each group except for one were working for the experimenter, and they all intentionally gave the same wrong answer. About one-third of the real subjects yielded to the group judgment even though they did not see it as representing the right answer. They yielded because they either questioned their own judgment ("I must need glasses; all these people can't be wrong") or did not want to stand out and be different ("I know they're wrong, but I don't want to seem the oddball"). In other words, the informal norm was to go along with the group, to acquiesce to the group judgment or action.

The fact that behavior can be influenced by norms is further illustrated in research by Milgram (1963) on obedience. Subjects watched a confederate of the experimenter whom they believed to be another subject like themselves deliver an electric shock to someone. Actually, no real shock was being delivered, but they did not know that. When they were asked to deliver a painful and perhaps even harmful shock to someone, many of them complied. The norm to obey commands or even requests from someone in authority is for many people both powerful and compelling. Teachers must remember that they

Figure 10.3 🍎 Examples of Classroom Norms
Schmuck and Schmuck, 1988, p. 186.

	FORMAL	INFORMAL
STATIC	Rules followed with little prompting: 1. No cheating 2. Asking permission to leave the room 3. Addressing teacher when seeking permission to change something in the room	Procedures and routines: 1. How students enter the room 2. Who talks to whom for how long 3. Saying "Good morning," "Thank you," etc., to the teacher
DYNAMIC	Rules in need of at least occasional enforcement: 1. No talking during story time or individual study time 2. Turning work in on time 3. Using correct grammar in talking and writing	Interpersonal actions that involve active monitoring: 1. Addressing the teacher in a nasty fashion 2. Wearing hair in a style extremely different from that of other students 3. Acting abusively toward others

have this power, particularly when children are in early stages of moral development (see Chapter 9) and tend to react in an absolute fashion to adult authority.

Factors That Affect the Influence of Norms.   When the group is (1) a highly close-knit one like a club or team, (2) a source of gratification for its members, (3) one in which members share group goals or aims, and (4) one in which norms are highly relevant to group functioning, then norms will be very influential and will affect the feelings and behaviors of the members. In most cases, classroom communities do not have these characteristics, so their norms will be less influential than those of other groups or communities of which students are members.

Jackson (1960) has shown that when the *range of tolerable behavior* approved of by a group is narrowly defined, then both the probability of transgression and its ensuing punishment are increased. Teachers who demand a narrow range of tolerable behavior, therefore, are more likely to be spending time disciplining students than those whose range of tolerable behavior is broader.

Norms also differ in *intensity* depending on how important they are to persons of a given age. Among teen-agers, for example, norms that govern dress and dating are very important and therefore intense, while among nursery-school or kindergarten children the more intense norms are those that govern sharing of toys.

Particularly strong are norms that are agreed upon by virtually all members of a group, called *highly crystallized* norms by Jackson (1960). However, norms that are highly crystallized for each subgroup in a classroom community but that are different or in disagreement are considered *ambiguous* norms and may lead to conflict. If the more serious students want to pay attention but the less serious students want to talk, the result may be some unpleasant interaction between the two subgroups.

Sometimes, norms are not well *integrated*, in which case they can easily lead to confusion. If the teacher tries to establish a norm for working independently *and* a norm for attending to his or her every word, then there may be confusion when the teacher tries to interrupt individual work sessions to give out general instructions.

Finally, people are all members of many groups, each of which has its own norms. When a norm is shared by all groups, such as being quiet when someone else is talking, then that norm has *congruence*. Congruent norms are easier to follow than incongruent ones. If one teacher expects students to raise their hands and be recognized before they may speak, while another teacher permits students to speak out spontaneously, students may forget when they are supposed to raise their hands and when they need not.

Normative Goal Structures.   These are shared expectations about the best or proper way to attain desired goals, such as achieving knowledge or developing skills in a classroom. Johnson and Johnson (1975) identify and describe three normative goal structures for instruction that are particularly relevant for teachers: cooperative, competitive, and individualistic.

When working within a *cooperative* goal structure, each member seeks an outcome that will be beneficial to all members. In other words, the members share the same goal and can attain it only interdependently and to the same degree. On a baseball team, for example, a victory is a victory for all and a loss is a loss for all, even though some players may have gotten more hits than others or made more errors. Hits and errors are individual outcomes. The cooperative goal is winning. In a classroom, the use of the cooperative goal structure is rare, even though research findings indicate that this is the most effective goal structure in promoting achievement (Johnson, Maruyama, Johnson, Nelson, & Skon, 1981).

In the *competitive* goal structure, by comparison, students seek not only to succeed but also to make other students fail — what economists call a *zero-sum* situation. In order for there to be a winner, there must be a loser. When a teacher gives only a fixed percentage of A's to a class, the goal structure becomes competitive because for someone to get an A, others must get B's, C's, etc. (The baseball example above, while cooperative within a team, is obviously competitive between teams, where there will be a winner and a loser. However, it is considered to be primarily cooperative.)

Finally, an *individualistic* goal structure is one in which the goals of individuals are independent of one another. Thus, whether or not one person attains his or her goal has nothing to do with the success or failure of anyone else. Typically, classrooms are structured in this way — each student being out for him- or herself and not affecting the goal attainment of others.

To restate, the possibilities are

- cooperation: If I win, you win; if I lose, you lose.
- competition: If I win, you lose; if I lose, you win.
- individualism: My winning or losing has nothing to do with you; your winning or losing has nothing to do with me.

Championing the increased use of cooperative learning structures in the classroom, in contrast to either competitive or individualistic ones, has been a central aim of Johnson and Johnson (1975) and Slavin (1983a). Slavin's approach to *student team learning*, called Student-Teams and Academic Divisions, or STAD, involves grouping students into four-member heterogeneous learning teams to study material initially presented by the teacher. Students then take a test on the material individually but are rewarded based on the average test performance of the four team members. The idea is to provide incentives for students to encourage and help one another to master academic materials. Slavin (1983b) has found that the student team learning model produces consistently more positive effects on student achievement, across all students, than the traditional or individualistic approach, and that these effects are primarily due to the idea of team incentives rather than individual ones.

Results from a study by Johnson, Johnson, and Stanne (1986) showed that COOPERATIVE group students did the best on worksheets, tests, bonus points, and all other achievement measures. COMPETITIVE group students did the next best and INDIVIDUALISTIC students did the worst.

But what could be the reason for the success of so-called cooperative groups? If we presume that within such groups, the less able students are likely to solicit help from the

Table 10.1 🍎 Critical Differences between Peer-Tutoring and Group-Investigation Methods of Cooperative Learning in Teams

Peer Tutoring	Group Investigation
Source and Variety of Information and the Nature of the Learning Task	
1. Information is transmitted by the teacher or a text.	1. Information is gathered by pupils.
2. Learning sources are limited to cards, a worksheet, or a lecture.	2. Learning sources are varied in number and kind.
3. Tasks emphasize information and/or skill acquisition.	3. Tasks stress problem-solving, interpretation, synthesis, and application of information.
Interpersonal Relations and Communication	
4. Peer communication in teams is primarily unilateral or bilateral (in pairs).	4. Communication in teams is primarily bilateral and multilateral (discussion).
5. Peer communication is for rehearsal of teacher-taught materials.	5. Peer communication is for interpretation and exchange of ideas.
6. Peer interactions frequently imply status distinctions ("I teach, you listen.").	6. Interactions are primarily based on mutual exchange.
7. Pupils interact sporadically or in pairs.	7. Group members coordinate activities on a group-wide basis.

more able students and, in turn, the more able students are likely to give help to less able students when they solicit it, then help would account for the greater achievement in such groups (Webb, 1982, 1983). Cooperative groups work best when the rewards are given out on a group basis, thus motivating less able group members to seek help and more able group members to provide it (Webb, 1982). In competitive and individualistic situations, there will be little motivation for students to help one another.

Based on Webb's findings, teachers are encouraged (1) to have students work in groups when possible, (2) to compose each group of students of all levels of ability rather than the more typical approach of segregating the "highs" from the "lows," and (3) to provide rewards and recognition on a group basis to stimulate students who need help to seek it and receive it from their more able groupmates.

Interactive learning and teaching offers teachers a variety of ways to proceed. Sharan (1980) has grouped these alternatives into two categories, called peer-tutoring and group-investigation. The rules for setting up both types are listed and compared in Table 10.1.

An example of the Johnson and Johnson approach (1975) to cooperative learning in comparison to the other types is given in Box 10.3, and a technique developed by Sharan and Hertz-Lazarowitz (1981) is given in Box 10.4.

Peer Tutoring	**Group Investigation**
Academic Product, Evaluation, and Rewards	
8. Academic product is independent (that is, there is cooperation in means but not in goals).	8. Academic product is interdependent (that is, there is cooperation in means and in goals).
9. Evaluation is primarily individual (individual tests, scores).	9. Evaluation is both individual and group (group report or project as collective product).
10. Rewards are extrinsic (reinforcement in the form of personal praise).	10. Rewards are primarily intrinsic (self-directed interest in topic).
Classroom Organization	
11. The class functions as an aggregate of teams that are uncoordinated or are engaged in a uniform task.	11. The class functions as a "group-of-groups" with between-group coordination and division of labor and tasks.

SOURCE: Sharan, S. (1980). Cooperative learning in small groups: Recent methods and effects on achievement, attitudes, and ethnic relations. *Review of Educational Research, 50,* 241–272.

Box 10.3

Comparing Cooperative, Competitive, and Individualistic Learning Methods, Johnson & Johnson Style

	Cooperative	Competitive	Individualistic
Basis for a Student's Grade on Worksheets and Final Test	Average performance of group members	Relative position in group	Individual performance compared to preset criteria
Basis for a Student's Bonus Points	Each student gets 10% of what total class earns	Given only to students first in class standing	Based on individual work
Basis for Daily Feedback	Group performance	Individual performance relative to group and class	One's own performance only
Interaction Pattern	Group members assigned specific roles; roles rotated daily	Everybody works alone	No interaction permitted
How Daily Worksheets Are Completed	Individually	Individually	Individually
How Final Tests Are Taken	Individually	Individually	Individually
Resulting Achievement	The best	The next best	The worst

Leadership

Leadership has typically been thought about and described in two ways: (1) as a set of psychological characteristics of the person exerting influence and (2) as a set of behaviors that exert interpersonal influence on other people. The latter approach, *functional leadership*, has been more productive (Stodgill, 1974) and is more appropriate for describing the leadership of a teacher in the classroom. This is so because it views leadership as a transactional exchange or interpersonal event between the person exerting influence and those being influenced. Leadership can then be described as a set of behaviors that helps a group of people move toward a particular objective. In part, the effect of those behaviors will depend on such factors as the prestige and authority of the leader and the relationship between the leader and the followers.

Box 10.4

🍎

Planning and Carrying Out a Group Project

In their handbook for using cooperative learning procedures, Sharan and Hertz-Lazarowitz (1981) describe five steps for students to follow in planning and carrying out a group project:

1. The topic is selected and students are grouped into teams of six to research it.

2. The topic is divided into subtopics; pairs of individuals within groups select subtopics for study and decide what to study, how to study, and the purpose of the study.

3. The investigation is carried out by pairs first; later the group integrates everyone's contributions into a single outline.

4. A final report is presented to the whole class, including activities and total class discussion.

5. An evaluation is made of the final reports and of the work done to construct the reports. Achievement tests can be given, but it is equally important to carry out a cooperative evaluation, involving both students and teacher, that includes peer reactions and may lead to revisions in subsequent group procedures.

Bases of Leadership. French and Raven (1959) identified five bases for influence. In terms of teacher/student relationships, they can be illustrated in the following ways:

1. *Expert power*—Students perceive the teacher as having much knowledge and skill; as a consequence, they believe they can learn from such an individual.

2. *Referent power*—Students perceive the teacher as someone they like and with whom they can identify; as a consequence, they attempt to imitate or be like that individual.

3. *Legitimate power*—Students perceive the teacher as the boss; as a consequence, they believe that the teacher is entitled to tell them what to do.

4. *Reward power*—Students perceive the teacher as one who is empowered to hand out rewards; as a consequence, they do what the teacher wants in order to get rewarded.

5. *Coercive power*—Students perceive the teacher as one who is empowered to hand out punishments; as a consequence, they do what the teacher wants in order to stay out of trouble.

The position of teacher automatically carries with it three of the five bases for influence: legitimate power, reward power, and coercive power. However, Kounin (1970) and others have shown that the most successful teachers develop expert and/or referent bases for power. To develop expert power and referent power, teachers should create conditions in the classroom that facilitate academic work and a positive learning environment. This means taking steps to encourage independence, stimulate open communication, and make oneself liked by students. Being the absolute ruler in the classroom leads either to student dependency and apathy or to resistance and friction. Teachers who rely too heavily on coercive power to deal with individual students, particularly ones who are seen as having high power themselves, create what Kounin and Gump (1958) called the "ripple effect," or a spread of tension and disaffection among the entire class. Coercion may yield short-term compliance but may reduce long-term student interest and respect.

Leadership for Classroom Management.   Research has shown that the key to classroom management lies not in merely disciplining students who are misbehaving (Kounin, 1970), but in maintaining student involvement in work activities and resolving minor disruptions. Good classroom management serves to *prevent* major problems.

In the classroom, the teacher is the legitimate leader, with the power to reward and punish. The teacher's power will be even greater if he is liked and respected by his students.

The keys to effective leadership for classroom management, according to Good and Brophy (1984), are these:

1. Make sure students clearly understand and accept classroom rules.
2. Try to maximize classroom work time rather than stressing control of misbehavior.
3. Get students to develop inner self-control rather than trying to control them by coercive power.
4. Gear classwork to students' interests and aptitudes.

To accomplish or implement these keys to classroom management, say Good and Brophy (1984), the teacher must place great stress on *planning* and *organizing* lessons and classroom activities and having them go on without delay or disruption. Clear rules should be established and students should have the responsibility for carrying them out. Work assignments should also be clear, and *positive language* should be used to reinforce appropriate behavior. In other words, students should be told what to do rather than what not to do.

Good and Brophy (1984) also emphasize the *pacing* of lessons as a key to maintaining students' *attention* and thereby avoiding disruptions. Teachers should gain attention at the start of a lesson, stimulate and monitor it throughout the lesson, and terminate a lesson when student attention can no longer be held.

When a problem does occur, Good and Brophy (1984) recommend eliminating it as quickly as possible and with as little distraction of other students as possible. Specific techniques they suggest using to cause the disruptive student to behave are (1) eye contact, (2) touch and gesture, (3) physical closeness to the offender, (4) asking the offender a lesson-related question, and (5) praising the desirable behavior of a student sitting near the offender. Some additional suggestions are given in Box 10.5.

Leadership Styles.   Do all leaders perform the same way? Are all types of leadership appropriate in every situation? The answer to both questions is "no," especially for teachers. Two contrasting styles of leadership have been named *task leadership* and *social–emotional leadership*. Task leaders focus on successful performance of the activity a group is dealing with. Task leaders present and elicit information, opinions, and suggestions (Bales, 1970). As teachers, they teach content, present lectures, give tests, and concentrate on helping students acquire information. Social–emotional leaders focus on encouragement, harmony, compromise, and morale-building. As teachers, they manage, control, discipline, and motivate. Obviously, teachers have to be part task leader and part social–emotional leader.

Leadership style can also vary from *autocratic* — with the teacher serving as the sole authority and making all the rules and decisions — to *democratic* — the teacher giving everyone a fair chance to participate in rule- and decision-making — to *laissez-faire* — the teacher not being involved at all in the process of making either rules or decisions. Lewin, Lippitt, and White (1939) discovered in their classic experiment that while autocratic leadership might be more productive in the short term, its long-term effects were quite deleterious. Group members learned very little self-control in autocratically led groups and did very little useful work in those led by laissez-faire leaders. For a teacher, the best course appears to be the more moderate one of being a democratic leader and involving students in some classroom rule- and decision-making.

Box 10.5

Techniques from Effective Classroom Managers

To be an effective classroom manager, master these proven techniques (Kounin, 1970; Emmer & Evertson, 1981).

With-itness

Let students know that you are aware of everything that is happening in the classroom. Develop "eyes in the back of your head." Don't become preoccupied with a few students. When there is a disruption, don't make a *target error* by blaming the wrong student or a *timing error* by waiting too long before doing something. Don't waste your time on minor infractions while ignoring or being unaware of major ones. When there is an infraction, deal with it immediately, clearly, assertively but in a friendly, not a hostile, way.

Overlapping

Keep track of and supervise more than one activity at the same time. Monitor everything that is going on in the classroom constantly. Deal with individual and small-group work simultaneously.

Group Focus

Keep as many students as you can (all, if possible) involved in class activities at the same time. Don't concentrate on or involve just a few students while the rest are left to their own devices. Set a series of activities in motion at the same time so that everyone has something to do. Don't have some work and others watch.

Movement Management

Create a constant sense of movement and pace or tempo in the classroom by creating smooth transitions from activity to activity. Always keep things moving smoothly. Don't take too much time to start a new activity. Don't start a new activity in the middle of something else or when you don't have the attention of all the students. Don't create confusion yourself by bad timing.

Since the teacher is the legitimate leader in the classroom, the way he or she chooses to run that classroom at any given moment constitutes both a leadership style and a *model of teaching*. Some teachers establish a routine style or model by always informing, involving, and controlling students in the exact same way. But does that make sense? Might it not make better sense for teachers to adapt their leadership style to the situation at hand?

Joyce and Weil (1980) describe four basically different leadership or teaching styles that teachers can choose from depending on what it is they are trying to accomplish. When their principal purpose is to transmit information to students, they should adopt an *information-processing* style or model. They should function like a TV documentary or newspaper and present information in the way that is easiest for their students to understand. When their purpose is to help students learn to get along with and help one another, they should adopt a *social interaction* style using small-group and other interactive techniques. When their purpose is to help students develop a sense of identity, they should adopt a *focus-on-the-individual-person* style and use discussions and personal contact. Finally, when their purpose is to control behavior and maintain discipline, they should adopt a *behavior modification* model (see Chapter 3) and use rewards and shaping to achieve acceptable classroom behavior. (There are also four different styles of relating to others, described on pages 357–358 in Chapter 13.)

Finally, there exists the possibility of picking the style that fits or matches the way students learn (Hunt & Sullivan, 1974). Some students like structure and control. They like being given information and being told what to do. They should be taught using a *teacher-directed* or *structured* style with methods such as lecture and seatwork-recitation. Other students prefer controlling their own learning and are mature enough to do so. They should be taught by a more *self-directed* or *unstructured* style in which the teacher functions more as guide and adviser and meets with students individually or in small groups. (See the different instructional models described in Chapter 5 and the discussion of matching instructional styles with cognitive styles in Chapter 13.)

Clearly, as a teacher you do not always have to use the same approach or style to lead your classroom. You can pick the style that best fits the situation and the students, provided you have learned to use more than one style and have enough self-awareness and self-control to change from one style to another. Another set of styles you might consider is described in Box 10.6.

Communication

The effectiveness or influence of a communication is based on a number of factors, each of which will be considered in turn. Taken together, they deal with *who* says *what to whom* and with *what effect*.

The Role of the Communicator. How effective or opinion-changing a communication is depends on *who* says it—in particular, how *credible* or believable the audience perceives the source of the communication to be. Hovland (1963) reports that the more similar the source's position on an issue is to one's own, the more credible one is likely to perceive the source to be and the more fair one is likely to perceive the message. In other words, people interpret a communication in the light of their own position on the issue.

In addition, the more the communicator is respected, the more the communication is likely to change the audience's opinion (Hovland, 1963). That is why advertisements and commercials use people who are trusted and believed in to deliver the intended message. Therefore, the words of a respected teacher will carry more weight with students than the words of a lightly regarded teacher, unless the message deviates too much from the students' current views. Sports heroes may be more effective than law enforcement officials in convincing students of the dangers of drugs—but only if the students are *not* already totally committed to drug use.

Box 10.6

Teaching Styles:
From Command to Problem Solving

Mosston (1972) has created a *spectrum* or continuum of six teaching styles. At one end of the spectrum, the teacher makes all of the decisions about what and how to teach, and attempts to totally control the classroom environment and all the students in it. At the opposite end of the spectrum, many of the decisions and much of the control are in the hands of students. Each style, starting at the teacher-control end, is described briefly below.

Command Style

The teacher chooses the lesson goals and the exact procedures for meeting them. In other words, the teacher is in command. The lecture-and-demonstration format is used because with it the teacher can best control what is taught and how students behave while it is being taught. This is perhaps the most traditional teaching style.

Task Style

Students are allowed to choose where and at what pace they will complete each task, as they typically do in a laboratory, gymnasium, art studio, or music studio.

Reciprocal Style

This involves using the small-group method or tutor method, in which students take turns functioning as teachers of other students under the supervision of the teacher. It is a partnership approach (see Boxes 10.3 and 10.4) in which students have more control over what and how to teach than in the preceding styles.

Individual Style

This involves teaching by using individualized or programmed instruction (see Chapter 5). The teacher chooses the instructional material, but students have control over when and how they complete it. The timing may be under student control, but the intellectual content is still completely under teacher control.

Guided-Discovery Style

The teacher creates a learning environment in which the students themselves find the information or explanations they need, rather than being told to them by the teacher. The teacher may ask the questions, but the students must find the answers. This style closely fits the Piagetian approach covered in Chapter 8.

Problem-Solving Style

This is like independent study, in which students choose what to study while the teacher functions as an adviser. Students are encouraged to invent multiple solutions to their problems.

The Content of the Communication.   A communication's effectiveness or influence in changing opinions also depends on *what* it says. Developing communication skills means knowing how to prepare effective communications. But what should be contained in an effective communication? Should it arouse the emotions of the audience? Can you frighten people into changing their opinion, as, for instance, in telling people about how they may lose their teeth if they don't brush them or about how they may lose their lives if they take drugs? Not according to research findings. Hovland (1963) found that people tend not to believe pronouncements of "gloom and doom" or tend not to take them as seriously as they do more factual, less emotional messages, and so are not much influenced by them. (Witness, for example, the fact that nations often do not take seriously the threats of overpopulation or global warming.) Sometimes, in fact, highly emotional messages cause the audience to "tune out" or even become hostile toward the communicator. It is better to just communicate the facts.

But, of course, there are often facts that support one position and facts that refute it. Should both be presented? Again, Hovland (1963) reports relevant findings. If the audience is on your side to begin with, then just presenting your side is better than presenting both sides — unless someone else is likely to come along later and present the other side. Then, presenting both sides is better. Since teachers do not know whether their students agree with them, or who will be trying to convince their students next, it is better for teachers to present both sides of an issue. However, the side of the issue that is presented first is likely to be more influential (Hovland, 1963) than the side presented second.

Congruent communication uses the language of acceptance rather than the language of rejection. It never derogates or "puts down" a child's character.

What should be done if the purpose of the message is simply to inform rather than to influence? Box 10.7 and Box 10.8 contain some concrete suggestions.

Audience Predisposition.   The next factor affecting the influence of a communication is the audience, the people *to whom* the message is sent. It has already been said that if the audience is made up of people who think like the speaker, they will pay much more attention to what the speaker is saying. Of equal importance are the norms of the groups of which these people are members. The more the members of the audience value the groups they belong to and hence accept their norms, the less likely they are to be influenced by the message if it goes against those norms (Hovland, 1963). Telling youngsters who are members of gangs about the dangers of violence has little effect because they have already accepted the gang's norm that pronounces violence to be acceptable. In order to change the members' beliefs and attitudes about violence, efforts must be made through the gangs and their leaders to change the norms of the gangs.

Box 10.7

How to Be a Skillful Communicator

Schmuck and Schmuck (1988) offer the suggestions below for sending and receiving a message:

Sending a Message

- MAKE CLEAR STATEMENTS and make them short (three or four sentences). The receiver should be able to successfully paraphrase them.
- DESCRIBE ONE'S OWN BEHAVIOR both as an illustration and to communicate empathy.
- DESCRIBE FEELINGS directly in order to establish trust (for example, "I feel pleased," "I like your sense of humor").
- AIM STATEMENTS at the audience's level of experience, expertise, and understanding.

Receiving a Message

- PARAPHRASE IDEAS that you hear the other person say to show that you are listening (for example, "Did I hear you say . . . ?").
- DESCRIBE OTHERS' BEHAVIOR rather than trying to describe their character or motivation, neither of which you can see (for example, "That's the fourth time you've interrupted" rather than "You're a rude little boy").
- CHECK IMPRESSIONS to determine whether you are accurately perceiving the feelings of the message-sender toward you, rather than just assuming what those feelings are or condemning them (for example, "I gather from the look on your face that you're angry. Is that right?" rather than "What right do you have to be angry?").

Hovland (1963) also reports on the effects that a particular personality characteristic may have on the ease with which a person can be persuaded. That personality characteristic is *self-esteem*. Persons low in self-esteem are more easily influenced than those high in self-esteem. (This can be related to the concept of self-efficacy described in the next chapter.)

Audience predisposition is also influenced by seating arrangements, particularly by how much access to communication each person has by virtue of his or her physical relationship to the other participants. People like to have more access to information; even though giving it to them may not maximize efficiency, it will maximize satisfaction. When every participant has equal access to information being passed in the form of notes, as they do in a circle pattern, or almost equal access, as they do in a line pattern, they

---

Box 10.8

Congruent Communication

Ginott (1972) calls communication that is harmonious and authentic, and where words fit feelings, congruent. Congruent communicators substitute a language of ACCEPTANCE for a language of rejection. Congruent communication acknowledges a child's situation; incongruent communication derogates and degrades a child's character and personality.

Congruent	Incongruent
1. I see the paint spilled. We need a rag to clean it up.	1. Why are you so clumsy and careless?
2. I am concerned about your work in English. It needs improvement.	2. You're smart enough to do better. Isn't it time to buckle down?
3. I am appalled at your behavior.	3. You are so stupid.
4. I get angry when I see food on the floor. This room needs to be cleaned.	4. You boys are slobs. You belong in a pigsty. Clean it up now.
5. The noise is annoying.	5. Stop the noise.
6. I would like to finish my statement.	6. You are rude.
7. You seem upset about the homework. It does seem like a lot.	7. It's your own fault for being lazy and not finishing it in class.
8. You forgot your book. Here it is.	8. Scatterbrain! You'd forget your head if it weren't attached to your shoulders.
9. Get right to the point. Start with your facts.	9. You write as though you had verbal diarrhea.
10. We have a problem. What's the solution?	10. Why are you never ready to take a test?
11. You've raised an important question.	11. How would I know? That's beside the point.

tend to like what they are doing more than when one person has more access than all the others, as in an X or Y configuration (Leavitt, 1951).

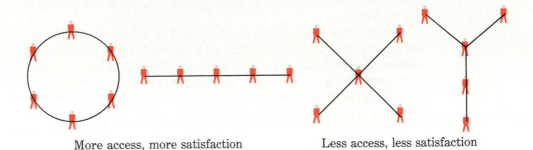

More access, more satisfaction   Less access, less satisfaction

Teachers need to ensure that all of their students are in the flow of communication, even though doing so may occasionally require that specific communications be repeated.

Audience Response.   An active audience is much more likely to be influenced than a passive one. King and Janis (1956) had students not merely listen to a communication but play a role that required them to deliver a persuasive communication to others. The role players changed their opinions more than those who just listened to the same communication. Perhaps the desire to be consistent in one's thoughts and actions is what causes a change in action to result in a change in thought (Festinger, 1957).

It is, therefore, very important for students to participate in the communication process. They can do this by answering or asking questions of the teacher, by interacting with other students in discussion groups, or by participating in other forms of small-group instruction (such as cooperative learning). Over time, students may forget the source of a message, but they are much less likely to forget its content, particularly if they paid close attention to it (Hovland, 1963).

Friendship and Liking

An important group outcome is friendship or the liking that individuals have for one another. In a group setting, friendship and liking between members manifests itself as *cohesiveness*—the attraction and attachment that group members feel toward their group. Members of cohesive groups (1) share a common group identity (they think of themselves as members of the group; (2) share a common sense of purpose; (3) communicate differently with one another than with nonmembers; (4) share and follow common norms of acceptable behavior; (5) accept specific roles, including that of leader; and (6) establish a status system or a hierarchy of worth (that is, a chain of command, a pecking order) for the group. These characteristics are much less true of groups that lack cohesiveness.

The groups a person likes the most and identifies with the most come to be that person's *reference groups*. These are the groups whose influence and judgment that person is most willing to accept. People compare and judge themselves relative to the other members of their reference groups, and they conform to the norms of these groups. Clubs, gangs, fraternities, organizations, and even particular classes can become the reference groups that young people choose to identify with and follow. When they do, they will adhere to the norms of these groups.

What Makes a Group Attractive?   The better able a group is to fulfill someone's needs, the more attractive the group will be to that person (Wright & Duncan, 1986). In other words, if someone stands to gain a lot from belonging to a particular group, membership in that group will be most valued and appealing. Consequently, the norms of that appealing group will be most influential on that person's behavior and opinions.

One factor that affects a group's ability to fulfill someone's needs is its *prestige*. The more important a group is, the greater the satisfaction of its members (Meir, Keinan, & Segal, 1986). Being in a highly regarded social club, sorority, or fraternity or in an honors class or honor society will make a student feel important and, hence, will increase the appeal that group has for him or her. Successful groups or teams are much more appealing to their members than unsuccessful ones.

The *climate* of a group also influences its attractiveness. Interestingly, group members find cooperative groups more appealing than competitive groups (Worchel, Andreoli, & Folger, 1977). This is particularly true in racially integrated or cross-ethnic groups (Johnson & Johnson, 1985). In part, the climate of these racially mixed groups, and consequently their attractiveness, was increased because students *interacted* more within them than within competitive groups.

Size is another factor that influences a group's appeal. Smaller groups tend to be more appealing than large ones (Wicker, 1969) because it is easier to get to know the other members and because there is more chance to participate. Smaller classes have this appealing quality as well, except perhaps for students who would prefer the protection of anonymity afforded by a larger class. Which brings up another factor that makes a group appealing: its *protectiveness*. Often the attraction of gangs is their ability to protect their members against aggression by other gangs.

The primary *activity* or *task* that the group is engaged in is another factor that influences its appeal. Stamp collectors like stamp clubs, athletes like sports teams, and good students like highly motivated academic groups. It will take effort to make school groups attractive to students who do not like academic work. However, a class will become more attractive to students when the class activity is more gamelike and thus more likable. (Review the illustration on page 15 of Chapter 1 of how to make classroom activities more appealing.)

The *social structure* of a group or class also affects its appeal. *Centrally structured* groups that have powerful and controlling leadership and narrow and defined friendship patterns are less attractive to the majority of their members than are *diffusely structured* groups that have a wide range of support and less focus on interpersonal acceptance and rejection (Marshall, 1978).

Another important feature of social structure is the *opportunity for member participation*. In classrooms and schools where students have more opportunity to interact with one another—the so-called "open" classrooms (described at the end of Chapter 8) in contrast to the traditional ones, or in the cooperative learning model (described earlier)—there are more friendship choices (Epstein, 1983). *Self-reliance*, too, seems to be an influential factor: Where there is more self-reliance built into the classroom structure, there is more opportunity for friendships to form (Epstein, 1983).

Finally, an important determinant of the attractiveness of a classroom group is the *behavior of the teacher*. Students who are satisfied with their teachers usually feel good about school, learning, and themselves. Pepitone (1964) proposed that persons are attracted to those who assign them a position of high status or who help them feel secure. They tend to feel hostile toward those who demean them in their own eyes or in the eyes of others. Students who are valued by their teachers, therefore, tend to find their classroom experiences satisfying, while students who are devalued by their teachers tend to find their classroom experiences unsatisfying (Stensaasen, 1970).

What Happens in Attractive Groups?   Attractive groups tend to improve the *self-esteem* of their members by making them feel more important. They also produce a sense of *trust* and *openness* among their members that leads not only to more *communication*, but to more open communication. Luft (1969) proposed the framework shown in Figure 10.4 known as the *Johari Window* (named by combining the first names of *Joe* Luft and *Harry* Ingram). In attractive groups, the first quadrant—the area of sharing and openness—is expanded, while the other three areas of blindness, avoided information, and unconscious activity contract. Teachers can use the Johari Window concept to help students reveal more about themselves from quadrants 2 and 3, which will result in the development of greater emotional closeness and lead to yet more openness and spontaneity.

Attractive groups are also productive groups if the norms of the groups support productivity (Kafer, 1976). When friends as a group endorse academic performance as a mutual goal, then the academic performance of each member will be enhanced. Teachers

Figure 10.4 🍎 The Johari Window of Awareness in Interpersonal Relations From Luft, 1969.

	KNOWN TO SELF	NOT KNOWN TO SELF
KNOWN TO OTHERS	1. Open Area of sharing and openness	2. Blind Area of blindness
NOT KNOWN TO OTHERS	3. Hidden Area of avoided information	4. Unknown Area of unconscious activity

would do well to encourage their students to work together (as in cooperative learning) on academic tasks in order to help them develop group norms conducive to productivity. Teachers can develop a sense of camaraderie and group cohesion within their own class-rooms by applying the Japanese approach known as the *quality circle* (Wood, Hull, & Azumi, 1983), described in Box 10.9.

How to Determine Liking Patterns Among Students.   It can be helpful to determine liking patterns among students in order to provide unpopular students with social support or special assistance, or to solicit the cooperation of popular and influential students. In setting up work groups or teams, knowledge of individual student popularity and friendship choices can help the teacher create new combinations (1) to foster new friendships or (2) to help less popular children interact with more popular ones. It can also

---

Box 10.9

Using Quality Circles
in the Classroom

The quality circle utilizes *participative management*, a technique for involving group members in group decision making. In a classroom this means (1) increasing student involvement and (2) using work teams. A teacher can have the whole class meet in a quality circle once or twice a week for 30 minutes to an hour each time. At each meeting there should be an agenda, such as a discussion of classroom rules, homework, disruptive behavior, use of classroom material, or any classroom problem or issue that is current, that concerns students, and that relates to the quality of life and work in the classroom. Agenda items may be student-initiated or teacher-initiated, and more than one item may be on the agenda for any meeting. A teacher can also appoint a student steering committee to set the agenda for each meeting and to conduct each meeting. Steering committee membership should be rotated from month to month.

In conducting the meeting (which is carried out, of course, with members sitting in a circle), the first step is to *identify problems*. The steering committee may provide a short list of problems, but group members should be allowed to add others to it. Then each problem should be described by those who have identified it. The group should *generate solutions* to each problem by brainstorm-ing (see Box 7.7), and then evaluate these solutions by combining individual judgments or voting to try to achieve a consensus. During the meetings, emphasis should be placed on (1) giving everyone a chance to participate and to candidly express his or her opinion; (2) listening to what others say (and repeating it, if necessary), keeping an open mind, and looking for merit in others' ideas; (3) giving feedback to one another and credit where due; (4) not engaging in personal attacks (criticiz-ing ideas but not people); and (5) maintaining a climate of friendship and cooperation but resolving conflict when it does arise. This means being a skillful communicator, as described in Box 10.7.

Remember this is not merely a discussion group. It is a problem-solving group and its recom-mended solutions must be tried out in the classroom. In this way students will become committed to quality in their classroom life and activities.

help teachers detect any biases — say, racial or gender — that exist in the classroom and may be deterring smooth interaction. Measuring student popularity makes it possible to identify selected, rejected, and neglected students.

One way to proceed in determining liking patterns is to ask each student to choose or *nominate*, in writing and in private, the three students he or she likes most. (The nomination procedure often includes also asking each student to name the three he or she likes least, though this question may be avoided to avoid causing hurt feelings.) Another approach is to ask class members to write down the names of the person or persons they would most like to sit next to and those they would least like to sit next to (again, with caution exercised in using the second question). No prespecified number is requested and no names need to be given for least favorite(s) if none apply. Schmuck and Schmuck (1988) provide a sample diagram of the resulting patterns of choice among a class of 15, shown in Figure 10.5.

Figure 10.5 🍎 A Sample Sociogram of Seating Choices Among 15 Students

Eight girls (numbers 1 through 8 or circles) and seven boys (numbers 9 through 15 or squares); solid lines represent positive choices and dashed lines represent negative choices. (Adapted from Schmuck and Schmuck, 1988, p. 171.)

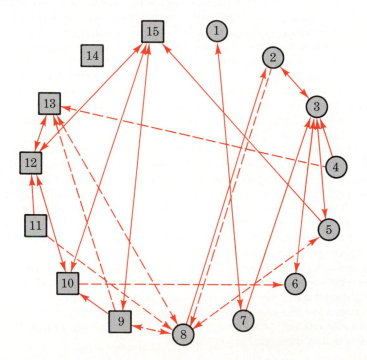

This diagram of liking patterns is called a *sociogram*. The sociogram in Figure 10.5 shows that all the boys (numbers 9 through 15) chose to sit next to boys and all the girls (numbers 1 through 8) except one (number 5) chose to sit next to girls. Among the girls, number 3 was the most popular while number 8 was specifically rejected by five class-mates. Moreover, the girl she chose rejected her. Girl number 8 may be a candidate for the teacher's help, as may be boy number 13 who also received three negative choices. Both are probably experiencing rejection. Boy number 14 is an isolate who neither chose anyone nor was chosen by anyone. He will also need teacher assistance to be integrated into the class social structure. "Stars" like girl number 3 and boy number 15 who are chosen by many classmates should be called upon to help overcome the rejection and isolation of other students.

Classroom Climate

What is classroom climate? It is the product of all the factors that affect groups and that have been described in this chapter: expectations, norms, leadership, communication, and friendship. Taken together, these social and interpersonal dimensions produce an overall point of view or *ideology* in a classroom or school, along with a consistent *organizational structure*, which gives rise to a set of *instructional practices*.

Climates have been described as *open* and *closed* (Halpin, 1966) or *effective* and *ineffective* (Brookover et al., 1982). In an open or effective climate, teachers believe and expect that

- all students are worthwhile and can learn and reach high standards of achievement based on their own ability and on the commitment and efforts of teachers.

In an open or effective climate, the organizational structure and norms provide

- recognition and rewards for high achievement;
- opportunities for students to express themselves and be treated with fair-ness and dignity;
- cooperative and supportive interaction between students and between teachers and students;
- nondiscrimination, meaning equal interactional and instructional oppor-tunities for all students regardless of gender, race, or ethnicity.

A good example of a technique that contributes to effective classroom climate is the quality circle (described in Box 10.9).

This does not mean that in an effective climate the teacher will always teach and behave the same way. Sometimes the teacher will provide more structure, sometimes less; sometimes the teacher will use direct instruction, sometimes small-group or coop-erative instruction; sometimes the teacher will lead with a firm hand, sometimes with

Box 10.10

Like People, Groups Grow

Groups deal with two tasks or domains at the same time: (1) their job, or what they are there to accomplish, such as learning; and (2) the interpersonal or social relationships among their members. Tuckman (1965) has described groups as going through four stages of development as they deal with both their job and their social sphere. He called these stages *forming, storming, norming, and performing*, and knowing about them can help a teacher produce an effective classroom climate.

In the beginning, groups *form*. They come together for the first time. They seek structure, guidance, and direction. They are dependent on their leader to tell them what to do. A teacher should provide some direction and guidance, but it should be neither total nor absolute, or else students will not be motivated to take some responsibility for their own learning and social development.

When group members discover what the rules are, or when they discover that part of the responsibility for making the rules is theirs, they may become hostile and dissatisfied. They may even rebel. That is to say, they *storm*. An effective leader or teacher, rather than becoming threatened and trying to stamp it out, permits this expression of feelings and helps students understand it. More freedom rather than less freedom is often the key to further development.

The group members are now ready to establish both rules and a sense of trust. It is at this time that they *norm*. A pattern of relationships and interpersonal rules begins to develop that will enable the group to be an effective learning and teaching medium.

If the teacher has given the class the freedom and opportunity to grow through the first three stages, they will now begin to *perform*. A few months of the school year may have to pass before this last stage develops, but if it does develop, the teacher's patience will be rewarded. Students will finally work together productively and harmoniously to learn the subject matter and to enjoy the chance of being together as a classroom group.

less control and discipline (see the different teaching styles in Box 10.6). At all times, the teacher's goal will be to maximize the gains that a class can make, both as individuals and as a group, in knowledge and in feelings or attitudes. (The fact that how this is done will have to vary as the classroom group develops is illustrated in Box 10.10.)

In sum, there are climates that are positive and desirable, that students enjoy being in, and that they learn in. Maximizing all the group processes described in this chapter, which include being open, positive, and accepting in (1) expectations, (2) classroom norms or rules, (3) style of leadership, and (4) communication style, will lead to group cohesiveness as well as to a sense of satisfaction and accomplishment among students. Students will want to come to school and will feel that they can have some direct influence on what goes on there. They will feel accepted and respected by their teachers and their classmates. There will be a positive classroom climate.

Summary of Main Points

1. Class members interact as a group, subject to the principles of *group dynamics*. The teacher, as classroom *leader*, is influenced by *member characteristics* such as *expectations* and by *group characteristics* such as norms, which also influence other *group processes* such as *communication* and, in turn, affect *group outcomes* such as *attraction* to the group and *climate* of the classroom.

2. *Expectations* are beliefs people hold about themselves and others. When they act on these beliefs, they influence their own behavior and the behavior of others in ways that cause the beliefs to come true. This is called the *self-fulfilling prophecy*. When teachers believe that certain students will gain or bloom academically, research shows that this actually comes to pass, reflecting the power and the reality of the self-fulfilling prophecy.

3. Teachers communicate their expectations to students by *praising* and *helping* the ones they believe to have high ability and giving them *more time to answer questions*, reflecting a concern with their *performance*; this is in contrast to a concern with simply *controlling* the ones they believe to have low ability. *Encouragement* is much more likely to be offered to the former group than to the latter.

4. *Norms* are *shared agreements* by group members on world views, beliefs, likes and dislikes, and standards of behavior. They can be *formal* or *informal*, *static* or *dynamic*. Group influence can be strong enough to cause people to see things differently than they really are, or at least to say they do.

5. Norms describe the *range of behavior* tolerable to the group. They vary across groups in their levels of *intensity* or importance, *crystallization* or degree of endorsement, *ambiguity* or clarity, degree of *integration* or confusion, and *congruence* or consistency.

6. *Normative goal structures* are shared expectations about the best way to attain goals. When each member seeks an outcome that is beneficial to all, the goal structure is called a *cooperative* one, in contrast to a *competitive* goal structure, in which each member seeks a goal that will cause all others to fail. When members' goal attainments are independent, the goal structure is *individualistic*. Much research has shown the cooperative structure to be both the most pleasurable and the most enhancing of academic performance.

7. In the *functional* approach, leadership is thought of as a set of influential behaviors rather than a set of personal traits. The basis of functional leadership can be *expertise* or the leader's possession of knowledge, *reference* or the degree to which the leader is identified with, *legitimacy* or a part of the leadership job, or the leader's power to *reward* or punish (or *coerce*). Teachers automatically have the last three but must earn the first two.

8. To be an effective classroom manager, a teacher must be able to *plan*, *organize*, and *pace* lessons to gain student attention and should use *positive language*. The teacher can control or avoid disruptiveness through eye contact and physical closeness as well as by being *with-it* or aware, *overlapping* classroom activities, keeping a *group focus*, and *managing movement* or tempo.

9. Leadership can be focused on the *task* or work goal of the group or on the *social–emotional* climate. Leaders can use a *democratic*, *autocratic*, or *laissez-faire* style. Effective teachers can use more than one style or model of teaching—ranging from *teacher-directed* to *student-directed*—depending on the task and the circumstances.

10. The effectiveness of classroom communication that is intended to persuade depends on *who* says *what to whom* and with *what effect*. *Credible* communicators are more influential than noncredible ones. Highly *emotional* messages are not as influential as less emotionally charged ones. *Two-sided* messages are more effective for general audiences than *one-sided* ones.

11. Messages that *conflict* with *group norms* are not very effective, nor are *setting patterns* that isolate individuals from information. When the audience *participates* in the communication process, such as by role playing, the influence of the communication is greatest.

12. Important group outcomes are friendship and liking. Groups whose members share these feelings are *cohesive*, which makes them *attractive*. Such groups often serve as *reference groups* in that their influence and judgment are accepted.

13. The factors that help make certain groups more attractive to certain people, and hence make them reference groups, are their *prestige* or importance, their *climate* or opportunity for interaction, their *size* (or smallness), their *protectiveness* or ability to protect their members from harm, their *activity* or task focus, and their *social structure* or how broad they are in terms of individual acceptance and influence. In classroom groups, the *behavior of the teacher* also affects the attraction for students.

14. Attractive groups are characterized by *trust* and *openness* in the *communication process*, reflected in a *sharing* rather than a hiding of one's feeling and ideas. They are also characterized by *productivity* if that is consistent with the norms of the group. One approach to using such groups for problem-solving processes is called the *quality circle*.

15. Teachers can determine liking or friendship *patterns* in classroom groups by privately asking students who they like and dislike or who they would like or not like to sit next to. Choices can then be diagrammed in the form of *sociograms* to reveal patterns of bias or to pinpoint students who may need special social assistance and support. Influential students can also be identified this way.

16. The sum total of group factors results in a group or classroom *climate* that represents the *ideology*, *structure*, and *practices* of the group. It may be *open* or *closed*, *effective* or *ineffective*, and it will grow or *develop* through a set of *stages* over time.

Suggested Resources

Ginott, H. (1972). *Teacher and child*. New York: Macmillan.

Good, T. L., & Brophy, J. E. (1984). *Looking in classrooms* (3rd ed.). New York: Harper & Row.

Johnson, D. W., & Johnson, R. T. (1975). *Learning together and alone: Cooperation, competition, and individualization*. Englewood Cliffs, NJ: Prentice-Hall.

Joyce, B., & Weil, M. (1980). *Models of teaching* (2nd ed.). Englewood Cliffs, NJ: Prentice-Hall.

Kounin, J. S. (1970). *Discipline and group management in classrooms*. New York: Holt, Rinehart & Winston.

Schmuck, R. A., & Schmuck, P. A. (1988). *Group processes in the classroom* (5th ed.). Dubuque, IA: Brown.

Chapter
11

Social Foundations of Behavior

Objectives

1. Identify three limitations of behaviorism as an explanation of social behavior.
2. Describe the basic principles of Bandura's social cognitive theory, including (a) reciprocal determinism, (b) symbolizing capability, (c) forethought capability, (d) vicarious capability, (e) self-regulatory capability, and (f) self-reflective capability.
3. Identify the five effects of modeling, that is, the five things an individual can learn by watching others.
4. Describe the process of learning from models, including attention, retention, production, and motivation.
5. Describe the effects of the outcomes of models on vicarious learning — in particular, how vicarious reinforcement, vicarious punishment, model attributes, vicarious motivation, and vicarious emotion influence observer behavior.
6. Define self-efficacy and describe its role in behavior as proposed by Bandura.
7. Describe four sources of efficacy information — enactive attainment, vicarious experience, verbal persuasion, and physiological state — and their impact on self-efficacy.
8. Describe the impact of school and teachers on a student's self-efficacy.
9. Define self-regulation and describe its relation to self-efficacy as proposed by Bandura.
10. Describe the impact of four factors on the enhancement of self-regulatory efficacy: goal setting, commitment, incentives, and personal control.

Table 11.1 🍎 Comparing Direct and Indirect Learning

Type of Learning	How It Happens
Direct (instantaneous matching; enactive learning)	Learner performs or enacts the response him- or herself and directly experiences the consequences. $S^D \rightarrow R \rightarrow S^R$ (from Chapter 3) (S^D may be provided by model.)
Indirect (delayed matching; vicarious learning)	Learner observes the model perform the behavior and observes the model being reinforced. Later the learner performs the behavior. S^D (model) $\rightarrow R$ (model) $\rightarrow S^R$ (model) (from Chapter 3) later S^D (similar situation) $\rightarrow R$ (modeled response)

Basic Principles

Limitations of Behaviorism

Behavioral theories that explain the acquisition of behavior by the law of effect or reinforcement have been encountered in Chapters 2 and 3. These theories posit that behaviors followed by positive reinforcement are learned, while those lacking such consequences are extinguished. This explanation has been challenged on a number of grounds, particularly the following three, by Bandura (1977).

1. *Behaviorism is not representative of what happens in natural settings.* No one is present on a day-to-day basis to provide people with rewards for desirable behaviors in order to increase their frequency of occurrence. Usually, people must manage and control their own behavior.

2. *Behaviorism does not account for the acquisition of novel responses.* There are times when people behave in a way they never have before. If behavior requires reinforcement to occur, how could it possibly occur the first time?

3. *Behaviorism accounts for direct learning only* (where the consequences immediately follow the act), *not for delayed matching* (where the consequences do not occur until later). Often, a behavior is learned but is not performed immediately; the effects of learning may not occur until some later time. A comparison of direct and indirect learning is shown in Table 11.1.

Social Cognitive Theory

To overcome these limitations, Bandura (1977, 1986) has proposed an alternative theory called *social learning theory* or *social cognitive theory*. It has six basic principles.

Reciprocal Determinism.   The first basic principle of social cognitive theory is that *behavior*, *personal factors*, and *environmental events* all operate together as interactive determinants or causes of each other in what Bandura (1978) calls the *self-system*.

Figure 11.1 🍎 **Reciprocal Determinism: The Three-Way Relationship Between Personal Factors (P), Behavior (B), and Environmental Events (E)**

Adapted from Bandura, 1978.

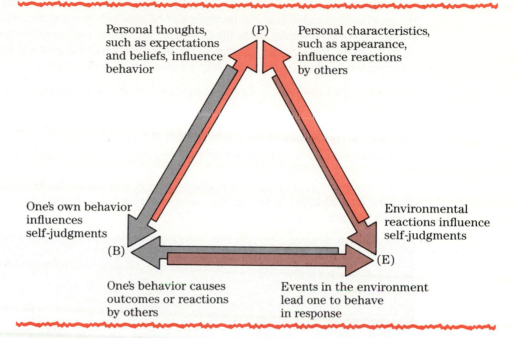

Personal thoughts, such as expectations and beliefs, influence behavior

(P)

Personal characteristics, such as appearance, influence reactions by others

One's own behavior influences self-judgments

(B)

Environmental reactions influence self-judgments

(E)

One's behavior causes outcomes or reactions by others

Events in the environment lead one to behave in response

This interlocking system, shown in Figure 11.1, represents the three factors — P or personal ones, E or environmental ones, and B or behavior — as points of a triangle. The double arrows between each factor indicate that each may affect or determine each of the others in a reciprocal way — hence reciprocal determinism.

Imagine how this would work. You are a person (P) with expectations and values as well as a personal style or personality. You like intellectual challenges and social interaction. Consequently, you like going to school, and when you get there your behavior (B) is positive and gregarious. Your friends know your personality (P), and they react with environmental events (E) or friendliness. They also react (E) to your behavior (B). If you do something strange or unexpected, they will react to it. Their reactions (E), in turn, influence your behavior (B) as well as affecting your personality (P). If they stop being nice to you (E), you may become moody (P). So, the self is a system and the factors in it — personal, behavioral, and environmental — affect one another.

Symbolizing Capability.   Bandura (1986) proposed that people view the world *symbolically*, by *cognitive representation*, and that it is these cognitive representations, rather than the world itself, to which people often react. What does this mean? It means that because human beings have the power to think and to use language to think with, the past can be "carried around" in one's head, and the future can be "tested out" as well. At any moment in time, reality consists of only those people, objects, and events that can be seen and heard. All the other people one has known and all the experiences one has ever had can exist only as thoughts, or cognitive representations, in one's head. It is as if people had video recorders in their heads and were recording everything that happened to them, except that their "videotape" is their capability to remember or make symbolic or cognitive representations of each experience.

The same is true of the future. What has not yet happened can be represented in the mind nevertheless. Possible behavior can be anticipated, expected, worried about, and tested out symbolically, in the mind, without necessarily ever being carried out physically. *Thoughts*, the symbolic or cognitive representations of the past and future, therefore, are the "materials" that influence or cause subsequent behavior.

Forethought Capability.   In addition to being used to represent the past, thinking or symbolic capability can also be used to *plan for the future* (Bandura, 1986). People can anticipate how others will react to them, can set goals, and can plan courses of action. They can, in short, *think ahead*—because *thoughts precede action*. Sometimes, as will be seen, thoughts may be helpful; sometimes they may be a hindrance.

People react to your personality and your behavior. You, in turn, are affected by how they react to you. This is called reciprocal determinism, *and it makes you feel good about yourself when someone likes you.*

Vicarious Capability.   People, especially children, can and often do learn *by observing others behave* and seeing the consequences of that behavior (Bandura, 1986). This is called *vicarious learning*. Of course, people can learn by doing things themselves and seeing their own consequences, but life would be quite limited if this were the only way to learn. It helps to be able to learn through others' experiences. Much more will be said about vicarious learning since it is a distinct principle of social learning.

Self-Regulatory Capability.   A basic principle of social cognitive theory is that people have the *ability to control their own behavior*. How hard people work, how many hours they sleep, what they eat, whether they use alcohol or drugs, whether they gamble, how they deport themselves in public, how much they talk, whether they do their homework, and on and on, are behaviors that they control. These behaviors do not *have* to be done, necessarily, to suit others. People do them based on their own internal standards and their own motivation (Bandura, 1982). Of course, people will be influenced by the way others react to them, but the principle responsibility will be their own.

Self-Reflective Capability.   Last, and perhaps of greatest importance, Bandura (1977) proposed that people often *think about or reflect upon themselves*. Individuals monitor their ideas and judge the adequacy of their thoughts, and thus of themselves, by the results of their acts. Of all the judgments people make of themselves, the most important, according to Bandura (1977), is how competent or capable they think they are to perform a task successfully. He calls this judgment *self-efficacy*, and it affects choice of activity, amount of effort invested in an activity, length of perseverance in the face of difficulty, and likelihood of approaching a task with anxiety and apprehension versus self-assurance (Bandura, 1982). This important concept will be returned to later in the chapter.

Observational Learning from Models

A highly efficient characteristic of social learning is that it can be done *vicariously,* through the observation of others. Those people who are imitated or whose behavior others learn from are called *models*, and from their behavior and its consequences a variety of different things can be learned.

Effects of Modeling

According to Bandura (1986), there are five things that observers can learn from models.

1. Observers can learn *new cognitive skills*, such as reading, and new *behaviors*, such as how to swing a golf club, by watching others perform.
2. Watching models can *strengthen* or *weaken* observers' previously learned *inhibitions* over their own behavior. In other words, observers can learn what they can and cannot get away with. When observers see models perform an act, they decide (a) whether they too have the ability to perform that act, (b) whether the model was rewarded or punished for performing the act, and (c) whether they are likely to experience the same consequences if they perform the act. If an observer decides not to perform an act after seeing a model perform it and suffer unpleasant consequences, then the modeling effect is known as *inhibition*. If the observer

was unlikely to perform the act before but then becomes less restrained after seeing the model do it and not suffer any adverse consequences, the influence of modeling is known as *disinhibition* and the observer will probably perform the act too. If, for example, one child sees a second child punished for playing with a particular toy, the first child will be inhibited from playing with the toy. But if the second child is seen playing with the toy and not being punished, then the first child will be more likely to want to play with that same toy.

3. Models can also serve as *social prompts* or *inducements* for observers. In other words, observers can learn what the benefits of performing an act are. Sometimes an act is performed not because of any disinhibition not to avoid it, but because it is worth doing. Seeing the gratitude and good feeling someone else provokes by doing a good deed, for example, may stimulate or induce an observer to behave in a similarly altruistic way (Bandura, 1969).

4. From watching models, observers can learn how to *use their environment* and the *objects* in it. An observer might not have thought of using a ladder as a bench, for example, or a shoe as a paper weight, until first seeing a model do it.

5. Seeing models express emotional reactions often causes observers to *become aroused* and *express the same emotional reaction*. Children often display delight, for example, when they see it in others or distress when others display that feeling.

The Process of Learning from Models

Observational or vicarious learning is governed by four processes, listed in Figure 11.2 and briefly described below.

Attention.   People cannot learn by observation unless they attend to and accurately perceive the modeled activities. This will depend on how *simple* and *conspicuous* the modeled acts are (simpler and more conspicuous acts being easier to attend to than more obscure ones). It will also depend on whether or not the observer is *set* or *disposed* to look for these acts, especially when many acts are competing for the observer's attention. This will depend, in part, on their *relevance* to the observer. Student teachers, when observing classroom teachers in action, may attend to the less significant teaching acts because there are so many teaching acts going on at the same time, but they may be attending to them all more than are the students being taught because these acts have great relevance to the future career of these prospective teachers. Finally, attention will depend on what activities and models are most readily available to be attended to. For example, someone is more likely to attend to aggressive acts if constantly surrounded by them than if aggression is rare in the environment (Short, 1968).

Attention is also influenced by whether the observed action produces a noticeable effect (Yussen, 1974). Actions without *functional value*—without apparent results or usefulness for dealing with the environment—are often ignored. People pay little attention to much of what they see everyday because it has no noticeable outcome.

Figure 11.2 🍎 Processes Governing Observational Learning
Adapted from Bandura, 1986, p. 52.

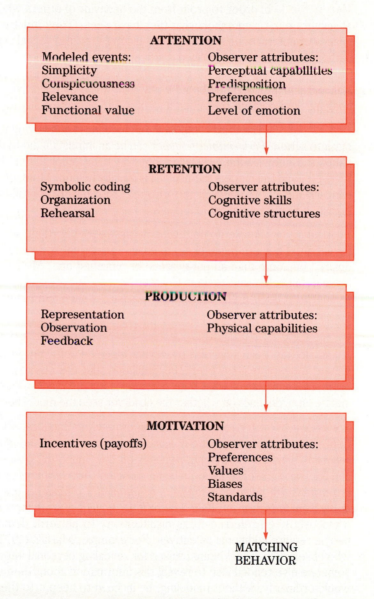

MODELED
EVENTS

ATTENTION

Modeled events: Observer attributes:
Simplicity   Perceptual capabilities
Conspicuousness   Predisposition
Relevance   Preferences
Functional value   Level of emotion

RETENTION

Symbolic coding   Observer attributes:
Organization   Cognitive skills
Rehearsal   Cognitive structures

PRODUCTION

Representation   Observer attributes:
Observation   Physical capabilities
Feedback

MOTIVATION

Incentives (payoffs)   Observer attributes:
                           Preferences
                           Values
                           Biases
                           Standards

MATCHING
BEHAVIOR

Attractive models, like those in advertisements or on television programs, attract considerable attention. Television, in general, is an effective attention-getting device for modeling purposes, though that is not its prime intention, except perhaps for advertisements.

To gain student attention for observational learning, teachers should try (1) *accentuating* the *essential features* of the performance to be learned, (2) *subdividing* activities into parts, (3) *highlighting* the component skills, and (4) *giving* the students *opportunities between observations to practice* what they have seen.

Retention.   In order to profit from the behavior of others who are no longer present, observers must remember what they have seen. They must *code* the information into images or abstractions such as mental pictures, or into verbal symbols, and then store it in their memories (as described in Chapter 6). It is very helpful if the modeled activities are *rehearsed* or practiced immediately after they are seen (Bandura & Jeffrey, 1973). Rehearsal or practice need not be physical; it can be cognitive, that is, with the person imaging or visualizing the action in contrast to actually doing it.

Production.   The third component of modeling is converting the idea, image, or memory into action. *Performance feedback* can be an important aid to this process. Self-observation through videotape replays is one way to accomplish this. Feedback from coaches, teachers, and the models themselves is equally helpful. Most effective is corrective modeling (Vasta, 1976), in which performance problems are identified and the correct performance is then remodeled.

Motivation.   People do not enact or carry out everything they have learned from observation. They are more likely to enact a modeled behavior if it results in a valued or desired outcome than an unrewarded or punished one. Motivation will be dealt with in more detail below and again in Chapter 12.

The sequence of observational learning is shown in Figure 11.3.

Learning from the Outcomes of Models

It has already been said that observing modeled acts can, in itself, lead individuals to imitate those acts. However, the likelihood that the observed acts will be imitated is primarily a function of what their outcome is for the model. The choice to imitate or not imitate often depends on whether the observer sees the model being rewarded or punished.

Vicarious Reinforcement.   Research results (Bandura, 1986) show, beyond question, that *rewarded modeling is more effective than modeling alone in fostering imitative behavior*. This effect, though, depends on how much the observer values the outcome and on what type of behavior is being modeled. *Acts that involve effort and other unpleasant aspects are much more likely to be imitated if a model is observed being rewarded for doing them than if no one does them or if the model's consequences are not positive*. This has previously been referred to as disinhibition. To perform demanding or effortful acts, people require additional incentives. For example, Marlatt (1972) reported that persons who observed a model being praised for revealing personal information about himself to someone else tended also to reveal this information about themselves even though they would ordinarily, without modeling, be inclined to keep it to themselves.

The effect of vicarious reinforcement is particularly important in situations where it is difficult to otherwise judge the quality of a particular act or behavior. When someone is

Figure 11.3 🍎 The Sequence of Observational Learning

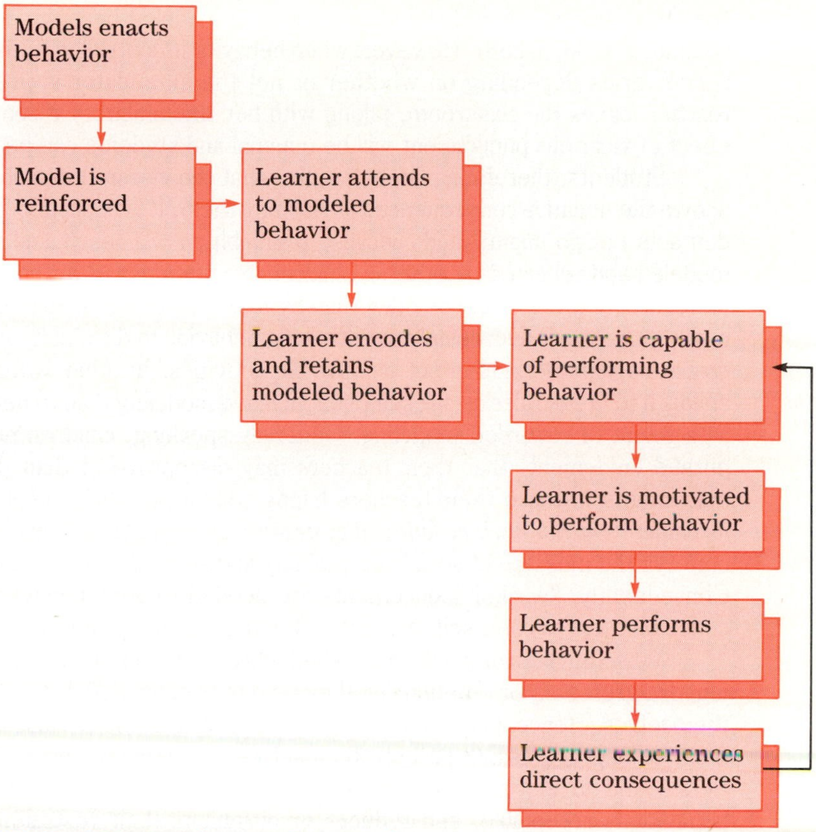

```
Models enacts
behavior
    │
    ▼
Model is          →   Learner attends
reinforced            to modeled
                      behavior
                          │
                          ▼
                      Learner encodes   →   Learner is capable   ◄──┐
                      and retains           of performing           │
                      modeled behavior      behavior                │
                                                │                   │
                                                ▼                   │
                                            Learner is motivated    │
                                            to perform behavior     │
                                                │                   │
                                                ▼                   │
                                            Learner performs        │
                                            behavior                │
                                                │                   │
                                                ▼                   │
                                            Learner experiences ────┘
                                            direct consequences
```

shooting a basketball and the ball goes in the basket, it is evident that the behavior was effective. However, when the quality of behavior is harder to judge, as when a student is giving a classroom talk or answering a teacher's question, the outcome of the behavior for the model provides considerable information for the observer. In those cases, teacher praise as an outcome for the model would foster modeling by an observer.

Finally, there is the old adage that "nothing succeeds like success." When a model achieves a valued outcome, there is no shortage of imitators. When one television network came out with a successful program format, such as situation comedy before a live audience, the other networks were quick to follow suit (Brown, 1971). When one student "gets away" with something, others are sure to follow.

Vicarious Punishment.   *When models are seen experiencing negative outcomes, the inclination of others to behave in similar way is diminished or inhibited.* This provides a mechanism for any group or society to acculturate its members to the rules of behavior and the sanctions that follow unacceptable behavior. Wilson, Robertson, Herlong, and Haynes (1979) found, for example, that students did not act aggressively in the classroom when a peer's aggressive acts were punished by the teacher, but they did behave aggressively when they saw that the aggressive acts of their peer went unpunished. Clearly, "observers who have seen modeled behavior punished are much less likely to act on what they have learned than if they have seen the modeled behavior rewarded or ignored" (Bandura, 1986, p. 288). However, when behavior is controlled by intimidation, its occurrence varies depending on whether or not the intimidator is present. So, when the teacher leaves the classroom, taking with her the inhibitory threat of punishment, the effect of vicarious punishment will be minimal and students can be expected to act out.

Students, therefore, can be taught what the classroom prohibitions are by being shown the negative consequences of violating them. It is especially important that forbidden acts not go unpunished, because disinhibition will result and then the acts will be modeled and repeated by others. Children can often get what they want more easily by disregarding prohibitions or rules than by following them. Therefore, it will not require much modeling of successful rule-breaking behavior to disinhibit or reduce vicarious restraints against forbidden but pleasurable activities. In other words, it is easier to get children to break rules as a result of unpunished modeling than to get them to follow rules as a result of rewarded modeling. Generally speaking, children need less influence to pursue enjoyments that their teachers may disapprove of than they need to forsake enjoyments to make their teachers happy (Bandura, 1986). That is why *prohibited or forbidden behavior must be followed by negative consequences*. The absence of punishment conveys the message of social acceptability and so weakens the restraints of observers. Consequently, "weaker inducements are needed to goad behavior that violates social codes but serves one's self-interests" (Bandura, 1986, p. 290).

When aggression goes unpunished, children tend to imitate it. When they are punished aggressively or emotionally, they tend to become aggressive, emotional punishers themselves. Hence, punitive and aggressive parents tend to raise children who become punitive and aggressive parents themselves. In addition, the portrayal of violence in movies and on television as permissible and successful leads children to believe that such behavior is acceptable, and reduces or disinhibits their restraints against it (Larsen, 1968). Some effects of the consequences of performing prohibited acts is shown in Table 11.2.

Table 11.2 🍎 Effects of the Consequences for Performing Prohibited Behavior

Model's Consequences	Effects on Observer
Punishment	Conveys social unacceptability
	Inihibits or restrains imitation (in presence of punisher)
Excessive punishment	Causes identification
	Legitimizes punishment as solution
Lack of punishment	Conveys social acceptability
	Disinhibits or weakens restraint
	Increases functional value
	Makes imitation likely (especially of pleasant act)

Model Attributes.   To predict the effects of vicarious consequences, teachers must consider not only the outcomes but also the characteristics or attributes of the model. *The more similar in characteristics the model is to the observer, the greater is the likelihood that similar actions by the observer will yield the same results as they did for the model.* However, in stark contrast to this is the fact that models with high status, competence, and power are more effective in influencing others to behave similarly than models of less stature. Why this seeming contradiction?

The answer may lie in the fact that "a model's attributes exert greatest influence when the modeled behavior is observable, but its consequences remain unknown" (Bandura, 1986, p. 209). In this case, the functional value of the modeled behavior must be judged from outward appearance, and the success of the model causes the observer to infer or expect that the behavior actually contributed to that success. However, if the observer imitates the behavior modeled by the successful and attractive model and the consequences for the observer are unsatisfactory, not only will the imitation of that behavior cease, but also the model will lose some of its attractiveness for the observer. The model will then be less influential for the observer.

The combined effects of model status and consequences on imitation look like this:

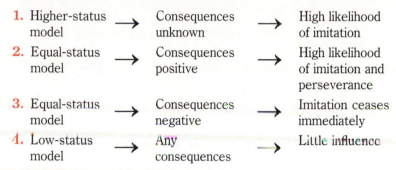

1. Higher-status model → Consequences unknown → High likelihood of imitation

2. Equal-status model → Consequences positive → High likelihood of imitation and perseverance

3. Equal-status model → Consequences negative → Imitation ceases immediately

4. Low-status model → Any consequences → Little influence

In the first instance (the higher-status model), the observer is lured by the expectation of becoming as successful as the model by imitating him or her. If you wear the same sneakers as your favorite basketball star, for example, you may think you will become a great player too. Or, use the beauty model's face cream and you too will become beautiful enough to adorn the cover of a fashion magazine.

In the second instance (the equal-status model), the observer believes that if the model can do it, he or she can do it too (Brown & Inouye, 1978). Of course, with an equal-status model, the question of whether or not the modeled behavior can be imitated successfully is important. The consequences to the model are critical because they are the basis by which the observer decides whether the behavior is worth trying. The similarity of the model to the observer is what helps the observer decide whether or not he or she can carry out the behavior too. In the classroom context, both high-status and equal-status models will be influential.

Vicarious Motivation.   Observed outcomes not only inform, they also motivate; but they only motivate someone who values those particular outcomes. If an observed behavior results in a valued outcome, the observer will be motivated to imitate that behavior. The observer must also believe, however, that he or she can reproduce the behavior. Seeing others succeed or fail helps people judge their own capability for carrying out the behavior.

The magnitude and frequency of the reward the model receives dictates the observer's motivation to persevere at the same act. Gamblers see the large amounts of money that can be won and the frequency with which they are won, and so are motivated to persevere in their gambling activity. In the classroom, seeing sustained hard work and study yield hard-to-come-by rewards demonstrates to the observer the usefulness of perseverance (Bandura, 1986). In such cases, observers may be willing to tolerate initial failures because the expectation for success is buoyed by the success of the model. If, however, successes come easily to others but rarely to oneself, the result is loss of self-confidence and despondency (Davis & Yates, 1982). We will return to this later, in the discussion of self-efficacy.

Box 11.1

The Teacher as Manager of Observational Learning

Identify the Behaviors to Be Modeled

Cognitive and motor skills (for example, reading, handwriting)

Common sense

Manners (for example, courtesy, respect for personal property)

Emotional displays (for example, anger)

Treatment of others (for example, meting out rewards and punishments)

Identify the Model

Self

Other students (of equal status)

Other live models: community visitors

Symbolic models: "heroes," videotapes, movies

Present the Modeled Behavior

Gain student attention—make it simple, conspicuous; break it down

Help them remember—coding and rehearsal

Help them produce—practice

Motivate them to imitate—provide incentives

Create Functional Value of Model's Behavior

Reward positive performance and positive behavior of model

Punish negative performance and negative behavior of model

Do not overreact or react personally to model's behavior

Do not display indifference to or ignore model's behavior

Vicarious Emotion.   Many emotions, such as fears, are acquired through observation. Sometimes people are afraid of, say, snakes, dogs, or tests, even though they have never been personally injured by them. Observers can get aroused and communicate their feelings through their voices, postures, and facial cues in addition to what they say. Or, they may scream, yell, or cry. Subsequent to such vicarious experiences, direct experiences with the same things may provoke the same emotion displayed by the model.

Some techniques for the teacher to use to manage observational learning are described in Box 11.1.

Self-Efficacy

Self-efficacy is Bandura's major concept in terms of its projected influence on behavior. Technically called *perceived self-efficacy*, it is defined as *"people's judgments of their capabilities to organize and execute courses of action required to attain designated types of performances"* (Bandura, 1986, p. 391). In other words, it is a personal belief about how successfully one can deal with a prospective difficult situation, such as a test, an interview, a contest, teaching a class, or a gathering of family members. Self-efficacy is *not* a function of a person's skills but of the *judgments* a person makes of what he or she can do with those skills. Self-efficacy is a self-belief in the capability to cope or excel in different situations.

Role of Self-Efficacy in Behavior

Bandura (1977) distinguishes between *self-efficacy* expectations, or *the conviction that one can successfully execute a behavior*, and *outcome expectations*, or the *estimate that a behavior will lead to certain outcomes*. Their relationship is shown in Figure 11.4. As the figure shows, performing the behavior depends on the *belief* that the behavior can be performed successfully, not on the estimated likelihood that performing the behavior will produce a particular outcome. It is not the value of the outcome or its likelihood that motivates behavior, according to Bandura; it is the belief that the behavior can be performed successfully. (Of course, having the skill necessary to perform it successfully is also a requirement.)

Figure 11.4 🍎 **The Difference Between Efficacy Expectations and Outcome Expectations as They Affect Behaviors and Outcomes**   From Bandura, 1977, p. 193.

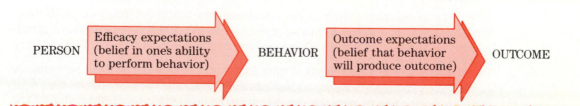

PERSON → Efficacy expectations (belief in one's ability to perform behavior) → BEHAVIOR → Outcome expectations (belief that behavior will produce outcome) → OUTCOME

The distinction between self-efficacy and outcome expectations, and the secondary role afforded outcome expectations as a predictor of behavior, has been challenged by Kirsch (1985) and others.

Effects of Self-Efficacy.   Self-efficacy theory predicts that people will (1) avoid situations that they believe exceed their coping skills, but (2) get involved in situations that they believe themselves capable of handling. In other words, self-efficacy beliefs will affect the *choice* of whether or not to attempt a behavior or task (Bandura, 1977). Judgments of efficacy will also affect the amount of energy or *effort* someone chooses to expend, and the degree of *persistence* in expending that effort, in the face of obstacles or over extended periods of time. Salomon (1984) found that children having high perceived self-efficacy as learners expended a lot of effort and experienced better consequent learning in situations they perceived as tough, but expended less effort and consequently experienced poorer learning in situations they perceived as easy. A strong sense of self-efficacy helps someone withstand failure in challenging situations.

Bandura (1986) also proposed that self-efficacy beliefs produce feelings or emotions in anticipation of performing. In other words, thinking that you are likely to succeed or cope gives rise to good feelings, such as pleasure, while expecting failure produces bad feelings, such as anxiety. These feelings then affect the performance itself. Thus, thoughts are the source of feelings. To change or eliminate certain negative feelings like anger, fear, or depression, you must first change your thoughts, particularly thoughts about being able to cope with difficult situations. For an illustration, see Box 11.2.

Characteristics of Self-Efficacy.   The impact of self-efficacy on behavior depends on three characteristics of self-efficacy (Bandura, 1977). First, it depends on the *magnitude* or *level* of efficacy expectations or beliefs, whether the beliefs apply to only the easy tasks within a domain, to the tasks of moderate difficulty, or to the really difficult tasks as well. For example, a student is given a book to read. Does she believe that she can read the book? If her self-efficacy for reading were of a low level or magnitude, then she would believe that she could read the book only if it were an easy one. However, if her self-efficacy for reading was at a high enough level or magnitude, then she would believe that she could read the book no matter how difficult it was.

The second characteristic is *generality*, or the breadth of the domain to which self-efficacy judgments apply. If a child's self-efficacy for bike riding were general enough, then he would believe that he could ride any kind of bike under almost any set of conditions. The third characteristic is *strength*, or how strongly specific efficacy beliefs are held. Strongly held beliefs of skillfulness or mastery capability would be less easily changed by a few unsuccessful experiences than would weaker beliefs.

Sources of Efficacy Information

How do people develop self-efficacy or the beliefs they hold about their own capabilities? Bandura (1977, 1986) proposes four sources of information that cause perceptions of self-efficacy to develop and change. These are described below and shown in Figure 11.5.

Enactive Attainment.   The most influential source of information about performance capabilities is actual *performance accomplishments*, or *personal mastery experiences*. What more convincing way to learn that something can be done than to actually try to do it and succeed. Success teaches people that they can succeed, and repeated early successes provide a cushion against occasional later failures. Moreover, when the basis for the sense of self-efficacy is someone's own actions and attainments, it tends to generalize to a range of similar activities.

Success enhances self-efficacy less when the task is easy than when it is hard, because the easy task did not require as much capability as the hard one. When one's success requires receiving help from someone else, self-efficacy is not enhanced as much as when success is accomplished by oneself. However, people with strong fears or inhibitions are not likely to do what is terribly hard for them or what they dread, especially by themselves. A child with a strong fear of speaking in class, for example, is not likely to speak out on his or her own. In such cases, methods must be used to induce or help that person perform the task, because there is little chance that it will be performed otherwise.

How can a teacher help or induce a student to perform a task, and consequently enable that student to experience the sense of self-efficacy that comes from success? One technique is called *participant modeling*: The student is helped (or prompted) to

---

Box 11.2

"Squeezing an Orange"

Wayne Dyer, the noted psychologist, often asks his audiences: *"What would you get if you squeezed an orange?"* *"Orange juice"* is the usual reply. "But what if you squeezed it at night?" is his next question. Again, the reply is "Orange juice." "And if your mother squeezed it?" "Orange juice." "If you squeezed with two hands or one?" Same answer: "Orange juice."

The next question to be asked is *"Why do you always get orange juice when you squeeze an orange?"* Think about that for a moment and see what you would say. The answer the audience gives is *"Because that's what's inside."*

Now ask yourself this next question. *"What do you get when you get squeezed? What comes out?"* Not orange juice, silly, because that's not what's inside you. What you get is *whatever's inside you*. And that is where self-efficacy theory comes into the picture. It looks like this:

When you're "squeezed" by mom or by your teacher or by your students, what comes out of you will be what is inside you, based on your *thoughts* about whether you can deal with the situation and how those thoughts make you feel. Do you want "sweetness" to come out of you the next time you're "squeezed"? Then you'd better start thinking positive thoughts about yourself and your ability to cope.

Figure 11.5 🍎 Major Sources of Efficacy Information and Ways of Providing This Information
Adapted from Bandura, 1977, p. 195.

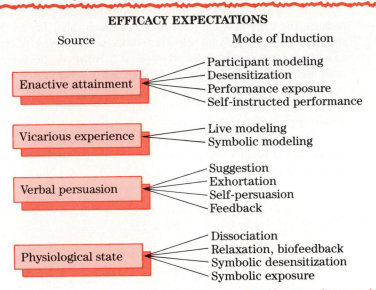

EFFICACY EXPECTATIONS

Source   Mode of Induction

Enactive attainment
- Participant modeling
- Desensitization
- Performance exposure
- Self-instructed performance

Vicarious experience
- Live modeling
- Symbolic modeling

Verbal persuasion
- Suggestion
- Exhortation
- Self-persuasion
- Feedback

Physiological state
- Dissociation
- Relaxation, biofeedback
- Symbolic desensitization
- Symbolic exposure

carry out or model one small step of the task at a time, or to complete the task starting with the easiest version and graduating to progressively harder versions (as in shaping). Another way is to have the student complete the task jointly with another, more capable student or even with the teacher as a partner. As the student progresses, supplementary aids are gradually withdrawn (or faded) so that the student can eventually perform successfully unassisted. Participant modeling, therefore, means doing it oneself with all the needed help, and then having that help gradually withdrawn.

A second approach, especially to reduce fear, is called *desensitization*. Gradually exposing students to fear-provoking experiences while trying to get them to relax helps them learn that they can cope with that situation (Wolpe, 1974). A third approach, called *performance exposure*, involves putting the student in the situation repeatedly so that he or she can adapt to the threat. This is somewhat akin to repeatedly throwing a person who is afraid of water into the deep end of a swimming pool. If the person is fished out right away, the result may be the elimination of the fear. Of course, this procedure is risky, depending on whether or not the exposure carries with it a sense of success (Rabavilas, Boulougouris, & Stefanis, 1976).

Finally, performance can be aided through the use of *self-instructions*, such as thinking about the performance of a task beforehand or viewing one's prior performance of it on videotape and telling oneself exactly what to do differently to improve. This process can be stimulated by having students verbalize aloud their thought processes during mastery experiences (Bandura, 1983). Seeing or otherwise being aware of one's successful performances strengthens self-beliefs in the capability to perform.

Personal accomplishment—the experience of success—or what Bandura calls enactive attainment, is the best way for someone to learn to believe in herself. With success like this, this young woman will have her sense of self-efficacy enhanced.

Vicarious Experience.   People do not rely on personal experience as the *sole* source of information about their level of self-efficacy. If they did, they would have to try everything themselves. *Seeing others who are similar perform activities successfully* can raise perceptions of one's own level of self-efficacy (Bandura, 1986). In other words, people say to themselves: "If they can do it, I can do it too." By the same token, seeing others who are similar fail at a given task causes judgments of one's own capabilities to be lowered (Brown & Inouye, 1978).

The reliance on others' experiences for one's own judgments of self-efficacy is especially great when *uncertainty* exists about one's own capability to perform a given task. This is particularly true when the uncertainty comes from a lack of relevant prior experience, or when factual evidence for judging performance is lacking. When one has never done something before, or when the quality of performance is difficult to judge, dependence on observing the performance of others to judge one's own capability is particularly great. How, for example, did you know what score to expect to get when you took the Scholastic Aptitude Test (SAT)? The probable answer is that you used other people's scores as a basis for formulating your self-judgment.

Generally, vicarious experiences are weaker than actual experiences (or enactive attainment) in affecting self-efficacy judgments. However, repeatedly seeing a model successfully complete a task that you have failed at will tend to sustain your desire to perform despite your own personal experience (Brown & Inouye, 1978).

To whom do people compare themselves? They compare themselves to *live models*, or people actually there, and to *symbolic* models, or people seen on television, in movies, or in magazines. Most often, people select models of capability equal to their own, but sometimes they choose models whom they aspire to be like. Judgments of similarity in choosing models apply only to those attributes or qualities judged to be of predictive significance for the task at hand. For example, in making judgments about stamina and physical efficacy, women chose other women as models, rather than choosing men, because they viewed themselves as dissimilar to men on the attribute of physical stamina (Gould & Weiss, 1981).

How should a teacher model performances to enhance the self-efficacy of students? First, the teacher should always engage in a difficult activity in ways that exemplify what that activity is like so that students can learn to *predict* the capabilities that will be required to perform that activity. In doing a math problem, for example, a teacher should not use shortcuts and thus cause students to think that the problem is easier to do than it will actually turn out to be. Second, the teacher should demonstrate highly effective techniques for handling the threatening aspects of the activity, so that students can learn to *control* their fears in that situation and cope with it in a capable fashion (Miller, 1981). For example, if there are ways for students to check their work as they try to complete a difficult math problem, the teacher should show them what these are.

Verbal Persuasion.   This is an attempt to *talk people into believing* that they have the capabilities they need to achieve what they seek. Often, what is accomplished through verbal persuasion is to convince people that they have the capability to do the job *if* they put in enough effort. However, it is probably easier to undermine self-efficacy by persuasion than to enhance it.

The effectiveness of verbal persuasion depends on the perceived credibility and expertness of the persuader; just as the effect of any communication depends on these qualities in the communicator (see Chapter 10). The more the persuader is believed, the more likely the recipient is to change his or her self-perception of capability. However, if someone is persuaded to believe that he can do something, and then tries it and fails, his regard for the opinion of the persuader is likely to go down.

Most persuaders rely on *suggestion*, a more casual form of persuasion as used, for example, in television commercials ("Be all you can be"), or on *exhortation*, a more intense form of persuasion as used, for example, by athletic coaches ("You can do it"). There is also the persuasion people use on themselves (*self-persuasion*) and, finally, there is *feedback*, the kind that tells someone that she is doing a good job (or, perhaps, a poor job) at some task, as a reflection of her capability. Encouraging feedback that leads to higher self-efficacy leads children to work harder and to accomplish more (Schunk, 1982, 1983).

In using persuasion, teachers are encouraged (1) to link it to self-efficacy, and (2) to provide it in the form of specific task feedback (for example, "Your performance on this task shows me that you know what you are doing and that you're capable of doing it well").

Physiological State.   People rely partly on their *emotional state* or *state of arousal* to judge whether or not they are capable of doing something successfully. People are much more likely to expect success on a task when they are not nervous about doing it than when they are. Fear and anxiety create the anticipation of stress in an upcoming task and thus reduce the sense of self-efficacy. Techniques that eliminate this anticipatory fear increase self-efficacy and lead to improvements in performance (Barrios, 1983).

Physiological states of fear can be reduced by *dissociation*, or convincing people that the fear comes from their thoughts and not from the feared object or situation. Other techniques include *relaxation* exercises, particularly when paired with *biofeedback* or actual evidence of one's emotional state (such as pulse rate), so that one can learn to control one's emotional reaction. Finally, mental exercises that combine visualization of the feared situation with resulting feelings of calmness rather than fear (*symbolic desensitization* and *exposure*) help to get rid of the feelings that signal the expectation of danger and the impending failure to cope.

The combined sources of efficacy information are illustrated by the anecdote in Box 11.3.

Self-Efficacy and School

In school, children's knowledge and thinking skills are continually tested and evaluated, and children are often compared to one another. Good students quickly develop a strong sense of self-efficacy. Poorer students find their self-efficacy judgments to be undermined, leading to a continuing downward spiral of performance. This is particularly true when (1) classroom instructional practices are lockstep, requiring that everyone be taught the same thing at the same time; (2) students are grouped by ability, thereby diminishing the self-efficacy judgments of those cast into the lower ranks; or (3) performance is competitive, dooming many to fail in order to provide success for a relative few (Bandura, 1986).

Teachers who endure frustrations due to the repeated failures of their low-achieving students also experience a loss of what has been called *instructional efficacy* (Dembo & Gibson, 1985). Thus, teachers also suffer losses in self-efficacy when they perceive themselves as unable to cope with the stresses and demands of teaching. Teachers must be sensitive to the needs of their students, but they also need success experiences themselves in order to feel good as teachers.

Is there a solution? Since self-perceptions of cognitive ability are based in large part on social comparison or comparisons between students, teachers are encouraged

- to have students engage in diversified activities;
- to tailor instruction to individual student skills;
- to use a cooperative rather than a competitive approach;
- to avoid making comparative evaluations.

The above techniques stimulate students to compare their progress to personal standards and, hence, to expand their competencies, rather than facing demoralizing social comparison (Rosenholtz & Rosenholtz, 1981). A more personalized classroom structure produces higher perceived efficacy and decreases students' dependence on the

Box 11.3

🍎

The "Lost Boy" on the Bridge

At the end of the boardwalk was an old, abandoned railroad bridge that looked like the one in the movie *The Lost Boys*. It stood on huge concrete "feet" and spanned a narrow channel of water about 30 feet below it. A boy of about 10 or 11 stood on the inside edge of the platform, at the edge of the rusty tracks, holding onto a pillar and looking down. Wearing a bathing suit, he was shivering and obviously trying to decide whether or not to jump the 30 feet into the water below to join his two friends who were already there. A group of onlookers gathered around him, waiting to see what he would do. Landing in the water meant jumping clear out over the base of one of the cement feet, a challenging act no doubt, and one that gave the boy great pause, as his shivering body revealed.

He was obviously asking himself: "Can I make it?" (or, in terms of the concepts of this chapter, "Do I have the *self-efficacy*?") His body, his *physiological state*, was answering him NO, as evidenced by the fear in his face and the goose bumps on his skin. As a result, he held firmly to the pillar. But his friends below were looking to change his level of self-efficacy through *verbal persuasion — exhortation*, to be exact. "You can do it." "It's easy." "We did it." "Don't be afraid." "Come on." "You'll make it," were the shouts coming up from below, but to no avail. The boy held fast.

So the other two boys decided to try a better method of enhancing self-efficacy: *vicarious experience*. They would serve as *live models*. They climbed out of the water and ran to the middle of the bridge where the boy and the onlookers were congregated. "Look, we'll show you how easy it is." And they both popped off the bridge like buttons on a shirt and landed safely in the water 30 feet below.

But even modeling didn't work, because the boy still held fast to the pillar and refused to jump. Only *enactive attainment*, actually jumping and living to tell of it, would convince him that he could do it, but his fear blocked him from trying. So the two friends came back again to the middle of the bridge and each took a hand of the lost boy. "Close your eyes and imagine jumping and landing in the water," they told him. "Now give us each a hand, and jump out as far as you can, but don't look down."

And so the frightened boy closed his eyes and tried to see himself being capable enough to complete the leap successfully, in order to be willing to try it. But would having his friends on either side offer enough reassurance? The onlookers waited in great anticipation. And then, "Frankie!" It was his mother's angry voice calling him. "Frankie, you come here this instant." Little Frankie no longer had thoughts about fear of the jump in his head. They were replaced by thoughts of fear of his mother. For a brief instant he thought: "I can do it." And poof, he was gone — 30 feet down into the water below.

opinions of teachers and classmates. Students' success in such a personalized and accepting classroom environment enhances teachers' sense of success or instructional efficacy.

Some specific techniques that teachers can use to enhance student self-efficacy and performance are offered in Box 11.4.

Self-Regulation

Self-regulation, or *the exercise of influence over one's own behavior*, is a fact of human existence. If actions were determined solely by external circumstances, people would be

Box 11.4

🍎

What Teachers Can Do to Enhance Students' Self-Efficacy and Self-Regulated Performance

Tuckman (1990) reports that the following teacher behaviors help students, particularly those low in self-efficacy, increase their self-efficacy and, as a result, perform more persistently.

1. Keep the tasks small. Require that more assignments be done but keep the length of each assignment as small and manageable as possible. This encourages proximal goal setting and task completion.

2. Use preset criteria for evaluating student task performance, and inform the students of the criteria prior to their undertaking the task (so they know exactly what they have to accomplish).

3. Provide specific numerical feedback to students after each assignment and test, to help them know exactly where they stand relative to the performance criteria.

4. Provide encouragement in response to student performance, by telling students what they have done well rather than what they have done poorly.

5. Have students participate in formal, written goal setting prior to undertaking specific tasks and tests, and urge them to set attainable goals.

6. Have students plan, in writing, when, where, and how they will complete assignments and what they will do to overcome obstacles that may arise.

7. Provide incentives for performance, beyond the normal grades, such as bonus points that can be accumulated to elevate a grade.

8. Use a cooperative learning approach to instruction (as described in Chapter 10), but have students submit their work individually for evaluation.

9. Get students into the performance "habit" by using the above guidelines.

like "weathervanes" (Bandura, 1986, p. 335), shifting direction at a moment's notice to conform to whatever outside influence was impinging on them. Self-regulation, however, is not achieved solely by willpower. People do possess "*self-directive capabilities* that enable them to exercise some control over their thoughts, feelings, and actions by the consequences that they produce for themselves" (Bandura, 1986, p. 335). However, people who are skeptical of their ability to exercise control over their behavior tend to undermine their own efforts to deal effectively with situations that tax or challenge their capabilities.

Self-Regulation and Self-Efficacy

The ability to control oneself—to choose, persist, persevere, and succeed in attempting to study, to diet, to exercise, to be in a good mood, to get up in the morning, to go to work, or to carry out any behavior that is taxing or challenging—depends, in part, on the belief in one's capability to do it. In short, self-regulation depends on self-efficacy. Barrios and Niehaus (1985) have shown that efficacy and, consequently, self-control to resist the use of drugs is undermined by inability to cope with negative emotions, social pressure to use drugs, and interpersonal conflict. People who have the necessary sense of self-efficacy to cope are able to produce the effort needed to succeed in high-risk situations. Success, in turn, further strengthens self-regulatory efficacy, while slip-ups, even when only occasional, may create a disbelief in one's coping efficacy and a tendency to relapse. Once a person sees him- or herself as powerless, further coping efforts are abandoned, resulting in a total loss of self-control.

Necessary coping skills and the belief in one's ability or efficacy to self-regulate are built, in large measure, through enactive attainment or mastery experiences. Persons with high self-regulatory efficacy were more likely to resist the urge to smoke following treatment, even after an occasional relapse, than persons with low self-regulatory effi-

Box 11.5

The Story of Johnny and Sarita

"Johnny Lingo's the sharpest trader in this part of the Pacific."

The simple statement made the villagers choke with muffled laughter and almost fall off the veranda steps.

"What goes on?" I demanded. "Everybody tells me to get in touch with Johnny Lingo and then breaks up. Is there no such person or is he the village idiot?"

"Not idiot," said Shenkin. "Only one thing. Five months ago Johnny came to Kiniwata and found himself a wife. He paid her father eight cows!"

He spoke the last words with great solemnity. Two or three cows would buy a fair-to-middling wife, four or five a highly satisfactory one.

"Eight cows!" I said. "She must have beauty that takes your breath away."

"That's why they laugh," Shenkin said. "It would be kindness to call her plain. She was little and skinny with no—ah—endowments. She walked with her shoulders hunched and her head ducked, as if she was trying to hide behind herself. She was scared of her own shadow, frightened by her own voice. She was afraid to laugh in public. The cousins urged Sam to ask for three cows and hold out for two until he was sure Johnny'd pay one. But Sam was so afraid that there'd be some slip in this marriage chance for Sarita that he wouldn't hold out for anything, so the cousins resigned themselves to accepting one cow. Then Johnny came in and said 'Sam Karo, father of Sarita, I offer eight cows for your daughter,' and delivered the cows."

This story interested me, so I decided to investigate. The next day, I reached the island where Johnny lived, went to his home, and was welcomed by him with a grace that made me feel the owner. I told him that his people had told me about him, that they said he was a sharp trader, that the marriage settlement he had made for his wife was eight cows, and that the local people wonder why he paid so much.

His chest expanded with satisfaction. "When they speak of marriage settlements, it will be remembered that Johnny Lingo paid eight cows for Sarita."

I was disappointed. I guess he felt he had to make himself famous for his way of buying a wife. I was tempted to deflate him by reporting that in Kiniwata he was laughed at for a fool.

cacy (Condiotte & Lichtenstein, 1981). College students with high self-efficacy were more inclined to participate in a voluntary homework program, and so gain the potential bonuses that were offered, than were those with low self-efficacy (Tuckman & Sexton, 1991). Recovering heart attack victims who saw themselves as high in physical efficacy expended more effort in exercising than did those who saw themselves as low (Ewart, Taylor, Reese, & DeBusk, 1983).

Thus, it would be fair to conclude that "believing is seeing" (rather than the other way around—as the customary saying goes). If you *believe* in your ability to control yourself, then you are likely to behave in a manner that enables you to *see* the results that you expect. If you *believe* you cannot do something, the result you *see* will be consistent with that belief: You will fail. (This is nicely illustrated by "The Story of Johnny and Sarita" in Box 11.5.) The key to self-regulation is believing in your capability to control yourself in difficult, risky, or challenging situations.

And then I saw her. She was the most beautiful woman I have ever seen. Not with the common, earthbound beauty of the girl who carries fruit. This woman had an ethereal loveliness that was at the same time from the heart of nature. The lift of her shoulders, the sparkle of her eyes spelled a pride to which no one could deny her the right. She moved with a grace that made her look like a queen who might turn into a kitten.

"She—she's glorious. Who is she?" I asked.

"My wife."

I stared at him. Do they practice polygamy here? He, for his eight cows, bought both Sarita and this other?

"There is only one Sarita," Johnny said, in reply to my puzzlement. "Perhaps you wish to say she does not look the way they say she looked in Kiniwata."

"She doesn't." The impact of the girl's appearance made me forget tact. "I heard she was homely. They all make fun of you because you let yourself be cheated by Sam Karo."

"You think eight cows were too many? Do you think anyone will make fun of us when they see her now? Much has happened to change her, particularly the day she went away."

"You mean she married you?"

"That, yes. But most of all, I mean the arrangements for the marriage. Do you ever think what is the lowest price for which she can be bought? And then later, when the women talk, they boast of what their husbands paid for them. One says four cows, another six. How does the woman feel who was sold for one or two? This could not happen to my Sarita."

"Then you paid that unprecedented number just to make your wife happy?"

"Happy? Yes, I wanted Sarita to be happy, but I wanted more than that. You say she's different from the way they remember her in Kiniwata. This is true. Many things can change a woman. Things that happen inside, things that happen outside. *But the thing that matters most is what she thinks about herself.* In Kiniwata, Sarita believed she was worth nothing. Now she knows she is worth more than any other woman on the islands."

"Then you wanted . . . "

"I wanted to marry Sarita. I loved her and no other woman."

"But—" I was close to understanding.

"But," he finished softly, "I wanted an eight-cow wife."

SOURCE: McGerr, Patricia. (1988, February). Johnny Lingo's Eight-Cow Wife. *Reader's Digest.*

Enhancing Self-Regulatory Efficacy

The three elements or components of self-regulation (Zimmerman, 1989) are the following:

1. *Self-monitoring*—knowing what you are doing; being aware; perceiving things accurately, not simply acting out of habit. This provides you with the information you need to set realistic performance standards and to evaluate ongoing changes in behavior.

2. *Self-evaluation*—deciding whether a given performance should be regarded favorably or unfavorably based on internal standards and comparisons with others. This provides you with the information you need to react to your own behavior.

3. *Self-reaction*—creating incentives for your own behavior; acknowledging and verifying your competencies and capabilities; feeling satisfied with yourself; increasing your interest in continuing. (The weaker the external demands for performance, the heavier the reliance on self-reaction.)

The procedures described below are recommended to make these three components contribute positively and maximally to self-regulation.

Goal Setting.   According to Bandura (1986, p. 469), "goals enhance motivation through self-reactive influences." When people commit themselves to an explicit goal, they are likely to do what they need to do to meet that goal. When they fall short of it, the resulting dissatisfaction usually serves as an incentive to make them work harder. Both knowledge of performance and a standard of comparison are needed to produce motivational effects (Bandura & Cervone, 1983), and goals provide such a standard of comparison. Goals not only help people judge how well they are doing, they also provide people with a basis for judging their capabilities. Hence, they contribute to self-efficacy.

What does Bandura (1986) recommend about the goals that are to be set? He says that goals should be

1. *specific* (rather than vague), so that you can hold yourself to them;

2. *challenging, yet attainable* (rather than too easy or too difficult), so that they will make you work hard but not be discouraged if you don't reach them;

3. *proximal*, or in the here-and-now (rather than distant or in the future), so that you can do something about them now;

4. *self-determined*, or chosen by you (rather than by somebody else), so that you will hold yourself responsible for progress toward the goal;

5. *incremental*, or made up of small, stepwise subgoals (rather than a single, overall, stable entity), so that the attainment of each can be satisfying and instrumental in your achieving subsequent ones, and also so that occasional failure can be taken in stride.

Subgoals do two things: They provide a *guide* and an *inducement* for present action. Subgoal attainments also do two things: They produce *efficacy information* and *self-satisfactions* that help sustain effort along the way. "Persistence that leads to eventual mastery of an activity is thus ensured through a progression of subgoals, each with a high probability of success" (Bandura, 1986, p. 475).

Commitment.   Once you have set your goals, you must make a commitment to them. It is your commitment that ensures that you will

- consider them important,
- pledge yourself to attain them,
- feel constrained to work toward them,
- not put off or postpone your effort,
- judge yourself unfavorably for failing to try,
- feel responsible for the outcome.

The stronger the commitment to a goal, the stronger the attempt to attain it. Bandura (1986) suggests making a public commitment to a goal — telling others — because that will likely make you work even harder in order to avoid any negative social consequences such as embarrassment.

Incentives.   Incentives, or payoffs for outcomes, help cultivate a sense of personal efficacy and enhance interest in the task. Bandura (1982) distinguishes between *task-contingent* incentives, which are given to someone merely for performing a repetitive and routine task over and over again, and *competence-contingent* incentives, which are rewards for task mastery that reflect on personal efficacy. Performance accomplishments that enable someone to fulfill personal standards, heighten task interest, and increase the sense of competence or efficacy should be accompanied by incentives. These can be both *internal*, such as feeling good about oneself, and *external*, such as winning a prize or giving oneself a present. External rewards also provide efficacy information because their attainment indicates having performed well.

It is important that a student view competent performance as the reason for the reward, rather than the reward being the automatic cause of competent performance (Karniol & Ross, 1977) as in Skinner's contingency management (see Chapter 3). In providing rewards for student performance, teachers should make it clear that the student's performance caused the reward, not vice versa. One way to do this is to have students make a verbal statement affirming their own competence at the time the reward is given. Doing this also increases students' interest in the activity (Sagotsky & Lewis, 1978).

Personal Control.   Self-regulation is not likely to happen unless people assume personal control over as many as possible of the events that affect their lives. A product of believing in one's capability to function and cope is being able to actually deal with the difficulties and challenges in life (Miller, 1980).

The two dangers to avoid are (1) finding someone else to run your life and relinquishing control of yourself to the other person (called *proxy control*) and (2) having another person relinquish control of him- or herself to you and having to assume proxy control of this other person. In the first case, you would lose all sense of self-efficacy; in the second case, you would be doing all the work and suffering all the distress of failure for someone else.

When a person relinquishes personal control, she gives up trying. Usually her reason is that she doubts her ability to succeed or that she doubts that her efforts will produce results because of the unresponsiveness or punitiveness of her environment. In either event, feelings of despondency and apathy are the result. As a teacher, it is important to provide students with an environment in which their performance accomplishments can be attained and recognized and rewarded, so that they can develop the personal control that self-regulation requires. (Refer back to Box 11.4 for a summary of relevant teacher interventions.)

A proposal for dealing with perhaps the greatest "enemy" of self-regulation, procrastination, is offered in Box 11.6.

Box 11.6

🍎

Procrastination "Busting"

Inside you, even at your most compulsive moments, lurks a little "demon" that seems to keep you from doing things you ought to be doing. Instead of encouraging you to study, for example, the little demon convinces you to go to the movies and leave the studying until later. But when "later" comes, the little demon uses the same arguments again, and so "later," perhaps, becomes "much later" or even "never." The little demon is your procrastinator-in-chief, and if you want to "bust" it you have to know how it works.

It starts off by appealing to your *pleasure principle*—your preference for ease over hard work—but it never warns you that pleasure now often means considerable pain later when the work is due. Then it becomes your center of *self-doubt*, telling you that you're not good enough to succeed at something so why bother to even try. Finally, it tries to get you to *externalize blame*—to get mad at whoever has given you the work and not do it, to spite that person or to show that the assignment is unfair. In brief, the procrastination demon lulls you into having fun, then steps on your self-confidence, and finally goads you into being angry at someone else.

But who is this demon? It's really you. It's really your irrational thoughts. So what can you do about it? Try these things:

- Pick out subgoals that you can realistically achieve. (Study for 30 minutes at a time, for example.)

- Write down both the positive and the negative consequences of doing what you should do and of doing what the demon would have you do. (This means think rationally. What turns out to make better sense—doing what you ought to do or what the demon says?)

- Promise yourself an immediate positive consequence for your effort. (Give yourself a break or even an ice cream after meeting your study time goal.)

- Provide yourself with social support for working. (Find some friends to study with.)

- Learn from your mistakes. Take aim, not blame, if your actions go awry. Get right back on track.

Try these five techniques and see if you can't "bust" your procrastination demon right out of your life. (And teachers can try them with their students.)

SOURCE: Tuckman, B. W. (1989). Thinking out loud: Procrastination "busting." *Educational Technology*, 29(3), 48–49.

Summary of Main Points

1. Bandura identified the following three limitations of behaviorism in explaining social behavior: (1) It is not representative of what happens in natural settings (often, no one is there to provide a reward); (2) it does not account for the acquisition of novel responses; (3) it accounts only for *direct learning* (instantaneous matching with immediate consequences), not for *indirect learning* (delayed matching, delayed consequences).

2. Instead, Bandura proposed *social cognitive theory*, with its six principles. The first is *reciprocal determinism*, the idea that behavior, personal factors, and environmental events operate together as interactive determinants or causes of each other (as the three vertices of a triangle) in the self-system.

3. The second is that people have a *symbolic capability* to view the world and to react to it. Experiences and people in the world are represented as thoughts in people's heads, and often these thoughts, rather than the people or experiences themselves, are what people react to.

4. The third principle is *forethought capability*, or the ability to plan for the future by thinking before acting. Thoughts, according to Bandura, always precede acts.

5. The fourth principle is *vicarious capability*: People are able to learn by watching others behave and seeing the consequences of others' behavior. Beyond learning by carrying out their own actions, people can learn vicariously, by observing others.

6. The fifth principle is *self-regulatory capability*. People have the ability to control their own behavior, such as working, eating, drinking, and studying, based on their own internal standards and motivation.

7. The sixth principle is *self-reflective capability*, or the ability to think about oneself. A person's most important self-thought is his judgment of his own competence or capability to perform a task successfully. This is called perceived *self-efficacy*.

8. People learn the following five kinds of social behavior vicariously, by observing others or *models*: (1) *new cognitive skills and behaviors*; (2) *strengthened or weakened previously learned inhibitions* over behavior (what can and cannot be gotten away with or succeeded at, depending on the consequences the model experiences; (3) *social prompts or inducements* to behave in a like manner; (4) *how to use the environment and the objects in it*; (5) *when to become aroused and what emotional reaction to express*.

9. How do people learn from models? First, they must pay *attention* to what the model is doing (which will be easier if the model's behavior is simple, conspicuous, relevant, and frequent, and if the model is attractive). Second, they must *retain* or remember what they see by coding the information into images and rehearsing. Third, they must convert the information into action, or *produce* it, for which feedback is helpful. Finally, they must be *motivated* to imitate it, because it leads to a desired outcome.

10. What is particularly important in vicarious learning is the observed impact of the outcome of the model's behavior (or the observed consequences to the model of his or her behavior). An observer is more likely to imitate a behavior if the model is

rewarded for it than if it has no consequences, especially when the behavior involves effort or other unpleasant aspects. Vicarious reinforcement is also important when it is otherwise difficult to judge the quality of a particular act. Moreover, when a model achieves a widely valued outcome, there is no shortage of imitators.

11. But when others are seen getting *punished*, the inclination of observers to behave similarly is diminished. This is particularly true when the punishing agent is present as a source of intimidation.

12. Forbidden acts should be punished, because ignoring them would simply invite others to imitate or repeat them by leading them to believe that such behavior is socially acceptable. However, highly punitive personal reactions to modeled, unacceptable behavior lead to identification with or subsequent modeling of the highly punitive reaction.

13. The more similar the model is to the observer, the more likely the observer is to conclude that he or she can obtain the same results by imitating the behavior. However, if the consequences of the model's behavior are uncertain or unknown, then high-status models will exert the greatest influence.

14. Observed outcomes not only inform, they also motivate. Observers will persevere longer and tolerate more failure themselves if they have seen a model get a larger, more frequent reward rather than a smaller, less frequent one. Emotional reactions are also learned, as observers watch models react to the consequences of their behavior.

15. *Self-efficacy* is one's *judgment* of one's own capability to carry out a particular behavior or course of action successfully. This is contrasted with *outcome expectations*, or the estimate that a behavior will lead to a certain outcome.

16. Self-efficacy theory predicts that people *choose*, *persist in*, and *expend effort on* tasks they believe themselves capable of handling and *avoid* situations they believe exceed their coping skills. Self-efficacy judgments also provoke emotions—pleasure in anticipation of success and fear or anxiety in anticipation of threat or failure—as a function of the *magnitude*, *generality*, and *strength* of efficacy expectations.

17. Where does the information on which self-efficacy judgments are based come from? There are four sources. *Enactive attainment*, or actual performance accomplishments or mastery experiences, are the most influential source of information. Doing it oneself, with help, to become convinced that one can do it is called participant modeling. Desensitization, repeated exposure, and self-instruction also help convince people of their self-efficacy by enabling them to do something themselves.

18. *Vicarious experience*, or the outcomes for others similar to oneself, can be used to judge whether or not one also can do something. Models can be live (actually there) or symbolic (on TV, in movies, or in books).

19. *Verbal persuasion*—ranging from the weaker suggestion to the stronger exhortation—can also be used to affect self-efficacy. Finally, *physiological state* helps tell people whether they should expect to succeed or fail at an oncoming task.

20. To enhance student self-efficacy, teachers are encouraged to diversify classroom activities, tailor instruction to individual needs, use cooperative approaches, and avoid comparative evaluations.

21. *Self-regulation*, or the exercise of influence over one's own behavior, is greatly affected by self-efficacy, or the *belief* that one can control oneself. *Belief* in oneself leads to self-control and hence to *seeing* improvements in one's life. Self-regulation requires *self-monitoring*, *self-evaluation*, and *self-reaction*.

22. To make these processes contribute to self-regulation by enhancing self-efficacy, the following techniques are recommended: *goal setting*, particularly of goals that are specific, challenging, proximal (in the here-and-now), self-determined, and incremental (subgoals provide guidance and inducement); *commitment* to ensure effort and perseverance; *incentives* or rewards for the attainment of competence, these rewards being both internal (satisfaction) and external (prizes); and *personal control* over one's behavior rather than that control being given to someone else (proxy control).

Suggested Resources

Bandura, A. (1982). Self-efficacy mechanism in social agency. *American Psychologist, 37*, 122–147.

Bandura, A. (1986). *Social foundations of thought and action*. Englewood Cliffs, NJ: Prentice-Hall.

Dyer, W. W. (1976). *Your erroneous zones*. New York: Avon.

Ellis, A., & Knaus, W. J. (1977). *Overcoming procrastination*. New York: New American Library.

Chapter
12

Motivating Students

Objectives

1. Describe the basic assumptions, principles, and model of the attribution theory of motivation.
2. Identify the antecedents, properties, and functions of causal inferences, the basic constructs of attribution theory.
3. Describe the role of emotions and persistent success or failure on attributions or causal inferences, including the pattern known as learned helplessness.
4. Describe the teacher's role in using attribution theory to motivate students.
5. Describe the need for achievement, its development, and techniques to enhance it.
6. Explain the drive theory of motivation as it applies to learning to avoid, learning to need, and resolving conflicts.
7. Describe self-actualization theory, the self-actualized person, and the hierarchy of needs as they relate to motivation.
8. Explain humanistic education, the procedure for enhancing students' self-actualization.

Introduction

To successfully perform an act, a person must have the pertinent skill knowledge or competencies. But these are not enough; they are necessary but not sufficient. The person must also be inclined to invest the energy that the act requires and to direct or focus that energy on performing that act. In other words, the person must be motivated to perform the act. (A student may know what and how to study and may realize that studying is important, yet she may not study because the motivation or drive is lacking.) Motivation refers to what *propels* and *directs* people to act.

Some concepts or ideas that can be applied to motivation have already been encountered in previous chapters of this book. One of these is *self-efficacy*, the belief in one's capability to perform successfully. As you discovered in Chapter 11, people who believe they can do an activity well will be inclined or motivated to perform that activity, while others, who believe that performing the activity is beyond their capability, will be fearful and will avoid undertaking it. This is particularly true of activities that people can choose to do or not do, namely, self-regulated activities. A person's motivation can also be enhanced or depressed if he observes someone else of similar ability and sees whether or not that model can successfully perform the activity. Seeing another person succeed increases the observer's sense of self-efficacy and inclination or motivation to try it him- or herself, while seeing another person fail has the reverse effect.

The concept of reinforcement, which represents the consequences or effect of performing an act, has also been encountered, in Chapter 3. Reinforcement, as shall be seen later in this chapter, can provide an incentive to induce someone to perform an act. Therefore, the desire to obtain reinforcement can serve as a potential motivator of behavior.

One key feature of motivation is having a goal. (Goal-setting was introduced in the previous chapter.) Being motivated means wanting to attain that goal and attempting to do so. The behaviors undertaken to reach that goal can be a function of what people think about themselves or a function of external incentives that cause them to act. In cognitive theories of motivation, goal-directed behaviors are a function of internal thoughts. In behavioral theories they are a function of external conditions. Teachers can use both conceptions of motivation to motivate their students.

In this chapter, some different notions or models of what motivates people to act will be contrasted. The first model described, like the one presented in the preceding chapter, focuses on what people believe about themselves, and so it represents a *cognitive* approach to motivation.

Attribution Theory

Attribution theory, proposed by Weiner (1972, 1980b), explains motivation on the basis of the perceived *causes* that a person might use to explain success or failure in a particular performance. Since every behavior has its consequences, the person who is acting to succeed experiences not only the act itself, but its outcomes as well. And according to attribution theory, he or she will *attribute* those outcomes to certain causal agents, seeking answers to such questions as, What made me succeed? What made me fail? To what cause do I attribute my success or my failure? Since the cause cannot be observed, it must be decided by inference. Hence, attribution theory is a theory about the *causal inferences* people make to explain their successes and failures, the *causal attributes* they choose to account for their outcomes.

Basic Assumptions and Principles

Every theory rests upon some necessary beliefs (witness those on pages 268–271, upon which Bandura's theory was based). Most notable in Weiner's theory are the five given below (Weiner, 1972, 1980b).

1. *Human beings are motivated to understand their own behavior* and, consequently, *to search for explanations.* Without this motivation for self-understanding, people would behave without ever really thinking about it. They would simply follow instincts as animals do.

2. *One-dimensional explanations (as proposed by a number of theorists) are inadequate* for explaining outcomes. Deci (1975), has proposed *intrinsic* versus *extrinsic* motivation, or motives coming from within ourselves (like the desire for self-satisfaction) compared to motives coming from outside ourselves (like the incentive of a high grade or some other reward). De-Charms (1968) has used the terms *origin* and *pawn*, respectively, to describe the individual who does the controlling for him- or herself versus the one who is controlled by someone else. Rotter (1966) calls the same dimension *locus of control* and distinguishes between self or *internal* locus or source of control and other or *external* locus or source of control. All three approaches use a single source of motivation or control as an explanation for behavior.

3. Weiner (1982), by contrast, believes that *explanations must be more complex; they must be multidimensional.* So he proposes *causal attributes* as a more complete explanation.

4. Weiner (1980b) also believes that *a person's future behavior is influenced by his or her belief system*—in particular, by *a cognitive analysis of perceived causes of prior outcomes.* In other words, first people figure out what caused their past outcomes and then they decide, on that basis, what to do next.

5. Thus, *information about cause, drawn from past or antecedent events, forms cognitive structures made up of causal inferences or beliefs about the cause of success or failure; and these beliefs or causal inferences influence subsequent behavior.*

Weiner (1972) proposed that people use the following causal attributes to explain their successes and failures: *ability, effort, task difficulty, luck,* and *help from others.* Outcomes depend on (1) how much ability or skill one has, (2) how much effort one puts in, (3) how difficult the task is, (4) how lucky one is, and (5) how much help one receives.

The Attributional Model

Weiner incorporated his ideas and beliefs about attribution into the model specified below and shown in Figure 12.1.

Step 1. Determine the relative success or failure of some activity that has been undertaken. (For example, "I just got a bad grade on another test in Professor Smith's course.")

Step 2. Determine the emotional consequences of the outcome: happiness for success and frustration or some other negative emotion for failure. (For example, "Getting lousy grades makes me so mad.")

Step 3. Look back or think about past experiences (what Weiner calls antecedent information) and the causal schemata already developed to explain these experiences. (For example, "Professors are usually the cause of my problem; their tests are often unfairly difficult.")

Step 4. Apply these past causal schemata to the present situation and, by analyzing the present situation itself, identify the causal attribute that explains the current success or failure. (For example, "This course and Professor Smith are just too tough for a student to survive.")

Step 5. Evaluate the causal attribute chosen as the explanation for the current outcome in terms of its properties (described below) to see what can be done about it. (For example, "This problem is out of my hands. Nothing I do will make this course any easier.")

Step 6. Decide exactly how to feel: proud, ashamed, angry, guilty about what happened. (For example, "This predicament I'm in sure makes me angry about this school.")

Step 7. Form expectations for the future in the form of beliefs about what is likely to happen next (as in one's sense of self-efficacy). (For example, "There's no way I can pass this course.")

Step 8. Choose the next or subsequent behavior and carry it out. (For example, "I think I'll drop this course.")

Then return to Step 1 and carry out all the steps again.

Thus, the general pattern looks like this (Weiner, 1980b):

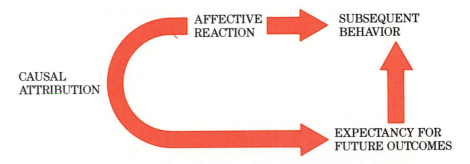

The belief in or inference about causal attribution gives rise to both an emotional reaction and an explanation, which together influence subsequent behavior. Will a person try again or not? That depends on what that person believes the cause of his prior outcomes has been, as elaborated below.

Figure 12.1 🍎 Steps in the Attributional Model of Motivation

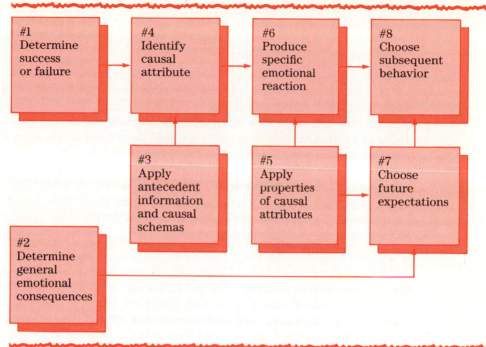

#1
Determine
success
or failure

#4
Identify
causal
attribute

#6
Produce
specific
emotional
reaction

#8
Choose
subsequent
behavior

#3
Apply
antecedent
information
and causal
schemas

#5
Apply
properties
of causal
attributes

#7
Choose
future
expectations

#2
Determine
general
emotional
consequences

Antecedents of Causal Inferences

How do people decide what is causing their successes and failures? How do they know whether it is effort or ability, luck or task difficulty, that has caused them to succeed or fail on a specific task? There are three general sources of information that help people decide why things have come out as they have, or the reasons for their successes and failures.

Specific Informational Cues.   In any situation, there are specific cues that help people decide why they have achieved a particular outcome (Weiner, 1977). The first of these is *past success history*. A consistent record of prior successes leads a person to conclude that high ability is the cause of a successful outcome. Similarly, a consistent record of failure leads to the inference that low ability is the cause. This conclusion will be moderated to some degree by a second cue, the *performance success of others*. When many others also succeed or fail at a task, the inferred cause may be task easiness or difficulty rather than ability. For example, if you are a person who typically succeeds, as on classroom tests, and you get a higher score than most others on a given test, your causal inference of choice will be high ability. If you get a lower score than you usually do, and everyone else does too, then task difficulty will be your likely explanation.

A third cue is *time-on-task*, which translates into how much effort has been put into task preparation and completion. If someone spends a lot of time preparing for a test and then gets a high grade, the causal inference of choice will probably be high effort. (But if the person gets a low grade, the likely inference would be task difficulty.) A fourth cue is *how much help was received*. If a person copied someone else's paper and then got an A, the copier would not be likely to conclude that either ability or effort was the key to success.

A final causal explanation is *randomness of outcome*. If individuals have no personal control over an outcome, as, for example, in the roll of the dice, then the likely conclusion will be that any outcome achieved is based on luck.

Causal Schemata.   These are relatively permanent cognitive structures that represent general beliefs about events and their causes (Weiner, 1977). For example, succeeding at an easy task would likely lead a person to conclude that success was based on either ability or effort. Clearly, it would not take both, since the task was easy. But if the task were hard, success would require both ability and effort. Exactly the opposite is true of failure. Failing at an easy task leads the person to conclude a lack in both ability and effort, since either alone would have been sufficient for success. In a hard task, the cause of failure might be either ability or effort since the lack of one alone would be enough to cause failure. (This is shown in Figure 12.2.) Beliefs like these are general and enduring and are often used to determine cause.

Individual Predisposition.   People differ in how they typically view themselves and the outcomes of their behaviors. Those who are high in the desire to achieve, for example, or who want and expect to succeed, blame any failure on their own lack of effort, rather than on lack of ability, and then increase their effort. Those lacking a strong desire to achieve are more inclined to blame their failure on task difficulty and luck and then decrease their effort (Weiner & Kukla, 1970). Children high in self-esteem credit their success to high ability rather than to outside sources such as help, luck, or task difficulty (Ames, 1978).

Figure 12.2 🍎 Causal Schemata for Explaining Success and Failure on Easy and Hard Tasks

	EXPLANATION FOR	
	SUCCESS	FAILURE
ON AN EASY TASK	High ability OR High effort	Low ability AND Low effort
ON A HARD TASK	High ability AND High effort	Low ability OR Low effort

Properties of Causal Inferences

Once the reason or causal attribute for success or failure at a particular task has been decided, the next step is to determine the consequences of that decision. Will people be affected differently if they infer ability as cause for success in contrast to effort, or effort in contrast to task difficulty, and so on? The answer is YES. Weiner (1979, 1982) has identified three dimensions of causal attributes—locus of causality, stability, and controllability—that lead people to react differently to the different causal attributes. (See Table 12.1 for a summary of the properties of each causal attribute on each dimension.)

Locus of Causality.   This refers to the location or *origin* of the perceived reason for the outcome. *Internal* causes come from within while *external* causes come from outside. Internal causes include ability, effort, mood, personality, and physical health. External causes include task difficulty, luck, and help. When success is perceived to be caused by internal attributes, it contributes to self-esteem; causes perceived to be external have no such effect (Weiner, 1982). If someone does well in a course because of ability or how hard she worked, she will feel good about herself. If someone does well because the teacher made it easy for him, he cannot give himself very much credit for his success. If he fails, though, he will feel better blaming that failure on the teacher (for making the course too hard) than blaming it on his own lack of ability or effort.

Stability.   This refers to the constancy or unchanging nature of a causal attribute. When a prior outcome is believed to be caused by a stable attribute (such as ability or task difficulty), then subsequent outcomes will be readily predicted to be the same. If someone lost a game of tennis today because she had little ability to play the game, she would expect to lose the game tomorrow as well because her ability would not be likely to change in such a short time.

Table 12.1 🍎 Properties of Various Causal Attributes on Each of the Three Dimensions

Causal Attribute	Property					
	Locus of Causality		Stability		Controllability	
	Internal	*External*	*Stable*	*Unstable*	*Controllable*	*Uncontrollable*
Ability	X		X			X
Effort	X			X	X	
Task difficulty		X	X			X
Luck		X		X		X
Help		X		X		X
Illness	X			X		X
Mood	X			X		X
Strategy	X			X	X	

Outcomes based on unstable causes (effort, luck, perhaps mood, or help) would not necessarily guarantee subsequent outcomes, as those based on stable causes do (Weiner, 1979). If a person lost a game of doubles because his partner had a bad day, he would not necessarily expect to lose again. People react with greater emotion to outcomes based on stable causes than to outcomes from unstable causes because they expect that such outcomes will continue. Hence, stability affects emotional reactions and expectations for future outcomes.

Controllability.   This refers to the extent to which a causal attribute is within a person's control and can be intentionally altered by choice, as opposed to being relatively unalterable. Among Weiner's dimensions, only effort is controllable. Effort is the only thing you can alter in order to change failure to success. Clifford (1984), however, has proposed *strategy*, or the way something is done, as a second controllable causal attribute.

Functions of the Causal Properties

The properties or functions of causal attributes are as follows:

1. They affect future goal expectancies (for example, failure attributed to a *stable* cause is expected to recur).
2. They generate particular emotional reactions: Failure attributed to *controllable* effort produces guilt or shame, while failure attributed to an *uncontrollable* lack of help, to poor luck, or to a difficult task produces anger.
3. They contribute to self-image: Success based on *internal* ability or effort produces pride and a positive self-image, while success based on *external* causes produces no emotional consequences.
4. They influence subsequent behavior.

In one research project, Weiner (1980a) exposed some people to a person falling down in the subway as a function of being drunk, a *controllable* circumstance (since people choose to drink). Others were exposed to a person falling down in the subway as the result of an *uncontrollable* infirmity or physical disability. The emotional reaction to the drunk person was disgust and the subsequent behavior was avoidance; the reaction to the disabled person was sympathy and the subsequent behavior was to offer help. People react not just to the occurrence of an event itself but to what they perceive or judge to be the cause of the event. They are more likely to pronounce blame on themselves and others when the cause is controllable than when it is uncontrollable.

Hence, effort emerges as a particularly important cause because it comes from within, is changeable, and is under one's control. It is hard to alter ability and impossible to do anything about luck. People can ask for help but are not guaranteed getting it, and they can seek out easier tasks but are never assured that the tasks will turn out to be that way. If you want to succeed, therefore, your best option is to choose to apply effort.

Some of the causal explanations sound like rationalizations, and indeed they are. They serve as a protective device against admitting to one's own lack of ability or unwillingness to apply effort. They allow students to dissociate themselves from the true causes. Teachers should focus students' attention on *effort* as a controllable cause that can lead to success.

The Role of Emotions

Remember that the attribution model looks like this:

PERCEIVED → EMOTIONAL → FUTURE → SUBSEQUENT
CAUSE   REACTION   EXPECTATION   BEHAVIOR

One's own emotional reaction and the emotional reactions of others influence what to expect and what to do. Similarly, one's own emotional reactions to others tells them how they should feel, what they can expect, and how they should behave. (This is similar to reciprocal determinism, described in the previous chapter.) For example, when people feel apathetic or resigned, what do they do? They usually stop trying, or they try something else, because they feel that it would be useless to continue on their present course. Feelings of gratitude or relief make people behave in a thankful manner or cause them not to proceed without help. Feelings of pride make them confident and lead them to take on or continue a task.

What about the feelings a person *receives*? What information do they convey? A teacher pitying or feeling sorry for a student may tell him that he is not very able or smart. A teacher's expression of anger toward a student and her work may tell the student that she has not put forth enough effort. Even teachers' expressions of sympathy may not make students feel good about themselves; they may instead suggest that the students are not able to do something on their own (Weiner, Russell, & Lerman, 1979).

Attributions for Persistent Success or Failure

Compare the student who succeeds on a consistent basis with the one who fails with equal regularity. What is the succeeder likely to infer as the cause for his or her success? The choice is usually ability—a stable, internal cause. And what about an occasional, and unexpected, failure? Here the choice will be an unstable or external cause such as luck or task difficulty (Weiner, 1979). In this way, self-esteem will be maintained and confidence will not be undermined. The result will be, more often than not, continued success. Moreover, when the tasks get harder, the succeeder will be inclined to exert more effort (a controllable cause) based on the expectation that effort expenditure and likelihood of success are related.

But what of those students characterized by persistent failure? No matter what some students do, they still seem to fail, academically or socially. They soon develop low self-esteem and the expectation to fail. Moreover, they come to believe that their outcomes are independent of their actions. In other words, they believe that no matter what they do, they still will fail. They see all causes as uncontrollable, stable, and external, and themselves as thus doomed to failure. Seligman (1975) has termed this state *learned helplessness*. Some children come to believe that they are helpless when they discover that they cannot seem to help themselves.

How do children with learned helplessness behave? According to Dweck (1975), *first, they give up easily*, especially in the face of failure, however minimal. They are quickly convinced that they are not capable of determining their own outcomes and so tend to regard any adverse circumstance as being insurmountable. *Second, they avoid taking personal responsibility for their failure* for as long as possible by not perceiving a relationship between their own behavior and their failure. As long as they can believe the cause of failure is external and uncontrollable, it is out of their hands. *Third*, when they must acknowledge that their failure is their fault, *they blame failure on a lack of ability* rather than a lack of effort. And *fourth, their failures are followed by a consistent deterioration in performance*. They go from bad to worse to worse yet.

Most teachers were good students themselves prior to becoming teachers, which means that they experienced success in school much more frequently than failure. This led to causal inferences of high ability (further supported by high effort) with its accompanying self-esteem and self-confidence regarding school-related tasks. As students, therefore, most teachers were motivated to succeed in school, and so they put forth the necessary effort.

However, upon venturing into the classroom again to teach, most teachers encounter some students, very unlike themselves, who are experiencing learned helplessness. These are the unmotivated students, the ones who are not inclined to put forth the effort because they believe it will be to no avail. Teachers must react to these students without really knowing (in most cases) what it is like to be in their shoes. What are teachers to do?

The Teacher's Role in Motivating Students

Being a motivated student means expending effort, and expending effort requires a belief that effort is a necessary prerequisite (or causal attribute) for success. Being motivated also means believing that you can help yourself succeed and being confident that you will succeed. Finally, being motivated requires that you believe that you have the ability to succeed.

Teachers Convey Attributional Information.   The task facing teachers is not only to help students succeed but also to *help students believe that it is their own ability and effort that is the cause of that success*. Figure 12.3 shows the three important ways that teachers influence students' beliefs about what has caused their successes and failures (Graham & Weiner, 1983). These are (1) specific performance feedback or what the teacher tells the student about the correctness of his or her work; (2) the teacher's nonverbal affective reaction to the student (for example, sympathy, anger, resignation, surprise); and (3) the subsequent behavior of the teacher toward the student (for example, giving help or extra work). Teachers need to become aware of the causal information they are conveying to students, particularly low-achieving students, by their words and manner, because students use this information to make inferences about their ability.

How Teachers Treat Low Achievers.   According to Good (1980), teachers treat low achievers differently from high achievers. Specifically, teachers are less demanding of, pay less attention to, and yet may give more unsolicited help to low achievers. These teacher behaviors, combined with a feeling of pity, convey to students the causal inference that their low achievement is caused by a lack of ability. Since ability is seen as an internal, stable, and uncontrollable cause of behavior, and hence something about which students can do little, they are likely to lapse into a pattern of learned helplessness. No one wants to believe that a lack of ability is the reason for their poor performance, so students react to such a message by assuming a helpless, uncontrollable stance.

Of particular concern is the use of praise and blame. When a teacher perceives a student as being of low ability and responds to this student's performance with excessive criticism, then it is clear to the student how negative the teacher feels. To avoid this critical behavior, many teachers adopt a different approach (described below) but one that sends out the same message equally strongly (Good, 1980): When a teacher gives a student *a noticeably easy task* and then *praises the student excessively for completing it successfully* (in an honest effort to provide praise for success), the student cannot help but perceive that the teacher believes he or she has *low ability*. Teacher overreactions to student performance often indicate to low-achieving students their lack of ability. "Oh, how wonderful you are for being able to complete this terribly easy task" tells students that their teacher expects very little from them.

What Can a Teacher Do?   First, a teacher can *emphasize learning* or the process of acquiring skills and knowledge *rather than achievement* or the product or result of that acquisition. Teachers should react to students' efforts rather than to just the results of

Figure 12.3 🍎 How Teachers Influence Students' Causal Inferences
From Bell-Gredler, 1986, p. 294.

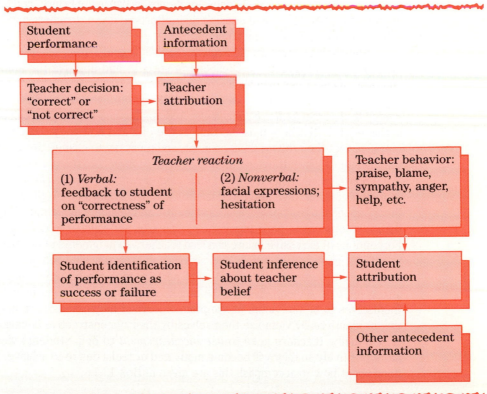

their work. Giving specific feedback to students on the correctness or incorrectness of their responses rather than merely grading their performance, reacting specifically to their performance rather than to their personality and upbringing, reacting to their performance without reference to the performance of other students — all these help students focus on learning.

Second, a teacher can improve the motivation or effort of students by *reducing the competitiveness* among them. The cooperative learning approach (as described in Chapter 10) and the mastery learning approach (as described in Chapter 5) are ways to help students avoid making negative causal inferences about their behavior as a result of contrasting it to that of other students. Cooperative learning and mastery learning are much more likely than the conventional classroom approach to yield success experiences for students who need them.

Third, a teacher needs to help students evaluate their outcomes on the basis of *causal attributes other than ability*. This is important because judgments of ability are tied to self-esteem and self-confidence, and negative judgments have the most harmful effect on a student's willingness to try to perform. As already mentioned, one way to do this is to reinforce *effort* rather than results, so that students will see effort, not ability, as the cause of success. Another way is to introduce a new causal attribute, *strategy*, as proposed by Clifford (1984). Strategy refers to the way you go about doing something. If a student does poorly on a test, it may not be due to ability or lack of effort in preparation. The problem may lie in poor study skills and poor test-taking skills, both of which are strategies. By helping students view strategies as causes of failure, and by helping them improve their strategies and praising their efforts to do so, teachers may be able to turn failure into success for many students.

Fourth, a teacher should *emphasize realistic goal-setting* (as discussed in Chapter 11) in order to increase the likelihood of success and improve the student's personal appraisal of his or her own ability.

Fifth, teachers should *monitor the attributional messages they send students* and *modify their verbal feedback statements*. Audiotaping and videotaping can be most helpful in this regard. Teachers must become aware of if and how they convey to students the message that they regard them as inept, and must try to change these expressions and the manner in which they use them (see Box 10.8 on congruent communications).

Sixth, teachers need to *avoid falling into a pattern of learned helplessness themselves* as a result of their own perceived failures and frustrations in the classroom. Attribution theory applies to teachers as well as students, and teachers make causal inferences about their own outcomes, particularly their successes and failures in helping students learn. Perceptions of excessive failure can lead teachers to judgments of low teaching ability or to a dissociation between their own actions and their teaching outcomes. Extreme cynicism and a progressive deterioration of performance can be the results. Teachers can also come to see themselves as the target of undesirable student behavior and believe themselves to be the victim (a symptom of learned helplessness), rather than realizing that students really victimize themselves by their unconstructive behavior.

Finally, teachers need to *use encouragement* to help students view themselves more positively so they will become motivated or feel a desire to achieve. Some suggestions about how to accomplish this are given in Box 12.1.

Box 12.1

Using Encouragement

1. Encouragement is based on a positive belief in your own ability and the ability of others; on accepting students as they are, not as they could be.

2. Encouragement is intended to help students believe in themselves and their own ability.

3. Encouragement helps students risk being imperfect by helping them realize that mistakes are not failures. Mistakes can promote learning.

4. Encouragement is different from praise. The student does not have to earn it by being first. It can be given for any positive movement. It means treating the student with acceptance and respect.

5. Encouragement focuses on effort. (It does not place a value judgment on the student like praise does.)

6. Encouragement begins by finding students' assets: their talents, positive attitudes, and goals, not their faults. Every student has strengths.

7. Encouragement is the opposite of discouragement. *Do not* discourage students by providing
   - negative comments and expectations ("put-downs"),
   - unreasonably high and double standards,
   - competition and overambition.

8. Encouragement affirms that the student is trying and that trying is worthwhile.

Need for Achievement

McClelland (1985; McClelland, Atkinson, Clark, & Lowell, 1953) has proposed that some individuals develop a motive for success that affects their drive for accomplishments. He designated it as the *need for Achievement* or, more simply, *n Ach*. And though it is one of many possible motives (Murray, 1938, had originally proposed 20), it is especially important to success in educational and business settings.

To determine the presence of this need, McClelland used a test called the *Thematic Apperception Test*, or TAT, in which people look at pictures and make up stories about what they see. Individuals high in n Ach created stories that focused on the imagined accomplishments, or strivings for accomplishments, of the characters in the pictures rather than on other aspects of their lives and personalities, such as wielding power or taking care of others.

In contrast to this need for achievement, McClelland believed that some people possess a need to avoid failure. While those with a high need for achievement tend to choose tasks of moderate difficulty, people with a need to avoid failure choose either exceptionally easy tasks, for which success is virtually guaranteed, or exceptionally hard

Figure 12.4 🍎 A Comparison of the Reactions to Success and Failure Experienced by High Need Achievers and High Failure Avoiders

CHANGE IN MOTIVATION

	FOLLOWING SUCCESS	FOLLOWING FAILURE
BY NEED ACHIEVERS	Diminished (They have proven they can do it and are ready for a new challenge.)	Heightened (They want to prove they can do it.)
BY FAILURE AVOIDERS	Heightened (They want to continue in this safe situation.)	Diminished (They find this to be too risky.)

tasks, for which failure is expected and, therefore, not a matter of personal responsibility (Atkinson, 1964). A contrast between how people high in need for achievement and people high in need to avoid failure react to success and failure on tasks of unspecified difficulty level is shown in Figure 12.4. Note that failure stimulates need achievers to try harder, while high failure avoiders prefer the safety of sure success.

Developing a Need for Achievement.   How do people get to be high in need achievement? Winterbottom (1958) has shown that childrearing practices are important influences, particularly parents' attitudes toward independence, mastery, and caretaking. Parents of children high in n Ach tended to expect "self-reliant mastery" at earlier ages than expected by parents of children lower in n Ach. While the parents of high need achievers placed restrictions on their children, they did so only after self-reliance training, so that when restrictions occurred the children had to "police" themselves. Parents of low need achievers encouraged their children to remain dependent on them longer for both achievement help and the enforcement of restrictions.

Stipek (1984) studied elementary-school children and concluded that the competitiveness of the later grades encourages students to shift from a task focus to an outcomes focus and to become more concerned with avoiding failure. As elementary-school children progress through the grades, the performance they expect from themselves is increasingly influenced by the performance feedback they receive from teachers (Eshel & Klein, 1981). Excessively harsh feedback and poor grades can quickly turn a high need achiever into a high failure avoider.

Training a Need for Achievement.   McClelland (1965, 1985) proposed a technique for increasing people's motivation to seek achievement. His technique centers on four principles, the first of which is to *take moderate risk*. This means avoiding both the sure success and the sure failure. To implement this principle teachers must meet the two following conditions:

- Students must be permitted to choose their own tasks (or their own difficulty levels within tasks).
- The consequences of failure must not be harsh.

If all students are given the same tasks with the same difficulty levels, as is often the case in school, then individual students cannot learn to choose the level of challenge that is right for them. If failure causes pain or embarrassment, children will always be motivated to choose the easiest tasks they can. Teachers need to create learning situations involving choice while at the same time minimizing personal consequences, so that students can learn to pursue the motivating choice of challenging themselves.

The second principle is to *take personal responsibility for your outcomes*. This means that people should not attribute either failure or success to forces outside themselves. People should look at themselves as the cause of their outcomes. To implement this principle, teachers must meet the following two conditions:

- Students must have to rely on themselves to accomplish a task.
- The consequences of failure must not be too harsh.

Like the previous principle, this requires that failure not be severely penalized, so that students will be willing to recognize and accept their own role in the achievement process.

The third principle is to *search the environment* and the fourth is to *use feedback*. Both place great emphasis on getting and using information. The first directs students to find out everything they can about the task and about the resources, including human ones, available to accomplish it. The second tells them to pay particular attention to the results of their actions in deciding what to do next. Both require

- an information-rich environment within which the student can move freely,
- information that is provided without threat,
- the opportunity to choose and change direction,
- that the consequences of failure not be too harsh.

Obviously, to teach students to be motivated to achieve, a teacher must create an open, information-rich environment with the opportunity for choice and nonpunitive consequences for making mistakes. McClelland found simulations and games very useful for this purpose (see Box 12.2 for an example).

Drive Theory

Recall that in the discussions of how people learn knowledge and skills, two different approaches were examined: the behavioral one (Chapter 3) and the cognitive one (Chapter 6). The difference between the two was that the behavioral model explains learning as the result of reinforcement and the cognitive model explains learning as the result of information processing or mental encoding and decoding.

Box 12.2

🍎

The Darts–Dice Game

This game requires a dart board (with possible scores of 10, 20, 30, 40, 60, 80, 100), six darts, and a pair of dice. (A ring toss may be substituted for the dart board.) Students may play individually or in teams. For each round (the number of rounds should be decided in advance), the following steps are taken.

Step 1. Each player decides whether to throw the six darts or roll the dice six times. Once made, the choice may not be changed for that round.

Step 2. Before each throw or roll, the player *bids* or predicts how many points he or she will earn on that throw or roll.

Step 3. The player then throws the first dart or rolls the first roll of the dice. If the player makes or exceeds his or her bid, the player receives *the number of points bid*. If the player falls short of the bid, *no points* are awarded.

Step 4. The player repeats the procedure for each throw or roll, first bidding and then throwing or rolling. After six turns, the next player follows the same procedure.

Step 5. The whole procedure is then repeated for a second and, if desired, a third round. Scores are kept so that winners and losers can be determined.

This game embodies the four achievement principles. Bidding levels represent levels of risk so students can learn to take moderate risks. Throwing darts, a skill, reflects taking responsibility for one's actions, in contrast to the luck of rolling dice. Searching the environment means watching others and learning how to maximize one's own gains. Using feedback means adjusting bids to fit one's actual performance.

Following the game, gather the class to discuss what the game was about; what students learned from it, particularly about how to succeed; and how it relates to real life.

The same distinction can be made in the attempt to explain motivation. So far, the focus has been on two cognitive approaches to motivation, attribution theory and need achievement theory, both of which explain motivation in terms of how people think about themselves and their experiences. The focus will now turn to drive theory, which explains motivation in behavioral terms — as doing what needs to be done to satisfy basic drives or other drives that have been associated with one of the basic drives.

Learning to Avoid and Escape.   Dollard and Miller (1950) describe the following experiment with rats that illustrates the drive theory explanation of motivation. A rat is placed in the white compartment of an apparatus that has two compartments, a black one and a white one, separated by a door. The animal receives shock and quickly learns to escape it by running through the door to the black box. Now the animal is placed in the white box without shock but continues to run out of it immediately into the black box, which suggests that the white box produces fear. Next, in order to see whether fear will motivate, and escape from fear will reinforce, the learning of a new habit, researchers again place the animal in the white box without shock. This time, however, the door between compartments is closed, and the rat can open it only by rotating a little wheel above it. After trial-and-error, the animal bumps the wheel, which turns and opens the door, through which the animal immediately escapes to the black box. With each trial, the animal learns to move the wheel faster and faster, based on the *externally induced motivation* to escape the fear associated with the white compartment.

Children learn to be afraid too, but through naturally occurring events. After being bitten by a dog, for example, a child who was not previously afraid learns to fear dogs and is motivated to learn a whole new set of responses, such as climbing over fences, staying in the house, or avoiding certain streets, in order to avoid dogs. Schools and teachers can also be the object of learned fears after they provoke negative, painful, or embarrassing experiences. Truancy can be a reinforcing event (what was called *negative reinforcement* in Chapter 3) by enabling an unhappy or fearful student to avoid the source of his or her fear or distress.

According to Dollard and Miller (1950), fear is learned because it is associated with cues that were previously neutral, such as the white compartment, dogs, or school. This association is based on the animal or human having experienced pain in the presence of these cues. Thus, fear functions as a *drive* because it motivates an effort to reduce, eliminate, or avoid it, and its reduction can *reinforce* learning responses that accomplish these goals. When a previously neutral cue (such as a dog) becomes associated with attraction or dislike, it becomes a discriminative stimulus for the learned drive of avoiding it to obtain negative reinforcement. (These concepts were described in Chapter 3.) People develop a learned drive to acquire money because of the many positive things they can buy with it, just as they develop a learned drive to avoid the things that raise their anxiety level or frighten them.

In simplest terms, drive theory says that individuals learn to want, or are motivated to get, things that feel good and avoid things that feel bad. If teachers want to motivate students to learn something or perform some act, they should follow the student's response or act with something that increases students' good feelings (positive reinforcement) or decreases students' bad feelings (negative reinforcement). Since reinforcement is an external phenomenon, drive theory sees the source of motivation as being outside the person (or extrinsic) rather than inside (or intrinsic). Remember that cognitive theories like attribution theory and social learning theory see motivation as intrinsic.

Dollard and Miller (1950) also proposed that punishment can be an effective drive-related technique. Because punishment can produce fear, if one simply imagines the punished act and simultaneously experiences the fear, the anticipation of punishment can successfully deter one from actually performing the act. *Fear* is a powerful motivator: (1) It is unpleasant, (2) it can become attached to a wide variety of situations, (3) any behavior that reduces fear is automatically reinforced simply *because* it reduces the fear (this is negative reinforcement), and (4) any behavior that causes or increases fear is automatically punished simply *because* it increases the fear (this is punishment type 1 in Table 3.3).

Moreover, when a person experiences fear in a new situation, that fear serves as a cue to elicit responses that have been learned previously in other frightening situations, and it also reinforces the learning of any new response that accompanies it. Therefore, when a child becomes afraid in school, he or she will perform many of the same responses that have accompanied fear at home as well as some new and perhaps strange ones that are discovered in school by trial-and-error or by imitation. Any response that reduces the fear will be reinforced and thus learned.

One final point about fear as a motivator: Since punishment can provoke fear, any punishment a teacher uses may produce fear in the student on whom it is used. If that student is trying his best to be successful and gain a positive reward, and yet is punished for that behavior, the resulting fear will decrease the drive or motivation to perform the reward-seeking behavior because it will now be accompanied by fear. Teachers must be very careful not to punish students' well-intended behaviors and thus cause them to be afraid to try. Many students, for example, will not volunteer to answer questions in class, despite the potential rewards for giving the correct answer, because of their fear of humiliation. This fear is not just imagined. It has been learned through experiences with thoughtless, insensitive, or imperceptive teachers.

Learned Needs.   Although some of the things people are motivated to get, like food and water, are the result of biological needs, many of our needs are learned. Any object or experience that is found to be reinforcing becomes the basis for a learned need, because people will be motivated to attain that object or have that experience. They will have learned to need it. When a youngster receives money for doing his chores, and uses it to buy himself something, he will want to get more money. He will be learning to need money and will be driven or motivated to do the things necessary to acquire it. Monkeys can be trained to work for poker chips if the poker chips can be traded in for grapes (Wolfe, 1936). Poker chips, like dollars, become *incentives* for behavior because they satisfy learned needs.

Grades in school have the potential to become learned needs, and they do become that for many children. For others, though, the attempt to get high grades can be punished by failure and thus become associated with fear. In such cases, what is learned is avoidance behavior rather than the drive to succeed.

Conflict.   When a person is motivated to carry out two mutually incompatible acts at the same time, then that person is in a state of conflict. The most common conflict, what Dollard and Miller (1950) call an *approach–avoidance conflict*, occurs when a person is motivated to approach something and at the same time avoid it. Going to school, for example, can provoke an approach–avoidance conflict. A student who wants to go to school to see her friends, but also wants to stay home because she has difficulty sitting still in school or getting along with her teachers, has an approach–avoidance conflict toward school. While by going to school she will be rewarded by being able to socialize, she will also be punished by having to sit still and study.

What do we know about such conflicts? According to Dollard and Miller (1950),

1. the tendency to approach a desired goal gets stronger the closer someone gets to the goal (called the *gradient of approach* or the *goal gradient*);
2. the tendency to avoid a feared object gets stronger the closer someone gets to the object (called the *gradient of avoidance* or the *fear gradient*);
3. the fear gradient increases more than the goal gradient as the object is approached (see Figure 12.5);
4. the strength of the tendency to either approach or avoid depends upon the strength of the drive on which it is based.

Figure 12.5 🍎 Approach–Avoidance Conflict

Adapted from Dollard and Miller, 1950, p. 356.

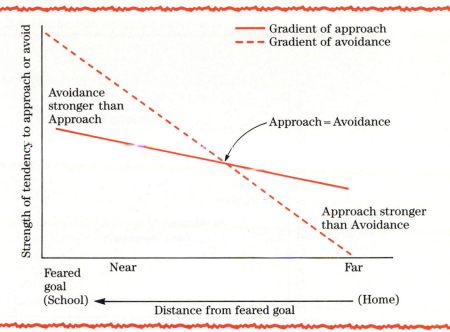

As shown in Figure 12.5, the individual will start out approaching the goal but will stop at the point where the two gradients cross because it is at that point that the tendencies to approach and to avoid are equal. The student may start off for school but never reach it. He may go halfway and then stop because of the approach–avoidance conflict.

What can be done to resolve this conflict? Dollard and Miller (1950) evaluate two possibilities: (1) *increasing the motivation to approach the goal* and (2) *decreasing the motivation to avoid the goal*. The results of these two possibilities are shown in Figure 12.6. Note that both approaches move the person with the conflict equally close to the feared goal. However, increasing the strength of approach increases the elicited fear while decreasing the strength of avoidance decreases the elicited fear. In the example of going to school, if a mother threatens her child or takes him by the hand and leads him to school, she will be heightening the fear and displeasure associated with school. Then it will become harder rather than easier to get him to go back. But if school can be made less painful (perhaps by making it a more successful experience), and the tendency to avoid it can thereby be decreased, the child will likely approach it with less fear.

For teachers, the message here is not to focus on increasing the motivation of students to approach feared goals but to focus on reducing the fears motivating avoidance. Motivational talks and potential rewards may not be nearly as effective as trying to find out what the student is afraid of and then acting to reduce that fear. If the student is afraid of failure, then the teacher should make every effort to minimize the consequences of failure so the student will not be afraid to try.

Sometimes the student is faced with two equally undesirable alternatives, what Dollard and Miller (1950) call an *avoidance–avoidance conflict*. In this case, the student

Figure 12.6 🍎 The Effect of Increasing the Strength of Approach (above) and Decreasing the Strength of Avoidance (below) on the Approach–Avoidance Conflict

Adapted from Dollard and Miller, 1950, pp. 358–361.

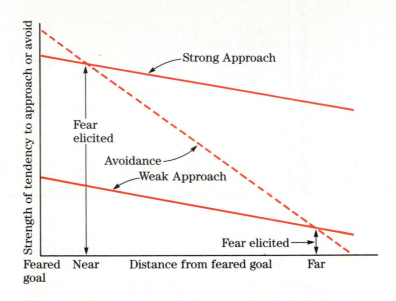

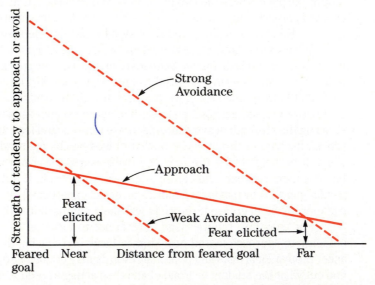

will resolve the conflict by doing neither of the undesirable alternatives, instead pursuing an entirely different course of action unless all other possibilities are blocked. In dealing with, for example, giving a student a choice between staying after school or having an extra assignment, the teacher must first ensure that the student cannot avoid both possibilities and then must try to reduce the strength of the tendency to avoid one of them. Perhaps the extra assignment can be made easier or more interesting.

Also, conflicts can sometimes be avoided and can often be resolved if the teacher sets up a series of *graded tasks* through which students can get progressively closer to a desirable goal without experiencing a steep increase in anxiety along the way. By being able to complete easier, more approachable tasks at the start of a learning sequence, students can be rewarded for their successes, thus increasing their motivation to continue. When the original activity is more difficult, the likelihood of failure increases, as does the tendency to avoid. Reducing the tendency to avoid by using a shaping strategy (as described in Chapter 3) is a way for teachers to enhance student motivation.

When you want to do something but are afraid to try, you have an approach–avoidance conflict. The boy in the middle may want to try to answer the teacher's question (like his classmates on either side) but is afraid of answering it wrong. Rather than pushing him to volunteer an answer, the teacher should try to reduce the fear associated with trying.

Misbehavior can be viewed as the result of a conflict between teacher goals and student goals. Students who seek to meet their own goals or satisfy their own needs will experience conflict with teachers when they behave in ways that interfere with teacher goals. Teachers can reduce the conflict by acting to reduce the students' tendency to avoid meeting teacher goals. This will work better than escalating the conflict by trying to push these students harder to approach teacher goals, which means challenging the students' own goal-directed behavior, however dysfunctional it may be. The goals of student misbehavior and the conflicts they are likely to produce are illustrated in Box 12.3.

Box 12.3

The Four Goals of Misbehavior

Student's Faulty Belief	Student's Goal	Teacher's Feelings	Teacher's Reactions	Student's Response to Teacher's Reaction	Guidelines for Redirecting Misbehavior
"I belong *only* when I'm noticed or served."	Attention	Annoyed	Remind, coax	Temporarily stops misbehavior; later resumes same behavior or seeks attention in another way	Recognize that reminders and warnings only reinforce the goal. Ignore behavior when possible. Give attention in unexpected ways. Notice positive behavior.
"I belong *only* when I'm in control or when I'm proving that no one can make me do anything."	Power	Angry, provoked	Give in or fight power with power	Intensifies power struggle or submits with defiant compliance	Withdraw from conflict. Help students use power constructively by enlisting their help.

Self-Actualization Theory

In contrast to drive theory, which focuses on the drive or motivation to gain external rewards and avoid punishments, self-actualization theory focuses on tapping internal resources to enable personal growth to occur. Drive theory can be called *deficiency theory* because it focuses on being motivated to gratify deficiencies and needs; self-actualization theory can be called *growth theory* because it focuses on going beyond equilibrium and safety to attain new levels of growth. It focuses on *becoming* and *being*, on ends rather than means, on attainment rather than frustration.

Student's Faulty Belief	Student's Goal	Teacher's Feelings	Teacher's Reactions	Student's Response to Teacher's Reaction	Guidelines for Redirecting Misbehavior
"I belong *only* when I hurt others and get even. I can't be liked."	Revenge	Hurt	Retaliate, get even	Seeks further revenge	Avoid punishment, retaliation, feeling hurt. Build trusting relationship.
"I belong *only* when I convince others that I am unable and helpless."	Display of inadequacy	Despairing, hopeless, discouraged	Agree with student that nothing can be done, give up	Shows no improvement	Recognize student's deep discouragement. Don't give up, pity, or criticize. Encourage all positive effort.

To identify the student's goal,

1. examine your own feelings and reactions to the misbehavior;
2. analyze the student's response to what you do and say.

SOURCE: Dinkmeyer, D., McKay, G., & Dinkmeyer, D., Jr. (1980). *Systematic training for effective teaching (STET): Teacher's handbook* (p. 18). Circle Pines, MN: American Guidance Services.

Table 12.2 ✎ Need Hierarchy and Levels of Personal Functioning

Need Hierarchy	Condition of Deficiency	Fulfillment	Illustration
Physiological	Hunger, thirst	Relaxation	Feeling satisfied after a good meal
	Sexual frustration	Release from tension	
	Tension	Experiences of pleasure from senses	
	Fatigue	Experiences of pleasure from senses	
	Illness	Physical well-being	
	Lack of proper shelter	Comfort	
Safety	Insecurity	Security	Being secure in a full-time job
	Yearning	Comfort	
	Sense of loss	Balance	
	Fear	Poise	
	Obsession	Calm	
	Compulsion	Tranquillity	
Love	Self-consciousness	Free expression of emotions	Experiencing total acceptance in a love relationship
	Feeling of being unwanted	Sense of wholeness	
	Feeling of worthlessness	Sense of warmth	
	Emptiness	Renewed sense of life and strength	
	Loneliness	Sense of growing together	
	Isolation	Sense of growing together	
	Incompleteness	Sense of growing together	
Esteem	Feeling of incompetence	Confidence	Receiving an award for an outstanding performance on some project
	Negativism	Sense of mastery	
	Feeling of inferiority	Positive self-regard	
		Self-respect	
		Self-extension	
Self-actualization	Alienation	Healthy curiosity	Experiencing a profound insight
	Metapathologies	Peak experiences	
	Absence of meaning in life	Realization of potentials	
	Boredom	Work that is pleasurable and embodies values	
	Routine living		
	Limited activities	Creative living	

SOURCE: DiCaprio, N. S. (1974). *Personality theories: Guides to being* (p. 411). Philadelphia: Saunders.

Maslow (1962, p. 45) portrays self-actualization theory, or the motivation to realize and actualize one's inherent potential, this way:

Enhance the dangers   Enhance the attractions

Safety   Growth

Minimize the attractions   Minimize the dangers

PERSON

Healthy growth is a never-ending series of free-choice situations, facing each person throughout life, in which each must regularly choose between growth and safety. To choose growth, the person must find it more attractive and less dangerous than its alternative, safety. If growth is either too unattractive or too dangerous, a person will retreat to safety.

Hierarchy of Needs.   Maslow (1962) proposes that we have, inherent within us, the following hierarchy of needs (arranged in order of priority):

1. physiological needs (food, water, sleep),
2. safety or security needs (freedom from danger and anxiety),
3. love or belonging needs (acceptance by others),
4. respect or self-esteem needs (mastery, self-confidence),
5. self-actualization need (ongoing realization of potential).

The needs are elaborated in Table 12.2. People begin by satisfying the lower needs, ensuring that they can eat, sleep, and be free from danger. For most people, these needs are easily satisfied; for some, they are not. When safety is more attractive and less dangerous than growth, especially when total effort is required to maintain safety, people will not proceed beyond this level of the hierarchy. They will not be motivated to grow. Once they feel safe, people will reach out for acceptance from others and will then attempt to attain mastery and self-esteem through their own actions and performances. When they have experienced success, they will finally proceed to the challenge of the pinnacle of growth — self-actualization.

Motivation, according to self-actualization theory, is striving to satisfy all the needs in the hierarchy, culminating with self-actualization. The goal in self-actualization theory is to *become* a self-actualized person.

The Self-Actualized Person.   What are the characteristics or hallmarks of the self-actualized person? According to Maslow (1962, 1968), they are

1. an accurate perception of reality,
2. increased acceptance of self and others,
3. increased spontaneity,
4. increased focus on solving problems,
5. increased detachment and desire for privacy,
6. increased autonomy and resistance to cultural influence,

7. greater freshness of appreciation,

8. greater richness of emotional reaction,

9. improved interpersonal relations,

10. increased satisfaction with the human condition,

11. more democratic character structure,

12. greatly increased creativeness,

13. more humanistic values (called the values of being),

14. higher frequency of peak experiences.

Key to the concept of the self-actualized person is the notion of a *peak experience*, a moment of rapture, wonder, or creativity. These peak experiences are characterized by what Maslow (1962) calls *cognition of being*, or wholeness of thought, and by *values of being* such as beauty, goodness, playfulness, truth, simplicity, and self-sufficiency. Peak experiences are moments of maturity and fulfillment during which a person becomes a self-actualizer. (For a more detailed description of a peak experience, see Box 12.4.)

Self-actualization is not a static process, so it is not technically accurate to talk about a self-actualized person. Instead, self-actualization is a process comprising episodes or spurts of openness, spontaneity, creativity, wholeness, and independence from the lower needs. During this time a person becomes more truly him- or herself, actualiz-

Box 12.4

What Is a Peak Experience?

Maslow (1962) gave college students the following instructions: Think of the most wonderful experiences of your life: the happiest, most ecstatic moments of rapture, perhaps from being in love, or from listening to music or suddenly being overwhelmed by the meaning of a book or a painting, or from some great creative moment. How did things look or feel at such moments, different from the way they look or feel at other times? In what ways are you, at such moments, a different person?

What were their answers? Here are a few:

1. Seeing the experience or object as a whole, detached from relations, usefulness, expediency, and purpose. Seeing it as if it were all there was in the universe.

2. Attending fully and exclusively to the object or experience (so that everything else "disappears"). Seeing it as marvelous, perfect, and unique.

3. Seeing its true nature or essence completely apart from human concerns. Seeing it in its own "being" rather than as something to be reacted to in some other human way.

4. Being fascinated by it and so looking at it repeatedly, intently, and with care.

5. Perceiving it as something that has a reality of its own, not dependent on you, the beholder. (This is called self- or ego-transcending perception.)

ing or realizing his or her potentialities and experiencing the core of his or her being. People are motivated to increase the frequency and intensity of peak experiences in order to function in a more self-actualized way.

Enhancing Self-Actualization—Humanistic Education.

Why should teachers be motivated to help students experience self-actualization? According to Maslow (1962), there are some very good reasons. Self-actualized students feel integrated, unified, capable of using all their capacities. In other words, they feel fully functioning, at the peak of their powers, and when they feel this way they experience less strain, less inhibition, and less self-doubt. This enables them to be spontaneous and creative, to express and to experience a more nearly pure expression of their own being or real self.

Can these capacities be taught in school? This is particularly challenging since most students have already learned that school is impersonal, boring, noncreative, irrelevant, and unpleasant—a place where punishment, discipline, humiliation, cheating, and conformity are the norms (Rogers, 1983). If the learning environment and the attitudes and beliefs of some teachers can be changed, then, according to Rogers (1983), students can be motivated to seek self-actualization. (See Box 12.5 for an example of what those humanistic teacher beliefs should be.)

The keys to *humanistic education*, or education that enhances self-actualization, are (1) teacher acceptance of the idea that all students have the capability to learn, (2) a

6. Having an end-experience, an end in itself, so valuable and such a great revelation as to be its own justification, to carry its own intrinsic value.

7. Experiencing a feeling of disorientation in time and space (in a daze; experiencing a loss in time).

8. Having a good or desirable feeling (as good as it should be) filled with awe, wonder, amazement, excitement, and even reverence.

9. Having a feeling of passivity and receptivity, an undemanding quality, a dreaminess, a peacefulness, a feeling of being given something; or humility, of surrendering before something great.

10. Feeling that this small piece of the world is, at that moment, all the world.

11. Feeling complete, uncondemning, compassionate acceptance and loving of the world and of the experience or object.

12. Experiencing a momentary loss of fear, anxiety, and inhibition and a giving up of restraint, critical judgment, and the need to understand.

13. Having a feeling of one's own being, of one's own perfection.

Have you ever had a peak experience? A recent one? Try writing it down and comparing the feeling to those on this list.

curriculum relevant to student interests, (3) a nonthreatening and nonhumiliating climate, (4) opportunities for student participation and self-initiation, (5) self-evaluation (as opposed to evaluation by others), and (6) a continuing openness to experience and to the process (rather than the product) of learning (Rogers, 1983). Humanistic education, therefore, embraces intrinsic rather than extrinsic motivation.

Although these key features seem as if they should be commonplace in schools, they are actually more the exception than the rule. To become more humanistic, schools need (1) more open scheduling, (2) more emphasis on active learning, (3) more oppor-

Box 12.5

Effective Characteristics of Teachers

Teacher's Belief	Teacher's Behavior	Results for Students
"I believe students can make decisions."	Permits choices. Encourages.	Feel self-confident. Try. Contribute. Solve problems. Become resourceful.
"I am equal to, not more or less than, others."	Believes in and respects students. Encourages independence. Gives choices and responsibility. Expects students to contribute.	Develop self-reliance, independence, responsibility. Learn to make decisions. Respect selves and others. Believe in equality.
"I believe in mutual respect."	Promotes equality. Encourages mutual respect. Avoids promoting guilt feelings.	Respect selves and others. Have increased social interest. Trust others.
"I am human; I have the 'courage to be imperfect.'"	Sets realistic standards. Focuses on strengths. Encourages. Is not concerned with own image. Is patient.	Focus on task at hand, not on self-elevation. See mistakes as challenge. Have courage to try new experiences. Are tolerant of others.
"I believe all people are important, including myself."	Encourages mutual respect. Invites contributions. Refuses to be "doormat." Knows when to set limits and say no.	Know and accept limits. Respect rights of others.

SOURCE: Dinkmeyer, D., McKay, G., & Dinkmeyer, D., Jr. (1980). *Systematic training for effective teaching (STET): Teacher's handbook* (p. 43). Circle Pines, MN: American Guidance Services.

Teachers who believe that all students can learn, who create an open and friendly climate, and who allow students to participate freely, without fear of judgment, are acting to enhance the self-actualization of their students.

tunity for student independence, (4) more focus on creativity, (5) more cooperative learning activities, (6) more use of self-evaluation, and (7) more focus on respecting personal integrity and dealing with the needs of the student than on following a preset curriculum (Patterson, 1973).

Some of these requirements are beyond the control of individual classroom teachers. Others are not. Teachers are certainly free to motivate the *self-discovery* process by allowing their students to bring aspects of themselves into the instructional process. Jones (1968) advocates using fantasy and feelings as valuable learning mediums by, for example, having elementary school children describe their daydreams. From this children learn that their feelings and images have a place in school. Teachers can use this personal input not only as an effective tool for communication but as a part of a specific learning task, such as a unit on the environment or on getting along with others.

Humanistic education, therefore, is education that focuses on how students feel about themselves and what motivates them. It is education that provides the opportunity for self-discovery and the development of self-awareness. It is education that stimulates affective development (see Chapter 9) and makes use of interpersonal or group processes (see Chapter 10). It is education that encourages the use of imagination and personal feelings in the process of teaching. It is education aimed at the goal of student self-actualization. (Some classroom activities for enhancing self-actualization are described in Box 12.6.)

Box 12.6

Some Self-Actualization Exercises

IALAC

Have students make a sign that reads "IALAC" (for *I Am Lovable And Capable*) and wear it on their shirts or blouses all day long. Any time during the day that something happens to make them feel less lovable and capable, they should rip off a piece of the sign; any time something happens to make them feel more lovable and capable, they should make a star on their sign. The next day, have them discuss their experiences.

My Time

Each student gets to lead the whole class, or a group of students, in any activity of his or her choice.

"I Can . . ." Statements

Have students write on the blackboard as many "I CAN . . ." statements as they can in two minutes.

Strength Lists

On sheets of paper, for five minutes, have students list as many of their strengths as they can. They can then share any they choose to with others. (Lists can also be done as collages.) They can also write down the strengths of classmates serving as partners, and then share them with one another.

Summary of Main Points

1. It has already been said (in Chapter 11) that people who have high *self-efficacy* believe they can do an activity well and will be motivated to perform that activity.

2. In this chapter, another *cognitive* approach is described. *Attribution theory* (developed by Weiner) focuses on the causes to which people attribute their successes and failures. These causes or explanations for outcomes are called *causal attributes* or *causal inferences* and are made, presumably, because people are motivated to understand and explain their behavior.

3. Previously offered, one-dimensional explanations of motivation were seen by Weiner as being inadequate, so he proposed a more complex model with at least five causes — *ability, effort, task difficulty, luck*, and *help from others* — that can be used to explain behavior based on information obtained from prior experiences.

4. The *proposed model* has eight steps, starting with a given success or failure outcome producing general emotional consequences, a causal inference to explain the out-

"Mirror, Mirror"

Mirror, mirror, say what you see,
Say what you like the best about me.

Each student holds the "mirror" up to his or her ear, and then tells the class or fellow group members what the "mirror" said.

A "Me Tree"

Have students draw large trees and, on the roots, draw symbols or paste pictures of their strengths, one per root. On the branches have them draw symbols or paste pictures of their accomplishments. Have them post their trees around the room and add to them as they develop new strengths or attain new accomplishments.

Animal Farm

Have each student choose the animal he or she likes best and answer the following questions: (1) What do I like best about this animal? (2) How am I most like this animal? (3) How would I like to be more (and perhaps less) like this animal? Students can then discuss or even act out their answers in small groups.

SOURCE: Howe, L. W., & Howe, M. M. (1975). *Personalizing education: Values clarification and beyond* (pp. 81–105). New York: Hart.

come, a specific emotional reaction, and expectations for the future, all of which culminate in the choice and execution of another behavior.

5. Causal inferences are based on *specific informational cues* such as past successes (an indication of ability), the performance of others (an indication of task difficulty), time-on-task (an indication of effort), amount of help received, and randomness of outcome (an indication of luck).

6. *Causal schemata* or general beliefs about outcomes and events surrounding them, also influence causal inferences (for example, success on an easy task can be explained by *either* high ability *or* high effort while success on a hard task requires *both*). Finally, *individual predispositions*, like desire to achieve or self-esteem, affect the likelihood of choosing one cause over another to explain a particular outcome.

7. Causal inferences have three properties: *locus of causality*, or whether the origin of the cause is *internal* to the person (like ability and effort) or *external* to or outside the person (like task difficulty, luck, or help); *stability*, or resistance to change, with ability and task difficulty being relatively *stable* and the others more changeable or *unstable*; and *controllability*, or being within a person's control, with effort being the

only *controllable* one. Effort turns out to be the only internal, unstable, controllable cause and, hence, the one most amenable to change by any individual person.

8. The causal properties affect future goal expectations, generate particular emotional reactions, contribute to self-image, and influence subsequent behavior. The most influential property is controllability; thus the key is effort, because it enables people to control their own outcomes.

9. *Emotional reactions* to outcomes help tell people what to expect and what to do. Feelings of resignation or apathy make people stop trying, for example, while feelings of pride create confidence and the inclination to proceed. *Persistent success* yields self-esteem and pride, while *persistent failure* leads to a syndrome called *learned helplessness*, characterized by giving up easily, not taking personal responsibility for failure or else blaming it on a lack of ability, and continuing to deteriorate in performance. This is not characteristic of many teachers in their student days but is characteristic of some of the students they will teach.

10. Teachers *convey attributional information* to their students via specific performance feedback, nonverbal reactions, and subsequent behavior. In particular, they often treat high-achieving and low-achieving students differently, leading low-achieving students to believe they are of low ability and to lapse into learned helplessness. Overreacting to a low-achieving student by giving high praise for success on an easy task sends that student the message that the teacher sees him or her as having little ability. Teachers generally demand less from low achievers, pay less attention to them, and give them unsolicited help.

11. Teachers are encouraged to emphasize learning (a process) rather than achievement (an outcome); to reduce classroom competitiveness; to emphasize effort (or strategy—the way something is done) rather than ability; to emphasize realistic goal setting; to monitor the attributional messages they send students and change their language, if necessary; to use encouragement; and to avoid falling into a pattern of learned helplessness themselves.

12. Another approach to motivation is to look at the individual predisposition to succeed—called *need for achievement* by McClelland and measured by the achievement content of stories that people make up in response to pictures.

13. A contrasting predisposition is *need to avoid failure*. People with this need prefer the safety of easy success to the challenge of more difficult undertakings. These predispositions are based in part on childrearing practices and early school experiences. High need for achievement seems to require opportunities for *independence* and *self-reliant mastery* in early development.

14. To encourage need for achievement to develop, teachers must help students learn to take *moderate* risks, to take *personal responsibility* for their own outcomes, to *search* the environment for information, and to *use feedback* to adjust behavior. Games and simulations can be very useful for teaching these principles.

15. *Drive theory* is a behavioral (in contrast to a cognitive) approach to motivation that explains behavior as an attempt to satisfy basic as well as *learned drives* by obtaining *reinforcement*, often from external sources. When a person experiences something unpleasant in a particular situation, that situation comes to evoke *fear*, and the person is motivated to *escape* from or *avoid* that situation in order to reduce the fear. Any successful avoidance behavior will be reinforced by the *reduction of fear*.

16. People learn to be motivated to perform any act that produces a positive result (positive reinforcement) or reduces a negative one (negative reinforcement). People, thus, develop *learned needs*.

17. Because *punishment* can produce fear, people will be motivated to avoid it and thus will learn to avoid performing punishable acts. Punishing a student for trying, therefore, however inadvert the punishment, will motivate the student to avoid trying. Positive reinforcements or incentives lead to the development of learned needs, just like negative effects lead to the development of learned fears.

18. The motivation to both approach and avoid the same goal at the same time, because that goal leads to both positive and negative outcomes, is called an *approach–avoidance conflict*. Trying to increase the tendency to approach (by "pushing" or "pulling") produces more fear and, thus, less positive results than trying to decrease the tendency to avoid (by making it safer), because the *fear gradient* increases faster than the *goal gradient* as a person gets closer to a feared goal.

19. Teachers are encouraged to avoid coaxing, fighting, retaliating, or giving up in resolving their conflicts with misbehaving students.

20. *Self-actualization theory* is a *growth* theory rather than a *deficiency* theory, because it posits an inherent motivation to grow and develop to a point of *realizing one's potential*. To choose growth, a person must find it to be more *attractive* and less *dangerous* to satisfy than other needs are.

21. Maslow proposes a *hierarchy of needs*, in priority order, of physiological gratification, safety, love, esteem, and self-actualization. Higher-order needs are not dealt with until lower-order ones are satisfied.

22. A self-actualized person is capable of having *peak experiences*, characterized by *cognition of being* or wholeness of thought and *values of being* such as beauty, goodness, and truth. An experience such as a truly creative or inspiring moment blocks all other perceptions and experiences and gives the person experiencing it a feeling of awe, rapture, compassionate acceptance, and perfection.

23. *Humanistic education* is intended to enhance students' self-actualization and is characterized by teachers who believe that their students can grow, a curriculum that is relevant to student interests, a nonthreatening atmosphere, student participation, self-evaluation, and an openness to experience. The focus is on meeting student needs, and much activity is focused on the *self-discovery* process and the development of self-awareness and self-esteem as prerequisites to self-actualization.

Suggested Resources

Dinkmeyer, D., McKay, G., & Dinkmeyer, D., Jr. (1980). *Systematic training for effective teaching (STET): Teacher's handbook*. Circle Pines, MN: American Guidance Services.

Maslow, A. H. (1968). *Toward a psychology of being* (2nd ed.). Princeton, NJ: Van Nostrand.

McClelland, D. C. (1985). *Human motivation*. Glenview, IL: Scott, Foresman.

Rogers, C. (1983). *Freedom to learn: For the 80's*. Columbus, OH: Merrill.

Weiner, B. (1980). *Human motivation*. New York: Holt, Rinehart & Winston.

Part Three

Testing
and
Evaluation

Chapter
13

Individual Differences

Objectives

1. Identify and describe intelligence as a general mental capability, a group of traits, a set of different mental abilities, and a process.
2. Describe the relationship of intelligence to age, heredity, environment, and achievement.
3. Identify the educational effects of grouping students by intelligence or ability.
4. Describe social class as an individual difference measure and as it relates to education.
5. Describe cognitive or learning style—in particular, structure-seeking versus independence-seeking—as an educationally relevant type of individual difference between students.
6. Identify the methodology and the educational effects of matching and mismatching students' cognitive or learning style with the style of instruction they receive.
7. Describe creativity and the related variable of brain hemisphere predominance as educationally relevant characteristics of individual students.
8. Describe and illustrate four interpersonal or relationship styles as individual differences between students.
9. Describe differences in moods, particularly anxiety, that can exist between students and explain the possible effects these have on school performance.

Introduction

Children are different from one another in a variety of ways. Many of these ways, such as how tall they are, how wealthy their parents are, what colors they like to wear, and what country their ancestors came from, ought not to have very much to do with how they learn or how they behave in school. Other differences, such as how smart they are, how much they have already learned, how they learn best, and how they feel about themselves and school, can be expected to affect their school behavior and performance.

This chapter will deal with some of the school-relevant ways in which children are different and, equally important, how these differences are determined. Because test scores are used and interpreted in determining these differences, this chapter will serve as a useful introduction to the topic of testing.

Intelligence

Intelligence or mental ability is a widely used and popular concept for explaining individual performance and performance differences in the school setting. In order to specify what intelligence is and how it develops to different degrees in different students, we will look at different conceptions of intelligence and at how intelligence testing first developed.

The Origin of Intelligence as a General Mental Capability

Alfred Binet, a French psychologist, was asked to identify schoolchildren in Paris who required special educational treatment, so that they could be separated from those who did not. To identify these children, he decided that first he needed to determine the *intelligence* or *general mental capability* of all schoolchildren. He defined intelligence as a combination of the following abilities: (1) reasoning and judgment, (2) comprehension, (3) maintenance of a definite direction of thought, (4) adaptation of thinking to the attainment of a desirable end, and (5) autocritical abilities or finding one's own mistakes (Binet & Simon, 1908; Binet, 1916). Despite the fact that he defined intelligence in terms of components, he believed that intelligence was a *single, complex process* and not a set of separate elements. Thus, he measured intelligence as a single score across a set of 30 different tasks that he believed reflected the process of intelligence. (These tasks, grouped by age level, are shown in Box 13.1.)

Binet's original conception of intelligence as a single process was later supported by Spearman (1927), who found an overlap between individual performances on a variety of intelligence subtests. He concluded that this reflected a common or *general factor* of intelligence that was a shared requirement of all the subtests. Beyond the general factor, Spearman (1927) also posited the existence of specific factors, unique to each mental activity, that combined with the more important general factor to constitute intelligence. Intelligence, therefore, was largely viewed as a general ability to solve mental problems.

Intelligence as a Group of Traits

Intelligence has also been viewed as a set of specific traits or factors. Thurstone (1938) identified the following as *primary mental abilities*:

1. *Number* — doing arithmetic calculations
2. *Verbal* — showing understanding of word passages

3. *Space* — manipulating an object in two or three dimensions
4. *Word Fluency* — thinking of the meaning of isolated words
5. *Reasoning* — discovering a rule or principle
6. *Rote Memory* — quick memorization

Many students are better at some of these tasks than they are at others, indicating a difference in proficiency or ability from one to the others.

Guilford (1967) has proposed a considerably more complex model of discrete intellectual abilities (shown in Figure 13.1) that features three dimensions: (1) *content* — the intellectual realm or area (such as figures or words), (2) *operation* — the nature of the performance required (for example, thinking or memorizing), and (3) *product* — the kind of outcome produced (for example, relationship or implications). The model produces 120 combinations, suggesting that there are that many discrete intellectual factors or small pieces that must be fitted together to make a whole.

One psychologist, upon hearing about this highly complex and very well-organized conception of intelligence, quipped: "If I were the Almighty, I wouldn't have made so many different boxes, and if I did, I wouldn't have stacked them that neatly." This reflects the difficulty in thinking about intelligence as such an incredibly organized system of minute components.

Figure 13.1 🍎 Guilford's Model of Intelligence
From Guilford, 1967.

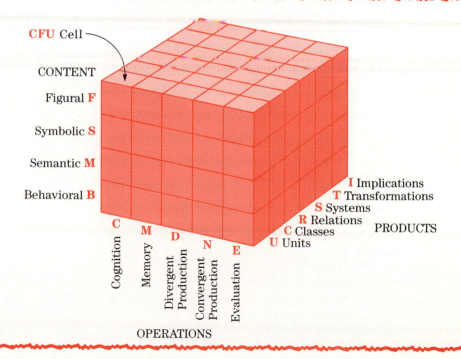

Box 13.1

The First Intelligence Test: The Binet–Simon Scale of 1908

The grouping of items at the appropriate age levels is shown below. Items are included that about 75% of the children of that age group could pass. Many of the items still appear in current intelligence tests.

Age 3
1. Points to nose, eyes, mouth
2. Repeats sentences of six syllables
3. Repeats two digits
4. Enumerates objects in a picture
5. Gives family name

Age 4
1. Knows own sex
2. Names certain family objects shown to him (key, knife, penny)
3. Repeats three digits
4. Perceives which is the longer of two lines 5 and 6 cm. in length

Age 5
1. Indicates the heavier of two cubes (3 and 12 grams; 6 and 15 grams)
2. Copies a square
3. Constructs a rectangle from two triangular pieces of cardboard, having a model to look at
4. Counts four coins
5. Repeats a sentence of ten syllables

Age 6
1. Knows right and left; indicated by showing right hand and left ear
2. Repeats sentence of sixteen syllables
3. Chooses the prettier in each of three pairs of faces (aesthetic comparison)
4. Defines familiar objects in terms of use
5. Carries out three direct instructions
6. Knows own age
7. Knows morning and afternoon

Age 7
1. Perceives what is missing in unfinished pictures
2. Knows numbers of fingers on each hand and on both hands without counting
3. Copies a written model ("The Little Paul")
4. Copies a diamond
5. Describes presented pictures
6. Repeats five digits
7. Counts thirteen coins
8. Identifies by name four common coins

Age 8
1. Reads a passage and remembers two items
2. Adds up the value of five coins

3. Names four colors: red, yellow, blue, green
4. Counts backwards from 20 to 0
5. Writes short sentences from dictation
6. Gives differences between two objects

Age 9

1. Knows the date: day of week, day of month, month of year
2. Recites days of week
3. Makes change: four cents out of twenty in playstore transaction
4. Gives definitions that are superior to use; familiar objects are employed
5. Reads a passage and remembers six items
6. Arranges five equal-appearing cubes in order of weight

Age 10

1. Names the months of the year in correct order
2. Recognizes and names nine coins
3. Constructs a sentence in which three given words are used (Paris, fortune, gutter)
4. Comprehends and answers easy questions
5. Comprehends and answers difficult questions (Binet considered item 5 to be a transitional question between ages 10 and 11. Only about one-half of the ten-year-olds got the majority of these correct.)

Age 11

1. Points out absurdities in statements
2. Constructs a sentence, including three given words (same as number 3 in age 10)
3. States any sixty words in three minutes
4. Defines abstract words (charity, justice, kindness)
5. Arranges scrambled words into a meaningful sentence

Age 12

1. Repeats seven digits
2. Gives three rhymes to a word (in one minute)
3. Repeats a sentence of twenty-six syllables
4. Answers problem questions
5. Interprets pictures (as contrasted with simple description)

Age 13

1. Draws the design made by cutting a triangular piece from the once-folded edge of a quarto-folded piece of paper
2. Rearranges in imagination the relationship of two reversed triangles and draws results
3. Gives differences between pair of abstract terms: pride and pretension

---

(It is interesting to speculate on how many of these age-graded tasks from 1908 could be passed by 75% of today's children of those respective ages. More than likely today's 4-year-olds could name objects like a key, a knife, or a penny, but how many 13-year-olds today could distinguish between the terms "pride" and "pretension"? Have we become less bright, or is it simply a matter of changing cultures? Such differences in standards certainly point up the importance of constantly updating tests.)

SOURCE: Binet, A., and Simon, T. (1908). "Le developpement de l'intelligence chez les enfants." *L'Année Psychologique*, 14, 1–94.

Different Kinds of Intelligence

Closely related to the conception of intelligence as a group of traits is the idea of different kinds of intelligence. Jensen (1968) proposed two: *associative intelligence*, requiring memory and the ability to build simple associations or connections, and *abstract intelligence*, requiring thinking and problem-solving. In many ways, the first probably serves as a prerequisite for the second, but having the first does not necessarily guarantee the development of the second.

More recently, Gardner (1983) proposed seven different intelligences:

1. *Linguistic* intelligence or the ability to use words (as might a writer),
2. *Musical* intelligence or the ability to write music or play an instrument (as might a musician),
3. *Logical–mathematical* intelligence or the ability to reason and use symbols (as might a scientist),
4. *Spatial* intelligence or the ability to arrange and rearrange objects in space (as might an architect),
5. *Bodily kinesthetic* intelligence or the ability to control one's body (as might a dancer or gymnast),
6. *Intrapersonal* intelligence or the ability to control one's inner thoughts and feelings (as might a spiritual leader),
7. *Interpersonal* intelligence or the ability to function well socially (as might a salesperson or politician).

Gardner sees these types of intelligence as being *modular* like the components of a stereo system. You can have some of these intelligences but not others, and you can lose some and gain or retain others. Schools often ignore many of these types of intelligence while focusing primarily on linguistic and logical–mathematical types. In so doing, they may unnecessarily cause some students to feel inferior to others.

Intelligence as a Process

It is also possible to view intelligence as a process rather than a trait or static characteristic. As we saw in Chapter 8, Piaget viewed intelligence as the result of the process of *adaptation*, itself made up of two subprocesses, *assimilation* and *accommodation*, governed by the process of *equilibration*. In other words, intelligence is what people use to cope with their experiences and is itself developed and enhanced by being so used. The reflection of intelligence is in the schemata that a person develops based on the experiences that he or she encounters in dealing with the environment.

Another way to view intelligence is as a reflection of the process of *learning*. In other words, intelligence is one's teachability or one's ability to learn. Feuerstein, Rand, Hoffman, and Miller (1980) determine intelligence by teaching someone how to do something and then measuring how much better he or she can do it after being taught than before. Feuerstein et al. (1980) call this process *mediated learning* or learning that is assisted by the teaching process. The question of how intelligent a person is then becomes a matter of how readily that person can learn as a result of being taught.

Sternberg (1982, 1985) has proposed that intelligence is a reflection of one's ability to *process information* (as described in Chapters 6 and 7). As such, it includes three components:

1. *Meta* components — the executive processes that regulate or control problem-solving (such as planning and monitoring strategies),
2. *Performance* components — the processes actually used to solve a problem (such as encoding and comparing),
3. *Knowledge Acquisition* components — the processes used for acquiring new information (such as elaborating and organizing).

When faced with a problem to solve, the individual must make decisions about what kind of a problem it is and how to solve it. To do this, he must first function like a good executive or controller, and then actually go about solving the problem. A problem-solver must be a good thinker or performer in the domain of the problem. A problem-solver must also have specific information relevant to the problem or must know how and where to get this information. A problem-solver must be a good knower or learner.

According to this view of intelligence, making a person smart means teaching her how to execute, perform, and learn in a wide variety of content areas. It also means that measuring how smart a person is requires that she be tested to see how well she solves problems (in practical as well as academic areas), rather than testing only what she already knows. It is a markedly different approach to intelligence than the one proposed by Binet (with which this chapter began), and it is more likely than Binet's to stimulate a broad conception about the kinds of things students should learn in school.

Despite these many and varied conceptions of what intelligence is, it is still typically measured as a set of primary traits or mental abilities, as illustrated by the test items shown in Box 13.2.

Intelligence and Age

The original method for scoring intelligence tests was based on the obvious fact that intellectual performance increases with age (Binet & Simon, 1908). To ensure that intelligence-test scores reflected the age of test-takers, the concept of *mental age* was created. A child's mental age was based originally on the age equivalence of the most difficult items a child was able to get right (see Box 13.1 for item groupings by age). Today, however, a child's mental age is based on the average age of children who get the same number of items right as that child does. For example, if a child, regardless of age, gets 30 items right and the average age of all children who get 30 items right is 6½, then that child has a mental age of 6.5. (This represents a norm-referenced approach to test-score interpretation, as described in Chapter 16.)

Box 13.2

Some Illustrative Intelligence-Test Items*

Verbal Items: Examples

Word Substitution
Which of the words below is the best substitute for the italicized word in the following sentence?
He was a good doctor, but alcohol was his *ruin*.

a. plague   *c.* fate
b. undoing   *d.* destiny

Synonyms
Which word means the same as the given?
TEMPERAMENT

a. angriness   *c.* hostility
b. popularity   *d.* disposition

Word Classification
Which word does not belong?

a. horse   *c.* mosquito
b. flower   *d.* snake

Verbal Analysis
Which word should go in the blank space to fulfill relationships that call for it?
COLD:HOT   UP:_____

a. down   *c.* low
b. high   *d.* under

Word Class
Into which one of the four classes does the given word best fit?
PALM

a. plant   *c.* tree
b. flower   *d.* leaf

Verbal Relations
Which alternative pair comes nearest to expressing the relation of the given pair?
BIRD:SONG

a. fish:water   *c.* pianist:piano
b. person:speech   *d.* horse:ranch

Figural Items: Examples

Recognition of Objects
What is the object?

Figure Matching
Which alternative (at the right) is most nearly like the test object (at the left)?

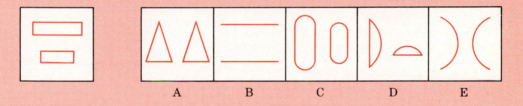

Figural Relations
What kind of figure should appear in the cell with the question mark?

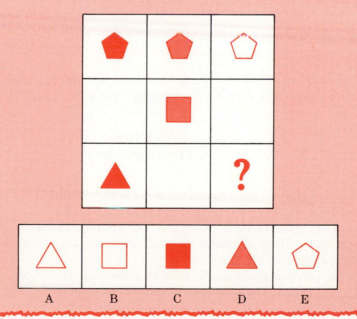

Box 13.2 continued

Spatial Visualization

Diagrams I and II show two steps in folding a square piece of paper and cutting a notch in a certain location. Which alternative shows how the paper would look when unfolded?

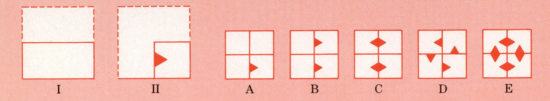

Hidden Figures

Which of the five simple figures at the top is concealed in each of the item figures?

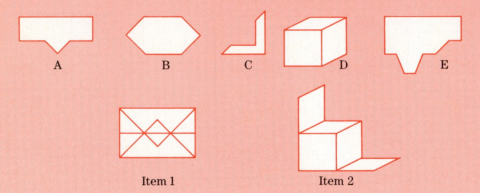

Item 1   Item 2

To convert mental age into a measure of intelligence, researchers created the *intelligence quotient* or *IQ* using the following formula:

$$IQ = \frac{\text{Mental age}}{\text{Chronological age}} \times 100$$

Thus, if the child who has a mental age of 6.5 is also 6½ years old, then that child would have an IQ of 100. Whenever a child scores exactly the same as the average child of his or her own age, then that child has an IQ of 100. Children scoring the same as those older than they are will have IQ's above 100, while children scoring the same as others younger will have IQ's below 100.

The cutoff scores originally used for classifying children based on IQ scores are shown in Box 13.3. These categories are used less commonly today.

Identical Figures

Which figure in the row is exactly the same as the one at the left?

A   B   C   D   E

Recognition of Figural Classes

Which figure does not belong to the class determined by the other three figures?

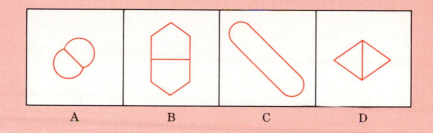

A   B   C   D

*Answers to these fictitious items appear on page 344 as footnote 1.

Nowadays, the IQ score is simply computed on the basis of how a child scores compared directly to children of different ages and is called the *deviation IQ*. (This will be discussed further in Chapter 16.)

Where Does Intelligence Come From?

The two potential sources of influence on intelligence are *heredity* and *environment*. Heredity refers to the extent to which a person's intelligence is based on the intelligence of his or her parents, while environment represents the contribution of that person's experiences, both at home and in school, to intelligence.

There is clear evidence to suggest that heredity is a highly influential factor on intelligence (Jensen, 1969; Mittler, 1971). If the level of intelligence of identical twins (born from the same egg) who are reared together in the same home at the same time by

Box 13.3

Suggested Classification of IQ's

IQ	Classification
Above 140	"Near" genius or genius
120–140	Very superior intelligence
110–119	Superior intelligence
90–109	Normal, or average, intelligence
80–89	Dullness
70–79	Borderline deficiency
Below 70	Definite feeblemindedness

SOURCE: Terman, L. (1916). *The measurement of intelligence*. Boston: Houghton-Mifflin.

the same parents is compared to the level of intelligence of identical twins reared apart (having been separated at birth and then reared by different "parents" in different homes), the differences are very small. In other words, twins, who have the same heredity, have very similar IQ's regardless of whether they have the same environment. Moreover, identical twins reared apart, meaning siblings with the same heredity but different environments, have IQ's much more similar to one another than ordinary siblings reared together, even though the latter have a similar environment but a somewhat different heredity.

These findings, of course, do not suggest that the impact of home environment and school on intelligence is inconsequential. No matter how great a child's inborn intellectual capacity is, that capacity will not be realized or actualized unless the home and school environments are reasonably supportive and stimulating. While teachers must recognize that each child has his or her own intellectual level, that level may represent only a partial degree of that child's potential. The teacher still has the opportunity to help all children reach their potential. School experiences, therefore, should not be discounted. (To put this issue into perspective, see Box 13.4.)

There is little certainty about exactly what intelligence is, what its properties are, how best to measure it, or what it should be a prerequisite for. Moreover, controversy is

---

[1]Answers for Box 13.2: *b, d, b, a, c, b,* airplane, C, A, C, 1-A, 2-D, D, C

Box 13.4

🍎

Testing and Teaching "Intelligence"

In the late 1960s, while many civil rights groups focused their efforts on elimination of tests as culturally biased, Ernie Green of the A. Phillip Randolph Institute took a different approach. He developed a program in Brooklyn's Bedford-Stuyvesant section to train potential apprenticeship candidates to take the screening test. The General Aptitude Test Battery (GATB) is a type of broad-based intelligence test that the United States Employment Service uses in screening and counseling job seekers. It is also used as a screening device for apprenticeship training programs. Because blacks tended to score lower than whites on this test, they were eliminated from competition for places in apprenticeship programs. Assuming that white candidates have had more specific training in taking such tests as the GATB, Green added relevant experience to the culture of minority candidates to overcome the cultural bias. Using mainly self-educated ex-convicts as teachers, he had black candidates spend six to eight weeks learning basic math and English. They practiced on items similar to those found on the current form of the GATB (a review process not unlike the College Board review or the "Regents review" in New York schools).

Their heads filled with vocabulary words, analogies, and math skills, Ernie Green's first group of graduates took the exams. The results were gratifying: Virtually all the students in the program were above the cut-off scores. "They're beating the system," shouted their critics, who were trying to maintain the status quo. "It's not fair to teach people to take a test." "But," responded Green, "isn't that what the middle-class school experience is all about?" The courts agreed and ruled that those who had never been taught what the test measured were entitled to be given the opportunity to learn it.

Test results may be a cause of school behavior and not just its effect. If children who have higher IQ scores are expected by their teachers to do better in school than children with lower scores (a not unreasonable supposition), and if teachers are nicer to these high-IQ test-scorers and help them more than they help the low scorers, it is evident that IQ test scores are not only the effect of school experiences but also their cause. (This effect of expectations, called the self-fulfilling prophecy, was described in Chapter 10.)

One benefit of the debate on intelligence testing is to make educators more careful in the use of IQ tests. Clearly, blacks and whites as groups do tend to score differently on IQ tests — perhaps, it could be argued, because blacks have had poorer schooling. Possibly, then, we should reconsider how tests should be used. Except for the diagnosis of marked deficiency, it would be wise to focus testing on what children have learned as a result of school experiences and to draw conclusions on this basis rather than on the basis of variations in native intelligence.

common over whether intelligence, as it is presently used, is universally applicable (as it might be if it were based on heredity) or culturally bound (as a result of environmental influences that vary from culture to culture). Using intelligence-test scores as a basis for life decisions for children, or even for adults (see Box 13.4), in all but extreme cases, may be unwise and unfounded.

Anne Anastasi, a former president of the American Psychological Association and an expert in differential psychology, offered the following five points on the way that intelligence may best be viewed (1982, p. 211):

1. as a descriptive rather than an explanatory concept, meaning as an expression of an individual's ability at a given point in time, in relation to current age norms (intelligence tests cannot indicate the reasons for someone's performance);
2. as amenable to modification by environmental interventions rather than fixed and unchanging;
3. as the end product of a vast and complex sequence of interactions between hereditary and environmental factors;
4. as a composite of several functions rather than a single, unitary ability, meaning the combination of abilities required for survival and advancement within a particular culture;
5. as a relative ability or one that will tend to increase with age in those functions whose value is emphasized in the culture or subculture, and will tend to decrease in those functions whose value is deemphasized.

Intelligence Versus Achievement

Intelligence can be described as a general mental ability or as a set of more specific mental abilities or traits. How, then, does it differ from achievement as measured by achievement tests? Perhaps we can best answer this question by looking at what it is that achievement tests measure and then contrasting that with the content of intelligence tests.

Achievement tests generally measure so-called *reading skills*, such as (1) vocabulary or identifying a synonym of a word or a word that fits a given definition, (2) word analysis or identifying the sound of a word or a part of a word, and (3) reading comprehension or answering a question based on a story or reading passage. Achievement tests also tend to measure *language skills*, like (1) spelling, (2) punctuation, (3) capitalization, and (4) grammar or word usage.

Mathematics is another area covered by achievement tests. It is usually divided into (1) computation, (2) concepts or basic rules, and (3) applications or solving problems. Achievement tests also cover *social studies*, *science*, and, occasionally, *study skills*.

The content of achievement tests is not very dissimilar from that of intelligence tests. Both seem to measure what students have learned, but intelligence seems to be less dependent upon specified prior experiences than does achievement (Anastasi, 1982). Also, intelligence tests often include the measurement of nonverbal skills, while achievement tests do not. Cronbach (1984) sees ability as a spectrum or continuum ranging from the broad ability to transfer what has been learned from one situation to another (or *intelligence*) to crystallized or specific learning resulting from direct training and instruction (or *achievement*). Intelligence, therefore, looks forward toward possible future learning, while achievement looks backward toward the measurement of past learning. Nevertheless, the overlap between the two concepts of intelligence and achievement, and the tests that measure them, is considerable.

Fitting Instruction to Ability: Ability Grouping

Ability grouping or homogeneous grouping means classifying pupils in terms of factors that are presumed to affect learning (such as intelligence or mental ability) and then forming instructional groups made up of pupils who are highly similar on these factors. Many elementary schools have gifted classes, remedial classes, special-education classes, reading groups and, sometimes, mathematics groups. Many high schools have honors classes, college preparatory classes, academic tracks, vocational tracks, general tracks, and special-education classes. In every instance, students of common ability are grouped together, separate from students of either greater or lesser ability. The rationale is that instruction will be more efficient if all students are equally capable than if the level of capability varies greatly from student to student. In other words, narrowing the range of capability among students in a class is presumed to improve the effectiveness of instruction and thereby increase achievement.

A major study of 86 fifth-grade classrooms in the New York City Public Schools over a two-year period (fifth grade to seventh grade) revealed that "narrowing the range

Experiences, interactions, and opportunities to learn help to nurture the budding intelligence of young children and help them develop the capability to adapt to their environment. Intelligence is not fixed and unchanging, but can grow—in fact, flourish—under the right circumstances.

of ability (on the basis of group intelligence tests) per se, without specifically designed variations in programs for the several ability levels, does not result in consistently greater academic performance for any group of pupils (Goldberg, Passow, & Justman, 1966, p. 161). In other words, ability grouping was not effective.

One reason for the lack of effectiveness was that most teachers were more successful in teaching a single subject to several ability levels at the same time than in teaching all subjects to narrow-range classes. Moreover, teachers did not necessarily alter what they taught when the range of ability of the students they were teaching changed, especially in the subject areas the teachers felt least competent to teach. Grouping students by ability does not tend to help them learn more *unless* their instruction is specifically designed and fitted to their ability level, a practice that is not typical, except perhaps in special-education classes.

A recent review of ability-grouping studies by Slavin (1987) reached a similar conclusion for between-class or self-contained ability grouping, namely, that it did not enhance achievement except in *reading*. Since reading is a prerequisite to most other learning, groups of similar ability seem to produce better results than groups of dissimilar ability. Slavin (1987) also found that *within-class* ability grouping was effective for teaching *mathematics*.

What about the effects of ability grouping on nonacademic variables, such as attitude toward self? Goldberg, Passow, and Justman (1966) found little effect, either positive or negative. The act of being grouped, however, can affect a student's self-expectations as well as the expectations of teachers, resulting in what has been called the self-fulfilling prophecy (See Box 10.2 on page 241). Ability grouping would appear, therefore, to be a poor educational strategy except when specific instructional approaches have been designed for a particular group. Alternatively, the cooperative-learning approach (see the section on normative goal structures in Chapter 10, and Box 10.3 in particular) would appear to be a good strategy for dealing with students with a range of abilities. Having brighter students work with less bright students can provide academic and nonacademic benefits to both groups (Webb, 1982).

Social Class

Social class or *socioeconomic status* (SES) is a function of parent's *education level* and *occupational status* as these affect *income level* or wealth. Children with college-educated parents who are engaged in professional occupations have higher SES, hence greater prestige, than children with uneducated parents who are engaged in unskilled jobs or are unemployed. While intelligence is a characteristic that is only partially outside of a child's control, social class, since it is based entirely on parental attainments, is wholly beyond a child's control.

Of what consequence is social class to education? Hess (1970) points out that high SES parents tend to be actively involved in the education of their children, not only in the home environment but also in their interactions with their children's schools. Low SES parents may value education for their children, but they are less comfortable than their high SES counterparts in dealing with the authority structure of the schools. However, recent efforts in New York City to provide low SES parents with real educational choices for their children has resulted in much greater parental involvement and a subsequent increase in student achievement.

About one out of five persons in the United States lives either on welfare or on an income that is below the subsistence level. An increasingly high percentage of low-income people are homeless. It is hard for people living with the disadvantage of poverty to provide for the basic needs of their children, much less their social and educational needs. Children of poverty frequently lack the educational stimulation and opportunity characteristically provided to children of higher social class by their parents. Moreover, many poor children are members of single-parent families and that single parent works, reducing even further the opportunities for educational stimulation in the home.

What can be done to improve the plight of low SES children? While not the panacea originally thought, early childhood enrichment programs for low income children provide

Grouping children by ability or by some other aspect of the way they have performed in school does not help them perform better. Many researchers and teachers have found that mixing students who are different into the larger group, rather than separating them, yields better results.

many benefits, not the least of which are health and nutritional benefits such as good meals (Lazar & Darling, 1982). They can also help to offset any lack of early stimulation in the home by providing the conversation, books, and educational toys that might otherwise be missing (Hess, 1970).

Cognitive or Learning Style

Quite apart from the question of a person's intelligence is the question of how that person typically goes about thinking and learning. Some people are very organized and structured, for example; others are disorganized and spontaneous. Some people see things in very concrete, black-and-white terms, while others differentiate many shades of gray. It is useful to look at differences between the ways different children think and learn and then to link these differences to different styles of teaching.

Structure-Seekers Versus Independence-Seekers

A distinction can be made between two types of learners: those who seek structure or guidance to assure their conformity and those who prefer independence and the opportunity to explore. The first group fears making errors, while the second group uses them as a way to learn. Hunt and Sullivan (1974) refer to the first group as *low conceptual level* and the second group as *high conceptual level*. Witkin (1962) calls the first group *field dependent* and the second group *field independent*. Also, to use Kagan's (1965) terms, the first group tends to be more *reflective*, the second more *impulsive*.

What do these different terms mean? Picture two students. Let's call them Alicea and Bev. Alicea is always on time for class and always sits in the same seat. Her notebooks are always perfectly divided and filled with notes. She likes it when the teacher lectures and gives explicit homework assignments. She likes to know exactly what is expected of her, which usually means what the test is going to cover. She works slowly but methodically and asks lots of questions to make sure she is doing what she is supposed to do. She likes following rules. She likes material to be organized for her. She is practical and predictable. She likes school and her teachers are very fond of her.

Now look at Bev. She gets bored with the predictability of school and the lack of opportunity to pursue her own intellectual interests. She likes to write poetry and to follow her own lead. She works quickly and with great spontaneity. She often scribbles on scraps of paper or on the backs of envelopes. Some of her teachers find her as trying as she finds them. But if you put her in an unstructured situation, she will figure it out on her own, whereas her classmate, Alicea, will need someone to help her structure the situation to make it look more like something with which she is familiar. While Alicea needs to get her directions from *outside* herself, Bev prefers to provide her own from *inside*. Alicea has a higher *need for conformity*, while Bev has a higher *need for independence*.

The point is not that either Bev or Alicea is a better student or a better person than the other — only that they are different, their differences representing disparate points on a continuum onto which all students fall. Joining Alicea are all her classmates who

- need explicit instructions to solve problem;
- require externally defined structure, goals, and reinforcement;
- conform to the prevailing pattern of thinking and acting;

- work methodically and systematically;
- see things in "either–or" terms;
- prefer not to work on their own.

Bev, on the other hand, is joined by her classmates who

- can generate their own problem-solving instructions;
- prefer to impose their own structure and define their own goals;
- generate their own unique pattern of thinking and acting;
- work quickly and intuitively;
- see things in subtle ways and nuances;
- prefer to do "their own thing."

Since Bev and Alicea are merely examples, or what you might call prototypes, they represent pure instances of the two types. In any classroom you will encounter many variations of these at the same time. (See Box 13.5 for another, familiar example of these two cognitive types.)

Matching Instructional Style with Cognitive Style to Meet Individual Learning Needs

Which type of learner is most likely to be taught in a way that is consistent with his or her cognitive style? Since most classrooms and curriculums are structured and controlled by

---

Box 13.5

The Odd Couple

Felix Unger and Oscar Madison, characters in a Neil Simon play, movie, and television series, lived together despite the fact that their personal styles were extremely different. Dubbed the "odd couple" because Felix was so neat, organized, and fastidious while Oscar was rambunctious, spontaneous, and carefree, their oddness or mismatch made for many laughs. Felix, for example, was always concerned that Oscar would miss an appointment or fail to carry out a responsibility, so he left him little notes on his pillow, on the bathroom mirror, on the refrigerator — to name just a few places. Oscar would stumble upon the notes, crumple them up, and throw them at Felix in a mock rage because he figured that anything he couldn't remember to do wasn't worth doing. Felix, by comparison, would never, knowingly, allow his schedule to be messed up.

When a teacher must deal with students who are very different from himself, the result is an "odd couple," a "Felix" and an "Oscar." The teacher may want order and explicit following of directions. The student may be more carefree — not just to give the teacher a hard time, but because that's the way that student is. Oscar and Felix, however, could never manage to avoid fighting with one another over their differences. If Felix cooked a gourmet meal and taunted Oscar about preferring to eat hot dogs, then Oscar would invariably end up throwing the food at Felix, or putting his dirty socks in Felix's bed. All this makes good theater, but it does not make good instruction. Teachers have to learn not only to tolerate their differences with some students but to respect and enjoy them as well.

rules and requirements external to the student, the structure-seeker is most likely to find himself in a learning situation that *matches* his own style. The choice of an instructional method to match individual learning needs has been dubbed a *matching model* by Hunt and Sullivan (1974). It has also been referred to by Cronbach and Snow (1977) as the *aptitude–treatment interaction* or ATI because the treatment or approach is chosen to match the inclination of the students.

How can matching models be implemented? Ideally, each student should be allowed to choose her preferred form of instruction, but in a class of 20 to 30 students allowing this much choice could be chaotic. A second possibility is for the teacher to vary the instructional model (using a continuum such as that shown in Box 10.6, p. 252) so that every student would experience times of match and times of mismatch. A third possibility is to offer so-called magnet classrooms or magnet schools, in which a particular model of teaching predominates, and let students (and their parents) choose their own match. A fourth possibility would be to measure individual style by test or interview and then assign students to classes taught in a way consistent with that style. This could be called cognitive-style grouping.

In sum, the alternatives for matching are

1. to provide instructional style choices within a classroom,

2. to alter instructional style from unit to unit within a classroom,

3. to offer alternative classes or schools with different instructional styles from which students can choose,

4. to offer alternative classes with different instructional styles and assign students based on their measured cognitive styles.

The typical occurrence is for classes and schools to employ different instructional styles (even though the structured, conformity-oriented one is the most common, it is not exclusive) and for students to either choose or be assigned to different instructional styles without regard to their learning styles. As a result, in every instructional setting, some students are experiencing a match and some a mismatch between the approach to instruction and the way they learn. Consider and compare some of the results of both match and mismatch situations described below. (Also see the description of leadership styles in Chapter 10.)

Match–Mismatch Studies.   Domino (1971) divided 100 college students into those who were high in or preferred *conformity* and those who were high in or preferred *independence*, based on personality test scores. He then assigned half of each group to a psychology class that was taught in a *conforming* or highly structured manner (with rules, requirements, and an emphasis on attendance and memorization) and half to a psychology class that was taught in an *independent* or less structured manner (using more of a seminar approach). As a result, half of each group experienced a match between their learning style and the teaching style used in the course and half experienced a mismatch. Students whose learning style matched the teaching style of the particular class they were placed in did better on the course exams, got a better course grade, and evaluated the course more positively than did students for whom the teaching style did not fit their learning style. One type of teaching, in and of itself, was neither better nor worse than the other in terms of its effect on student achievement or course liking. *How effective a teaching style* *was or how liked it was depended on the way the students who experienced it learned better*. When the teaching style fit the student learning style, it worked; when it did not fit, it did not work.

Similar results were obtained by Tuckman and Orefice (1973). They classified students as low conceptual and high conceptual (similar to Piaget's concrete and formal) and taught half of each group by a combination of programmed instruction and lecture and the other half by programmed instruction alone. High-conceptual students preferred programmed instruction alone and spent considerably more time at it than low conceptual students. Low-conceptual students preferred the lecture method. Tuckman (1968) studied the teacher preferences expressed by low-conceptual and high-conceptual vocational students and found that lows preferred directive teachers while highs preferred nondirective ones.

Thus there is a strong correlation between how students learn or think and how they prefer to be taught. Teaching everyone by lecture, for example, will work well for some students — those who need the structure of explicit, externally controlled instruction (or have a need for conformity) — but not for others who prefer more freedom to create their own structure (or have a need for independence). By comparison, self-study or independent study will work well for some (those with a need for independence), but will possibly be a disaster for others (those with need for conformity). The best solution may be to provide clear alternatives and allow students to choose between them.

Match and mismatch can also result when students with different cognitive styles read instructional materials that have different structures (recall the discussion of processing structures or levels on pages 126–127 of Chapter 6). Some students may find it easier to remember information that merely summarizes the main points that have been made in the text, or what Meyer (1984) calls the *collection* structure, while other students may remember more when similarities and differences between concepts are presented in what Meyer calls the *comparison* structure. (These two structures were used to analyze the Supertanker passage in Chapter 6.) In fact, the discovery by Rotton, Blake, and Heslin (1977) that "open-minded persons attended to the content and implications of a message, whereas closed-minded persons attended to the surface quality of information" (p. 81) supports that idea of match and mismatch in reading.

Further support for this idea comes from a study by Rickards and Slife (1987) comparing open-minded or low-dogmatic students to closed-minded or high-dogmatic ones on these two structures. They obtained the results shown in Figure 13.2. For high-dogmatic students, there apparently was no question of match or mismatch: They did equally well with both structures. However, low-dogmatic or open-minded students experienced a match when the comparison structure was used (they remembered more) and a mismatch when the collection structure was used (they remembered less). Thus, optimum recall may depend for some students on whether the structure of the material to be recalled matches their cognitive style.

Creativity

Creativity, as a cognitive process, was discussed in Chapter 7, along with useful procedures to enhance its occurrence in students. It will be discussed briefly here as a reflection of individual differences. As was said in Chapter 7, creativity is a different

Figure 13.2 🍎 **Amount of Free Recall from Passages Utilizing Two Different Kinds of Structure (Comparison and Collection) by High Dogmatic and Low Dogmatic Students**

Based on findings by Rickards and Slife, 1987.

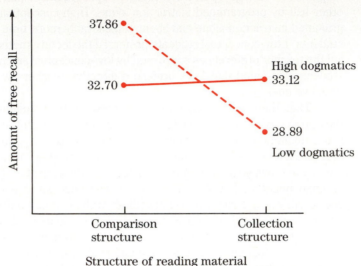

ability from intelligence (Wallach & Kogan, 1965). It is a *divergent* ability rather than a *convergent* ability, to use Guilford's (1967) terms. Creativity is primarily reflected in producing many novel yet appropriate solutions to a problem, while intelligence is primarily reflected in finding the one correct solution. Creativity is used to expand the possibilities, while intelligence is used to narrow them.

Generally, researchers measure creativity in test situations by giving people objects, situations, or lines and asking them to generate as many acceptable alternatives as they can in terms of uses, consequences, or drawings. More-creative persons are able to generate more alternatives than less-creative persons. Moreover, many of the alternatives they generate are novel or are less obvious than the ones generated by their less creative peers.

Brain Hemisphere Predominance. It has been suggested that creativity may be related to the side or hemisphere of the brain that predominates in an individual. Galin and Ornstein (1972) proposed that persons with left-hemisphere or *left-brain predominance* specialize in language and logic and in dealing systematically and sequentially with details and features. Such people are thought to be more *analytic* in their orientation. Persons with right-hemisphere or *right-brain predominance* were said to be more visually and spatially oriented (as opposed to being verbally oriented), more holistic in their thinking (as opposed to analytic), and, as a result, more creative (Torrance, 1982).

School, with its emphasis on speaking, listening, reading, writing, and arithmetic — all left brain functions — would seem to be "lopsided" in its neglect of the development of right-brain functions (Bogan, 1975). Students favoring right-brain functioning tend to predominate among (1) those failing school; (2) those with learning disabilities and other types of poor readers; (3) dyslexics; (4) those with behavior problems; and (5) low achievers (Stellern, Marlowe, & Jacobs, 1983).

Suggested remedies for right-hemisphere neglect in classrooms include (1) using more laboratory and field experience in place of some lectures and seminars (Bogan, 1975); (2) using more experiential approaches to the teaching of reading; and (3) providing more opportunities for drawing, music, and other creative activities. In addition, based on the observed connection between exercise and creativity (Tuckman & Hinkle, 1986), more physical activities may also help overcome right-brain neglect.

Interpersonal Style

In addition to the way a person typically thinks or processes information, which was referred to as cognitive style, it is also possible to characterize someone by the way he or she typically *relates to other people*. This may be called the interpersonal style or the relationship style. There are many ways to categorize or classify people based on how they relate to others, such as how much they like to be with others, how much they like to control or be controlled by others, and how much they like to give and receive affection. (One such system for classifying students, generated by teachers themselves, is shown in Box 13.6.)

An interesting way to describe interpersonal style has been proposed by Allessandra (1987) under the rubric of *relationship strategies*. It is based on the idea that people need to understand how other people like to be treated, if they want to treat them in a way that will enhance their relationships. The alternative is for people to treat everyone the way they themselves like to be treated, erroneously assuming that everyone is just like them, which would interfere with their relationships.

To categorize someone's relationship strategy, according to Allessandra (1987), it must be first determined whether they are more *self-contained* or more *open*. Self-contained people tend to keep their distance and maintain their territory. In other words, they like their privacy. They are not usually "touchers." In addition, they are likely to be task-oriented, and well-organized, and all business, so to speak. By contrast, open people tend to get close (physically and emotionally) to and be more accessible to others. It may be accurate to say that open people "can be read like a book" or "wear their hearts on their sleeves" because they often show and tell how they feel. They tend to not be very well-organized, and they seem to operate on their own personal time clock.

The second relationship dimension is *indirect* versus *direct*, which is different from openness. *Indirect* people tend to be cautious, careful, and slow at making decisions. They usually try to avoid risks, decisions, change, and failure. They generally speak slowly and softly without looking in the eyes of the person to whom they are speaking. They typically take the roundabout route in dealing with others, rather than being confrontive. They believe in following rules, and when they find themselves in a gray area without well-defined rules, they seek permission to proceed.

Contrast them with *direct* people, who tend to be risk-takers and usually come at others head-on. More often than not, they speak loud and fast, seek success, and are quick to take action. Unlike indirect types, they tend to believe that rules are made to be

Box 13.6

Teachers Describe Four Major Types of Students

A. Good Types

1. Natural leaders
2. Autonomous and self-directed
3. Interdependent, high achievers
4. Interdependent, low achievers
5. Nonconforming but work-oriented
6. Nonconforming, creative
7. Conforming and dependent
8. Submissive

B. Indifferent Students

9. Happy-go-lucky
10. Beauty queen
11. Gone on athletics
12. Duck-tail haircut
13. Prig
14. I-don't-need-an-education

C. Bad Students

15. Teacher impressers
16. Short-cutters
17. Clowns and attention seekers
18. Misdirected superior
19. Social climbers
20. Monopolizers
21. Hero worshipers and blind followers
22. Antisocial and destructive

D. Lost Souls

23. The rejected
24. The dreamers
25. The sufferers
26. The passive

SOURCE: Thelen, H. A. (1967). *Classroom grouping for teachability*. New York: Wiley.

broken, and when they find themselves in a gray area, they can be expected to push on ahead. While indirect people are often characterized as wishy-washy, direct people are more likely to be seen as pushy, aggressive, and overbearing.

These two dimensions — self-contained (or private) versus open, and indirect versus direct — can be combined to produce the four interpersonal types or relationship strategies shown in Figure 13.3 and described below (based on Allessandra, 1987).

1. The Director (Self-Contained but Direct).   This is the type who likes to be the leader, or the boss. The director can be all business and is usually in a hurry ("Don't waste my time"). The director tends to be competitive, bossy, critical, and decisive — the person to get the job done — and does the job with conviction and efficiency. Among students, the directors usually want to be in charge and independent of the teacher. They may challenge the teacher's authority, but only because they believe "directors" can do a task better. They are a challenge to teach, particularly if the teacher is a "director" himself.

2. The Thinker (Self-Contained and Indirect).   If the director can be described as a "bull," then the thinker is an "owl." Thinkers characteristically are accurate fact-gatherers and problem-solvers. They tend to make excellent accountants or scientists, working by themselves, slowly but methodically, to solve the problem at hand. Where the director may be hurried and decisive, the thinker is more likely to be deliberate. Where the director may become critical and bossy under stress, the thinker is more likely to become withdrawn. The thinker's bywords are apt to be "plan," "prepare," and "proceed with accuracy." When teachers can draw them out, thinkers can be a pleasure to teach (even the teacher's "pets").

3. The Socializer (Open and Direct).   Picture the talker, the persuader, the exaggerator, the overpowering social dynamo, the person who craves recognition, and you are likely to have the socializer. Always in "fifth gear," the socializer can be sarcastic and superficial when stressed. Usually, though, the socializer is spontaneous in decision-making, with the decisions changing easily and often. The socializer is likely to be upbeat, seeking fun, and doing everything with a flair. Like the director, the socializer is a

Figure 13.3 🍎 Four Interpersonal Types or Relationship Strategies
Based on Allesandra, 1987.

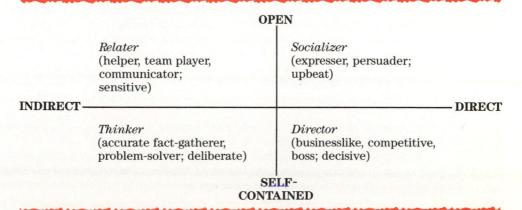

teacher's challenge—but for a different reason: The socializer tends to go for the lime-light, and as a result is hard to keep on-task.

4. The Relater (Open but Indirect).   The relater tends to be the team player, the communicator, the one who holds in her own feelings but encourages others to express theirs. If the socializer is likely to be the salesperson or the TV personality, the relater is likely to be the nurse, the social worker, or the counselor. The relater is usually casual and at ease but can be submissive and indecisive under stress. Usually, though, the relater is warm and sensitive and makes decisions in a consultative way. It is hard for teachers not to favor relaters, because they extend their relating skill to teachers as well.

A scenario of the four types reacting to the same school situation is shown in Box 13.7. By being aware of and able to detect the four types, teachers can alter their own expectations and reactions to facilitate the learning and development of each type of student.

Mood (Anxiety)

Mood represents a feeling of well-being or ill-being. However, the label is most often used to describe negative feelings or feelings of ill-being such as depression, anger, and,

---

Box 13.7

Four Personality Types Relate to a Case of False Witness

Students at Broadview High were leaving the building at lunchtime without proper passes and then either not coming back or getting into trouble, so the principal decided to assign a four-student "honor guard" to cover the main entrance. As chance would have it, each of the four seniors the principal selected for the honor guard had a different relationship style: one was a director, one a thinker, one a socializer, and one a relater.

Everything went well with the honor guard plan for about two months and then a disaster happened. A student went out into the schoolyard and apparently got into a fight. Rather than admit having fought and get into trouble, the student pretended to have a scuffle with the honor guard upon his reentry into the building. He then claimed that the honor guard beat him up. Another student who saw the apparent "scuffle" with the honor guard, although from a distance, supported the story, and at a subsequent hearing held by the principal, the honor guard members were found guilty and expelled from school.

Luckily though, very soon thereafter, students who had seen the real fight in the schoolyard came forward and convinced the principal that he had made the wrong decision. So he summoned the four honor guard students to his office, one at a time, to tell them that they were exonerated.

The relater came in first and, upon hearing the new decision, gently proclaimed: "It was an honest mistake, Mr. Principal. I won't hold it against you."

Next in was the thinker, who slowly pondered this new decision and then reasoned out loud: "I can see how you might have been misled. I suggest you mount a TV camera at the entrance from now on."

The socializer bounded in next, breathed an enormous sigh of relief upon hearing the new decision, fell to his knees, and shouted: "I'm saved. Let's party."

Last in came the director, who strode forcefully up to the principal's desk, listened to the new decision, looked the principal in the eye, and announced: "Mister, I told you all along I was innocent. I'm going to sue you and this school for all you're worth."

in particular, anxiety. Anxiety in conjunction with test-taking or *test anxiety* was first identified by Sarason and Mandler (1952). Mandler and Sarason (1952) proposed that test anxiety was composed of two drives: (1) *task-directed drives* that stimulate the person to reduce the drive by completing the task and (2) *anxiety drives* that interfere with task completion by producing feelings of inadequacy and helplessness. It is the anxiety drives that cause people to carry out task-irrelevant behaviors and hence impair performance. So, while task-directed drives may be thought of as *facilitating* performance, anxiety drives would be considered as *debilitating* performance.

Liebert and Morris (1967) separated debilitating anxiety drives into two components: (1) *worry* or the "cognitive expression of concern about one's own performance" (p. 975) and (2) *emotionality* or the body's reaction to the situation, such as perspiration and an accelerated heartbeat.

Spielberger (1972) distinguished between two aspects of anxiety: (1) *state* — the anxiety one feels in a specific anxiety-provoking situation and (2) *trait* — one's tendency to be anxiety-prone in a wide range of situations. An important examination, for example, will induce most students to experience the *state* of anxiety. At the same time, some students feel anxious in any school situation because they possess the *trait* of anxiety. Trait anxiety, therefore, represents an individual difference much like intelligence or cognitive or interpersonal style because it is a continuing and enduring characteristic of individuals.

What is the effect on a student of being typically high in anxiety as opposed to typically low? Based on Hembree's (1988) review of 562 studies, it is known that anxiety tends to interfere with or have a debilitating effect on school performance, particularly for students of average ability. The debilitating effect alters performance on tests seen as difficult but not on tests seen as easy, and teachers can mitigate it by giving characteristically high-anxiety students (1) low-stress instructions (such as telling them the test is just for practice and won't count toward their grade, or that it can be retaken, if necessary, or disregarded if their score is too low), (2) memory support (such as letting them use a "cheat" sheet or a book for reference), or (3) performance incentives (such as rewarding them for doing well). Students who are typically low in anxiety do better when teachers give them ego-involving instructions, such as telling them that the test results will have an important effect on their grade.

What are the implications of individual differences in students' anxiety levels for teachers? This question can be answered in terms of the match–mismatch model discussed previously. If a teacher stresses the importance of a test, that stress (a) matches the needs of low-anxiety students who will then be motivated to do well but (b) mismatches the needs of high-anxiety students whose resulting stress and consequent elevated anxiety will debilitate their performance. If a teacher minimizes the importance of a test, then the needs of high-anxiety students will be matched (they will feel less stressed) but the needs of low-anxiety students will be mismatched (they will feel less motivated).

The best approach to this problem would be to help high-anxiety students reduce their characteristic anxiety level. There are many treatment programs that seem capable of doing this effectively (Hembree, 1988). Since being anxious in school is something that students learn (it is not present until after the third grade), treatments to reduce it focus on unlearning and relearning. These treatments, however, are out of the classroom teacher's range since they require intensive counseling. A second possibility would be to give separate test instructions to high-anxiety and low-anxiety students, but this requires

Figure 13.4 🍎 The Mood Thermometers:
Measuring Tension (or Anxiety), Confusion, Anger,
Fatigue, and Depression

From Tuckman, 1988. (Note: Some thermometers are inverted and out of line on the page to keep students from simply marking them all at the same level.)

HOW I FEEL RIGHT NOW

There are five thermometers to measure your feelings.
Mark a line on each one to show the "high" or "low" you feel.
Each one measures a different feeling. Don't just mark them
all the same. For two of them you have to turn the paper over.
Give your real, honest feeling. Don't just make something up.

knowing who they are, being able to separate them, and instructing each group independent of the other. This is impractical.

A good policy to follow is to try to provoke as little anxiety as possible among students (Tobias, 1979), assuming (1) that tests are so inherently anxiety-provoking that the low-anxiety students will be automatically motivated and the high-anxiety students equally automatically overstressed, and (2) that means other than provoking anxiety can be used to motivate low-anxiety students. If teachers were to make a conscious effort to reduce the threatening nature of many school situations, particularly testing, high-anxiety students would suffer many fewer debilitating effects. The test performance of high-anxiety students would become a much better reflection of what they have learned rather than merely showing the degree to which they are experiencing test anxiety.

What about other negative moods, such as depression or anger? Researchers know little about how students develop these mood traits or what effect they have on academic performance, either as mood traits or mood states, other than to recognize that they can influence students' reactions to instructional materials and their recall of information contained in these materials (Hettena & Ballif, 1981).

Box 13.8

🍎

Eagles and Ducks

Dr. Wayne Dyer divides the world into two performance or motivational types: eagles and ducks. How can you tell them apart, other than by the fact that eagles "soar" and ducks "quack"? Eagles choose success; they find ways to get things done. They go the extra distance to help people and win them over. They believe in themselves. Ducks maintain the status quo; they rigidly enforce the rules; they protest about being overworked. Ducks are the bureaucrats, the people behind the desks and counters who tell those waiting in line to see them what they can and can't do. Eagles help people do what they want to do if they possibly can. When you're trying to get out into a line of traffic, ducks frown at you and don't let you in. Eagles stop and wave for you to get in front of them. In the supermarket, baggers who are ducks can never keep up with the check-out person and always manage to put the bread underneath something heavy so that it gets squished. Baggers who are eagles are ready when you are with a smile and a friendly word, and they take your groceries out to your car.

Teachers who are eagles try to help students solve their problems, even if it means extending themselves or putting themselves out. Teachers who are ducks tell a student with a problem, "If I do it for you, I'll have to do it for every student," as a reason for ignoring a special request. Such teachers need to be reminded that "every student" isn't asking them for special help, and doesn't either need it or merit it.

Think of the last time you were an eagle or a duck or when you last encountered one. When did someone last ask you for a favor or ask you to go out of your way for them (perhaps to drop something off or help them with something)? Were you a duck or an eagle? Did you make up an excuse to avoid doing it or did you go out of your way to help them out? Did you "quack" or did you "soar"? Next time, try being an eagle instead of a duck and see what happens.

It may be helpful for teachers to be aware of the mood states of their students in response to particular classroom activities. Also, knowing which students are chronically anxious (or tense), depressed, or angry may help teachers know which students to give special attention to or refer for special counseling. A simple instrument for measuring moods, including anxiety (or tension), is shown in Figure 13.4.

Another example of individual differences, this in terms of differences in what might be called motivational style, is shown in Box 13.8.

Summary of Main Points

1. Albert Binet conceived of intelligence as a *general mental ability*, made up of a single, underlying process or general factor.

2. Intelligence can also be defined as a *group of traits* such as number, verbal, space, word fluency, reasoning, and rote memory, or as a *group of abilities* such as associative and abstract or linguistic, musical, logical–mathematical, spatial, bodily kinesthetic, intrapersonal, and interpersonal.

3. Intelligence can be defined as a *process* such as adaptation, or the ability to learn, or the ability to process information (to control, solve problems, and acquire information).

4. Researchers originally reported intelligence as the *intelligence quotient* or IQ by (a) determining the *mental age* of the person being tested based on the average age of students having the same raw score, (b) dividing this result by the test-taker's *chronological age*, and (c) multiplying this answer by 100. (This way the average IQ came out to be 100.) Intelligence is now computed directly as *deviation IQ*.

5. Intelligence is a joint function of a person's *heredity* and his or her *environment*. Studies with identical twins reared apart show that heredity is a highly consequential factor. However, the impact of school experiences should not be discounted.

6. In school, the emphasis is on the effect of the specific application of mental ability on what is learned — or *achievement* in reading, language arts, mathematics, social studies, science, and study skills.

7. Intelligence has been used to group students for instruction; classes homogeneous on intelligence represent what is called *ability grouping*. Research findings show that ability grouping does not have a very great influence on how much students learn unless instruction is specifically designed and fitted to each ability group level. The use of within-class grouping has had better results than between-class grouping.

8. *Social class* or socioeconomic status (SES) is a function of parents' education level, occupational status, and income level. This variable is wholly outside of a child's control. High SES parents tend to be more involved in the education of their children both at home and in school. But many children grow up under conditions of poverty. Early childhood enrichment programs can help these children overcome early deficits.

9. How a person thinks or learns represents his or her *cognitive style*. *Structure-seekers* desire highly organized and structured learning environments with substantial external control, while *independence-seekers* prefer to provide their own structure and control. The first group has need for conformity and explicit directions; the second group needs independence and opportunity.

10. To facilitate each group's learning, the type of instruction should be *matched* to the learning style, as opposed to *mismatched*, so that structure- or conformity-seekers are taught by formal, teacher-controlled methods and independence-seekers are taught by informal, student-controlled methods.

11. To accomplish matching, teachers must have instructional alternatives available and students must be able to choose between them. Research has shown that for learning, matching (or aptitude–treatment interaction) is more effective than mismatching.

12. *Creativity*, the ability to generate multiple problem-solutions, is another individual difference measure. It has been related to *brain hemisphere predominance*, with *right*-brained individuals tending to be more creative and *left*-brained individuals tending to be more analytic and verbal. Experiential and artistic experiences are recommended to strengthen right-brain tendencies.

13. People characteristically relate to other people according to their *interpersonal* (or relationship) *style*. By combining judgments about whether a person is (a) self-contained or open and (b) direct or indirect, teachers can define four styles: (1) the self-contained but direct *director*, (2) the self-contained and indirect *thinker*, (3) the open and direct *socializer*, and (4) the open but indirect *relater*.

14. The director tends to be bossy; the thinker, deliberative; the socializer, persuasive; and the relater, sensitive in relating to other people. Teachers must learn how to deal with their own style plus each of the other styles as they appear in their students.

15. *Mood* represents the "feeling" side of people, a common negative aspect being *anxiety*. For many students, anxiety is provoked by tests (called *test anxiety*). Depending on the individual student, test anxiety is composed of *task-directed drives*, which facilitate task completion, or *anxiety drives*, which debilitate or interfere with task completion.

16. Anxiety drives have a cognitive or thinking component called *worry* and a feeling component called *emotionality*, which provokes bodily reactions. Anxiety can be both a *state*—a reaction to a provocative situation—and a *trait*—a chronic, typical characteristic of a person.

17. Teachers can help high-anxiety students by giving them (a) *low-stress instructions*, (b) *memory assistance*, and (c) *incentives*. While low-anxiety students are motivated by high stress or ego-involving instructions, this level of personal involvement is too anxiety-provoking for students already high in test anxiety.

18. Students should be helped to overcome their test anxiety, and, whenever possible, test instructions and procedures should be designed to minimize the creation of additional anxiety.

Suggested Resources

Anastasi, A. (1982). *Psychological testing* (5th ed.). New York: Macmillan.

Cronbach, L. J., & Snow, R. L. (1977). *Aptitudes and instructional methods*. New York: Irvington.

Sternberg, R. J. (1985). *Beyond IQ: A triarchic theory of human intelligence*. New York: Cambridge University Press.

Chapter
14

Constructing a Test

Objectives

1. Describe the procedures involved in making a content outline, preparing objectives, and writing test-item specifications.
2. Identify the relationship between a content outline, objectives, test-item specifications, and test items.
3. Identify advantages and disadvantages of and techniques for writing completion items to measure knowledge.
4. Identify advantages and disadvantages of and techniques for writing multiple-choice items to measure knowledge.
5. Identify advantages and disadvantages of and techniques for writing true–false, other two-choice, and matching items to measure knowledge.
6. Describe translation, interpretation, and extrapolation as components of comprehension and explain the use of multiple-choice items to measure each.
7. Describe application, analysis, synthesis, and evaluation as higher cognitive processes.
8. Identify techniques for writing essay items to measure application, analysis, synthesis, and evaluation.
9. Identify the characteristics of a performance test and the steps involved in its construction.

Making a Content Outline

Test construction begins with course planning. For most teachers this means making a content outline of the unit to be taught. *A content outline is a list of the concepts, ideas, and skills to be covered in the instructional unit that the test will measure.* A content outline is normally developed as a prerequisite to building a lesson plan. The existence of one facilitates building a test because it also serves as a plan for what the test should measure.

Thus, the teacher's first decision is determining the segment of instruction—a lesson, a unit, a group of units—to be covered by the test. The second decision is identifying the content of the segment, because that content is what will be covered in the test. The content should be outlined as briefly as possible, because it is intended only as a guide to the material that must be covered on the test.

Two sample content outlines, one for a group of units in reading and one for a group of units in mathematics, are shown in Table 14.1.

Preparing Objectives

The preparation of objectives has already been described, in Chapter 5, in conjunction with the design of instruction. Of course, objectives are not limited to the design of instruction; they are also used in the construction of test items. They provide specific information about how a concept, an idea, or a skill that has been taught can be measured. They also help the teacher in selecting test-item type, constructing items, and scoring. A brief review of what objectives are and how they are written is provided below.

Table 14.1 🍎 Sample Content Outlines

Reading Content Outline	Mathematics Content Outline
final consonant digraphs	place value (1's, 10's, 100's)
initial consonant blends	addition without carrying
final consonant blends	associative principle
vowels modified by *r* in words	subtraction without borrowing
vowel diphthongs in words	distributive principle
singular and possessive nouns	common fractions
adjective endings	improper fractions
irregular verbs and verb endings, present tense	place value (1,000's, 10,000's)
compound words	decimal fraction values
contractions	decimals
synonyms and antonyms	decimals to fractions
personal pronouns	fractions to decimals
context and configuration clues	adding with regrouping
sequences of details	multiplication facts
main ideas	multiplication of two-digit numbers

What Is an Objective?   An objective is an *intended outcome* or *learner capability* resulting from instruction, stated in an *observable* and *measurable* way. The measurability of an objective is what makes it a useful guide for test construction.

The second step in test construction (after a content outline is prepared) is to precede each entry in the content outline with the appropriate *action verb*, to produce a list of *shorthand objectives* describing intended learner behaviors. Doing this enables the teacher to specify in measurable or observable form the concepts, ideas, and skills covered in the lesson or unit. Here are some examples of abbreviated objectives made from the entries in the content outlines shown in Table 14.1.

- Recognizing the sound of final consonant blends
- Identifying vowel diphthongs in words
- Classifying adjective endings
- Stating main idea
- Identifying common fractions
- Converting decimals to fractions
- Stating multiplication facts

Starting with a content outline makes it easy to prepare a list of shorthand objectives by attaching the appropriate action verb to each entry in the outline. But a decision must be made about which action verb to use. The verb chosen should be one that describes the exact behavior the students will be expected to perform. Will the students point to the correct answer? Then the verb should be *identify*. Will they put things in categories? If so, they will be classifying. The verb must describe the action the student is taking in using the concept, idea or skill listed in the content outline. (Refer to Section 5.1 and Table 5.1 for examples and definitions of action verbs.)

Formal objectives also contain (1) a statement of the *conditions* (or givens) necessary for performing the intended behavior and (2) a statement of the *criteria* for evaluating the correctness or acceptability of the intended behavior. These two components of an objective are combined with the action statement in the process of test construction. This is accomplished through the development of test item specifications as a prerequisite to the construction of a test.

Writing Test Item Specifications

Test-item specifications describe the *action* or behavior a student is expected to be able to carry out, the *conditions* under which that behavior is to be carried out, and the *criteria* for determining whether or not the behavior has been carried out correctly or acceptably (Tuckman, 1988a). Let's say a teacher wants students to measure the length of something. She must give them or tell them precisely what she wants them to measure. In addition, she must give them something to measure with and specify the unit of measurement. Can they use a ruler? Should they measure in inches or centimeters? These issues must all be determined in the test-item specifications.

Hively (1973) has referred to the conditions of measurement as the *content limits* that define the prospective item's *domain*. For any given objective, there are potentially many test items that could be written, and these items will range in difficulty. A simple objective like adding numbers covers a very wide domain of possible items depending on how many numbers are added, how large the numbers are, how much carrying is required, whether or not the numbers are whole as opposed to decimals or mixed numbers, and whether the numbers are all positive or some positive and some negative. The conditions or content limits define the acceptable range for the particular students to be tested. In the early elementary grades, the content limits might include only two whole, positive numbers with no more than two digits each and carrying only on the last digit. Following this restriction would still result in a large number of test-item possibilities, but all would be in the domain the students are expected to deal with.

There is also the issue of scoring criteria. For objectively scored items (those for which there is only one right answer), correctness is predetermined and need not be specified. However, it might be useful to specify the number of times or percentage of times the student will be expected to demonstrate the capability of producing the correct answer (for example, three out of four or nine out of ten).

On items that require that the correctness of the student's answer be judged (for example, essay questions), it is necessary to provide some indication of the basis upon which that judgment is to be made, such as a listing of several issues or topics. Item-scoring will be described more fully at the end of the next chapter.

The third step in the construction of a test is to expand the objectives into the kinds of test-item specifications shown in Table 14.2. These specifications describe the conditions for performing the action (or what the student will be given), the action or performance itself, and the criteria for evaluating the correctness of the action. Test-item specifications are elaborations of objectives that help teachers decide exactly how to write test items that will measure the objectives.

What Kinds of Items and How Many?   Before actually writing test items, it is necessary to decide what kind or kinds of items to write and how many of each to include. The question of the number of items to write will be considered first.

There is no automatic way to decide how many items a test should contain. The number will depend on the number and type of objectives to be measured, the type of items being used, the amount of time available for testing, and the age of the students. While there should be at least two items per objective, the more items there are to measure an objective the greater the accuracy. (Accuracy or reliability will be described in the next chapter.) Therefore, teachers should try to write enough items to fill the time allotted for testing and have as many items as possible per objective.

All objectives, however, are not necessarily equal in importance. More instructional time is spent on more important objectives. Therefore, the more important objectives should have more items on the test to measure them than the less important objectives. The importance of each objective should be weighed against the importance of other objectives, and items for each objective should be allocated in reference to this weighting.

Selection of types of items is perhaps easier because it is based on the action verb used in each objective. Verbs such as *name, list*, and *state* require that a person provide or generate a short answer, as in a completion item, while verbs such as *identify, distinguish*, and *recognize* require that a person choose a correct answer from among choices, as in item types such as multiple-choice and matching. The verb *classify* requires putting things into categories, which generally means the two-choice item format. Those types of verbs would exhaust the short-answer item formats since short-answer items measure whether someone can point to the right answer or make up a very short one.

Longer answers that are descriptive, analytic, or interpretive require essay tests for their measurement. While identification choices (as in a multiple-choice item) are made up by the test-builder, and the test-taker is asked to select a particular one, in an essay item the test-builder indicates what is to be described and the test-taker makes up the description.

Some verbs, such as *demonstrate* and *construct*, call for an actual performance. Many objectives in mathematics, science, or the arts, for example, call for students to

Table 14.2 ✎ Some Sample Test-Item Specifications

A. **Objective:** *Given a sequence of fractional expressions, the student will demonstrate a procedure for determining their correct sum.*

Conditions	Action	Criteria
Four fractional expressions (fractions and mixed numbers) with denominators between 2 and 8 (except for 7). At least three different denominators.	Find the sum. (Also, show your work.)	a. Conversion of fractions to least common denominator should be shown. b. Answers should be reduced and converted to mixed numbers. c. Three out of four correct.

B. **Objective:** *Given a paragraph without capitalization, the student will demonstrate proper placement of all capital letters.*

Conditions	Action	Criteria
Paragraph with four sentences, each of which contains proper nouns and the word "I."	Mark a circle around all the letters that need to be capitalized.	a. Circles first letter of each sentence. b. Circles first letter of each proper noun. c. Circles the word "I."

C. **Objective:** *Given instructions to do so, the student will describe Skinner's theory of learning.*

Conditions	Action	Criteria
Instructions: In no more than a page, describe Skinner's theory of learning.	Write an essay on the topic.	Answer includes mention and accurate description of reinforcement, contingency management, and extinction and clearly differentiates it from Pavlovian conditioning.

Table 14.3 🍎 Item Types to Test Various Actions

Action	Item Type
Name	Completion
State	
List	
Identify	Multiple-choice, Matching
Distinguish	
Recognize	
Classify	Two-choice
Describe	Essay
Analyze	
Interpret	
Demonstrate	Performance
Construct	

demonstrate a procedure. Objectives of this type would call for a test item that requires students to carry out a computational or physical performance.

Thus, test objectives contain the information needed to decide which kinds of items to use. (A summary of action verbs and the kinds of items to measure them appears in Table 14.3.) If the item type chosen reflects the action verb in the objective but not the type of performance the teacher desires, then the objective should be rewritten to contain the action verb that would measure the desired performance. Both the test objectives and the items to measure them must correspond very closely in action, conditions, and scoring criteria.

The Taxonomy.   In Chapter 5 the taxonomy of the cognitive domain (pages 94–96) (Bloom's taxonomy; see Figure 5.2) was introduced. The taxonomy includes six major categories — (1) knowledge, (2) comprehension, (3) application, (4) analysis, (5) synthesis, and (6) evaluation — all of which are useful for planning, classifying, and sequencing both instructional objectives and test items.

The remainder of this chapter will describe the construction of test items to measure objectives that are classified into each of the six categories of the taxonomy. For the first two categories, knowledge and comprehension, short-answer items will be described (as the type most commonly used); for the remaining four categories essay and performance items will be described (as the typical form of measurement). In this way, testing for the entire cognitive domain will be covered.

Writing Short-Answer Items to Measure Knowledge

There are basically two types of short-answer test items to measure knowledge: (1) those for which the test-taker must *generate* an answer (completion type) and (2) those for which the test-taker must *choose* an answer (choice type). The bases for constructing each of these two types of items will be discussed in turn. This section also will focus on the measurement of *knowledge* or what a test-taker knows; the measurement of *comprehension* or what a test-taker understands will be the focus of the next section. Although a number of different types of short-answer items for measuring knowledge will be described, the two that are recommended as most practical in terms of writing and scoring are the completion item and the multiple-choice item.

Completion-Type Items

Completion items are single-sentence questions for which a test-taker must produce a free-choice short answer (usually a word or a phrase). Sometimes a word or phrase is left out of a sentence and the test-taker must supply it. Answer choices are *never* given in this type of item. Answers must always be generated by the test-taker based on his or her recall. In other words, the test-taker must remember the correct answer in order to state it.

Below are some examples of completion items.

- The nineteenth president of the United States was _____.
- The gland of the body that secretes the hormone epinephrine is _____.
- The poem "Leaves of Grass" was written by _____.
- Two fractions cannot be added unless they have the same _____.
- The plural form of the noun *moose* is _____.
- The form of conditioning described by Skinner is called _____ conditioning.

(The answers to these questions appear in footnote 1, page 372.)

Advantages and Disadvantages.   Completion items are generally easy to construct but occasionally hard to score. They work best when they are written to measure recall of specific, discrete facts one or two words long. If a teacher tries to make a completion item too tricky or too clever, it will become ambiguous and produce many possible answers, more than one of which may be correct. This will make scoring difficult and highly subjective. Restricting this item type to the measurement of facts can help the test-builder avoid this problem.

Writing the Item.   Listed below are the rules to follow in writing completion-type items.

1. Keep the item clear, unambiguous, and narrow in scope so that there will be only one correct answer.
2. Do not provide so much information in the item that the correct answer becomes obvious.
3. Make sure the correct answer is short and does not include extraneous words.
4. Do not let the grammar of the sentence serve as a clue to the correct answer.
5. Make sure that the missing part is exactly what the test-taker should be expected to remember.
6. Place the blank at or near the end of the statement.

Consider the following alternative items that, presumably, all measure the same point:

- The assumption that organisms will behave to gain _____ is the basis of the behavioristic theory of _____.
- The assumption that organisms will behave to gain reinforcement is the basis of the behavioristic theory of _____.
- The behavioristic theory of Skinner is based on the assumption that organisms will behave to gain _____.
- The _____ theory of Skinner is based on the assumption that organisms will behave to gain reinforcement.

In this example, which piece of information should the test-taker be able to remember? Should the test-taker be able to name Skinner as the theorist of reinforcement, or reinforcement as the theory of Skinner, or behaviorism as the kind of theory that Skinner's reinforcement theory is? Asking the test-taker to name more than one fact in the same item invites ambiguity. In this case Pavlov or Thorndike might be paired with their appropriate theory (which would not be "correct" on the test if the purpose of the item was to measure knowledge of Skinner). The best version of the item is the third, in which the essential feature to be remembered is the principle of *reinforcement*, on which Skinner's behaviorism is based.

A good way to construct a completion item is to write an entire statement first, without leaving anything out. Then, refer to the objective that the item is intended to measure and block out the one word or phrase that represents the essence of what the test-taker will be expected to recall. This procedure should produce a clear, meaningful, and easily scored item, and it can also be applied to writing completion items that measure information in textbooks.

Look at the first sentence in the above paragraph. It could be used directly to produce the following completion item:

- Writing an entire statement without leaving anything out at first is a good way to write a (an) _____ item.

(The word *an* has been added to keep the grammar of the sentence from providing a clue to the answer.) The item measures whether a test-taker can name the kind of item represented by a statement from which something has been left out.

Multiple-Choice-Type Items

The most widely used choice-type item is the multiple-choice item. It is like a completion item except that, instead of a blank, it has a set of, usually, four or five potential answer choices. Instead of having to recall or remember the right answer, in a multiple-choice item the test-taker must identify or recognize the right answer by distinguishing it from the wrong answers or *distractors*. The distinction between the right answer and the

---

[1]Answers: Rutherford B. Hayes, adrenal, Walt Whitman, denominator, moose, operant.

distractors should be based on the objective. If the objective, for example, were to identify the basic principle of Skinner's theory, namely, reinforcement, then a possible item might be

- According to Skinner, learning occurs because of the pairing of a response and
  a. a stimulus.
  b. a drive.
  c. a reinforcer.
  d. another response.

Since many of the end-of-chapter tests in textbooks and many teachers' tests contain multiple-choice questions, there is no shortage of examples of this type of item. In addition, some examples of multiple-choice items are given in Box 14.1.

Box 14.1

Sample Multiple-Choice Items to Measure Knowledge*

1. Which of the following is part of an objective?
   a. knowledge to be understood
   b. appreciation to be felt
   c. action or behavior to be performed
   d. awareness or sensitivity to be developed

2. Which of the following is *not* a criterion of a good objective?
   a. measurable
   b. reliable
   c. specific
   d. challenging
   e. none of the above

3. For which one of the following areas is it possible to prepare test items with answers that are completely right or wrong?
   a. values
   b. higher cognitive processes
   c. knowledge acquisition and comprehension
   d. creative processes

4. Piaget has labeled the process by which the young infant makes interesting spectacles last as
   a. accommodation.
   b. reproductive assimilation.
   c. recognitory assimilation.
   d. generalizing assimilation.

---

*Answers to Box 14.1 are in footnote 2, page 374.

Advantages and Disadvantages.   The major advantages of a multiple-choice item are the ease of scoring it, the ease of analyzing its results (discussed in the next chapter), and its potential use for measuring comprehension (described later in this chapter). A final advantage is its capability for testing whether students can distinguish between the correct answer and common misconceptions or erroneous lines of thought. By constructing particular answer choices, the test-builder can set up the requirement to distinguish between the right answer and frequent wrong answers.

Multiple-choice items also have their disadvantages. These include the following:

1. They are difficult to write since they require not only the right answer but three or four plausible distractors.
2. If the distractors are not truly wrong, there will be more than one right answer.
3. If the distractors are obviously wrong, everyone will be able to figure out the right answer (by process of elimination).
4. Even if the item is good, some people will get the right answer by guessing.

Overcoming these disadvantages requires not only developing some skill at writing multiple-choice items, but also testing out the items and rewriting them, if necessary, on the basis of the results. This latter aspect will be dealt with in the next chapter. Here the topic will be item-writing rules.

Writing the Item.   A useful technique for writing a multiple-choice item is to start out by writing a statement of fact or knowledge based on an objective (just as was suggested for writing a completion item). If, for example, the objective says,

GIVEN THREE FRACTIONS, IDENTIFY THEIR LEAST COMMON DENOMINATOR

then a possible statement of knowledge would be

THE LEAST COMMON DENOMINATOR OF ½, ¼, AND ⅙ IS 12.

The next step would be to convert this statement of knowledge into a multiple-choice test item. The item or *stem* would be

THE LEAST COMMON DENOMINATOR OF ½, ¼, AND ⅙ IS

and the right answer choice is 12. All that remains is to write three or four distractors. The third rule for how not to write multiple-choice items in Table 14.4 says: "Don't choose distractors that are unrelated to the kinds of mistakes test-takers are likely to make," which means the test-builder should determine the kinds of mistakes students are likely to make and use them as a basis for constructing distractors. In calculating the least common denominator, one kind of mistake students might make is to calculate a common denominator other than the least or lowest one. To test this, 24 would be a good distractor. Another common mistake might be to compute a denominator common to two of the fractions but not to the third, so 8 would be a good distractor. A third common mistake might be to assume that the largest denominator of the three given fractions will work as a common denominator, so that 6 might be a good distractor.

---

[2]Answers to Box 14.1: 1-c, 2-e, 3-c, 4-b.

Try another example. If the objective were

IDENTIFY THE FUNCTIONS OF DIFFERENT COURTS IN THE AMERICAN SYSTEM OF JUSTICE

one statement of fact would be

AN APPELLATE COURT REVIEWS THE DECISIONS OF OTHER COURTS.

The item stem could then be

WHEN A COURT IS CALLED AN APPELLATE COURT, THAT MEANS THAT IT

and the correct answer is

REVIEWS THE DECISIONS OF OTHER COURTS.

Table 14.4 🍎 The Don'ts and Do's of Writing Multiple-Choice Items

Don'ts	Do's
1. Don't write distractors that are totally implausible or obviously wrong.	Write distractors that are plausible.
2. Don't write distractors that are actually correct.	Write distractors that are wrong.
3. Don't write distractors that are unrelated to the kinds of mistakes test-takers are likely to make.	Write distractors that represent likely mistakes.
4. Don't write distractors that are different from the correct answer in length or grammar.	Make all answer choices comparable in appearance and structure.
5. Don't write distractors that overlap one another or that overlap the correct answer.	Make all answer choices independent.
6. Don't use words that test-takers won't understand.	Use common words.
7. Don't use statements that have more than one meaning.	Use statements with only one meaning.
8. Don't use absolute terms such as *always, never,* and *all.*	Make items and answer choices of indeterminate degree.
9. Don't write long answer choices.	Write short answer choices.
10. Don't build clues into the item statement or answer choices.	Use words in answer choices that are as different as possible from words used in the item statement.
11. Don't test more than one point at a time.	Test only one point at a time.
12. Don't let one item give a clue to the answer to another.	Make items independent and nonoverlapping.
13. Don't always assign the correct choice to the same letter.	Randomize the letter of the correct choice from item to item.

Think of what misconceptions students might have so that they can be used to write the distractors. Students might confuse appellate courts with lower courts, which MUST HAVE A JURY and CAN CONDUCT THE ORIGINAL TRIAL, or they might confuse them with supreme courts, which CAN DECLARE LAWS UNCONSTITUTIONAL. Thus, there are three possible distractors, all of which resemble the correct answer in length and grammar and are not only plausible but are likely mistakes. Yet all three choices are clearly wrong.

Another point about answer choices for this item must be made. It would have been equally correct to say that appellate courts HEAR APPEALS OF THE DECISIONS OF OTHER COURTS, but the word *appeals* is a clue for the "appellate" function (one word is derived from the other). The word *appeals*, therefore, is best avoided to eliminate the possibility of an extra clue.

As a final example, consider the objective below:

IDENTIFY THE FORM OF THE VERB "TO BE" THAT CORRECTLY FITS THE PRONOUN AND TENSE OF THE SENTENCE.

One statement of fact would be

FOR THE PAST TENSE, USE "WAS" OR "HAVE BEEN" WITH "I."

Now the item can be

WHICH SENTENCE IS CORRECT?

A right answer choice will be I WAS LATE. I HAVE BEEN LATE cannot be used as a distractor because it is also correct grammar. But there are many common mistakes in forming the past tense of the verb "to be" that will form good distractors. For example:

I BEEN LATE.
I BE LATE.
I WERE LATE.
I IS LATE.

Being around children and knowing the speaking mistakes they make will help teachers construct distractors for this kind of grammar item.

When writing multiple-choice items, remember to

1. start with the objective,
2. write statements of fact that fit the objective,
3. write distractors that reflect common mistakes,
4. avoid the 13 "don'ts" listed in Table 14.4.

Other Choice-Type Items

There are three other types of choice items: *true–false* items, *other two-choice* or *classi-fication* items, and *matching* items. The construction of each will be described briefly.

True–False Items.   These are statements that the test-taker must judge to be either true or false. Here are some examples.

- The capitol of Florida is Orlando.   TRUE   FALSE
- The plural of *ox* is *oxes*.   TRUE   FALSE
- The branch of government charged with making
  the laws is the executive.   TRUE   FALSE
- Colorado produces more copper ore than any
  other state.   TRUE   FALSE
- ACTH is a hormone secreted by the pineal gland.   TRUE   FALSE

All of the above items are false, but on an actual test it would be preferable to mix true items and false items together. As in writing the other types of short-answer items, begin with an objective, derive from it statements of fact, and then, in the case of true–false items, change some of the statements of fact to make them false.

OBJECTIVE:	IDENTIFY THE CHARACTERISTICS OF SUBATOMIC PARTICLES.
STATEMENT OF FACT:	"ELECTRONS HAVE A NEGATIVE UNIT CHARGE AND NEGLIGIBLE MASS."
TRUE ITEM:	USE THE STATEMENT OF FACT.
FALSE ITEM:	"ELECTRONS HAVE A NEUTRAL CHARGE AND A MASS OF ONE."

In the case of the false item, the definition of a different subatomic particle, a neutron, has been substituted for the correct definition.

True–false items are usually easy to write, at least for the measurement of recognition of facts, a use for which they are best suited. The difficulty in writing these items lies in generating plausible false statements, particularly in deciding which aspect of the fact to make false. In deciding this, just as in choosing distractors for multiple-choice items, consider the misconceptions and likely mistakes of students and embody them in the false statement. Think of a false item as a distractor.

If the statement of fact, for example, were

FRANKLIN DELANO ROOSEVELT, IN HIS FIRST INAUGURAL SPEECH, SAID: "WE HAVE NOTHING TO FEAR BUT FEAR ITSELF."

decide what the important mistake would be. Would it be (1) attributing the quote to someone else, (2) attributing someone else's quote ("blood, sweat, and tears," for example) to FDR, or (3) realizing that FDR said it but thinking he said it in his second, third, or fourth inaugural speech rather than his first? Once the important mistake has been decided upon, a false statement can be written, such as

WINSTON CHURCHILL, AT THE START OF WORLD WAR II, SAID: "WE HAVE NOTHING TO FEAR BUT FEAR ITSELF."

The biggest problem with true–false items, apart from their possible ambiguity, is that since there are only two answer choices the probability of guessing the correct answer is 50%. This probability is twice as large as for a multiple-choice item with four answer choices; moreover, a multiple-choice item tests three or four misconceptions rather than one. But multiple-choice also requires the test-builder to write three or four distractors for each item, compared to only one for a true–false item.

Other Two-Choice Items.   These items are like multiple-choice items in a series but they have only two choices: a correct one and a distractor. However, in any item there may be many correct answers and many distractors. Some examples:

- Use *a* or *an* before each word: _____ cat, _____ elf, _____ arm
- Circle all the *even* numbers: 12 6 19 11 1 10 7 21 34
- Check all the cities below that are state capitols.

Pierre	St. Louis
San Francisco	Santa Fe
Milwaukee	Olympia

- Circle all the words below that are used in Skinner's theory of learning.

emotion	cognition	discrimination
reinforcement	efficacy	assimilation
extinction	contingency	generalization

This type of item, described as being in a classification format, is useful for measuring whether a student can distinguish items that fit a category (or exemplars) from items that do not fit a category (or nonexemplars). The above illustrations have (1) nouns that begin with vowels versus those that begin with consonants, (2) even numbers versus odd numbers, (3) capitols versus big cities, and (4) Skinnerian terms versus non-Skinnerian terms. Whenever the task is to determine whether students can distinguish between exemplars and nonexemplars of a given category, other two-choice items can be constructed.

Like most of the various short-answer item types, other two-choice items work best for assessing factual knowledge, but are susceptible to guessing and are often ambiguous. It is important to include in other two-choice items only terms that very clearly either fit or do not fit the classification category. In other words, (1) the classification category itself must be clear and distinct from other potentially confusable categories, and (2) the terms to be classified must be clear examples or nonexamples of that category.

As in writing the other types of short-answer items, begin with the objective, such as

GIVEN A LIST OF ORGANISMS THAT LIVE IN WATER, DISTINGUISH BE-
TWEEN MAMMALS AND NONMAMMALS (FISH, AMPHIBIANS, AND
REPTILES).

Then, produce a statement of fact, such as

SOME MAMMALS THAT LIVE IN WATER ARE WHALES, DOLPHINS, OT-
TERS, AND SEALS.

Distractors or nonmammals that live in water and that may be confused with mammals must then be identified. They may include tuna, sharks, frogs, eels, and water moccasins. From this list of mammals and nonmammals that live in water, a two-choice item can easily be written:

CIRCLE THE MAMMALS BELOW.

OTTERS	DOLPHINS	TUNA
SHARKS	EELS	FROGS
WHALES	WATER MOCCASINS	SEALS

Remember that choices for categories and for nonexemplars should be based on the distinctions made in the objectives of the lesson. If, in the above example, the objective is to teach students to distinguish between mammals and fish only, then the nonexemplars would be limited to fish.

Matching Items.   These are the most difficult short-answer items to construct. They are multiple stems with multiple choices, and each choice is a distractor for the other choices. Their biggest shortcoming, beyond their difficulty to write, is that as a test-taker gets closer to completing the item, the number of distractors is steadily reduced — which increases the success rate of guessing. It is also difficult to write an item as complex as a matching item without giving any extra clues. Here is an example of a matching item.

In items 1 through 5, match each of the following *statements* to a particular *person*.

Statement	**Persons**
1. The only president to resign.	a. Hubert Humphrey
	b. John Kennedy
2. The last Democratic president.	c. Jimmy Carter
	d. George Bush
3. This president was never elected.	e. Gerald Ford
	f. Ronald Reagan
4. He served two full terms as president.	g. Richard Nixon
	h. Herbert Hoover
5. He was never president.	

(The answers to these questions appear in footnote 3, page 380.)

As can be seen from the above example, matching items work best as measures of a test-taker's knowledge of facts. This item could be used to measure the objective

DISTINGUISH BETWEEN RECENT PRESIDENTS ON THE BASIS OF VARIOUS CHARACTERISTICS.

The characteristics described in the item are some of the ones that are appropriate for distinguishing between these presidents. (Note: To make the item more difficult, the test-builder *should give three more choices* than are necessary to match each description.)

In writing a matching item, the test-builder must ensure that each component deals with common elements of a *single* category (such as all president's characteristics). If categories are mixed, it becomes impossible to decide which choices go together. In addition, each choice must *uniquely* fit each stem, or else there will be more than one correct answer. Suppose, in the previous example, that one of the stems was "A Republican president." Since five of the choices were Republican presidents, any one of them would be a correct choice. Consequently, a student could not choose *the* correct answer, and the item-writer could not be sure that there would be enough correct choices for each stem.

It is important, therefore, that the response choices be (1) nonoverlapping, (2) uniquely fitted to one of the stems, (3) plausible distractors to one another in terms of their connection to the other stems, (4) focused on the critical characteristics set forth in the objective, and (5) greater in number than the descriptions.

Conclusions About Measuring Knowledge

Of all the short-answer item types, completion items are the easiest to write. Multiple-choice items are the easiest to score and analyze, and have the added advantage of being able to tap a number of student misconceptions and misunderstandings at the same time. It is no wonder, then, that virtually all published tests that measure knowledge utilize multiple-choice items for that purpose. Teachers are encouraged to spend the time and expend the effort constructing multiple-choice items to measure knowledge.

Writing Short-Answer Items to Measure Comprehension

For the measurement of comprehension, item use will be restricted to multiple-choice items because they afford the item-writer greater flexibility than the other short-answer types.

Differentiating Between Knowledge and Comprehension

Bloom (1956) relates the following story about the famous educational philosopher and creator of progressive education, John Dewey:

> John Dewey . . . asked a class, "What would you find if you dug a hole in the earth?" Getting no response, he repeated the question; again he obtained nothing but silence. The teacher chided Dr. Dewey, "You're asking the wrong question." Turning to the class, she asked, "What is the state of the center of the earth?" The class replied in unison, "Igneous fusion." (p. 29)

What does this story illustrate? It illustrates the distinction between rote knowledge, which is memorized ("The state of the center of the earth is igneous fusion") and comprehension, which means understanding ("If you dug a hole in the earth, eventually you would come to molten rock"). Both statements are the same, but one comes out of memory while the other reflects an understanding of what is in memory.

An item that measures knowledge, therefore, is an item that can be answered from memory, assuming that the necessary knowledge has been learned and is in long-term memory (see Chapter 6). If the necessary knowledge is not in long-term memory, the item cannot be answered. An item that measures comprehension, on the other hand, cannot necessarily be answered even if the prerequisite knowledge is present in memory. Comprehension requires more than memory. It requires thinking and understanding. If the exact answer to an item can be found in a textbook or in lecture notes, it is a knowledge item. It calls for a specific fact. If an item requires thinking to figure out the

[3]Answers: 1-g, 2-c, 3-e, 4-f, 5-a.

"But Professor Dewey, I don't understand the question." When students learn by rote or by memorization, they can only restate what they have committed to memory. To use information in a range of situations, students must comprehend it.

answer, it is a comprehension item. It calls for understanding. Some sample comprehension items are given in Box 14.2. Compare them to the sample knowledge items in Box 14.1.

Measuring Comprehension

Comprehension, according to Bloom's (1956) taxonomy, can be divided into three categories: translation, interpretation, and extrapolation. Each will be described in turn.

Translation.   Everyone is familiar with the term *translation* as it applies to the process of changing statements from one language into another, such as Russian into English or English into Spanish. But in a more general sense, translation means putting a statement into another set of terms so that someone can understand what it means. If someone told you that he had a "ubiquitous comestible" in a bag and asked you if you would eat it on a piece of bread, you might be hesitant to answer, not knowing whether the substance represented by these strange words was something you would dare put in your mouth. But if you were able to "translate" these words into the familiar ones — commonplace, edible substance (such as butter or margarine) — your understanding of what you were being asked would overcome your hesitancy to answer.

Hence, translation means

1. putting a communication into another language, into other terms, or into another form of communication;

2. transforming the abstract or technical to the concrete or everyday;

3. transforming something into a briefer form;

4. giving an illustration or example of the meaning or use of a principle or abstraction;

5. transforming words into symbols, illustrations, maps, tables, diagrams, graphs, or formulas — or vice versa.

Look at item 5 in Box 14.2. The paragraph is difficult to understand because its language and phrasing are different from those that are used today. To *understand* its

---

Box 14.2

Sample Multiple-Choice Items to Measure Comprehension*

1. The following test item, "With a set of blocks, construct a model of the street on which your school is located and then position your school on it," is a measure of which of the following objectives:
   a. Use a given material to create a representation of a specified area.
   b. Identify map symbols on an outline map.
   c. Use geographical directions to designate the route between given locations on a map.
   d. Identify objects that correspond to symbols on a map.

2. Debbie's standard score on a standardized achievement test in English was 82. Which of the statements below tells us what that score means?
   a. Debbie's score was higher than 82% of the students in the norming group at the same grade level.
   b. Although Debbie is in the seventh grade, her test score was higher than the average eighth-grader's.
   c. Debbie's score was above the norming group average for her grade by twice as much as the other scores deviated from the mean.
   d. Debbie's test score fell into a band of scores of the norming group that was represented by the score of 8.

3. Which of the following would you consider the most appropriate instructional strategy, given the class performance on the Stanford Achievement Test shown in Figure 16.4 (p. 446) of this book?
   a. Spend more time teaching math applications and less time teaching reading comprehension.
   b. Spend more time teaching social science and less time teaching math computation.
   c. Spend less time teaching language sensitivity and more time teaching conventions.
   d. Spend less time teaching phonetic analysis and more time teaching structural analysis.

meaning, a reader must *translate* it into more familiar words and phrases. Some additional examples of translation items are given in Box 14.3.

The rules for writing translation items are basically the same as those for writing any multiple-choice item (shown in Table 14.4), except that the information the item calls for must reflect one of the five aspects of translation given above (rather than reflecting knowledge of facts). In other words, the item stem must present words, numbers, or pictures, and the answer choices must present translations of these into another form or level of understanding, with one answer choice being the correct translation and the others, the distractors, being plausible mis-translations. The student's answer choice will then reveal whether he or she is able to translate what is given in the item stem into another, corresponding form and, hence, whether he or she understands the given information.

A typical translation item might involve giving an unfamiliar example of a principle or concept and then asking the student to identify, from among a set of four choices, the

4. Consider the following statement of an intended objective: The student will be able to know well the cardinal rules of grammar. Would you say that this statement includes
   a. action only
   b. action + conditions
   c. action + criterion
   d. none of the above

5. For what men say is that, if I am really just and am not also thought just, profit there is none, but the pain and loss on the other hand are unmistakable. But if, though unjust, I acquire the reputation of justice, a heavenly life is promised to me. Since then appearance tyrannizes over truth and is lord of happiness, to appearance I must devote myself. I will describe around me a picture and shadow of virtue to be the vestibule and exterior of my house; behind I will trail the subtle and crafty fox. (Machiavelli, *The Prince*)

   Which of the following best expresses the main topic of this selection?
   a. What is justice?
   b. How to attain eternal life
   c. How to be successful
   d. What is the nature of virtue?
   e. What is truth?

*Answers to Box 14.2 appear in footnote 4, page 384.

Box 14.3

Sample Items to Measure Translation*

1. A group of examiners is engaged in the production of a taxonomy of educational objectives. In ordinary English, what are these persons doing?
    a. Evaluating the progress of education
    b. Classifying teaching goals
    c. Preparing a curriculum
    d. Constructing learning exercises

2. "The idea systems of primitive groups of people are highly restricted and traditional in content and, in addition, have been transmuted into customary ways of doing things." This best illustrates
    a. the stability of the primitive social organization.
    b. how primitive people evaluate the worth of ideas.
    c. the change of ideas to action.
    d. the repetition of customary ways of doing things.
    e. the slow progress of primitive peoples.

3.

--after Darling

The above cartoon best illustrates which statement?
    a. Social problems are relative to time, place, and culture.
    b. The process of inventions is cumulative.
    c. Social problems are more prevalent in a dynamic society.
    d. There are differences in the rates of change between different phases of a culture.

*Answers to Box 14.3 appear in footnote 5, page 386.

SOURCE: Bloom, B. S. (1956). *Taxonomy of educational objectives: Cognitive domain* (pp. 99, 101). New York: David McKay.

principle or concept of which it is an example. The student must "translate" the example into the concept or principle that fits it. Answering item 1 in Box 14.2 requires translating a test item example into the objective for which it is a measure.

Interpretation.   To comprehend or understand also means to be able to interpret. Interpretation, according to Bloom (1956), means the following:

1. grasping the thought or the main idea of a work as a whole,
2. separating what is essential from what is not essential,
3. distinguishing warranted conclusions from unwarranted ones,
4. making an inference or generalization from data.

A sample item to measure interpretation is shown in Box 14.4. (Also, see Boxes 15.1 and 16.1 as examples of exercises that require interpretation, particularly making inferences and generalizations from data.)

To write interpretation items, create or find a paragraph (such as the one in item 5 in Box 14.2), a data set (such as the one in Box 14.4), or an outcome (such as the one in item 2 in Box 14.2), and ask the students to interpret it based on one of the four meanings of interpretation given above. One answer should be the correct interpretation—the correct main idea, the essential point, a warranted conclusion, or an accurate inference or generalization—while the distractors should be plausible but incorrect alternatives. The act of interpretation, therefore, is not to tell exactly what something means in other terms; that is translation. The act of interpretation is to identify meaning by drawing conclusions based on what is given. Those conclusions, though, are not predetermined and available in memory. Instead, they are thought out logically on the basis of the information that is given.

Extrapolation.   This third aspect of comprehension refers to predicting, extending the meaning, or determining the implications, consequences, or effects of something in the future. The test-builder constructs typical items by providing a data set (similar to the types used to measure interpretation) and asking the test-taker to use that data set to identify outcomes or effects in the future or under a different set of circumstances.

Look at item 3 in Box 14.2. The test-taker is given a data set, specifically a set of achievement-test scores for a class of fourth-graders (shown in Chapter 16 of this book). From this data set the test-taker must determine the best instructional strategy to use to help the class overcome deficiencies that the test-taker has located in the given test scores. So, the test-taker must

1. locate the relevant information in the data set;
2. determine, by extrapolation, the best strategy to use next;
3. identify the answer choice that expresses that strategy.

The item-writer must provide distractors that express strategies that, while still plausible, are not truly consistent with and do not truly follow from (as a natural consequence) the relevant information in the data set. By selecting the correct strategy (or next step, consequence, or implication), the test-taker shows that he or she understands the information presented in the data set.

Box 14.4

🍎

Sample Items to Measure Interpretation*

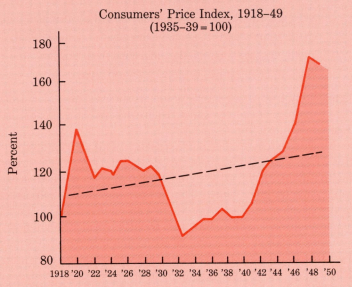

Consumers' Price Index, 1918–49
(1935–39 = 100)

Source: U.S. Dept. of Labor, Bureau of Labor Statistics.

Making your judgments only in terms of the information given in the graph, classify each of the items on the next page by writing A, B, C, D, or E next to it.

Writing Essay Items to Measure the Higher Cognitive Processes

Essay items can be used to measure the higher cognitive processes represented in the taxonomy (shown in Figure 5.2). In other words, if the purpose is to measure knowledge or comprehension, short-answer items work better, but if the purpose is to measure application, analysis, synthesis, or evaluation, essay items would be the better choice.

Application.   The general objective for an application item is this:

> Given an appropriate *problem* situation in which no mode of solution is specified, demonstrate the use of an *abstraction* by solving the problem correctly.

---

[5]Answers to Box 14.3: 1-b, 2-c, 3-d.

A. if the item is *definitely* true,
B. if the item is *probably* true,
C. if the information given is not sufficient to indicate any degree of truth or falsity in the item,
D. if the item is *probably false*,
E. if the item is *definitely false*.

1. People were better off in 1932 than in 1949.

2. Since 1918 to the present, the dollar was most valuable in 1933.

3. More prices went up than went down between 1932 and 1940.

4. Men in the age group of 30–40 made the most income gains in the past decade.

5. In 1940–46 some loss in real income was most probably incurred by people living on interest from bonds.

6. More prices went down than went up between 1926 and 1929.

7. Anyone living on a fixed income was much worse off in 1949 than in 1940.

*Answers to Box 14.4 appear in footnote 6, page 388.

Note: To determine if the test-taker is "going beyond the data" to arrive at a decision requires a count of B items incorrectly marked A; C items marked A, B, D, or E; and D items marked E. "Overcaution" requires a count of A items marked B; B and D items marked C; and E items marked D. Evaluation of "crude errors" requires a count of A and B items marked D or E and D or E items marked A or B.

SOURCE: Bloom, B. S. (1956). *Taxonomy of educational objectives: Cognitive domain* (p. 109). New York: David McKay.

The "abstraction" in the objective refers to a general idea, rule of procedure, generalized method, technical term, concept, principle, theory, or law.

Consider the following example of an essay item (taken from Tuckman, 1988a, p. 81):

- You are in charge of planning meals and ordering food at a small summer camp. There are one hundred campers—boys aged twelve to fifteen years—and a staff of fifteen adults. You must be concerned with both cost and nutritional value since these will be the criteria for judging your menus. Write out menus for five days of breakfasts, lunches, and suppers and explain why you made the choices you did.

In this item, principles of the cost and nutritional value of various foods must be applied to solve the problem of planning menus. Specifically, knowledge of the principles of the different food groups, and how foods can be combined to form balanced meals, must be applied to solve the menu-planning problem.

Before you write the item, it is useful to consider the steps, listed below, that a test-taker must go through to complete it successfully.

1. Search for familiar elements in the problem.
2. Restructure the problem in a familiar context.
3. Classify the problem as to type.
4. Select the suitable abstraction.
5. Use the abstraction to solve the problem.

To write the item, select a concrete situation that contains a problem to be solved (or think of a problem and then identify the situation in which it occurs). The problem must be one that the test-takers have not seen before in its exact form, but its solution must rely on knowledge and abstractions that the test-takers have already been taught. The concrete situation can be either an entirely new one or an old one with new elements. In the menu-planning illustration above, for example, the students should already have learned about foods and nutrition, and even about planning menus for themselves at home. Then, in the item, the situation could be changed to a camp of 115 campers.

How can you determine a concrete situation in order to write an application item? Try one of the following:

1. a fictional situation,
2. a situation that will come up later in instruction but has not been encountered yet,
3. an old situation with a new slant (like the camp illustration).

It is usually easiest to come up with a new slant for an old situation.

In addition to the *situation* and *problem*, essay items often contain specific *response instructions*, covering things like

1. minimum or maximum number of words or pages to write,
2. specific points to be covered,
3. requirements for explanations and/or details,
4. number of solutions required,
5. special criteria for evaluating performance (for example, neatness, clarity),
6. number of points the item is worth or amount of time to spend on it.

Such response instructions may be provided for any essay item to help structure the student's response.

Also, it is recommended that at the time an essay question is written, teachers compose an answer key or a model answer in order to ensure that the question is written appropriately to elicit what is deemed the correct response.

Analysis.   This involves breaking down material into its constituent parts — its (1) *elements* (such as assumptions, facts, hypotheses, beliefs, conclusions, or supportive statements); (2) *relationships* (such as cause and effect, sequence, assumptions and conclusions, or details and main idea), or (3) *organizational principles* (such as form, pattern, materials and their connection to point of view, meaning, purpose, or bias).

---

[6]Answers to Box 14.4: 1-d, 2-a, 3-a, 4-c, 5-b, 6-e, 7-a.

Consider this objective as a representation of analysis:

Given unique material, demonstrate a procedure for breaking it down into its component elements, relationships, or organizational principles.

Here are two examples of essay items to measure analysis:

- State four reasons why Hamlet did not kill King Claudius until the end of the play despite his commitment to do so at the beginning. Describe how you determined what these reasons were.
- Consider the ways Jean Piaget and B. F. Skinner might teach a child to ride a bike. In what ways might their techniques be different? In what ways the same? How can you tell?

In writing an analysis item, determine the information or experience to be analyzed, compared, or contrasted and the aspects or components of that information or experience. The information or experience is usually something that is read, observed, or listened to (for example, a story, painting, piece of music, or other kind of direct experience), and the student is asked to analyze what he or she has seen or heard or learned in terms of elements, relationships, or organizational principles. Presumably the student has already learned how to conduct an analysis and has already acquired the information or had the experience, but has never had to conduct an analysis of the specific information or experience given in the item. Carrying out that analysis demonstrates the use of a higher cognitive process.

Like application items, analysis items may include response instructions such as asking students to supply details or explanations or reasons for their answers. This enables the teacher to see and evaluate the mechanics of the analysis process used by the student. Without these response instructions, students may produce "short answers" (as they would in completion items) rather than demonstrating the process of analysis as the teacher or test-builder intends.

Synthesis.   This is the putting-together of elements to form a unique whole. The product of synthesis may be

1. a unique communication intended to inform, describe, persuade, impress, or entertain (like a story or poem);
2. a plan or proposed set of operations (like a lesson plan or problem-solving plan);
3. a set of abstract relations (like a theory of learning).

An example of a synthesis item appears below:

- Suppose you have been put in charge of developing a day-care program for your school. Plan and describe how you would go about this task and what your intended result would be. Do not omit the details.

Synthesis is a creative and inventive process. As such, it has some unique testing requirements. In testing for synthesis, try

1. to provide conditions suitable for creative work, including no time pressure, few controls, and minimal restrictions (as, for example, in a take-home, open-book, or untimed test);

2. to require more than one performance sample (because the synthesis skill may vary from problem to problem);

3. to break the typical pattern of test administration with its limits on time, place, and resources, rather than choosing not to measure creative performance and resorting instead to short-answer items;

4. to use competent judges for the evaluation of products (see Chapter 15).

Synthesis is an important cognitive skill. Despite the difficulty in measuring it, teachers are encouraged to try. But to do so they must pose problems outside the range of the familiar so that students will be required to generate novel solutions. In particular, asking students to write a creative piece, formulate a theory, design a novel piece of equipment, or propose a new procedure gives them an opportunity to synthesize. Make sure, however, that the problem is one for which students have not seen the solution before, or else they will rely on memory rather than synthesizing skill to solve it.

Evaluation.   This involves *making judgments (not opinions) about the value of ideas, works, solutions, methods, or materials for some particular purpose*. These judgments may be either *quantitative* (that is, numerical) or *qualitative* (that is, in terms of quality). In addition, the evaluative judgments are made using *criteria* and *standards* that are either determined by the students themselves or given to them. These criteria and standards are used to appraise or evaluate the extent to which the work, idea, or particular solution is *accurate*, *effective*, *economical*, or *satisfying*, using two kinds of judgment:

1. judgment in terms of *internal* evidence such as logic, exactness, consistency, documentation, and clarity;

2. judgment in terms of *external* evidence such as comparison with other works or ends to be satisfied, application of given rules or standards, and consistency with known facts.

Here are two examples of evaluation items:

- An important function of the National Labor Relations Board (NLRB) is to help settle disputes between labor and management. Describe how one such dispute between teachers and school boards was handled successfully, pointing out how the settlement illustrates a general strength of the NLRB. Your essay should be about two to three pages long.

- You have just received a third-grade reading textbook in the mail from a publisher. Describe how you would go about evaluating whether or not the textbook you have received is a good one, good enough for you to recommend to others. Give at least four different ways that you might evaluate the textbook.

In writing an evaluation essay item, choose something about which students can be expected to have extensive knowledge and understanding. Students must know the criteria used in judging the idea or object, and they must have skill in the application of these criteria. The evaluation item is intended to measure whether or not students know and can use the appropriate evaluative criteria.

To write the item, select a work or an idea to which specific internal or external (or both) evaluative criteria can be applied and then ask the students to evaluate it as a member of a given class or category, in comparison with another given work or idea, or against other predetermined criteria. Remember that the process of judging is often as important as the final judgment; include response instructions that specify that students write about the evaluative process as well as supplying their final judgment. When asked to evaluate something, students may simply say that it is "good" or "bad." Require them to explain how they arrived at their decision, what criteria they used and why, how the work or idea came out on each criterion, and how they figured out how it came out.

It is important to distinguish evaluation from a student's opinion. By explaining, defending, and supporting an evaluative position, students are able to demonstrate a higher cognitive ability rather than merely render an opinion.

Constructing a Performance Test

A performance test is one on which students actually have to construct a product or demonstrate a procedure such as writing a letter, repairing an automobile engine, bisecting an angle, doing a swan dive, making a bookcase, or drawing a flag. Performance testing can sometimes be done with paper and pencil (such as in writing a letter) but often requires different kinds of tools (such as laboratory tools in preparing a slide of a tissue specimen in a biology lab or carpentry tools in building a bookcase). Performance testing is sometimes done by itself and sometimes done in conjunction with essay or short-answer item testing. Sometimes students are performance-tested individually and sometimes they are tested in groups.

Essential Considerations.   Most performance testing has the following essential requirements:

1. a hands-on exercise or problem to solve (the student must actually be asked to do something, such as a construction or demonstration);
2. a material outcome or product at the end of the testing process (the student must make an actual product);
3. access to the solution process by the teacher (the teacher must observe not only the end result or product but also how that result or product was arrived at);
4. that students use specific skills (often psychomotor or physical) in producing the final product;
5. that students apply their understanding or knowledge and comprehension (knowing how to do something) in producing the final product.

Constructing the Test.   The first step is to *specify the desired performance outcome*, which means writing an objective requiring an actual performance, such as a construction or demonstration. Below are some examples:

- Construct a collage that expresses how you feel about the environment.
- Demonstrate a procedure for baking a lemon meringue pie.
- Construct a picture of a pueblo that was used by the Hopi Indians.
- Demonstrate a procedure for tuning a piano.

All of the above examples require hands-on performance, yield a product (a collage, a pie, a picture, a tuned piano), and make use of a process (finding, selecting, cutting, arranging, and gluing, for example, in the case of the collage).

A performance test can be used to determine whether a student can carry out a specific activity to achieve a desired result. This student is making a presentation on her chosen topic to demonstrate her ability to present information in a succinct, accurate manner.

The second step is to *specify the test situation*, which is the set of givens or conditions under which the student will attempt to produce the desired performance. Here are the test situations or givens for the above examples:

- Collage: given a group of specific magazines, a large piece of fiber paper, a scissors, and glue.
- Pie: given all necessary ingredients (for example, flour, fruit, sugar), measuring implements, cookware, oven.
- Drawing: given paper, ruler, and crayons.
- Piano tuning: given an out-of-tune piano and a set of tuning forks.

The third step is to *specify the response instructions*, such as the following:

- Show all your work.
- Don't leave anything out.
- Product should be tasty.
- You will get 10 points for creativeness and 10 points for technical accuracy.
- The display should be able to be mounted on the wall.
- You have 30 minutes to complete the task.

If there are any particular performance requirements, they should be specified as part of the response instructions.

The fourth step is to *specify process and product criteria* in the form of a *performance checklist*. The checklist will be used to score the performance test by providing a basis for judging both the performance and the product. Performance checklists are described in the next chapter.

A sample performance test is shown in Box 14.5.

Box 14.5

A Performance Test in Science for Fourth-Graders
Units of Force

(Objective 1) 1–3

Provide the child with four containers, each of which weighs one newton; a spring that he or she has not seen before mounted on a tripod (for example, Macalester Tripod Spring with centimeter tape on plastic cylinder); a pencil and some graph paper. Tell him or her, "Each one of these containers weighs one newton. Use them and the graph paper to calibrate the spring so that you can use the stretch of the spring to measure forces." One check should be given in the acceptable column for task one if the child plots one point correctly, one check in the acceptable column for task two if he or she plots two points correctly, and one check in the acceptable column for task three if he or she plots three or more points correctly.

(Objective 2) 4

Using your hand, pull on the spring until it is stretched to some length within the range of calibration. Tell the child, "Measure the force that I am exerting on the spring with my hand. Draw an arrow on your graph to show me where you are reading the force, and tell what the reading is." One check should be given in the acceptable column for task four if the child indicates the correct point on the graph with an arrow and states the measure of the force in newtons. If he or she merely gives a value (say, 3.5), it is allowable to prompt with the question "3.5 what?" Allow an error of 0.2 newtons.

SOURCE: Adapted from American Association for the Advancement of Science. (1968). *Science—A process approach* (Part E). Lexington, MA: Ginn & Company.

Summary of Main Points

1. The first step in constructing a test is to make a *content outline* or list of concepts, ideas, and skills covered in the instructional segment or unit that the test is intended to measure. Teachers normally do this prior to teaching the unit.

2. The second step is to prepare *objectives*, or statements of intended student outcomes in measurable or observable form. (The key element of the objective is the *action verb*, which helps provide the basis for the selection of the proper test-item form.) Teachers often prepare these prior to instruction as well.

3. The third step is the preparation of *test-item specifications*, which describe the action, conditions, and criteria, in some detail, for each of the objectives to be covered by the test. The conditions or content limits specify the prospective domain or range of possibilities for items measuring a given objective.

4. Next, the test-builder must decide the type and number of items to write. There should be at least two items per objectives, and, at most, as many as can reasonably be answered in the allotted time.

5. The type of item should be based on the action verb, with *stating* measured by completion items, *identifying* by multiple choice, *describing* by essay, and *constructing* and *demonstrating* by performance testing. The types of items are also connected to Bloom's taxonomy, with short-answer items measuring knowledge and comprehension and essay and performance items measuring the higher cognitive processes.

6. *Completion* items are single-sentence questions or fill-ins for which a free-choice word or phrase answer must be supplied. No answer choices are given; test-takers must *recall* the correct answer. Completion items are easier to write than multiple-choice but are harder to score.

7. A completion item must be clear enough to ensure that there is only one correct answer but should not provide so much information that the test-taker can determine the correct answer simply by reading the question. Also, the correct answer should be short. A good way to write a completion item is to write an entire statement without leaving anything out and then block out the one word or phrase that represents the critical essence of the statement.

8. *Multiple-choice* items are stems with a set of four or five answer choices, one of which is correct. The other, wrong ones are called distractors. Test-takers must *recognize* the correct answer.

9. The test-builder writes multiple-choice items by starting out with a statement of fact based on an objective and then, from it, creating an item stem and a correct answer choice. Distractors that are truly wrong but *plausible*, in that they represent possible wrong avenues of thought, are then generated. It is important in writing multiple-choice items to have only one right answer but to have distractors that are plausible to minimize the likelihood that test-takers can figure out the right answer from the item itself.

10. *True–false* items are statements or misstatements of fact that the test-taker judges to be true or false. These items are easy to write but also easy to answer by guessing, since the test-taker has a 50–50 chance of being right.

11. Other *two-choice* items are like multiple-choice items in a series but only have two answer choices (for example, "is an example of," "is not an example of") and are used to measure *classification* or the student's ability to distinguish whether something does or does not fit a given category. The choices for classification category and for distractors or nonexemplars should be based on the distinctions that teachers are trying to teach students to make.

12. *Matching* items have multiple stems and multiple answer choices and are difficult to write. Response choices should be nonoverlapping, unique (for the stem they fit), and plausible (for the stems they do not fit).

13. The above item types are used to measure knowledge, though multiple-choice items can also be used to measure *comprehension*. Knowledge items can be answered from memory; comprehension items require thinking.

14. Comprehension items measure the ability to *translate* or convert a communication from one form to another. To understand the meaning of something unfamiliar the student must first be able to translate it into a more familiar form. Translation items typically provide an example and ask the test-taker to identify the principle or concept of which it is an example.

15. Comprehension items also measure *interpretation* or getting the main idea or the essential or warranted conclusion. Typically, test-takers are provided with a paragraph, a data set, or an outcome and are asked to identify the correct meaning. Finally, comprehension items measure *extrapolation* or the ability to predict or extend the meaning of a given set of data.

16. Essay items are used to measure *application* or the ability to solve an unfamiliar problem correctly by applying or using the correct abstraction (abstractions may be ideas, methods, rules, principles, or the like). Writing the item means identifying or creating a *concrete situation* and then making up a *problem* within that situation to be solved. *Response instructions* (for example, specific requirements looked for in the answer) may also be provided.

17. Essay items also measure *analysis* or the ability to break down materials into constituent elements, relationships, or organizational principles. In writing these items, teachers must determine the material or experience they want analyzed and present it to the students along with any special response instructions.

18. Essay items can be used to measure *synthesis* or the putting-together of elements to form a unique whole. Synthesis is a creative and inventive process and, as such, has some unique testing requirements. It should be measured without either time or information-source constraints.

19. Essay items can also measure *evaluation*, the ability to make judgments about the value (accuracy, effectiveness, or satisfaction) of some work or method using either *internal* (for example, logic) or *external* (for example, comparison with other work) standards. The test-builder selects something to be evaluated that students know about and to which internal and/or external criteria can be applied, and then asks students to judge it against the criteria. Evaluative criteria may be provided, or students may be asked to provide them themselves. Students should be asked not only to provide the evaluative outcome or result but also to describe their evaluative process.

20. A *performance test* is one in which students actually have to *construct* a product or *demonstrate* a procedure, rather than just write about it. These tests require a hands-on problem to solve, a material outcome or product, a solution process that the teacher can access, the use of specific skills, and the application of both knowledge and comprehension. In constructing a performance test, test-builders must specify (a) the *desired performance outcome*, (b) the *test situation*, (c) the *response instructions*, and (d) the *process and product criteria*.

Suggested Resources

Bloom, B. S. (1956). *Taxonomy of educational objectives. Cognitive domain*. New York: David McKay.

Bloom, B. S., Hastings, J. T., & Madaus, G. F. (1971). *Handbook on formative and summative evaluation of student learning*. New York: McGraw-Hill.

Gronlund, N. E. (1982). *Constructing achievement tests* (3rd ed.). Englewood Cliffs, NJ: Prentice-Hall.

Tuckman, B. W. (1988a). *Testing for teachers*. San Diego: Harcourt Brace Jovanovich.

Chapter
15

Evaluating
and Improving
Tests and Scoring

Objectives

1. Define content validity and describe its use in test evaluation.
2. Demonstrate procedures for evaluating the content validity of a test.
3. Describe factors that make tests valid.
4. Define reliability and describe its use in test evaluation.
5. Demonstrate procedures for computing the mean and standard deviation of a set of scores.
6. Demonstrate two contrasting procedures for determining the reliability of a test.
7. Describe factors that make tests invalid.
8. Demonstrate the use of item analysis for identifying poor test items and diagnosing their weaknesses.
9. Describe three procedures for scoring essay-test responses.
10. Describe procedures for improving the reliability of test scoring.
11. Demonstrate the technique of developing a checklist to evaluate performance.

Why Evaluate a Test?

Tests are used to make important judgments about students and their performance. Results are used to assign students to special classes, to recommend or require additional assignments, and to assign grades. Teachers should not want to make such important decisions on the basis of faulty test results. They should build the best tests they can, and they should also examine the results on those tests as a way of improving them. In other words, if teachers want good tests they have to (1) follow the rules of good item-writing given in the preceding chapter, (2) be willing to take extra time to evaluate their tests, and (3) use techniques and principles described in this chapter to improve their tests (after they have given them) based on test results. Teachers need to use their test results not only to evaluate their students but to evaluate their tests as well. To evaluate their tests, teachers have to plan to use their tests more than once.

No measurement is perfect; each one contains errors. If a test is too hard, a teacher may erroneously conclude from its results that students have learned little, and as a result give them low grades. Conversely, a test that is too easy may result in grade inflation. Because item-writing is a task that requires skill and practice, items may be written that have nothing to do with the lesson, that are ambiguous, that have more than one right answer, or that have an obvious right answer. Bad items introduce error into a test and cause teachers to make mistaken judgments. This chapter will focus on how to determine the errors made in test construction so that they may be both corrected and avoided.

A Test Should Have Validity

The first criterion of a good test is *validity*. Validity is based on *whether the test measures what it is supposed to measure* or whether data from the test can be used to draw conclusions based on the test's intended purpose.[1] How can the judgment of what a test is supposed to measure be made so that its validity can be determined? The answer is based on an examination of the *objectives* for the lessons that have been taught and for which students are being tested. The instructional objectives for the lessons should also be the objectives for the test of achievement resulting from those lessons since that is what the test is intended to measure. The relationship between objectives, instruction, and testing should look like this:

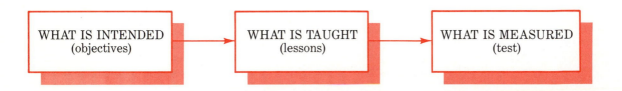

WHAT IS INTENDED (objectives) → WHAT IS TAUGHT (lessons) → WHAT IS MEASURED (test)

---

[1]This type of validity is called *content-related validity*. There are other forms of test validity, but they do not apply well to teacher-built achievement tests.

A test should fit or match the instructional objectives (just as the instruction should fit or match those same objectives) because that is what the test is *supposed to* measure.

How Can a Test's Validity Be Determined?   The measure of a test's validity is the degree to which its test items fit or match the objectives of the lessons that they are testing. By laying test items alongside objectives, the teacher can determine whether there are (1) test items to measure each objective (so that no objective goes unmeasured) and (2) objectives to match each test item (so that no test item measures something other than what was supposed to have been taught).

In doing this matching teachers must take specific considerations into account. These considerations are enumerated below.

1. *Do items that measure a particular objective actually require students to carry out the action specified by that action verb in that objective?*

If, for example, an objective uses the verb *identify*, test items measuring that objective should require the student to point to the right answer, as in a multiple-choice item. If an objective uses *state* or *name* or *list*, test items should call for this behavior, as in a completion item. The verb *describe* would require a free response as on an essay test, and *demonstrate* or *construct* would require actual performances, at least in paper-and-pencil form. Valid items require the same kind of performance specified in the objectives they measure. Items that require performances that differ from those called for in the objectives they measure are invalid.

2. *Do items that measure a particular objective cover that same content called for in the objective?*

To be valid, test items must correspond in content to the objective they measure. The fact, concept, or rule named in the objective must be the one measured by the test item. The correspondence must be as exact as possible. If, for example, the objective says "identify mammals," then the items must measure the identification of mammals, not the identification of fish or the distinction between potentially confusable mammals and fish.

3. *Do items that measure a particular objective provide the same conditions and require the same scoring criteria as those called for in that objective?*

Objectives written in long form contain conditions and criteria. The *conditions* indicate what materials and information the students must be given to perform the objective. The *criteria* indicate how that performance will be evaluated. Valid test items provide students with the "givens" called for in the objective they measure, and they are scored according to the criteria called for in the objective they measure. If the objective says, "Given a list containing the names of fish and fishlike mammals," that list must appear in the item in order for it to be valid. If the objective indicates that "students' descriptive responses will include mention of the differences in breathing and in bone structure," then the scoring key for that item must include that description in order for the item to be valid.

4. *Does the number of items that measure a particular objective accurately reflect the relative importance of that objective?*

All objectives are not equally important. An objective's importance is reflected in the amount of instructional time devoted to teaching it. The teacher may spend two or three class periods on an important objective but only a single class period on a less important objective. A valid test should contain a minimum of two items per objective for the least important objectives and more than two items as a function of the importance of the objective. An objective three times as important, for example, would have six items testing it, in contrast to two for the objectives of lesser importance.

Determining a Test's Validity.   Imagine that a teacher just finished teaching a social studies unit on the deserts of Africa. She started with a list of seven objectives and taught all of them to her students. She taught her class, through lecture and discussion, (1) the location of the deserts, (2) their names, (3) the plants that grow there, (4) the animals that live there, (5) how the people there satisfy their basic needs, (6) what it is like to grow up there, and (7) the culture of the people who live there. (These seven objectives appear in Figure 15.1.)

The teacher constructed a test for measuring her unit objectives on African deserts. Then she matched up her test items to her list of objectives to see where there was (and was not) a correspondence. Figure 15.1 shows this as it would be done for two tests. The content map at the top of Figure 15.1 shows that the test in question has high validity. It has met all validity criteria in that (1) the content of all objectives has been measured, (2) all items measure objectives, (3) all items fit the action, conditions, and criteria called for by the objective they measure, and (4) the number of items per objective fits the relative importance of that objective. The test measured in the top half of Figure 15.1 fits its objectives.

By contrast, the content map at the bottom of Figure 15.1 shows a lack of correspondence between objectives and test items. One objective (#2) has not been measured at all, while two items have been included that measure content not included in any of the given objectives (listed as "objective" 8 in Figure 15.1). Moreover, one item fits the content of an objective (#4) but not the action of that objective. Finally, the correspondence between the number of items per objective and the importance of each objective is not exact. Objective 3 has been overmeasured by one item and objectives 5 and 6 undermeasured by one item each. The test measured in the bottom of Figure 15.1 lacks validity and the teacher should revise it in order to improve the correspondence to its objectives.

What Makes Tests Invalid?

The three factors that make tests invalid are described below.

Testing What Was Never Taught.   At the two extremes of achievement testing are "teaching for the test" and "testing what was never taught." A valid achievement test is one that tests for what was taught, with both instructional content and test items a function of the same set of objectives. However, although based on the same objectives, a test must in some respects be independent of what was taught. On a test, students must demonstrate their ability to transfer or apply what was learned to unfamiliar material. Learning must have taken place prior to testing, but the test items on which that learning is to be demonstrated must be new. Those test items must not have been seen or practiced during instruction.

Teachers may occasionally feel a mischievous urge to spring some surprises in a test, but too many surprises will result in a test that has little to do with what was taught. This situation is shown in Table 15.1. A test need not be mundane or ordinary; it can be

Figure 15.1 🍎 A Content Map Compared for Two Tests: One High in Validity and One Low in Validity

High Validity

	Objectives for Unit on Deserts of Africa Given a map of North Africa, students can	Units of Importance*					
		1	2	3	4	5	6
1	Mark in the location of three major deserts	◉	◉				
2	Recall and write in the names of these deserts	◉	◉				
3	Identify indigenous plant life	◉	◉				
4	Identify indigenous animal life	◉	◉				
5	Describe how humans satisfy their basic needs there	◉	◉	◉			
6	Describe what it is like to grow up there	◉	◉	◉	◉		
7	Describe the culture (that is, the rules of getting along together)	◉	◉	◉			
8							

Low Validity

	Objectives for Unit on Deserts of Africa Given a map of North Africa, students can	Units of Importance*					
		1	2	3	4	5	6
1	Mark in the location of three major deserts	◉	◉				
2	Recall and write in the names of these deserts	X	X				
3	Identify indigenous plant life	◉	◉	◉			
4	Identify indigenous animal life	◉	✳				
5	Describe how humans satisfy their basic needs there	◉	◉	X			
6	Describe what it is like to grow up there	◉	◉	◉	X		
7	Describe the culture (that is, the rules of getting along together)	◉	◉	◉			
8		⊗	⊗				

* Based on time spent on each.

◉ Single test item or point of credit on a test item that measures a given objective.

⊗ Test item that does not measure a given objective.

X Given objective for which test item is missing.

✳ Given objective for which test item measures wrong action.

Table 15.1 🍎 Relation Between Testing and Teaching

Similarity Between Test and Instruction			
Same Objectives, Same Items	Same Objectives, New Items That Fit	Same Objectives, New Items That Don't Fit	New Objectives, New Items That Fit
Practice as part of instruction ("teaching to the test")	Valid test of what was taught	Failing to test what was taught	Testing what was never taught

creative; and students must not be shown the test items in advance. But students' instructional experiences should bear directly on the material to be covered in an achievement test or it cannot be considered a content-valid measure of what students have learned.

Failing to Test What Was Taught.   Testing what was never taught is testing performance on objectives that are new and different from those on which the lesson was based. The reciprocal of this testing what was never taught is failing to test what was taught. It does not matter what the objectives of testing are if they are not even measured. If a test is given at the completion of instruction, and the items test in whole or in part what was never taught (or new objectives), then there will be less room to test the instructional objectives that were actually taught. This is also shown in Table 15.1. The solution is to use the instructional objectives to build the test so that no instructional objective goes unmeasured.

Bias.   Sometimes, test items that appear to measure performance on instructional objectives actually do not. They may measure how well students read, how familiar they are with white, middle-class culture, or how closely their outside interests correspond to the context of the test items. If test items are written with a context that goes beyond the specifics of the objective they are measuring, performance on them may be the result of bias. Bias represents *a relative advantage or disadvantage of test-takers based on some lasting characteristic they have that is unrelated and irrelevant to the purpose of the test and the test's objectives*. For example:

- A test item that uses a cooking recipe as a context for measuring mathematics skills may be biased against boys, while one that uses baseball averages may be biased against girls. This is called a gender stereotype.
- A test item that uses bank accounts or stocks and bonds as a context may be biased against children of the poor while one that uses city streets may be biased against rural-dwellers.
- A test item that unnecessarily uses "big" words or irrelevant technical terms may be biased against poor readers, while one that unnecessarily uses unrelated facts or abstractions may be biased against test-takers possessing less knowledge.

Test-builders must make every effort to avoid introducing any unnecessary bias. The context should be made general enough and the wording simple enough for all students to understand. In this way, the item will measure only what it is intended to measure, or its objective.

A Test Should Have Reliability

If a test does not provide a reliable picture of what students have learned, then those students who have come to every class, paid attention, done the assignments, and studied for the test may not earn higher scores than students who have done none of these things. Failure of a test to distinguish between constructive learning behavior and its absence casts a great shadow on the educational process.

Thus, the second criterion of a good test is *reliability*. Reliability is based on *whether a test measures something accurately or consistently* (Tuckman, 1988a). Regardless of what quality a test measures, it must measure it in a way that reflects as closely as possible the degree to which it is present in each test-taker. In other words, the *measured* amount of a test-taker's quality must correspond as closely as possible to the *true* or actual amount.

Technically, a test's reliability is based on the correspondence of the scores it measures to true or actual scores, but this correspondence is hard to determine directly because it is not possible to know the true scores. One way to overcome this problem would be to give the same test over and over to the same students and actually see how much their scores varied from testing to testing (using a measure called the standard error of measurement), but this is impractical. Therefore, less direct methods have been invented, some of which are described below.

Since no test can be perfect — meaning that no test can measure every true score with exact precision — reliability coefficients, which are estimates of true variability in a test's scores, can never attain a value of 1.00. However, the more closely this ideal is approached, the more reliable or accurate a given test is. Soon, two procedures for estimating the reliability of a test, one mathematical and one not, will be described. But first consider how a set of test scores can be described.

The Mean and the Standard Deviation.   Since determining a test's reliability requires that the teacher examine an actual set of test scores, a way is needed to describe the scores in that set without simply listing them all. What is needed are *descriptive statistics* or terms that describe a set of test scores.

The first descriptive statistic describes the arithmetic middle or center of the set of scores. It is called the *mean* and is represented by the symbol $\overline{X}$ (or X-bar). To compute it we add together each individual test score (or X) and divide that sum (Σ) by the number of scores (N). The formula for the mean is

$$\overline{X} = \frac{\Sigma X}{N}$$

Suppose the following 10 scores were obtained on a test:

9	7
9	7
8	6
8	5
7	4

These 10 scores add up to 70 points, so the calculation for the mean would be

$$\overline{X} = \frac{70}{10} = 7.0$$

The mean is equal to 7.0. The "average" score on the test would therefore be 7.

The mean, however, is not enough to describe a set of scores. The mean tells where the arithmetic center of a set of scores is, but it does not tell the degree to which the individual scores vary. The scores can be spread out very far or more concentrated in the middle, as the two typical or *normal* distribution curves, shown below, are. (The normal distribution is described in considerably more detail in the next chapter; see pages 428–429.)

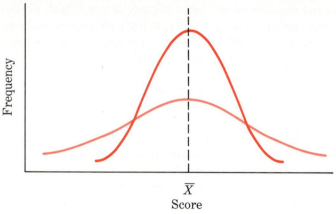

One way to describe the dispersion of a set of scores is to use a measure that tells how much each score deviates from the mean. The *standard deviation* (represented here by the lowercase letter s) indicates how much the scores in a set deviate from the mean. Its formula is

$$s = \sqrt{\frac{\Sigma(X - \overline{X})^2}{N - 1}}$$

To compute the standard deviation, we calculate the difference or deviation of each score from the mean $(X - \overline{X})$, squaring each difference to make each score positive, adding the results (as indicated by the Greek capital letter sigma or Σ), dividing by the number of scores minus one $(N - 1)$, and then taking the square root of the result (to compensate for having squared each deviation score). For the set of data given above, for which the mean of 7.0 was computed, the process of computing the standard deviation looks like this:

Score	$(X - \overline{X})$	$(X - \overline{X})^2$
9	+2	4
9	+2	4
8	+1	1
8	+1	1
7	0	0
7	0	0
7	0	0
6	−1	1
5	−2	4
4	−3	9
Σ 70	0	24

$$s = \sqrt{\frac{24}{10 - 1}}$$

$$= \sqrt{2.67}$$

$$= 1.63$$

So this set of 10 scores can be described as having a mean of 7.0 and a standard deviation of 1.63.

How Can a Test's Reliability Be Determined?   In determining reliability, the first procedure we will examine is a mathematical one that uses what is called the Kuder-Richardson Formula 21 (K–R 21):

$$\text{K–R 21} = \frac{n}{n-1}\left(1 - \frac{\overline{X}\,(n - \overline{X})}{ns^2}\right)$$

$\overline{X}$ represents the mean score of the class members on the test, which we obtain by (1) adding all the individual scores together and (2) dividing by the number of scores or test-takers. The s represents the standard deviation of scores around the mean, obtained by (1) subtracting each individual test score from the mean to get a set of deviation scores, (2) squaring each deviation score, (3) adding the squared deviation scores to get a sum of squared deviation scores, (4) dividing that sum by the number of scores or test-takers minus one, and (5) taking the square root of the result. The letter n stands for the number of items on the test.

Suppose a class of 10 students was given a 12-item test on which *each item is scored as right or wrong* (a necessary requirement for the use of the K–R 21 formula). Therefore, the scores can range from a low of 0 to a high of 12. Suppose the 10 students obtained the following scores:

Test 1

12	9
11	9
10	8
10	7
9	5

These scores add up to 90 and, since there are 10 scores, the mean score is 9. Subtracting 9 from each score, squaring each result, and adding the squares gives a total of 36, which, when divided by 9 (the number of scores minus one), yields 4.0. This is the value of s^2, the variance.[2] Plugging $n = 12$ (items), $\overline{X} = 9$, and $s^2 = 4.0$ into the K–R 21 formula gives a resulting reliability coefficient of 0.48. This reliability is unacceptably low. Reliability coefficients should not fall below 0.50 and preferably not below 0.65 (Tuckman, 1988b).

It is important to realize that the K–R 21 formula is based on the assumption that performance by students on a test is normally distributed or fits the bell-shaped curve. (A normal curve is shown in Figure 15.2 and again in Figure 16.1 on page 429.) For the values on K–R 21 to be accurate, scores must be distributed across the entire score range with the majority in the middle and a decreasing number at each end. This requires test items that are similar in terms of difficulty, neither too easy nor too hard. The above score distribution (of Test 1) is concentrated at the high end of the score range with a relatively small amount of variation between scores.

---

[2]Since the K–R 21 formula actually calls for s^2 rather than s, it is not necessary to perform the last step of taking the square root in the computation of s. The term s^2 is called the *variance*.

Figure 15.2 🍎 Distribution of Scores on Test 1 and Test 2 and for an Ideal Normal Curve

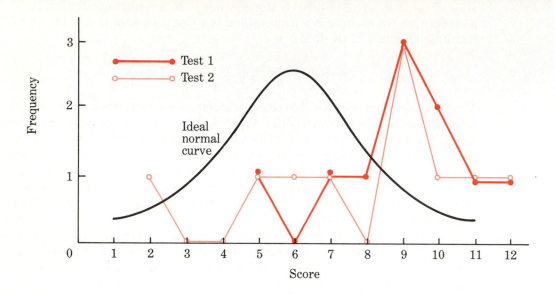

When the measure of variation, s^2, in the K–R 21 formula goes up, the resulting reliability coefficient goes up as well. (That happens because the fraction that is subtracted from one in the K–R 21 formula gets smaller as its denominator, ns^2, gets larger.)

Compare the results above with those reported by Tuckman (1988a) for the following 10 scores on another 12-item test:

Test 2	
12	9
11	7
10	6
9	5
9	2

The distribution of scores on the two tests is shown in Figure 15.2. On Test 2 (above), the mean score ($\overline{X}$) is 8 (being farther away from the ceiling of 12 than the mean of 9 in the previous example). The variance (s^2) is 9.1 (compared to 4.0 in the previous example). The resulting reliability coefficient for this test based on the above set of scores is 0.77. Thus, in these examples the broader, more normally distributed set of scores yielded the higher K-R 21 reliability coefficient.

All test scores do not necessarily approach the pattern of a normal distribution. On some tests, especially those with few items, or very easy or very difficult items, or those taken by equally well-prepared students, test scores may be clustered at the high end or low end of the distribution. In such cases, the approach to reliability described next should be used.

Parallel-Item Reliability.   This type of reliability is suitable for use on those class-room tests on which a large segment of the class is expected to demonstrate proficiency (referred to as criterion-referenced tests in the next chapter). *Parallel-item reliability is based on the determination of consistency of performance by students across items that are intended to measure the same objective.*

Say, for example, that the 12-item test referred to first (Test 1 on page 405) is an attempt to measure performance on four objectives, with three items having been written for each objective. Then, each item in each three-item set can be considered to be a measure of the same thing—the particular objective that that three-item set has been written to measure. If students have acquired proficiency on a given objective, they should get right all three items that measure that objective. If they have not acquired proficiency on that objective, they should get wrong all three items that measure that objective. This expectation is based on the assumption that all three items in a set measure the same objective and have approximately the same degree of difficulty. When the characteristic pattern is for students to get one or two items of the three right and the remaining two or one wrong, that indicates that the three items do not all measure the same objective or are not equal in difficulty. In either case, the mini-test of that objective can be considered to be low in parallel-item reliability.

We can assess parallel-item reliability by simply counting. Examine the performance of the 10 students on the first 12-item test (Test 1), item scores of which have been arrayed in Table 15.2. It can be seen from the array that there is considerable consistency of performance across the first and third three-item sets.

Table 15.2 🍎 An Array of Item Scores by 10 Students on 12-Item Test 1*

Student/Items	Objective One			Objective Two			Objective Three			Objective Four			Total Correct
	1	2	3	4	5	6	7	8	9	10	11	12	
1						X	X	X	X				8
2						X					X		10
3							X	X	X				9
4						X							11
5							X	X	X				9
6						X	X	X	X		X		7
7						X				X	X		9
8			X			X	X	X	X	X	X		5
9													12
10						X					X		10

*X's indicate incorrect responses; blanks indicate correct responses.

On the first set (Objective One) all students got all items right, suggesting that the items were parallel or measured the same thing and that the objective was well taught. On the third set (Objective Three) half the students got all three items wrong and half got all three right, a clear indication that the items are parallel. On the second and fourth sets, the results are not so clear-cut. On Objective Two, item 6 is probably too hard or does not measure the same thing as items 4 and 5. Item 6 should be rewritten. On Objective Four, item 12 may be too easy or item 11 too hard, or they may not measure the same thing. Both items should be examined and perhaps rewritten.

After minor modifications Test 1 should have sufficiently high parallel-item reliability.

What Makes Tests Unreliable?

In order to create more reliable tests, the test-builder must identify the factors that affect test reliability. These are described below.

Number of Test Items.   The more items, the greater the sample of student performance and thereby the greater the accuracy of assessment. Evaluation of performance to determine knowledge of an objective would be much less accurate on a single item than on 10 items. Of course, there is a limit to the number of test items students can complete before fatigue sets in, but within limits, the teacher can increase a test's reliability by adding items.

Item Difficulty.   Poorly written items may turn out to be too easy or too hard. When students can determine the answer to an item from the item itself, then virtually all of them will get the item right. A whole test made up of such items will be very unreliable. The teacher cannot gain an accurate picture of what students know if they can all figure out the right answers from the items themselves. The same can be said of items that are too hard. For example, when items have more than one acceptable answer, students will have to guess at which answer is right, thereby making the test result an inaccurate picture of what students know. By writing high quality items of moderate difficulty, and not including too many items that are excessively easy or difficult, teachers can improve the reliability of their tests.

Item Discrimination.   An accurate test item is consistent with other test items that are measuring the same thing. In other words, each item is considered to be a mini-test of whatever the whole test is measuring. Then, to the extent that the results on each item are the same as the results on the total test, the test is more reliable. Put another way, an accurate test item discriminates or distinguishes between test-takers who do well on the total test and those who do poorly. A test is unreliable when many of the items are inconsistent in what they are measuring. Item discrimination, like item difficulty, is greatly affected by the quality of test items. By writing high-quality items, teachers can maximize the potential of these items to discriminate between high scorers and low scorers.

Conditions of Test Administration.   If the room in which the test is given is hot or noisy or poorly lighted, the accuracy of the test as a measure of individual performance may suffer. Testing conditions should be kept as constant and comfortable as possible across all testings.

Conditions of Scoring. On tests that require scoring judgments, such as essay tests, there are many factors that may affect the accuracy of the results. Inconsistencies in the scorer or judge brought on by fatigue, biases for and against particular students, and changes in the scoring criteria will all have an adverse affect on reliability. Scoring criteria and model answers should be developed in advance, and multiple judges or multiple scorings should be used to overcome this problem (see pages 413–421).

Summary. To build more reliable tests, teachers should

- include enough test items (to combat the effects of individual item inaccuracy and guessing);
- write high-quality items — following the rules of item-writing covered in Chapter 14;
- write items of intermediate difficulty — avoiding writing items that seem too hard or too easy;
- administer tests consistently and under comfortable conditions;
- when scoring requires judgment, use preset scoring criteria, score all tests twice, and score without seeing the name of the student whose response it is.

Improving a Test's Reliability

As hard as teachers try to follow the above rules, they still will not necessarily build acceptably reliable tests. Even the experts must rely on their own best judgments in writing test items and cannot be sure that the results are acceptable. The best way to determine the quality of test items is not to rely on personal judgment but to look at the way students actually perform on them. The students' pattern of right and wrong answers on test items can be used effectively to provide information on item quality and accuracy. There are two ways this can be done.

Parallel-Item Agreement. When a test is given to a small number of students all of whom are expected to have attained mastery of the objectives measured by the test, then agreement or lack of agreement between items measuring the same objective can be used as a basis for identifying poor items. (This procedure has been described on pages 407–408 and illustrated in Table 15.2.) If student performance on some items is not consistent with performance on other items that have been written to measure the same objective, the former can be considered nonparallel and should be rewritten. When virtually all students get right, or wrong, all but one of the items written to measure the same objective, then that one item on which results differ is nonparallel. Rewriting these nonparallel items will increase the parallel-item agreement of the entire test.

Item Analysis. The principle procedure for distinguishing between good and poor items is item analysis. In item analysis *the performance of a test-taker on each of the items of* *a test* is compared to the performance of other test-takers and to the individual's performance on the total test. The purpose of item analysis, as applied to performance on a multiple-choice test, is fourfold:

1. to determine the degree of *difficulty* of each item based on how many students got it right;
2. to determine the *discrimination* of each item based on how many more high performers than low performers got it right;
3. to determine the *distractibility* of the distracters based on which distracters were ignored; and
4. to determine the *reason that an item lacks quality*, namely, whether it has more than one right answer, is miskeyed, taps a common misconception, or contains some "trick."

The teacher can accomplish each of the above four purposes by completing the steps that follow.

1. *Score the test and compute a total score for each student.* (This needs to be done anyway, to give each student a grade.)

To improve a test's reliability, you must first give it to a class of students. When you look at the results, you will discover which items were too hard or too easy.

2. *Divide the class into two halves, the UPPER half* (or *U*, the half who got the higher total scores on the test) *and the LOWER half* (or *L*, the half who got the lower total scores).

3. *Record the percentage of students in each half, U and L, who chose each of the answer choices on each item.* (The percentage is the number who chose an answer divided by the total number in the class times 100.)

4. *Compute the Difficulty Index for each item* as the percentage (%) of the whole class combined $(U + L)/2$ who chose the right answer (designated by an *) on that item.

5. *Compute the Discrimination Index for each item* as the percentage of the upper half who got the item right minus the percentage of the lower half who got the item right $(U - L)$.

Consider the examples below.[3] Remember the basic formulas

$$\text{Difficulty Index} = \%^*(U + L)/2$$
$$\text{Discrimination Index} = \%^*(U - L)$$

where $\%^*$ signifies percent correct, U is upper half, L is lower half, and the * marks the correct answer. Here's an example:

		A*	B	C	D	
1. Upper ½	U	95	5	0	0	DIFF = (95 + 45)/2 = 70 Good
Lower ½	L	45	20	20	15	DISC = (95 − 45) = 50 Good

How should this item be judged? A difficulty level of about 70% is advantageous because if 70% is obtained for all items, it will be the percentage correct for the test as a whole, putting the average grade at the level of C (see page 447 for a related discussion of letter grades). Items with difficulties below 50 are generally too hard; those much above 80 are too easy. Regarding discrimination, higher is better if the goal is to spread out the scores on the test, and 50 is quite high. (Actually, anything above 20 is generally regarded as adequate.) The above item appears satisfactory in terms of both difficulty and discrimination. Moreover, each of the distracters (B, C, and D) was chosen by approximately the same percentage of the lower group, that being close to the guessing percentage of one out of four or 25%. This item is worth keeping.

		A*	B	C	D	
2. Upper ½	U	98	0	2	0	DIFF = (98 + 62)/2 = 80 OK
Lower ½	L	62	13	10	15	DISC = (98 − 62) = 36 Good

Item 2 was easier than item 1, but some easier items are good to retain for motivational purposes. The distracters seemed to work for poorer students. This item should be retained as well.

---

[3]The author is indebted to Harold J. Fletcher for providing these examples.

```
                     A*   B   C   D
3. Upper ½   U   60   0  40   0   DIFF = (60 + 80)/2 = 70   Good
   Lower ½   L   80  10   5   5   DISC = (60 − 80) = − 20   Terrible
```

Something was wrong with item 3 since it resulted in a negative discrimination. The recommendation is to rewrite choice C because it distracted too many of the good students. Chances are that choice C is almost as good an answer as the one keyed correct (A), but subtly enough so that only the better students were "fooled" by it.

```
                     A*   B   C   D
4. Upper ½   U   72  13   8   7   DIFF = (72 + 68)/2 = 70   Good
   Lower ½   L   68  12   6  14   DISC = (72 − 68) = 4   Poor
```

Very many of the poorer students got item 4 right relative to the better students. Perhaps it failed to discriminate what was taught from what was already known through common sense. While not a perfect item, it may still be good enough to use again, if enough of the other items are good.

```
                     A*   B   C   D
5. Upper ½   U   64  20  16   0   DIFF = (64 + 52)/2 = 58   So-so
   Lower ½   L   52  22  26   0   DISC = (64 − 52) = 12   So-so
```

Item 5 is another item of marginal quality because too few of the better students got it right relative to the poor students. Also, choice D is not working as a distracter (no one chose it). Item 5 can probably be retained after choice D is rewritten.

```
                     A*   B   C   D
6. Upper ½   U   86   0   0  14   DIFF = (86 + 8)/2 = 47   Poor
   Lower ½   L    8   0   0  92   DISC = (86 − 8) = 78   Great???
```

Item 6 discriminates too well, but the problem would seem to be in the instruction that preceded it rather than in the item itself. Why do almost all of the poorer students pick answer D? They may have acquired a common misconception as a result of instruction. If so, the teacher had better go back and teach them that D is wrong. Distracters B and C should also be rewritten because they are not working. No student chose either one.

```
                     A*   B   C   D
7. Upper ½   U   98   0   2   0   DIFF = (98 + 76)/2 = 87   Easy
   Lower ½   L   76   9   7   8   DISC = (98 − 76) = 22   OK
```

Item 7 is an easy item with some ability to discriminate. Some items like this are worth keeping because they balance out hard items and help keep down test anxiety.

```
                     A*   B   C   D
8. Upper ½   U   98   0   2   0   DIFF = (98 + 96)/2 = 97   Too easy
   Lower ½   L   96   4   0   0   DISC = (98 − 96) = 2   Poor
```

A test can occasionally stand an item as easy as item 8, but not too often. Such easy items are motivational at best but contribute little to test reliability because they cannot discriminate well between different levels of performance.

The results of item analysis help the teacher decide what items to keep, what items to discard, what items to change, and how to change them. You can try your own hand at item analysis by answering the questions in Box 15.1.

Scoring an Essay Test Reliably

Thus far, the discussion of reliability has been limited to the reliability of short-answer items, particularly multiple-choice items. There is also an issue of reliability in regard to essay tests. For essay tests, reliability is based not on the items, as it is in multiple-choice tests, but on the scoring. In other words, the error or inaccuracy in essay testing is not in the writing of items, as it is for short-answer items, but in the writing of answers. Therefore, essay-test scoring must be done systematically and consistently, as de-scribed below.

Scoring Criteria

There are three kinds of criteria for scoring an essay item response: (1) content criteria, (2) process criteria, and (3) organization criteria. *Content criteria* refer to *the informa-tion, knowledge, or facts that must be present in order for the student to answer the question adequately*. Although essay items are not written primarily to measure knowledge, they usually require that some be presented. The scorer should specify, before scoring essay responses, exactly what content must be present in the response for the response to be adequate. The scorer may want to identify both necessary knowledge and optional knowledge, the latter depending on the particular direction the essay writer has taken.

Process criteria are used to evaluate the solution or recommendation presented in the response in terms of (1) *its accuracy or workability*, (2) *the reasons given to support it*, and (3) *the logic or rationale used to arrive at it*.

For example, suppose the test-scorer defines the appropriate problem-solving pro-cess to include the following six steps:

1. defining the problem,
2. generating alternative solutions,
3. weighing the alternative solutions against criteria,
4. choosing what seems to be the best solution,
5. applying the solution to the problem,
6. evaluating the extent to which the solution fits the problem.

Using the above list, the teacher can score students' essay responses by judging whether or not (or to what degree) each of the six problem-solving steps are reflected in the response. In other words, essay responses would be judged in terms of (a) the correct-ness of the given solution and (b) whether the process of finding that solution was accom-plished using the above problem-solving steps.

In items that measure analysis, students are expected to determine the compo-nents or elements of an object or experience and their relationship, and to explain how these were determined or what they mean. The scorer must specify, in advance, what elements should be found in the response, what kind of reasoning should have been used to identify an element, how elements relate to one another, and how these relationships relate to the solution. Essays cannot be scored unless scorers predetermine what they are looking for in scoring them. Lists of criteria or model answers enable scorers to judge whether or not (or to what degree) the predetermined requirements are present in the answer by giving them something to which each answer can be compared.

Suppose students were presented with a piece of abstract art or poster art and asked (1) what they thought the artist was "trying to say" and (2) what elements of the art led them to that conclusion. Before scoring their answers, the teacher should first decide what answers would be acceptable for the first part and what elements must be cited as satisfactory explanations in the second part. In other words, to score an essay test

---

Box 15.1

🍎

Test-Item Analysis*

In the tables below are percentages of Upper (*U*) and Lower (*L*) scoring students who selected each of four options (A, B, C, D) on eight test items. Asterisk indicates correct (keyed) answer. Compute difficulty and discrimination indices for each item and then answer the questions.**

		A	B*	C	D	
1.	U	0	98	0	2	DIFFICULTY =
	L	26	32	20	22	DISCRIMINATION =

		A	B	C*	D	
2.	U	0	2	96	2	DIFFICULTY =
	L	8	6	82	4	DISCRIMINATION =

		A*	B	C	D	
3.	U	60	40	0	0	DIFFICULTY =
	L	20	60	10	10	DISCRIMINATION =

		A	B	C	D*	
4.	U	25	25	20	30	DIFFICULTY =
	L	26	28	24	22	DISCRIMINATION =

		A*	B	C	D	
5.	U	100	0	0	0	DIFFICULTY =
	L	20	0	0	80	DISCRIMINATION =

		A	B	C*	D	
6.	U	5	35	60	0	DIFFICULTY =
	L	25	20	30	25	DISCRIMINATION =

reliably, the teacher must decide in advance not only what answers are acceptable but also what justifications or explanations are required in support of those answers.

The third kind of criteria are *organization criteria*. As the name implies, these criteria refer to the manner in which an essay response is organized or structured. Does the essay follow a logical pattern? Does it have an introduction, arguments, and a conclusion, or does it ramble along in a disorganized fashion?

Essay responses are far easier to score when they have a coherent structure. Students should be encouraged to prepare an outline before writing an essay response. To foster this, response instructions can indicate that the organization of the response will be taken into account when the essay is scored.

Essay-scorers may also want to take into account *originality* and *creativity* in scoring essay responses. To do so, they should include judgments of these qualities in the scoring procedure.

		A	B	C	D*	
7.	U	0	80	0	20	DIFFICULTY =
	L	5	5	10	80	DISCRIMINATION =

		A*	B	C	D	
8.	U	10	0	90	0	DIFFICULTY =
	L	10	10	70	10	DISCRIMINATION =

1. Which item was probably not covered in lecture or text?
2. Which item was probably keyed wrong?
3. Which item is best in terms of measurement principles?
4. Which item could be considered "tricky"?
5. Which item serves a motivational goal if not a measurement goal?
6. Which item should be stressed more in the future to overcome an apparently strongly held misconception?
7. Which item seems to have an answer that appears correct but upon careful analysis is judged wrong?
8. Which item can be improved with the simplest revision?
9. Which item has useless distractors?
10. Which item is probably invalid?

*The author is indebted to Harold J. Fletcher for providing this material.

**Answers can be found in footnote 4 at the bottom of page 416.

Doing the Scoring

There are three different ways to score an essay response.

Criterion Point Scoring.   This is the most detailed way to score an essay response. To do it, the teacher generates as detailed a set of criteria as possible, and then assigns a number of points for each criterion, using a response scoring sheet such as the one shown in Figure 15.3. In this scoring procedure, which would be applied to a problem-solving essay, criteria are scored on either a 10-point scale or a 5-point scale and partial credit may be given. Rather than judging the essay as a whole, the scorer scores each aspect of the essay by itself against the appropriate criterion. Breaking down the scoring process this way tends to make it more reliable.

In this illustration (Figure 15.3), spaces are provided for two judges to score each essay. Since this is usually not realistic or practical for classroom teachers, each essay, or some proportion of all essays, can be scored twice by the same teacher to determine whether scoring is being done consistently or reliably.

Sometimes the criteria for which points are awarded in scoring an essay include specific ideas that the essay writer is expected to cover in answering the essay question. An example of this approach, along with its application to a sample essay response, is shown in Box 15.2. Note that in this example, as in all instances of criterion point scoring, detailed scoring criteria are specified in advance, and points are awarded based on the extent to which each individual criterion is met. This is the most reliable way to score an essay response.

Wholistic Scoring.   In this procedure, read the entire essay response and assign it a grade based on how closely it fits a prespecified or ideal response. To use this procedure reliably, the teacher should actually prespecify five model responses: an A response, a B response, a C response, a D response, and an F response, or one for each of the five grades. The best way to achieve this, in scoring a set of essay questions, is to read over the whole set of answers and find a *model* for each of the five grades (in other words, a

---

[4]Answers to Box 15.1.

	1	2	3	4	5	6	7	8
DIFF	65	89	40	26	60	45	50	10
DISC	66	14	40	8	80	30	− 60	0

Question	Item	Answer
1.	4	All answers are at guess level (about 25%).
2.	8	C is actually the right answer. Change your scoring key.
3.	1	Best on both difficulty and discrimination.
4.	7	Those in the "know" chose B. Or
	3	Choice B is subtly wrong.
5.	2	It's a giveaway (89% got it right).
6.	5	Poorer students believe D. Or
	3	Too many students believe B.
7.	5	D appears correct to poor students, but better students judge it wrong.
8.	6	Rewrite only choice B so that more *U*'s get it right.
9.	5	Only item with two: B & C.
10.	4	Same as question 1. "Invalid" means "not taught."

model A answer, a model B answer, and so on). Then the teacher would use the models for comparison to classify every student's response as an A, B, C, D, or F. Hence, *the scorer scores the whole essay against a set of model responses.*

Further, it is recommended that teachers score a single essay question across all students' essay tests rather than scoring each whole test at a time. Doing this makes comparison scoring possible and helps maintain a focus on given model responses. Scoring an essay response is a matter of judgment, but the intention should be to make the judging process as reliable or accurate as possible. Unlike using specific criteria to aid the scoring process, wholistic scoring relies on the use of model responses to which any given response can then be compared. The result is the direct assignment of a grade.

Ranking.   In this procedure, individual essay responses are not assigned a number of points or a wholistic letter grade, but are ranked in order of how complete or creative they are or how well they match other criteria. In other words, the best response goes on top, the next best goes next, the third best next, then fourth, fifth, and so on right down to the worst response. Once ranking is completed, a grade or a number of points is assigned to each response. Hence, *the scorer scores the whole essay by assigning it a position relative to the other essays.* (The next chapter, on test-score interpretation, will

Figure 15.3 🍎 A Sample Essay Response Scoring Sheet
From Tuckman, 1988a, p. 97.

Student _____   Test _____
Date _____   Item _____

Criterion	Weight	Points Possible	(Judge A) Points Obtained	(Judge B) Points Obtained	(Average) Points Obtained
Content	1	10			
Organization	1	10			
Process					
Solution					
Accuracy	½	5			
Consistency	½	5			
Originality	½	5			
Argument					
Accuracy	½	5			
Consistency	½	5			
Originality	½	5			

Total Points Possible = 50

Total (Average) Points Obtained =

Percent Score = $\dfrac{\text{Total Points Obtained}}{\text{Total Points Possible}} \times 100 =$

Comments:

Box 15.2

🍎

**A Sample Third-Grader's Essay Response and
Its Criterion Point Scoring**

Have you ever been an eagle or a duck? When? Which would you rather be? Why?*

I would rather be a
eagle because they fly
through the air. One time
I was a duck. I got mad an
I open the door to fast an
I hit my face on it.
I am a eagle all the
time now. I clean the house.
pick up my room. My sister
is a duck she never helps
me.

Scoring:

Category	Max Points	Points Earned
1. Spelling	20	15
2. Grammar	20	15
3. Reason for choice	20	15
4. Illustration of eagle	20	20
5. Illustration of duck	20	20
Total	100	85

---

*See Box 13.9 for a description of "eagles" and "ducks."

Scoring an essay test reliably can be a difficult task. But this teacher makes the job easier and the results more accurate by using a set of prespecified criteria against which to judge each student's answer.

provide a basis for deciding how many answers to assign an A or full credit, how many a B or minus one, how many a C, and so on. This represents relative or norm-referenced scoring, as described in the next chapter.)

So, in criterion point scoring, points are assigned on the basis of the essay response that meets each preset criterion; in wholistic scoring, the whole essay is assigned a grade through comparison to a preset model; and in ranking, responses are placed in rank order of "goodness" and then a certain number are given A's, a certain number B's, and so on.

Improving Reliability of Essay Scoring

On essay tests the teacher reads the responses and makes judgments about students' competency or proficiency. What would happen if the teacher were to read that essay a second time? Would the same judgments of performance be made? If the second-round judgments are different from the first, who is to say which is more accurate? Maybe some of the essays were read late at night when the teacher was tired, and the remainder were read in the morning when the teacher was more alert. Or perhaps the teacher read the name of the students before reading their response and, because of the difficulty in making the judgments that essay-response scoring requires, was influenced by expectations based on students' past performances and abilities. When unconscious biases or expectations affect scoring consistency, reliability suffers.

To assure the reliability of scoring, responses should be rescored (Tuckman, 1988b). Responses to every essay item, or some proportion of them, should be read twice. The minimum number of essays that is usually read twice to establish reliability is one out of five. Teachers should try to read one out of every five essay responses twice to see how closely the judgment determinations agree. If scoring criteria are established or model answers are prespecified, scoring can be done much more quickly. Knowing exactly what to look for, and how much the different criteria will be weighed, can help the teacher score and rescore all the essays efficiently.

Here are some suggestions about how to improve reliability as a scorer. First, cover the students' names before scoring in order to avoid being influenced by expectations based on prior performance. This is called *scoring blind*. (This procedure was also described in Chapter 1.)

Second, structure the response key in terms of the ideal answer and the number of points given for organization, content, creativity, problem solution, and rationale. The more scoring specifications there are, the more likely it is that the scoring will be consistent, time after time, student after student. Communicating these criteria to students also helps them write better, easier-to-score essay responses.

Scoring Performance Tests Reliably

An aid to scoring a performance test reliably is the *performance checklist*. The last step in constructing a performance test, as described in the previous chapter, is specifying process and product criteria. Operationally, these criteria are set forth in a performance checklist, which is a list of every feature or characteristic of the performance process or resulting product that must be observed in order to certify the quality of the performance. In the sample performance test, for example, shown in Box 14.5, the teacher is instructed in what to look for and how many points to award if it occurs. Such performance steps include plotting one, two, or three points correctly; indicating the correct point on the graph; and stating the measure of the force in newtons.

In other words, a performance checklist is a list of prespecified behaviors for evaluating the process of performing a given task successfully. To construct a performance checklist, the teacher must first separate the correct performance into its component behaviors and then list them. Then, when observing the performance of students on the task, the teacher marks all the checklist behaviors that are observed and uses them as the basis for scoring the performance.

Suppose a performance for fourth-graders was, after they completed a project on trees, to turn in a report that contained (1) pictures of local trees and their leaves, (2) information about trees in terms of their contributions to ecology and quality of life, and (3) recommendations to help protect trees. The teacher could create a performance checklist like this:

Performance Checklist: Project on trees

    a. Report is neat.

    b. At least three different types of trees are drawn and labeled.

    c. Each type of tree is described.

    d. Value of trees is described.

    e. Ways to protect trees are described.

The teacher would then use the checklist to evaluate each student's report by checking whether or not each of the five criteria was met. Hence, a performance checklist is a technique for specifying, in detail, the criteria by which a performance is to be evaluated.

Some additional examples of performance checklists are provided in Box 15.3.

Box 15.3

Some Sample Performance Checklists

Bisecting an Angle

_____ a. Compass is used.

_____ b. Point placed on vertex; arc is made between sides.

_____ c. Point placed on each intersection between arc in (b) and side; equal arcs are made.

_____ d. Line is drawn from vertex to intersection between arcs in (c).

_____ e. Two resulting angles are equal when checked with protractor.

_____ Overall quality of performance on a 0–5 scale.

Constructing a Rock Display

_____ a. All three kinds of rocks—igneous, sedimentary and metamorphic—are represented.

_____ b. Rocks are cleaned and polished.

_____ c. Rocks are attractively mounted.

_____ d. Rocks are labeled (including name and where found).

_____ e. Display can be placed on wall.

_____ Overall quality of performance on a 0–5 scale.

Weighing Objects of Unknown Weight on a Laboratory Balance

_____ a. Objects of known weight combined to try to match object of unknown weight.

_____ b. Weights added or subtracted to compensate for underbalance and overbalance.

_____ c. As balance is approached, smaller weights added systematically.

_____ d. When balance is achieved, total value of known weights is computed by adding.

_____ e. Correct result is achieved.

_____ Overall quality of performance on a 0–5 scale.

Summary of Main Points

1. Because no measurement can be perfect, all tests will contain some errors. Since test results are important to teachers and students alike, efforts to minimize these errors are worth undertaking. Such efforts can be made not only in building tests but also in revising them based on student performance prior to using them again.

2. Tests can be evaluated in terms of their validity, the extent to which they measure what they are intended to measure. A test's validity may be determined relative to its objectives, if that is what the test is intended to measure. If objectives are used to guide both what is taught and what is tested, then the resulting test is likely to be valid in that it will differentiate between students who have learned the lessons and those who have not.

3. One way the teacher can determine a test's validity is by matching its items to the objectives that it is testing. It is important that no objectives are missing test items and that no test items are missing objectives.

4. In determining the validity of a test based on the correspondence between items and objectives, the test-builder should make the items specifically match the objectives in terms of the objectives' (a) action (as specified by the action verb), (b) content, and (c) conditions and criteria. Moreover, the number of items measuring each objective should correspond to the objective's relative importance. The teacher can facilitate the matching process by building a content map.

5. Tests will not be content-valid if they test what was never taught or do not test what has been taught. In addition, validity will be lacking if bias is introduced into test items through their having a high reading level, interest-based content, or cultural background requirements.

6. Another basis for evaluating a test is its reliability or its accuracy or consistency across items. Technically, reliability means the extent to which measured scores on a test correspond to "true" scores.

7. One way to determine the reliability of tests on which the scores fall on a normal or bell-shaped curve is to calculate the mean and standard deviation of a set of test scores and then use these descriptive statistics to compute Kuder-Richardson Formula 21 (K–R 21). With this formula, the greater the standard deviation or variance or dispersion of a normally-distributed set of test scores, the more likely the reliability is to approach an ideal value of 1.00.

8. When scores on a test are all expected to approach the high end of the distribution (based on total mastery), the teacher can judge reliability by examining student performance on parallel items, those that are intended to measure the same objective. High parallel-item agreement reflects high reliability.

9. The factors that tend to affect a test's reliability are (a) its length, the number of items; (b) the difficulty level of its items; (c) the extent to which its items discriminate between students who do well on the total test and those who do poorly; (d) the conditions of test administration; and (e) the conditions of scoring. Writing a large enough number of test items that are of high quality, consistent with one another, and of intermediate difficulty is likely to result in a reliable test.

10. Since the teacher cannot accurately judge a test's reliability just by looking at it (or by comparing it to its objectives, as in the case of validity), it must be tried out and the results examined to determine its reliability. Performance on items that are intended to measure the same objective can be compared and those that are found not to be parallel can be rewritten.

11. More intensively, the teacher can conduct an item analysis of test results by examining (a) the indexes of item difficulty and item discrimination for each item and (b) the

number of students in the upper and lower halves of the class who chose each answer choice on each item. The teacher can compute item difficulty by finding the percentage of students in the whole class who got the item right, and can compute item discrimination by finding the difference between the percentage of students in the upper and lower halves of the class who got the item right.

12. The purpose of item analysis is to discover and rewrite items that (a) are too easy or too difficult, (b) fail to discriminate between those who have learned and those who have not, and (c) contain some trick, common misconception, more than one right answer, or distracters that are ignored. Making the necessary revisions can greatly improve the reliability of a test.

13. When tests are of the essay type, rather than short-answer, then it is of primary importance to try to maximize the reliability or accuracy of scoring. Scoring can be improved if the teacher uses (a) content criteria to evaluate the presentation of facts or information; (b) process criteria to evaluate the solution or recommendations, their justification, and the means by which they were arrived at; and (c) organization criteria to evaluate the structure or comprehensiveness of the essay. Originality and creativity should also be taken into account.

14. Essay-test responses may actually be scored any one of three ways. In *criterion point scoring*, specific scoring criteria are listed on a scoring sheet, the essay response is evaluated on each criterion, and points are awarded for each evaluation. The points are then totaled to arrive at the total score for the essay. In *wholistic scoring*, sample responses for each scoring grade — A, B, C, D, F — are created or identified and then each essay response is compared to each model to yield a grade. In *ranking*, the essays are put in rank order of quality, and a certain number are assigned each grade.

15. Teachers can improve the reliability of the scoring procedure by (a) scoring a part of each test twice; (b) scoring the tests blind, by covering up the name of the student whose essay is being read; and (c) structuring the response key in advance as much as possible to reflect scoring criteria and to guide subsequent evaluative judgments.

16. Performance tests can be reliably scored if the teacher first prepares a *performance checklist* that lists each criterion by which the performance of a particular task is judged. The checklist lists necessary behaviors or necessary features of the appropriate performance, and the teacher checks all that are observed in each student's performance to produce a performance score.

Suggested Resources

Baker, F. (1977). Advances in item analysis. *Review of Educational Research, 47,* 151–178.

Kubiszyn, T., & Borich, G. (1984). *Educational testing and measurement.* Glenview, IL: Scott Foresman.

Mehrens, W., & Lehmann, I. (1978). *Measurement and evaluation in education and psychology* (2nd ed.). New York: Holt, Rinehart & Winston.

Tuckman, B. W. (1988a). *Testing for teachers* (2nd ed.). San Diego: Harcourt Brace Jovanovich.

Chapter
16

Interpreting and Evaluating Test Scores

Objectives

1. Identify reasons for interpreting test scores.
2. Describe criterion-referenced test interpretation and the computation of the percent-correct score.
3. Identify reasons for going beyond criterion-referenced test interpretation, and distinguish between criterion-referenced and norm-referenced test interpretation.
4. Identify aspects of norm-referenced test interpretation, including the norming group and the normal curve.
5. Demonstrate procedures for computing the following norm-referenced scores and converting from one to the other — z-score, SAT score, percentile rank, and stanine score — and describe the relation between these scores and the normal curve.
6. Describe the meaning of the grade-equivalent score and its limitations.
7. Identify the characteristics of standardized tests.
8. Demonstrate procedures for interpreting and evaluating a set of student test scores.
9. Identify the interpretation and evaluative meaning of test-score results from standardized tests provided in score reports.
10. Demonstrate the procedures for absolute grading, grading "on the curve," and standardizing scores as techniques for assigning grades on tests.

Why Do Test Scores Require Interpretation?

Test scores must be interpreted to determine what they indicate about the characteristics or capabilities of the test-takers who are being measured. Interpretation helps educators understand the information a test score conveys; otherwise, a test score is just a number or a set of numbers. Test scores tell us little unless some basis is used for determining their meaning.

The score that a student or test-taker gets on a test is called a *raw score*, usually designated by the letter "X." It represents the number of points the student has earned on the test (say, the number of items answered correctly), but what does this raw score actually mean? Is it high? Is it low? Does it reflect competence or mastery? Is it worthy of an A, a B, or what? Is it average? Is it acceptable? Suppose a student got 60 points on an algebra test? Should the student pass the course, or go on to the next unit, or get a grade of C, or receive extra help from the teacher? Without a basis for interpreting the test score, the results are difficult to use for any purpose, including grading.

The teacher needs something to relate the test scores to: *reference points* or benchmarks that can be used to give the test scores meaning, or to which the test scores can be compared for interpretation. There are two such referencing systems available. One is called *criterion-referencing* and the other *norm-referencing*. Criterion-referencing utilizes *absolute* evaluative criteria and norm-referencing utilizes *relative* evaluative criteria. Criterion-referencing, the simpler of the two approaches, will be described first.

Criterion-Referenced Test Interpretation

As the name implies, criterion-referenced test interpretation means that test scores are interpreted in terms of predesignated criteria or standards. Since the standards are decided in advance, and remain the same, they are considered *absolute*.

The Percent-Correct Score. The score that is most typically used for criterion-referencing is the *percent-correct score* (% correct). It is computed by the following formula:

$$\% \text{ Correct} = \frac{\text{Raw score}}{\text{Maximum possible score}} \times 100$$

To convert a raw score into a %-correct score, the teacher must know the maximum possible score on the test.

On a 50-point test, for example, a raw score of 40 would represent 80% correct. On a 20-point test, a raw score of 16 would also represent 80% correct. The two scores, 40 and 16, are the same in terms of % correct since one was obtained on a 50-point test and the other on a 20-point test. However, a set of criteria for interpreting the %-correct score is still needed because, by itself, the %-correct score means little.

Preset Criteria for Score Interpretation. Is an 80%-correct score high and, if so, how high is it? Criterion-referenced interpretation requires a set of preset criteria for interpreting and evaluating the %-correct score. Many teachers simply decide that any score above 65% correct is a passing score and any score below 65% is a failing score, or they may use more detailed, but still arbitrary, cutoff criteria, such as

90%–100% is an A

80%–89% is a B

70%–79% is a C

65%–69% (or, alternatively, 60%–69%) is a D

0%–64% is an F

Where do these criteria or cutoff scores come from? Who says that 90% is an A and 80% is a B and so on? These criteria simply represent the judgment of the teacher, but when many teachers tend to use the same cutoff scores or predesignated criteria, they have become part of the common practice of test interpretation.

Why Not Always Use Criterion-Referencing?

Why is any other way of interpreting test scores needed? Why not always use the absolute basis of judging according to preset standards or criteria? One reason is that some teachers may *not accept these preset criteria* because they are, after all, quite arbitrary. Yet these teachers may *not have any criteria to substitute for them*. Why shouldn't an A be 95% to 100% or 85% to 100%? What is so magical about 90% to 100%? Maybe 50% or 75% should be the passing grade, rather than 65%? To use criterion-referencing, a teacher must accept the common preset criteria or have a better set of his or her own. There is really no way to know whether the common set is appropriate or not, or whether any other particular set is better.

Another problem with criterion-referencing has to do with *test difficulty*. What if the test for which scores are being interpreted is a very easy test? Then every student may get an A or a B. Does that mean that all the students have achieved high mastery of what was taught? Not necessarily. It is just as likely that the uniformly high scores are the result of the easiness of the test. High scores at any time may reflect an easy test rather than great student competence, and without clear preset criteria, interpretation is difficult. Thus, arbitrary criteria may yield inaccurate interpretations.

The same problem of interpretation exists when mostly low scores are obtained on a test. Should everyone fail? Not necessarily, because the test may have been too hard. Even with content-valid tests, the range of difficulty levels on a test can vary greatly. Only when most of the test items are of intermediate difficulty will preset criteria yield accurate interpretations. It is difficult to tell whether test scores have been unduly influenced by test difficulty.

Another problem with criterion-referenced test interpretation is that *no test is perfect in validity and reliability*. Consequently, arbitrary preset criteria may be inaccurate or inappropriate since the test scores will partly reflect test error. Unfortunately, all test interpretation is somewhat affected by this problem, which is a good reason to try to build accurate tests (as described in Chapter 15).

Finally, the standardized tests that are given to students nationwide are difficult to interpret on an absolute basis in terms of preset criteria because all students have not been taught the same material at the same time. Moreover, when arbitrary criteria are inaccurate or do not fit a test well, then students, parents, and teachers could mistakenly think that someone did even worse (or better) than his or her test scores showed.

For all of these reasons, an alternative to criterion-referencing was developed and, when appropriate, may be used by teachers. This alternative is also used to interpret published test results.

Norm-Referenced Test Interpretation

Background

Instead of interpreting test scores by comparing them to preset criteria, teachers can interpret them by comparing them to one another (for example, by comparing the scores of all the students in a class) or by comparing them to another set of test scores (for example, by comparing them to those of another class or another group of test-takers). This relative approach to test interpretation is known as *norm-referencing*, and the *set of scores* to which any single score is compared is referred to as the norms. Norm-referencing represents using relative scoring criteria rather than the absolute ones used in criterion-referencing.

Norms.   These are the test scores used to interpret a given test score. Test scores are interpreted relative to norms. For published tests, norms must be obtained prior to the commercial use of the test so that test-users can be supplied with norms tables for converting raw scores to the various norm-referenced scores described below. To obtain norms, the test-builders administer published tests to a large group of representative test-takers, called the *norming group*, the members of which are selected to be representative of students whose scores will subsequently be evaluated by being compared to scores of the norming group. Hence, norming-group members represent all ages, all grade levels, all sections of the country (geographically as well as in terms of urban, suburban, and rural), all ethnic groups, and all socioeconomic levels in order to give the resulting norms the widest applicability. Moreover, norming is done fairly often so that norms can be as recent as possible.

For teacher-built tests, norm-referencing can be done on the basis of a single class or group of classes, either current or recent. It is often easiest to use a single class (if it is large enough) as the basis for generating norms to interpret the raw scores of all the students in that class.

The Normal Curve.   The normal curve was introduced briefly in the previous chapter and appears again in Figure 16.1. It represents an expected but ideal (or theoretical) distribution of a set of test scores on any measure that is independent and random. Measurements of height, weight, intelligence, self-esteem, or many other variables for a group of people would result in the "normal" or symmetrical bell-shaped distribution in Figure 16.1.

The normal curve follows a predictable pattern. First, it is perfectly symmetrical, with the mean raw score for the norming group at its center. Second, approximately two-thirds of the test-takers are clustered toward the center of the distribution (under the "hump") with half of the remaining third "strung out" at each end. It is "normal," in other words, for the majority of test-takers to be in the average range on the variable being tested, regardless of what that variable is (so long as it is independent and random), and the minority to be at either extreme. (This description is based on what statisticians call the central limit theorem.) Most people are average on most measures; fewer people are extreme.

Figure 16.1 ❦ The Normal Curve (Including Various Kinds of Standard Scores and Percentile Scores)

From *Test Service Bulletin No. 48*, January 1955. San Antonio, TX: The Psychological Corporation.

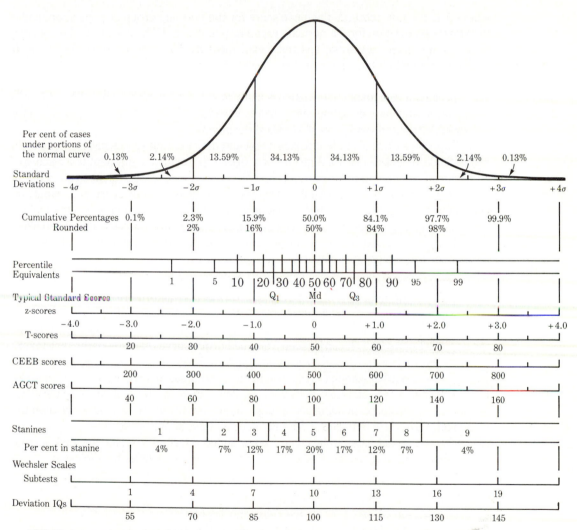

NOTE: *This chart cannot be used to equate scores on one test to scores on another test. For example, both 600 on the CEEB and 120 on the AGCT are one standard deviation above their respective means, but they do not represent "equal" standings because the scores were obtained from different groups.*

Norm-Referenced Scores

Standard Score: The *z*-Score.   The most basic norm-referenced score is the standard score, and the most basic standard score is the *z-score*. The *z*-score is computed using the formula

$$z = \frac{X - \overline{X}}{\sigma}$$

where X is the raw score, $\overline{X}$ the mean score for the norming group or population, and σ the standard deviation for the norming group or population.[1] The *z*-score is the distance between any given raw score and the mean, measured in standard deviation units. It indicates how much bigger or smaller a given raw score is than the mean of a set of comparison scores in standard deviation units. If the comparison scores or norms are very spread out (the standard deviation is quite large), a given raw score will be closer to the mean in standard deviation units than it would be if the set of scores were more narrowly distributed (with a small standard deviation).

Suppose a class of students takes a test and the resulting scores have a mean of 70 and a standard deviation of 15. A given raw score of 70 would be equivalent to a *z*-score of 0 (because it is equal to the mean), a raw score of 85 would be equivalent to a *z*-score of $+1.0$ (because it is one standard deviation above the mean), a raw score of 55 would be equivalent to a *z*-score of -1.0 (because it is one standard deviation below the mean), and a raw score of 65 would be equivalent to a *z*-score of -0.33 (because it is one-third of one standard deviation below the mean). These results are easily computed with the formula for the *z*-score given above.

Percentages of Each Standard Score.   We can interpret any specific *z*-score by determining approximately what percentage of the test-takers are above it and what percentage are below it. To do this, we use the percentages within the normal curve shown in Figure 16.1 or, more easily, the rounded cumulative percentages given below the curve in Figure 16.1. It can be seen from the normal curve that *34%* of the test-takers fall between the mean (0) and minus one standard deviation (-1σ), *14%* fall between minus one standard deviation (-1σ), and minus two standard deviations (-2σ), and *2%* fall below minus two standard deviations (-2σ). Since the normal curve is perfectly symmetrical, the corresponding percentages above the mean are also *34%* between the mean and $+1\sigma$, *14%* between $+1\sigma$ and $+2\sigma$, and *2%* above $+2\sigma$.

These percentages can be cumulated or added, starting from the low end, so that the total percent of test-takers below each *z*-score can be identified, as follows:

$z = -3$ 0% are below this score
$z = -2$ 2% (2) are below this score
$z = -1$ 16% (2 + 14) are below this score
$z = \ \ \ \ 0$ 50% (2 + 14 + 34) are below this score
$z = +1$ 84% (2 + 14 + 34 + 34) are below this score
$z = +2$ 98% (2 + 14 + 34 + 34 + 14) are below this score
$z = +3$ 100% (2 + 14 + 34 + 34 + 14 + 2) are below this score

---

[1]The letter *s* is used for the standard deviation of a sample group's scores and the Greek letter σ is used for the standard deviation of a population's scores.

For z-scores with decimals, such as $+0.33$, interpolation can be done between the whole-number z-scores above and below, and the resulting percentage can then be added on to the total for the z-score below.[2] For $+0.33$, for example, about one-third of the people in the $z = 0$ to $z = +1$ range must be added to the percentage for $z = 0$. One-third of 34% (the percent in this range) is approximately 12%, and adding 12% to 50% means that about 62% of the test-takers are below the z-score of $+0.33$.

Other Standard Scores: The SAT Score.   There are other standard scores[3] that we can compute by transforming the z-score in order to eliminate both negative scores and decimals. The z-score can be transformed using the formula

$$\text{Standard score} = M + S(z)$$

where M is any arbitrary number chosen to be the mean and S is any other arbitrary number chosen in advance to be the standard deviation.

As an illustration, consider the scoring of the Scholastic Aptitude Test (SAT) used by many colleges for entrance screening purposes. (It is shown in Figure 16.1 under the letters CEEB for College Entrance Examination Board.) For each half of the test, the verbal portion and the quantitative portion, the preset mean (M) is 500 and the preset standard deviation (S) is 100 (as shown in Figure 16.1 under "CEEB scores"). Considering the *total* score, or both halves of the test together, then $M = 1000$ and $S = 200$.

So, if a student gets a total SAT score of 1000, that student is average compared to other students who take the SAT, and 50% of the test-takers in the norming group fall below that student's score. To be in the top 84% requires a z-score of $+1$, which means an SAT score of 1200 (computed as $1000 + (1 \times 200)$). If a student gets a combined or *total* SAT score of 800 (400 on both halves), which is the entrance requirement at many colleges, this score will have below it only 16% of the test-takers in the norming group. If a student gets a combined or *total* SAT score of 700, the percentage of test-takers in the norming group who are below this score will be about 9%.[4]

It can be seen from this example that norm-referencing or comparison or relative scoring can be helpful in test-score interpretation. This helpfulness is based on determining the percentage of students below a given score. There is a specific, norm-referenced score that can be used for this purpose, and it is described next.

Percentile Rank.   This "score," often represented as *%ile rank*, is the percentage of persons in the norming or comparison group scoring lower than or equal to a given person. It can be computed with the following formula[5]:

$$\text{\%ile Rank} = \frac{\text{No. below } (+ \text{ equal to})}{\text{Total no. in norming group}} \times 100$$

---

[2]Linear interpolation along the normal curve is approximate at best because the curve is not a straight line. However, approximations are sufficient for interpretation purposes.

[3]Other standard scores are often referred to as *scaled scores*.

[4]The z-score for a total SAT score of 700 will be -1.5 since 700 is 1½ standard deviations below the mean of 1000, and a z-score of -1.5 exceeds 9% of the scores (or 2% $+ (½ \times 14\%)$).

[5]For large samples, the numerator of the formula usually is "number below $(+ ½$ equal to)," but for calculations on a single class the two formulas yield approximately the same result.

The %ile rank indicates the percentage of people a given student's score exceeds. To determine a student's %ile rank requires either (1) that student's rank or relative position in the comparison group; or (2) all of the scores in the comparison group, to compute that rank via the formula above. The student's rank cannot be used in the formula because rank tells how many scores are above the student's score (by counting down from the top) while the formula uses the number below (by counting up from the bottom). Given rank, the determination of %ile ranks requires first finding the difference between rank and the total number of students (or counting down from the rank to the bottom), to find out the number that are below, and then using the formula.

Remember that the %ile rank and % correct are very different scores. The %ile rank indicates relative standing in comparison to other students, while the % correct reflects absolute test performance in relation to the maximum possible test score. Look at this example:

Raw Score	Rank	%ile	% Correct (out of 20)
18	1	90	90
16	2	80	80
15	3	70	75
14	4.5*	60	70
14	4.5	60	70
13	7.5	40	65
13	7.5	40	65
13	7.5	40	65
13	7.5	40	65
11	10	0	55

*To compute rank for tied scores, average what the ranks would have been for each of the scores had they not been tied.

The table above represents a class of 10 students with raw scores on a 20-item test. Since all the scores are available, we can rank them (but we must correct for ties by using average ranks). A student with a score of 14, for example, has six students below or equal to her (five below plus one equal to). Using the formula results in 6 out of 10, times 100, or the 60th %ile. For % correct, the student got 14 out of 20 (times 100) or was 70% correct. Thus, the percentile rank and the %-correct score can each be calculated.

Percentile Ranks and the Normal Curve.   When it comes to determining percentile ranks on published tests, the above computational procedures cannot be used because the total set of comparison scores (from the norming group) is vast, unavailable, and has already been collected—prior to the commercial use of the test. Instead, norms tables and conversion tables are available and can be used for determining percentile ranks, as shall be seen later in this chapter. Therefore, computation of percentile ranks will be facilitated by use of the normal curve.

The percentages of test-takers under each part of the normal curve and the cumulative percentages as shown in Figure 16.1 have already been referred to. A raw score equal to the mean has already been shown to exceed 50% of all scores in the norming group, while a raw score one standard deviation above the mean has already been shown to exceed 84% of all scores in the norming group. Percentile ranks represent the percentages of people exceeded by a given z-score because a percentile rank is based on the percentage of test-takers below (and equal to) a given score. Thus, if the *z*-score to which a given raw score corresponds is known, then we can determine its percentile rank equivalent either by using the cumulative percentages, which can be calculated, or by looking it up in Figure 16.1. (Figure 16.1 also has a percentile equivalent scale underneath the cumulative percentages.)

It can be seen from the normal curve (in Figure 16.1) that the percentile ranks for the different *z*-scores are as follows:

z	%ile Rank
-3	0
-2	2
-1	14
0	50
$+1$	84
$+2$	98
$+3$	100*

*Technically, 99 is the highest percentile rank. Since the highest person cannot count him- or herself, he or she can only be ahead of 99 out of 100. Also, percentile ranks are rounded down to the nearest whole number.

For *z*-scores that fall in between whole numbers, we can use interpolation to approximate percentile rank equivalent. (For example, a *z*-score of $+1.5$ would be about halfway between 84 and 98 or about 91.) Thus, given a *z*-score, we can determine its percentile rank equivalent (and, given a %ile rank, can determine the equivalent *z*-score).

Stanine Score.   A stanine score is a single-digit standard score with a mean of 5 and a standard deviation of 2. Actually, a stanine is a band into which a number or range of scores fall (see the row marked "Stanines," third from the bottom, in Figure 16.1). There are only nine stanines, and each band covers an equal "distance" under the normal curve—except for stanines 1 and 9, which are open-ended.

On most published tests, stanine scores are reported because of their ease of interpretation. Students scoring at the average level will end up in stanine 5, while those one standard deviation above the mean will have a stanine score of 7, and one standard deviation below the mean a stanine score of 3. The fact that there are only nine possible scores, spread out equally across the normal curve, gives the stanine score its easy interpretability.

Stanines and Percentile Ranks.   It has already been shown how we can convert *z*-scores to percentile ranks using the normal curve. It is also possible to convert stanine scores to percentile ranks using the normal curve. The percentages of test-takers falling into each stanine are listed in the second column of Table 16.1. (Notice that these percentages are completely symmetrical and have been "rounded" to be multiples of 4 in the following pattern: 4, 8, 12, 16, 20, 16, 12, 8, 4.) From these percentages, the range of percentile ranks of each stanine can be determined (shown in the fourth column of Table 16.1) as well as the percentile rank equivalent of the point at which each stanine band begins and each stanine band ends (shown in the third column of Table 16.1). This can be done because percentages of scores below a given score represent percentile ranks and percentages are cumulative as they proceed along the normal curve.

Table 16.1 🍎 Stanine–Percentile Rank Conversion Table

Stanine	Approx. % of Ranked Raw Scores	%ile Rank Equivalents	%ile Rank Range
9	4		96–99
		99	
		96	
8	8*		88–95
		88	
7	12		76–87
		76	
6	16*		60–75
		60	
5	20		40–59
		40	
4	16*		24–39
		24	
3	12		12–23
		12	
2	8*		4–11
		4	
1	4		0–3
		0	

*Note that these numbers are slightly different from those in Figure 16.1. They have been adjusted here to make them easier to remember.

Let's start with stanine 1, which contains 4% of the norming group. The lowest person in the first stanine will have a percentile equivalent of 0, while the upper limit of the first stanine (which is also the lower limit of the second stanine) will have a percentile equivalent of 4. It is customary to assign the person at the upper limit of one stanine band and the lower limit of the next highest stanine band to the higher one, so the fourth percentile will begin the second stanine, which includes 8% of the test-takers. Adding 8 to 4 (4 being the lowest percentile in stanine 2) gives 12, meaning that the twelfth percentile will be the dividing line between stanines 2 and 3. Thus, stanine 2 will range from 4th %ile to 11th %ile and stanine 3 will begin with 12th %ile. Add 12, the percent of test-takers in stanine 3, to this to get the upper limit of stanine 3 and the lower limit of stanine 4 — which will be 24 (4 + 8 + 12). Similarly, by adding or accumulating each additional percent of test-takers in each subsequent stanine band, we can compute the percentile limits and ranges for each stanine band (as shown in Table 16.1).

Grade-Equivalent Scores.   These scores, sometimes labeled GES, are computed only for published tests based on the results of the norming group. The GES of a given raw score represents the *average grade level of all students in the norming group who obtained the same raw score as the given raw score*. It is reported in school years and months, with the school year divided into 10 months. Hence, a GES of 6.5 would represent a test score equal to the average sixth-grader after he has completed five months (or half) of the sixth grade. Since teachers do not have data from the norming group, they cannot compute the GES; they must rely on tables and reports supplied by the testing company.

Grade-equivalent scores were invented to aid teachers and parents in interpreting published test scores, but they may produce misinterpretation because *they cannot always be taken literally*. Since it is impossible to cover all the material to be learned in all grades in one test, the testing companies have created separate tests, usually for every pair of grade levels. Therefore, first- and second-graders might take one test and third- and fourth-graders another. Students at each grade level would take a test covering the work at their grade level and an adjacent grade level, and only students at their grade level and the adjacent grade level would take the same test.

Students who score very high or very low on the test (plus or minus two or more standard deviations) may not have any counterparts in the norming group who scored as high (or as low), so a literal grade-equivalent score cannot be computed. In these cases, the testing companies extrapolate by going farther up or down on the grade scale to compute a GES. Hence, a third-grader could conceivably be given a GES of 6.5 on mathematics or a sixth-grader a GES of 9.2 on language arts. This does not necessarily mean that the third-grader can do sixth-grade work in mathematics or that the sixth-grader can do ninth-grade work in language arts, because (1) neither level of work was included on the test they took and (2) few, if any, students at those higher grade levels took the same test they did.

Therefore, teachers should interpret the GES in a literal fashion only for the grade-level range that the test covers. Above or below that grade range, the actual GES number should be interpreted with caution.

Standardized Tests

Before we go into examples of score conversion and interpretation, techniques that are commonly used on standardized tests, it would be helpful to look at what standardized tests are and to identify their principal characteristics. Standardized tests are published tests, used nationwide, that teachers administer and for which they receive the results. Later on in this chapter, score reports from some of these tests will be presented and their interpretation will be described. First, the features of standardized tests are listed below.

1. *They are mostly achievement tests*. Except for an occasional intelligence or mental ability test, these are tests that are intended to measure what students have learned in school as a result of instruction. They are designed to measure achievement based on what students are expected to learn.

2. *Their content does not fit the curriculum perfectly*. Since standardized tests are given across many school districts, nationwide, and are often administered in October or May of the school year, their content cannot, in every instance, fit the curriculum as closely as teachers' own tests do. Standardized tests must be designed to fit a fictitious or ideal national curriculum (often based on textbooks) and so will overlap individual curricula somewhat but not perfectly (Freeman et al., 1983). To use a term

introduced in the last chapter, it would be appropriate to say that these tests are *less valid* than teacher-built tests.

3. *Their items have been tested and refined.* Beside being written by professional item-writers, the items on standardized tests have been tried out, the results have been subjected to item analysis (as described in the previous chapter), and the tests have been revised when necessary. As a result of this process, these tests have *higher reliability* than teacher-built tests. In fact, their reliabilities are almost always between 0.90 and 0.97 (out of a possible 1.00). Hence, these tests are accurate and consistent, and their results closely fit the normal curve.

4. *Their instructions for administration are formalized.* The way these tests are given is as standardized as the tests themselves (another reason they are called "standardized" tests), so that teachers all over the country are required to administer them the same way. Instructions for administration are written out in detail.

5. *They are accompanied by national norms for score interpretation.* As described earlier in this chapter, before being made commercially available, these tests are typically administered to a large, national sample of students, broadly representative of the population, who serve as a norming group. The test-builders convert the raw scores to norm-referenced scores by using these norming groups for comparison purposes. (Local norms are also often provided for comparison purposes.) These tests are typically scored by the testing companies and the results are provided on forms or printouts (to be described later). Manuals are also available containing norms tables that can be used for purposes of score conversion and interpretation, based on the results of the norming group. A sample norms table is shown in Table 16.2.

The results that test companies provide will be discussed further, but first the score conversion and interpretation process itself will be described.

Teachers can use test score results to identify those students who may need some extra help to overcome deficiencies in basic skills.

Table 16.2 🍎 An Excerpt of a Norms Table from the Metropolitan Achievement Tests*

TOTAL READING

RS	PR	S	GE	SS	RS	PR	S	GE	SS
105	99	9	PHS	734	52	22	3	1.9	529
104	99	9	PHS	711	51	20	3	1.9	527
103	99	9	9.7	686	50	20	3	1.9	526
102	99	9	8.0	671	49	19	3	1.9	524
101	98	9	7.2	660	48	17	3	1.8	522
100	97	9	6.8	652	47	17	3	1.8	521
99	96	9	6.1	644	46	16	3	1.8	519
98	95	8	5.8	638	45	15	3	1.8	518
97	93	8	5.6	633	44	14	3	1.8	516
96	92	8	5.2	628	43	13	3	1.7	514
95	90	8	4.9	623	42	13	3	1.7	513
94	88	7	4.8	619	41	12	3	1.7	511
93	86	7	4.6	615	40	11	3	1.7	509
92	85	7	4.4	612	39	11	3	1.7	508
91	83	7	4.1	608	38	10	2	1.7	506
90	81	7	3.9	605	37	9	2	1.6	504
89	79	7	3.7	602	36	8	2	1.6	502
88	77	7	3.6	599	35	8	2	1.6	501
87	76	6	3.5	597	34	7	2	1.6	499
86	74	6	3.4	594	33	7	2	1.6	497
85	72	6	3.3	591	32	6	2	1.5	495
84	70	6	3.2	589	31	6	2	1.5	493
83	68	6	3.1	586	30	5	2	1.5	491
82	66	6	3.1	584	29	5	2	1.5	490
81	65	6	3.0	582	28	4	2	1.5	488
80	62	6	3.0	579	27	4	2	1.5	486
79	60	6	2.9	577	26	4	2	1.4	484
78	59	5	2.9	575	25	3	1	1.4	481
77	57	5	2.9	573	24	3	1	1.4	479
76	55	5	2.8	571	23	3	1	1.4	477
75	54	5	2.8	569	22	2	1	1.4	475
74	52	5	2.7	567	21	2	1	1.3	473
73	50	5	2.7	565	20	2	1	1.3	470
72	48	5	2.6	563	19	2	1	1.3	468
71	47	5	2.6	561	18	1	1	1.3	465
70	45	5	2.5	559	17	1	1	1.2	463
69	44	5	2.5	558	16	1	1	1.2	460
68	42	5	2.4	556	15	1	1	1.2	457
67	41	5	2.4	554	14	1	1	1.1	454
66	39	4	2.3	552	13	1	1	1.1	451
65	38	4	2.3	551	12	1	1	1.1	447
64	36	4	2.2	549	11	1	1	1.0	443
63	35	4	2.2	547	10	1	1	K.9	439
62	33	4	2.1	545	9	1	1	K.8	435

*Primary 2 (Spring) — Form L Raw Scores (RS) and Equivalent Percentile Ranks (PR), Stanines (S), Grade Equivalents (GE), and Standard Scores (SS). Note that raw scores of 53–61 and 1–9 have been omitted from the full table.

SOURCE: The Psychological Corporation, 1986.

An Example of Converting and Interpreting Scores[6]

The Class.   Consider a fictitious group of four standardized tests with the characteristics listed below. (The population referred to is the norming group, used for comparison purposes.)

Standardized Tests

		IQ	MATH	SCI	LANG
Given:	Population Mean	100	500	100	50
Given:	Population Stand. Dev.	15	100	10	10

Assume that these tests were administered to a class of 20 students ($N = 20$) with the following class results:

	IQ	MATH	SCI	LANG
Given: Class Mean	100	550	100	45
Computed: Class z-Score	0	+0.5	0	−0.5

A class interpretation obtained by computing the class z-score as shown above reveals that the class is average in both intelligence and science achievement since the class mean and population or norming group mean are the same on both these tests. In math, the class is doing quite well (one-half a standard deviation above the population mean or better than about two-thirds of the norming group), while in language the class is doing quite poorly (one-half a standard deviation below the population mean or better than only about one-third of the norming group). After seeing these results, the teacher may be inclined to increase the time spent teaching language arts and decrease the time spent teaching mathematics.

Consider the scores on four more tests, this time teacher-made tests, for the same class of 20.

Teacher-Made Tests

	HIST	MATH	ENG	PE
Given: Maximum Score	100	50	50	100
Given: Class Mean	70	25	40	90
Computed: Class % Correct	70%	50%	80%	90%

The %-correct score, a criterion-referenced score, has been computed for the class's performance on each test. Since it is already known that the class is good in math and poor in language arts, an examination of class performance on the four tests leads to the

---

[6]The author is indebted to Harold J. Fletcher for providing this example.

conclusion that the math test was very hard and the English test fairly easy. As for the PE test, it was either very easy or the class is very good in PE.

Three Students.   We will continue this example of score interpretation by looking at how three students in the class (Bill, Dora, and Tanya) did on these eight tests and then interpreting the results. These students' raw scores (X) are given below.

| | | **Standardized Tests** | | | | | **Teacher-Made Tests** | | | |
		IQ	*MATH*	*SCI*	*LANG*		*HIST*	*MATH*	*ENG*	*PE*
Bill	X	115	300	82	40	X	20	15	40	85
						Rank	20	20	10	17
Dora	X	105	600	112	64	X	80	35	45	95
						Rank	3	2	1	1
Tanya	X	100	500	102	51	X	79	33	44	94
						Rank	4	3	2	2

For the teacher-made tests, rank in class is given in addition to raw score.

To interpret these scores, we'll start with the first student, Bill, and convert his raw scores on the standardized tests to three norm-referenced scores (z-score, percentile rank, and stanine) using the z-score formula (on page 430) and the conversion information in Figure 16.1, in Table 16.1, and in the section on percentiles and the normal curve (pages 432–433). Remember that the mean and standard deviation for the population or norming group above have already been given (see page 438). Then we convert his individual ranks on the four teacher-made tests into percentile ranks (using the formula on page 431) and convert the raw scores into %-correct scores (using the formula on page 426 and the maximum scores given above). These calculations yield the following results:

| | **Standardized Tests** | | | | | **Teacher-Made Tests** | | | |
	IQ	*MATH*	*SCI*	*LANG*		*HIST*	*MATH*	*ENG*	*PE*
X	115	300	82	40	X	20	15	40	85
z	+1.0	−2.0	−1.8	−1.0	rank	20	20	10	17*
%ile	84	2	4	16	%ile	0	0	50	15
stanine	7	1	2	3	% cor	20	30	80	85

*To compute %ile rank given class rank, determine how many students are below or behind the given student. Since class rank tells how many are ahead, the student's rank must be subtracted from the number of students in the class (in this case 20) to get the number below or behind (3). Then divide 3 by 20 and multiply by 100.

Clearly, Bill could be called a classic *underachiever*, since his high intelligence (IQ) score of 115 would lead his teacher to expect him to do much better in school. Bill's IQ exceeds 84% of the norming group, but his achievement on the standardized tests in math, science, and language exceeds only 2%, 4%, and 16%, respectively, of the norming-group members.

How well did Bill do on the teacher's tests? The pattern is consistent on all—except, perhaps, the PE test, which may reflect Bill's greater interest in PE or the fact that it may have been a test of physical skill. Thus, Bill is not doing as well on school tests as his teacher might have expected. His teacher may want to talk to Bill and his parents to see if anything can be done to bring his school performance (as reflected on published

Box 16.1

Data from Seven Sixth-Grade Students Tested in Mid-Year*

Standardized Tests

TEST 1 = Intelligence test with Mean = 100 and sd = 15; raw score given
TEST 2 = test of Mathematics Achievement; percentile rank given
TEST 3 = test of Language Achievement; stanine score given
TEST 4 = test of Science Achievement; Grade Equivalent Score given

Teacher-Made Tests (different teacher for each course and test)

TEST 5 = Math, 20 division problems; score (number correct) and grade given
TEST 6 = English essay, 1 question read and assigned score ranging from 1 (low) to 10 (high); score and grade given
TEST 7 = PE test, students given 3 chances to perform each of 10 exercises as demonstrated; number successfully passed and grade given

Student	Test 1 IQ	Test 2 MATH	Test 3 LANG	Test 4 SCI	Test 5 MATH	Test 6 ENG	Test 7 PE
1	140	52	5	6.7	14/C	6/C	8/B
2	102	51	5	6.6	14/C	6/C	10/A
3	104	54	5	6.4	18/A	9/A	4/D
4	115	84	4	6.2	16/B	6/C	8/B
5	130	96	3	7.8	19/A	3/D	10/A
6	120	90	6	9.6	17/B	8/B	7/C
7	140	85	7	8.4	19/A	10/A	10/A

1. The academic achievement of which student is as predicted?

2. After seeing the GES, parents of student 6 request that he be transferred to the ninth-grade science class. How do you respond?

3. Which student appears to be an "overachiever" who works very hard for course grades?

4. The parents of student 7 ask you to tell them what the Language stanine score of 7 means in terms of relative achievement. What do you say?

5. Which student appears to be an "underachiever"?

6. Which student apparently has a learning problem in one academic area?

7. On the basis of IQ scores, can you predict better academic achievement of student 3 relative to student 2?

8. The IQ score of student 4 is equivalent to a z-score of _____.

9. The IQ score of student 5 is equivalent to a percentile score of _____.

10. The IQ score of student 6 is approximately equal to which of the following percentile scores? 80, 85, 90, 95

---

*The author is indebted to Harold J. Fletcher for providing this material. Answers to questions 1–10 are given in footnote 7 on page 442.

achievement tests and teacher tests) up to a level more consistent with his mental ability as reflected by his high IQ.

Doing the same computations for the second student, Dora, produces the results shown below.

	Standardized Tests					Teacher-Made Tests			
	IQ	*MATH*	*SCI*	*LANG*		*HIST*	*MATH*	*ENG*	*PE*
X	105	600	112	64	X	80	35	45	95
z	+ .33	+ 1.0	+ 1.2	+ 1.4	rank	3	2	1	1
%ile	62	84	88	92	%ile	85	90	95	95
stanine	6	7	7	8	% cor	80	70	90	95

Dora might be called an *overachiever* based on her pattern of test results. On both standardized achievement tests and class tests, Dora achieves levels that exceed what might be expected of her on the basis of her slightly above-average IQ score (62nd %ile rank). Her only "low" score was the 70% correct on the teacher's math test, but this was a difficult test (its class mean percent correct was only 50%). Moreover, on a relative basis, even her math score was high (ranking at 90th %ile). Dora is apparently a motivated student and the results of her effort are good.

The last student for whom there are data, Tanya, is represented below.

	Standardized Tests					Teacher-Made Tests			
	IQ	*MATH*	*SCI*	*LANG*		*HIST*	*MATH*	*ENG*	*PE*
X	100	500	102	51	X	79	33	44	94
z	0	0	+ 0.2	+ 0.1	rank	4	3	2	2
%ile	50	50	58	54	%ile	80	85	90	90
stanine	5	5	5	5	% cor	79	66	88	94

Tanya displays a pattern of results quite different from either Bill or Dora. Like Dora, Tanya has only an average IQ; unlike Dora, she does very average work on the standardized achievement tests, as one might expect from her IQ score. However, in her class work, Tanya does well (from the 80th to the 90th %ile rank) — almost as well as Dora. Tanya is getting high grades but, unlike Dora, she is not getting similar results on her standardized tests.

Two hunches or hypotheses may be offered to explain Tanya's performance on this battery of tests, specifically the discrepancy between her high scores on the classroom tests and her low scores on the standardized tests. One hunch is that in class she is learning only enough to get good grades, and she does not really understand or retain information or skills. That is why she does so poorly on the broader, more comprehensive standardized tests. An alternative hunch is that Tanya has test anxiety and generally does poorly on standardized tests. If the second hunch is right, then even her IQ test score would be an underestimate of her mental ability. Based on these test results, it is impossible to tell which hunch is correct. The teacher would have to bring in other evidence about Tanya's performance and talk to Tanya about her work and her feelings to decide which hunch, if either, is correct.

Standardized tests are administered in the same, standardized way every time and everywhere they are given. The results will help teachers diagnose student deficiencies.

Test scores, like those for the three students in this example, can give teachers a lot of information if they know how to interpret them. Of course, even test scores do not provide all the answers about a student's performance and the reasons behind it. Test patterns, however, often do provide clues about how to help students improve their school performance.

Try to answer the questions in Box 16.1 by interpreting the test scores given for seven students.

[7]Answers to questions in Box 16.1:

1. Student 2 is average in IQ and average on everything else (except PE — which cannot be predicted by IQ). Student 7 is close to performing as predicted but should have done even better on the standardized achievement tests.
2. No! Do not take GES literally. Student 6's science test did not measure ninth-grade work and was not taken by ninth-graders.
3. Student 3 has an average IQ but does A work in academic courses (tests 5 and 6).
4. Tell them their child did better than about 82% of the other students.
5. Student 1 has a very high IQ and does average work on all academic achievement tests.
6. Student 5 does well on everything but English/Language.
7. No! The small difference is well within the test's error range.
8. $+1.0$ (it is one standard deviation above the mean).
9. 98 (two standard deviations above the mean is above 98% of test-takers).
10. 90 ($z = 1.3$ is above about 89% of test-takers).

Interpreting Standardized Test Scoring Reports

Standardized or published test results are provided to students, parents, and teachers in the form of scoring reports. These scoring reports contain the kinds of scores that have already been described with little or no conversion required by the teacher. It will be useful to see examples of these reports and to examine the information they contain and the interpretations that can be made from this information.

Individual Student Score Reports.   Two sample individual score reports for the same student are presented in Figures 16.2 and 16.3. Both reports cover the same tests and subtests. The simpler report, shown as Figure 16.2, provides percentile ranks and stanine scores for each subtest in the test battery as well as for mental ability (or intelligence), represented by the last test entry in the list. In addition, this report includes national percentile bands that indicate the range within which each test score falls. Such bands are appropriate since test scores are not exact. Hence, individual test scores may more properly be considered to fall within a band of possible scores. (This is already true for the stanine score, which is itself a band.)

An examination of the results shown in Figure 16.2 for the fictitious student Charles Ballard, a fourth-grader, reveals that his weakest areas are (l) the concepts of number and (2) science; his greatest strengths are (l) social science and (2) using information. In all other areas he is average, despite having a percentile rank of 82 in mental ability.

Figure 16.3 provides an elaboration of the information on Charles Ballard, beyond what was shown in Figure 16.2. In Figure 16.3 his raw scores, scaled scores, and grade-equivalent scores can also be seen for each subtest. In addition, the report in Figure 16.3 explicitly compares his scores on each test and what might be expected based on his ability.

Of particular interest is the information conveyed in the bottom half of the form in Figure 16.3. This is a combination of a criterion-referenced report (raw score/number of items) and a norm-referenced report (below, at, or above average) for each specific skill test in the achievement test battery. From these results, his teacher can see exactly what skills this student needs help to master: the ones that are checked in the "below average" column.

The combination of criterion-referenced and norm-referenced results on a skill-by-skill basis, shown in the score report in Figure 16.3, provides teachers with information they can use for diagnostic and prescriptive purposes. Not just a set of numbers, this kind of report gives teachers the information necessary to decide what additional help, if any, each individual student may need.

Class Score Reports.   Also available to teachers are score reports for the entire class, such as the one shown in Figure 16.4. This class score report is the same as the individual report shown in Figure 16.3, but the data represent the average or distribution of scores of all the students in the class rather than of just one student. It can be seen that Ms. Wellen's fourth-grade class (actually 4.2, because they were tested in October) has done very poorly in science and concepts of number, just as the individual student, Charles Ballard, did (his data were shown in Figure 16.2). A possible conclusion is that the second- and third-grade teachers in Ms. Wellen's school have not spent enough time in these two areas. Perhaps they need to be emphasized more in the school's curriculum.

Figure 16.2 🍎 Individual Pupil Profile Report on the Stanford Achievement Test From The Psychological Corporation, 1982.

Stanford ACHIEVEMENT TEST
WITH OTIS-LENNON SCHOOL ABILITY TEST

PUPIL PROFILE
CHARLES A BALLARD

TEACHER MS WELLENS
SCHOOL LAKESIDE ELEMENTARY
SYSTEM NEWTOWN PUBLIC SCHOOLS

GRADE 4
TEST DATE 10 12 82
STANFORD NORMS GR 4 1
OLSAT NORMS GR 4 FALL

NATIONAL PERCENTILE BANDS

TESTS	NATIONAL PR	S
WORD STUDY SKILLS 	50	5
READING COMPREHENSION	50	5
VOCABULARY	52	5
LISTENING COMPREHENSION	44	5
SPELLING	40	5
LANGUAGE	60	6
CONCEPTS OF NUMBER	32	4
MATH COMPUTATION	50	5
MATH APPLICATIONS	50	5
SOCIAL SCIENCE	82	7
SCIENCE	34	4
USING INFORMATION	77	7
TOTAL READING	50	5
TOTAL LISTENING	48	5
TOTAL LANGUAGE	52	5
TOTAL MATHEMATICS	44	5
OTIS-LENNON SCHOOL ABILITY TEST	82	7

BELOW AVERAGE 1 5 10 20
AVERAGE 30 40 50 60 70
ABOVE AVERAGE 80 90 95 99

1 5 10 20 30 40 50 60 70 80 90 95 99
BELOW AVERAGE AVERAGE ABOVE AVERAGE

D. HOW TO INTERPRET THESE SCORES

The report above shows the Percentile Rank (PR) and Stanine (S) scores this student obtained on the Stanford Achievement Test

Stanine scores range from a low of 1 to a high of 9 Stanines 4, 5, and 6 are considered average. Stanines 1, 2, and 3 below average, and Stanines 7, 8, and 9 above average.

Percentile Ranks range from a low of 1 to a high of 99. If a student has a Percentile Rank of 70, for example, it means that this student obtained a score that is higher than 70 percent of the students in the comparison group

The group with which the student is compared is shown in the heading "National" means that the student is compared with a nationally representative sample of students in the same grade

The Percentile Bands to the right show that scores are approximate indicators of achievement By comparing the bands you can see whether the student did better in some subjects than in others If two bands do not overlap, you may conclude that the difference between those two scores is indeed meaningful

The skills measured by each of the tests are described on the back

LEVEL FORM-PRIM 3 E OLSAT LEVEL FORM-ELEM S COPY 1

DATA SERVICES DIVISION   THE PSYCHOLOGICAL CORPORATION
HARCOURT BRACE JOVANOVICH PUBLISHERS

Figure 16.3 🍎 Individual Skill Analysis Scoring Report on the Stanford Achievement Test From The Psychological Corporation, 1982.

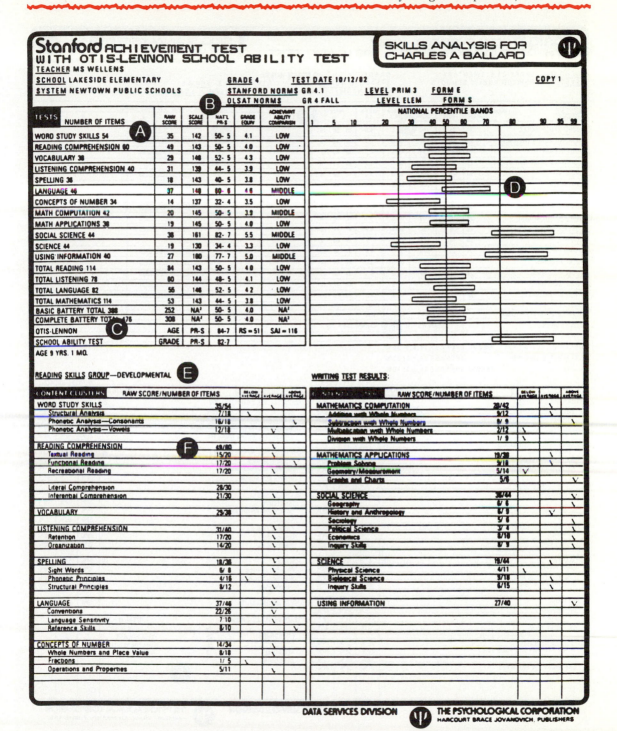

Stanford ACHIEVEMENT TEST WITH OTIS-LENNON SCHOOL ABILITY TEST

SKILLS ANALYSIS FOR MS WELLENS

SCHOOL SYSTEM: LAKESIDE ELEMENTARY, NEWTON PUBLIC SCHOOLS
GRADE 4 TEST DATE 10/12/82
STANFORD NORMS GR 4 1 LEVEL PRIM 3 FORM E
OLSAT NORMS GR 4 FALL LEVEL ELEM FORM S
COPY 1

TESTS	NUMBER TESTED FOR AAC	MEAN RAW SCORE	MEAN SCALE SCORE	NAT'L GROUP PR-S	GE OF MEAN SS	AAC PERCENT L M H
WORD STUDY SKILLS	28	34	140	5	4.0	40 50 10
READING COMPREHENSION	28	47	137	46-5	3.7	36 46 18
VOCABULARY	28	26	135	48-5	4.2	38 40 22
LISTENING COMPREHENSION	28	30	140	38-4	3.7	30 62 8
SPELLING	28	20	141	42-5	3.5	42 50 8
LANGUAGE	28	35	145	56-5	4.4	44 44 12
CONCEPTS OF NUMBER	28	13	130	28-4	3.3	48 30 22
MATH COMPUTATION	28	19	142	48-5	3.6	46 36 18
MATH APPLICATIONS	28	18	140	44-5	4.1	42 40 18
SOCIAL SCIENCE	28	26	150	54-5	4.4	31 41 28
SCIENCE	28	18	127	26-4	3.1	38 60 2
USING INFORMATION	28	29	135	52-5	4.4	37 40 23
TOTAL READING	28	81	140	46-5	3.9	38 48 14
TOTAL LISTENING	28	56	142	48-5	4.1	30 50 20
TOTAL LANGUAGE	28	63	145	52-5	4.0	43 47 11
TOTAL MATHEMATICS	28	51	140	42-5	3.8	45 36 20
BASIC BATTERY TOTAL	242	NA²	NA²	NA²	NA²	
COMPLETE BATTERY TOTAL	286	NA²	NA²	NA²	NA²	

NATIONAL GROUP STANINE BANDS 1 2 3 4 5 6 7 8 9

OTIS-LENNON MEAN RS = 46 MEAN SAI = 107
SCHOOL ABILITY TEST N = 28

OLSAT GRADE NORM STANINE SUMMARY N = 28
ABOVE AVERAGE (7,8,9) 30%
AVERAGE (4,5,6) 52%
BELOW AVERAGE (1,2,3) 18%

CONTENT CLUSTERS	NUMBER TESTED	BELOW AVG RANGE	AVG RANGE	ABOVE AVG RANGE
WORD STUDY SKILLS	28	21%	44%	35%
Structural Analysis		40%	40%	20%
Phonetic Analysis—Consonants		7%	40%	53%
Phonetic Analysis—Vowels		17%	52%	31%
READING COMPREHENSION	28	21%	50%	28%
Textual Reading		23%	54%	23%
Functional Reading		12%	48%	40%
Recreational Reading		18%	44%	38%
Literal Comprehension		19%	50%	31%
Inferential Comprehension		32%	52%	16%
VOCABULARY	28	20%	56%	24%
LISTENING COMPREHENSION	28	8%	68%	24%
Retention		4%	58%	38%
Organization		12%	78%	10%
SPELLING	28	23%	61%	16%
Sight Words		10%	60%	30%
Phonetic Principles		28%	62%	10%
Structural Principles		30%	62%	8%
LANGUAGE	28	18%	57%	25%
Conventions		7%	64%	29%
Language Sensitivity		32%	52%	16%
Reference Skills		15%	55%	30%
CONCEPTS OF NUMBER	28	26%	55%	19%
Whole Numbers and Place Value		22%	58%	20%
Fractions		34%	58%	8%
Operations and Properties		21%	50%	29%

CONTENT CLUSTERS	NUMBER TESTED	BELOW AVG RANGE	AVG RANGE	ABOVE AVG RANGE
MATHEMATICS COMPUTATION	28	23%	51%	26%
Addition with Whole Numbers		23%	51%	26%
Subtraction with Whole Numbers		23%	54%	23%
Multiplication with Whole Numbers		25%	48%	27%
Division with Whole Numbers		21%	52%	27%
MATHEMATICS APPLICATIONS	28	12%	65%	23%
Problem Solving		18%	60%	22%
Geometry/Measurement		10%	65%	25%
Graphs and Charts		8%	71%	21%
SOCIAL SCIENCE	28	22%	56%	22%
Geography		32%	60%	8%
History and Anthropology		24%	55%	21%
Sociology		20%	60%	20%
Political Science		22%	58%	20%
Economics		16%	56%	28%
Inquiry Skills		18%	52%	30%
SCIENCE	28	27%	59%	14%
Physical Science		30%	62%	8%
Biological Science		28%	60%	12%
Inquiry Skills		24%	54%	22%
USING INFORMATION		19%	55%	26%

READING SKILLS GROUPS TOTAL N = 28

	N	%		N	%
ENRICHMENT	7	25	VOCABULARY	2	7
DEVELOPMENTAL	14	50	COMPREHENSION	3	11
REMEDIAL	0	0	INCOMPLETE	0	0
DECODING	2	7			

DATA SERVICES DIVISION

THE PSYCHOLOGICAL CORPORATION
HARCOURT BRACE JOVANOVICH PUBLISHERS

Based on these results, Ms. Wellen may be inclined to spend more of her mathematics teaching time on concepts (class GES of 3.3) and computations (class GES of 3.6) and less on applications (class GES of 4.1). The most specific class weakness in mathematics, as revealed by the content area cluster report on the bottom half of the form, is in fractions, where 34% of the class scored below average. (Compare this to "Graphs and Charts," where only 8% scored below average.) It is possible that, in this school district, the topic of fractions is taught later in the fourth-grade year. If so, and if the testing had been done later, it might have reflected greater class competence in fractions.

Another suggestion for Ms. Wellen based on the results in Figure 16.4 would be to spend more time teaching science (class GES of 3.1) and less time teaching social science (class GES of 4.4). This may result in her class performing up to grade level in science.

Class reports, such as the one illustrated in Figure 16.4, can provide teachers with useful information to guide their overall teaching strategy and dictate the amount of time they allocate to different subject areas, sub-areas, and specific content clusters or skills within areas. Knowing that a class is performing far below grade in a specific area, especially if instruction in that area has already been provided, tells a teacher that more instructional effort must be directed to that area during the ensuing school year. The more detailed or specific the information, the easier it will be for the teacher to know exactly which skill to focus the extra instruction on. Class performance on specific content clusters relative to a national sample, as shown in the bottom half of the score report in Figure 16.4, represents specific information that can be used for this purpose.

Grading

There are more ways than one to assign grades based on test performance. These are described, and compared, below.

Absolute Grading.   If a teacher wants to use criterion-referenced grading, he or she should decide what percentage of items on a given test a student needs to get right to earn an A, what percentage to earn a B, a C, and so forth. Arbitrary judgments are sometimes necessary to set these criteria. (A sample scale was shown on page 427, with a %-correct score in the 90's an A, in the 80's a B, in the 70's a C, between 65 and 69 a D, and below 65 an F. Alternatively, a numerical grade system, as opposed to a "letter" grade system, simply reports the %-correct score as the grade.)

Preset scoring, however, can greatly misrepresent student competence when the test being used is too easy or too hard. An alternative procedure is described below.

Grading "On the Curve."   The curve referred to is the normal curve (shown in Figure 16.1). Grading on it means assigning some proportion of the students each letter grade based on the *relative* position of their score on the test. On the normal curve, the most frequently occurring grades would be the ones in the middle — B and C; the more extreme grades — A, D, and F — would occur less frequently since on the normal curve extreme scores are much less frequent than more central or average ones.

One way to fit grades to the normal curve would be to use the scale given below (which has been arbitrarily designed to use whole-number z-scores and yield a symmetrical distribution of grades):

A is any score greater than $z = +1.0$
B is any score greater than $z = 0$ or the mean (and below A)
C is any score greater than $z = -1.0$ (and below B)
D is any score greater than $z = -2.0$ (and below C)
F is any score equal to or below $z = -2.0$

(Each unit of z equals one standard deviation, so to apply this scale we must calculate the mean and standard deviation of a set of test scores.) From the normal curve it can be determined that the above scoring scale would yield the following distribution of scores:

16%   A's
34%   B's
34%   C's
14%   D's
2%   F's

An example of the use of this scale is shown in Box 16.2. Of course, we can move the grade scale either up or down the normal curve (that is, to the left or the right) by using fractional z-scores as cutoff points, thereby increasing or decreasing the percentage of A's, D's, and F's.

One way to approximate the above procedure of grading on the curve, based on the likelihood of any set of test scores being normally distributed, is (1) to compute the actual %-correct score for each student and the actual mean percent correct for the entire class, (2) to choose a predetermined or adjusted class mean that represents the level desired for the class (80% works well), (3) to add to or subtract from each individual actual %-correct score the difference between the actual class mean %-correct score and the adjusted class mean to get an adjusted individual %-correct score, and (4) to use a letter-grade scale like the one on page 427, assigning a letter grade to each student based on his or her %-correct score. For example, if the test was hard and the class mean %-correct score was 70%, add 10% to each individual %-correct score and then use the grading scale on which 90–100% is an A, 80–89% a B, 70–79% a C, 65–69% a D, and 0–64% an F to convert adjusted %-correct scores to letter grades. For numerical scores, just use each %-correct score with the 10% adjustment added on.

There is another way to use a grading scheme based on the actual distribution of scores on a test. (Normally we would expect a large class to produce the same number of A's as D's plus F's, about twice as many B's as A's, and about the same number of C's as B's.) If the grade distribution of %-correct scores is displaced upward because the test was too easy, resulting in a preponderance of high grades, we can adjust the score to 75% or 77% (rather than 80%) by adding to (or subtracting from) each individual %-correct score the difference between the actual class mean %-correct score and 75% (or 77%). The resulting distribution of grades will be an approximate fit to the normal distribution.

Box 16.2

Using the Normal Curve to Assign Grades

Three classes with a combined total of 97 students took a test containing 100 multiple-choice questions, each worth one point. The following descriptive statistics were computed for the raw score distribution:

$$\overline{X} = 78$$

$$sd = 11$$

Based on the above statistics, the following arbitrary grade scale was developed:

$$
\begin{aligned}
A &= 90 - 100 \quad (\text{starts at next score above } \overline{X} + 1 \text{ sd})\\
B &= 78 - 89 \quad (\text{starts at next score above } \overline{X})\\
C &= 68 - 77 \quad (\text{starts at next score above } \overline{X} - 1 \text{ sd})\\
D &= 56 - 67 \quad (\text{starts at next score above } \overline{X} - 2 \text{ sd})\\
F &= 0 - 55 \quad (\text{ends at } \overline{X} - 2 \text{ sd})
\end{aligned}
$$

Below are the actual frequencies of scores for the grades (off somewhat from the predicted frequencies because the mean and standard deviation have been rounded).*

A	13%
B	37%
C	37%
D	9%
F	3%

---

*The above grade scale was specifically chosen to produce this grade distribution. Note that the percentage of A's is about the same as the percentage of D's + F's, and the percentage of A's is about one-third the percentage of B's. Rather than choosing the test to be an absolute indicator of student performance, we chose the grade distribution arbitrarily and then adjusted the grading scale to produce this grade distribution. This is an alternative to criterion-referenced scoring.

Standardizing Scores. Another method to generate norm-referenced numerical scores that correspond to actual raw scores on a test is to standardize them the way testing companies do, by (1) converting every raw score to a z-score and (2) converting z-scores to scaled scores (SS) using the formula SS $= M + S(z)$, where M is a preset mean and S is a preset standard deviation. One scaled score that is sometimes used is the T-score, where M is preset at 50 and S at 10. Another scale, previously described, is the SAT (CEEB) score, where $M = 500$ and $S = 100$ for each half of the test. IQ scores are scaled scores (called deviation IQ's) and have a preset mean of 100 and a standard deviation of 15. All three of these kinds of scores are shown in Figure 16.1.

Two scaled scores that fit the typical academic grading scale rather well are (1) scores for which the mean is preset at 80 and the standard deviation at 10 and (2) scores for which the mean is preset at 78 and the sd at 12 — so that A's are scores in the 90's, B's in the 80's, C's in the 70's, and so on. Call these a *G*-score and a *G*[1]-score, respectively,

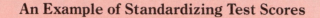

Box 16.3

An Example of Standardizing Test Scores

Below are a set of 30 raw test scores with a mean of 74 and a standard deviation of 14, along with the conversion of these scores into *z*-scores, *G*-scores = $80 + 10(z)$, G^1-scores = $78 + 12(z)$, stanine scores, and percentile ranks. A frequency distribution of these scores is also shown.

Raw Score	*z*-Score	*G*-Score	*G*[1]-Score	Stanine Score	%ile Rank*
99	+1.7	97	98	9	97
97	+1.6	96	97	8	93
95	+1.4	94	95	8	90
92	+1.2	92	92	7	87
90	+1.1	91	91	7	83
88	+1.0	90	90	7	80
85	+0.8	88	88	7	77
83	+0.6	86	85	6	73
82	+0.5	85	84	6	70
80	+0.4	84	83	6	65
80	+0.4	84	83	6	65
79	+0.3	83	82	6	60
76	+0.1	81	79	5	55
76	+0.1	81	79	5	55
75	+0.1	81	79	5	46
75	+0.1	81	79	5	46
75	+0.1	81	79	5	46
74	0	80	78	5	40
72	−0.1	79	77	4	37
70	−0.3	77	74	4	31
70	−0.3	77	74	4	31
68	−0.4	76	73	4	27

*Computed from formula (*not* from normal curve).

with the letter "G" standing for grade. To compute a G-score and a G^1-score, first convert raw scores to z-scores and then convert z-scores to G-scores or G^1-scores using the formulas

$$G = 80 + 10(z)$$

$$G^1 = 78 + 12(z)$$

Raw Score	z-Score	G-Score	G^1-Score	Stanine Score	%ile Rank*
65	−0.6	74	71	4	23
63	−0.8	72	68	3	20
60	−1.0	70	66	3	17
57	−1.2	68	64	3	13
54	−1.4	66	61	3	10
50	−1.6	64	59	2	7
47	−1.8	62	56	2	3
43	−2.1	59	53	1	0

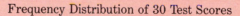

Frequency Distribution of 30 Test Scores

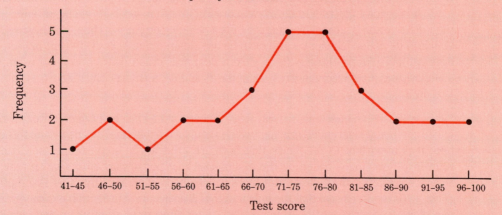

There are many ways to assign test grades, but whichever way a teacher uses, students will always be as interested in the results as these two are.

If necessary, these scores can then be converted into letter grades, as described above.

It is a good practice to plot raw scores before standardizing them, to ensure that their distribution is normal or somewhat fits a bell-shaped curve. Then, the mean (M) and standard deviation (S) can be preset to be any desired numbers. Different preset numbers can be experimented with to yield a desirable grade distribution. An example of standardizing a set of raw scores using the G and G^1 formulas given above is shown in Box 16.3.

Comparing Approaches to Grading.   Faced with a choice between criterion-referenced and norm-referenced grading, which should a teacher use? In answering this question, it is important to recognize that both are arbitrary in some respects. Criterion-referenced grading is based on the assumption that performance on a given test is an accurate reflection of mastery. But there is usually no assurance that this assumption is correct. (It has been said that the only test that is an accurate reflection of mastery is the one given to paratroopers—in which they must jump from an airplane and survive to demonstrate that they have mastered the required skills.) In addition, criterion-referenced grading requires the use of an arbitrary scale to convert numerical scores to letter grades.

Norm-referenced scoring requires that test scores be normally distributed and then generates scores that have meaning on a relative basis only. The teacher is still faced with the arbitrary task of converting numerical scores to letter grades, which requires an arbitrary setting of the curve to determine how many students will receive each grade.

What if most of the students have achieved reasonable mastery of the topics covered in the test? Norm-referenced grading will spread the grades out so that some students will receive low grades. (After all, the curve must have a bottom.) This would be inaccurate. If, however, the test were very hard, criterion-referenced grading would result in some students who had mastered the material receiving low grades. This would be inaccurate.

If a teacher is highly confident that his or her test is an accurate reflection of the criteria for mastery of the topics covered, then criterion-referenced scoring may be used with a sense of assurance of its appropriateness. If a teacher has more confidence in the normal distribution of his or her students on knowledge of the topics covered by the test than in the accuracy or acceptability or difficulty of the test itself, then norm-referenced scores would be the more appropriate choice.

Summary of Main Points

1. Test scores are interpreted to determine what they mean. Actual or *raw* scores on a test cannot be interpreted without reference points or benchmarks that tell how high or low (or good or bad) they are.

2. Benchmarks or criteria for test interpretation can be preset on an absolute basis (such as 90's are A's, 80's B's, 70's C's, and so on) and then raw scores fitted into these ranges. This is called *criterion-referencing* and its principle score is the *percent-correct score*, the raw score divided by the maximum possible score times 100.

3. When preset criteria do not seem appropriate because of uncertainty about a test's difficulty, validity, or reliability, test scores can be interpreted on a relative basis — specifically, relative to one another. This is called *norm-referencing*.

4. The scores to which we compare a given score in order to interpret it are called *norms*, and the groups that generate these scores are called *norming groups*. The distribution of scores of any group tends to approximate a symmetrical, *normal curve* with the preponderance of scores in the middle and a decreasing number toward either end.

5. The basic norm-referenced score is the *z-score*, equal to the difference between the raw score and the mean divided by the standard deviation. In other words, it is a score's distance from the mean in standard deviation units.

6. We can scale z-scores by setting any predesignated mean (M) and standard deviation (S) and using the formula Scaled score $= M + S(z)$. The SAT score uses a preset mean of 500 and an sd of 100 for each half (verbal and quantitative) of its total score.

7. We compute the *percentile rank (%ile)* using either the percentages under the normal curve or the formula Number below and equal to ÷ Total number × 100. This rank indicates the percentage of scores below a given score or the percent of people

behind a given person in the score distribution. We can convert *z*-scores to percentile ranks using the cumulative percentages under the normal curve.

8. The *stanine score* is a one-digit band of scores with a mean of 5 and a standard deviation of 2. There are nine stanines containing, respectively, about 4, 8, 12, 16, 20, 16, 12, 8, and 4 percent of the population. By cumulating these percentages, we can convert stanine scores to percentile ranks.

9. The *grade-equivalent score* (GES) of a given raw score is the average grade level of students in the norming group who obtained the same score as the given one. At the extremes, these scores should not be taken literally because they are computed by extrapolation (since only students in one or two grade levels take each test, and each test covers the work of only those one or two grade levels). Students who score beyond the grade level range of the test, therefore, cannot necessarily do the work at the higher grade level.

10. *Standardized tests* are published tests, usually of achievement, that are given nationwide. Their content does not fit the curriculum of each individual classroom, school, or school district perfectly, so these tests may lack validity for classroom purposes. Because they are tested and refined, though, they are high in reliability. The administrative instructions are formalized and the tests are accompanied by national norms for score interpretation.

11. To interpret a set of test scores, we can convert standardized test results (raw scores) to *z*-scores, percentile ranks, and stanine scores and can convert teacher-made test results to %-correct scores and percentile ranks (the latter requiring data on class rank).

12. To look for a pattern in a class or in an individual compare standardized achievement results and class achievement results to each other and to IQ score. Look at individual subject-matter areas. Try to detect evidence of such things as over- and under-achievement, and try to determine if, and in what area, a specific student needs help based on that student's score pattern.

13. Published tests provide score reports containing a variety of scores for ease of interpretation. *Individual student score reports* usually provide percentile ranks, stanine scores, and scaled scores for each test area and sub-area. Often, more detailed information, such as performance on individual skills, can help teachers pinpoint the weaknesses and strengths of each individual student. Knowledge of deficiencies can serve both a diagnostic and a prescriptive function.

14. *Class score reports* provide the same information as individual reports but are averaged across all students in a class. Just as individual reports help teachers know the skill areas in which specific students need help, class reports help teachers know where they may want to place more or less curricular emphasis in order to capitalize on class strengths and overcome class deficiencies.

15. To assign grades, teachers can use an *absolute preset grading scale*, such as 90% correct and above is an A, 80–89% a B, 70–79% a C, 65–69% a D, and below 65% an F. Such absolute grading requires that tests be suitably criterion-referenced or fitted to absolute standards.

16. Lacking absolute assurance that their tests fit exact criteria for mastery, teachers often choose to *grade "on the curve,"* that curve being the normal curve. One way to

do this is to compute the class mean and standard deviation on the test and then label any score more than 1 sd above the mean an A, any score above the mean and below 1 sd a B, any score above -1 sd but equal to or below the mean a C, any score equal to or below -1 sd but above -2 sd a D, and any score equal to or below -2 sd an F.

17. Alternatively, we can approximate the above grade distribution by computing the class mean %-correct score and then adding to (or subtracting from) every individual %-correct score the difference between the class mean and 80% (or 78% or 75%) to produce a distribution of scores that will fit the grading model of 90+ equals an A, 80+ a B, 70+ a C, 65+ a D, and below 65 an F.

18. Finally, teachers can grade numerically by standardizing each individual score using the formula

$$\text{Scaled score} = \text{Preset mean} + \text{Preset sd} \times z\text{-Score}$$

By presetting the mean at either 80 or 78 and presetting the standard deviation at either 10 or 12, we can convert raw scores to z-scores and then to norm-referenced scaled scores that can be either used numerically as they are or converted to letter grades again with a grading scale of 90+ equals an A, 80+ equals a B, and so on.

19. Each type of grading is arbitrary in some respect. When teachers believe their tests to be accurate reflections of mastery of the topics covered, then criterion-referenced grading would be their choice. When they are more confident that their students are normally distributed on their knowledge of the topics covered by the test than they are in the properties of their test, then norm-referenced grading would be their choice.

Suggested Resources

Cronbach, L. J. (1984). *Essentials of psychological testing* (4th ed.). New York: Longman.

Hopkins, K. D., & Stanley, J. C. (1981). *Educational and psychological measurement and evaluation* (6th ed.). Englewood Cliffs, NJ: Prentice-Hall.

Levy, P., & Goldstein, H. (1984). *Tests in education*. Orlando, FL: Academic Press.

Linn, R. L. (1989). *Educational measurement* (3rd ed.). New York: Macmillan.

Mehrens, W. A., & Lehmann, I. J. (1987). *Using standardized tests in education* (4th ed.). New York: Longman.

Tuckman, B. W. (1988). *Testing for teachers* (2nd ed.). San Diego: Harcourt Brace Jovanovich.

Bibliography

Alessandra, T. (1987). *Relationship strategies*. Paper presented at the Fourth Annual Conference on Creative Management in Higher Education, New Orleans.

Ames, C. (1978). Children's achievement attributions and self-reinforcement: Effects of self-concept and competitive reward structure. *Journal of Educational Psychology, 70*, 345–355.

Amidon, E., & Hunter, E. (1966). *Improving teaching: The analysis of classroom verbal interaction*. New York: Holt, Rinehart & Winston.

Anastasi, A. (1982). *Psychological testing* (5th ed.). New York: Macmillan.

Anderson, J. R. (1985). *Cognitive psychology and its implications* (2nd ed.). New York: Freeman.

Anderson, R. (1984). Role of the reader's schema in comprehension, learning and memory. In R. Anderson, J. Osborn, & R. Tierney (Eds.), *Learning to read in American schools: Basal readers and content texts*. Hillsdale, NJ: Lawrence Erlbaum.

Armbruster, B. B., & Anderson, T. H. (1984). Mapping: Representing informative text diagrammatically. In C. D. Holley & D. F. Dansereau (Eds.), *Spatial learning strategies*. Orlando, FL: Academic Press.

Armbruster, B. B. & Brown, A. (1984). Learning from reading: The role of metacognition. In R. Anderson, J. Osborn, & R. Tierney (Eds.), *Learning to read in American schools: Basal readers and content texts*. Hillsdale, NJ: Lawrence Erlbaum.

Asch, S. E. (1952). *Social psychology*. Englewood Cliffs, NJ: Prentice-Hall.

Atkinson, J. W. (1964). *An introduction to motivation*. Princeton, NJ: Van Nostrand.

Ausubel, D. P. (1960). The use of advance organizers in the learning and retention of meaningful verbal material. *Journal of Educational Psychology, 51*, 267–272.

Ausubel, D. P. (1968). *Educational psychology: A cognitive view*. New York: Holt, Rinehart & Winston.

Ausubel, D. P., & Robinson, F. (1969). *School learning: An introduction to educational psychology*. New York: Holt, Rinehart & Winston.

Azrin, N. H., & Holz, W. C. (1966). Punishment. In W. K. Honig (Ed.), *Operant behavior: Areas of research and application* (pp. 380–447). New York: Appleton–Century–Crofts.

Baker, F. (1977). Advances in item analysis. *Review of Educational Research, 47*, 151–178.

Bales, R. F. (1970). *Personality and interpersonal behavior*. New York: Holt, Rinehart & Winston.

Bandura, A. (1969). Social-learning theory of identificatory processes. In D. A. Goslin (Ed.), *Handbook of socialization theory and research* (pp. 213–262). Chicago: Rand-McNally.

Bandura, A. (1977). Self-efficacy: Toward a unifying theory of behavioral change. *Psychological Review, 84*, 191–215.

Bandura, A. (1978). The self system in reciprocal determinism. *American Psychologist, 33*, 344–358.

Bandura, A. (1982). Self-efficacy mechanism in human agency. *American Psychologist, 37*, 122–147.

Bandura, A. (1983). Self-efficacy determinants of anticipated fears and calamities. *Journal of Personality and Social Psychology, 45*, 464–469.

Bandura, A. (1986). *Social foundations of thought and action*. Englewood Cliffs, NJ: Prentice-Hall.

Bandura, A., & Cervone, D. (1983). Self-evaluative and self-efficacy mechanism governing the motivational effects of goal systems. *Journal of Personality and Social Psychology, 45,* 1017–1028.

Bandura, A., & Jeffrey, R. W. (1973). Role of symbolic coding and rehearsal processes in observational learning. *Journal of Personality and Social Psychology, 26,* 122–130.

Bangert, R., Kulik, J. A., & Kulik, C. C. (1983). Individualized systems of instruction in secondary schools. *Review of Educational Research, 53,* 143–158.

Barrios, B. A. (1983). The role of cognitive mediators in heterosocial anxiety: A test of self-efficacy theory. *Cognitive Therapy and Research, 7,* 543–554.

Barrios, F. X., & Niehaus, J. C. (1985). The influence of smoker status, smoking history, sex, and situational variables on smokers' self-efficacy. *Addictive Behaviors, 24,* 13–19.

Becker, W. C. (1986). *Applied psychology for teachers: A behavioral cognitive approach.* Chicago: Science Research Associates.

Becker, W. C., Engelmann, S., & Thomas, D. R. (1975). *Teaching 1: Classroom management.* Chicago: Science Research Associates.

Bell-Gredler, M. E. (1986). *Learning and instruction: Theory into practice.* New York: Macmillan.

Binet, A. (1916). *The development of intelligence in children* (E. S. Kite, Trans.). Baltimore: Warwick & York.

Binet, A., & Simon, T. (1908). Le developpment de l'intelligence chez les infants. *L'Année Psychologique, 14,* 1–94.

Blitz, B. (1973). *The open classroom: Making it work.* Boston: Allyn & Bacon.

Bloom, B. S. (1956). *Taxonomy of educational objectives. Handbook I: Cognitive domain.* New York: David McKay.

Bloom, B. S. (1976). *Human characteristics and school learning.* New York: McGraw-Hill.

Bloom, B. S., Hastings, J. T., & Madaus, G. F. (1971). *Handbook on formative and summative evaluation of student learning.* New York: McGraw-Hill.

Bogan, J. E. (1975). Some educational aspects of hemispheric specialization. *UCLA Educator, 17,* 16–21.

Bourne, L. E., Jr., Dominowski, R. L., & Loftus, E. F. (1979). *Cognitive processes.* Englewood Cliffs, NJ: Prentice-Hall.

Bradshaw, J. L., & Nettleton, N. C. (1981). The nature of hemispheric specialization in man. *The Behavioral and Brain Sciences, 4,* 51–91.

Brookover, W. Beamer, L., Efthim, H., Hathaway, D., Lezotte, L., Miller, S., Passalacqua, J., & Tournatzky, L. (1982). *Creating effective schools.* Holmes Beach, FL: Learning Publications.

Brophy, J. E. (1988). Research linking teacher behavior to student achievement: Potential implications for instruction of Chapter 1 students. *Educational Psychologist, 23*(3): 275–276.

Brophy, J. E., & Good, T. L. (1972). Teacher expectations: Beyond the Pygmalion controversy. *Phi Beta Kappan, 54,* 267–278.

Brown, A. L. (1980). Metacognitive development and reading. In R. Spiro, B. Bruce, & W. Brewer (Eds.), *Theoretical issues in reading comprehension.* Hillsdale, NJ: Lawrence Erlbaum.

Brown, A. L., & Kane, M. J. (1988). *Cognitive flexibility in young children: The case for transfer.* Paper presented at the annual meeting of the American Educational Research Association, New Orleans.

Brown, I., Jr., & Inouye, D. K. (1978). Learned helplessness through modeling: The role of perceived similarity in competence. *Journal of Personality and Social Psychology, 36,* 900–908.

Brown, L. (1971). *Television: The business behind the box.* San Diego: Harcourt Brace Jovanovich.

Bruner, J. S. (1960). *The process of education.* New York: Vintage.

Bruner, J. S. (1964). The course of cognitive growth. *American Psychologist, 19*, 1–15.

Burchard, J. D., & Barrera, F. (1972). An analysis of time out and response cost in a programmed environment. *Journal of Applied Behavior Analysis, 5*, 271–282.

Carrier, C. A., & Titus, A. (1981). Effects of notetaking, pretraining, and test-made expectations on learning from lecture. *American Educational Research Journal, 18*, 385–397.

Carroll, J. B. (1963). A model of school learning. *Teachers College Record, 64*, 723–733.

Carroll, J. B. (1985). The "model of school learning": Progress of an idea. In C. Fisher & D. C. Berliner (Eds.), *Perspectives on instructional time* (pp. 29–58). New York: Longman.

Carter, K. (1984, November–December). Do teachers understand principles for writing tests? *Journal of Teacher Education*, pp. 57–60.

Chall, J. S. (1983). Literacy: Trends and explanations. *Educational Researcher, 12*, 3–8.

Chase, W. C., & Simon, H. A. (1973). Perception in chess. *Cognitive Psychology, 4*, 55–81.

Clement, J. (1989). Nonformal reasoning in physics: The use of analogies and extreme cases. In J. Voss, D. N. Perkins, & J. Segal (Eds.), *Informal reasoning*. Hillsdale, NJ: Lawrence Erlbaum.

Clifford, M. M. (1984). Thoughts on a theory of constructive failure. *Education Psychologist, 19*, 108–120.

Condiotte, M. M., & Lichtenstein, E. (1981). Self-efficacy and relapse in smoking cessation programs. *Journal of Consulting and Clinical Psychology, 49*, 648–658.

Cook, L. K. (1982). *The effects of text structure on the comprehension of scientific prose*. Unpublished doctoral dissertation, University of California, Santa Barbara.

Cooper, H. M. (1979). Pygmalion grows up: A mode for teacher expectation communication and performance influence. *Review of Educational Research, 49*, 389–410.

Cossairt, A., Hall, R. V., & Hopkins, B. L. (1973). The effects of experimenter's instructions, feedback, and praise on teacher praise and student attending behavior. *Journal of Applied Behavior Analysis, 6*, 89–100.

Covington, M. V., Crutchfield, R. S., Davies, L. B., & Olton, R. M. (1974). *The productive thinking program*. Columbus, OH: Merrill.

Cronbach, L. J. (1984). *Essentials of psychological testing* (4th ed.). New York: Longman.

Cronbach, L. J., & Snow, R. L. (1977). *Aptitudes and instructional methods*. New York: Irvington.

Davis, F. W., & Yates, B. T. (1982). Self-efficacy expectancies versus outcome expectancies as determinants of performance deficits and depressive affect. *Cognitive Therapy and Research, 6*, 23–35.

deCharms, R. (1968). *Personal causation*. New York: Academic Press.

Deci, E. (1975). *Intrinsic motivation*. New York: Plenum.

deGroot, A. D. (1965). *Thought and choice in chess*. The Hague: Mouton.

Dembo, M. H., & Gibson, S. (1985). Teachers' sense of efficacy: An important factor in school improvement. *Elementary School Journal, 63*, 210–219.

DiCaprio, N. S. (1974). *Personality theories: Guides to being*. Philadelphia: Saunders.

Dick, W., & Carey, L. (1985). *The systematic design of instruction* (2nd ed.). Glenview, IL: Scott, Foresman.

Dick, W., & Reiser, R. A. (1989). *Planning effective instruction*. Englewood Cliffs, NJ: Prentice-Hall.

Dinkmeyer, D., McKay, G., & Dinkmeyer, D., Jr. (1980). *Systematic training for effective teaching (STET): Teacher's handbook*. Circle Pines, MN: American Guidance Services.

Dollard, J., & Miller, N. E. (1950). *Personality and psychotherapy*. New York: McGraw-Hill.

Domino, G. (1971). Interactive effects of achievement orientation and teaching style on academic achievement. *Journal of Educational Psychology, 62*, 427–431.

Dooling, D., & Lachman, R. (1971). Effects of comprehension on retention of prose. *Journal of Experimental Psychology, 88*, 216–222.

Dweck, C. S. (1975). The role of expectations and attributions in the alleviation of learned helplessness. *Journal of Personality and Social Psychology, 31*, 674–685.

Dyer, W. W. (1976). *Your erroneous zones*. New York: Avon.

Edmonds, R. R. (1986). Characteristics of effective schools. In U. Neiser (Ed.), *The school achievement of minority children*. Hillsdale, NJ: Lawrence Erlbaum.

Eisman, J. W. (1981). What criteria should public school moral education programs meet? *The Review of Education, 7*, 213–230.

Ellis, A., & Knaus, W. J. (1977). *Overcoming procrastination*. New York: New American Library.

Emmer, E. T., & Evertson, C. (1981). Synthesis of research on classroom management. *Educational Leadership, 38*, 342–347.

Epstein, J. (1983). Selection of friends in differently organized schools and classrooms. In J. Epstein & N. Karweit (Eds.), *Friends in school*. New York: Academic Press.

Erikson, E. H. (1963). *Childhood and society* (2nd ed.). New York: Norton.

Erikson, E. H. (1968). *Identity: Youth and crisis*. New York: Norton.

Eshel, Y., & Klein, Z. (1981). Development of academic self-concept of lower-class and middle-class primary school children. *Journal of Educational Psychology, 73*, 287–293.

Ewart, C. K., Taylor, C.B., Reese, L. B., & DeBusk, R. F. (1983). Effects of early post-myocardial infarction exercise testing on self-perception and subsequent physical activity. *American Journal of Cardiology, 51,* 1076–1080.

Ferster, C. B., & Skinner, B. F. (1957). *Schedules of reinforcement*. New York: Appleton–Century–Crofts.

Festinger, L. (1954). A theory of social comparison processes. *Human Relations, 7*, 117–140.

Festinger, L. (1957). *A theory of cognitive dissonance*. Stanford, CA: Stanford University Press.

Feuerstein, R., Rand, Y., Hoffman, M., & Miller, R. (1980). *Instrumental enrichment: An intervention program for cognitive modifiability*. Baltimore: University Park Press.

Flavell, J. H. (1963). *The developmental psychology of Jean Piaget*. Princeton, NJ: Van Nostrand.

Freeman, D., Kuhs, T., Porter, A., Floden, R., Schmidt, W., & Schwille, J. (1983). Do textbooks and tests define a national curriculum in elementary school mathematics? *Elementary School Journal, 83*, 501–513.

French, J., & Raven, B. (1959). The bases of social power. In D. Cartwright (Ed.), *Studies in social power*. Ann Arbor, MI: Institute for Social Research.

Gagné, E. D. (1985). *The cognitive psychology of school learning*. Boston: Little, Brown.

Gagné, R. M. (1985). *The conditions of learning* (4th ed.). New York: Holt, Rinehart & Winston.

Gagné, R. M., & Briggs, L. J. (1979). *Principles of instructional design* (2nd ed.). New York: Holt, Rinehart & Winston.

Gagné, R. M., & Driscoll, M. P. (1988). *Essentials of learning for instruction* (2nd ed.). Englewood Cliffs, NJ: Prentice-Hall.

Galin, D., & Ornstein, R. (1972). Lateral specialization of cognitive model: An EEG study. *Psychophysiology, 9*, 412–418.

Gardner, H. (1983). *Frames of mind: The theory of multiple intelligences*. New York: Basic Books.

Geiger, K., & Turiel, E. (1983). Disruptive school behavior and concepts of social convention in early adolescence. *Journal of Educational Psychology, 75*, 677–685.

Gelman, R., & Gallistel, C. R. (1978). *The child's understanding of number*. Cambridge, MA: Harvard University Press.

Getzels, J. W., & Jackson, P. W. (1962). *Creativity and intelligence: Explorations with gifted students*. New York: Wiley.

Ginott, H. (1972) *Teacher and child*. New York: Macmillan.

Glenberg, A. (1976). Monotonic and nonmonotonic lag effects in paired-association and recognition memory paradigms. *Journal of Verbal Learning and Verbal Behavior, 15*, 1–16.

Glover, J. A., Ronning, R. R., & Bruning, R. H. (1990). *Cognitive psychology for teachers*. New York: Macmillan.

Glynn, S. M., & DiVesta, F. J. (1977). Outline and hierarchical organization as aids for study and retrieval. *Journal of Educational Psychology, 69*, 89–95.

Goldberg, M, L., Passow, A. H., & Justman, J. (1966). *The effects of ability grouping*. New York: Teachers College Press.

Good, T. L. (1980). Classroom expectations: Teacher–pupil interactions. In J. H. McMillan (Ed.), *The social psychology of school learning* (pp. 79–122). New York: Academic Press.

Good, T. L., Biddle, B. J., & Brophy, J. E. (1975). *Teachers make a difference*. New York: Holt, Rinehart & Winston.

Good, T. L., & Brophy, J. E. (1984). *Looking in classrooms* (3rd ed.). New York: Harper & Row.

Good, T. L., & Brophy, J. E. (1988). *Looking in classrooms* (4th ed.). New York: Longman.

Good, T. L., & Grouws, D. (1979). The Missouri Mathematics Effectiveness Project: An experimental study in fourth-grade classrooms. *Journal of Educational Psychology, 71*, 355–362.

Good, T. L., Grouws, D., & Ebermeier, H. (1983). *Active mathematics teaching*. New York: Longman.

Goodlad, J. I. (1984). *A place called school*. New York: McGraw-Hill.

Gould, D., & Weiss, M. (1981). Effects of model similarity and model self-talk on self-efficacy in muscle endurance. *Journal of Sport Psychology, 3*, 17–29.

Gould, R. L. (1978). *Transformations: Growth and change in adult life*. New York: Simon & Schuster.

Graham, S., & Weiner, B. (1983). Some educational implications of sympathy and anger from an attributional perspective. In R. Shaw & M. Farr (Eds.), *Cognition, affect, and instruction*. Hillsdale, NJ: Lawrence Erlbaum.

Gronlund, N. E. (1982). *Constructing achievement tests* (3rd ed.). Englewood Cliffs, NJ: Prentice-Hall.

Guilford, J. P. (1967). *The nature of human intelligence*. New York: McGraw-Hill.

Halpin, A. W. (1966). *Theory and research in administration*. New York: Macmillan.

Hayes, J. R. (1989). *The complete problem solver* (2nd ed.). Hillsdale, NJ: Lawrence Erlbaum.

Hayes-Roth, B., & Thorndyke, P. W. (1979). Integration on knowledge from text. *Journal of Verbal Learning and Verbal Behavior, 18*, 91–108.

Hembree, R. (1988). Correlates, causes, effects, and treatment of test anxiety. *Review of Educational Research, 58*, 47–77.

Hess, R. (1970). Class and ethnic influences upon socialization. In P. Mussen (Ed.), *Carmichael's manual of child psychology* (3rd ed., Vol. 2). New York: Wiley.

Hettena, C. M., & Ballif, B. L. (1981). Effects of mood on learning. *Journal of Educational Psychology, 73*, 505–508.

Hively, W. (1973). Domain-referenced curriculum evaluation. *UCLA Center for the Study of Evaluation Monograph Series in Evaluation*, No. 1.

Holland, J. G., & Skinner, B. F. (1961). *The analysis of behavior*. New York: McGraw-Hill.

Hopkins, K. D., & Stanley, J. C. (1981). *Educational and psychological measurement and evaluation* (6th ed.). Englewood Cliffs, NJ: Prentice-Hall.

Hovland, C. I. (1963). Yale studies of communication and persuasion. In W. W. Charters & N. L. Gage (Eds.), *Reading in the social psychology of education* (pp. 239–253). Boston: Allyn & Bacon.

Howe, L. W., & Howe, M. M. (1975). *Personalizing education: Values clarification and beyond*. New York: Hart.

Hunt, D. E., & Sullivan, E. V. (1974). *Between psychology and education*. Hinsdale, IL: Dryden Press.

Inhelder, B., & Piaget, J. (1958).*The growth of logical thinking*. New York: Basic Books.

Jackson, J. M. (1960). Structural characteristics of norms. In N. Henry (Ed.) *The dynamics of instructional groups* (59th yearbook, part 2). Chicago: National Society for the Study of Education.

Jensen, A. R. (1968). Social class, race, and genetics: Implications for education. *American Education Research Journal, 5*, 1–42.

Jensen, A. R. (1969). How much can we boost IQ and scholastic achievement? *Harvard Educational Review, 39*, 1–123.

Jensen, A. R., & Rohwer, W. D., Jr. (1963). Verbal mediation in paired-associate and serial learning. *Journal of Verbal Learning and Verbal Behavior, 1*, 346–352.

Jewell, L. N., & Reitz, H. J. (1981). *Group effectiveness in organizations*. Glenview, IL: Scott, Foresman.

Johnson, D. W., & Johnson, R. T. (1975). *Learning together and alone: Cooperation, competition, and individualization*. Englewood Cliffs, NJ: Prentice-Hall.

Johnson, D. W., & Johnson, R. T. (1985). Relationships between black and white students in intergroup cooperation and competition. *Journal of Social Psychology, 125*, 421–428.

Johnson, D. W., Maruyama, G., Johnson, R. T., Nelson, D., & Skon, L. (1981). The effects of cooperative, competitive, and individualistic goal structures on achievement: A meta-analysis. *Psychological Bulletin, 89*, 47–62.

Johnson, R. T., Johnson, D. W., & Stanne, M. B. (1986). Comparison of computer-assisted cooperative, competitive and individualistic learning. *American Educational Research Journal, 23*, 382–392.

Jones, E. E., and Gerard, M. B. (1967). *Foundations of social psychology*. New York: Wiley.

Jones, K. (1984). *Success factors among inner-city college students*. Paper presented at the annual meeting of the American Educational Research Association, New Orleans.

Jones, R. M. (1968). *Fantasy and feeling in education*. New York: New York University Press.

Joyce, B., & Weil, M. (1980). *Models of teaching* (2nd ed.). Englewood Cliffs, NJ: Prentice-Hall.

Kafer, N. (1976). Friendship choice and performance in classroom groups. *The Australian Journal of Education, 20*, 278–284.

Kagan, J. (1965). Reflection–impulsivity and reading ability in primary-grade children. *Child Development, 36*, 609–628.

Kamii, C., & DeVries, R. (1978). *Physical knowledge in preschool education*. Englewood Cliffs, NJ: Prentice-Hall.

Karniol, R., & Ross, M. (1977). The effect of performance-relevant and performance-irrelevant rewards on children's intrinsic motivation. *Child Development, 48*, 482–487.

Katona, G. (1940). *Organizing and memorizing*. New York: McGraw-Hill.

Keller, J. M. (1983). Motivational design of instruction. In C. M. Reigeluth (Ed.), *Instructional-design theories and models: An overview of their current states*. Hillsdale, NJ: Lawrence Erlbaum.

Kiewra, K. (1985). Investigating notetaking and review: A depth of processing alternative. *Educational Psychologist, 20*, 23–32.

King, B. T., & Janis, I. L. (1956). Comparison of the effectiveness of improvised versus non-improvised role playing in producing opinion changes. *Human Relations, 9*, 177–186.

Kirsch, I. (1985). Self-efficacy and expectancy: Old wine with new labels. *Journal of Personality and Social Psychology, 49*, 824–830.

Kohlberg, L. (1969). Stage and sequence: The cognitive-developmental approach to socialization. In D. Goslin (Ed.), *Handbook of socialization theory and research*. Chicago: Rand-McNally.

Kohlberg, L. (1975). The cognitive-developmental approach to moral education. *Phi Beta Kappan, 56*, 670–677.

Kohlberg, L. (1981). *The philosophy of moral development*. New York: Harper & Row.

Köhler, W. (1959). *The mentality of apes*. New York: Vintage.

Kounin, J. S. (1970). *Discipline and group management in classrooms*. New York: Holt, Rinehart & Winston.

Kounin, J. S., & Gump, P. V. (1958). The ripple effect in discipline. *Elementary School Journal, 59*, 158–162.

Krathwohl, D. R., Bloom, B. S., & Masia, B. B. (1964). *Taxonomy of educational objectives. Handbook II: Affective domain*. New York: David McKay.

Kubiszyn, T., & Borich, G. (1984). *Educational testing and measurement*. Glenview, IL: Scott, Foresman.

Kulik, J. A., Kulik, C. C., & Cohen, P. A. (1979). A meta-analysis of outcome studies of Keller's Personalized System of Instruction. *American Psychologist, 34*, 307–318.

Lampert, M. (1986). Knowing, doing, and teaching multiplication. *Cognition and Instruction, 3*, 305–342.

Larkin, J. H. (1982). The cognition of learning physics. *American Journal of Physics, 49*, 534–541.

Larsen, O. N. (Ed.). (1968). *Violence and the mass media*. New York: Harper & Row.

Lazar, I., & Darling, R. (1982). Lasting effects of early education. *Monographs of the Society for Research in Child Development, 47*(No 2. 2–3, Serial No. 195).

Leavitt, H. J. (1951). Some effects of certain communication patterns on group performance. *Journal of Abnormal and Social Psychology, 46*, 38–50.

Lehman, D. R., Lampert, R. O., & Nisbett, R. E. (1988). The effects of graduate training on reasoning: Formal discipline and thinking about everyday-life problems. *American Psychologist, 43*, 431–442.

Levin, J. R., & Kaplan, S. A. (1972). Imaginal facilitation of paired-associate learning: A limited generalization? *Journal of Educational Psychology, 63*, 429–432.

Levy, P., & Goldstein, H. (1984). *Tests in education*. Orlando, FL: Academic Press.

Lewin, K., Lippitt, R., & White, R. (1939). Patterns of aggressive behavior in experimentally created social climates. *Journal of Social Psychology, 10*, 271–299.

Lewis, A. (1988). *Effects of representation training on students' comprehension of arithmetic word problems*. Unpublished doctoral dissertation, University of California, Santa Barbara.

Lickona, T. (1977, March). How to encourage moral development. *Learning*, pp. 38–42.

Liebert, R., & Morris, L. (1967). Cognitive and emotional components of test anxiety: A distinction and some initial data. *Psychological Reports, 20*, 975–978.

Linn, R. L. (1989). *Educational measurement* (3rd ed.). New York: Macmillan.

Lockwood, A. (1978). The effects of value clarification and moral development curricula on school-age subjects: A critical review of recent research. *Review of Educational Research, 48,* 325–364.

Loftus, G. R., & Loftus, E. F. (1976). *Human memory: The processing of information.* Hillsdale, NJ: Lawrence Erlbaum.

Luft, J. (1969). *Of human interaction.* Palo Alto, CA: National Press Books.

Madsen, C. H., Jr., Becker, W. C., Thomas, D. R., Koser, L., & Plager, E. (1968). An analysis of the reinforcing function of "sit down" commands. In R. K. Parker (Ed.), *Readings in educational psychology* (pp. 265–278). Boston: Allyn & Bacon.

Mager, R. F. (1984). *Preparing instructional objectives* (2nd ed.). Belmont, CA: Pitman.

Mandler, G., & Sarason, G. (1952). A study of anxiety and learning. *Journal of Abnormal and Social Psychology, 47,* 166–173.

Mansfield, R. S., Busse, T. V., & Krepelka, E. J. (1978). The effectiveness of creativity training. *Review of Educational Research, 48,* 517–536.

Marcia, J. E. (1980). Identity formation in adolescence. In J. Adelson (Ed.), *Handbook of adolescent psychology.* New York: Wiley.

Marlatt, G. A. (1972). Task structure and the experimental modification of verbal behavior. *Psychological Bulletin, 78,* 335–350.

Marshall, R. E. (1978). *The effect of classroom organization and teacher–student interaction on the distribution of status in the classroom.* Unpublished doctoral dissertation, University of Chicago.

Marx, R. W., & Walsh, J. (1988, January). Learning from academic tasks. *Elementary School Journal,* pp. 207–219.

Maslow, A. H. (1962). *Toward a psychology of being.* Princeton, NJ: Van Nostrand.

Maslow, A. H. (1968). *Toward a psychology of being* (2nd ed.). Princeton, NJ: Van Nostrand.

Mayer, R. E. (1979). Twenty years of research on advance organizers: Assimilation theory is still the best predictor of results. *Instructional Science, 8,* 133–167.

Mayer, R. E. (1984). Aids to prose comprehension. *Educational Psychologist, 19,* 30–42.

Mayer, R. E. (1987). *Educational psychology: A cognitive approach.* Boston: Little, Brown.

McClelland, D. C. (1965). Toward a theory of motive acquisition. *American Psychologist, 20,* 321–333.

McClelland, D. C. (1985). *Human motivation.* Glenview, IL: Scott, Foresman.

McClelland, D. C., Atkinson, J. W., Clark, R. A., & Lowell, E. L. (1953). *The achievement motive.* New York: Appleton–Century–Crofts.

McConkie, G. (1977). Learning from text. In L. Shulman (Ed.), *Review of research in education* (Vol. 5). Itasca, IL: Peacock.

McDaniel, M., & Pressley, M. (1984). Putting the keyword method in context. *Journal of Educational Psychology, 76,* 598–609.

Mehrens, W. A., & Lehmann, I. J. (1978). *Measurement and evaluation in education and psychology* (2nd ed.). New York: Holt, Rinehart & Winston.

Mehrens, W. A., & Lehmann, I. J. (1987). *Using standardized tests in education* (4th ed.). New York: Longman.

Meichenbaum, D., & Asarnow, J. (1979). Cognitive–behavioral modification and metacognitive development: Implications for the classroom. In P. Kendall & S. Hollon (Eds.), *Cognitive–behavioral intervention: Theory, research, and procedures.* Orlando, FL: Academic Press.

Meir, E. I., Keinan, G., & Segal, Z. (1986). Group importance as a mediator between personality–environment congruence and satisfaction. *Journal of Vocational Behavior, 28*, 60–69.

Merton, R. (1949). *Social theory and social structure*. New York: Free Press.

Meyer, B. J. F. (1975). *The organization of prose and its effects on memory*. New York: American Elsevier.

Meyer, B. J. F. (1984). Text dimensions and cognitive processing. In H. Mandl, N. L. Stein, & T. Trabasso (Eds.), *Learning and comprehension of text* (pp. 3–51). Hillsdale, NJ: Lawrence Erlbaum.

Meyer, B. J. F., Brandt, D. M., & Bluth, G. J. (1980). Use of top-level structure in text: Key for reading comprehension of ninth-grade students. *Reading Research Quarterly, 16*, 72–103.

Milgram, S. (1963). Behavioral study of obedience. *Journal of Abnormal and Social Psychology, 67*, 371–378.

Miller, G. A. (1956). The magical number seven, plus or minus two: Some limits to our capacity for processing information. *Psychological Review, 63*, 81–97.

Miller, S. M. (1980). Why having control reduces stress: If I can stop the rollercoaster I don't want to get off. In J. Garber & M. E. P. Seligman (Eds.), *Human helplessness: Theory and research* (pp. 71–95). New York: Academic Press.

Miller, S. M. (1981). Predictability and human stress: Toward a clarification of evidence and theory. In L. Berkowitz (Ed.), *Advances in experimental social psychology* (Vol. 14, pp. 204–256). New York: Academic Press.

Mittler, P. (1971). *The study of twins*. Middlesex, England: Penguin.

Mosston, M. (1972). *Teaching: From command to discovery*. Belmont, CA: Wadsworth.

Mowrer, O. H. (1938). Enuresis: A method for its study and treatment. *American Journal of Orthopsychiatry, 8*, 436–459.

Murray, H. (1938). *Explorations in personality*. New York: Oxford University Press.

Newell, A., & Simon, H. A. (1972). *Human problem solving*. Englewood Cliffs, NJ: Prentice-Hall.

Newman, T. R. (1976). *Changeover: Breakthrough to individualization*. Wayne, NJ: Wayne Township Public Schools.

O'Day, E. F., Kulhavy, R. W., Anderson, W., & Malezynski, R. J. (1971). *Programmed instruction: Techniques and trends*. New York: Appleton–Century–Crofts.

Ormrod, J. E. (1990). *Human learning*. Columbus, OH: Merrill.

Oser, F. (1986). Moral education and values education: The discourse perspective. In M. C. Wittrock (Ed.), *Handbook of research on teaching* (3rd ed.). New York: Macmillan.

Paivio, A. (1979). *Imagery and verbal processes*. Hillsdale, NJ: Lawrence Erlbaum.

Palincsar, A. S., & Brown, A. L. (1984). Reciprocal teaching of comprehension-fostering and comprehension-monitoring activities. *Cognition and Instruction, 1*, 117–175.

Pasnak, R. (1987). Accelerated cognitive development of kindergarteners. *Psychology in the Schools, 24*, 358–363.

Pasnak, R., Brown, K., Kurkjian, M., Triana, E., & Yamamoto, N. (1987). Cognitive gains through training on classification, seriation, and conservation. *Genetic, General and Social Psychology Monographs, 113*(3), 293–321.

Patel, V. L., & Groen, G. J. (1986). Knowledge-based solution strategies in medical reasoning. *Cognitive Science, 10*, 91–116.

Patterson, C. (1973). *Humanistic education*. Englewood Cliffs, NJ: Prentice-Hall.

Pavlov, I. P. (1927). *Conditioned reflexes*. London: Oxford University Press.

Pavlov, I. P. (1960). *Conditioned reflexes*. New York: Dover.

Pepitone, A. (1964). *Attraction and hostility*. New York: Atherton Press.

Perkins, D., & Salomon, G. (1989). Are cognitive skills context-bound? *Educational Researcher, 18*(1), 16–25.

Peterson, P., & Walberg, H. (1979) *Research on teaching: Concepts, findings, and implications*. Berkeley, CA: McCutchan.

Phillips, D. (1971). Applications of behavioral principles in classroom settings. In W.C. Becker (Ed.), *An empirical basis for change in education*. Chicago: Science Research Associates.

Piaget, J. (1932). *The moral judgment of the child*. New York: Harcourt, Brace & World.

Piaget, J. (1950). *The psychology of intelligence*. New York: Harcourt Brace Jovanovich.

Piaget, J. (1951). *Play, dreams and imitation in childhood*. New York: Norton.

Piaget, J. (1952). *The origins of intelligence in children*. New York: International Universities Press.

Piaget, J. (1954). *The construction of reality in the child*. New York: Basic Books.

Piaget, J. (1958). Principal factors determining intellectual evolution from childhood to adult life. In E. L. Hartley & R. E. Hartley (Eds.), *Outside readings in psychology* (2nd ed., pp. 43–55). New York: Crowell.

Piaget, J. (1961). The genetic approach to the psychology of thought. *Journal of Educational Psychology, 52*, 275–281.

Piaget, J. (1967). *Six psychological studies*. New York: Vintage Books.

Piaget, J. (1970). *Science of education and the psychology of the child*. New York: Viking Press.

Piaget, J. (1972). Intellectual evolution from adolescence to adulthood. *Human Development, 15*, 1–12.

Piaget, J. (1973). *To understand is to invent: The future of education*. New York: Grossman.

Piaget, J. (1977). *The development of thought: Equilibrium of cognitive structures*. New York: Viking Press.

Piaget, J., & Inhelder, B. (1969). *The psychology of the child*. New York: Basic Books.

Polya, G. (1973). *How to solve it: A new aspect of mathematical method* (2nd ed.). Garden City, NY: Doubleday.

Premack, D. (1965). Reinforcement theory. In D. Levine (Ed.), *Nebraska Symposium on Motivation* (pp. 123–188). Lincoln, NE: University of Nebraska Press.

Pressley, M., Snyder, B. L., & Cariglia-Bull, T. (1987). How can good strategy use be taught to children? Evaluation of six alternative approaches. In S. M. Cormier & J. D. Hagman (Eds.), *Transfer of learning* (pp. 81–120). Orlando, FL: Academic Press.

Psychological Corporation (1986). *Metropolitan achievement tests manual*. San Antonio, TX: Psychological Corporation.

Purpel, D., & Ryan, K. (Eds.). (1976). *Moral education . . . it comes with the territory*. Berkeley, CA: McCutchan.

Pyke, S. W., & Agnew, N. M. (1991). *The science game: An introduction to research in the social sciences* (5th ed.). Englewood Cliffs, NJ: Prentice-Hall.

Rabavilas, A. D., Boulougouris, J. C., & Stefanis, C. (1976). Duration of flooding sessions in the treatment of obsessive–compulsive patients. *Behavior Research and Therapy, 14*, 349–355.

Rabinowitz, M., & Glaser, R. (1985). Cognitive structure and process in highly competent performance. In F. D. Horowitz & M. O'Brien (Eds.), *The gifted and talented: Developmental perspectives* (pp. 75–98). Washington, DC: American Psychological Association.

Rathbone, C. (1974). *Open education: The informal classroom*. New York: Citation Press.

Reder, L. M. (1976). *The role of elaboration in the processing of prose*. Unpublished doctoral dissertation, University of Michigan, Ann Arbor.

Reimer, J., Paolitto, D. P., & Hersh, R. M. (1983). *Promoting moral development: From Piaget to Kohlberg* (2nd ed.). New York: Longman.

Reiser, R. A., & Gagné, R. M. (1983). *Selecting media for instruction*. Englewood Cliffs, NJ: Educational Technology Publications.

Resnick, L. B. (1987). Learning in school and out. *Educational Researcher, 16*, 13–20.

Reynolds, R., & Anderson, R. (1982). Influence of questions on the allocation of attention during reading. *Journal of Educational Psychology, 74*, 623–632.

Rickards, J. P., & Slife, B. D. (1987). Interaction of dogmatism and rhetorical structure in text recall. *American Educational Research Journal, 24*, 635–641.

Robin, A. L. (1976). Behavioral instruction in college classrooms. *Review of Educational Research, 46*, 313–355.

Rogers, C. (1983). *Freedom to learn: For the 80's*. Columbus, OH: Merrill.

Rogers, V. R. (1970). *Teaching in the British primary school*. New York: Macmillan.

Rosenholtz, S. J., & Rosenholtz, S. M. (1981). Classroom organization and the perception of ability. *Sociology of Education, 54*, 132–140.

Rosenshine, B. (1979). Content, time and direct instruction. In P. Peterson & H. Walberg (Eds.), *Research on teaching: Concepts, findings and implications*. Berkeley, CA: McCutchan.

Rosenthal, R. (1973, April). The Pygmalion effect lives. *Psychology Today*, pp. 56–63.

Rosenthal, R., & Fode, K. L. (1963). The effect of experimenter bias on the performance of the albino rat. *Behavioral Science, 8*, 183–189.

Rosenthal, R., & Jacobson, L. (1968). *Pygmalion in the classroom*. New York: Holt, Rinehart & Winston.

Rothkopf, E. Z. (1970). The concept of mathemagenic activities. *Review of Educational Research, 40*, 325–336.

Rotter, J. B. (1966). Generalized expectancies for internal versus external control of reinforcement. *Psychological Monographs, 80*(1, Whole No. 609).

Rotton, J., Blake, B. F., & Heslin, R. (1977). Dogmatism, trust and message acceptance. *Journal of Psychology, 96*, 81–88.

Rubovits, P. C., & Maehr, M. L. (1971). Pygmalion analyzed: Toward an explanation of the Rosenthal–Jacobson findings. *Journal of Personality and Social Psychology, 19*, 197–204.

Sageria, S., & DiVesta, F. (1978). Learner expectations induced by adjunct questions and the retrieval of intentional and incidental information. *Journal of Educational Psychology, 17*, 280–288.

Sagotsky, G., & Lewis, A. (1978). *Extrinsic reward, positive verbalizations, and subsequent intrinsic interest*. Paper presented at the meeting of the American Psychological Association, Toronto.

Salomon, G. (1984). Television is "easy" and print is "tough": The differential investment of mental effort in learning as a function of perceptions and attributions. *Journal of Educational Psychology, 76*, 647–658.

Sarason, S., & Mandler, G. (1952). Some correlates of test anxiety. *Journal of Abnormal and Social Psychology, 47*, 810–817.

Schachter, S. (1959). *The psychology of affiliation*. Stanford, CA: Stanford University Press.

Schlaefli, A., Rest, J. R., & Thoma, S. J. (1985). Does moral education improve moral judgment? A meta-analysis of intervention studies using the Defining Issues Test. *Review of Educational Research, 55*, 319–352.

Schmuck, R. A., & Schmuck, P. A. (1988). *Group processes in the classroom* (5th ed.). Dubuque, IA: Wm. C. Brown.

Schoenfeld, A. H. (1979). Explicit heuristic training as a variable in problem-solving performance. *Journal for Research in Mathematics Education, 10*, 173–187.

Schoenfeld, A. H. (1985). *Mathematical problem solving*. Orlando, FL: Academic Press.

Schunk, D. H. (1982). Effects of effort attributional feedback on children's perceived self-efficacy and achievement. *Journal of Educational Psychology, 74*, 548–556.

Schunk, D. H. (1983). Ability versus effort attributional feedback: Differential effects of self-efficacy and achievement. *Journal of Educational Psychology, 75*, 848–856.

Schwebel, M. (1975). Formal operations in first year college students. *Journal of Psychology, 91*, 133–41.

Schwebel, M., & Raph, J. (1973). *Piaget in the classroom*. New York: Basic Books.

Seligman, M. E. P. (1975). *Helplessness*. San Francisco: W. H. Freeman.

Selman, R. L. (1978). Education for cognitive development. In *Stage theories of cognitive and moral development* (Reprint No. 13). Cambridge, MA: Harvard Educational Review.

Sharan, S. (1980). Cooperative learning in small groups: Recent methods and effects on achievement, attitudes and ethnic relations. *Review of Educational Research, 50*, 241–272.

Sharan, S., & Hertz-Lazarowitz, R. (1981). A group investigation method of cooperative learning in the classroom. In S. Sharan et al. (Eds.), *Cooperation in education*. Provo, UT: Brigham Young University Press.

Short, J. F. (Ed.) (1968). *Gang delinquency and delinquent subcultures*. New York: Harper & Row.

Sigel, I., Brodzinsky, D. A., & Golinkoff, R. M. (1981). *New directions in Piagetian theory and practice*. Hillsdale, NJ: Lawrence Erlbaum.

Simon, H. A. (1978). Information-processing theory of human problem solving. In W. Estes (Ed.), *Handbook of learning and cognitive processes: Volume 5. Human information processing*. Hillsdale, NJ: Lawrence Erlbaum.

Skinner, B. F. (1938). *The behavior of organisms*. New York: Appleton–Century–Crofts.

Skinner, B. F. (1953). *Science and human behavior*. New York: Macmillan.

Skinner, B. F. (1954). The science of learning and the art of teaching. *Harvard Educational Review, 24*, 86–97.

Skinner, B. F. (1968). *The technology of teaching*. New York: Macmillan.

Skinner, B. F. (1969). *Contingencies of reinforcement*. New York: Appleton–Century–Crofts.

Skinner, B. F. (1978). *About behaviorism*. New York: Knopf.

Skinner, B. F., & Epstein, R. (1982). *Skinner for the classroom*. Champaign, IL: Research Press.

Slavin, R. E. (1983a). *Cooperative learning*. New York: Longman.

Slavin, R. E. (1983b). When does cooperative learning increase student achievement? *Psychological Bulletin, 94*, 429–445.

Slavin, R. E. (1987). Ability grouping and student achievement in elementary schools: A best-evidence synthesis. *Review of Educational Research, 57*, 293–336.

Smith, L. M., & Geoffrey, W. (1968). *The complexities of an urban classroom*. New York: Holt, Rinehart & Winston.

Spearman, C. (1927). *The abilities of man*. New York: Macmillan.

Spielberger, C. D. (1972). Anxiety as an emotional state. In C. D. Spielberger (Ed.), *Anxiety: Current trends in theory and research* (Vol. 1, pp. 23–49). New York: Academic Press.

Stellern, J., Marlowe, M., & Jacobs, J. (1983). The relationship between cognitive mode and right hemisphere test performance. *Journal of Psychoeducational Assessment, 1*, 395–404.

Stensaasen, S. (1970). *Interstudent attraction and social perception in the school class*. Oslo, Norway: Universitelsforlaget.

Sternberg, R. J. (1982). Reasoning, problem solving, and intelligence. In R. J. Sternberg (Ed.), *Handbook of human intelligence*. New York: Cambridge University Press.

Sternberg, R. J. (1985). *Beyond IQ: A triarchic theory of human intelligence*. New York: Cambridge University Press.

Sternberg, R. J., & Wagner, R. K. (1986). *Practical intelligence: Nature and origins of competence in the everyday world*. New York: Cambridge University Press.

Stipek, D. J. (1984). The development of achievement motivation. In R. Ames & C. Ames (Eds.), *Research on motivation in education* (Vol. 1). Orlando, FL: Academic Press.

Stodgill, R. M. (1974). *Handbook of leadership: A survey of theory and research*. New York: Free Press.

Sulzer-Azaroff, B., & Mayer, G. R. (1986). *Achieving educational excellence: Using behavioral strategies*. New York: Holt, Rinehart & Winston.

Taylor, B. M., & Samuels, S. J. (1983). Children's use of text structure in the recall of expository material. *American Educational Research Journal, 20*, 517–528.

Terman, L. (1916). *The measurement of intelligence*. Boston: Houghton Mifflin.

Thelen, H. A. (1967). *Classroom grouping for teachability*. New York: Wiley.

Thorndike, E. L. (1911). *Animal intelligence*. New York: Macmillan.

Thorndike, E. L. (1913). *The psychology of learning* (Educational Psychology II). New York: Teachers College Press.

Thorndike, E. L. (1923). The influence of first-year Latin upon the ability to read English. *School Sociology, 17,* 165–168.

Thorndike, E. L. (1931). *Human learning*. New York: Century.

Thorndike, R. (1968). Review of Rosenthal & Jacobson, Pygmalion in the classroom. *American Educational Research Journal, 5*, 708–711.

Thorndyke, P. W. (1977). Cognitive structures in comprehension and memory of narrative discourse. *Cognitive Psychology, 9,* 77–110.

Thurstone, L. L. (1938). Primary mental abilities. *Psychometric Monograph No. 1*. Chicago: University of Chicago Press.

Tikunoff, W., Berliner, D. C., & Rist, R. (1975). *An ethnographic study of the 40 classrooms of the Beginning Teacher Evaluation Study known sample* (Technical Report No. 75-10-5). San Francisco: Far West Laboratory.

Tobias, S. (1979). Anxiety research in educational psychology. *Journal of Educational Psychology, 71*, 573–582.

Torrance, E. P. (1982). Hemisphericity and creative functioning. *Journal of Research and Development in Education, 15*, 29–37.

Torrance, E. P. (1984). *Torrance tests of creative thinking: Directions manual and scoring guide*. Bensenville, IL: Scholastic Testing Service.

Tuckman, B. W. (1965). Developmental sequence in small groups. *Psychological Bulletin, 63*, 384–399.

Tuckman, B. W. (1968). *A study of the effectiveness of directive versus nondirective vocational teachers as a function of student characteristics and course format* (Final Report). Washington, D.C.: U.S. Office of Education.

Tuckman, B. W. (1988a). *Testing for teachers*. San Diego: Harcourt Brace Jovanovich.

Tuckman, B. W. (1988b). *Conducting educational research* (3rd ed.). San Diego: Harcourt Brace Jovanovich.

Tuckman, B. W. (1988c). The scaling of mood. *Educational and Psychological Measurement, 48*, 419–427.

Tuckman, B. W. (1989). Thinking out loud: Procrastination "busting." *Educational Technology, 29*(3), 48–49.

Tuckman, B. W. (1991). Motivating college students: A model based on empirical evidence. *Innovative Higher Education, 15*, 167–176.

Tuckman, B. W., & Bierman, M. (1971). *Beyond Pygmalion: Galatea in the schools*. Paper presented at the meeting of the American Educational Research Association, New York.

Tuckman, B. W., & Hinkle, J. S. (1986). An experimental study of the physical and psychological effects of aerobic exercise on school children. *Health Psychology, 5*, 192–207.

Tuckman, B. W., & Orefice, D. S. (1973). Personality structure, instructional outcomes, and preferences. *Interchange, 4*, 43–48.

Tuckman, B. W., & Sexton, T. L. (1990). The relation between self-beliefs and self-regulated performance. *Journal of Social Behavior and Personality, 5*, 465–472.

Turiel, E. (1973). Stage transition in moral development. In R. M. W. Travers (Ed.), *Second handbook of research on teaching*. Washington, DC: American Educational Research Association.

Vasta, R. (1976). Feedback and fidelity: Effects of contingent consequences on accuracy of imitation. *Journal of Experimental Child Psychology, 21*, 98–108.

Wadsworth, B. J. (1989). *Piaget's theory of cognitive and affective development* (4th ed.). New York: Longman.

Wagner, R. K. (1987). Tacit knowledge in everyday intelligent behavior. *Journal of Personality and Social Psychology, 52*, 1236–1247.

Walker, H. M., & Buckley, N. K. (1974). *Token reinforcement techniques: Classroom applications for the hard-to-teach child*. Eugene, OR: E-B Press.

Wallach, M. A., & Kogan, N. (1965). *Modes of thinking in young children*. New York: Holt, Rinehart & Winston.

Wason, P. C. (1968). Reasoning about a rule. *Quarterly Journal of Experimental Psychology, 20*, 273–281.

Webb, N. M. (1982). Student interaction and learning in small groups. *Review of Educational Research, 52*, 421–445.

Webb, N. M. (1983). Predicting learning from student interaction: Defining the interaction variables. *Educational Psychologist, 18*, 33–41.

Weiner, B. (1972). *Theories of motivation from mechanism to cognition*. Chicago: Markham.

Weiner, B. (1977). An attributional approach for educational psychology. In L. Shulman (Ed.), *Review of Research in Education* (Vol. 4, pp. 179–209). Itasca, IL: Peacock.

Weiner, B. (1979). A theory of motivation for some classroom experiences. *Journal of Educational Psychology, 71*, 3–25.

Weiner, B. (1980a). A cognitive (attribution)–emotion–action model of motivated behavior: An analysis of judgments of help-giving. *Journal of Personality and Social Psychology, 39*, 186–200.

Weiner, B. (1980b). *Human motivation*. New York: Holt, Rinehart & Winston.

Weiner, B. (1982). The emotional consequences of causal ascriptions. In M. S. Clark & S. T. Fiske (Eds.), *Affect and cognition: The 17th annual Carnegie symposium on cognition* (pp. 185–208). Hillsdale, NJ: Lawrence Erlbaum.

Weiner, B., & Kukla, A. (1970). An attributional analysis of achievement motivation. *Journal of Personality and Social Psychology, 15*, 1–20.

Weiner, B., Russell, D., & Lerman, D. (1979). The cognition–emotion process in achievement-related contexts. *Journal of Personality and Social Psychology, 37*, 1211–1220.

Weinstein, C. E. (1982). Training students to use elaboration learning strategies. *Contemporary Educational Psychology, 7,* 301–311.

Weinstein, C. E., & Mayer, R. E. (1985). The teaching of learning strategies. In M. C. Wittrock (Ed.), *Handbook of research on teaching* (3rd ed.) (pp. 315–327). New York: Macmillan.

Wenger, E. (1987). *Artificial intelligence and tutoring systems: Computational and cognitive approaches to the communication of knowledge.* Los Altos, CA: Morgan Kaufmann.

Wertheimer, M. (1945). *Productive thinking.* New York: Harper.

White, R. W. (1959). Motivation reconsidered: The concept of competence. *Psychological Review, 66,* 297–333.

Wicker, A. W. (1969). Size of church membership and members' support of church behavior settings. *Journal of Personality and Social Psychology, 13,* 278–288.

Wilson, C. C., Robertson, S. J., Herlong, L. H., & Haynes, S. N. (1979). Vicarious effects of time-out in the modification of aggression in the classroom. *Behavior Modification, 3,* 97–111.

Winterbottom, M. R. (1958). The relation of need for achievement to learning experiences in independence and mastery. In J. W. Atkinson (Ed.), *Motives in fantasy, action, society* (pp. 453–478). Princeton, NJ: Van Nostrand.

Witkin, H. A. (1962). *Psychological differentiation.* New York: Wiley.

Wittrock, M. C., Marks, C., & Doctorow, W. (1975). Reading as a generative process. *Journal of Educational Psychology, 67,* 484–489.

Wixson, K. (1984). Level of importance of postquestions and children's learning from text. *American Educational Research Journal, 21,* 419–433.

Wolfe, J. B. (1936). Effectiveness of token rewards for chimpanzees. *Comparative Psychology Monographs, 12*(60).

Wolpe, J. (1974). *The practice of behavior therapy.* New York: Pergamon.

Wood, R., Hull, F., & Azumi, K. (1983). Evaluating quality circles: The American application. *California Management Review, 26,* 37–53.

Wood, W. S. (1971). The Lincoln Elementary School projects: Some results of an in-service training course in behavioral psychology. In W. C. Becker (Ed.), *An empirical basis for change in education.* Chicago: Science Research Associates.

Worchel, S., Andreoli, V. V., & Folger, R. (1977). Intergroup cooperation and intergroup attraction: The effect of previous interaction and outcome of combined effort. *Journal of Experimental Social Psychology, 13,* 131–140.

Wright, T. L., & Duncan, D. (1986). Attraction to group, group cohesiveness, and individual outcome: A study of training groups. *Small Group Behavior, 17,* 487–492.

Yussen, S. R. (1974). Determinants of visual attention and recall in observational learning by preschoolers and second-graders. *Developmental Psychology, 10,* 93–100.

Zimmerman, B. J. (1989). A social cognitive view of self-regulated academic learning. *Journal of Educational Psychology, 81,* 329–339.

Copyrights and Acknowledgments

Text Credits

ALLYN & BACON   for excerpts from *Planning Effective Instruction* by W. Dick and R. A. Reiser. Copyright © 1989 by Prentice-Hall. Reprinted by permission of Allyn & Bacon.

AMERICAN GUIDANCE SERVICE   for table titled "Four Goals of Misbehavior" (p. 18) and table titled "Effective Characteristics of Teachers" (p. 43) from *Systematic Training for Effective Teaching (STET): Teacher's Handbook* by Don Dinkmeyer, Gary D. McKay, and Don Dinkmeyer, Jr. © 1980, American Guidance Service, Inc., Circle Pines, MN 55014. Reproduced with permission of publisher. All rights reserved.

AMERICAN PSYCHOLOGICAL ASSOCIATION   for excerpt from Lehman, D. R., Lempert, R. O., and Nisbett, R. E. (1988). The effects of graduate training on reasoning: Formal discipline and thinking about everyday life events. *American Psychologist*, *43*, 431–442. Copyright 1988 by the American Psychological Association. Reprinted by permission.

BASIC BOOKS   for excerpts from *The Construction of Reality in the Child*, by Jean Piaget. Translated by Margaret Cook. © 1954 by Basic Books, Inc. Reprinted by permission of Basic Books, Inc., Publishers, New York.

HAROLD FLETCHER   for materials on test-item analysis, data from sixth-grade students tested in midyear, and miscellaneous testing examples. Reprinted with permission.

HARCOURT BRACE JOVANOVICH   for adapted table from *Personality Theories: Guides to Being* by N. S. DiCaprio, copyright © 1974 by Saunders College Publishing, a division of Holt, Rinehart and Winston, Inc., reprinted by permission of the publisher.

INTERNATIONAL UNIVERSITY PRESS   for excerpts from *The Origins of Intelligence in Children* by Jean Piaget. Copyright 1952 International University Press. Reprinted by permission of the publisher.

INTERNATIONAL READING ASSOCIATION   for material from "Appendix: Supertankers" from Meyer, Bonnie J. F., Brandt, D. M., and Bluth, G. J. (1980). Use of top-level structure in text: Key for reading comprehension of ninth-grade students. *Reading Research Quarterly*, *16*(1), 102–103. Reprinted with permission of Bonnie J. F. Meyer and the International Reading Association.

ALICIA WOLFGANG KEMPER   for "A Personal Scenario: Learning in My Father's Workshop" (unpublished) by Alicia Wolfgang Kemper. Reprinted by permission of the author.

DR. DARRIN R. LEHMAN   for excerpt from Lehman, D. R., Lempert, R. O., and Nisbett, R. E. (1988). The effects of graduate training on reasoning: Formal discipline and thinking about everyday life events. *American Psychologist*, *43*, 431–442. Reprinted by permission of the authors and the American Psychological Association.

LONGMAN PUBLISHING GROUP   for excerpt from *Taxonomy of Education Objectives: The Classification of Educational Goals. Handbook I: Cognitive Domain* by Benjamin S. Bloom et al. Copyright © 1956 by Longman Publishing Group; for excerpt from *Active Mathematics Teaching* by Thomas L. Good, Douglas A. Grouws, and Howard Ebermeier. Copyright © 1983 by Longman Publishing Group; for excerpt from *Piaget's Theory of Cognitive and Affective Development* by Barry J. Wadsworth. Copyright © 1989 by Longman Publishing Group. All reprinted by permission of Longman Publishing Group.

MACMILLAN PUBLISHING COMPANY   for tables and excerpt reprinted by permission of Macmillan Publishing Company from *Teaching 1: Classroom Management* by Wesley C. Becker, Siegfried Englemann, and Don R. Thomas. Copyright © Science Research Associates, 1975; for material reprinted with permission of The Free Press, a Division of Macmillan, Inc., from Jean Piaget, *The Moral Judgment of the Child*, translated by Marjorie Gabian. New York: The Free Press, 1965; for excerpt from Wood, W. D. (1971). The Lincoln Elementary School projects: Some results of an in-service training course in behavioral psychology. In W. C. Becker (Ed.), *An empirical basis for change in education*. Copyright Science Research Associates, 1971.

PATRICIA MCGERR   for "Johnny Lingo's Eight-Cow Wife," copyright 1965 by Patricia McGerr. Published in *Woman's Day* Magazine, Nov. 1965; reprinted in *Reader's Digest*, Feb. 1988.

MCGRAW-HILL   for excerpt from Holland, J. G., and Skinner, B. F. (1961). *The Analysis of Behavior*. New York: McGraw-Hill. Reprinted by permission of McGraw-Hill, Inc.

W. W. NORTON   for table adapted from *Identity, Youth, and Crisis* by Erik H. Erikson, by permission of W. W. Norton & Company, Inc. Copyright © 1968 by W. W. Norton & Company, Inc.

THE PSYCHOLOGICAL CORPORATION   for excerpt of norms table from the *Metropolitan Achievement Test*, 6th ed. Copyright © 1986 by Harcourt Brace Jovanovich, Inc. Reproduced by permission. All rights reserved.

ROUTLEDGE AND KEGAN PAUL, LTD.   for excerpt from *The Mentality of Apes* by W. Köhler. Reprinted by permission of the publisher, Routledge and Kegan Paul, Ltd.

Photo and Figure Credits

Chapter 1 Opener © Jeffry W. Myers/Stock Boston. **5** © Michael Weisbrot & Family/Stock Boston. **6** © Elizabeth Crews/Stock Boston. **10** © Elizabeth Crews/Stock Boston.

Part 1 Opener © Jim Conk/Lightwave. **Chapter 2 Opener** Copyright © 1985 by Blair Seitz. All rights reserved. **25** Culver Pictures. **Chapter 3 Opener** © Lawrence Migdale/Stock Boston. **49** © MCMXC Peter Menzel/Stock Boston. **55** © Elizabeth Crews/Stock Boston. **57** Copyright © 1987 by Blair Seitz. All rights reserved. **Chapter 4 Opener** © Elizabeth Crews/Stock Boston. **71** Courtesy of author. **74** © Jean Claude LeJeune/Stock Boston. **82** © George Whiteley/Photo Researchers, Inc. NY. **84** © Barbara Rios/Photo Researchers, Inc. NY. **87 & 89** From *The Systematic Design of Instruction*, 2/e, by Walter Dick and Lou Carey. Copyright © 1985, 1978 by Scott Foresman and Company. Reprinted by permission of Harper-Collins Publishers. **Chapter 5 Opener** © Barbara Rios/Photo Researchers, Inc. NY. **95** B. S. Bloom, *Taxonomy of Educational Objectives. Handbook I: Cognitive Domain*. New York: David McKay, 1956. **106** © Jean Claude LeJeune/Stock Boston. **107** © Rhoda Sidney/PhotoEdit. **110** © Elizabeth Crews, 636 Vincente Avenue, Berkeley, CA 94707. **Chapter 6 Opener** © Elizabeth Crews/Stock Boston. **118** From *Cognitive Psychology of School Learning* by Ellen D. Gagné. Copyright © 1985 by Ellen D. Gagné. Reprinted by permission of HarperCollins Publishers. **121** © Ulrike Welsch 1989/PhotoEdit. **122** © Photo: Elizabeth Crews. **132** © Photo: Elizabeth Crews. **136** © Rhoda Sidney/PhotoEdit. **Chapter 7 Opener** © Bob Daemmrich/Stock Boston. **145** © Photo: Elizabeth Crews. **153** © Tim Davis/Photo Researchers, Inc. NY. **161** Ursula Markus/Photo Researchers, Inc. NY.

Part 2 Opener © Blair Seitz. All rights reserved. **Chapter 8 Opener** © Elizabeth Crews/Stock Boston. **170** AP/Wide World Photos. **177** © 1981 Suzanne Szasz/Photo Researchers, Inc. NY. **181** © Mary Kate Denny 1991/PhotoEdit. **188/89, 191/93** Adapted from *The Growth of Logical Thinking: From Childhood to Adolescence* by Barbel Inhelder and Jean Piaget. Copyright © 1958 by Basic Books, Inc. Reprinted by permission of Basic Books, Inc., a division of HarperCollins Publishers. **190** © Elizabeth Crews/Stock Boston. **195** © Bohdan Hrynewych/Stock Boston. **196** © Ulrike Welsch 1988/Photo Researchers, Inc. NY. **Chapter 9 Opener** © Oscar Palmquist/Lightwave. **211** © Michael Weisbrot & Family/Stock Boston. **223** © Elizabeth Crews/Stock Boston. **226** © Hazel Hankin/Stock Boston. **228** Richard Hutchings/InfoEdit. **Chapter 10 Opener** © Bob Daemmrich/Stock Boston. **248** © David Powers, 1985/Stock Boston. **253** © Abraham Menashe 1991/Photo Researchers, Inc. NY. **260** From Richard A. Schmuck and Patricia A. Schmuck, *Group Processes in the Classroom*, 5th ed. Copyright © 1988 Wm. C. Brown Publishers, Dubuque, Iowa. All rights reserved. Reprinted by permission. **Chapter 11 Opener** © Bob Daemmrich, Austin, Texas. **270** © Elizabeth Crews. **273** Albert Bandura, *Social Foundations of Thought and Action: A Social Cognitive Theory*, © 1986, p. 52. Adapted by permission of Prentice-Hall, Englewood Cliffs, NJ. **279** Albert Bandura, Self Efficacy: Toward a Unifying of Behavioral Change. *Psychological Review, 84*, 1977, pp. 191–215. © 1991 by the American Psychological Association. Adapted by permission. **282** Albert Bandura, Self Efficacy: Toward a Unifying of Behavioral Change. *Psychological Review, 84*, 1977, p. 195. © 1991 by the American Psychological Association. Adapted by permission. **283** Cathy Cheney/Stock Boston. **Chapter 12 Opener** © Bob Daemmrich/Stock Boston. **307** Reprinted by permission of MacMillan Publishing Company from *Learning and Instruction: Theory into Practice*, by M. E. Bell-Gredler. Copyright © 1985 by Margaret Bell. **317** © Elizabeth Crews/Stock Boston. **317** Photo Researchers, Inc. NY.

Part 3 Opener © Bob Daemmrich/Stock Boston. **Chapter 13 Opener** © 1991 Jim Conk/Lightwave. **335** J. P. Guilford, *The Nature of Human Intelligence*, 1967, McGraw-Hill, Inc. Used with permission of the publisher. **347** © 1988 Laimute E. Druskis/Stock Boston. **349** © Michael Weisbrot & Family/Stock Boston. **354** Copyright 1991 by the American Educational Association. Adapted by permission of the publisher. **Chapter 14 Opener** © Bob Daemmrich/Stock Boston. **384** B. S. Bloom, *Taxonomy of Educational Objectives. Handbook I: Cognitive Domain*. New York: David McKay, 1956. **381** © Elizabeth Crews. **392** © Elizabeth Crews. **Chapter 15 Opener** © Oscar Palmquist 1991/Lightwave. **410** © 1977 Peter Menzel/Stock Boston. **419** © Elizabeth Crews. **Chapter 16 Opener** © Jeffrey W. Myers/Stock Boston. **444–46** From *The Stanford Achievement Test*, 7th edition, Copyright © 1982, 1983, 1984, 1986 by Harcourt Brace Jovanovich, Inc. Reproduced by permission. All rights reserved. **436** © Elizabeth Crews. **442** © 1988 by Blair Seitz. **452** © Elizabeth Crews.

Author/Subject Index

A 1
B 2
C 3
D 4
E 5
F 6
G 7
H 8
I 9
J 0